T0180075

Lecture Notes in Computer Science   13762

More information about this series at https://link.springer.com/bookseries/558

Mirjam Vosmeer ·
Lissa Holloway-Attaway (Eds.)

Interactive Storytelling

15th International Conference
on Interactive Digital Storytelling, ICIDS 2022
Santa Cruz, CA, USA, December 4–7, 2022
Proceedings

 Springer

Editors
Mirjam Vosmeer (ID)
Amsterdam University of Applied Sciences
Amsterdam, The Netherlands

Lissa Holloway-Attaway (ID)
University of Skövde
Skövde, Sweden

ISSN 0302-9743   ISSN 1611-3349 (electronic)
Lecture Notes in Computer Science
ISBN 978-3-031-22297-9   ISBN 978-3-031-22298-6 (eBook)
https://doi.org/10.1007/978-3-031-22298-6

This Springer imprint is published by the registered company Springer Nature Switzerland AG
The registered company address is: Gewerbestrasse 11, 6330 Cham, Switzerland

Preface

This volume constitutes the proceedings of the 15th International Conference on Interactive Digital Storytelling (ICIDS 2022). ICIDS is the premier conference for researchers and practitioners concerned with studying digital interactive forms of narrative from a variety of perspectives, including theoretical, technological, and applied design lenses. The annual conference is an interdisciplinary gathering that combines technology-focused approaches with humanities-inspired theoretical inquiry, empirical research, and artistic expression.

This year's conference was built around the central theme of 'Speculative Horizons'. With this theme we were motivated to consider the future and its relationship to interactive digital storytelling. In our contemporary times where we are confronting global disasters, from war to pandemics, and where we are challenged by the ever-increasing impacts of climate change and the toll of other human interventions on our worlds and cultures, we focus on critical questions: What can we foresee and foretell about what is next on the horizon? How can interactive digital storytelling be a call to action, a mode for healing and peace, or a method of intimate communication to help us visualize, empathize, and consider what might be at stake in our worlds and how we can intervene? With this theme we encouraged authors to explore the ways that narratives, technologies, systems, cultures, and creators can situate and motivate us, attuning us to a present reality, while looking forward to an unknown and uncertain future that we may, or may not, be able to change. What should we know now to aid us in the journey forward?

These proceedings represent the latest work from a wide range of researchers, with representation from around the world. Authors of submitted papers came from 29 different countries, with a similar range of representation in terms of the Program Committee. The program was divided into six main areas: Applications and Case Studies; Interactive Narrative Design; Social and Cultural Contexts; Theory, History and Foundations; Tools and Systems; and Virtual Worlds, Performance, Games and Play. Each subject area represents an important domain for exploring the theories, contexts, histories, practices, and designs for interactive digital storytelling. Collectively the papers in this volume present a range of intriguing and thoughtful reflections on how these unique digital narrative forms may be critiqued, developed, and designed.

ICIDS 2022 was hosted at University of California, Santa Cruz, but organized as a hybrid event, with participants either attending on-site, or joining the conference remotely through a number of different online platforms. Care was taken to ensure that all aspects of the program were equally accessible to those who were attending physically and virtually.

This year, we received 79 paper submissions (50 full papers, 19 short papers, and 10 posters/demos). Following the review process, the Program Committee accepted 30 full papers, 10 short papers, and 5 posters/demos. The total acceptance rate was 0.57.

As in the past, the review process was strictly double-blind and used a structured and detailed review form. A minimum of three reviews per paper were requested before the decision, with additional reviews solicited on the recommendations of reviewers. In addition, we included a rebuttal phase, and final decisions were made at a virtual program chairs meeting, which included the area chairs. However, we still welcome feedback from both authors and reviewers to help us continue to refine and strengthen the way that we run the conference. We want to thank our area chairs for their hard work and participation in the meta-review process: Elin Carstensdottir, Colette Daiute, Elizabeth Goins, Hartmut Koenitz, Jonathan Lessard, Ilaria Mariani, Chris Martens, Ulrike Spierling, Christian Roth, and Rebecca Rouse.

Finally, we want to thank the members of the ICIDS community who served as reviewers this year. The commitment of our reviewers to provide high-quality reviews and constructive and insightful discussions is a credit to our community, and helps to maintain the rigor and integrity of our ongoing development of this exciting and growing field.

December 2022

Mirjam Vosmeer
Lissa Holloway-Attaway

ARDIN, The Association for Research in Interactive Digital Narratives

ARDIN's purpose is to support research in Interactive Digital Narratives (IDN), in a wide range of forms, be that video and computer games, interactive documentaries and fiction, journalistic interactives, art projects, educational titles, transmedia, virtual reality and augmented reality titles, or any emerging novel forms of IDN.

ARDIN provides a home for an interdisciplinary community and for various activities that connect, support, grow, and validate said community. The long- term vision for the suite of activities hosted by ARDIN includes membership services, such as a community platform, job postings, and support for local gatherings, but also conferences, publication opportunities, research fellowships, and academic/professional awards. ARDIN publishes a monthly newsletter and holds a monthly online social, where both established researchers and graduate students share their ongoing work in an informal setting. A new journal (Journal for Interactive Narrative Research), published in collaboration with ETC press, is currently being prepared, with a first issue planned to be available soon. There are also several committees and task forces, listed below.

ICIDS is the main academic conference of ARDIN. Additional international and local conferences are welcome to join the organization. The Zip-Scene conference, focused on eastern Europe, is the first associated conference.

Diversity is important to ARDIN. The organization will strive towards gender balance and the representation of different people from different origins. Diversity also means to represent scholars at different levels of their careers.

No ARDIN member shall discriminate against any other ARDIN member or others outside of the organization in any way, including but not limited to gender, nationality, race, religion, sexuality, or ability. Discrimination against these principles will not be tolerated and membership in ARDIN can be withdrawn based on evidence of such behavior.

The association is incorporated as a legal entity in Amsterdam, the Netherlands. First proposed during the ICIDS 2017 conference in Madeira, Portugal, the association was officially announced at ICIDS 2018 in Dublin, Ireland. During its foundational year, members of the former ICIDS Steering Committee continued to serve as the ARDIN board as approved by the first general assembly at ICIDS 2018. The current board structure and membership were approved at the second general assembly at ICIDS 2019 in Utah, and, as of October 2022, ARDIN has more than 160 members.

More information about ARDIN can be found at https://ardin.online/. ARDIN is also on Facebook (https://www.facebook.com/ARDINassociation), Twitter (@ARDIN_online), and Discord (https://discord.gg/jNg5b5dWP4).

Committees

The Promotion and Advancement committee is led by Hartmut Koenitz and Josh Fisher with the help of Luis Bruni and Colette Daiute. The aim of this committee is to create a tenure equivalency document and recruit a team of expert reviewers for tenure and examination. Those interested should reach out to Hartmut Koenitz (hkoenitz at gmail.com).

The IDN in Education committee is led by Jonathon Barbara. This committee will be looking into how IDN can become a part of school (K-12) curricula and will be producing a white paper with recommendations. Students are also welcome to join as task force members! Those interested should reach out to Jonathon Barbara (barbaraj at tcd.ie).

Task Forces

The Task Force on Inclusive Pricing Structure is led by Agnes Bakk. This task force will be looking into how to adjust registration for membership and conference registration according to GDP. Those interested should reach out to Agnes Bakk (bakk at mome.hu).

The Task Force on ARDIN Outreach is led by Maria Cecilia Reyes. Aims of this task force are to create awareness about IDN and around ARDIN, and to build partnerships with industry, art, and education institutions, among others key stakeholders. Contact Maria Cecilia Reyes (mariaceciliareyesr at gmail.com) for more information or to get involved.

Organization

Organization Committee

General Chairs

Michael Mateas	UC Santa Cruz, USA
David Lamas	Tallinn University, Estonia

Program Committee Chairs

Mirjam Vosmeer	Amsterdam University of Applied Sciences, The Netherlands
Lissa Holloway-Attaway	University of Skövde, Sweden

Art Exhibits Chairs

Nick Montfort	Massachusetts Institute of Technology, USA
Clara Fernández-Vara	New York University, USA

Workshop Chair

Mirjam Vosmeer	Amsterdam University of Applied Sciences, The Netherlands

Doctoral Consortium Chairs

Hartmut Koenitz	Södertörn University, Sweden
Sherol Chen	Google, USA

Publicity Chair

Shi Johnson-Bey	UC Santa Cruz, USA

ARDIN Officers and Board

Executive Board

Hartmut Koenitz (President)	Södertörn University, Sweden
Frank Nack	University of Amsterdam, The Netherlands
Lissa Holloway-Attaway	University of Skövde, Sweden
Alex Mitchell	National University of Singapore, Singapore
Rebecca Rouse	University of Skövde, Sweden

General Board

Ágnes Bakk   Moholy-Nagy University of Art and Design,
                                        Hungary
Luis Bruni   Aalborg University, Denmark
Clara Fernandez-Vara   NYU, USA
Josh Fisher   Columbia College Chicago, USA
Andrew Gordon   University of Southern California, USA
Mads Haahr   Trinity College Dublin, Ireland
Michael Mateas   UC Santa Cruz, USA
Valentina Nisi   University of Madeira, Portugal, and Carnegie
                                        Mellon University, USA
Mirjam Palosaari Eladhari   Södertörn University, Sweden
Tess Tanenbaum   UC Irvine, USA
David Thue   Carleton University, Canada, and Reykjavik
                                        University, Iceland

Program Committee Area Chairs

Applications and Case Studies

Colette Daiute   City University of New York, USA
Joshua Fisher   Ball State University, USA

Interactive Narrative Design

Elin Carstensdottir   UC Santa Cruz, USA
Jonathan Lessard   Concordia University, Canada

Social and Cultural Contexts

Ilaria Mariani   Politecnico di Milano, Italy
Rebecca Rouse   University of Skövde, Sweden

Theory, History and Foundations

Hartmut Koenitz   Södertörn University, Sweden
Ulrike Spierling   RheinMain University of Applied Sciences,
                                        Germany

Tools and Systems

Max Kreminski   UC Santa Cruz, USA
Chris Martens   North Carolina State University, USA

Virtual Worlds, Performance, Games and Play

Elizabeth Goins	Rochester Institute of Technology, USA
Christian Roth	HKU University of the Arts Utrecht, The Netherlands

Program Committee

David Antognol	Columbia College Chicago, USA
Ruth Aylett	Heriot-Watt University, UK
Julio Bahamon	UNC Charlotte, USA
Paulo Bara	ITI-LARSyS, Portugal
Jonathan Barbara	St. Martins Institute of Higher Education, Malta
Dan Barnard	Independent
Pippin Barr	Concordia University, Canada
Miguel Barreda-Ángeles	University of Amsterdam, The Netherlands
Mattia Bellini	University of Tartu, Estonia
Wolfgang Broll	Ilmenau University of Technology, Germany
Luis Emilio Bruni	Aalborg University, Denmark
Rogelio Cardona-Rivera	University of Utah, USA
Elin Carstensdottir	UC Santa Cruz, USA
Chiara Ceccarini	University of Bologna, Italy
Fanfan Chen	National Taipei University of Business, China
Yun-Gyung Cheong	SKKU, South Korea
Laureline Chiapello	Université du Québec à Chicoutimi, Canada
Kenny Chow	The Hong Kong Polytechnic University, China
Marc Christie	Inria, France
Sharon Lynn Chu	University of Florida, USA
Leonardo Codamo	Politecnico di Milano, Italy
Shauna Concannon	University of Cambridge, UK
Colette Daiute	City University of New York, USA
Rossana Damiano	Università di Torino, Italy
Melanie Dickinson	UC Santa Cruz, USA
Simon Dor	UC Santa Cruz, USA
Maria Engberg	Malmö University, Sweden
Riccardo Fassone	Università di Torino, Italy
Jamie Fawcus	University of Skövde, Sweden
Clara Fernandez Vara	New York University, USA
Maria José Ferreira	Universidade de Lisboa, Portugal
Joshua Fisher	Columbia College Chicago, USA
Caitlin Fisher	York University, Canada
Lucas Friche	University of Lorraine, France
Pablo Gervás	Universidad Complutense de Madrid, Spain

Michael Nitsche	Georgia Institute of Technology, USA
Renata Ntelia	Lincoln University, USA
Neil O'Dwyer	Trinity College Dublin, Ireland
Ethel Ong	De La Salle University, Philippines
Jennifer Palilonis	Ball State University, USA
Sofia Peracchi	Politecnico di Milano, Italy
Derek Reilly	Dalhousie University, USA
María Cecilia Reyes	Vilnius University, Lithuania
Justus Robertson	Rochester Institute of Technology, USA
Remi Ronfard	Inria, France
Christian Roth	HKU University of the Arts Utrecht, The Netherlands
Rebecca Rouse	University of Skövde, Sweden
Jonathan Rowe	North Carolina State University, USA
Anastasia Salter	University of Central Florida, USA
Ben Samuel	University of New Orleans, USA
Bobby Schweizer T.	Texas Tech University, USA
Sabrina Scuri	ITI-LARSyS, Portugal
Hélène Sellier	Université Paris-Est Marne-la-Vallée, France
Yotam Shibolet	Utrecht University, The Netherlands
Alexander Shoulson	Bungie, USA
Mei Si	Rensselaer Polytechnic Institute, USA
Andy Smith	North Carolina State University, USA
Ulrike Spierling	RheinMain University of Applied Sciences, Germany
Anne Sullivan	Georgia Institute of Technology, USA
Alina Striner	University of Maryland, USA
Adam Summerville	Cal Poly Pomona, USA
Torbjörn Svensson	University of Skövde, Sweden
Steven Sych	Concordia University, Canada
Cristina Sylla	University of Minho and ITI - LARSyS, Portugal
Nicolas Szilas	University of Geneva, Switzerland
Mariet Theune	University of Twente, The Netherlands
Mattia Thibault	Tampere University, Finland
David Thue	Carleton University, Canada
Elise Trinh	Concordia University, Canada
Romana Turina	Arts University Bournemouth, UK
Mirjam Vosmeer	Amsterdam University of Applied Sciences, The Netherlands
Hui-Yin Wu	Centre Inria d'Université Côte d'Azur, France
Huiwen Zhao	Bournemouth University, UK
Jan de Wit	Tilburg University, The Netherlands

Contents

Interactive Narrative Design

Theory, History and Foundations

Tools and Systems

Virtual Worlds, Performance, Games and Play

Applications and Case Studies

Using Storytelling to Teach Children Biodiversity

Maria José Ferreira[1,2,3(✉)] (iD), Raul Benites Paradeda[5], Raquel Oliveira[2,4], Valentina Nisi[1,3], and Ana Paiva[1,2]

[1] Instituto Superior Técnico - University of Lisbon, Lisbon, Portugal
{maria.jose.ferreira,valentina.nisi,ana.s.paiva}@tecnico.ulisboa.pt
[2] INESC-ID, Lisbon, Portugal
[3] Interactive Technologies Institute, LARSyS, Funchal, Portugal
[4] Iscte-Instituto Universitário de Lisboa (Cis-IUL), Lisbon, Portugal
rsaoa@iscte-iul.pt
[5] State University of Rio Grande do Norte, Natal, Brazil
raulparadeda@uern.br

Abstract. This paper is about improving children's learning of biodiversity and preservation of the environment through interactive storytelling and gaming. We conducted a user study with a between-subjects design with eighty-three children aged 6 to 10 years from the South of Brazil. We analysed the role of the agent's embodiment (embodied vs not embodied), the presence (or absence) of storytelling, and children's previous knowledge of biodiversity, in children's performance and engagement with the application. Our results demonstrate that: a) children seeing familiar biodiversity were more engaged with our system than those seeing non-familiar biodiversity, and b) children with a higher level of knowledge (3rd and 4th school years) performed better in the species identification task than those with a lower level of knowledge (1st and 2nd school years).

Keywords: Human-agent interaction · Virtual robot · Storytelling · Learning · Biodiversity

1 Introduction

In 2015, the international community established 17 Sustainable Development Goals (SDGs) [47] as part of the United Nations (UN) 2030 Agenda for Sustainable Development, as a commitment to execute actions to face the global

This work was supported by national funds through Fundação para a Ciência e a Tecnologia (UIDB/50021/2020 and PD/BD/150286/2019), LARSyS (UIDB/50009/2020), and Agência Regional para o Desenvolvimento e Tecnologia (M1420-09-5369-000001). We would like to acknowledge Funchal Natural History Museum, Lisbon city hall, António F. Aguiar, Fernando Louro Alves and Heide Vanessa Santos for the biodiversity information validation. Furthermore to Sandra Olim (3D manipulation), Ana Pires (feedback) and Marta Bubicz (connections with Brazilian schools), the Secretary of education from Horizontina city and to Bela União Municipal Elementary School.

M. Vosmeer and L. Holloway-Attaway (Eds.): ICIDS 2022, LNCS 13762, pp. 3–27, 2022.
https://doi.org/10.1007/978-3-031-22298-6_1

challenges the world encounters. The 15th SDG intends to stop biodiversity loss. For this reason, educating and motivating future generations to learn about and protect endemic species and wildlife while maintaining the balance of biodiversity is essential.

Following this line of reasoning, Interactive Storytelling (IS) researchers have utilised different strategies to support biodiversity conservation investigation, from transmedia tools [22], to games [25,38,49], and Interactive location-based stories [15,22]. From those strategies, IS has been shown to be an efficient way for children to expand their creativity, unfold narrative thinking, improve language and communication skills, and develop their social and emotional abilities [2,4, 26,37,64]. Besides increasing engagement, storytelling also carries educational benefits and increases the children's curiosity about different topics [29].

Several studies report on the effectiveness of storytelling, being fun, engaging, and highly memorable, increasing students' interest in hearing stories, as well as talking, writing, and reading about them (e.g., [5,40]). Digital storytelling is beneficial not only in developing teachers' content, pedagogical and technological knowledge, but also in improving the students' learning as it increases the understanding of the content catering to their intelligence [18].

However, IS effectiveness in this context still demands further investigation. The use of virtual robotic agents in education is a relatively new area of research and quite a desired one by teachers and educators. For example, [1] performed a study comparing the effects of a physical and virtual robotic agent on enjoyment, immersion, and vocabulary retention in adult participants who had to learn a new language. Although, significant differences were found in pleasure and immersion for participants without previous experience with social robots, the learning outcomes were similar in both groups.

[23] compared a physical robot with a virtual one in a task intended to assess cognitive skills and concluded that virtual robots are a viable alternative, overcoming the limitations of physical robots, such as cost, reliability and the need for on-site technical support.

In addition to presenting similar learning outcomes to physical robots and providing a cost-effective alternative, virtual agents have proved to be valuable tools in efforts to manage and conserve biodiversity [69], education in biodiversity [11,24], and to raise awareness of the importance of conservation of biodiversity [38,45].

Moreover, combining storytelling and social agents allows more interactivity and attractiveness (e.g., [25]). Additional factors influencing the child's learning outcomes are the child's familiarity with the technological resources, prior knowledge of the content to be addressed, the child's intellectual development, approach to the narrative content, and the interactive scenario, among others (e.g., [7,10]).

Familiarity with a given topic can impact children's perceptions. Previous research has shown that familiarity with a topic is positively associated with comprehension and increased knowledge sharing [43], with peer influence to improve children's choices [9], with linguistic stress in different dialects [32] and encouragement when working with young children [57].

In this paper, we investigate whether children's performance and engagement with biodiversity are influenced by: a) the narrative channel; b) the presence of a virtual agent; c) familiarity with biodiversity; and d) prior knowledge of biodiversity. We based our work on the Constructivism and the Cognitive Development Theories of Piaget [50,51]. These theories argue that the acquisition of knowledge and familiarity with a subject is facilitated by children's personal experiences.

This paper describes the results of a study conducted with children between 6 and 10 years old who interacted with a virtual robotic agent through interactive storytelling activity designed to teach them about local and non-local flora and fauna. Overall our results show that children familiar with biodiversity were more engaged with our system, and those with higher biodiversity experience performed better.

2   Technological Approaches to Biodiversity Education

In the biodiversity education context, technology has been shown to play a central role by bridging the gap between formal and informal education and between school-specific digital tools and simple digital tools [67].

Studies using a mobile-learning digital app demonstrated that identifying plant species was a successful strategy to promote students' knowledge of Botanics [36]. Serious games are also an excellent strategy to inspire sustainable and eco-friendly attitudes [3].

Collaborative digital storytelling has been used to create awareness about biodiversity in school settings [52], but also in other educational contexts (with tourists learning about local biodiversity, with positive outcomes both in terms of attitudes and knowledge outcomes [15,16,22,48]. Moreover, several studies recognise virtual agents as important digital educational tools in other areas of learning, such as mathematics [30] and languages [41].

In addition to interactive narratives, some studies have investigated the use of virtual or robotic agents playing different roles, such as apprentice, teacher, companion, assistant or even as a character in the story [28,35,37,39,60] in children's learning outcomes.

However, to the best of our knowledge, there is a lack of easy-to-use digital tools using virtual characters to exercise younger children's (at a primary level of education) skills and knowledge about local species of animals and plants in a classroom context.

The existing tools, for instance, [49,58,62,69], although promising, focus primarily on teenage children and adults and are limited in the kind of experience they provide, see Table 1.

Based on these advantages, we decided to use the storytelling strategy to support children learn about biodiversity. The story is told through a virtual robotic agent, thus providing more interactivity, attractiveness, and engagement.

Table 1. Comparison of literature work and our work, with PA and VA meaning Physical and Virtual Agent.

Age Groups	Studies	Sample Characteristics	Activity & Agent	Goal Objectives	Limitations
Preschooler (3–5)	[28]	N = 10 (3–3.6) 5 females 5 males	Storytelling PA	Teach new concepts using prerecorded stories; Tool for constructive learning.	Small Sample
	[35]	N = 20 (4–6)	Storytelling Game PA	Language education; New vocabulary words	Wizard is needed
Middle Childhood (6–11)	[24]	Young children	Interactive Story PA	Education in biodiversity	Hypothetical scenario; Black and white scenarios mislead to errors.
	[25]	N = 105 (6–10) 49 females 56 males	Digital educational tools Storytelling (multimedia application) VA		
	[39]	N = 34 (10)	Interactive narratives PA	Learn second language; English Materials in language learning; Expand vocabulary; Single vs group interactions of children.	Robot movements are limited; No cooperation with child and robot; Teacher controls the robot; Conditions might have been benefited by the interaction with 2 robots.
	[60]	N = 20	Storytelling Tool PA and VA		
	[37]	N = 40 (6–8) 22 females 18 males	Interactive stories PA		
Young Teens (12–14)	[3]	N = 52 (13–14) 19 females 33 males	Serious games PA	Sustainable, eco-friendly attitudes	Predominant male sample.
	[41]	N = 44 (12)	Digital educational tools VA	Teach foreign language vocabulary	Agent was not intelligent; No interaction among user and agent;
	[30]	N = 23 13 females 10 males	Digital educational tools VA	Learning Algebra	One-on-one and/or group interviews.
Teenagers (15–17)	[36]	N = 165 (15–18) 57% females 43% males	Mobile-learning digital app –	Botanics	Unbalanced conditions, (102 indoor and 63 outdoor).
	[15]	N = 13 (15–17)	Co-design Games –	Prototype of game and story plots	Games visualisation can lead to user to disengage with the physical exhibit of the museum.
	[16]	Teenagers	Mobile interactive technologies and Digital storytelling VA	Seals Endangered species	Description of the storyfied game and gamified story.
	[45]	Players Students	Role-playing game VA	Education and conservation of biodiversity; Information about UNESCO protected forest; Raise awareness; Video interviews about nature and biodiversity preservation; Local environment to assess their problems and propose solutions.	Unclear what age group the tool is proposed to; Experience prototype; Sample had predominant domain expert players; Targets tourists users; Tool for teacher; Difficulties on editing process in 60% of the participants;
Adults (>18)	[38]	N = 14 (21–30) 7 females 7 males	Game –	Learn a new language.	Researchers had to use Wizard of OZ when there were system errors.
	[69] [11]	N = 10	Serious games VA		
	[22]	N = 11 (25–50)	Transmedia story –		
	[48]	N = 12 (23–88)	Platform (web and mobile)		
	[52]	N = 155	Collaborative digital storytelling PA and VA		
	[1]	N = 55 (18–29) 21 females 34 males	Role-playing game PA versus VA		
Middle Childhood (6–11)	Our work	N = 83 (6–10) 45 females 38 males	Digital educational tool and Storytelling (multimedia application) VA	Education in local and non-local biodiversity.	Sample size unbalanced; One geographic location.

3   Goal and Hypotheses

This study aimed to test the effectiveness of our tool as well as to understand how children's performance and engagement would be affected when they interacted with: a storytelling scenario, a virtual agent with and without embodiment, their familiarity and their existing experience with biodiversity. To achieve these purposes, we designed a study with young children around an agent-driven interactive storytelling application and tested the following hypotheses:

– **H1** - When comparing an agent telling a story with an agent not telling a story, children will have: a) higher performance and b) higher engagement.
– **H2** - When comparing an agent that mediates the interaction instead of a non-present agent (narrator), children will have: a) higher performance and b) higher engagement.
– **H3** - When comparing learning about familiar biodiversity with unfamiliar biodiversity, children will have: a) higher performance and b) higher engagement.
– **H4** - Children with some existing experience with biodiversity (3rd and 4th school years) will be able to correctly identify elements of biodiversity more frequently when compared with younger children with less or no experience with biodiversity (1st and 2nd school years).

4   Research Methods

To validate our hypotheses, we conducted a between-subjects study with children who interacted with a virtual agent through an interactive scenario. In this study, the presence or absence of the embodiment of a robotic agent (virtual model of a Pepper robot), the narrative plot (present vs absent), and the type of biodiversity (local vs foreign) were manipulated. Also, information about the children's school year, geographic location and their performance in a biodiversity identification task were collected.

4.1   Sample

A convenient sample of eighty-three children enrolled in elementary school in a city in southern Brazil participated in our study. Children's age ranged from 6 to 10 years old, and our sample had 45 girls and 38 boys. Participants were randomly assigned to one of the conditions based on the following between-subjects design: 2 (Embodiment: virtual agent vs narrator) x 2 (Story: present vs non-present) × 2 (type of Biodiversity: local vs foreign), see Table 2.

4.2   Procedure

Children were recruited from a public school, and the data collection occurred during regular daily classes over multiple days. Before the experiment began,

Table 2. Children's school year and gender distribution by the type of biodiversity seen and interacted condition.

Biodiversity type	Condition	School year				Gender		Total
		1	2	3	4	Male	Female	
Local	Robot and Story	4	2	1	2	4	5	9
	Robot and No Story	2	3	0	2	2	5	7
	No robot and Story	1	3	5	2	4	7	11
	No Robot and No Story	1	5	2	3	4	7	11
	Total	8	13	8	9	14	24	38
Foreign	Robot and Story	2	1	2	6	9	2	11
	Robot and No Story	4	2	3	5	6	8	14
	No robot and Story	4	3	1	3	6	5	11
	No Robot and No Story	3	1	0	5	3	6	9
	Total	13	7	6	19	24	21	45
Total	Robot and Story	6	3	3	8	13	7	20
	Robot and No Story	6	5	3	7	8	13	21
	No robot and Story	5	6	6	5	10	12	22
	No Robot and No Story	4	6	2	8	7	13	20
	Total	21	20	14	28	38	45	**83**

we collected the parents, the university Ethical Commission and the Secretary of Education from Horiziontina city approvals. Children interacted with the developed scenario using the school's computers. They were told to engage in a dynamic science class to learn and teach an agent about biodiversity. The activity took approximately 25 min to complete and followed the flow described in Fig. 1.

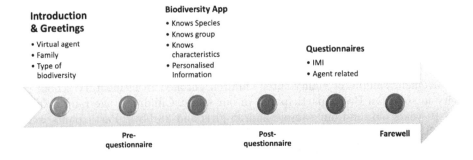

Fig. 1. Procedure flow performed.

At first, the virtual agent (named *Flor*; meaning Flower) introduces itself. In the embodied condition, the agent starts by describing that in the year 3000, families have a robot or virtual assistant to help them in their tasks. In the voice-only condition, the child is informed that the application was developed to learn about her surroundings. Afterwards, the child is asked to indicate their name, gender, school year, and geographic area.

Then, *Flor* introduces John, a young boy and his family who are planning to take a walk around nature. Conversely, the non-storytelling system, *Flor* informs the children's that they will take a virtual walk around nature to learn more about it. After this, *Flor* questions the child about what is a *trilha* (Brazilian expression for hiking); and then proceeds to explain what it is.

Fig. 2. Scenario replica with white representing the path's beginning and end, yellow birds, blue flowers and mammals, orange invertebrates, green trees, and pink the repeated species placements.

Next, the forest environment is introduced, see Fig. 2, with the characters (family and/or agent) at the beginning of the path. At this stage, *Flor* informs the children that the path is full of proximity sensors that trigger information about the surrounding species.

Before starting the adventure, the agent requests the children to tell her what they know about biodiversity (pre-questionnaire with four questions about species and one about liking nature, based on a 5-point emoticon scale [53]). Regarding the species-related questions, we asked children to identify the veracity (true, false, or do not know) of information related to the species that they would later see in the application.

At this point, children received a first badge for their accomplishment within the application (Fig. 3). Then exploration starts (with or without the storytelling) until children reach the first sensor marking the presence of a bird, (Fig. 2 yellow path). The camera circles the bird showing its 3D representation. After, the agent asks the children if:

a) They know the species (showing them a picture of the species in its natural environment) see Fig. 4 b). If children know the species, the agent asks them to recognise their name from a list of four options. Otherwise, it will tell them the answer;

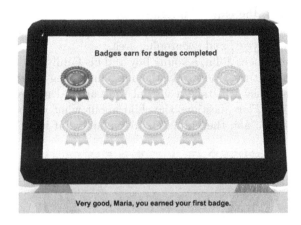

Fig. 3. Badges screen presented to children.

b) If children know the group that the specie belongs to; the child can choose from a list of eight icons;
c) From a list of eight options, children can identify the species' characteristics (physical features, food, need to live and habitat).

 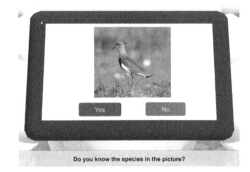

(a) 3D species.   (b) Picture in natural environment.

Fig. 4. Children's visualisation of a species, with a 3D model and its picture in a natural environment.

This interaction follows the same approach as in [25] with children encountering four different species of flora and fauna, complemented with scientific information; one of the four species children have encountered is repeated (explained in Sect. 4.4). After children report on their knowledge about the species, the application shows again the 3D model of that species and *Flor* shares the specie's further details (see Fig. 5 for an example). Children will then receive a second badge for completing another level. The path progresses encountering the following species represented in blue, orange, green and pink from Fig. 2, probing the children's knowledge and sharing more information about the species and assigning additional badges as they progress.

Did you know that the Parrot Charão is a species that is distributed over a wide area, mainly in the northeast, center and southeast of Rio Grande do Sul.

Fig. 5. Children's visualisation of a 3D Bird while receiving more information about it.

The walk ends up at the starting point. Here, children fill in a post-questionnaire (the same questions as in the pre-questionnaire, but in reverse order), the Intrinsic Motivation Inventory (IMI) [55,56] and the Robotic Social Attributes Scale (RoSAS) [14] questionnaires, with badges earned in between questionnaires. Afterwards, the characters and the agent will say goodbye, and the game ends.

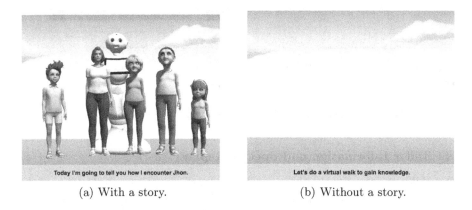

Today I'm going to tell you how I encounter Jhon.	Let's do a virtual walk to gain knowledge.
(a) With a story.	(b) Without a story.

Fig. 6. Children's interaction with the application in the introduction phase.

4.3   Application

A Unity application was developed with a natural scenario as the central theme and run in a WebGL environment. This application included several characters, a 3D model of the Pepper robot, five persons (adults and children) and the 3D models of all species to be studied. The individuals were created using the Daz 3D studio software [21], see Fig. 6 a) for illustration. The remaining characters, robot and species, were all obtained from websites that contain free 3D models (e.g., [13,17,27,31,68]). In some situations, we had to adapt the species models (e.g., changing colours and size) to make them as similar as possible to the species we chose to use in the study.

Besides including characters, we have also used several free and paid plugins to customise a 3D environment where we could generate our forest and meadow [59] (Fig. 2 shows a preview of the general scenario), and text-to-speech [20] and WebGL Speech [65] solution to give a voice to the virtual agent.

With the tools used, we could customise our application to include plants, trees, bushes and water areas to simulate a scenario for learning about biodiversity. In addition, it allowed us to have scenes narrated more naturally regardless of the embedded agent (virtual robot or only narrator, see Fig. 7). Along with these customisation's, we added subtitles of everything the agent said and visual cues to enhance clarity and help children better comprehend the task.

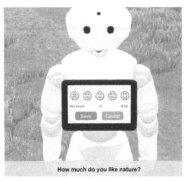
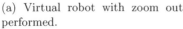

(a) Virtual robot with zoom out performed.

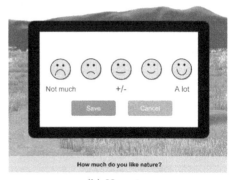

(b) Narrator.

Fig. 7. Children's interaction with the virtual agent conditions.

4.4 Tailor Information and Species Replay

After children answered the three questions regarding their understanding of the encountered species, they would see the specie 3D representation and receive tailored information according to their performance. The performance is determined based on the calculation presented in the work of [25] that considers the answers given for the three questions and the proportion of characteristics for each species the children saw. Furthermore, in [25] the performance was categorised on three levels, and we kept the personalisation of information in the same range. In the first level, children received information about where they could find that species and their habitat (this information is later asked in the post-questionnaire). In the second level, children received details about physical characteristics, like the size of certain parts of the species' body and differences among males and females species, among others. Lastly, in the third level, children were shown curiosities about each specie. All children reach at least level one; however, they can choose to either see more information about the encountered species or continue with the scenario. This process is reiterated for each species until the children see all three levels of personalised information or choose to continue.

In [25], the authors observed how children's feelings changing (e.g., sad to happy) according to the virtual agent telling them their answers were correct or incorrect. We explored this behaviour by randomly repeating one of the species from the four they have seen towards the end of the path. Our goal was to: a) boost children's motivation, especially those that did not have a good knowledge of species and b) understand how much attention they were paying to the information being conveyed (not analysed in the scope of this paper).

4.5 Measures

We have calculated the following composite variables based on the data collected through the interaction with the application:

- The performance that children had using the application;
- Children's engagement;
- Children's existing experience;
- Children's familiarity with biodiversity;
- Agent type of embodiment;
- The correct and incorrect answers in the pre and post-questionnaires;
- The differences in the answers given between pre and post-questionnaires for all questions.

We computed children's performances based on the data collected with the application following the guidelines of [25]. Since children's performance was computed iteratively by recalculating or updating the data each time they saw a new species with data from that species, we focused on the performance after children had seen the four different species and when they saw one repeated species. Several researchers have analysed performance differences among assessments of a task to understand if an activity is effective or not, for instance, [63]. First, we computed the differences between seeing a repeated species and without a repeating species. Afterwards, a sign test with continuity correction was conducted to determine the effect of children's performance when they saw four species without repetitions and one repeated species. Our data reveal a statistically significant median increase in performance scores (.014) when children saw one repeated species (.287) when compared with when they did not repeated species (.270), $z = -4.536$, $p < .001$. Given this outcome, we will consider the performance (PF) when children did not repeat species (PF_NRS) and when they repeated one species (PF_RS).

Children's engagement was assessed based on their answers to the IMI questionnaire by following the guidelines of [55].

Children's previous experience was evaluated based on Piaget's theory of cognitive development, which remarks that young children ($4 - 7$ years) still have immature reasoning [51]. Given this outcome, we focus on the school year that generally connects with the children's age to perform the split among older and younger children. This way, older children with ages around $8 - 10$ (3rd and 4th school years) were classified as having high previous experience. While younger ones, $6 - 7$ years old (1st and 2nd school years), were classified as having low previous experience.

The correct and incorrect answers to the questions from the pre and post-questionnaires were assessed based on the veracity of the statements for each species. First, children that replied "*I do not know*" regardless of the question were categorised as having an incorrect answer. Secondly, children that replied "*True*" and the correct answer was true, or that replied "*False*", and the correct answer was false, were classified as correct; otherwise, they were classified as incorrect.

The differences among pre and post-questionnaires for the species questions were made according to each question's correct and incorrect veracity described above. Children with correct or incorrect answers in both questionnaires for the same question were classified as "*Maintain answer*". Those children that had a correct answer in the pre-questionnaires but then had an incorrect one in the Post-questionnaire were classified as "*Pre correct and Post incorrect*". Lastly, those with correct answers in the Post-questionnaire and incorrect in the Pre-questionnaires were classified as "*Pre incorrect and Post correct*". At the same time, the question about children liking nature was classified similarly to the one done for the species; instead of correct and incorrect, we analysed if their scores were higher, lower, or the same among the questionnaires. This way, we classify children's answers as "*Maintain answer*"; "*Pre higher and Post lower*", and "*Pre lower and Post higher*".

5   Data Analysis

The data was analysed with the SPSS (v.28) program. We performed a Shapiro-Wilk test to assess the normality of the variables considered in our analysis. Since our data did not conform with a normal distribution, with p-values $< .001$, we used non-parametric tests to evaluate our assumptions.

6   Results

6.1   H1 - Storytelling

Performance: A Kruskal-Wallis H test was run to determine if there were differences in the performance score between four groups of participants, namely, those that saw: the "robot and story" ($n = 20$), "robot and no story" ($n = 21$), "no robot and story" ($n = 22$) and "no robot and no story" ($n = 20$). Table 3 presents the aforementioned distributions per type of biodiversity.

The mean ranks (MR) of PF_NRS scores, increased from the condition with no robot and no story (49.10), to robot and story (45.95), to no robot and story (37.14), to robot and no story (36.57), but the differences were not statistically significant, $\chi^2(3) = 4.233$, $p = .237$. Likewise, the MR of PF_RS scores, increased from the condition no robot and no story (45.93), to robot and story (44.40), to robot and no story (39.64.), to no robot and story (38.50), but the differences were not statistically significant ($\chi^2(3) = 1.393$, $p = .707$).

Table 3. Distribution of type of biodiversity per condition for performance (PF_NRS and PF_RS).

Biodiversity Type	Condition	PF_NRS			PF_RS		
		Mean	Min.	Max.	Mean	Min.	Max.
Local	Robot and Story	.38	.22	.57	.43	.20	.68
	Robot and No Story	.26	.23	.32	.31	.23	.51
	No robot and Story	.33	.20	.57	.40	.23	.63
	No Robot and No Story	.33	.18	.71	.38	.20	.78
	Total	.33	.18	.71	.38	.20	.78
Non-Local	Robot and Story	.34	.18	.66	.36	.18	.69
	Robot and No Story	.31	.22	.74	.35	.21	.81
	No robot and Story	.24	.18	.29	.26	.20	.31
	No Robot and No Story	.42	.26	.71	.46	.23	.77
	Total	.32	.18	.74	.35	.18	.81
Total	Robot and Story	.36	.18	.66	.39	.18	.69
	Robot and No Story	.30	.22	.74	.34	.21	.81
	No robot and Story	.29	.18	.57	.33	.20	.63
	No Robot and No Story	.37	.18	.71	.42	.20	.78
	Total	.33	.18	.74	.37	.18	.81

Engagement: We performed a Kruskal-Wallis H test to analyse the differences among each condition where we manipulated the agent embodiment and its ability to tell a story (or not) with children's engagement. Our results reveal that the MR distribution of engagement scores was not statistically significantly different between groups ($\chi^2(3) = 962$, $p = .810$), with engagement scores, increasing from the condition no robot and story (46.00, $n = 22$), to no robot and no story (41.58, $n = 20$), to robot and no story (41.02, $n = 21$), to robot and story (39.05, $n = 20$).

6.2   H2 - Agent Embodiment

Performance: We conducted a Mann-Whitney test to examine the differences between agent embodiment and children's performance. In Table 4 we report the performance scores distribution by the agent embodiment type. Our results did not reveal statistically significant differences ($U = 826.000$, $z = -.319$, $p = .750$) in the PF_NRS scores, for the virtual agent (MR = 41.15) and the narrator (MR = 42.83). Similarly, there were no statistical significant differences ($U = 859.500$, $z = -.014$, $p = .989$) in the PF_RS scores, for the virtual agent (MR = 41.96) and the narrator (MR = 42.04).

Table 4. Distribution of type of biodiversity per agent embodiment for children's performance (PF_NRS and PF_RS).

Biodiversity Type	Agent Embodiment	PF_NRS			PF_RS		
		Mean	Min.	Max.	Mean	Min.	Max.
Local	Virtual Agent	.33	.22	.57	.38	.20	.68
	Narrator	.33	.18	.71	.39	.20	.78
	Total	.33	.18	.71	.38	.20	.78
Non-Local	Virtual Agent	.33	.18	.74	.35	.18	.81
	Narrator	.32	.18	.71	.35	.20	.77
	Total	.32	.18	.74	.35	.18	.81
Total	Virtual Agent	.33	.18	.74	.36	.18	.81
	Narrator	.33	.18	.71	.37	.20	.78
	Total	.33	.18	.74	.37	.18	.81

Engagement: Our assessment of children's engagement while interacting with a virtual agent and a narrator did not reveal significant differences while performing a Mann-Whitney U test ($U = 781.500$, $z = -.730$ $p = .465$). Our data also unveils that the MR of engagement scores were higher when children interacted with a narrator (43.89) than with the virtual agent (40.06).

6.3 H3 - Biodiversity Familiarity

Performance: A Mann-Whitney U test was used to assess differences in children's performance while identifying familiar and non-familiar biodiversity, see Table 5 for more details.

Our findings did not uncover a statistically significant difference among children's PF_NRS ($U = 728$, $z = -1.161$, $p = .246$) and PF_RS ($U = 714$, $z = -1.289$, $p = .197$), among familiar ($n = 38$) and non-familiar ($n = 45$) biodiversity. Plus, the MR distributions of PF_NRS and PF_RS revealed that familiarity with biodiversity was higher in both situations (45.34 and 45.71 respectively) than in non-familiarity with biodiversity (39.18 and 38.87 respectively).

Table 5. Distribution of biodiversity familiarity for children's performance (PF_NRS and PF_RS).

Biodiversity Familiarity	PF_NRS			PF_RS		
	Mean	Min.	Max.	Mean	Min.	Max.
Familiar	.33	.18	.71	.38	.20	.78
Non-Familiar	.32	.18	.74	.35	.18	.81
Total	.33	.18	.74	.37	.18	.81

Engagement: A Mann-Whitney U test was performed to uncover differences in children's engagement and familiarity with biodiversity. Overall the test revealed that the engagement scores for familiar biodiversity (MR = 47.93) were significantly higher compared with non-familiar (MR = 36.99) biodiversity ($U = 629.500$, $z = -2.078$, $p = .038$).

6.4   H4 - Previous Experience

After performing a Mann-Whitney U test, our results revealed significant differences for children with high existing experience ($MR_{PF\_NRS} = 48.42$, $MR_{PF\_RS} = 49.49$) being able to correctly identify the biodiversity elements more than those with low existing experience ($MR_{PF\_NRS} = 35.43$, $MR_{PF\_RS} = 34.33$), ($U = 1452.500$, $z = -2.445$ $p = .014$, and $U = 1407.500$, $z = -2.865$ $p = .004$ for PF_NRS and PF_RS respectively). In Table 6 we report the distribution of the aforementioned variables.

Table 6. Distribution of the type of biodiversity, existing experience and children's performance (PF_NRS and PF_RS).

Biodiversity type	Existing experience	PF_NRS			PF_RS		
		Mean	Min.	Max.	Mean	Min.	Max.
Local	Low	.29	.18	.48	.31	.20	.60
	High	.38	.21	.71	.47	.24	.78
	Total	.33	.18	.71	.38	.20	.78
Non-Local	Low	.26	.18	.57	.29	.18	.69
	High	.37	.20	.74	.40	.20	.81
	Total	.32	.18	.74	.35	.18	.81
Total	Low	.28	.18	.57	.30	.18	.69
	High	.38	.20	.74	.43	.20	.81
	Total	.33	.18	.74	.37	.18	.81

6.5   Pre and Post-questionnaires

A McNemar's test with continuity correction was run to determine if there was a difference in the proportion of children's knowledge between the pre and post-questionnaires. In Table 7, we report the differences among each question as well as their corresponding test result. Overall our data revealed that children, after interacting with the application:

- increased their number of correct answers after seeing a Bird, $\chi^2(1) = 7.26$, $p = .007$.
- increased their number of wrong answers after seeing a Flower or Mammal, $p = .648$.
- increased their number of wrong answers after seeing an Invertebrate, $p = 1.000$.
- increased their number of correct answers after seeing a Tree, $\chi^2(1) = 4.45$, $p = .035$.

Table 7. McNemar's test results for the pre and post-questionnaires, with **I** and **C** meaning incorrect and correct answers, respectively, **(a)** meaning binomial distribution used, and * significant results.

Question		Pre	Post		Chi-Square	Asymp. Sig.
			I	C		
1	I		10	21	7.23	**.007***
Birds	C		6	46		
2	I		56	8	–	.648 (a)
Flowers & Mammals	C		11	8		
3	I		59	10	–	1.000 (a)
Invertebrates	C		9	5		
4	I		12	26	4.45	**.035***
Trees	C		12	33		

A Wilcoxon signed-rank test was conducted to determine the effect that interaction with our application had on children liking of nature by comparing their pre and post-scores. However, our results did not demonstrate a statistically significant median change (0) in children liking nature when comparing their scores on the pre (5) and post-questionnaire (5), $z = -.762$, $p = .446$.

6.6   Children's Assessment of the Virtual Agent (Robot and Narrator)

Figure 8 shows children's answers for each of the four conditions manipulated in our study (embodiment and story presence) when children answered the question

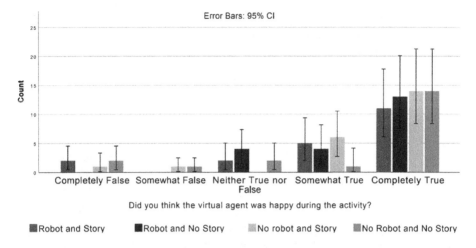

Fig. 8. Children's assessment if the agent was happy during the activity.

about the agent's happiness during the activity. Our results revealed that 62.7% ($n = 52$) of the children reported that the agent seemed happy during the interaction.

When questioned about how clearly the agent communicated throughout the activity, 65.1% agreed (completely true, $n = 54$) that the agent communicated clearly, see Fig. 9.

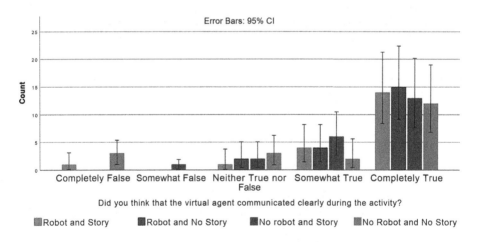

Fig. 9. Children's assessment if the agent communicated clearly during the activity.

When questioned about how well the agent responded during the activity, see Fig. 10, 73.5% of the children reported that they agreed (completely true, $n = 61$) with the statement.

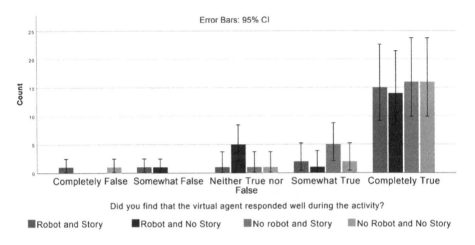

Fig. 10. Children's assessment if the agent responded well during the activity.

6.7   Correlations

In order to understand if there was any association between engagement and children's performance (PF_NRS and PF_RS) scores, we performed a Spearman's rank-order correlation, see Table 8. Our data reveal that there was a statistically significant strong positive correlation between PF_NRS and PF_RS scores, $r_s(81) = .860$, $p < .001$.

Table 8. Spearman's rank-order correlation results for the engagement and performance (PF_NRS and PF_RS) scores, with * meaning significant results at 0.01 level.

		Engagement	PF_NRS	PF_RS
Engagement	Correlation Coefficient	1.000	.143	.043
	Sig. (2-tailed)		.198	.702
	N	83	83	83
PF_NRS	Correlation Coefficient	.143	1.000	**.860****
	Sig. (2-tailed)	.198		<.001
	N	83	83	83
PF_RS	Correlation Coefficient	.043	**.860****	1.000
	Sig. (2-tailed)	.702	<.001	
	N	83	83	83

7   Discussion

In this work, we investigate if children's performances and/or engagement with nature and biodiversity were influenced by the storytelling activity, the story-teller agent's embodiment, children's familiarity and their existing experience with biodiversity. To achieve these goals, we have proposed four hypotheses, and through a user study, we found evidence to validate **H3b** and **H4**.

In **H1** we predicted that interacting with a storyteller agent (vs. a voice-only narrator) would help children perform better in the species identification activity (**H1a**) and be more engaged (**H1b**) with it. We did not find evidence to support this hypothesis with children's performance being relatively stable across conditions.

Interestingly, the condition where the information is presented without the virtual robot intervention and no storytelling shows slightly better results (mean .37 and .42 without and with repeated species) among all conditions. However, these results are almost identical to the ones observed in the condition in which children interacted with a virtual robot and a story (mean .36 and .39 without and with repeated species). Moreover, children's engagement was generally higher for all conditions, with a mean of 4.01 out of 5 (ceiling effect). On the one hand, the results can be influenced by the novelty effect of the application, versus children's day-to-day traditional activities. This alone can generate enthusiasm and engagement. On the other hand, maybe our application sensorially overloaded children, with the amount of visuals and information delivered for each species? Is using four different species belonging to different groups too much variation? Or is the number of details provided in the tailored information excessive? Researchers have found that heavy cognitive load can negatively affect [12] or create some interference in tasks [33]. We need further investigation to understand if the influencing factors mentioned above contributed to our results, and if yes to what extent.

We have also predicted in **H2** that the presence of agent embodiment would contribute to improved performance (**H2a**) and greater engagement (**H2b**) in the activity when compared with a narrator (voice-only), which was not confirmed. The performance exhibited by our participants exposed identical results while interacting with a virtual agent (ceiling effect). Our findings align with the work of [34] that argues about the novelty effect of the agent embodiment causing a generalised excitement of children while making them pay more attention to the activity, which could reduce any potential differences in performance across conditions.

The engagement scores unveiled a similar effect as the performance, with mean scores of 4.02 for the virtual agent and 4.01 in the narrator conditions out of a maximum of 5 (ceiling effect). These results seem to align with the work of [19] that analysed the effects of a storyteller agent with different embodiment (human voice, virtual agent and robot), which revealed higher engagement of participants towards the end of the story. However, given their experimental design, the authors could not infer which agent was a more effective storyteller.

Our findings regarding the agent embodiment seem to be coherent with the results obtained with H1, highlighting the need to expose children to multiple interactions to understand whether the novelty effect influences the tasks or not. Several authors have argued that exposing children for longer periods of time to a task has helped to decrease the novelty effect (e.g., [54]).

Our results partially support **H3** as children's engagement (**H3b**) was revealed to be associated with their familiarity with biodiversity. However, the same relationship was not found regarding children's performance (**H3a**). Children that interacted with familiar biodiversity had significantly higher engagement scores (mean of 4.18 out of 5) than those who saw non-familiar (mean of 3.88 out of 5) biodiversity. At the same time, children's performances when exposed to familiar and non-familiar biodiversity were similar. These findings can result from the similarities among animals and plants, which are hard to identify visually, even for experts in biodiversity. They argue that *"the determination of plant species from field observation requires substantial botanical expertise, which puts it beyond the reach of most nature enthusiasts"* [70]. This effect could have been exacerbated by children's naive awareness or lack of exposure to biodiversity. Results from the pre and post-questionnaires assessment hint in that direction, where children demonstrated a better understanding of species before engaging with our activity. Particularly when answering questions regarding flowers or mammals ($n_{pre} = 11$, $n_{pos} = 8$) and invertebrates ($n_{pre} = 9$, $n_{pos} = 5$) but not for birds ($n_{pre} = 6$, $n_{pos} = 46$) and trees ($n_{pre} = 12$, $n_{pos} = 33$).

The results gathered with our system highlight the need to educate children about certain species more than others, as is the case of mammals, flowers and invertebrates. In research studies, teaching children about birds and tree elements is more common (e.g., [6,42]).

In **H4**, we predicted that children with existing experience with biodiversity would be able to perform better in our activity. Our results supported this hypothesis as children with more experience with biodiversity (3rd and 4th school years) performed significantly better than those with less experience (1st and 2nd school years) with biodiversity. This result seems to be coherent with prior findings as described by [8] that uncovered a tendency in which older children remembered more easily of the moment they learned something than younger children.

8   Conclusion

Promoting children's knowledge about nature and how the world is interconnected has become an essential subject given the climate change crisis and biodiversity losses the planet is suffering. For this purpose, we can take advantage of storytelling combined with Human-Computer Interaction and Human-Robot Interaction, which have positive influences on children's education [44,46,61,66]. Our work presents the design and the results from the study of a learning application combining Virtual Agent and storytelling activity to help children comprehend their environment and its biodiversity. We have compared the agent embodiment, the presence of storytelling, and children's familiarity and experience with biodiversity to children's performance and engagement with the application. The results show that children familiar with biodiversity were more engaged with our system, and those with higher biodiversity experience performed better.

Our limitations with this study are the small sample size and the restriction to only one geographic location. On the one hand, our data revealed a balanced number of children in our main conditions (e.g., embodiment x story presence); however, when analysing the distribution of children per school year, the numbers are significantly unbalanced. This fact might have biased the main findings here reported. On the other hand, having just one geographic location does not allow us fair comparisons of differences among measures. In the future, exploring other geographic locations and having a more balanced distribution of children by school year per condition would be essential.

Our final argument is that learning about biodiversity should not be grounded only on local biodiversity experiences and knowledge. It is paramount to use innovative, attractive and interactive strategies that allow children to acquire knowledge of global biodiversity and learn to preserve it for their own and future generations.

References

1. Ali, H., et al.: Virtual or physical? social robots teaching a fictional language through a role-playing game inspired by *Game of Thrones*. In: Salichs, M.A., Ge, S.S., Barakova, E.I., Cabibihan, J.-J., Wagner, A.R., Castro-González, Á., He, H. (eds.) ICSR 2019. LNCS (LNAI), vol. 11876, pp. 358–367. Springer, Cham (2019). https://doi.org/10.1007/978-3-030-35888-4_33
2. Alves-Oliveira, P., Arriaga, P., Paiva, A., Hoffman, G.: YOLO - Your own living object. In: ACM/IEEE International Conference on Human-Robot Interaction, p. 638. IEEE Computer Society, March 2020. https://doi.org/10.1145/3371382.3378395
3. Alves-Oliveira, P., Sequeira, P., Paiva, A.: The role that an educational robot plays. In: 2016 25th IEEE International Symposium on Robot and Human Interactive Communication (RO-MAN), pp. 817–822. IEEE (2016)
4. Angel-Fernandez, J.M., Vincze, M.: Introducing storytelling to educational robotic activities. In: IEEE Global Engineering Education Conference, EDUCON. vol. 2018-April, pp. 608–615. IEEE Computer Society, May 2018. https://doi.org/10.1109/EDUCON.2018.8363286
5. Atta-Alla, M.N.: Integrating language skills through storytelling. Engl. Lang. Teach. **5**(12), 1 (2012)
6. Bartoszeck, A.B., Vandrovieski, W., Tratch, V., Czelusniak, F., Tunnicliffe, S.D.: What do Brazilian school children know about birds in their country. Eur. J. Educ. Res. **7**(3), 485–499 (2018). https://doi.org/10.12973/eu-jer.7.3.485. http://www.eu-jer.com/
7. Belpaeme, T., Kennedy, J., Ramachandran, A., Scassellati, B., Tanaka, F.: Social robots for education: a review. Sci. Robot. **3**, 5954 (2018). https://doi.org/10.1126/scirobotics.aat5954. http://robotics.sciencemag.org/

8. Bemis, R.H., Leichtman, M.D., Pillemer, D.B.: 'i remember when i learned that!'developmental and gender differences in children's memories of learning episodes. Infant Child Dev. **20**(4), 387–399 (2011)

9. Bevelander, K.E., Anschütz, D.J., Engels, R.C.: The effect of a fictitious peer on young children's choice of familiar v. unfamiliar low- and high-energy-dense foods. British J. Nutrition **108**, 1126–1133 (2012). https://doi.org/10.1017/S0007114511006374.   https://www.cambridge.org/core/journals/british-journal-of-nutrition/article/effect-of-a-fictitious-peer-on-young-childrens-choice-of-familiar-v-unfamiliar-low-and-highenergydense-foods/F75A926E6EAB1D0EF160FD2C72CB2DB3

10. Ángela Bravo Sánchez, F., Correal, A.M.G., Guerrero, E.G.: Interactive drama with robots for teaching non-technical subjects. J. Hum.-Robot Interact. **6**, 48 (2017). https://doi.org/10.5898/JHRI.6.2.Bravo. http://humanrobotinteraction.org/journal/index.php/HRI/article/view/317

11. Briot, J.P., et al.: A serious game and artificial agents to support intercultural participatory management of protected areas for biodiversity conservation and social inclusion. In: 2011 Second International Conference on Culture and Computing, pp. 15–20. IEEE (2011)

12. Paas, F.G.W.C., Van Merriënboer, J. J. G.: Instructional control of cognitive load in the training of complex cognitive tasks. Educ. Psychol. Rev. **6**(4), 351–371 (1994). https://www.jstor.org/stable/23359294

13. CadNav: 3d models & 3d objects free download - cadnav (2022). https://www.cadnav.com/3d-models/

14. Carpinella, C.M., Wyman, A.B., Perez, M.A., Stroessner, S.J.: The Robotic Social Attributes Scale (RoSAS): development and validation. In: ACM/IEEE International Conference on Human-Robot Interaction. vol. Part F127194, pp. 254–262. IEEE Computer Society, New York, March 2017. https://doi.org/10.1145/2909824.3020208

15. Cesário, V., Coelho, A., Nisi, V.: Co-designing gaming experiences for museums with teenagers. In: Brooks, A.L., Brooks, E., Sylla, C. (eds.) ArtsIT/DLI -2018. LNICST, vol. 265, pp. 38–47. Springer, Cham (2019). https://doi.org/10.1007/978-3-030-06134-0_5

16. Cesário, V., Olim, S., Nisi, V.: A natural history museum experience: memories of carvalhal's palace – turning point. In: Bosser, A.-G., Millard, D.E., Hargood, C. (eds.) ICIDS 2020. LNCS, vol. 12497, pp. 339–343. Springer, Cham (2020). https://doi.org/10.1007/978-3-030-62516-0_31

17. CGTrader: Free 3d models | cgtrader (2022). https://www.cgtrader.com/free-3d-models

18. Choo, Y.B., Abdullah, T., Nawi, A.M.: Digital storytelling vs. oral storytelling: an analysis of the art of telling stories now and then. Universal J. Educ. Res. **8**(5A), 46–50 (2020)

19. Costa, S., Brunete, A., Bae, B.C., Mavridis, N.: Emotional storytelling using virtual and robotic agents. 15, June 2018. https://doi.org/10.1142/S0219843618500068

20. Crosstales_LLC: Home - your partner for video interactive solutions, games and unity assets | crosstales (2022). https://www.crosstales.com/en/

21. Daz_Productions_Inc: Daz 3d–3d models and 3d software | daz 3d (2022). https://www.daz3d.com/

22. Dionisio, M., Nisi, V., Nunes, N., Bala, P.: Transmedia storytelling for exposing natural capital and promoting ecotourism. In: Nack, F., Gordon, A.S. (eds.) ICIDS 2016. LNCS, vol. 10045, pp. 351–362. Springer, Cham (2016). https://doi.org/10.1007/978-3-319-48279-8_31

23. Encarnação, P., Alvarez, L., Rios, A., Maya, C., Adams, K., Cook, A.: Using virtual robot-mediated play activities to assess cognitive skills. Disabil. Rehabil. Assist. Technol. **9**(3), 231–241 (2014)
24. Ferreira, M.J., Nisi, V., Melo, F., Paiva, A.: Learning and teaching biodiversity through a storyteller robot. In: Nunes, N., Oakley, I., Nisi, V. (eds.) ICIDS 2017. LNCS, vol. 10690, pp. 367–371. Springer, Cham (2017). https://doi.org/10.1007/978-3-319-71027-3_45
25. Ferreira, M.J., Oliveira, R., Olim, S.C., Nisi, V., Paiva, A.: Let's learn biodiversity with a virtual "robot"? In: Wagner, A.R., Feil-Seifer, D., Haring, K.S., Rossi, S., Williams, T., He, H., Sam Ge, S. (eds.) ICSR 2020. LNCS (LNAI), vol. 12483, pp. 194–206. Springer, Cham (2020). https://doi.org/10.1007/978-3-030-62056-1_17
26. Fletcher, K.L., Reese, E.: Picture book reading with young children: a conceptual framework. Dev. Rev. **25**(1), 64–103 (2005). https://doi.org/10.1016/j.dr.2004.08.009
27. Free3D: Free 3d models download - free3d (2022). https://free3d.com/3d-models/
28. Fridin, M.: Storytelling by a kindergarten social assistive robot: a tool for constructive learning in preschool education. Comput. Educ. **70**(Suppl. C), 53–64 (2014). https://doi.org/10.1016/j.compedu.2013.07.043. http://www.sciencedirect.com/science/article/pii/S036013151300225X
29. Garzotto, F., Paolini, P., Sabiescu, A.: Interactive storytelling for children. In: Proceedings of the 9th International Conference on Interaction Design and Children, pp. 356–359 (2010)
30. Gilbert, J.E., et al.: Teaching algebra using culturally relevant virtual instructors. IJVR **7**(1), 21–30 (2008)
31. Inc., S.: Explore 3d models - sketchfab (2022). https://sketchfab.com/3d-models
32. Jacewicz, E., Fox, R.A.: Perception of local and non-local vowels by adults and children in the south. J. Acoustical Soc. Am. **47**, 627 (2020). https://doi.org/10.1121/10.0000542
33. Karthikeyan, C.: Evaluative study on consequences of cognitive and sensory overload: a socio-psychological perspective. Int. J. Manage. IT Eng. **7** (2017). http://www.ijmra.us
34. Kennedy, J., Baxter, P., Belpaeme, T.: Comparing robot embodiments in a guided discovery learning interaction with children. Int. J. Soc. Robot. **7**, 293–308 (2015). https://doi.org/10.1007/S12369-014-0277-4/FIGURES/7. https://link.springer.com/article/10.1007/s12369-014-0277-4
35. Kory, J., Breazeal, C.: Storytelling with robots: learning companions for preschool children's language development. In: 2014 RO-MAN: The 23rd IEEE International Symposium on Robot and Human Interactive Communication, pp. 643–648. IEEE (2014)
36. Laganis, J., Prosen, K., Torkar, G.: Classroom versus outdoor biology education using a woody species identification digital dichotomous key. Natural Sci. Educ. **46**(1) (2017)
37. Leite, I., et al.: Narratives with robots: the impact of interaction context and individual differences on story recall and emotional understanding. Front. Robot. AI **4**, 29 (2017). https://doi.org/10.3389/frobt.2017.00029. http://journal.frontiersin.org/article/10.3389/frobt.2017.00029/full
38. Loureiro, P., Prandi, C., Nunes, N., Nisi, V.: Citizen science and game with a purpose to foster biodiversity awareness and bioacoustic data validation. In: Brooks, A.L., Brooks, E., Sylla, C. (eds.) ArtsIT/DLI -2018. LNICST, vol. 265, pp. 245–255. Springer, Cham (2019). https://doi.org/10.1007/978-3-030-06134-0_29

39. Lu, Y.T., Chang, C.W., Chen, G.D.: Using a programmable storytelling robot to motivate learning second language. In: Seventh IEEE International Conference on Advanced Learning Technologies (ICALT 2007), pp. 841–844. IEEE, July 2007. https://doi.org/10.1109/ICALT.2007.274. http://ieeexplore.ieee.org/document/4281172/

40. Lucarevschi, C.R.: The role of storytelling on language learning: a literature review. Working Papers of the Linguistics Circle 26(1), pp. 24–44 (2016)

41. Macedonia, M., Groher, I., Roithmayr, F.: Intelligent virtual agents as language trainers facilitate multilingualism. Front. Psychol. **5**, 295 (2014)

42. Madden, L., Liang, J.: Young children's ideas about environment: perspectives from three early childhood educational settings. Environ. Educ. Res. **23**(8), 1055–1071 (2017). https://doi.org/10.1080/13504622.2016.1236185

43. Marr, M.B., Gormley, K.: Children's recall of familiar and unfamiliar text. Reading Res. Quart. **18**, 104 (1982). https://doi.org/10.2307/747539

44. Master, A., Cheryan, S., Moscatelli, A., Meltzoff, A.N.: Programming experience promotes higher stem motivation among first-grade girls. J. Exp. Child Psychol. **160**, 92–106 (2017)

45. Mathevet, R.: Butorstar: a role-playing game for collective awareness of wise reedbed use. Simul. Gaming **38**(2), 233–262 (2007)

46. Mikropoulos, T.A., Katsikis, A., Nikolou, E., Tsakalis, P.: Virtual environments in biology teaching. J. Biol. Educ. **37**(4), 176–181 (2003)

47. Nations, U.: The 17 goals — sustainable development. https://sdgs.un.org/goals

48. Nisi, V., Dionísio, M., Silva, C., Nunes, N.J.: A participatory platform supporting awareness and empathy building between tourists and locals: The Há-vita case study. In: Proceedings of the 13th Biannual Conference of the Italian SIGCHI Chapter: Designing the next Interaction, pp. 1–10. Association for Computing Machinery, New York, September 2019. https://doi.org/10.1145/3351995.3352049

49. Nisi, V., Prandi, C., Nunes, N.J.: Towards eco-centric interaction: urban playful interventions in the anthropocene. In: Nijholt, A. (ed.) Making Smart Cities More Playable. GMSE, pp. 235–257. Springer, Singapore (2020). https://doi.org/10.1007/978-981-13-9765-3_11

50. Piaget, J.: Part i: Cognitive development in children: Piaget development and learning. J. Res. Sci.Teach. **2**, 176–186 (1964). https://doi.org/10.1002/tea.3660020306

51. Piaget, J.: Piaget's theory (1976). https://doi.org/10.1007/978-3-642-46323-5_2

52. Putri, I.G.A.P.E.: Critical environmental education in tertiary english language teaching (elt): a collaborative digital storytelling project. Indonesian J. Appl. Linguist. **8**(2), 336–344 (2018)

53. Read, J., Macfarlane, S., Casey, C.: Endurability, engagement and expectations: measuring children's fun. In: Interaction design and children, pp. 1–23. Eindhoven: Shaker Publishing (2002). https://www.researchgate.net/publication/228870976

54. Rodrigues, L., et al.: Gamification suffers from the novelty effect but benefits from the familiarization effect: findings from a longitudinal study. Int. J. Educ. Technol. High. Educ. **19**, 1–25 (2022). https://doi.org/10.1186/S41239-021-00314-6/FIGURES/3. https://educationaltechnologyjournal.springeropen.com/articles/10.1186/s41239-021-00314-6

55. Ryan, R.M.: Control and information in the intrapersonal sphere: an extension of cognitive evaluation theory. J. Personality Soc. Psychol. **43**(3), 450–461 (1982). https://doi.org/10.1037/0022-3514.43.3.450. /record/1983-07280-001

56. Ryan, R.M., Rigby, C.S., Przybylski, A.: The motivational pull of video games: a self-determination theory approach. Motivation Emotion **30**, 347–

363 (2006). https://doi.org/10.1007/S11031-006-9051-8/TABLES/9. https://link.springer.com/article/10.1007/s11031-006-9051-8

57. Sawyers, J.K., Moran, I.J.D., Fu, V.R., Milgram, R.M.: Familiar versus unfamiliar stimulus items in measurement of original thinking in young children. Perceptual Motor Skills **57**, 51–55 (1983). https://doi.org/10.2466/PMS.1983.57.1.51

58. Sébastien, D., Conruyt, N., Courdier, R., Tanzi, T.: Generating virtual worlds from biodiversity information systems: requirements, general process and typology of the metaverse's models. In: 2009 Fourth International Conference on Internet and Web Applications and Services, pp. 549–554. IEEE (2009)

59. Shapes: Nature starter kit 2 | 3d environments | unity asset store (2016). https://assetstore.unity.com/packages/3d/environments/nature-starter-kit-2-52977

60. Shih, C.F., Chang, C.W., Chen, G.D.: Robot as a storytelling partner in the English classroom - preliminary discussion. In: Seventh IEEE International Conference on Advanced Learning Technologies (ICALT 2007), pp. 678–682. IEEE, July 2007. https://doi.org/10.1109/ICALT.2007.219. http://ieeexplore.ieee.org/document/4281125/

61. Shim, K.C., Park, J.S., Kim, H.S., Kim, J.H., Park, Y.C., Ryu, H.I.: Application of virtual reality technology in biology education. J. Biol. Educ. **37**(2), 71–74 (2003)

62. Silva, C., et al.: Há-vita: a transmedia platform about madeira's nature and culture. In: 5th IFIP Conference on Sustainable Internet and ICT for Sustainability, SustainIT 2017, pp. 1–2. Institute of Electrical and Electronics Engineers Inc., June 2018. https://doi.org/10.23919/SustainIT.2017.8379813

63. Spitale, M., et al.: Design patterns of technology-based therapeutic activities for children with language impairments: a psycholinguistic-driven approach, pp. 1–7. Association for Computing Machinery (5 2021). https://doi.org/10.1145/3411763.3451775

64. Stork, M.G.: Supporting twenty-first century competencies using robots and digital storytelling. J. Formative Des. Learn. **4**(1), 43–50 (2020). https://doi.org/10.1007/s41686-019-00039-w

65. They_Love_Games: Webgl speech | audio | unity asset store (2019). https://assetstore.unity.com/packages/tools/audio/webgl-speech-105831

66. Tobar-Muñoz, H., Baldiris, S., Fabregat, R.: Augmented reality game-based learning: enriching students' experience during reading comprehension activities. J. Educ. Comput. Res. **55**(7), 901–936 (2017)

67. Torkar, G.: 2 biodiversity and digital technologies in school. TEALEAF, p. 13 (2017)

68. TurboSquid: 3d models for professionals : Turbosquid (2022). https://www.turbosquid.com/

69. Vasconcelos, E., Lucena, C., Melo, G., Irving, M., Briot, J.P., Sebba, V., Sordoni, A.: A serious game for exploring and training in participatory management of national parks for biodiversity conservation: Design and experience. In: 2009 VIII Brazilian Symposium on Games and Digital Entertainment, pp. 93–100. IEEE (2009)

70. Wäldchen, J., Mäder, P.: Plant species identification using computer vision techniques: a systematic literature review. Arch. Comput. Methods Eng. **25**(2), 507–543 (2017). https://doi.org/10.1007/s11831-016-9206-z

Button Portraits: Embodying Queer History with Interactive Wearable Artifacts

Alexandra Teixeira Riggs$^{(\boxtimes)}$ ⓘ, Noura Howell ⓘ, and Anne Sullivan ⓘ

Georgia Institute of Technology, Atlanta, GA 30332, USA
{ariggs8,nhowell8,unicorn}@gatech.edu

Abstract. *Button Portraits* is a tangible narrative (TN) that represents queer history using artifacts from the Gender and Sexuality Collections at Georgia State University. The experience tells the stories of queer activists who influenced and produced Atlanta's patchwork of LGBTQ + organizations from the mid 1970s to the present. As a case study, this project offers insights on how wearability, embodiment, and queer archival methods can shape the design and experience of tangible historical narratives and their ability to call for reflection on our relationships to archival materials and history. This paper argues that queer methods can develop and reveal embodied, liminal stories in TNs in the following ways: 1. Using queer methods and queer archival scholarship to understand and design tangible narratives engenders experiences that resist binary narrative categories. 2. Designing queer history tangible narratives requires understanding the sociocultural context and the ways the experience itself can be *queered*. 3. Embodiment through wearability in a queer TN experience *troubles* the relation of bodies, spaces, selves, and stories—reinforcing our queer theoretical framing. Overall, this design case study illustrates how tangible storytelling design can be deepened through attention to queer methods, especially when used alongside embodiment and wearability.

Keywords: Tangible narrative · Archival materials · Oral histories · Interactive narrative · Queer history · Queer south · Wearable artifacts

1 Introduction

Tangible narratives (TNs or TINs) are storytelling experiences told through interaction with physical objects embedded with digital capabilities [31]. Beyond the traditional fictional stories, we posit that TNs can also be powerful experiences for reflection and reimagination when experiencing historical narratives. The potential of TNs lies in their ability to draw palpable connections between bodies and their environments, which can be extended to include archival materials and historical subjects. Our project specifically focuses on queer history narratives, in which reflection plays an important role in the experience. To tell these stories, we examine how the relationships between body, environment, archival materials, and historical subjects can be queered—or thought of as intentionally fluid, fluctuating, and in process. To do so, we use queer archives scholarship, coupled with queer methods, to reflect on the design process and experience of tangible narratives.

M. Vosmeer and L. Holloway-Attaway (Eds.): ICIDS 2022, LNCS 13762, pp. 28–47, 2022.
https://doi.org/10.1007/978-3-031-22298-6_2

Specifically, our project *Button Portraits* explores Southern queer history as an under-represented subject matter in archival and storytelling efforts. Narratives about Southern queer history are continually (and increasingly) unearthed as part of concerted efforts by activist organizations, archivists, and storytellers. These stories are told in a variety of forms, including podcasts, online articles, books, workshops, and panel discussions, that push to make this history more visible [22, 25, 43, 57, 58]. As part of that body of work, *Button Portraits* is a tangible, non-linear portrait of two prominent Southern lesbian activists in the 1970s that uses replicas of the activists' own buttons—the type that are pinned to a garment (Fig. 1)—as vehicles through which to experience their stories.

Fig. 1. Photograph of "March on Washington for Lesbian and Gay Rights" button [13].

Through the embodied interaction of pinning on these buttons and listening to a narrative fragment, participants intimately relate to archival materials, the queer activists who owned them, and their stories (Fig. 2). We argue that the intimacy engendered by interacting with wearable tangible archives allows participants to draw connections between themselves and historical subjects, as well as *trouble*, or intentionally entangle and unsettle, these relationships through embodied experience.

This paper presents *Button Portraits* as a case study and offers reflections on how queer archival scholarship and methods can enrich the design and experience of historical narratives and artifacts. We further examine how wearable tangible narrative design can *queer* an individual's relationship to historical artifacts and their spatial and sociocultural context, methodologically refusing to define or categorize the subjects of history.

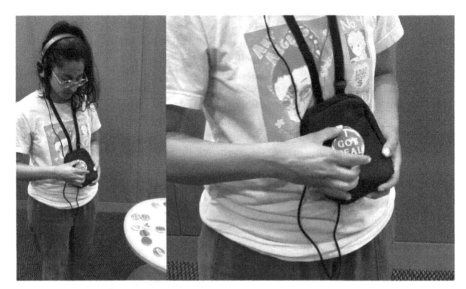

Fig. 2. *Button Portraits* interaction: A participant selects a button to wear on their audio player, places it on a magnetized area, and listens to a corresponding oral history.

Finally, we look at how embodiment through wearability can be used in the design of a queer TN experience to trouble the relationship between bodies, spaces, selves, and stories, reinforcing our queer theoretical framing. As illustrated by our case study, our reflections contribute approaches to advance tangible narrative design that is itself fluid, fragmentary, and experienced nonlinearly. We consider these approaches to tangible narrative design to be especially relevant not only to queer storytelling, an underrepresented and much needed area, but also to storytelling that largely eludes solid linear narratives.

2   Related Work

Button Portraits builds on existing work in several areas, including tangible interactive narratives (TNs or TINs) and the role of embodiment, historical artifacts as TNs, queer interactive narratives, and queer archives. With the exploration of queer historical artifacts through TNs, we rely on queer methods and the notion of queering the archive as a mode of storytelling interaction.

2.1   Tangible Narrative and Embodiment

In proposing a TN as a case study, our work draws specifically from Harley et al.'s framework for tangible narratives [31] as well as Tanenbaum et al.'s exploration of tangible non-linear storytelling in "The Reading Glove" [54], while acknowledging the larger body of recent work that supports narrative design using tangible interfaces [6–9, 16, 29, 32, 37–39, 51, 53]. Harley notes that tangible user interfaces, specifically diegetic tangible objects, allow for participants to "bridge the gap between the world of the story and the world of the user. The physical characteristics of the objects carry narrative meaning that the user interprets virtually and through tangible interaction" [31]. This makes tangible narratives well positioned to explore queer archives, particularly for this emphasis on "making strange," "negotiating differences," and "resisting categorization," which are core to queer methods [29]. Furthermore, these diegetic tangibles allow participants to develop "not only a personal relationship to the unfolding story, but also personal responsibility" [31] which invites self-reflection on the participant's role in the story, the history, the artifacts and key figures, and the larger sociocultural context.

This framing of object interaction producing narrative meaning also recalls Grosz's "Bodies-Cities", where she argues for a troubling of the relationship between the body and space, and that bodies and environments produce each other in a complex feedback loop that continually transforms reality. Similarly, participants and physical narrative objects produce and reflect one another, allowing for bodies to "reinscribe and project themselves" onto the narrative space and for the tangible narrative to "reflect the form and interests of the body" [28].

Inspired by these two approaches, we use tangible buttons in our experience, which are worn on the body and trigger stories, allowing participants to further embody their relationship to queer history. Additionally, the embodied interactions of choosing a button, wearing it, and listening to the oral history further produce the environment, which influences the interactions.

2.2 Historical Artifacts and Tangible Narrative

Button Portraits also draws upon research of TNs and cultural artifacts, including in co-design [3], and design toolkits [45]. In this paper, we explore Chu and Mazalek's Tangible Embodied Narrative Framework (TENF) which is a conceptual structure for "designing tangible and embodied narrative interaction with cultural heritage artifacts" in museum contexts [10]. They argue the TN design must present cultural aspects of an artifact to support visitors in "drawing connections between the digital replica and the original artifact." They also maintain that interactions must refer to the original context of the artifact or cultural practice, while providing simultaneous digital feedback. In other words, for visitors to understand the meaning of a historical artifact, the form of the tangible experience design, their interactions with it, and any digital feedback must be grounded in the artifact's cultural context. We draw from and build on this framework, crafting the experience of *Button Portraits* around the cultural context of Atlanta's queer history.

Chu and Mazalek [10] also develop spectra on which to map a tangible narrative interaction for cultural artifacts, building on Ryan's original framework [46] and Murray's characterization of "threshold objects," which exist in physical and virtual space, providing immersion and participation in the narrative [42].

In their framework, Chu and Mazalek propose three spectra: (1) diegetic vs. non-diegetic, determining whether the interactor can physically situate themselves within the story; (2) internal vs. external, describing a first person versus omniscient perspective; and (3) ontological vs. exploratory, determining whether the interactor directly alters the outcome of the story or simply explores its parts. TENF offers a powerful starting point for understanding the narrative dimensions of tangible interactions with respect to grasping an artifact's historical meaning. However, we posit that it is equally important to examine the archival process surrounding historical artifacts, and in doing so we arrive at a more nuanced framing for our experience. In the discussion section we return to how *Button Portraits* as a case study can expand and enrich TENF.

2.3 Queer Interactive Narrative and Archives

In interactive digital narrative (IDN), queering of narratives has primarily been explored through storytelling methods [33, 47, 49]. However, queering an archive and its use in TNs is underexplored and is particularly challenging due to the inherently fluid and fragmentary nature of queerness relative to archival work.

Beyond storytelling methods, IDN research has explored the role of queer communities in interactive narratives, which speaks to the broader sociocultural context of storytelling. Salter et al. examine the visual novel engine Ren'Py and discuss how it engenders not only queer gameplay, but queer storytelling and related communities through open-source design, principles of inclusivity, and attention to stories "on the margins" [47]. We similarly seek to elevate queer stories, while referring to the broader social, collective involvement in framing and sharing such narratives outwardly.

With respect to context, we further look to queer archives scholarship to situate this work not only within TN design, but also within archival research. Even beyond queer archives, the nature of archival work is largely fragmentary and piecemeal: we are continually working "ad hoc and ad interim," piecing histories together into a "grand contraption," as Geertz notes [24]. Similarly, as Darnton echoes, "History is tentative. Just as archives provide evidence for arguments, they undo them" [11]. The narratives that we construct from and through history are often arbitrary, as we piece together "endless fragments from countless lives" [11].

With queer archives specifically, this work becomes even murkier when we acknowledge that queerness itself is inherently resistant to categorization. Avery H. notes the tension between "containing and protecting specific versions of the past," queer theory's claim that "archives feign reproductivity," and that queerness must embrace "ahistoricity" in resistance of misrepresentative narratives or categorization [2]. This tension between the framing and categorizing common in archival practice and the inherent fluidity of the queer experience presents a paradox in representing queer history [1, 35, 36].

As with bodies and environments [28], we also acknowledge that our stories are collectively produced, that there is a "constant reweaving of the social fabric" [12], that we exist "in transmission, in communication," and so do our histories as continual evidence. Therefore, we must similarly approach archiving as a collective process, along with the archive and individuals who make it as co-producing one another. Building on these practices, much work has been done to queer the archive [35, 36, 55], to document queer history, and to examine the nature of a queer archive. However, we must equally consider how archives are viewed and experienced. We describe drawing from these considerations and engaging queer archives in more detail in Sect. 4.1.

3 Methods

3.1 Design Research Methods

This work draws from design research approaches that foreground reflection, knowledge production through design, embodiment, and self-reflexivity, including research through design [21, 23, 56] and reflective design [48]. These approaches employ the "methods, practices and processes of design practice with the intention of generating new knowledge," where both output and process build on each other [21].

Reflective design encourages designers to "use reflection to uncover and alter the limitations of design practice," ultimately questioning their role in the design process, supporting critical reflection, and rethinking underlying assumptions of technology [48]. This reflection becomes an integral part of the design process, and "dialogic engagement between designers and users through technology" enhances this activity [48]. By drawing from reflective design and research through design, we engage a self-reflexive approach that builds knowledge through the design process, while reflecting on the context and underlying forces at work.

3.2 Queer Methods

We also draw from queer methods, reflecting on and reinforcing the design of tangible narratives by attending to their queer theoretical context. Using queerness as a methodology, *Button Portraits* positions queer physical spaces as multidimensional. By placing ourselves in these spaces through tangible narrative, we implicate our own bodies and identities in history, further adding to and complicating the archive. For context, we look to Ghaziani and Brim's *Queer Methods* [5, 26]. They apply aspects of queer theory, such as fluidity, instability, and that which is perpetually becoming, to the research of queer subjects [26]. They argue for "embracing as methodology their refusal to clearly define or isolate their objects of investigation," which characterizes how we might complicate or trouble our histories, relationships, and locales [6].

Similarly, Migraine-George and Currier's "Querying Queer African Archives," calls for approaches to the archive that shift focus from "the archive as repository to the archive as process" [40]. This approach calls into question the "institutionalization of knowledge" along with the practices and methods of archiving [40]. By introducing movement into queer methods, Migraine-George and Currier's work parallels Grosz's framing of bodies and environments as continually producing one another [28]. Together, these approaches speak to embodiment, queerness, and archival practice as ongoing processes [26]. *Button Portraits* acknowledges movement in queer methods, along with the co-production of bodies and environments, by specifically drawing attention to the gestures and corporeality in tangible narrative interactions.

Using queer methods in conjunction with our chosen design methods, we seek to resist taxonomic modes of archiving and trouble histories through design and self-reflection. Our resistance of traditional archival categorization is referred to by Brim and Ghaziani, quoting Hennen, as a "scavenger method," and speaks to a fluid and purposefully queer traversal of the archive [26]. Applying this to design, we similarly build knowledge through a nonlinear, "scavenger" process. Specifically, we traversed archival materials nonlinearly, deliberately taking a relational approach that not only looked at oral histories and objects, but also included conversations with archivists and the activists themselves.

We lastly refer to Shaw and Sender's characterization of queer technologies and their affordances, which considers how "hacking and resistance of heteronormative technologies offer alternative forms of engagement and experience" [49]. Our efforts in queering design methods similarly composed of "hacking" or piecing together and taking apart fragments of oral histories, archival materials, and our own self-reflexive interpretations, to arrive at an experience that moves through narrative in a manner just as abstract, partial, and liminal as our archival practices.

4   Narrative and Artifact Design

Button Portraits tells a non-linear story of Atlanta's queer history, using oral histories of two prominent lesbian activists, Maria Helena Dolan and Lorraine Fontana, paired with historical artifacts from their collections as storytelling objects to frame the narrative. These activists were crucial in establishing a foundation for the city's LGBTQ + community, and specifically lesbian rights movement, through their writing, publishing, community organizing, and work with activist groups from the 1970s until the present. In representing their stories, we portray "portraits" of their lives and work through interactions with replicas of their own objects. We intend to continue to expand our efforts to include additional Southern queer activists who helped shape the movement, while acknowledging the work of countless others that are still underrepresented in our archival efforts.

4.1   Engaging the Archive

Button Portraits began with the Gender and Sexuality Collections at Georgia State University that chronicles much of Atlanta's LGBTQ + activism from the 1960s to the present. We approached the collection with a wide lens, sifting through periodicals about the city's gay and lesbian scene in the 1970s and 80s, reading firsthand accounts of organizing activities, and examining photographs of early pride marches. The research started first with an *inhale*: taking in the archive and wading through, rather than starting with a purpose of aiming to categorize, or tell a linear story, as alluded to in *Queer Methods* [5, 26].

We chose to focus on primarily physical artifacts, specifically "ephemera" and wearables in the collection, as our research question centered around applying queer methods to wearable tangible narrative design. Additionally, in queer archives scholarship, "ephemera" are considered an integral dimension of chronicling queer stories, as these are objects typically left out of traditional records [35]. In the Gender and Sexuality Collections, wearable ephemera consisted of items such as t-shirts, armbands, bags, bandanas, name tags, scarves, and most notably, buttons and pins. Out of the wearable objects in the collection, buttons and pins (Fig. 3) were not only commonly collected amongst several of the activists, but they also revealed rich stories of their lives through their visual and textual links to social causes, identities, events, and locations. Buttons also lent themselves to wearable tangible interaction, as they could be easily pinned to clothing, as well as physically handled, eliciting the intimacy of a worn experience.

Fig. 3. Photographs of selected buttons and pins [4, 13, 14, 17, 18].

By understanding the archival button collections as *portraits* of their originators' lives, we aimed to reveal their stories *through* their objects, pairing artifacts with oral histories. We specifically focused on buttons belonging to Fontana and Dolan, as their collections also contained oral histories, which would comprise the second piece of our project. Linking the artifacts directly to their originators' oral histories further served as an aspect of narrative continuity [15, 19, 20]. Additionally, their writing, work, and activist involvements represent key pieces of Atlanta's LGBTQ + rights movement. In manifesting their stories with this initial project however, we acknowledge that theirs are not the only stories to tell when chronicling Southern LGBTQ + history, and that we intend to expand this project to involve additional individuals and artifacts.

4.2   The Artifacts and Oral Histories

While considering Dolan and Fontana's collections, we investigated the ways that a tangible interactive narrative, created using their buttons and oral histories, could craft portraits of their lives and legacies. Dolan and Fontana's buttons (see Fig. 3 for a sampling of the collection) had originated from an array of sources throughout their lives and spanned themes of activism, identity, activities, political causes, events, and locations among many others. Some of the buttons pointed to known historical events, but many were of unknown origin or reference, left up to interpretation by the curator or archivist, and subsequently the researchers and authors of this paper.

As a body of artifacts, the buttons themselves told a nonlinear story: revealing fragments of identities, events, and communities in piecemeal portraits. Similarly, the activists' oral histories referenced these themes, but they nevertheless digressed, following a wayward, nonlinear path [15, 19, 20]. By pairing the two together, we aimed to evoke this nonlinearity, alluding to the fragmentary nature of not only historical narratives, but also of their traversal in archival work. This wayward traversal itself is a queer method: in doing so, we trouble the nature of taxonomical categorization or linear historical narratives. Furthermore, we self-reflexively acknowledge our roles as researchers and curators as we interpret and frame history, understanding that even our own categorization of queer archives, or queerness itself, poses a paradox.

With this fluid, self-reflexive aim, our ensuing design project elicited a nonlinear narrative through the tangible experience of interacting with and wearing these buttons, linking each to a relevant, evocative fragment of the originator's oral history. The choice of a button as a tangible interface worked particularly well, as the design metaphorically alludes to a continual opening and closing, a link between past and present, and a connection point between individuals. Buttons serve as signifiers of our identities, causes, and communities. They communicate solidarity or support, and as symbols, they "turn on" or "activate," as in activating knowledge or connection.

When considering Chu and Mazalek's TENF framework [10], the button artifacts in this case are nondiegetic objects, in that they are not referenced in the narrative of the oral histories. However, in their framework, nondiegetic interactions are useful in "reasoning about abstract concepts that underlie the story" [10], and these interactions heighten a participant's sense of involvement in the story and situate them in the narrative by virtue of their physicality [31, 32].

Not only do the buttons situate participants in the narrative, but they also refer to spatial situations beyond the tangible interaction. For instance, buttons are meant to circulate in space, to be passed and linked between individuals. Once in circulation, they are read by others, and in the specific case of LGBTQ + history, they are often coded and meant to be recognized by other members of the queer community, signifying solidarity or kinship [59]. In this way, buttons refer once again to Grosz's characterization of the coproduction of bodies and their environments; and to the collective, fragmented nature of these continual relationships [28].

In this vein, buttons also represent an important aspect of the larger historical context, as they are central to queer activism, identity, and community formation, though they are not directly referenced in Dolan or Fontana's anecdotes. Referring to the larger contextual meaning of these objects in queer archives scholarship adds a dimension of queer methodology that moves beyond the narrative framework, refers to, and troubles the objects' position within the archive and history.

4.3 Designing the Experience

In constructing the tangible interactive experience, we listened to oral histories given by Dolan and Fontana [15, 19, 20], identifying key fragments that paired with their buttons in the collection.

As we listened to their autobiographical accounts, we chose buttons that represented themes discussed in the oral histories, creating thematic affinity maps, such as the one pictured in Fig. 4. We applied these maps to identify and pair artifacts to story themes for use in the final experience. To associate narrative segments to buttons, we used keywords, phrases, and images from 233 total buttons in Dolan and Fontana's collections to their counterparts in 10 h of oral history transcripts, as part of an emergent, co-productive process. In some instances, keywords such as "The March on Washington" were easily identified in oral histories. For other cases, we imposed a more curatorial hand, such as associating a button with the slogan "I Got Real" to an anecdote about gender presentation, alluding to the concept of "realness" in drag and queer culture [60]. We actively resisted creating a linear story or guided narrative structure from the buttons and oral histories, as is traditionally done in museum exhibitions. Instead, in our design, the effect of nonlinearly discovering stories from the artifacts is meant to parallel both the messy entanglements of archival practice and of queer stories and relationships.

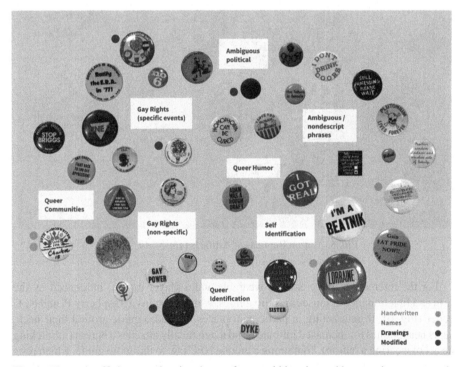

Fig. 4. Thematic affinity map showing themes from oral histories and buttons that correspond.

As per the requirements of the collection, artifacts cannot be removed or modified in any way. We instead produced replicas of the buttons, shown in Fig. 5, using a button maker and hi-res photographs of the artifacts (allowing us to retain any aging, marks, or modifications), which were digitally enhanced to increase legibility.

Fig. 5. Button Replicas of Artifacts [13, 14, 17, 18].

For the interaction, we created a wearable audio player device, influenced by the form and functionality of museum audio guides, which contains a Raspberry Pi and NFC reader (Fig. 6). In interacting, a participant places the audio guide around their neck, wears headphones for increased intimacy, and magnetically attaches a button (mimicking the act of wearing a button), containing a unique NFC tag, to the audio guide, which rests at approximately chest level. Placing the button on the audio guide allows it to read the unique NFC identifier attached to the button, which then causes the audio guide to play the corresponding fragment of oral history. Each button is mapped to a unique narrative fragment, so the story is experienced entirely nonlinearly: a participant can choose any given button, in any order, and listen to the corresponding anecdote.

Fig. 6. A second view of the *Button Portraits* interaction: A participant chooses a button to wear on their audio player, places it on a magnetized area, and listens to an oral history story fragment corresponding to that button. Each button has a unique NFC tag read by the audio player.

Experientially, this physical gesture of holding a button to one's chest and intimately listening to an interview with the button's original owner serves to not only implicate participants in this history, but also to reframe their relationships to the stories through attention to their own bodily experience.

In an exhibition context, *Button Portraits* would be situated adjacent to the archives space, referring to the collection and inviting further exploration. However, *Button Portraits* can be experienced outside of the archive while referencing the original collection through signage and wall text. The exhibition will comprise a table with the buttons clustered together, the audio player, a mirror to view oneself wearing the button, and instructions for how to experience the piece (Fig. 7).

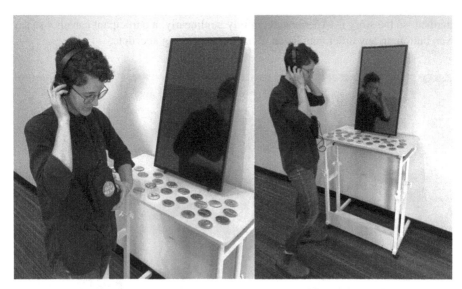

Fig. 7. An exhibition view of *Button Portraits*, where button artifacts are placed on a table with a mirror, and participants choose any button to interact with.

While listening to oral histories, participants may stay close to the table or walk around the space, which can include the archive, evoking the spatial and corporeal connection to both the buttons and the participants' surroundings.

Initial informal feedback on the experience, aiding our design iterations, focused on increasing accessibility for the wearer and visibility of the buttons while being worn. For instance, we chose a more universally wearable button for our design, as opposed to a jacket or more fitted piece of "ephemera," which would unnecessarily limit participants based on size. Additionally, we aim to provide a mirror within the exhibition space to increase visibility of the button for the wearer, and to further implicate participants in their embodied experience of queer history.

5   Discussion and Implications: Queering Tangible Narrative

Button Portraits is a case study in applying queer methods and queer archival scholarship to the design of tangible narrative experiences, while exploring dimensions of wearability to heighten and trouble relationships between participants, history, and their spatial context. The experience purposefully draws out a fragmentary, nonlinear narrative experience, evoking the partial and entangled nature of archives scholarship, while troubling or *queering* participants' relationships to historical events by physically situating them alongside archival materials and subjects. In this way, the work builds on tangible narrative scholarship to heighten participants' involvement in a story through wearability and to examine this interaction through a queer lens. Through this embodied interaction and contextualization within a queer theoretical frame, the work destabilizes and troubles relationships between participants' bodies, narratives, and histories.

5.1 Beyond Narrative Binaries

We argue that queer methods and queer archival scholarship can influence the way we understand and design tangible narratives for historical artifacts by allowing us to resist binary narrative design categories. Returning to the TENF framework [10], *Button Portraits* may at first be categorized in the following ways: non-diegetic, as the participant is not a character within Dolan or Fontana's stories; external, as the participant's perspective is partially third-person; and exploratory, as the interactor does not influence the story but rather explores it. However, in the experience of *Button Portraits*, none of these characterizations are categorically fixed. The buttons may seem at first non-diegetic, but they slip into diegetic if either of the activists mentions a reference from a button's text, thereby heightening the wearer's involvement in the story. Second, though a participant's perspective may seem external, by virtue of wearing the button and listening intimately, this embodied interaction may suggest a dialogue with the activist, implicate the wearer in the story, and cause their perspective to shift internally. Third, though a participant may not influence the story in a direct narrative interaction, by understanding that bodies and environments co-produce one another [28], and by implying the social and collective dimensions of the button objects, wearers may influence stories and relationships beyond those of the immediate interaction.

In describing the fluidity of these narrative categories, we find that though TENF's categories are referred to as spectra, their analysis foregrounds the binary ends of these narrative elements. Indeed, binary, categorical descriptions of narrative elements are prevalent throughout TN and IDN frameworks [34, 41], and Chu and Mazalek acknowledge this fixity as a limitation of TENF [10]. We interpret this as a generous invitation to build on and enrich their work and take this as an opportunity to expand approaches to interactive narrative largely. We suggest expanding TENF to further invest in holding space for narratives that exist in between points, within multiple places on continuous spectra. By offering reflections on how binary framings structurally overlook the fluidity and liminality inherent in queer narratives, we work to expand and enrich tangible narratives to support more diverse storytelling. *Button Portraits'* experiential fluidity and resistance to categorization highlight a potential path for queer methods and theoretical framing to impact the broader understanding and design of tangible narratives.

5.2 Beyond Narrative: Queering, Contextualizing, and Embodying the Experience

When designing tangible narratives around queer historical artifacts, we must also think about the sociocultural context and how the experience can be queered. This highlights one dimension in which Chu and Mazalek's TENF [10] can be expanded—adding representation for the sociocultural context of the narrative within the framework. Building on this, we call for attending to the structural, methodological, and social dimensions of working with archival subject matter, as well as framing and understanding how a tangible narrative experience exists in that space.

In *Button Portraits*, our design process critically examines the larger context of archival work, using queer archives as a lens, along with the social and collective dimensions of space when experiencing an embodied narrative interaction. Not only does the experience of the work explore the relationship between bodies, stories, and environments, but it also sits within and is produced by an existing community of Southern LGBTQ + activists, archivists, and individuals. The project is more than a narrative and experience; it began as a relationship between the authors and archivists and continues to evolve to include the activists represented, along with other members of the community, inviting discussion and reflection on the role of archives in our present and future.

Based on our research in designing *Button Portraits*, we suggest that a tangible narrative that chronicles queer history cannot only be *about* queer subjects, but it must also be framed and experienced queerly, with attention to the inherent fluidity and fragmentation of all aspects of the design process. *Button Portraits* embodies the fluidity of a queer tangible narrative experience by resisting the binary categories typically used to describe narrative design. It moves between diegetic and non-diegetic sensibilities, implicates participants in a story through embodiment while allowing them to remain at a distance, and invites them to understand their role in a larger, collective relationship to archival subjects and history. In addition to narrative design and experience, *Button Portraits* foregrounds queer archival scholarship and methods as foundational considerations, arguing for tangible narrative design that acknowledges its artifacts' archival and sociocultural context, alongside its narrative framing. Beyond queer tangible narratives, we argue that this consideration can apply to any form of storytelling, where individuals must consider and "do justice to" the contextual and dialogical understanding of a narrative [44], collapsing boundaries between storyteller and subject, between story and setting.

Embodiment drawn out through wearability in this queer tangible narrative also powerfully troubles the relation of bodies, spaces, and stories [28]—and this troubling reinforces our queer theoretical framing. Wearing artifacts allows participants to embody their relationship to queer history: the gesture of choosing a button, pinning it on, and listening to the voice of an activist foregrounds a relationship between the interactor, the object, and the narrative. Further, this relationship speaks to the co-production of bodies, objects, environments, and stories, which parallels the movement and liminality discussed in queer methods [26, 40], and adds additional theoretical dimensions to our understanding of tangible narrative.

5.3   Queer Methods for Queer Archives

In designing *Button Portraits*, the act of creating replicas of buttons for the purposes of interactive storytelling is notable in that it evokes and critically examines the sentiment of curating. It alludes to the notion that histories and artifacts are continually selected, mediated, and framed by the archivist, researcher, and in this case, designer of the storytelling interface. In reframing, retelling, and replicating artifacts and stories, we self-reflexively acknowledge our own roles as researchers and mediators, recognizing the always partial and incomplete framing of historical narratives.

The work invites us to question and reflect on our own identities in relation to one another, as well as to our communities both past and present. It evokes the sensation of "trying on"–as with a button– an identity and story, but it nevertheless alludes to our inability to perceive one's interior life or history [27]. In exploring and interacting with the fragmented narrative, participants will only ever discover pieces of history, reflecting the unknowable and always partial, collective nature of historical framing.

In presenting archival objects, *Button Portraits* also self-reflexively alludes to themes of equity, context, and power: who is represented in queer history, which stories are told, which communities are portrayed, how is that history retold, and by whom? In equitably representing stories in a digital or tangible interactive format, we look to Parvin's "Doing Justice to Stories" [44], Tuhiwai Smith's "Decolonizing Methodologies" [50], and TallBear's "Standing With and Speaking as Faith" [52] for insight. To practice equitable representation, we embrace "telling stories back," being in and of the communities within which these stories live, and dialogical forms of storytelling and listening. We trouble "assumptions, dominant narratives, and predefined modes of action inclusive of those that animate digital storytelling initiatives" [30, 44], especially by virtue of the interactions we design. As mentioned, *Button Portraits* exists in and of Atlanta's LGBTQ + community and has been conceptualized by its members. Our aim as authors is to continue to work within this context to dialogically share and reflect on the stories presented, and to argue for this continued broader approach to tangible narrative design for archival materials and stories.

Button Portraits also has implications that extend beyond queer storytelling to museums and archives largely. As a case study, *Button Portraits* reflects on how embodiment, wearability, and queering the archive through queer methods can shape the design and experience of tangible historical narratives. In archives and museums, visitors would benefit from these tangible experiences that allow for a deepened understanding of history through embodied interaction and nonlinear exploration.

5.4 Limitations and Future Work

Currently, *Button Portraits* focuses on only two activists and the artifacts within one archive, and we acknowledge that this work does not seek to represent queer history universally. Additionally, we intend to extend our research beyond specific stories, fostering ongoing dialogue and relationships with queer spaces, communities, and activists both established and burgeoning.

As this design project is meant to evolve within Southern queer communities, future iterations will seek to work with and dialogically tell stories of underrepresented members, especially QTBIPOC (queer, trans, Black, Indigenous, People of Color) and other marginalized voices. As part of an ongoing archival effort, QTBIPOC oral histories are currently being added to the Gender and Sexuality Collections under the Transgender Oral History project [25], and this design project will evolve to collectively tell those stories. It is our hope that this project continues to grow within and through its members, that histories continue to be shared, and that the dialogical nature of our engagement persists.

Lastly, while this paper discusses the theoretical contributions and design process of *Button Portraits*, further work is needed to explore how participants interact with and reflect upon the experience. We plan to conduct a user study as our immediate next step, and in our next publication, we will report on findings from this study, focusing on how the artifact and interactions engender embodiment and a deepened understanding of queer history.

6   Conclusion

Button Portraits as a case study builds on the existing body of tangible narratives of historical artifacts by adding dimensions of queer archives scholarship and queer methods to design and experience considerations. Our design suggests that a queer design research methods approach, coupled with dimensions of wearability and consideration of queer archival process, seek to not only place participants in relation to historical narratives and figures but to trouble, reframe, and *queer* these relationships. By virtue of this design, the intimacy and physicality garnered by wearability, paired with an abstract nonlinear narrative, evokes the paradox of being close to and yet distant from individuals and their interior lives and stories. It alludes to the opacity and ever shifting, fragmentary, and fluid nature of both history and its actors. Further, it presents a powerful opportunity to reshape participants' experiences of the archive, calling for intimacy, reflection, and collective involvement in understanding our histories.

References

1. Arondekar, A., et al.: Queering archives: A roundtable discussion. Radic. Hist. Rev. **2015**(122), 211 232 (2015). https://doi.org/10.1215/01636545-2849630
2. Avery, H.K.: Thoughts on Queering the Archive, http://www.metatron.press/alpha/work/kit-avery-h/, last accessed 06 May 2022
3. Avram, G., et al.: Creating tangible interactions with cultural heritage: lessons learned from a large scale, long term co-design project. CoDesign **16**(3), 251–266 (2020). https://doi.org/10.1080/15710882.2019.1596288
4. Ball, M.C.: Artifacts 1
5. Brim, M., Ghaziani, A.: Introduction: queer methods. WSQ Womens Stud. Q. **44**(3–4), 14–27 (2016). https://doi.org/10.1353/wsq.2016.0033
6. Catala, A., Theune, M., Sylla, C., Ribeiro, P.: Bringing Together Interactive Digital Storytelling with Tangible Interaction: Challenges and Opportunities. In: Nunes, N., Oakley, I., Nisi, V. (eds.) ICIDS 2017. LNCS, vol. 10690, pp. 395–398. Springer, Cham (2017). https://doi.org/10.1007/978-3-319-71027-3_51
7. Chenzira, A., et al.: RENATI: recontextualizing narratives for tangible interfaces. In: Proceedings of the 2nd international conference on Tangible and embedded interaction - TEI '08, p. 147. ACM Press, Bonn, Germany (2008). https://doi.org/10.1145/1347390.1347423
8. Chu, J.H.: Designing tangible interfaces to support expression and sensemaking in interactive narratives. In: Proceedings of the Ninth International Conference on Tangible, Embedded, and Embodied Interaction, pp. 457–460. ACM, Stanford California USA (2015). https://doi.org/10.1145/2677199.2693161
9. Chu, J.H., et al.: Universal threshold object: designing haptic interaction for televised interactive narratives. In: Proceedings of the Ninth International Conference on Tangible, Embedded, and Embodied Interaction, pp. 285–292. ACM, Stanford California USA (2015). https://doi.org/10.1145/2677199.2680563
10. Chu, J.H., Mazalek, A.: Embodied engagement with narrative: a design framework for presenting cultural heritage artifacts. Multimodal Technol. Interact. **3**(1), 1 (2019). https://doi.org/10.3390/mti3010001
11. Darnton, R.: The Good Way to Do History | Robert Darnton, https://www.nybooks.com/articles/2014/01/09/good-way-history/

12. Dewey, J.: Democracy and Education: An Introduction to the Philosophy of Education. Macmillan (1916)
13. Dolan, M.H.: Buttons 1
14. Dolan, M.H.: Buttons 2
15. Dolan, M.H., Hayward, D.: Maria Helena Dolan and Dave Hayward Oral History Interview 2018-10-22 (2018)
16. Echeverri, D., Wei, H.: Letters to José: A Design Case for Building Tangible Interactive Narratives. In: Bosser, A.-G., Millard, D.E., Hargood, C. (eds.) ICIDS 2020. LNCS, vol. 12497, pp. 15–29. Springer, Cham (2020). https://doi.org/10.1007/978-3-030-62516-0_2
17. Fontana, L.: Buttons 1
18. Fontana, L.: Buttons 2
19. Fontana, L.: Lorraine Fontana Oral History Interview March 14, 2019 (2019)
20. Fontana, L.: Lorraine Fontana Oral History Interview October 29, 2012 (2012)
21. Frayling, C.: Royal College of Art: Research in art and design. Royal College of Art, London (1993)
22. Fulton, Jr, P.: Gay Atlanta Flashback, https://gayatlflashback.com/, last accessed 06 July 2022
23. Gaver, W.: What should we expect from research through design?. In: Proceedings of the SIGCHI Conference on Human Factors in Computing Systems, pp. 937–946. ACM, Austin Texas USA (2012). https://doi.org/10.1145/2207676.2208538
24. Geertz, C.: After the Fact: Two Countries, Four Decades. Harvard University Press, Cambridge, Mass, One Anthropologist (1996)
25. Gerrard, M.: GSU Library Research Guides: Georgia Transgender Oral History Project: About the Georgia Transgender Oral History Project, https://research.library.gsu.edu/c.php?g=112 3948&p=8198040, last accessed 23 July 2022
26. Ghaziani, A., Brim, M. (eds.): Imagining queer methods. New York University Press, New York (2019)
27. Glissant, É.: Poetics of Relation. University of Michigan Press (1997)
28. Grosz, E.: Bodies-Cities. In: Sexuality & space. Princeton Architectural Press, New York, N.Y (1992)
29. Gupta, S., Tanenbaum, T.J.: Shiva's Rangoli: tangible interactive storytelling in ambient environments. In: Companion Publication of the 2019 on Designing Interactive Systems Conference 2019 Companion, pp. 29–32. ACM, San Diego CA USA (2019). https://doi.org/10.1145/3301019.3325145
30. Haraway, D.: Situated Knowledges: The Science Question in Feminism and the Privilege of Partial Perspective. Fem. Stud. 14(3), 575 (1988). https://doi.org/10.2307/3178066
31. Harley, D., et al.: Towards a Framework for Tangible Narratives. In: Proceedings of the TEI '16: Tenth International Conference on Tangible, Embedded, and Embodied Interaction, pp. 62–69. Association for Computing Machinery, New York, NY, USA (2016). https://doi.org/10.1145/2839462.2839471
32. Holmquist, L.E., et al.: Every object tells a story: Physical interfaces for digital storytelling. Presented at the Proceedings of the NordiCHI (2000)
33. Howard, K.T.: A Design Framework for Learning About Representation in Video Games Through Modification of Narrative and Gameplay. In: Cardona-Rivera, R.E., Sullivan, A., Young, R.M. (eds.) ICIDS 2019. LNCS, vol. 11869, pp. 422–426. Springer, Cham (2019). https://doi.org/10.1007/978-3-030-33894-7_46
34. Koenitz, H., Haahr, M., Ferri, G., Sezen, T.I.: First Steps towards a Unified Theory for Interactive Digital Narrative. In: Pan, Z., Cheok, A.D., Müller, W., Iurgel, I., Petta, P., Urban, B. (eds.) Transactions on Edutainment X. LNCS, vol. 7775, pp. 20–35. Springer, Heidelberg (2013). https://doi.org/10.1007/978-3-642-37919-2_2
35. Kumbier, A.: Ephemeral Material: Queering the Archive. Litwin Books, Sacramento, CA (2014)

36. Marshall, D., et al. (eds.): Queering Archives: Historical Unravelings. Duke University Press, Durham (2014)

37. Mazalek, A.: Tangible narratives: emerging interfaces for digital storytelling and machinima. In: Lowood, H., Nitsche, M. (eds.) The Machinima Reader, pp. 91–110. The MIT Press (2011). https://doi.org/10.7551/mitpress/9780262015332.003.0007

38. Mazalek, A., et al.: Tangible viewpoints: a physical approach to multimedia stories. In: Proceedings of the tenth ACM international conference on Multimedia - MULTIMEDIA '02, p. 153. ACM Press, Juan-les-Pins, France (2002). https://doi.org/10.1145/641007.641037

39. Mazalek, A., Davenport, G.: A tangible platform for documenting experiences and sharing multimedia stories. In: Proceedings of the 2003 ACM SIGMM workshop on Experiential telepresence - ETP '03, p. 105. ACM Press, Berkeley, California (2003). https://doi.org/10.1145/982484.982505

40. Migraine-George, T., Currier, A.: Querying queer african archives: methods and movements. Womens Stud. Q. **44**(3/4), 190–207 (2016)

41. Murray, J.: The Last Word on Ludology v Narratology in Game Studies (2005)

42. Murray, J.H.: Hamlet on the holodeck: the future of narrative in cyberspace. MIT Press, Cambridge, Mass (1998)

43. Padgett, M.: A night at the Sweet Gum Head: drag, drugs, disco, and Atlanta's gay revolution. W. W. Norton & Company, New York, NY (2021)

44. Parvin, N.: Doing justice to stories: on ethics and politics of digital storytelling. Engag. Sci. Technol. Soc. **4**, 515–534 (2018). https://doi.org/10.17351/ests2018.248

45. Petrelli, D., et al.: Envisioning, designing, and rapid prototyping heritage installations with a tangible interaction toolkit. Human–Computer Interact. 1–41 (2021). https://doi.org/10.1080/07370024.2021.1946398

46. Ryan, M.-L.: Avatars of story. University of Minnesota Press, Minneapolis (2006)

47. Salter, A., et al.: "Just because it's gay?": transgressive design in queer coming of age visual novels. In: Proceedings of the 13th International Conference on the Foundations of Digital Games, pp. 1–9. ACM, Malmö Sweden (2018). https://doi.org/10.1145/3235765.3235778

48. Sengers, P., et al.: Reflective design. In: Proceedings of the 4th decennial conference on Critical computing between sense and sensibility - CC '05, p. 49. ACM Press, Aarhus, Denmark (2005). https://doi.org/10.1145/1094562.1094569

49. Shaw, A., Sender, K.: Queer technologies: affordances, affect, ambivalence. Crit. Stud. Media Commun. **33**(1), 1–5 (2016). https://doi.org/10.1080/15295036.2015.1129429

50. Smith, L.T.: Decolonizing methodologies: research and indigenous peoples. Zed Books. University of Otago Press; Distributed in the USA exclusively by St. Martin's Press, London; New York: Dunedin, N.Z.: New York (1999)

51. Sylla, C., Gonçalves, S., Brito, P., Branco, P., Coutinho, C.: A Tangible Platform for Mixing and Remixing Narratives. In: Reidsma, D., Katayose, H., Nijholt, A. (eds.) ACE 2013. LNCS, vol. 8253, pp. 630–633. Springer, Cham (2013). https://doi.org/10.1007/978-3-319-03161-3_69

52. TallBear, K.: Standing with and speaking as faith: a feminist-indigenous approach to inquiry. J. Res. Pract. 10, (2014)

53. Tanenbaum, K., Hatala, M., Tanenbaum, J., Wakkary, R., Antle, A.: A case study of intended versus actual experience of adaptivity in a tangible storytelling system. User Model. User-Adap. Inter. **24**(3), 175–217 (2013). https://doi.org/10.1007/s11257-013-9140-9

54. Tanenbaum, T.J., et al.: The reading glove: designing interactions for object-based tangible storytelling. In: Proceedings of the 1st Augmented Human International Conference, pp. 1–9. Association for Computing Machinery, New York, NY, USA (2010). https://doi.org/10.1145/1785455.1785474

55. Zepeda, L.: Queering the Archive: Transforming the Archival Process. (2018). https://doi.org/10.13023/DISCLOSURE.27.14

56. Zimmerman, J., et al.: Research through design as a method for interaction design research in HCI. In: Proceedings of the SIGCHI Conference on Human Factors in Computing Systems, pp. 493–502. ACM, San Jose California USA (2007). https://doi.org/10.1145/1240624.124 0704
57. ALFA 50 Reunion, https://events.zoom.us/ev/AtAlerlF6u5GrDXNRc67hnHxMvq5HlDFw R7Yi9kgi-6LGFxy6zzb~AggLXsr32QYFjq8BlYLZ5I06Dg, last accessed 26 July 2022
58. Out Down South Showcase: https://www.atlantalgbtqhistoryproject.org/events/outdownsouth showcase, last accessed 26 July 2022
59. Secret Symbols and Signals: https://www.lgbtculturalheritage.com/secret-symbols, last accessed 26 July 2022
60. Underground Ball Culture – Subcultures and Sociology, https://haenfler.sites.grinnell.edu/ subcultures-and-scenes/underground-ball-culture/, last accessed 07 October 2022

Interactive Digital Storytelling in Cultural Heritage: The Transformative Role of Agency

Dimitra Petousi[1] , Akrivi Katifori[1,2(✉)] , Katerina Servi[1,2] , Maria Roussou[2] ,
and Yannis Ioannidis[1,2]

[1] ATHENA Research Center, Artemidos 6 & Epidavrou, 15125 Maroussi, Greece
{vivi,yannis}@di.uoa.gr, dpetousi@athenarc.gr
[2] Department of Informatics and Telecommunications,
National and Kapodistrian University of Athens, Panepistimioupolis, Ilissia, Greece
mroussou@di.uoa.gr

Abstract. Digital storytelling has been established as an effective approach for promoting visitor engagement in cultural heritage contexts. Interactive digital storytelling is however not as prevalent in this field. In this work we attempt to gain insight for the added value that interaction in the form of enhanced user agency brings to a cultural heritage experience in terms of supporting its ultimate objectives: engagement with the cultural content as well as reflection, meaning making and historical empathy. Through a user study with 67 participants experiencing a historical "choose your own adventure" type of IDN on-line, we examine the user experience in general and, in particular, correlations of user perceived agency with the dimensions of immersion and transformation. Our results are promising as to the use of this type of IDN for the wider audiences and reveal a concrete effect of user perceived agency on the aforementioned two user experience dimensions.

Keywords: Interactive digital storytelling · Cultural heritage · Visitor experience · Agency · Interactivity

1 Introduction

Digital storytelling has been established as an effective approach for promoting visitor engagement in cultural heritage contexts [1–5] and has been shown to function as "an incentive to delve deeper into history" [6]. Pujol et al. [7] provide a thorough account of the importance of storytelling for cultural heritage and comment that, following the constructivist theories of learning, "stories are more easily remembered than raw facts because they contain an underlying structure and can be linked with prior experiences" [7]. Coerver et al. [8] discuss the importance of shifting from facts to stories that cultural heritage consumers may relate to, promoting emotions and curiosity and claim that, "what most visitors really need is a story—a memorable, emotionally resonant way to connect with a fundamentally foreign object". Amongst the variety of experience types that have been applied in a heritage setting, digital storytelling has the advantage of simplicity and appeal to wider audiences, adults and children.

© The Author(s), under exclusive license to Springer Nature Switzerland AG 2022
M. Vosmeer and L. Holloway-Attaway (Eds.): ICIDS 2022, LNCS 13762, pp. 48–67, 2022.
https://doi.org/10.1007/978-3-031-22298-6_3

In many cases in this domain, the term "interactive" has been used to characterize digital storytelling apps [9], "when in fact they simply offer options that allow the users to control their navigation around the site and to select informational content". Leaving aside serious games, interactive digital storytelling (IDN) in its branching narrative, visual novel or gamebook forms has not yet been established as a practice in heritage. Interestingly, however, the request for "more interaction" has been a recurrent theme in the evaluation of different digital storytelling apps for museums [4, 6]. Although these stories might have featured several branching and decision points, if those "revolved around information content that the visitors could access or the path they could follow on-site", users felt that the story was "too guided and too linear", offering "no actual control on the plot" and "no possibility to actually interact in a meaningful way [9]. As Crawford [10] would explain, these experiences lacked "richness", which "depends on the functional significance of each choice and the perceived completeness of choices offered".

Authoring, however, and IDN experience involves a significantly higher level of challenges for the story creators in comparison to linear stories. Creating a quality IDN experience requires a deep understanding of the concept of interactive storytelling and its best practices, which might be commonplace in the sector of gaming, but they are not in heritage practice and cultural institutions and digital storytelling authors are often reluctant to make the effort.

In this work we attempt to gain insight on the added value IDN brings to a cultural heritage experience in terms of its ultimate objectives: engagement with the cultural content as well as reflection, meaning making and historical empathy. Through a user study with 67 participants experiencing a historical "choose your own adventure" type of IDN on-line, we examine the user experience in general and, in particular, correlations of user perceived agency with the dimensions of immersion and transformation. Our results reveal a concrete effect of user perceived agency to both of these dimensions.

In Sect. 2 we present in more detail the background research on agency in IDN that has been the foundation for this work, relevant evaluation frameworks, as well as the definition of historical empathy as transformational experience objective, while in Sect. 3 we briefly present the objectives and methodology for our study, including a description of the IDN used. Section 4 focuses on the results of the study, Sect. 5 discusses the results and 6 concludes the paper.

2 Background

2.1 Interactivity and Agency

Creating an interactive digital narrative experience is a challenging practice. Writers, content creators and designers often have to compromise between the interactivity complexity and the quality of the storytelling. Most efforts at increasing interactivity rely on emergent narrative but at the expense of authorial control and/or quality [11]. Interactivity is a long contested term, approached from different perspectives. Murray in [12] views interactivity as a combination of the procedural and participatory properties and immersion as a combination of their spatial and encyclopedic qualities. Crawford [13] frames it in terms of a conversation between participants in which both actors alternately "listen, think, and speak". Zimmerman [14] describes interactivity in terms of different modes of engagement with a media artifact, whereas Ryan [15], proposes four types of interactivity based on user functions and perspectives in cybertexts. Murray examines in detail the way narratives produced in digital formats have begun to simulate imaginary worlds in which one can become immersed as an agent who has the power to transform a course of action.

One of the domains where agency has been studied is interactive movies. Murakami [16] mentions that the potential of the agency of the user as an interactor of the narrative is necessary to keep the audience interested in telenovelas and might affect the future design of such experiences. Kolhoff and Nack [17] investigate the impact of agency in interaction and experience based on the interactive movie "Bandersnatch". According to the authors, engagement elements such as agency, curiosity and challenge were appreciated as positive, whereas sensory appeal and aesthetics were considered weaker [17]. They conclude that once novelty wears off, the interest drops due to low levels of perceived control, positive effect and endurability. Therefore, the future design of such experiences has to consider these implications and improve drastically [17].

Vermeulen et al. [18] studied the impact on engagement and interactivity through a study on the adventure game "Fahrenheit" and found that the effectance scale was related to interactivity.

Agency plays a major role in interactivity. The term originates from Murray who describes agency as "the satisfying power to take meaningful action and see the results of our decisions and choices" [12]. Mateas and Stern [19] introduce the temporality of meaning production, and they distinguish between local and global agency. Local agency is the experience attendant to a specific user action or choice and is defined as "when the player's actions cause immediate, context specific, meaningful reactions from the system. Global agency can be defined as: "at the end of the experience the player can understand how her actions led to this storyline" [19]. Another distinction was introduced by Tanenbaum and Tanenbaum [20] and differentiates true or unrestricted agency, and limited or restricted agency.

Agency has been studied in interactive media such as video games, however due its complexity as a concept, its understanding remains still a subject for research. Some works have investigated different forms of agency and their impact on player engagement or the understanding of internal narrative [21, 22, 38]. Generally, agency is considered an innovative design element of video games, essential to the experience and interactivity of the game [39].

2.2 Evaluating IDN Experiences

There are several evaluation approaches for assessing user experience in IDN [23, 24]. One of the initial approaches is Murray's [12] with a high level interpretation of user experience focusing on three main aspects (Immersion, Agency and Transformation).

Roth's and Koenitz [25] connect research in psychology based on entertainment theory with a humanities-based perspective to design a comprehensive conceptual framework to support evaluation. The framework identified twelve concrete user experience dimensions categorized under three main aspects: (1) Agency, with the sub-categories of usability, effectance and autonomy, (2) Immersion, differentiated between perceptual (flow and presence) and narrative (role identification, curiosity, suspense and believability) and (3) Transformation, with the sub-categories of eudaimonic transformation, appreciation affect (positive, negative) and enjoyment.

We apply this framework by focusing its transformation aspects on the transformative learning and historical empathy objectives. We chose the perspective of Murray [12] and Roth and Koenitz [25] for interactivity and agency as it aligns better with the objectives of our context of use for IDN. Murray's [12] views not only define the term in accordance with the informal education, cultural heritage perspective and needs and also expand on the notion of agency. Murray's [12] definition of agency and interactivity go beyond active participation in the narrative to concepts of engagement and transformation which align well with history education and the perspective taking and affective connection aspects of historical empathy.

2.3 Agency and Transformative Learning

Educators and scholars have long stated that critical reflection is key to enabling students to gain the full benefits from their learning experience. Developed by Mezirow [26] Transformative Learning Theory has three fundamental components, critical reflection, the centrality of experience and rational discourse.

Mezirow's theory of transformative learning presupposes agency. Agency is the means by which the limitations of an inadequate meaning perspective are transcended. This implies that transformation cannot be achieved only from within the existing meaning perspective but rather it should also be exercised outside that constellation of constructs. This depends on the person dissociating from their perspective to enter a groundless state where original thought is possible. A central concept in transformative learning theory is that individuals make meaning of their experiences and revise that meaning based on new experiences that are discrepant with their previous points of view. This, combined with the fact that we make sense of our lives through stories, implies a clear intersection between transformative learning and interactive storytelling.

Transformative Learning places critical reflection front and center. Critical reflection involves challenging habits and expectations and reassessing one's own orientation to knowledge, attitudes, beliefs, and actions. Critical reflection is also crucial for a meaningful history education, especially if viewed through the lens of historical empathy. The mere transmission of historical facts and events is ineffective without a transformative component. The model of Historical Empathy [27] has the potential to act as a transformative learning method. The model aims to facilitate critical reflection and affective engagement with the past, beyond basic memorization of facts. It foresees three aspects, starting from historical contextualization as the basic learning of historical facts, moving to perspective-taking, as the understanding of the views of past people, and, finally, to affective connection, prompting users to understand past people as individuals with their own emotions, values and worldview [28]. The combination of historical empathy and transformative learning in history education involves not just the ability to think critically about a specific event of the past but to also understand the multiple perspectives on that event, recognise these understandings and apply them into events today. As authors in [29] noted "transformative history teaching attempts a critical understanding of the confictual past through the cultivation of historical thinking, empathy, an overcoming of ethnocentric narratives and the promotion of multiperspectivity".

3   Research Objectives and Method

In this section we briefly present our research objectives and the design of the study, including the questionnaire, the IDN experience we employed as well as the description of the study participants.

3.1   Research Questions and Study Design

As already noted, existing research has confirmed the effects of digital storytelling on the immersion and transformation aspects of the user experience, and its potential to promote visitor engagement with heritage. At the same time, the key role of agency has been recognized for transformative learning. In this work we aim to examine the effect of agency on a cultural heritage digital storytelling experience. Our focus in the wider IDN field is interactive fiction in the form of a digital narrative composed of dialogue-based episodes. At the end of each brief episode, the user is prompted to make choices that will affect the story plot. This type of experience can be addressed to a wider and more diverse audience than that of an approach where the gaming aspect is more pronounced. Serious games for heritage are mostly appealing to gamers. Whereas a simpler choice-based approach can be consumed by non-gamers as well, for on-site visits or as a virtual experience. In this work we opt to examine (a) the effectiveness of IDN as virtual content, decoupled from a physical visit to an archaeological site and (b) the role of user perceived agency to the components of the user experience. Thus, we formulate the following two research questions:

- RQ1 - Could a "choose your own adventure" type of IDN be effective as a virtual experience in a digital heritage context, with the objective to promote transformational aspects such as historical empathy and engagement with a specific archaeological site or historical period?
- RQ2 - Is there an effect of the user's perceived sense of agency on the user experience (immersion and transformation) in this type of IDN for cultural heritage?

In order to explore these research questions, we designed a user study that took place on-line with invited adult participants. They would be asked to experience an IDN set in the historical context of Ancient Athens (see Sect. 3.3) and then fill-in a questionnaire in Google Forms format (Sect. 3.2).

We prepared an invitation which briefly presented the digital narrative concept, the study objectives and the process the participants would have to follow. It was clarified to the users that the study was anonymous and they were asked to fill-in an on-line consent form.The invitation was circulated on-line to different academic and project mailing lists as well as through organization, project and personal social media accounts. Interested individuals were sent the relevant instructions and were asked to view the experience and fill-in the questionnaire at their own time before the given dead-line.

3.2 Questionnaire

The questionnaire consisted of open and close ended questions grouped in two main parts, (a) participant profile and (b) captivation, affective engagement and reflection questions.

The first part recording the participant profile contains 11 questions including demographics (age, gender) as well the participant interest in history and archaeology as well as general interest in literature and films, including preferred genres. We decide to record this information to examine if it affects in any way the general user experience and time spent with the virtual tour.

The second part focused on user experience aspects, roughly grouped into the three broader categories of Agency, Immersion and Transformation, aligned with the framework by Roth and Koenitz [25] (See Sect. 2.2). Taking into account that our context and objectives are focused on informal education and the Transformation aspects of the user experience, we further divide our Transformation questionnaire statements to those related to "Sensory delight" as the pleasurable experience derived from design and aesthetics [25] and "Eudaimonic appreciation" as the "experiential dimension is linked to users' construction of personal meaning". The latter includes statements related to the historical empathy model [27] and, more specifically, its three constituents, historical contextualization, perspective taking and affective connection. This part of the questionnaire was composed of 25 statements, 22 in a 5-point Likert scale from Completely disagree to Completely agree and 3 multiple choice ones. The Agency aspect contained 5 Likert- scale statements (Table 1) and 2 multiple choice ones attempting to elaborate on the nature of the users' decision making process. The Immersion aspect included 6 statements (Table 2) and the Transformation 11, plus one multiple choice one recording the participants' emotions during the experience.

3.3 The IDN Experience

The IDN experience in this study follows an approach of the gamebook, "Choose your own adventure" type [30], and its digital equivalent, the visual novel [31, 32]. It is a narrative driven experience written from a second-person point of view, with the reader assuming the role of the main character and making choices that determine this character's actions and the plot's outcome. The narrative consists of a series of dialogue episodes, presented in text and audio and combined with brief narrative parts setting the time and location as well as offering additional historical information about specific topics, upon user request. This information takes the form of a brief list of "frequently asked questions" at the end of each episode, such as "What is Tholos", "What is the

Peloponnesian War?" or "What is the exposure of infants?". Illustrations of the characters and locations are also offered as visual aids. After each episode, choices are offered in text format to the user on how they would like to proceed with a specific activity or what are their plans. After the end of the main story, there is the possibility to find out what happened to the main characters after.

This IDN is an adaptation of an IDN experience created for a mobile-based visit to an outdoors archeological site [33]. We added additional content and instructions to the story to make it suitable for off-site viewing. Another adaptation of this experience has been used as a collaborative informal learning activity for history education in [34], and used in a relevant study with teenagears examining the effects on historical empathy of conversation inspired by the decision points.

The main character of the story is an enslaved person of a relatively well-off household of ancient Athens. Slavery in ancient Athens during the classical period (480–323 BC) is considered a controversial institution for a city and time period that has beencharacterised as the "cradle of Democracy". This controversy as well as the well-known, but, at times, simplistic view of this society from the wider public creates an opportunity for interesting historical fiction. Especially during the specific period of the story setting, after the defeat of Athens has been defeated in the Peloponnesian War and the deep crisis of its aftermath, several of the story themes and topics are relevant also today: the financial crisis and its implications, ethical, political and social issues of distribution of wealth, and more personal issues of coping in times of crisis, fear for the future of the individual and their family and loved ones, feelings of trust, or lack of, towards others, etc. The different endings lead to various outcomes for the main character, all plausible in the specific historical context. They are a direct or indirect result of the users' choices, and some are more favorable than others. Being a branching narrative, the experience does not have a fixed time duration and it may range from 17 to 22 min.

The interactive storytelling experience features 7 decision points at each story path and 15 alternative endings defined by combinations of these decision points. To address the issue of "functional significance" [10] of the choices, some of the decision points are decisive about how the story unfolds later on. For example, already at the start of the experience, the user is asked to decide whether the main character should wear or not his protective amulet, which has been with him since he was a child (Fig. 1).

Some decision points are of a more ethical or emotional nature and are designed to provoke reflection rather than having any functional significance.

7th day of Skirophorion. The year when Euthycles was the so-called "eponymous archon" - meaning the ruler and lord. One hour before sunrise. You are about to accompany your master to the market. You are washing your face in the basin. You are wearing your tunic and sandals. On your way out, you see your amulet with the head of Hermes hanging on the door. You've had this amulet since you were an infant. What do you decide to do?

You carry the amulet with you. This is your lucky charm. You feel that it can help you.

You leave it behind. You feel like something could happen and you could lose it.

Fig. 1. Beginning of the story - example of decision point.

Following existing design approaches for IDN experiences, we decided to implement an approach to agency where the outcomes of the user choices are not directly evident to the user. These choices are not solely based on ethics but rather also on other behavioral criteria that the user decides to convey in place of the main character, such as the willingness to take risks. These ethical or attitude choices become the incentive for reflection on the perspective of the main characters, which are people of that historical period. Would it be realistic for me to make this choice, being an enslaved person in Athens of that time? Would it be beneficial for me to react in this way in the specific context? And what would be the consequences of my choices? This type of reflection on the choices may promote promote learning objectives related to historical empathy An example of a choice would be the following:

Eukratis: Maybe… But I want something in return…;
Nikoklis: What?
Eukratis (pointing at you): Him! Your slave! I have an idea on how to use him!
Eukratis' proposal comes as a shock. You..
are aware of your position and do not react at all.
forget your place and respond insolently.

In this type of choice users have to either consider the historical context and make a pragmatic choice, i.e. not react to being sold, or consider previous choices they made that imply certain character traits for the protagonist. The learning objective in this choice aims to promote reflection on the point of view of an enslaved person at that historical period, by not just presenting a series of facts, but rather attempt to help the users participate and understand that specific perspective.

The interactive experience has been implemented as a web-based multimedia application using the [35, 36] authoring tool.

3.4 Participants

67 participants responded to our open call for participation in the study. Of them, 45 were women, 22 men and 2 preferred not to disclose. In terms of age distribution, the majority fell in the range of 36 to 55. More specifically, the participants had the following age distribution: > 65 - 6 participants, 56–65 - 7 participants, 46–55 - 24 participants, 36–45 - 18 participants, 26–35 -7 participants, 19–25 - 5 participants.

The majority of the responders reported to already be somewhat or significantly knowledgeable in the history of Ancient Athens before the IDN experience (26 participants reported "much knowledge" on the topic and 29 "some") and professed an interest in history (AV = 4.3 and STD = 0.76 in a 1 to 5 Likert scale) and archaeology (AV = 3.88 and STD = 0.95). Similarly, the majority of the participants gave a high score to the statement "I love literature" (AV = 4.37 and STD = 0.88).

4 Analysis and Results

To explore RQ1, we firstly calculated the average and standard deviation for each of the Likert-scale statements, attempting to gain insight as to the effectiveness of the IDN experience in relation to the three aspects of Agency, Immersion and Transformation (Tables 1, 2 and 3). In Sect. 4.1, we present these results along with the rest of the close ended statements in each category and the analysis of the user comments, focusing on RQ1.

We then performed tests to explore correlations between the Agency related statements and those of the other two categories (RQ2). In the case of Agency, apart from using each of the E11, E12, E13 and E14 statements individually, we also calculated a combined "agency" score as the average of these four statements' scores. We employed this measure also in the statistical analysis. In each case the Pearson r correlation coefficient was calculated. This is a measure of linear correlation between two sets of data, which has a value between − 1 and 1, A value of 0 implies that there is no linear dependency between the variables. The results are presented in Sect. 4.2, which focuses on RQ2.

4.1 RQ1: IDN and Visitor Experience

Agency
Table 1 presents the average and standard deviation for the statements related to perceived user agency. It can be noted that the average for all statements is around 3.5, indicating that most users agreed to a certain level of perceived agency. Their responses to whether they would have liked the story to be linear, without choices, are mostly negative.

Table 1. Participants responses to the statements related to Agency - average score and standard deviation in a 5-point likert scale from 1 to 5.

Statement	Category	AV/STD
E11 - The experience gave me precisely those options to influence the storyline in the way that I had in mind	Autonomy	3.42/0.9
E12 - My choices had a direct impact on the events in the story	Effectance	3.7/0.93
E13 - I felt that my choices could affect the overall story outcome	Effectance	3.66/1
E14 - I could understand how my choices affected the events later on in the story	Effectance	3.53/1.15
E17 - I would have liked this experience to be linear (without choices)	Preference for Agency	1.66/0.86

In terms of their decision making approach (Fig. 2), 45% of the users made choices based on their own character whereas 34% attempted to think like the main character and decide as he would. 12% aimed for the optimum ending whereas 9% claimed to have made decisions randomly.

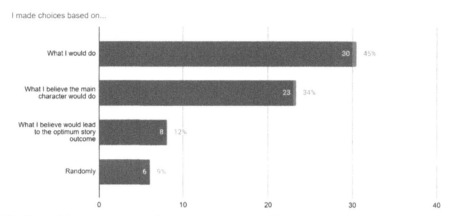

Fig. 2. Participant responses to the statements "The experience was…" Number of participants and percentage is shown. The participants could select only one option.

Immersion

In the case of Immersion, as shown in Table 2, the flow and believability aspects are closer to 4, indicating that the users did find the story characters and setting realistic and were absorbed by the experience. The suspense and role identification statements scored a bit lower, with an average closer to 3 ("Neither agree nor disagree").

Table 2. Participants' responses to the statements related to Immersion - average score and standard deviation in a 5-point Likert scale from 1 to 5.

Statement	Category	AV/STD
E3 - I hardly noticed the time passing	Flow	3.9/1
E8 - The story characters seemed realistic	Believability	3.88/0.88
E9 - Sometimes I felt anxious about how the story would develop	Suspense	3.3/1.11
E10 - I found myself wishing for a particular story outcome	Suspense	3.05/1.17
E22 - The experience brought the past to life for me	Believability	3.94/1.03
E25 - During the experience I identified with one or more of the characters	Role identification	3.03/1.25

Transformation

The participants' responses in most statements related to the Transformation aspects of the experience are positive, with an average score in most cases between 3.5 - 4 (Table 3). Participants reported to have enjoyed the experience with an average score of 3.94, and, similarly, liked the story plot (AV = 3.97). Especially in the case of meaning making, we note higher scores in statements E24 (AV = 4) and E31 (AV = 3.7) related to perspective taking and affective connection respectively. Taking into account that the ultimate objective of the experience is to promote informal learning in a cultural heritage context, and historical empathy, in particular, the experience seemed to be effective in that respect: Most participants felt that they learnt something new (E19) and are inspired to learn more (E21), as well as saw the past "through the eyes of its people".

Table 3. Participants responses to the statements related to Transformation - average score and standard deviation in a 5-point Likert scale from 1 to 5.

Statement	Category	AV/STD
E1 - I enjoyed the experience	Enjoyment	3.94/0.93
E4 - I will be thinking about this experience for some time to come	Eudaimonic appreciation	3.42/1.06
E5 - I would like to talk to others about this experience	Eudaimonic appreciation	3.69/1.13
E6 - I liked the story plot	Sensory delight	3.97/0.86
E7 - I liked the story visuals/images	Sensory delight	3.39/1.23
E19 - I learnt something that I did not know about Ancient Athens	Meaning making - Historical contextualization	3.37/1.28
E20 - The experience has changed my perception of the people of Ancient Athens	Meaning making - Historical contextualization	2.62/1.17
E21 - I am now inspired to want to learn more about Ancient Athens and its people	Meaning making - Affective connection	3.7/1.17
E23 - The experience made me think about issues and ideas that usually do not concern me	Meaning making - Perspective taking	3.09/1.13
E24 - The experience helped me see the past through the eyes of its people	Meaning making - Perspective taking	4/0.87
E26 - I felt that the life and the dilemmas of the characters have things in common with my own life	Meaning making - Affective connection	3.07/1.28

Participants were also asked to assign characteristics to both immersion and transformation aspects of the experience. As it can be seen from Fig. 3, 76% of the users characterized the story as "interesting" and 51% found it pleasant, followed by "innovative" (24%), "simple" (24%) and "concise" (19%).

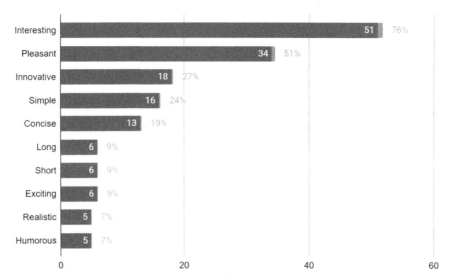

Fig. 3. Participant responses to the statements "The experience was…" Number of participants and percentage is shown. The participants could select more than one option.

4.2   RQ2: The Effect of User Perceived Agency on Immersion and Transformation

In this section we focus on the results of the analysis on possible correlations between the aspect of Agency and the other two visitor experience dimensions. Table 4 lists correlations between each of the statements and the agency measure we have defined (second column) as well each individual agency-related statement (third column). When there is a detected correlation with the Agency measure, the Pearson coefficient (Z) and significance (p) are provided. If there is not, a "-" is noted. Correlations with specific agency related statements are also noted.

Examining the results in Table 4, we observe correlations of the user-perceived sense of agency with the majority of Immersion and Transformation statements. In the 4 cases that no such correlation is detected, there are correlations with one or more of the Agency-related statements. These correlations are all less than 0.5 and thus can be characterized as "weak".

Figure 4 provides an additional indication on the participants' outlook on the choices. 61% users found them "interesting" as well as helpful to "immerse in the story" (33%), "reflect" (36%) or feel like "the main character" (21%). There were few users (9%) that found the choices "disruptive for the story flow" or "distracting".

Table 4. Identified correlations between the questionnaire statements related to Immersion and TRansformation and the combined Agency score (second column) and individual agency-related statements (third column).

Statement	Correlation with Agency	Correlations with Agency statements
Immersion		
E3 - I hardly noticed the time passing	$Z = 0.244$, $p = 0.047$	E14: $Z = 0.274$, $p = 0.026$
E8 - The story characters seemed realistic	$Z = 0.284$, $p = 0.02$	E12: $Z = 0.329$, $p = 0.007$, E13: $Z = 0.362$, $p = 0.003$
E9 - Sometimes I felt anxious about how the story would develop	-	E11: $Z = 0.348$, $p = 0.004$, E12: $Z = 0.428$, $p < 0.001$
E10 - I found myself wishing for a particular story outcome	$Z = 0.254$, $p = 0.04$	E11: $Z = 0.340$, $p = 0.006$, E12: $Z = 0.485$, $p < 0.001$, E14: $Z = 0.277$, $p = 0.025$
E22 - The experience brought the past to life for me	$Z = 0.299$, $p = 0.014$	E11: $Z = 0.327$, $p = 0.007$, E12: $Z = 0.333$, $p = 0.006$, E13: $Z = 0.3$, $p = 0.015$
E25 - During the experience I identified with one or more of the characters	-	E14: $Z = 0.302$, $p = 0.01$
Transformation		
E1 - I enjoyed the experience	$Z = 0.370$, $p = 0.002$,	E11: $Z = 0.300$, $p = 0.016$, E12: $Z = 0.384$, $p = 0.002$, E13: $Z = 0.337$, $p = 0.007$, E14: $Z = 0.354$, $p = 0.004$
E4 - I will be thinking about this experience for some time to come	$Z = 0.347$, $p = 0.004$	E11: $Z = 0.395$, $p = 0.001$, E12: $Z = 0.329$, $p = 0.007$, E13: $Z = 0.360$, $p = 0.003$, E14: $Z = 0.334$, $p = 0.006$
E5 - I would like to talk to others about this experience	$Z = 0.287$, $p = 0.019$	E12: $Z = 0.373$, $p = 0.002$, E13: $Z = 0.324$, $p = 0.008$
E6 - I liked the story plot	$Z = 0.422$, $p < 0.001$	E11: $Z = 0.398$, $p = 0.001$, E12: $Z = 0.375$, $p = 0.002$, E13: $Z = 0.383$, $p = 0.002$, E14: $Z = 0.405$, $p = 0.001$
E7 - I liked the story visuals/images	$Z = 0.317$, $p = 0.10$	E11: $Z = 0.284$, $p = 0.022$, E12: $Z = 0.389$, $p = 0.001$, E13: $Z = 0.358$, $p = 0.004$, E14: $Z = 0.257$, $p = 0.039$
E19 - I learnt something that I did not know about Ancient Athens		

(*continued*)

Table 4. (*continued*)

Statement	Correlation with Agency	Correlations with Agency statements
E20 - The experience has changed my perception of the people of Ancient Athens	-	E11: Z = 0.243, p = 0.049
E21 - I am now inspired to want to learn more about Ancient Athens and its people	-	E11: Z = 0.285, p = 0.021, E13: Z = 0.284, p = 0.022
E23 - The experience made me think about issues and ideas that usually do not concern me	Z = 0.266, p = 0.033	E11: Z = 0.408, p = 0.001, E12: Z = 0.426, p < 0.001
E24 - The experience helped me see the past through the eyes of its people	Z = 0.342, p = 0.005,	E11: Z = 0.353, p = 0.004, E12: Z = 0.340, p = 0.005, E13: Z = 0.308, p = 0.012, E14: Z = 0.259, p = 0. 036
E26 - I felt that the life and the dilemmas of the characters have things in common with my own life	-	E13: Z = 0.337, p = 0.007

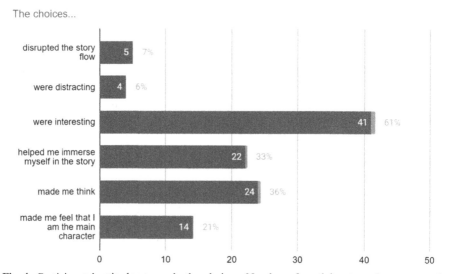

Fig. 4. Participants' attitudes towards the choices. Number of participants and percentage is shown. The participants could select more than one option.

5 Discussion and Conclusions

Based on the premise that digital storytelling has been a well-established practice for cultural heritage and the informal learning of history, we set out to explore whether addressing the additional design challenge of interactivity in the form of user agency to create an IDN is really worth it in this field. Previous evaluations of digital storytelling approaches with visitors have hinted at the need to offer "more interactivity". To this end, in this work we design a user study where we attempt to evaluate a historical "choose your own adventure" IDN, based on the Roth and Koenitz framework [26], which is combined with the historical empathy model for the education of history [27]. We focus on examining (a) the users' perspective on an IDN offered as a virtual experience for remote visitors, in terms of its immersion and transformation aspects, and (b), the user perceived agency this IDN offers and its correlations with the other experience dimensions.

Our results indeed reveal that the experience has been effective to an extent in both the immersion and transformation directions and the role of agency seems to have been an important contributing factor. Although in our study the identified correlations of Agency with Immersion and Transformation are characterized as weak, for the domain of cultural heritage they provide a strong indication that Agency can indeed play a key role in transformative learning. Agency contributes to the development of awareness of personal and social contextual influences via the storytelling experience. As seen in the results in Sect. 4.2 the role of feelings, context and reflection are significant in fostering transformation. Results reveal that if IDN experiences support agency, with historical empathy as the ultimate objective, users are willing to engage in perspective taking, affective connection, critical thinking and reflection and then change can be initiated which is indeed a crucial part of transformation and transformative learning. Regarding immersion, agency and choices seem to act as a path to implementing a specific type of immersion. Immersion and choices exist as related and distinct elements in storytelling. Examining their effects on interaction within the story, immersion is evident in realism, plot development and identification regarding historical events and figures. Therefore immersion is important in order to project the past through the story and the choices given are important to determine how users move within the story, in other words how they would "exist" in the past, as characters.

Schnepfleitner and Ferreira [37] take Mezirow's core elements of transformative learning and apply them to storytelling. The Role of Critical Reflection in storytelling can be used to examine values and beliefs which transcends superficial learning. The Role of Dialogue, as the dialogue that occurs between the conscious and the unconscious, can help us understand or become aware of our internal self and how we project that to the world. The Role of Individual Experience in storytelling involves the first-person perspectives of current or previous experiences which are conditioned and formed by the lens through which we interpret and make sense and meaning of the world. The IDN experience presented in this study attempted, and up to a point, succeeded to align with these three elements. However, it is important to conduct more follow-up studies focusing on qualitative data and delving deeper on the function of specific design elements on the transformative learning process. As an example, role identification seems to be a key dimension of immersion that may promote the perspective taking and affective connection aspects of historical empathy and its exact function in this context needs to be further examined, combined with methods to enhance it.

Our results support the hypothesis that agency is appropriate for the implementation of transformative learning in digital storytelling experiences for cultural heritage sites. The design implications in this case require an IDN experience design that allows users to make decisions freely and also respond to these decisions well. It is up to the authors/ designers at which points of the narrative/story plot these decisions can be implemented and evaluated and at which points the risk and behavior patterns of users will bear consequences. Agency is still underexplored in IDNs for cultural heritage, however it is a promising direction for research. Research could also explore more in-depth the functionality of agency in transformative learning and how to implement it correctly in order to avoid deviations which will affect user experience, i.e. users trying to manipulate the direction of the plot to achieve the optimum outcome irrespective of role-identification. Examining more closely in this context types of agency that have been defined in the wider IDN and gaming field, such as "illusory" agency [38] and "invisible" agency [21] is also a possible direction for future research.

As Şengün [21] states [through invisible agency "the direction of the narration becomes extremely personal – and almost subconscious. Then the final impact of the overall experience becomes deeply imposing and sometimes even a bit disturbing".

For this study we opted not to use a second, linear digital storytelling as a control condition. One reason was addressing the complex issue of what would be the linear equivalent of this interactive story with alternative endings and the question of whether the two would be really comparable, as well as the need to have as many participants evaluating the IDN version. We plan however to follow up with a new study focusing on how the interactive version would compare with a linear one.

Understanding how users relate to IDN experiences for cultural heritage informs experts on what pieces of information are important and how authors will write these stories. By defining guidelines for the use of agency and the types of choices and their relation to immersion and transformation in order to achieve informal learning objectives. This type of research could be crucial in order to better understand the strengths and the weaknesses of such approaches and trigger reflective dialogue on the use of storytelling techniques framed by the historical empathy model, different point of views, identifications etc. and how these shape the affective connection of the user to characters of the past (real or fictional), in interactive media.

References

1. Bedford, L.: Storytelling: The Real Work of Museums. Curator: The Museum Journal **44**, 27–34 (2001)
2. Lombardo, V., Damiano, R.: Storytelling on mobile devices for cultural heritage. New Review of Hypermedia and Multimedia **18**(1–2), 11–35 (2012). https://doi.org/10.1080/13614568. 2012.617846
3. Pau, S.: Audio that moves you: experiments with location-aware storytelling in the SFMOMA app. In: MW17: Museums and the Web 2017, Archives & Museum Informatics, https://mw17.mwconf.org/paper/audio-that-moves-you-experiments-with-location-aware-storytelling-in-the-sfmoma-app/, last accessed 30 July 2022
4. Roussou, M., Katifori, A.: Flow, staging, wayfinding, personalization: evaluating user experience with mobile museum narratives. Multimodal Technologies and Interaction **2**(2), 32 (2018). https://doi.org/10.3390/MTI2020032

5. Poole, S.: Ghosts in the Garden: locative gameplay and historical interpretation from below. Int. J. Herit. Stud. **24**(3), 300–314 (2018). https://doi.org/10.1080/13527258.2017.1347887
6. Liarokapis, F., Voulodimos, A., Doulamis, N., Doulamis, A. (eds.): Visual Computing for Cultural Heritage. SSCC, Springer, Cham (2020). https://doi.org/10.1007/978-3-030-37191-3
7. Pujol, L., Roussou, M., Poulou, S., Balet, O., Vayanou, M., Ioannidis, Y.: Personalizing interactive digital storytelling in archaeological museums: the CHESS project. In: Earl, G., Sly, T., Chrysanthi, A., Murrieta-Flores, P., Papadopoulos, C., Romanowska, I., Wheatley, D. (eds.) 40th Annual Conference of Computer Applications and Quantitative Methods in Archaeology (CAA), pp. 77–90. Amsterdam University Press, Southampton (2012)
8. Coerver, C.: On (Digital) Content Strategy (2016), https://www.sfmoma.org/read/on-digital-content-strategy/, last accessed 19 July 2022
9. Katifori, A., Karvounis, M., Kourtis, V., Perry, S., Roussou, M., Ioanidis, Y.: Applying Interactive Storytelling in Cultural Heritage: Opportunities, Challenges and Lessons Learned. In: Rouse, R., Koenitz, H., Haahr, M. (eds.) ICIDS 2018. LNCS, vol. 11318, pp. 603–612. Springer, Cham (2018). https://doi.org/10.1007/978-3-030-04028-4_70
10. Crawford, C.: Interactive storytelling. In: Wolf, M.J., Perron, B. (eds.) The Video Game Theory Reader. Routledge, New York (2003)
11. Vosmeer, M., Schouten, B.: Interactive Cinema: Engagement and Interaction. In: Mitchell, A., Fernández-Vara, C., Thue, D. (eds.) ICIDS 2014. LNCS, vol. 8832, pp. 140–147. Springer, Cham (2014). https://doi.org/10.1007/978-3-319-12337-0_14
12. Murray, J.: Hamlet on the Holodeck. Free Press, New York (1997)
13. Crawford, C.: Chris Crawford on game design. New Riders, Indianapolis (2003)
14. Zimmerman, E.: Narrative, interactivity, play, and games: Four naughty concepts in need of discipline. First person: New media as story, performance, and game, 154 (2004). https://static1.squarespace.com/static/579b8aa26b8f5b8f49605c96/t/5992108bf7e0 ab87779d3dc0/1502744715814/Four_Concepts.pdf
15. Ryan, M.L.: Narrative as Virtual Reality: Immersion and Interactivity in Literature and Electronic Media. Johns Hopkins UP, Baltimore (2001)
16. Murakami, M.H.: November. Narrative agency and user experience in transmedia narratives: Brazilian telenovelas case. In: Proceedings of the Latin American Conference on Human Computer Interaction (CLIHC '15), Article 20, pp. 1–4. Association for Computing Machinery, New York (2015). https://doi.org/10.1145/2824893.2824911
17. Kolhoff, L., Nack, F.: How Relevant Is Your Choice? In: Cardona-Rivera, R.E., Sullivan, A., Young, R.M. (eds.) ICIDS 2019. LNCS, vol. 11869, pp. 73–85. Springer, Cham (2019). https://doi.org/10.1007/978-3-030-33894-7_9
18. Vermeulen, I.E., Roth, C., Vorderer, P., Klimmt, C.: Measuring User Responses to Interactive Stories: Towards a Standardized Assessment Tool. In: Aylett, R., Lim, M.Y., Louchart, S., Petta, P., Riedl, M. (eds.) ICIDS 2010. LNCS, vol. 6432, pp. 38–43. Springer, Heidelberg (2010). https://doi.org/10.1007/978-3-642-16638-9_7
19. Mateas, M., Stern, A.: Interaction and narrative. In: Tekinbas, K.S., Zimmerman, E. (eds.) The game design reader: A rules of play anthology 1, pp. 642–669. MIT press, Massachusetts (2005)
20. Tanenbaum, K., Tanenbaum, T.J.: Agency as commitment to meaning: communicative competence in games. Digital Creativity **21**(1), 11–17 (2010). https://doi.org/10.1080/146262610 03654509
21. Şengün, S.: Silent hill 2 and the curious case of invisible agency. In: Koenitz, H., Sezen, T.I., Ferri, G., Haahr, M., Sezen, D., Çatak, G. (eds.) ICIDS 2013. LNCS, vol. 8230, pp. 180–185. Springer, Cham (2013). https://doi.org/10.1007/978-3-319-02756-2_22
22. Ryabova, A.: The Games that Play with Us: How Invisible Agency Affects the Player's Experience and Changes Narrative? University of Dublin, Master of Science Interactive Digital Media (2021)

23. Hannesson, H.J., Reimann-Andersen, T., Burelli, P., Bruni, L.E.: Connecting the Dots: Quantifying the Narrative Experience in Interactive Media. In: Schoenau-Fog, H., Bruni, L.E., Louchart, S., Baceviciute, S. (eds.) ICIDS 2015. LNCS, vol. 9445, pp. 189–201. Springer, Cham (2015). https://doi.org/10.1007/978-3-319-27036-4_18

24. Bruni, L.E., Baceviciute, S., Arief, M.: Narrative Cognition in Interactive Systems: Suspense-Surprise and the P300 ERP Component. In: Mitchell, A., Fernández-Vara, C., Thue, D. (eds.) ICIDS 2014. LNCS, vol. 8832, pp. 164–175. Springer, Cham (2014). https://doi.org/10.1007/978-3-319-12337-0_17

25. Roth, C., Koenitz, H.: Evaluating the user experience of interactive digital narrative. In: Proceedings of the 1st International Workshop on Multimedia Alternate Realities (AltMM '16), pp. 31–36. Association for Computing Machinery, New York (2016). https://doi.org/10.1145/2983298.2983302

26. Mezirow, J.: How critical reflection triggers transformative learning. Fostering critical reflection in adulthood **1**(20), 1–6 (1990)

27. Endacott, J., Brooks, S.: An updated theoretical and practical model for promoting historical empathy. Soc. Stud. Res. Pract. **8**(1), 41–58 (2013). https://doi.org/10.1108/SSRP-01-2013-B0003

28. McKinney, S., Perry, S., Katifori, A., Kourtis, V.: Developing digital archaeology for young people: a model for fostering empathy and dialogue in formal and informal learning environments. In: Hageneuer, S. (ed.) Communicating the Past in the Digital Age: Proceedings of the International Conference on Digital Methods in Teaching and Learning in Archaeology, pp. 179–195. Ubiquity Press, London (2020). https://doi.org/10.5334/bch.n

29. Psaltis, C., Carretero, M., Čehajić-Clancy, S. (eds.): History Education and Conflict Transformation. Springer, Cham (2017). https://doi.org/10.1007/978-3-319-54681-0

30. Jenkins, K.M.: Choose your own adventure: Interactive narratives and attitude change. Master of Arts in the Department of Psychology (Social), The University of North Carolina, Chapel Hill (2014)

31. Cavallaro, D.: Anime and the Visual Novel: Narrative Structure, Design and Play at the Crossroads of Animation and Computer Games. McFarland & Company, Jefferson (2010)

32. Øygardslia, K., Weitze, C.L., Shin, J.: The Educational Potential of Visual Novel Games: Principles for Design. Replaying Japan 2, (2020). https://www.researchgate.net/publication/341380379

33. Katifori, A., Roussou, M., Kaklopoulou, I., Servi, K.: Mobile interactive storytelling in the Athens Ancient Agora: exploring the right balance between the Site and the App, in XVII. Culture and Computer Science (Berlin), pp. 47–60 (2019).

34. Petousi, D., Katifori, A., Servi, K, Roussou, M., Ioannidis, Y.: History education done different: a collaborative interactive digital storytelling approach for remote learners. Front. Educ. (12 August 2022). https://doi.org/10.3389/feduc.2022.942834

35. Vrettakis, E., Kourtis, V., Katifori, A., Karvounis, M., Lougiakis, C., Ioannidis, Y.: Narralive – Creating and experiencing mobile digital storytelling in cultural her-itage, Digital Applications in Archaeology and Cultural Heritage, Volume 15 (2019)

36. Vrettakis, E., et al.: The Story Maker - An Authoring Tool for Multimedia-Rich Interactive Narratives. In: Bosser, A.-G., Millard, D.E., Hargood, C. (eds.) ICIDS 2020. LNCS, vol. 12497, pp. 349–352. Springer, Cham (2020). https://doi.org/10.1007/978-3-030-62516-0_33

37. Schnepfleitner, F.M., Ferreira, M.P.: Transformative Learning Theory–Is It Time to Add A Fourth Core Element? Journal of Educational Studies and Multidisciplinary Approaches **1**(1), 40–49 (2021)
38. MacCallum-Stewart, E., Parsler, J.: Illusory agency in vampire: The masquerade–Bloodlines. Dichtung Digital. Journal für Kunst und Kultur digitaler Medien **9**(1), 1–17 (2007). https://doi.org/10.25969/mediarep/17706
39. Habel, C., Kooyman, B.: Agency mechanics: gameplay design in survival horror video games. Digital Creativity **25**(1), 1–14 (2014). https://doi.org/10.1080/14626268.2013.776971

Interactive Cartographic Storytelling with Complex Spatio-Temporal Structures and Social Connections

Ying Zhu[1]([✉]), Aylish Turner[2], Naomi Yonas[3], and Douglas Blackmon[1]

[1] Georgia State University, Atlanta, GA, USA
{yzhu,dblackmon}@gsu.ed
[2] University of Southern California, Los Angeles, CA, USA
aeturner@usc.edu
[3] University of California at Berkeley, Berkeley, CA, USA
naomi.yonas01@berkeley.edu

Abstract. In this paper, we describe the design of an interactive carto-graphic storytelling platform for the 1906 Atlanta Race Massacre, a hor-rific incident that had a profound impact on the civil and human rights movement in the United States. This four-day event happened at various locations in downtown Atlanta and involved many people. Although mul-tiple books and articles have been written about the 1906 Atlanta Race Massacre, they described the past events using conventional storytelling methods. We want to tell this story from a cartographic perspective because the locations are essential to this story. We also want to con-nect the past with the present because most people walking on the same streets today do not know the history and significance of the locations. Furthermore, most people are unaware that some major institutions are intricately connected to the people involved in the 1906 events. Telling the story this way requires us to handle a complex spatio-temporal struc-ture and an extensive social network, which is unusual in traditional car-tographic storytelling. In this paper, we discuss our design decisions and rationals. We believe our discussion will benefit other interactive story designers who deal with similar complex stories.

Keywords: Interactive narrative design · Cartographic storytelling · Historical event · Case studies

1 Introduction

Cartographic storytelling [8,9,12,18,20,21,26] is a type of visual storytelling [16,17,24]. Although there are different cartographic storytelling genres, almost all assume a linear narrative sequence [21]. However, in telling the 1906 Atlanta Race Massacre story, we encountered a more complex spatio-temporal structure and an extensive social network.

Supported in part by NSF Award #1852516.

M. Vosmeer and L. Holloway-Attaway (Eds.): ICIDS 2022, LNCS 13762, pp. 68–82, 2022.
https://doi.org/10.1007/978-3-031-22298-6_4

The Atlanta Race Massacre happened in September 1906 in Atlanta, Georgia, United States. For four days, White mobs roamed downtown streets, destroyed Black-owned properties, and beat and killed many Black people. Many prominent White politicians, journalists, and businessmen in Atlanta were directly or indirectly involved in the incident. These people had a complicated social network, and their legacies are still deeply connected to some major institutions today. Although the record of the ordinary Black people's experience in this period is hard to find, many Black business leaders and intellectuals were deeply affected by the incident. They took actions that profoundly impacted the civil and human rights movements in the US. In addition, many streets and buildings where the 1906 incident happened are still standing today. But most people are not aware of their history and significance.

Although this event made national and even international headlines at the time (Fig. 1b), it was largely forgotten until the 2000s.s. Since then, the story was told in many articles and several books [2,4,7,13,25,27]. All the publications about this event have used conventional storytelling methods, such as text and pictures. They mostly told what happened in 1906. Our work differs from the previous works in several ways. First, we want to tell the story from a cartographic perspective because locations are essential to this story. Much of the story happened on the streets, and most of the same streets and some key buildings still stand today, and they can be easily found on Google Earth. Second, we want our readers to connect the past with the present because most people are unaware of what happened in 1906 on these familiar streets. Third, we want our readers to explore the stories of the characters closely related to the 1906 event, their complicated social network, their legacies, and their deep connections to the major institutions around us today. Overall, we want to provide readers with a broader and deeper understanding of the 1906 event and its intricate connections to our surroundings.

Our story has a complicated structure. There is a location-driven story structure and a social-network-driven story structure. We also deal with three types of timelines: the timeline of the 1906 events, the timeline of a person's history and legacy, and the connection between a location in 1906 and the same location in the present day. Telling the story in such a way, we realize that our project differs from the existing interactive cartographic storytelling framework, which focuses mainly on the spatio-temporal structure. Therefore, we need to explore new techniques to tell the story.

In this paper, we describe our design decisions and rationals for the visual interface layout and user interactions. Our storytelling UI, built on the Google Earth Engine, has four synchronized components: locations, event narratives, characters narratives, and social networks. Each component allows readers to explore a different dimension of the story. The locations, event narratives, and character narratives each deal with a different timeline: locations for the past and present, event narratives for the chronology of the 1906 incident, and character narratives for the personal history and legacy of the characters.

The interactive story platform we are building will be an educational tool for learning the 1906 Atlanta Race Massacre, with a purpose similar to the New York Times' interactive story for learning the Tulsa Massacre [11]. The techniques discussed in this paper can benefit other storytellers who need to tell stories with similar complex structures.

2   Related Work

There have been several surveys and classifications of narrative visualization [16,17,19,24]. Segel and Heer [24] conducted a design space analysis of narrative visualization based on 58 examples. They divided the design space into three main features: genre, visual narrative tactics, and narrative structure tactics. They also placed narrative visualizations along a spectrum of author-driven and reader-driven approaches. Based on their framework, our project belongs to the "Annotated Graph/Map" genre, with a combination of linear and random access ordering in narrative tactics. Our story is primarily reader-driven.

Hullman and Diakopoulos [16] classified many rhetoric techniques used in narrative visualization. Based on their framework, our project used the rhetoric techniques of contrast and similarity. Ojo and Herav [19] analyzed the story typologies in 44 award-winning data stories. Our work relates to one of their story types: "Enable deeper understanding."

There have also been multiple reviews of cartographic storytelling [8,10,18, 20,21,26]. Phillips [20] identified eight basic plots of storytelling in earth sciences, but they are not related to our telling of historical events. Tally [26] explored the relationships between map and literature, and presented the idea that writers, readers, and critics are map creators and navigators. Caquard and Cartwright [8] identified two types of relationships between map and narrative: the narrative of map and the narrative of mapping. Our work belongs to the narrative of map, presenting spatio-temporal structures of our story and their relationships with places.

Mocnik and Fairbairn [18] compared cartographic and textual representations and concluded that texts have a stronger affordance of telling a story than maps because, although time and non-spatial aspects play an important role in stories, they are structurally underrepresented in a map. However, maps are good at depicting the relationship between locations. In our project, we use both cartographic and textual representations to tell the story. Spatial relationships are depicted in Google Earth, and the time structure is presented in texts. The synchronization of maps and texts establishes the spatio-temporal structure of the story.

Cortes [10] developed a conceptual framework for interactive cartographic storytelling that consists of two main components: visual narrative tactics and rhetoric devices.

Roth [21] pointed out the limitations of the taxonomy by Segel and Heer [24] for cartographic storytelling, proposed a different set of visual storytelling genres, and identified many visual storytelling tropes. He stated that visual storytelling genres differ by the visual or interactive technique used to enforce linearity in the narrative sequence. Given the non-linear structure of our story, we find it difficult to fit our work into Roth's genre framework. Perhaps the closest classification of our work is a combination of multimedia visual experiences and dynamic slide shows.

Many previous works have dealt with complex spatio-temporal structures in cartographic storytelling [3,5,6,9,15,22,23] but very few have dealt with both complex spatio-temporal and social network structure. Caquard and Fiset [9] developed a cybercartographic application for narrative cartography. They used it to visualize the spatio-temporal structure of the events in a movie. But the characters were not part of the visualization. Bogucka, et al. [5] described their cartographic narrative of cultural maps. It allows the comparison between Vienna, Paris, London, and New York. Also, it deals with multiple temporal dimensions, such as the city's spatial development, historical gender biases and modern responses to mitigate them, and the rise and fall of occupations throughout history. But there are no individual persons in the narrative.

Dos Santos, et al. [22] developed spatio-temporal storytelling techniques to analyze the relationships between violent events. The analysis focused on the location and time of the events but not on the connections between people. In another work, Dos Santos, et al. [23] used spatio-temporal storytelling techniques for intelligence analysis. Although social network data, such as Twitter, was used as an input into the system, the focus was on spatio-temporal analysis, and the social network itself was not explored.

Hewitt [15] created a cartographic narrative of the Battle of Hastings, showing the spatio-temporal nature of the events but not the relationship between the characters. Brown [6] developed a web-based cartographic narrative of the slave revolt in Jamaica in 1760–1761. The narrative is organized as interactive, animated slideshows of locations and timelines. The relationship between the characters is not explicitly explored or visualized.

The main difference between our work and the previous works is that we are dealing with a complicated spatio-temporal structure and a complicated social-network structure.

In terms of content, the New York Times' interactive story about the Tulsa Massacre [11] is the closest to our work. They used computer-generated 3D models, camera animations, maps, and historical pictures to help provide a guided tour of the event. But overall, it is largely based on a traditional journalism storytelling layout, and user interactivity is limited.

Our work was also inspired by two interactive media applications. One is the Google Earth-based game "Where on Google Earth is Carmen Sandiego?" [14]. The other is Arcade Fire's music video website "The Wilderness Downtown" [1].

3   1906 Atlanta Race Massacre and Its Legacy

A horrific event happened in Atlanta, United States, between September 22nd and 25th, 1906. White mobs roamed downtown streets, destroyed black-owned properties, and beat and killed Black people. At least 25 Black people were killed.

This incident was preceded by the 1906 Georgia governor's race between Hoke Smith and Clark Howell. Both candidates played to White fears of a Black upper class. Multiple newspapers of the time published articles about the unsubstantiated accounts of White women being attacked by Black men. White men were particularly enraged by these unjustified accounts and felt largely compelled to harm Black people. As thousands of White men gathered on Peachtree Street's Five Points during the afternoon of September 22nd, the tension from the articles and the growing economic competition between White and Black Atlantans reached a breaking point. Their violence continued up Peachtree Street where Black businessman Alonzo Herndon's barber shop was destroyed by the mob. Simultaneously, a large group of the mob moved through Marietta Street, where the US Post Office and Henry Grady statue were located. A couple of Black people were engulfed by the mob at the post office, and one Black man was killed and thrown on the steps of Grady's Statue as he tried to run away. That same night on Decatur Street, the White mob destroyed several Black businesses and harmed any Black person they saw on the street.

Many prominent White politicians, journalists, and businessmen were involved in the 1906 incident. James W. English, former Mayor of Atlanta and chairman of the City Police Commission at the time, did not prevent the riot from happening. Ernest Woodruff, the future owner of Coca-Cola, and many other business leaders signed a public petition that condemned the (mostly imaginary) alleged assaults on White women that supposedly triggered the attacks and blamed the situation on African-Americans. But the petition also expressed criticism of the Ku Klux Klan. This group of elite White citizens was closely connected, and their legacies are deeply connected to some major institutions today.

Although Black families hoped to defend themselves following the brutal events of Saturday, the Fulton County police arrested and disarmed them while the White mobs continued their rampage. In the aftermath of this event, there were several discussions between both communities to prevent any continued violence. Even though this stopped the massacre, additional issues arose that strengthened the racial segregation in the city for the long term [13].

The 1906 incident profoundly impacted the civil and human rights movement in the United States. Civil rights leaders, such as William E. B. Du Bois and Walter White, were deeply affected by the 1906 incident and advocated a more confrontational stance, which led to the founding of NAACP (The National Association for the Advancement of Colored People).

The 1906 Atlanta Race Massacre was largely buried and forgotten until 2000s s when several scholars published books on this event (Fig. 1a) [2,4,7,13]. There has been growing interest in this event and its legacy [25,27].

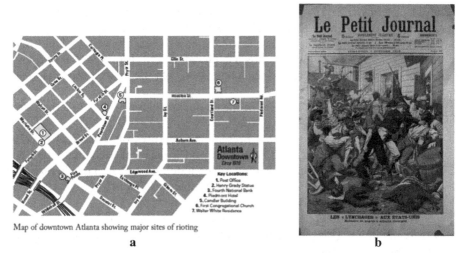

Map of downtown Atlanta showing major sites of rioting

a   b

Fig. 1. a. Key locations of the 1906 event [7]; b. The cover of Le Petit Journal (France), from October 7, 1906, is titled "Massacre of Negroes at Atlanta."

4   Interactive Narrative Design

A story event has four main components: location, time, character, and actions. Our interactive visual interface is divided into the following windows (Fig. 2).

- Window for the present day locations (Google Earth)
- Window for the past locations (showing old pictures)
- Event narrative window for the 1906 events
- Character narrative window for a character's history and legacy (a pop-up information window)
- A social network diagram (Fig. 4)

Our goal is to enable a deeper understanding of the 1906 Atlanta Race Massacre and its legacy. To achieve this goal, we need to handle the following tasks.

- Present the events of 1906.
  We decided to tell the story primarily based on locations rather than in chronological order. This is because the 1906 events mostly happened on the streets. The locations of the events are usually clear, but the timelines of some events are uncertain. In addition, some events happened simultaneously. Therefore, it is more logical to present the story by location. Readers explore the story by moving from location to location. The narrative of the events for each location is shown in the event narrative window (Fig. 2).
- Contrast the locations of the 1906 events to the same locations today.
  All the streets where the 1906 events happened are still there today. Some buildings, such as the Hurt Building, the Grady Statue, and possibly the Herndon Barber Shop, are still standing. The locations of the past are shown

in old pictures (Fig. 2). There are a few photos of the 1906 event and some drawings. We also have a collection of postcards from the 1900s s that show the streets and buildings of downtown Atlanta during that time. The same locations of the present day are shown in Google Earth (Fig. 2). We are exploring the possibility of superimposing and aligning old pictures on top of Google Earth.

– Present the histories and legacies of the characters closely related to the 1906 events.
  For each event and location, we present the pictures of characters closely related to the event (Fig. 2). The history and legacies of each character are displayed in a pop-up character narrative window (Fig. 3b). The character's legacy is also presented in a social network diagram (Fig. 4).
– Present the social connections between the characters.
  The social connections between the characters are described in the character narrative window (Fig. 3b). The social network diagram shows all the social connections in one picture (Fig. 4).
– Connect the characters to the institutions.
  The connections between characters and institutions are presented in the character's narrative window. When a past institution is clicked, an old picture is displayed in the past location window. When a current institution is clicked, the Google Earth window will display the location of the institution.
– Present the connections between the institutions, both past and present.
  The connections between the past and current institutions are presented in the social network diagram (Fig. 4). If an old picture is available, the old picture and the present-day location in Google Earth will be displayed.

Figure 3a shows the internal structure of our story.

4.1   Google Earth

Google Earth (Fig. 5) was selected for development due to its geolocation tools and accessibility. Google Earth's street view is a powerful visual tool that allows both the developer and the user to customize the perspective of a real-life location, allowing a simultaneous presentation of the past and present when placed alongside historical images of the same location. The ability to rotate 360°C within the location and "walk" virtually along the streets of downtown Atlanta also allows for greater user immersion and interactivity, effectively placing the user on the physical route of events during the 1906 Atlanta Race Massacre.

Additionally, Google Earth projects can be further customized using HTML, CSS, and JavaScript. By editing the Google Earth info box and creating an HTML/CSS template, an adaptable code framework that included location, non-linear movement, and character connections was formed. In combination with Google Earth's drag-and-drop UI, our project could be shared and edited to suit other complicated historical stories as necessary.

Fig. 2. The visual interface of our interactive narrative

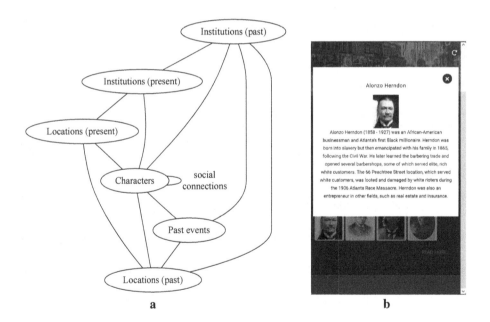

Fig. 3. a. Internal structure of our story; b. Character information window

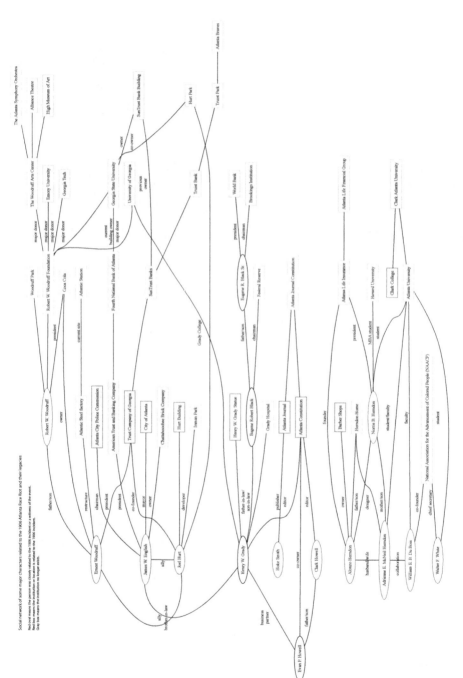

Fig. 4. The social network of selected people closely related to the 1906 Atlanta race massacre

Fig. 5. Google earth studio

4.2   Locations

The 1906 Atlanta Race Massacre happened around the streets of downtown Atlanta. The key locations include Five Points (where the mob congregated), the old Post Office (where a Black men was killed), Henry Grady Satue (a rallying point for the mob), Herndon's barber shop (Black-owned business), Candler Building, Fourth National Bank, Piedmont Hotel, etc. [7]

We have completed the narratives for four key locations: Five Points, Henry Grady Statue and the Old Post Office, Herndon's barber shop, and Candler Building. Our project is still a work in progress, and we are continuing to add more locations.

Figure 6 shows the visual interface for Five Points, including the Google Earth window, past location window, narrative about the 1906 events, and the related characters. When a character's picture is clicked, a window will display the narrative for that character (see Fig. 3b). Figure 2 shows the visual interface for the old post office and the Henry Grady Statue. The statue is still there today. Figure 7 shows the visual interface for Herndon's Barbershop. Figure 8 shows the visual interface for the Candler Building, which is still standing today.

Since this is a location-driven narrative, we provide two interfaces for readers to navigate the story. One is a slide show-based navigation where users can click the arrows in the Google Earth window to go to different locations (see Fig. 6). Another is a random access navigation control where readers can select locations on a Google Map view (Fig. 9).

Fig. 6. The visual interface for five points. This was where the riot started. The mob moved from this location in all directions.

4.3 Time

There are three types of timelines in our story. First, there is the timeline of the 1906 events, which contains some uncertainty. We present these events in the event narrative window (Fig. 2, Fig. 6, Fig. 7, and Fig. 8). As discussed earlier, we have adopted a location-driven structure. But for each location, the event is described chronologically. Second, there is the history and legacy of each character. This part of the story is told chronologically in the pop-up character narrative window (Fig. 3b). Third, there is the comparison between the location of the present day and the same location in the past. This is achieved by displaying the Google Earth (location of the present day) window and the "location of past" window side by side (Fig. 8).

4.4 Characters and Their Legacies

A key feature of our interactive narrative design is to let readers explore the intricate social connections between the characters and their connections to the major institutions in Georgia. This is the main difference between our work and the previous descriptions of the 1906 Atlanta Race Massacre. We want to show how the past is connected to the present, not just via locations but also through social connections because most people are unaware of such connections.

For example, the 1906 Atlanta Race Massacre was the key event that led William E. B. Du Bois co-founded NAACP. Walter White, who witnessed the 1906 events, later became the Chief Secretary of NAACP. Alonzo Herndon, whose barbershop was attacked by the White mob, founded Atlanta Life Insurance, whose successor Atlanta Life Financial Group is still operating today, with

Fig. 7. The visual interface for Herndon's barbershop. This business was attacked by the mob. Based on the old picture, it seems that the old building is still there. But we have not confirmed it.

Fig. 8. The visual interface for the candler building. This is a key landmark around which the riot happened. The building is still standing today.

Fig. 9. Key locations related to the 1906 Atlanta Race Massacre. A reader can click on a location and read the narrative.

its headquarter in downtown Atlanta. James W. English, a former Mayor of Atlanta and a key figure in the 1906 events, was the president of the Fourth National Bank of Atlanta (a key location of the 1906 events), whose building is now occupied by Georgia State University's Andrew Young School of Policy Studies.

Although such connections can be presented in texts, a more effective method is data visualization. We have created a social network diagram (Fig. 4) that shows the connections between the major characters, their legacies, and their connections to the major institutions in Georgia. The data visualization is created with GraphViz. We plan to convert it into an interactive social network diagram using Plotly so that a reader can click on a character or an institute to read the narrative and see the location.

5   Conclusion and Future Work

We have presented the design of interactive cartographic storytelling for the 1906 Atlanta Race Massacre. Our goal is to provide an educational platform that enables a deeper understanding of this event and its legacy. We not only want to tell what happened in the past but to connect the past with the present. We also want to explore the histories and legacies of the characters closely related to the 1906 event and their intricate connections with the institutions around us today. To achieve this goal, we must deal with a complex spatio-temporal story structure and an extensive social network. In this paper, we discussed our design decisions and implementations.

This project is still a work in progress. We will continue to add narratives for additional locations. Multimedia content such as audio and voices will be added. The social network will be expanded and converted to an interactive diagram. We also plan to conduct user studies to evaluate the project.

References

1. Arcade Fire: The Wilderness Downtown. http://www.thewildernessdowntown. com/. Accessed July 2022
2. Bauerlein, M.: Negrophobia: a race riot in Atlanta, 1906. Encounter Books (2002)
3. Bhatt, M., Wallgrun, J.O.: Geospatial narratives and their spatio-temporal dynamics: commonsense reasoning for high-level analyses in geographic information systems. ISPRS Int. J. Geo Inf. **3**, 166–205 (2014)
4. Blackmon, D.A.: Slavery by another name: the re-enslavement of black people in America from the Civil War to World War II. Anchor (2008)
5. Bogucka, E.P., et al.: Cartographic design of cultural maps. IEEE Comput. Graph. Appl. **40**, 12–20 (2020)
6. Brown, V.: Slave Revolt in Jamaica, 1760–1761: A Cartographic Narrative. http:// revolt.axismaps.com/. Accessed July 2022
7. Burns, R.: Rage in the Gate City: The story of the 1906 Atlanta Race Riot. University of Georgia Press (2009)
8. Caquard, S., Cartwright, W.: Narrative cartography: from mapping stories to the narrative of maps and mapping. Cartogr. J. **51**, 101–106 (2014)
9. Caquard, S., Fiset, J.P.: How can we map stories? a cybercartographic application for narrative cartography. J. Maps **10**, 18–25 (2014)
10. Cortes, N.A.L.: A conceptual framework for interactive cartographic storytelling. Master's thesis, University of Twente (2018). http://essay.utwente.nl/85868/
11. Daniels, N., Proulx, N.: Teaching About the Tulsa Race Massacre With The New York Times, Sept 2021. https://www.nytimes.com/2021/05/27/learning/teaching-about-the-tulsa-race-massacre-with-the-new-york-times.html. Accessed July 2022
12. Field, K.: The stories maps tell. Cartogr. J. **51**, 99–100 (2014)
13. Godshalk, D.F.: Veiled visions : The 1906 Atlanta race riot and the reshaping of American race relations. The University of North Carolina Press (2005)
14. Google Earth: Where on Google Earth is Carmen Sandiego? https://experiments. withgoogle.com/where-on-earth. Accessed July 2022
15. Hewitt, C.M.: The battle of hastings, a cartographic narrative. GeoHumanities **8**(1), 53–78 (2022)
16. Hullman, J., Diakopoulos, N.: Visualization rhetoric: framing effects in narrative visualization. IEEE Trans. Visual Comput. Graphics **17**, 2231–2240 (2011)
17. Kosara, R., Mackinlay, J.: Storytelling: the next step for visualization. Computer **46**(5), 44–50 (2013)
18. Mocnik, F.B., Fairbairn, D.: Maps telling stories? Cartogr. J. **55**, 36–57 (2017)
19. Ojo, A., Heravi, B.: Patterns in award winning data storytelling. Digit. J. **6**, 693–718 (2017)
20. Phillips, J.: Storytelling in earth sciences: the eight basic plots. Earth Sci. Rev. **115**, 153–162 (2012)
21. Roth, R.E.: Cartographic design as visual storytelling: synthesis and review of map-based narratives, genres, and tropes. Cartogr. J. **58**, 83–114 (2020)

22. Dos Santos, R.F., Boedihardjo, A., Shah, S., Chen, F., Lu, C.-T., Ramakrishnan, N.: The big data of violent events: algorithms for association analysis using spatio-temporal storytelling. GeoInformatica **20**(4), 879–921 (2016). https://doi.org/10.1007/s10707-016-0247-0
23. Santos, R.F.D., et al.: A framework for intelligence analysis using spatio-temporal storytelling. GeoInformatica **20**, 285–326 (2016)
24. Segel, E., Heer, J.: Narrative visualization: telling stories with data. IEEE Trans. Visual Comput. Graphics **16**, 1139–1148 (2010)
25. Suggs, E.: 115 years ago, a deadly race riot reshaped atlanta. The Atlanta Journal-Constitution, September 2021
26. Tally, R.T.: Introduction: Mapping narratives. Literary Cartographies, pp. 1–12 (2014)
27. Zainaldin, J.: The atlanta race riot of 1906: Why it matters 107 years later. https://www.georgiahumanities.org/2016/11/02/the-atlanta-race-riot-of-1906-why-it-matters-107-years-later/. Accessed July 2022

Carambola: Enforcing Relationships Between Values in Value-Sensitive Agent Design

Luis Garcia[(✉)] and Chris Martens

Northeastern University, Boston, MA 02115, USA
`garcia.lui@northeastern.edu`

Abstract. Carambola is a text-based strategy game that operational-izes the Theory of Basic Values (TBV) to model the motivations of its non-player characters (NPC) and the dilemmas it presents to players. The player takes on the role of the Emperor of a nation, making a series of executive decisions while noting the subsequent reactions of their NPC advisors. After a fixed number of rounds in which they choose actions, their NPC advisors vote on whether they should dethrone the player based on the affinity they have with the other subjects of the game. Advisor affinity is affected by the Emperor's actions, which each harm and promote a subset of their values. Our implementation of the TBV is a geometric interpretation that enforces restrictions on the attitudes that agents can have toward the values. We give a brief overview of the theory, and then describe our implementation and our plans for evaluating how this usage of the TBV affects the advisors' believability.

Keywords: Social simulation · Social psychology · Theory of basic values · Values · Value-sensitive narrative · Dilemma generation · Character generation · Believability · Affinity

1 Introduction

In the game *Tyranny*, the player is often presented with choices where the values of at least two opposing parties are at stake [1]. For example, after a successful siege of a city, the player may let one group, the Scarlet Chorus, loose so that they may raid and pillage as they please. On the other hand, the player may send in another group, the Disfavored, to impose martial law. The factions are representatives of sets of opposing values. The Scarlet Chorus represents, at least, hedonism, while the Disfavored represents conformity. In interactive narrative, this situation is a *dilemma*, or a moment wherein a player is presented with alternatives that each harm at least one value.

In the interactive narrative field, dilemmas have been utilized in order to generate stories that maintain some level of narrative interest by presenting players with hard choices [2,3,7]. In research and in video games, dilemmas are

M. Vosmeer and L. Holloway-Attaway (Eds.): ICIDS 2022, LNCS 13762, pp. 83–90, 2022.
https://doi.org/10.1007/978-3-031-22298-6_5

presented via non-player characters (NPCs) who represent the values at stake. We call this kind of character a *value-sensitive agent* [3].

Value-sensitive agents present a coherence problem. Coherence between the actions available to the player in a dilemma, the values they harm or promote, and the attitudes of the characters presenting the dilemmas through which the player interprets the alternatives is maintained solely by the author. With the current state of the art, if an author were to try to replicate *Tyranny*, they might accidentally write a situation wherein a character from the Scarlet Chorus acts disgusted when a player chooses to act hedonistically. Without extra writing to contextualize this reaction, this character appears to be acting inconsistently.

Toward reducing the possibility of inconsistent NPC behavior, we introduce a method of value-sensitive agent generation that enforces relationships between the values such that no values that are diametrically opposed can be cherished at once by the same agent. The values and the relationships between them are given by Schwartz's Theory of Basic Values [8]. We contextualize our implementation in our role-playing game, Carambola. Here, the player takes the role of an emperor making executive decisions, and is presented a sequence of dilemmas that lead either to them retaining their throne or losing it. Each choice the player makes elicits reactions from their NPC advisors based on the advisors' attitudes toward the values that the actions affect. Their reactions nudge them toward voting for either one of the player's possible outcomes (see Fig. 1). We hypothesize that our design improves the advisors' believability [4].

2   Theoretical Background

At the core of Carambola's design is an implementation of Schwartz's Theory of Basic Values (TBV), which posits that there is a shared set of values across cultures worldwide [8]. The theory has two facets which are relevant to our implementation: the values themselves and a geometric model for how the values are related to each other. According to the TBV, these universal values can be placed in a circular continuum in which the proximity of the values represents the amount of similarity their underlying motivations have (see Fig. 2).

In Carambola, we use this adjacency relationship from the TBV to enforce restrictions on the possible configurations of advisor attitudes toward the values. The advisors are each motivated to promote or maintain their empire's general wellness. However, that motivation manifests differently for each advisor through their personal attitudes toward the values that are promoted and harmed by the player's choices. Following the EGAD framework, the advisors can hold three attitudes: cherish, despise, or ambivalent about [5]. We extend the framework by ensuring that the values that advisors cherish (or despise) lie adjacent to each other on the continuum.

3   Related Work

Carambola's design is inspired by past interactive projects which feature value-sensitive agents [6,10]. Behind one of these projects [10] is one of the earliest

(a) A dilemma presented to the player. They must choose either one to progress the game.

On this day, **the Emperor** made the following mandate:

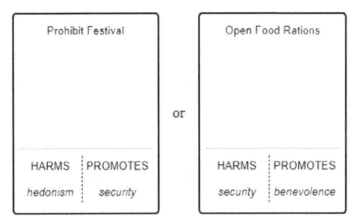

(b) The player's choice and the reactions of each of their advisors.

On this day, **The Emperor** chose to *Prohibit Festival* instead of *Open Food Rations*

Ivan likes this decision.

Dmitri abhors this decision.

Alyosha is unaffected by this decision.

(c) The "dethrone" ending of the game, one of two possible endings for the player.

...and the Emperor is Dethroned

Behind closed doors, the Emperor's advisors voted to dethrone them, ending a tumultuous rule.

Fig. 1. On each round, the player is presented with a dilemma (a). After a decision is made, the advisors react (b). At the end of the game, the advisors decide whether to retain the player as emperor by majority vote (c).

Fig. 2. The continuum of values introduced by Schwartz's Theory of Basic Values. The proximity of the values reflects how similar their underlying motivations are.

examples of value-sensitive narrative generation, IDTension [9]. Here, an author defines values via abstract keywords (e.g., *non-violence, law*). The author also configures both agents' attitudes toward each of these values and actions that are symbolic of the values. Carambola takes a similar approach to agent and action design. However, in Carambola the values are not defined by us, the designers, but are rather come directly from the TBV. Furthermore, our implementation enforces relationships between the values, precluding authorial mistakes that can produce situations in which agents can simultaneously hold positive attitudes toward diametrically opposed values, such as *violence* and *non-violence*.

The main mechanic of our game, dilemma resolution, is largely inspired by proposed frameworks for dilemma generation. To inform our NPC design, we follow the EGAD framework [5], which was proposed as a refinement over the GADIN system [2]. In this framework, agents may cherish, despise, or be ambivalent to each of the values, while actions may promote, harm, or do nothing to each. Like EGAD, we use the values from the TBV. However, the framework ignores the embedded relationships between the TBV's values. In Carambola, these relationships are central to the NPC design.

4   Game Design

To facilitate the player's ability to make reasoned decisions in the game, we sought to construct the advisors so that what their reactions and reasoning are consistent and clear to the player. We achieve consistency by ensuring that the values that the advisors cherish (or despise) are adjacent to each other on the value continuum. Clarity is achieved by plainly stating the advisors' reactions, their affinities toward the player, and by labeling actions such that there is a simple thematic link between what they represent and the values they promote.

4.1 Action Design

On each round, Carambola presents the player with a dilemma of two alternative actions (see Table 1). The action specifications were handwritten so that their effects fit in thematically with their labels. For example, *Authorize Military March* shows off the glory of Carambola's military (promoting their *achievements*) while reinforcing the force that the empire has over its citizens (harming *universalism*). Upon choosing an action, the player triggers its effects on the values, which elicit reactions from the advisors.

Table 1. A list of all available actions Carambola, along with their effects on the values. Every action has an opposite version, where its effects are flipped from the original.

Label	Value promoted	Value harmed
Maintain Barracks	Power	Universalism
Authorize Military March	Achievement	Universalism
Authorize Festival	Hedonism	Security
Maintain Art Museum	Stimulation	Conformity/tradition
Pardon Criminal	Self-Direction	Conformity/tradition
Maintain Hospital	Universalism	Power
Open Food Rations	Benevolence	Security
Enforce Mass	Conformity/Tradition	Stimulation
Maintain Prison	Security	Self-Direction

4.2 Advisor Design

To facilitate discussion about our advisor design, we will refer to Dmitri, an example advisor that can be generated in the game (see Fig. 3).

Value Attitudes. Like dilemma generation systems in the past, we designed advisors so that they each have values that they cherish, despise or are ambivalent toward [2] [3] [5]. At game start, we generate their attitudes toward the values according to the following rules:

1. The two values that an advisor cherishes (despises) are adjacent on the value continuum.
2. For an advisor to despise a value, it must be on the opposite half of the value continuum from the ones that they cherish.

Fig. 3. Value attitude configuration for Dmitri, an example advisor. Dmitri cherishes *power* and *security*, and despises *self-direction* and *universalism*. He is ambivalent toward the rest of the values.

Consistent with the TBV, with these two rules, adjacent values have similar motivations, while values that are opposite from each other on the continuum can conflict [8]. In our example, Dmitri cherishes *power* and *security*, but not *power* and *universalism* because the latter pair are on opposite sides of the continuum. For the purpose of ensuring that Dmitri's values are clear to the player, this is ideal: while *power* and *security* together emphasize control and the overcoming of threats, *universalism* invites diversity and self-expression.

Table 2. An illustration of how the effects (promote or harm) of the player's choice and an advisor's attitude (cherish or despise) interact to produce points.

		Player Choice Effect	
		Promote	Harm
Advisor	*Cherish*	+1	−1
Attitude	*Despise*	−1	+1
	Ambivalent	0	0

Reactions. After the player chooses one of the alternatives presented to them, each of their advisors takes a turn to react. Computationally, an advisor's reaction is the sum of points that the player's choice yields, with points being given according to Table 2. Thus, an advisor's reaction can range from being very positive (yielding 2 points) to neutral (yielding 0 points) to very negative (yielding −2 points). This sum is added to the advisor's overall affinity to the player.

To illustrate, suppose the player chooses *Maintain Barracks*. Because Dmitri cherishes *power* and this choice promotes it, the player receives +1 point. Because Dmitri despises *universalism* and this choice harms it, the player receives +1 additional point. Dmitri's overall reaction, then, is very positive, giving +2 points. His affinity toward the player moves in the positive direction.

5 Future Work

5.1 Evaluation of the Character Model

We plan on evaluating via user study the effect that Carambola's implementation of the TBV has on the believability of its NPCs. Our hypothesis is that our implementation makes the agents more believable than if their attitudes toward the values were randomized. To assess this, we will extend the list of actions in Carambola so that there are pairs of actions that affect the same values in the same way. For example, we may introduce the following two pairs:

1. *Increase Weapons Manufacturing* and *Occupy a Neighboring City*, which each promote *power* and harm *universalism*.
2. *Enforce Attendance to Mass* and *Close All Business for Holiday*, which each promote *tradition* and harm *self-direction*.

Our evaluation will have two study cases that differ in how the advisors would react to player choices. Our test case will be of the implementation detailed thus far, where advisors react according to their values. For each action pair, they will react exactly the same way for either action. In the control case, an advisor will favor one action in a pair, but disfavor the other one. Intuitively, if our hypothesis is correct, the control case would introduce a level of inconsistency in the advisors' reactions that will break players' suspension of disbelief.

To test our hypothesis, we will use the methods proposed in Gomes et al. [2013] to quantify the difference in character believability between the control and test cases [4]. Believability is split into a number of dimensions that describe different aspects of agent behavior. For example, one dimension is *behavior coherence*, which is the degree to which a human observer may deem an agent's actions to be logical according to their mental model of the agent's state. Part of our future work will be to find which subset of dimensions are appropriate for the limited context of our game.

5.2 Extending the Character Model

Currently, the advisors' attitudes toward the values are of a ternary set: cherish, despise, or ambivalent toward. This causes two issues: the advisors cannot hold positive attitudes toward conflicting values, and the advisors can only care about four of the values at a time. Even in Carambola, one can imagine space for characters who hold more complex attitudes. For example, a Robin Hood-esque character might seek more *power* in order to spread *benevolence* among Carambola's peasants. We speculate that switching from a discrete set of attitudes to a continuous one and allowing agents to have attitudes for all values on the continuum will be a step toward introducing such nuance.

5.3　Refining the User Interface

One relevant question to both the player experience and our described evaluation is that of how the presentation of each alternative action affects a player's ability to understand why their decisions elicit certain reactions from the NPCs. In Carambola's current iteration, we hand-wrote labels for each action (see Table 1). Whether the values that are promoted or harmed are appropriate for each action is highly subjective. Disagreement between the authors' and players' mappings between actions and values may weaken the data we gather in our evaluation.

References

1. Tyranny (2016). https://www.paradoxinteractive.com/games/tyranny/about
2. Barber, H., Kudenko, D.: Generation of adaptive dilemma-based interactive narratives. IEEE Trans. Comput. Intell. AI Games **1**, 309–326 (12 2009). https://doi.org/10.1109/TCIAIG.2009.2037925
3. Battaglino, C., Damiano, R., Lesmo, L.: Emotional range in value-sensitive deliberation (2013). http://hdl.handle.net/2318/147231
4. Gomes, P., Paiva, A., Martinho, C., Jhala, A.: Metrics for character believability in interactive narrative (2013)
5. Harmon, S.: An expressive dilemma generation model for players and artificial agents. In: The Twelfth AAAI Conference on Artificial Intelligence and Interactive Digital Entertainment (AIIDE-16), pp. 176–182 (2016)
6. Kybartas, B., Verbrugge, C., Lessard, J.: Subject and subjectivity: a conversational game using possible worlds. In: Nunes, N., Oakley, I., Nisi, V. (eds.) ICIDS 2017. LNCS, vol. 10690, pp. 332–335. Springer, Cham (2017). https://doi.org/10.1007/978-3-319-71027-3_37
7. Mateas, M., Mawhorter, P., Wardrip-Fruin, N.: Intentionally generating choices in interactive narratives, pp. 292–299 (2015). http://inform7.com/
8. Schwartz, S.H.: An overview of the schwartz theory of basic values. Online Readings in Psychology and Culture 2, December 2012. https://doi.org/10.9707/2307-0919.1116
9. Szilas, N.: Idtension: a narrative engine for interactive drama (2004)
10. Szilas, N.: The mutiny: an interactive drama on idtension, pp. 539–540 (2008)

A Demonstration of Loose Ends, A Mixed-Initiative Narrative Instrument

Max Kreminski[1,3]($\boxtimes$), Melanie Dickinson[2], Noah Wardrip-Fruin[3],
and Michael Mateas[3]

[1] Santa Clara University, Santa Clara, USA
[2] Nottingham, UK
[3] University of California, Santa Cruz, USA
{mkreminski,nwardrip,mmateas}@ucsc.edu

Abstract. We present a demonstration of Loose Ends, a mixed-initiative creative interface for playful storytelling that assists players in managing plot threads to achieve storytelling goals related to high-level story structure. From a design perspective, Loose Ends is an example of a *narrative instrument*: an expression-oriented playable system that can be played to produce narrative, in much the same way that musical instruments are played to produce music.

Keywords: Narrative instruments · Mixed-initiative co-creativity · Interactive emergent narrative · Story sifting

1 Introduction

One line of research in interactive storytelling aims to construct computational systems that assist the human interactor in making up a story of their own [9]—for instance by providing the interactor with a storytelling partner in the form of an artificially intelligent storytelling system, resulting in a *mixed-initiative co-creative* [10] approach to storytelling. Systems like Say Anything [13], Creative Help [11], and TaleBrush [1] enable collaborative human/AI storytelling at the level of the prose that constitutes a written story, while systems like *Writing Buddy* [12] and *Why Are We Like This?* [5,6] enable collaborative storytelling at the level of the plot events that constitute an abstract narrative structure.

Though these systems are in some ways successful at facilitating mixed-initiative storytelling (particularly by helping interactors to overcome short-term writer's block through the provision of suggestions as to how a story might be immediately continued), they have historically struggled to help users overcome a sense of long-term *structurelessness* in the stories they write. In terms of the creativity support needs experienced by creative writers [8], these systems are broadly effective at getting interactors unstuck, but less effective at helping them craft a satisfying overall plot arc.

M. Dickinson—Independent.

M. Vosmeer and L. Holloway-Attaway (Eds.): ICIDS 2022, LNCS 13762, pp. 91–97, 2022.
https://doi.org/10.1007/978-3-031-22298-6_6

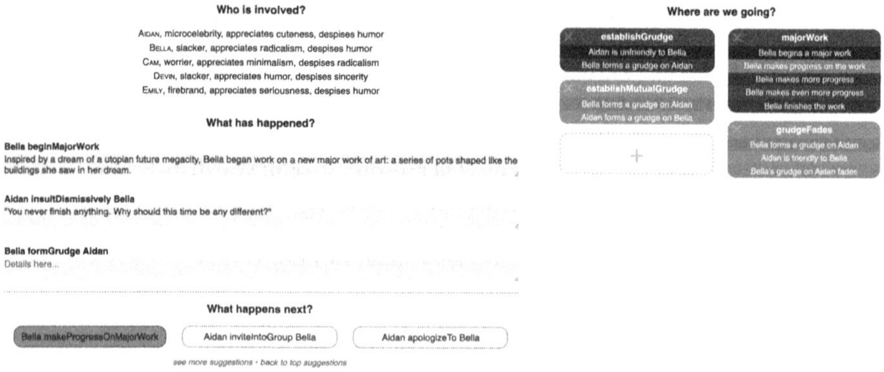

Fig. 1. The Loose Ends user interface. The **Who is involved?** section displays basic information about a generated cast of five characters. The **What has happened?** section lists plot events that have taken place in the story so far, along with player-written text giving more details about these events. The **What happens next?** section shows AI-generated suggestions for what might happen next in the story. The **Where are we going?** section shows active storytelling goals, including transparent goals that have been suggested by the AI system rather than added by the player. One action suggestion (highlighted in orange in the bottom left) is being hovered over by the player; consequently, the impact this suggestion would have on the active storytelling goals if accepted (i.e., advancement of the `majorWork` goal) is also highlighted in orange on the right.

Our new mixed-initiative storytelling system—Loose Ends—attempts to address this issue of long-term structurelessness in mixed-initiative co-creative storytelling through innovations in both AI system implementation and user interface design. In this paper, we briefly describe the design and implementation of Loose Ends, with a focus on the overall human/AI interaction loop that assists it in achieving this goal.

Loose Ends is open source[1] and can be played online in a web browser.[2] For a longer-form description of Loose Ends that also presents a preliminary evaluation of the system, see Kreminski et al. 2022 [7].

2   System Description

Loose Ends (Fig. 1) is a mixed-initiative creative interface [2] for playful storytelling. Much like several previous systems in this area of research [1,6,11–13], Loose Ends is an interactive system that assists users in producing non-interactive stories. We specifically conceive of Loose Ends as an AI-based *narrative instrument* [9]: a system that can be played to produce narrative, in much the same way that a musical instrument can be played to produce music.

---

[1] https://github.com/ItsProbablyFine/LooseEnds.
[2] https://itsprobablyfine.github.io/LooseEnds.

In the Loose Ends interaction loop, a human player repeatedly selects *action suggestions* furnished by the underlying AI system to continue the plot of a running story, using *storytelling goals* to steer the narrative toward player-desired long-term outcomes. Actions selected by the player are added to a running *story transcript*, and each action can be annotated with additional text by the player— for instance to narrate the action in greater detail.

The AI system that powers Loose Ends consists of two major components. First is a **storytelling goals tracker** that updates a pool of active and possible storytelling goals as new plot events are added. Second is an **action suggestion generator** that generates and ranks potential suggestions for the next plot event in the story based on the currently active storytelling goals.

2.1 Storytelling Goals Tracker

Storytelling goals in Loose Ends are used to set and maintain the high-level direction of the story. Every goal is an instance of a *goal template*: a story sifting pattern written in the domain-specific logic programming language Winnow [4].

Goals represent *plot threads* that the player wants to be included in the story they are writing. Since a story often consists of several parallel plot threads bound together, multiple goals are generally active at the same time. The current version of Loose Ends includes goal templates for plot threads that introduce or develop character relationships (e.g., friendship or rivalry); internal conflicts (e.g., artistic or career struggles); and high-level narrative themes (e.g., moral themes related to the virtues of persistence in the face of adversity). There are 12 goal templates total in the version of Loose Ends presented here.

As players select action suggestions (generated by the action suggestion generator) that advance these plot threads toward completion (or cut them off by making them impossible to complete), the storytelling goals tracker UI visibly updates to indicate the current completion progress of each goal. This allows players to see which goals are near completion, which goals are still a long way from being completed, and what kinds of actions should be taken next to advance various incomplete goals.

The Loose Ends user interface permits players to add goals manually (by selecting a goal template to instantiate as a goal, from a library of all available goal templates) and to remove goals that have already been established at any time. In addition, the AI system in Loose Ends constantly tracks and evaluates a pool of partial matches that the player has not established as goals. If one of these partial matches advances beyond a certain threshold (33% completion in the current version of Loose Ends), the system will automatically promote it to an active goal, rendered in a transparent style to indicate that this is a system-suggested goal rather than a player-added one. These goals can be removed by the player like any other (enabling the player to veto the system's suggestions of additional storytelling goals), or the player can click on them to remove the transparency effect and notionally "lock them in" as player-intended goals.

2.2 Action Suggestion Generator

Action suggestions in Loose Ends are drawn from two pools of actions. The *basic actions pool* contains actions that are possible for any character at any time, regardless of social state, and remains fixed at all times. The *dynamic actions pool* is recalculated whenever a new event is added to the story, and contains actions that are only possible because of active storytelling goals that are in an appropriate state. For instance, when a complete `establishGrudge` goal between the characters Cam and Devin is active, the dynamic actions pool will contain actions that Cam can only take toward Devin because of their active grudge on Devin (such as sabotaging Devin's most recent artwork). There are 32 action types total in the version of Loose Ends presented here: 20 basic actions and 12 dynamic actions.

Action suggestions are recalculated every time the set of active storytelling goals changes. When calculating action suggestions, the action suggestion generator first iterates over all possible next actions (in both the basic and dynamic action pools) and determines, for each action, which storytelling goals would be impacted (either advanced or cut off) by the addition of this action to the story. Each action is then given a priority score, which is the sum of three factors:

– The number of active storytelling goals that this action would advance
– A constant factor (0.5) if this action is from the dynamic actions pool—i.e., if it is only possible because of an active storytelling goal
– A random factor (between 0 and 0.5) to randomly permute the priority of actions with the same base score

Actions are sorted by their score and displayed in order, with the three highest-scoring actions being pulled to the top of the action suggestions list. In this way, actions that relate most strongly to the active storytelling goals are prioritized for display, with randomness ensuring a degree of alternation between suggestions that advance parallel plot threads. When the user hovers over an action suggestion to consider it, the precalculated information about which storytelling goals this action would advance or cut off is used to display the ramifications of accepting this action in the storytelling goals pane on the right side of the user interface.

3 Interaction Examples

In conjunction, the Loose Ends AI and user interface permit several desirable interactions that are not possible in other mixed-initiative creative interfaces for storytelling. Four especially interesting examples of novel mixed-initiative interactions enabled by Loose Ends are presented below.

Discovering New Storytelling Goals. Beyond simply suggesting action-level continuations to a running story in accordance with player-provided storytelling

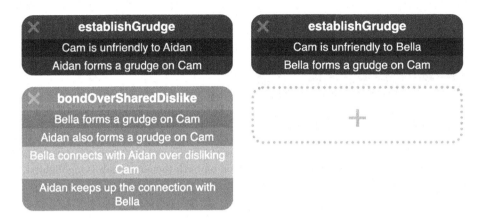

Fig. 2. Based on events that were added to the story to complete two `establishGrudge` goals, Loose Ends has automatically discovered and surfaced a suggestion for another author goal (the `bondOverSharedDislike` goal) to spin off a new plot thread initiated by these events.

goals, Loose Ends can also infer new storytelling goals that are consistent with the story so far and proactively suggest these goals to the player. This often results in interactions where a player who would otherwise become uncertain of what to do next is inspired by, and begins pursuing, a system-discovered storytelling goal instead.

For instance, in Fig. 2, the player has just completed two `establishGrudge` goals targeting the same character (Cam) have both been completed. At this point, Loose Ends automatically discovers and surfaces a successive character relationship development goal, in which Aidan and Bella (who both have grudges on Cam) bond over their shared dislike. The first two steps of this goal are already complete, because the system has been tracking the possibility of surfacing this goal in the background, but it has only just now progressed far enough to be displayed.

Discovering Thematic Conflicts. Loose Ends can make it apparent when a conflict has arisen between two active storytelling goals. For instance, in Fig. 3, the player is simultaneously working toward two distinct thematic goals for the story and considering an action that will reward Emily with career success after she completes a major artwork. This would support the theme that persistent work on a single major project leads to success (`slowAndSteady`) but undermine the competing theme that the way to success is to create a rapid succession of more minor artworks (`quantityOverQuality`). When the impact of the considered action on all active author goals is visualized, the conflict between these goals is revealed to the player.

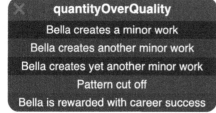

Fig. 3. As the player considers an action that would advance one of their thematic goals but undermine another, the impact of the action on both thematic goals is highlighted, making the conflict apparent.

Resurfacing Dormant Plot Threads. Because Loose Ends can maintain a larger set of active storytelling goals than the player can hold in their head all at once, action suggestions can serve to remind players of incomplete plot threads that they would otherwise forget to revisit. For instance, long-term storytelling goals like the `tryTryAgain` thematic goal (which requires a single character to repeatedly release artworks that are poorly received, before finally releasing one that is well-received) may temporarily fade into the background as the player focuses on another subplot that weaves together a few distinct storytelling goals at once—but once this more pressing subplot is complete, actions advancing the earlier thematic goal will again rise to the top of the action suggestions pool, reminding the player to return to the previously initiated thread.

Interleaving Parallel Plot Threads. When multiple parallel plot threads are active and none of these threads has storytelling priority, the slight random permutation of equally ranked action suggestions means that Loose Ends by default tends to promote actions that alternately advance different threads. This can help players escape fixation [3], in which they develop a narrow and premature focus on one plot thread or set of characters and forget about the possibility of developing others.

4   Conclusion

Loose Ends is a narrative instrument that can be played to produce narrative, much as musical instruments can be played to produce music. It includes several technical and design innovations aimed at helping players to achieve coherent long-term structure in the stories they produce, and the novel interaction patterns it enables can hopefully be retained and extended in other AI-based narrative instruments in the future.

Acknowledgements. Max Kreminski conducted part of this research while in residence at Stochastic Labs.

References

1. Chung, J.J.Y., Kim, W., Yoo, K.M., Lee, H., Adar, E., Chang, M.: TaleBrush: sketching stories with generative pretrained language models. In: CHI Conference on Human Factors in Computing Systems (2022)
2. Deterding, S., H., etal.: Mixed-initiative creative interfaces. In: Proceedings of the 2017 CHI Conference Extended Abstracts on Human Factors in Computing Systems, pp. 628–635 (2017)
3. Gero, J.S.: Fixation and commitment while designing and its measurement. J. Creative Behav. **45**(2), 108–115 (2011)
4. Kreminski, M., Dickinson, M., Mateas, M.: Winnow: a domain-specific language for incremental story sifting. In: Proceedings of the AAAI Conference on Artificial Intelligence and Interactive Digital Entertainment, vol. 17, pp. 156–163 (2021)
5. Kreminski, M., Dickinson, M., Mateas, M., Wardrip-Fruin, N.: Why are we like this?: exploring writing mechanics for an AI-augmented storytelling game. In: Proceedings of the 2020 Conference of the Electronic Literature Organization (2020)
6. Kreminski, M., Dickinson, M., Mateas, M., Wardrip-Fruin, N.: Why are we like this?: the AI architecture of a co-creative storytelling game. In: International Conference on the Foundations of Digital Games (2020)
7. Kreminski, M., Dickinson, M., Wardrip-Fruin, N., Mateas, M.: Loose Ends: a mixed-initiative creative interface for playful storytelling. In: Proceedings of the AAAI Conference on Artificial Intelligence and Interactive Digital Entertainment. vol. 18 (2022)
8. Kreminski, M., Martens, C.: Unmet creativity support needs in computationally supported creative writing. In: Proceedings of the First Workshop on Intelligent and Interactive Writing Assistants (In2Writing 2022), pp. 74–82 (2022)
9. Kreminski, M., Mateas, M.: Toward narrative instruments. In: Mitchell, A., Vosmeer, M. (eds.) ICIDS 2021. LNCS, vol. 13138, pp. 499–508. Springer, Cham (2021). https://doi.org/10.1007/978-3-030-92300-6_50
10. Liapis, A., Yannakakis, G.N., Alexopoulos, C., Lopes, P.: Can computers foster human users' creativity? theory and praxis of mixed-initiative co-creativity. Digital Cult. Educ. (DCE) **8**(2), 136–152 (2016)
11. Roemmele, M., Gordon, A.S.: Creative help: a story writing assistant. In: Schoenau-Fog, H., Bruni, L.E., Louchart, S., Baceviciute, S. (eds.) ICIDS 2015. LNCS, vol. 9445, pp. 81–92. Springer, Cham (2015). https://doi.org/10.1007/978-3-319-27036-4_8
12. Samuel, B., Mateas, M., Wardrip-Fruin, N.: The Design of *Writing Buddy*: a mixed-initiative approach towards computational story collaboration. In: Nack, F., Gordon, A.S. (eds.) ICIDS 2016. LNCS, vol. 10045, pp. 388–396. Springer, Cham (2016). https://doi.org/10.1007/978-3-319-48279-8_34
13. Swanson, R., Gordon, A.S.: Say Anything: using textual case-based reasoning to enable open-domain interactive storytelling. ACM Trans. Interac. Intell. Syst. (TiiS) **2**(3) (2012)

Social and Cultural Contexts

Teaching Literary Interactive Digital Narratives in Secondary Education: A French Study

Serge Bouchardon[1][(✉)] and Magali Brunel[2]

[1] Université de Technologie de Compiègne, Compiègne, France
serge.bouchardon@utc.fr
[2] Université Côte d'Azur, Nice, France
magali.brunel@univ-cotedazur.fr

Abstract. As part of a collaborative research project carried out in the Nice Academy (France) with a group of seven teachers in literature classes, the article aims to describe the various aspects and specificities of the teaching of literary interactive digital narratives in junior and senior high school classes. We focus on the treatment given by teachers to the different aspects of these digital works, the choices that the teachers make regarding didactic transposition, and the choices that the teachers offer pupils regarding writing practices.

Keywords: Literary interactive digital narrative · Didactics · Secondary education · Creative writing

In a recent roundtable at the ELO 2022 conference[1], Hartmut Koenitz urged teaching interactive digital narratives (IDNs), and teaching with IDNs. The question of teaching IDNs in universities has already inspired many studies (Dubbleman et al., 2018; Koenitz and Palosaari Eladhari, 2019; Barbara, 2020). However we lack empirical studies on the teaching of IDNs in secondary education (in both junior and senior high school classes).

We report here on a study on the teaching of a particular case of IDNs, namely literary IDNs (even if this name could of course be discussed). These are IDNs in which the verbal dimension plays not only an important role in the narration, but is worked in an aesthetic way (literature as art of language), and which claim a form of literariness (many examples are to be found in the Electronic Literature Collections, volumes 1 to 4[2]).

As part of a collaborative research project carried out in the South of France, with a group of 7 French teachers[3] in literature classes, this paper aims to describe the various aspects and specificities of the teaching of literary IDNs in junior and senior high school classes (see Fig. 1). In this project, the teachers approach literary IDNs as examples

---

[1] Jonathan Barbara, Hartmut Koenitz, Michael Schlauch, Mattia Bellini and Péter Kristóf Makai: *Interactive Digital Narratives in Education* (ELO 2022, Como, June 1st 2022).

[2] https://collection.eliterature.org/

[3] Each teacher chose a literary IDN from a corpus of 20 literary IDNs proposed by the two researchers (a researcher in didactics and a researcher in information and communication sciences). Eventually, three literary IDNs were selected by the teachers.

© The Author(s), under exclusive license to Springer Nature Switzerland AG 2022
M. Vosmeer and L. Holloway-Attaway (Eds.): ICIDS 2022, LNCS 13762, pp. 101–120, 2022.
https://doi.org/10.1007/978-3-031-22298-6_7

of digital literature, and more broadly of contemporary literature. We try to establish how teachers deal with the various aspects of literary IDNs, and identify the choices they make in terms of didactic transposition[4]. Working with a limited number of sample cases, the challenge consists in clarifying the ways in which the teaching of a literary IDN fits in with that of more traditional literary works, but also in showing how teachers use their scientific and professional skills to apprehend and teach the specificities of literary IDNs.

Fig. 1. French pupils studying an IDN in a junior high school class.

After establishing our theoretical framework (Sect. 1) and describing the context of our research (Sect. 2), we will present our analysis in four stages (Sect. 3). In this third section, we first analyze the process by which literary interactive digital narratives become part of a teacher's pedagogical project, and the different approaches teachers select to introduce these works to their pupils. Our attention subsequently turns to the objects of study, and particularly to the links created by teachers between digital works and literature, literacy or indeed the digital *milieu* specific to the pupils and the class in question. Renewing their traditional teaching methods based on the reading of an entire work, the teachers involved select various didactic options, which we then examine, along with the progression they envisage in order to enable their pupils to appreciate the chosen digital work. Finally we focus on writing practices, revealing the variety of writing practices proposed, as well as their firm connections with the studied works.

1 Theoretical Background

1.1 The Stakes Involved in the Teaching of Digital Literature

The literary IDNs are more broadly part of digital literature. But the teachers in secondary education face some difficulties:

---

[4] *Didactic transposition* is the deconstruction and reconstruction of science knowledge or practices in order to make them teachable.

- finding ways to make rather unusual literary works fit into the curriculum,
- accompanying the pupils who may feel a little disorientated in their reading of these works,
- even sometimes justifying their choices to parents who may be somewhat reluctant.

In spite of these difficulties, the teaching of digital literature offers many stimulating opportunities:

- Revisiting certain notions introduced in literature lessons (the author, the text, the narrative, etc.), and teaching pupils to question writing practices. This is what is referred to as the "heuristic value" of digital literature (Bouchardon, 2014).
- Developing teaching practices centered around digital literacy through the study of literature, thus endorsing the idea that "reading literature activates to the utmost the operations and codes which are susceptible to come into play in all reading activities" (Dufays et al., 2015). Similarly, we might claim that reading digital literature helps students to develop digital literacy skills in a pertinent way, challenging the traditional use of the Digital in French classes – not only is literature taught in a digital environment, but students also learn about the digital environment through the study of literature.
- Providing a partial solution for the type of pupil described by Marie-José Fourtanier as "the disarticulated reader" (2011), caught between their own cultural practices and references, and the works proposed for study in class.
- Discovering and exploring the creations of the "Extreme Contemporary" (Chaillou, 1987): introducing pupils to contemporary works, and therefore also to the corpus of contemporary digital literature, thus presenting them with the latest literary creations, inspired by contemporary existential, ethical and technological issues.
- Introducing pupils to creative digital writing practices, as we shall see below (Bouchardon, 2018).

Such are some of the very diverse stakes involved in the teaching of digital literature. These are similar to the goals of the teaching of French in high schools, notably developing in pupils a taste for both reading and writing practices, while inculcating in them a command of literary skills and a literary culture, as well as producing citizens capable of informed and pertinent digital practices.

1.2 Digital Literature

a. Digital Literature and its place in literary history

Digital literature has existed for more than six decades now, and descends from clearly identified lineages – combinatorial and constrained writing, fragmentary writing, sound and visual writing. It is important to place these literary practices in their context within literary history, and more particularly in that of the *avant-garde* movements of the twentieth century: Dadaism, Surrealism, Lettrism, the *Nouveau Roman*, or *OuLiPo*, thus approaching digital literature from the perspective of the continuity of literary history, in the same way as literature is traditionally taught in high schools, and particularly in French high schools.

b. The Specificities of Digital Literature

Most critics in the field are in agreement as to the two principal forms of literature relying on digital supports: **digitized literature** and true **digital literature**, even if the boundary between the two forms is sometimes blurred, perhaps increasingly so.

Digitized literature most often consists in adapting existing, initially printed works to digital forms, which are said to be enriched or augmented in that they include added functionalities (annotations, search or sharing options), or multimedia content (videos, or iconographic elements), which enhance the reader's appreciation and understanding. The nature of the text itself remains basically unchanged, however. It can or could still be printed without its signification being altered.

In the second of these two literary forms (*digital literature*), created and designed by and for digital media, the nature of a text would undergo profound changes were it to be printed. "Digital-born[5]" literary creation is currently flourishing in its various forms – hypertext fiction, animated poetry, works including automatic text generation or collaborative online creation. Authors invent and produce literary works specifically for digital media (computers, tablets and smartphones), and strive to exploit their characteristics, namely the multimedia or multimodal dimension, text animation, hypertext technology, and the potential for interactivity, but also geolocalization, notifications or even virtual reality. Digital literature is above all experimental. In an online exchange with Joe Tabbi, Scott Rettberg evokes "a fundamentally experimental practice, in the scientific sense of experimentation"[6]. This experimental dimension is often found in literary IDNs (Bouchardon, 2009; Rettberg, 2018). It particularly concerns narration: points of view, order and speed of the narrative.

1.3 Teaching Digital Works: The State of the Art

In the field of didactics, the teaching of digital literature has yet to produce any specific results, in spite of the fact that the way has been well-paved by several studies. Saemmer and Tréhondart (2014) show that digital works provide a new form of pleasure for the reader, due to their sensorial dimensions, their interactivity, and the fact that the technical possibilities offered by digital devices can lead to greater immersion of the reader in a work: the reader is invited to physically mimic the "manipulation" gesture evoked in the text.

Lebrun, Lacelle and Boutin insist on the need for formal teaching of multimodal literacy in a digital context (2012), pointing to the difficulties involved in reading such texts, which call on the reader to establish the links between the various pieces of information gathered. Lacelle and Lebrun specify the competencies which must be taught – being able to recognize the segmented nature of a message, to identify the coherence of information provided through different linguistic modes, to grasp the logic behind the meaning of a text (which is not necessarily presented in a linear fashion). Furthermore they recommend a better integration of digital texts in the teaching of traditional literacy,

---

[5] "Digital-born" (Hayles, 2008, 120).
[6] https://www.facebook.com/jill.rettberg/videos/522434064169.

"the starting-point for helping pupils to construct or enrich their multimodal comprehension/production skills, should be the classic comprehension/production processes." F. Cahen, analyzing his classroom experimentation with the reading of digital works in *Les Cahiers pédagogiques* (2016), brings to light the interest of confronting digital works with a more traditional corpus, thereby facilitating the study of literary language, or of the role of the reader, "the possibilties for interactivity lead to a debate on the place of the reader." (56).

And finally, Several studies in didactics focusing on the production of digital texts provide us with precious indications. Lacelle and Lebrun (2014) have pointed to the needs of pupils when learning production skills, especially with regard to the weakness of their competencis in the reading and interpretation of the iconic mode, which often leads to poor creations. Florey et al. (2020) have underlined that production and collaboration are called upon more than the analysis and the interpretation of the digital works. Other studies focus on digital writing practices instrumented by software (Petitjean, 2018); they explore the pragmatic and semiotic specificities of the format, and emphasize the extent to which this "architext" (Jeanneret and Souchier, 1999) conditions writing on the screen, constitutes a subjacent framework offering a constrained environment and structures what is written.

1.4 Introducing a New Object for Study into the Classroom: Defining a Pedagogical Process

In order to more clearly define what we mean by "digital works" as objects for study, we decided to analyse the work of teachers as a starting-point towards understanding how an object for study is constructed, following up on the methodologies put forward by the GRAFE group[7]. In this aim, we focused our attention more particularly on the notion of the teaching *"sequence"* or teaching plan (Ronveaux and Schneuwly, 2007), as the principal organizational element determining the object for study. On a more restricted scale (and particularly that of the teaching session), we also noted the pertinence of a secondary organizational element, the *"dispositif"*, i.e. a set of elements including teaching materials, instructions, and concrete conditions for the execution of a teaching situation designed with the aim of achieving a specific pedagogical objective (Cordeiro and Schneuwly, 2007). The two organizational elements (*sequence* and *dispositif*) guiding the activities of teachers described above will constitute the theoretical perspective from which we will analyze the processes of didactic transposition designed by the teachers (Fig. 2).

---

[7] https://www.unige.ch/fapse/grafe/

Fig. 2. Studying collectively an IDN in a classroom.

2 Presentation of Our Research

2.1 A Design-Oriented Research Group

Our research was carried out over a three-year period by a collaborative work team operating in the educational region of Nice in France. Teachers were invited to design and carry out teaching sequences in an autonomous manner, based on works and teaching resources suggested by researchers.

Our method was both descriptive and strategic. Our principal aim was to define and better understand the specificities of digital works as objects for study, and identify any observable phenomena occurring during the appropriation process, paying particular attention to the pupils' productions. Our long-term goals is to provide tools for the teaching of digital works, notably to contribute to the reflection around the opportunities which it offers, as well as to the didactic transposition process.

2.2 Presentation of the Sequences: Works Selected and Levels

For this study, we have based our analysis on the professional documents provided by 7 teachers having participated in the experimental teaching of three different literary interactive digital narratives. While this is not the place to give a detailed account of each work, we will briefly describe each of them.

Marietta Ren's *Phallaina*[8] is a huge horizontal "scrolling digital graphic novel[9]" for tablets and smartphones. It describes the itinerary of a young woman who is able

---

[8] http://phallaina.nouvelles-ecritures.francetv.frIn English: https://www.francetvlab.fr/en/posts/phallaina-a-new-kind-of-graphic-novel.

[9] In French, the author Marietta Ren created the neologism « bande défilée» in reference to « bande dessinée» (comic strip).

to interpret the speech of whales (see Fig. 3). The main character, Audrey, is a young woman who suffers from hallucinatory fits, during which she has visions of whales. Her neurological examinations reveal the existence of a physeter in her brain: an anomalous structure which enables its carriers to hold their breath for sustained amounts of time. Pedagogically, *Phallaina* is interesting in particular by the way in which a digital narrative can play with the conventions of a genre – in this case the comic strip with the comic strip boards, boxes, speech bubbles – to transform it by re-thinking its codes with the Digital (by breaking the strips, for example, and by introducing interactivity).

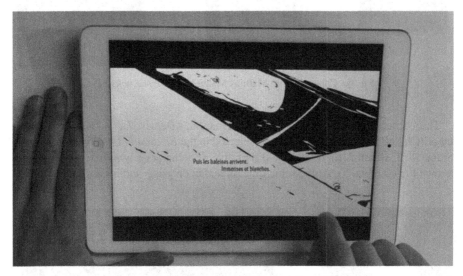

Fig. 3. *Phallaina*, by Marietta Ren.

L'homme volcan[10] is a multimedia narrative available as an app for iPad and iPhone. It tells the story of a little boy who is passionate about the universe of Jules Verne. He accidentally falls into the crater of a volcano, then reappears to his sister in the form of a little crimson supernatural being (see Fig. 4). Pedagogically, this interactive narrative is interesting in particular for the multimedia dimension (the role of the sound design, the graphic design and the animations). The author of the text, Mathias Malzieu, is also the singer of the pop band *Dionysos*, which created the sound design for the piece. The text *flies* above mists revealing the pictorial universe of the graphic designer Frédéric Perrin, composed of a series of animated and interactive drawings. These interactive paintings punctuate the text in the same way as the music of Dionysos and the whole digital narrative is an opportunity to make students think about the *intersemiotization* of the different media.

---

[10] https://www.dailymotion.com/video/xn1338.

Fig. 4. Captures from Mathias Malzieu's *L'homme volcan.*

The teachers also chose to teach Serge Bouchardon's *Déprise/Loss of Grasp*[11] (exhibited at *ICIDS Bournemouth 2020*[12] and selected in the *Electronic Literature Collection* volume 4[13]), which is the first-person narrative of a character who is losing grasp on his own life (see Fig. 5). At the same time, this play on grasp and loss of grasp mirrors

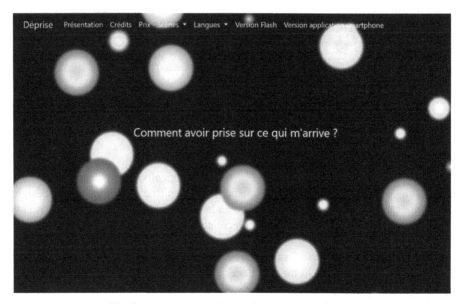

Fig. 5. *Déprise/Loss of Grasp,*by Serge Bouchardon.

---

[11] http://deprise.fr or http://lossofgrasp.com.

[12] https://icids2020.bournemouth.ac.uk/exhibition/

[13] https://collection.eliterature.org/4/, 2022.

the reader's experience of an interactive digital narrative. The reader experiences inter-actively the feeling of loss of grasp of the character. For instance, in the third scene, the character (who is also the narrator) is reading an ambiguous note from his wife. He speaks plainly about his loss of control. The reader can read the text either as a "love poem or a breakup note". The reader can experience this double interpretation with gestures. If the reader moves the mouse cursor to the top, the text will unfold as a love poem; but if the cursor is moved to the bottom, the order of the lines is reversed and the text turns into a breakup note. Pedagogically, this interactive narrative is interesting for the role of gestures: the reader's gestures fully contribute to the construction of the meaning of the narrative[14].

The pedagogical experimentation led by the teachers involved is composed of eight sequences, distributed as follows (Fig. 6):

Teachers	Title of the work	Author(s)	Date	Class level[15]	Code sequence
Hélène	*L'homme volcan*	M. Malzieu	2017	6ᵉ	S1
Hélène	*Phallaina*	M. Ren	2017	5ᵉ	S2
Hélène	*Phallaina*	M. Ren	2018	5ᵉ	S3
Claude	*L'homme Volcan*	M. Malzieu	2018	5ᵉ	S4
Samuel	*Phallaina*	M. Ren	2018	5ᵉ	S5
Caroline	*Déprise*	S. Bouchardon	2017	3ᵉ	S6
Virginie (replacing Caroline)	*Déprise*	S. Bouchardon	2017	3ᵉ	S7
Céline and Charline	*Déprise*	S. Bouchardon	2018	1ᵉ	S8

Fig. 6. Teaching sequences.

Almost all school levels were involved in the study of complete works, and *Déprise* was studied in both junior and senior high school classes.

2.3 Presentation of Data and Research Questions

For this article, the first stage in our research, the teachers' sequence plans constitute our principal source of data (see Fig. 7), enabling us to provide answers to the following research questions:

1) What treatment is given by teachers to the different aspects of digital works?
2) What choices do the teachers make regarding didactic transposition?
3) What choices do the teachers offer pupils regarding writing practices?

---

[14] Presentation: http://www.utc.fr/~bouchard/works/presentation_Loss-of-Grasp.pdf.

LECTURE ET COMPREHENSION DE L'ECRIT
Découvrir une œuvre de littérature numérique
Comprendre que l'écriture numérique nécessite d'anticiper les réactions du lecteur
Explorer le récit littéraire interactif c'est-à-dire l'interaction entre le lecteur et le récit
littéraire : étudier les gestes, attitudes et impressions du lecteur face à l'œuvre, expliciter les
différents "possibles" du lecteur
S'interroger sur le thème de la perte de contrôle sur les autres et sur soi-même
Lire un texte, le comprendre et se l'approprier de manière à pouvoir porter un jugement.

ECRITURE
Dans un diaporama, s'initier à l'écriture multimodale par le jeu des polices, l'insertion de sons,
d'images et de mouvements

MAITRISER LA LANGUE FRANCAISE : orthographe, conjugaison, grammaire et
vocabulaire
- travail autour du terme « déprise »
formation des mots et mots de la même famille, champ sémantique et lexical, antonymes et
synonymes

LANGAGE ORAL :
participer aux échanges en classe : justifier ses choix à l'oral, écouter, comprendre et pouvoir
expliciter le choix des autres.
mettre en voix les textes étudiés et les textes produits.
Participer à un débat argumentatif

AUTONOMIE et INITIATIVE : acquérir des méthodes de travail, apprendre à apprendre,
savoir travailler en équipe, assumer des rôles, prendre des décisions / savoir s'organiser.

Pblématique :
Qu'est-ce que la Déprise ? Comment prend-elle forme ?
Le lecteur prend -il le contrôle ?
Le lecteur guide-t-il la machine ou est-ce la machine qui guide le lecteur ?

Fig. 7. An example of a *sequence* or teaching plan.

3 Analysis

3.1 The Introduction of Digital Works

a. The integration of digital works in the curriculum and possible pedagogical
orientations

All the teaching sequences were based around complete digital works, generally
as part of a corpus of more traditional texts. The digital works in question were never
treated as secondary works, with between 9 and 14 teaching sessions devoted to
each one, proving that they were the object of detailed study within the respective
pedagogical projects.

During the study sequences, as is the case with traditional sequential organization,
reading and the interpretation of the written text is the dominant activity, while the
place given to interpreting images and to writing is also important. The sessions
devoted to the interpretation of images are justified by the fact that multimodal
works are, by nature, composed of static or moving images, which explains this

choice. However the importance of the sessions devoted to writing would seem to be the result of a pedagogical choice, these sessions bearing a close relation to the literary text studied (Tauveron and Sève, 2005), and constituting the final objective of the learning sequence, as we shall see at the end of our analysis.

Finally, we would like to draw your attention to one type of session which is inexistent in traditional learning sequences, and is devoted to the appropriation of the reading device or medium. Such sessions occupy a half-way position between technical discovery and discovery of the text, and seem to illustrate the interdependent relationship between reading practices and the medium involved (Goody, 2000; Chartier, 2012): the teachers seem to be aware of the fact that the media and devices used in interactive digital narratives require specific learning sessions, as we can observe in the following extract from our second sequence plan (S5), based on the study of *Phallaina*, "getting used to the tablet, discovering the application, learning how to navigate and how to use the table of contents, scrolling".

b. The approaches to studying digital works selected by the teachers

We were able to identify three main (combinable) approaches to digital works:

– the approach by (literary) genre

Samuel, working on *Phallaina*, gave the following title to one of his sessions: "At the crossroads between fantastic/marvelous literature and science fiction".

– the approach by media (in their capacity as communicational genres)

Caroline, working on *Déprise*, created a link between digital literature and video games, and gave the following title to one of her sessions: "The construction of 'playability'. The need for gradual learning with levels of difficulty as with video games". Céline, also working on *Déprise*, created a link between digital literature and art, taking her pupils to see an exhibition by a collective of digital artists.

– the approach through the senses (multimodality)

Caroline emphasized "the sensorial journey of the internet reader", insisting on the coordination between touching, seeing and hearing. Hélène called one of her sessions "*a multimodal language*". She worked with her pupils on *Phallaina* during two consecutive academic years, placing greater emphasis on multimodality during the second year (two different cohorts of students).

These different approaches are indicative of the ways in which teachers conceive the experience of the reading of a digital work by their pupils. Do they prefer to base this experience around cultural references, in order to avoid disorientating the pupils too much, or on other dimensions (such as the sensorial dimension) so as to more clearly emphasize the originality of such a reading experience?

3.2   What is Taught Through the Reading of Digital Works?

a.   Teaching about literature? About literacy? About the digital world?

When teachers propose digital works to their students, are they mainly interested by the literary dimension, or do they aim to help their pupils become digitally-literate citizens?

How is a link established with the history of literature? Is digital literature presented as an integral part of the vast history of literature, or rather as a form of expression for the extreme contemporary genre, its interest lying in the fact that it is a form which is currently being created? Some teachers begin by placing the digital creation for study on the timeline of literary history, or by emphasizing its intertextuality (e.g. Hélène with *l'Homme Volcan*). Others prefer to start by emphasizing the innovative reading experience the work offers (e.g. Virginie with *Déprise*). They all then endeavour to define what is meant by digital literature (what a digital work is, and how to read it).

Digital literacy requires the coordination of both technical and cultural (especially literary) knowledge. Do teachers place these resources in opposition, or do they recognize the need to combine the two? The technical aspect is by no means absent from the sequences conceived, as the teachers devote entire sessions to the appropriation of the tools (manipulation sessions). But if Samuel (S5) explicitly raises the question of the medium and the technical device, the coordination of the literary and digital dimensions is not always stressed (little emphasis is given to the "architextural" dimension of the writing tools, as if the tools were neutral). This no doubt remains one of the challenges for the teaching of digital literature, as the close links between cultural and technical knowledge are an aspect yet to be taken into consideration by teachers and institutions.

Does digital literature enhance our understanding of our digital *milieu* ("milieu" meaning that which lies both around and between us)? Do teachers place digital works in context in relation to their pupils' digital environment? No explicit links were established with usual writing practices, particularly those related to social media. However, several teachers insisted on the fact that these works make us think about the place of the Digital in our lives. A question raised by one of the teachers (working on *Déprise* with a class of sixteen-year-olds) about her sequence is emblematic in this respect: "In what manner does digital literature question our relationship to the digital world?" It is important to incite pupils to adopt a reflective attitude, and even to become enlightened users of the digital environment, a challenge which ties in with one of the stakes of digital literature.

b.   Which elements of digital literature and which textual aspects are generally studied?

Several types of objects for study are selected for digital literature classes, some of them relatively constant when studying complete works, such as the main character(s) or the *genre* of the work in question. Other aspects are less frequently covered in traditional literature classes; for example our corpus raises an interest for the identity of the readers and their emotions. Although a strong involvement of pupils with the studied work is not a phenomenon which is specific to digital literature, this aspect does however seem to be intensified by the technical processes involved, as Saemmer and Tréhondart point out when they speak of "immersive reception" (2014). Teachers working with eleventh grade students insisted on this point:

> "Even if they may be more disorientating for pupils than a traditional paper book, the choice of digital works captures the attention of the least-skilled readers (because digital works are relatively short, interactive, and have tactile and visual dimensions)." (S8)

Finally, certain new study objects are selected, first of all the multimodality of digital works. In accordance with the recommendations of Lebrun and Lacelle (2012), they identified the complexity of the interlinking of the various elements, as well as the specificity of the different communicational modes, along with the diversity of fonts and their animation as knowledge on which to focus their teaching, studying the signification of these aspects (S6, S2).

3.3   Text Analysis: Questions Around the Choice of Pedagogical Methods and Progressivity in Pupils' Appropriation of the Text

a. The pedagogical methods selected by the teachers

In the aim of more clearly defining the object for study, we shall focus at present on the reading methods selected by the teachers, so as to identify their pedagogical choices.

Our analysis firstly reveals certain elements of continuity – in more than 10 cases the digital works were studied in traditional text analysis sessions. What is most remarkable is that two new teaching methods emerged, as a response to a need for pupils to be accompanied in their reading of this new type of work. Indeed, even if pupils read them on devices with which they are very famliar, they are bewildered by and unsure of how to respond to digital works. Indeed, nearly all the teachers programmed an initial session devoted to accompanied reading at the beginning of their sequences. Thus pupils discovered the digital works in class, with teachers sometimes reading a text aloud at the same time as their pupils discovered it on their screens. The initial reading experience was in this way collective and shared. Additionally two teachers proposed "comprehension workshops" which involved pupils working on a passage, in the aim of not only more precisely grasping the literal sense but also understanding what the pupils identified in a very intuitive manner as the "atmosphere" (S5), that is to say the means used by the author for the reading of the text.

b. Two epistemological pathways

The progression within the sequences also reveals an itinerary allowing the teachers to define certain notions or to place emphasis on certain aspects of the work. Two alternative pathways can be observed in the teachers' sequences:

– the sequence begins by an analysis of the text before dealing with the multimodal and interactive dimensions;

– the sequence begins by an appreciation of the work in all its complexity (including the multimodal and interactive dimensions), followed by an analysis of the text (in the linguistic sense).

Are these two pathways representative of a strategy to reassure pupils (or even parents), sometimes disorientated by digital works? In both cases, the teachers endeavour to *reveal* the literariness of these works, helping their pupils to consider works which *a priori* do not meet the classic criteria of literariness (an unstable text, the multimodal dimension, material intervention by the reader) as literary. In the two pathways mentioned above, the teachers attempt to displace the notion of literariness in order to create *an interactive literary experience.*

3.4   The Writing Practices Developed in the Sequences

Once again our analysis of the characteristics of the sessions devoted to writing conceived by the teachers will remain a global one. We do not however wish to neglect this aspect, since, as we have emphasized, the important place given to writing activities was one of the specificities of the sequences studied (Fig. 8).

Fig. 8. Pupils creating a piece inspired by *Phallaina.*

a.   The evolution of the sessions and of the writing activities

   Whereas reports and studies about current writing practices stress that these often intervene only in the final evaluation session of a teaching sequence, writing activities in the sequences making up our sample were more frequent, and took place at different stages within the sequences. They were positioned after a number of reading sessions, the pedagogical project thus seeming to contribute to the aim of training pupils to be attentive to certain specificities when reading digital works in order to help them to constitute a pool of resources to be used in creative digital production activities. Indeed, it should be pointed out that the writing sessions were principally designed for the production of texts for the screen, even if this tendency was not an exclusive one in any of the sample sessions.

b. Characteristics of creative digital writing practices

The conduct of a pedagogical sequence, with its various sessions, shows that.
The written production:

- comes at the end of the sequence
- represents an important part of the sequence
- is directly linked to the resources worked on during the reading phase

The tools used are very different, and a considerable diversity of writing practices and formats can be observed: Ebooks, videos, slideshows, hierarchical or branching narratives created with Twine. But for each teacher, the chosen format is directly associated with the digital piece studied.

What is somewhat striking in the instructions given for writing, is that they do not invite pupils to reflect upon the role of the writing tool or software in the writing activity (the "architextural" dimension mentioned above). The tools used were however very different, and a considerable diversity of writing practices and formats can be observed: Ebooks in epub format (S4); vidéos in mp4 format (S3), diaporamas (S6), non-linear arborescences with Twine to write a scenario (S8). This led to the creation of an "interactive immersive work", with the help of multimedia professionals.

In the case of the Ebook, there were references to traditional paper books such as successive pages, but with illustrations and videos inserted into the pages. This is an example of an enriched work, or a work which is augmented by a multimodal dimension (see Fig. 9).

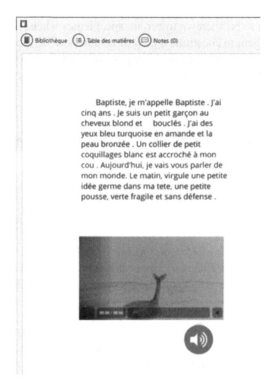

Fig. 9. Writing practice: a capture from the ebook of a junior school pupil, inspired by *L'Homme volcan*.

Here is a video capture of pupils working collectively on a production based on Phallaina: https://youtu.be/wxw-mOESfJs. The videos inspired by *Phallaina* reveal some very interesting experiments and reflections on the medium. Here the teacher does not intervene on the story, but on the tools available. She accompanies the pupils not on the narrative dimension (which would be in another context at the heart of her teaching), but by showing the possibilities of the tools.

Here is a production by 12 year old pupils having studied *Phallaina*: https://youtu.be/5UBYCiT_wfw. We have A4 sheets showing drawings with speech bubbles taped next to one another. The video sequence sweeps over the pages in a left-to-right movement to tell the story. In this animated video, the codes of the traditional paper cartoon book are revisited in the form of a "scrolling graphic novel", recreated using audio-visual and sound flows. We can see here how familiar pupils are with the entire universe of *Phallaina* (black and white graphic code, music/text articulation, play on fonts, even the scrolling rhythm). It is striking to see to what extent the pupils were able to integrate the world of *Phallaina*, including in terms of the emotion produced (see Fig. 10).

Fig. 10. Writing practice: a capture from a video inspired by *Phallaina*.

The slideshows used by the pupils to stage their own *Déprise/Loss of Grasp* invite the reader to participate in a tale which is partly narrative and partly poetic (see Fig. 11). These are examples of interactive animated multimedia presentations, playing on the notions of spatiality and temporality.

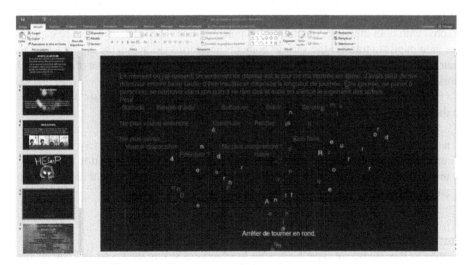

Fig. 11. Writing practice: a screen capture from a slideshow inspired by *Déprise*.

With Twine, the pupils could build a graph to create a non-linear interactive narrative (see Fig. 12).

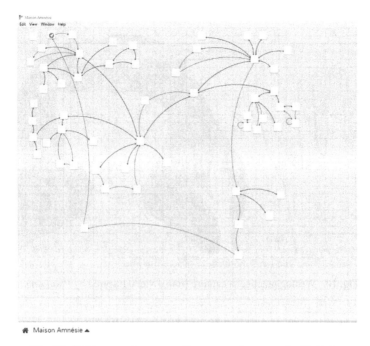

Fig. 12. Writing practice: a non-linear narrative created with *Twine*.

The interactive and multimedia solutions proposed produced very diverse forms of writing, using diverse formats (epubs imitating books, videos, slideshows, arborescent graphs) with both inherent constraints and potentialities. The teachers aimed to encourage their pupils to transfer the various contents and forms studied in the digital works to their writing activities, and to do this using similar writing forms to those of the studied works.

Overall, three main notions were transferred from the pupils' analysis of the works to their writing activities:

- a sensorial and multimedia universe,
- animation and temporality (the different ways of playing with the notion of time),
- interactivity and author-reader relationship (between control and loss of control, grasp and loss of grasp).

Further Reflection

Thanks to this study, we have been able to observe a strong desire on the part of the teachers involved to create a **continuum** between the teaching of literary interactive narratives and their more traditional practices. Moreover, the careful attention they paid to the **specificity** of these digital works inspired them to demonstrate genuine professional **creativity** and to pay close attention to the progression of their pupils in these new reading practices.

We have been able to observe the reinforcement of the **reading/writing links**. These links are highlighted by the study of stylistic **figures** specific to digital literature (whether related to sounds, images or gestures). These links sometimes go as far as **borrowing extracts** from the digital work studied (e.g. screen captures).

Conversely, we could point out that fewer links were established by the teachers between literary IDNs and the pupils' own private writing practices, which confirms that the teachers were uncomfortable with the idea of addressing this subject.

References

Barbara, J.: Authoring Tools in Teaching IDN: Design of LudoNarrative Dissonance. In: Interactive Storytelling 13th International Conference on Interactive Digital Storytelling. ICIDS, Bournemouth (2020)

Bouchardon, S.: Littérature numérique : le récit interactif. Hermès Science, Paris (2009)

Bouchardon, S.: La valeur heuristique de la littérature numérique, Hermann, Paris (2014). https://www.costech.utc.fr/CahiersCOSTECH/spip.php?article27

Bouchardon, S.: Pourquoi enseigner la littérature numérique?. In: Brunel, B., Quet, F. (eds) L'enseignement de la littérature avec le numérique. Bruxelles, Peter Lang, pp. 203–218 (2018)

Brunel, B., Quet, F.: L'enseignement de la littérature avec le numérique. Bruxelles, Peter Lang (2018)

Cahen, F.: Mais là, on sort un peu du cadre, non?. Les Cahiers pédagogiques **42** (2016). https://www.academia.edu/34974810/Mais_là_on_sort_un_peu_du_cadre_non

Chaillou, M.: L'extrême-contemporain, journal d'une idée. PO&SIE n°41. Paris (1987)

Chartier, R.: Qu'est-ce qu'un livre? Métaphores anciennes, concepts des lumières et réalités numériques. Le français aujourd'hui 2012/3 **178**, 11–26 (2012)

Cordeiro, G.S., Schneuwly, B.: La construction de l'objet enseigné et les organisateurs du travail enseignant. Recherche et formation **56**, 67–80 (2007)

Dubbleman, T., Roth, C., Koenitz, H.: Interactive Digital Narratives (IDN) for Change: Educational Approaches and Challenges in a Project Focused on Migration. In: Interactive Storytelling 11th International Conference on Interactive Digital Storytelling. ICIDS, Dublin (2018)

Dufays, J.-L., Gemenne, L., Ledur, D.: Pour une lecture littéraire. Histoires, théories, pistes pour la classe, [1996], 3^{e}ed. Bruxelles, De Boeck (2015)

Florey, S., Jeanneret, S., Mitrovic, V.: Lire des œuvres littéraires numériques en classe: quels apprentissages pour les élèves?. Numérique et didactique des langues et cultures (2020)

Fourtanier, M.-J.: Dislocation et "figurativisation" dans les dispositifs de lecteurs. Revue pour la recherche en éducation, Actes de colloque ACFAS 2010, Ottawa, pp. 48–54 (2011)

Goody, J.: The Power of the Written Tradition. Smithsonian Institution Press, Washington and London (2000)

Hayles, N.K.: Electronic Literature: New Horizons for the Literary. University of Notre Dame Press, Notre Dame (2008)

Jeanneret, Y., Souchier, E.: Pour une poétique de l'écrit d'écran. Xoana, images et sciences sociales 6/7, pp. 97–107. J.-M. Place, Paris (1999)

Koenitz, H., Palosaari Eladhari, M.: Challenges of IDN Research and Teaching. In: Interactive Storytelling: 12th International Conference on Interactive Digital Storytelling, ICIDS 2019. Little Cottonwood Canyon, UT, USA (2019)

Lacelle, N., Lebrun, M.: La littératie médiatique multimodale: réflexions sémiologiques et dispositifs concrets d'application. Forum lecture, Les apprentissages littéraciques avec les médias numériques (2014)

Lebrun, M., Lacelle, N.: Le document multimodal : le comprendre et le produire en classe de français. Œuvres, textes, documents: lire pour apprendre et comprendre à l'école et au collège, Repères, Élisabeth Nonnon and François Quet (dir.) **45**, 81–95 (2012). https://www.forumlect ure.ch/myUploadData/files/2014_2_Lacelle_Lebrun.pdf

Petitjean, A.M.: Écrits collaboratifs en classe de littérature, Expériences d'écriture sur pad au collège et au lycée". In: Brunel, M., Quet, F. (eds.) L'enseignement de la littérature avec le numérique, pp. 181–202. Bruxelles, Peter Lang (2018)

Rettberg, S.: Electronic Literature. Polity Press (2018)

Ronveaux, C., Schneuwly, B.: Approches de l'objet enseigné. Quelques prolégomènes à une recherche didactique et illustration par de premiers résultats. Éducation et didactique n°1 (2007)

Saemmer, A., Tréhondart, N.: Les figures du livre numérique augmenté au prisme d'une rhétorique de la reception. In: Paquienseguy, F., Bosser, S. (eds.) Études de communications, langages, information médiations : le livre numérique en question, no 4, pp. 107–128 (2014)

Schneuwly, B., Dolz, J. (eds.): Des objets enseignés en classe de français. Presses universitaires de Rennes, Rennes (2009)

Tauveron, C., Sève, P.: Vers une écriture littéraire, ou comment construire une posture d'auteur à l'école : de la GS au CM2. Hatier, Paris (2005)

Communication Features Facilitating Appreciation of Cultural Heritage Values for IDN

Srushti Goud[(✉)] and Vincenzo Lombardo

Universitá di Torino, Turin, Italy
{srushti.goud,vincenzo.lombardo}@unito.it

Abstract. Cultural heritage values are defined as a set of characteristics perceived in heritage by certain individuals or groups. Cultural heritage values highlight the motivations for the conservation of heritage properties by national and international organizations. These include value associations selected by experts and communities. Heritage values of communities are passed down over generations and help in conservation. Historic and traditional (pre-digital) narratives communicated values but not all sources were credible. Current efforts using digital technologies for the communication of cultural heritage disproportionately focuses on engagement and spectacularization. This has had a negative effect on research towards the sharing of cultural heritage values through Interactive Digital Narratives (IDN). We believe that a number of communication features can be beneficial to value appreciation especially when using IDN. In this paper, we discuss values included by the designer(s) and also appreciated by the user(s) of IDN in the communication of cultural heritage. We address four types of features that are suggested as being influential for the communication of cultural heritage values, namely 1) narrative significance, 2) multiperspectivity, 3) dialogue facilitation, 4) contextualization. We go through six case studies and show how to exploit these IDN features to effectively communicate the associated values of cultural heritage to a larger audience.

Keywords: Cultural heritage values · Cultural heritage communication · Communication features · IDN Design · Value appreciation

1 Introduction

Cultural heritage values can be defined as a set of characteristics perceived in heritage by certain individuals or groups [7] and different individuals or groups may have different typologies and ranges of values [2].

Researchers have been working on the concept of heritage value, its meaning, classification, and relevance. National and international charters concerning Cultural Heritage (CH) have also discussed the aspects of values pertaining to

© The Author(s) 2022
M. Vosmeer and L. Holloway-Attaway (Eds.): ICIDS 2022, LNCS 13762, pp. 121–138, 2022.
https://doi.org/10.1007/978-3-031-22298-6_8

it. The ICOMOS Venice Charter, 1964, states that it is our common responsibility to safeguard historic monuments in "the full richness of their authenticity" [10]. In particular, the Nara document, 1994, introduces authenticity as the "essential qualifying factor concerning values". The document points out that judgements of values must be done within their cultural contexts since it is not possible to "to base judgements of values and authenticity within fixed criteria". It acknowledges that both "the judgement of values" and "the credibility of related information" may vary across cultures and even within one culture. Hence, each culture must identify and assess the specific nature of its own heritage values and also understand the credibility and truthfulness of its related information sources [11].

All the values of a specific CH can be summarised under its 'Cultural Significance'. The Australia ICOMOS Charter for Places of Cultural Significance (The Burra Charter) defines cultural significance as the "aesthetic, historic, scientific, social or spiritual value for past, present or future generations". The charter explains that cultural significance "is embodied in the place itself, its fabric, setting, use, associations, meanings, records, related places and related objects". It also declares that the conservation of a place must not give "unwarranted emphasis on any one value" [2]. Hence, heritage properties can have many types of values that are equally significant and are built on various types of associations by the people.

Both the Burra Charter and the Nara Document point to a common idea that has shown up a bit more frequently in academic discussion of the late 20th to the early 21st century. It is the idea that the community may associate a set of heritage values to a heritage property (place, person or historical event) based upon their memories, their sense of place, or their intangible attachment to the events at a place. Research has shown that these are only quantifiable via a study and open acceptance of the 'community perspective'. The community perspective is something that may be under-appreciated in an official 'statement of significance' or in some cases may even be in opposition to what the expert or the administrative approach to a heritage property might be. This can be clearly seen by looking at literature where researchers have been interacting with members of a community to understand their perspectives [5,18,27].

The goal of this paper is to analyse cultural heritage communication projects to uncover communication features that bring about an appreciation of CH values in a digitally connected world by the use of Interactive Digital Narratives (IDN). The following section highlights the importance of values in the conservation and communication of CH along with the method by which IDN projects were selected for our analysis (supported by a table). In Sect. 3, we analyse the selected IDN case studies from the perspective of CH values, which have not only been included by the designers within the project but also have been perceived by the users. Further, in Sect. 4, we discuss what features enabled the value appreciation within the surveyed IDN projects. This discussion is accompanied by a table that shows the points where CH values were perceived in the selected projects. Finally, in Sect. 5 we conclude with a view towards the future.

2   Importance of Values in Cultural Heritage Conservation and Communication

Expert assessments are top-down processes, where value associations are provided to outstanding heritage properties. This can be seen in the 'statement of significance' attached with the properties on the world heritage list by UNESCO. These statements help with both conservation and communication of the heritage. A detailed body of research backs up expert perspectives and discussions. In contrast, individuals and communities perceive characteristics in any given CH which is then acknowledged as heritage values by the 'insiders' or the members of the community who associate the heritage property as part of their history and culture. Analysing these associations leads to a 'bottom-up' understanding of the concept of CH values. However, studies of the community perspectives on heritage are few and far-between [18].

Table 1. Search terms for the literature review and their evolution

Phase of search	Terms	Objectives of search	Remarks
Initial search	Values, Cultural Heritage Value, Cultural Heritage Communication, Collective Memory, Conservation, Framework for Cultural Heritage Conservation, Cultural Communication, Cultural Learning, Cultural Heritage Sites	Terms with large scope	Included many variations of studies - some were theoretical and some were research reports of surveys or projects
Filtered search	Edutainment, History Games, Serious Games, Memory Studies, Narrative, Storytelling, Digital Storytelling, Interactive Experience, VR/AR Phygital Experiences, UI/UX principles, Values in Design of CH Applications, Museum App, Visitor Experience Study, Value Transfer, Heritage Value Communication	Terms related to digital projects and theories on designing digital applications	Emphasis on technical strategizing and spectacularization is observed
Final search	Game Studies, Multimedia Information Systems, Interactive Digital Storytelling, Embodied Interaction, Tangible Interaction, Audio Design, Audio-Visual Narrative, Evocative Experience, Emotional Experience	Terms covering digital projects that communicate CH	Research reporting gives new search terms but CH value assessment in studies are noticeably under-represented

A study that looked into the community values of Akaroa landscapes in New Zealand uncovered that the Maori community associated their naming traditions, burial traditions, lookouts and signalling, whaling, fishing, and walking/trading routes, with the landscape. These values differed from the values associated to the same landscape by the later European inhabitants, such as, land clearance, saw-milling, cheese factories, and traditional farming activities [27]. The methods and model suggested in the study throw light on CH values from the community perspective. In a contemporary sense, such associations may not be immediately appreciated using an 'outstanding' or 'universal' approach to value assessment. Research shows that the statements made by the members of the community regarding their cultural associations and the communal sense of values have been interpreted with difficulty by practitioners. Experts show a tendency to 'correct' the people rather than to understand and evaluate them from their cultural viewpoint [18].

The communal perception of values presents a unique set of opportunities and challenges for the CH professional who wishes to conserve and communicate heritage. To better understand communication projects that convey information and values associated with CH properties, we have collected and reviewed published literature. The search terms used during different phases of searching and the evolution of the search objective over a period of two years are shown in Table 1. The search process organically led us to the understanding that digital applications communicating about CH properties do not see themselves as carriers of CH values. They are in effect a 'digitization' of information that is previously available with certain sources which are mostly curated by experts. Community perception of heritage properties are rarely accounted for, if ever. In the following section we shall discuss a few IDN projects that have presented community perspectives alongside expert associations. Cultural heritage communication (CHComm) projects should, in principle, account for the dimension of CH values because 'every act of heritage conservation is a communicative act' [12].

3   Analysis of Case Studies

The content for communication of CH requires historically accurate information that is presented in a manner which appeals to the user. In a survey covering the relationship between CH and storytelling, stories were described as 'vessels' for wisdom, beliefs and values. Storytelling itself is described as a tool to bridge the gap between people over time and across cultures, thereby becoming a means for the preservation and dissemination of CH [4]. Traditionally, CH values and information were communicated via oral tradition, folktales, performing arts, books, paintings, and inscriptions on built structures [14,24]. All these methods have created narratives that would be accessible across generations and across cultures over time.

In the last two decades, digital communication has assumed the mantle of carrier of CH values. Users in the younger age-groups are comfortable interfacing with digital applications but awareness of the existence of digital CHComm applications is not as good as it can be [9]. Studies regarding effectiveness of User Interface and User Experience (UI/UX) design are increasingly available [3,15]. Very few studies cover the process of content preparation, the emotional impact generated by the content and the appreciation for CH values seen from the end user [16].

Table 2. Details of case studies

Project	Heritage	Time period of coverage	Format	User Feedback method
Personalized mobile guide for Archaeological Museum of Tripolis, Greece [1]	Classical Greek Artefacts	~600 - 300 B.C	Mobile Application (Onsite and Offline)	Open ended group discussions
Audio narratives for a historic site of a World War I camp in the Alps, Italy [17]	Memories from World War I, Italy	1914–1918	Audio Guide (Onsite)	Observations and semi-structured interviews
ArkaeVision Archeo VR experience - Paestum archaeological site, Italy [19]	Temple of Hera II, Paestum, Italy	~500 B.C	Virtual Reality Application (Exhibition Setup)	Observations and questionnaire
Interactive website for the White Bastion Fortress in Sarajevo, Bosnia and Herzegovina [20–22]	White Bastion, Sarajevo, Bosnia & Herzegovina	Medieval period - 600–1300 Ottoman period - 1400 - 1800 Austro-Hungarian period - 1800 - 1900	4D Virtual Presentation (Website)	Online questionnaire and Semi-structured interview
Augmented tour through the Refugi 307 bomb shelter in Barcelona, Spain [23]	Bomb Shelter - Spanish Civil War era, Barcelona	1936–1939	Augmented Reality Experience (Onsite)	Open ended questionnaire
Serious historical video game- Czechoslovakia 38–89 [25]	Memories from the Occupation of erstwhile Czechoslovakia by Nazi Germany during WWII	1938–1989	Serious historic video game (Online)	Open ended comments from users both face to face and online through forums

In the last decade, CHComm projects have successfully used IDN as a tool for emotional engagement of users in various settings [8]. These innovations in technology and interactive narratives can be ably supported by content that inculcates CH value appreciation as one of its design pillars. Assessing the inclusion of values and uncovering their impacts on users of CHComm would mean answering two questions:

a. Designer intention - What heritage values are evidently included in the communication application?
b. User perception - Are there any identifiable impacts on users from the inclusion of the heritage values?

Published literature which documents the design, implementation and user evaluation of IDN projects for CH were studied to answer the above questions. Projects had to explicitly mention the terms 'value' or 'significance' and include qualitative or quantitative user feedback and discussion. Analysing the decisions that went into the design and implementation of an IDN project led to the understanding of the range of CH values that were included. Evaluating the reported user feedback allowed us to note the points that were appreciated by the users. Value associations that were included and appreciated were categorized for ease of understanding, based on previously published typologies seen in literature [6].

We have selected six projects in which we were able to identify CH value appreciation as reported by the researchers. All projects were designed and tested after 2015 and the research was published before 2021. Table 2 shows the specifics of the selected CHComm projects and their methodology of collecting user feedback. Two of these projects had their digital experiences online and we were able to interact with these projects first-hand in the course of our study [22,26]. In one case we were able to discuss the activities done during the project and its post-implementation impacts with the creator [1]. The other three projects were discussed in detail by the researchers in their respective publications. This enabled us to uncover value associations that were intentionally included in the design phase by the designers. Every project provided user feedback reports either through quotes from open-ended interviews, semi-structured interviews or through summaries of such assessments. Therefore, inclusion of CH values by the designer(s) and appreciation of the same by user(s) is assessed based on reported design procedure and user feedback. Following subsections analyse each selected case with regards to the two questions posed above.

1 - Personalized Mobile Guide for Archaeological Museum of Tripolis, Greece [1]. The archaeological museum of Tripolis, Greece, is described as a peripheral museum from which the most popular artefacts have been relocated to central museums, such as the National Archaeological Museum of Athens. The artefacts that are currently displayed at the museum are not closely linked to each other and therefore do not lend themselves to a narrative presentation. This project describes the creation of personalized narratives based on broader concepts as a solution to this problem.

Designer Intention: 'Thematic tours' were created which would guide the user along a predefined route. The designers included socio-cultural values of the ancient times as part of the thematic tour. For example, "women in antiquity" was a specific theme selected by the designer to base the narratives regarding artefacts. Users who shared their Facebook profiles were matched with tours that were determined to be relevant to their interests. Users who did not share their profiles could instead login as guests and receive a random thematic tour suggestion. The other tour options were also available for users to choose in case they did not want the suggested option. Every object that was part of a tour would have a short audio narrative based on the theme of the tour with subtitles for hearing impaired users. Visitors were free to pause and play the narratives and were also asked to provide an opinion at some points. This was done to encourage historical and social reflection.

User Perception: Post-visit the users were able to share their thoughts and reflections with other museum visitors, on a dedicated social media site as well as their personal social media. This method of personalised content delivery and post-visit social reflection was positively received by the users. Visitor comments showed individual and group reflection on different historical and/or social phenomena. Some themes on which reflections were invited included women's position in societies, the similarities between past and current societies, and the advances in art. Value associations that were perceived in this case study include historic, social and symbolic values.

2 - Audio Narratives for a Historic Site of a World War I Camp in the Alps, Italy [17]. A historic site of a World War I camp and trenches dug in the Alps is currently under the purview of Museo Storico Italiano della Guerra (Historical Museum of War in Italy). This project covers the design process of an on-site audio-based narratives system that looks to share the experiences of people from the times of World War I.

Designer Intention: The visitors of the Historical Museum of War in Italy are given guided tours through the camp and trenches from World War I era by the museum. The authors co-designed a system that can deliver audio-based narratives adapted from personal and historical records of the era. The system used custom made near-field communication devices to enable the user to choose what narratives they wanted to hear. The speakers were placed well above the line of sight of the visitors so that they could hear the audio but nothing would obstruct their vision. These narratives included perspectives of the soldiers in the trenches, common people living in the villages such as the wives of the soldiers during the war time, the administrative officer's perspectives and a poet's description of the time of war. These narratives were intended to add context to the site.

User Perception: The system delivered 'piecemeal' narratives that the visitors could choose to switch between on-site. This unique aspect contributed to the visitors appreciation of the narrative content, as observed by the researchers. Users appreciated how the community survived the war coping with fear and uncertainty all around. They stated that in many cases they felt a connection to the place because of the audio. Some users stayed silent as a mark of respect and to fully immerse themselves in the audio and in the place. Users commented that the disembodied sound in the location added more meaning and emotion to the content. Value associations that were perceived in this case study include historical and social values of the time.

3 - ArkaeVision Archeo VR Experience - Paestum Archaeological Site, Italy [19]. The ArkaeVision Archeo is a VR experience within a virtual reconstruction of the Paestum archæological site in the south of Italy where the ancient temple of Hera II is located. Hera was seen as the goddess of women and family in the ancient Greek religion and the VR experience provided a view into the everyday life in the ancient temple.

Designer Intention: Researchers created a narrative using the character of priestess 'Ariadne' and users could follow her along on an explorative path within the temple. They used scenography, dramaturgy, and other traditional film direction techniques to encourage user interest in life and culture during the 5th century BCE. Additional information was available to the user in the form of optional text that would be superimposed on top of the visualization. User profiling was done before the VR exploration categorizing users into groups such as children, common visitors and experts. The content was structured as a folk-tale, general narration or in-depth narration depending on the user type. The designers included interactions that highlighted the religious and socio-cultural values of the ancient times as part of the virtual reconstruction and guided experience.

User Perception: Users stated that they liked the experience within the VR environment and some users expressed interest in learning more about the 'priestess' character that guided them through the experience. Understanding the uses of the artefacts within a fully reconstructed VR temple, instead of the ruins that remain on the actual site today, was appreciated by the visitors. The true sense of wonder of the building in its full glory was impressed onto the minds of the visitors by the realistic lighting and colors. The recreation created a mental image which helped users relate to the religious practices of the time and were also shown to remember several aspects of it. Value associations that were perceived in this case study include religious, historic, aesthetic, social and symbolic values.

4 - Interactive Website for the White Bastion Fortress in Sarajevo, Bosnia and Herzegovina [20–22]. This project is a website that presents the evolution of the White Bastion Fortress in Sarajevo, Bosnia and Herzegovina across three distinct periods. The designers chose to call this as a 4D virtual reconstruction as the website included explorable 3D reconstructions of the fortress from three eras, thereby including the fourth dimension of time.

Designer Intention: Designers wished to present the historical evolution of the fortress over time. Videos discussing distinctive periods of existence of the fortress are shown after an introduction video. The videos are centred around an 'immortal soldier' character, who describes events that occurred in and around the fortress for each time period. In some sections of the video a narrator steps in to describe certain overarching events of the particular time-period that affected the fortress. For example the soldier character describing an extended period of peace in the Ottoman era video says that "I thought my name would be forgotten, that Sarajevo would never again need its soldier." Then after a brief musical interlude, the narrator steps in to say that "So it was until the campaign of Prince Eugene of Savoy in 1697...". Going through the entire series of videos allows users to form a mental image of the fortress from the medieval era to the 20th century. A corresponding interactive digital environment shows the structure of the fortress at the time. Finding an object within the fortress and clicking on it will open another tab where the object itself is highlighted and can be interacted with in more detail. Once all the interactive environments have been explored, users can view a final video meant as a closing comment. The designers conveyed historic values especially the political and military history perceptions of each era by creating the character of an 'eternal soldier' of the fortress who provided a voice to the 'will' of the fortress itself. The narrative structure placed the focus of the experience on the varying contextual cultural importance of the heritage.

User Perception: The user evaluation for this project was shared in three different publications. Non-expert users were asked questions relating to the historic information content that they saw and interacted with to test their learning. A majority of Bosnian users and all the non-Bosnian users answered questions correctly. They also commented that they felt immersed in the past while watching the videos [20]. Expert users from an interdisciplinary development team including a psychologist, communicologist and a film director among others commented on the content. Expert comments stated that the novel way of presenting information invoked curiosity and the application was attractive and engaging. Various improvements were also suggested to many aspects within the application [22]. In another evaluation to understand the usefulness of Interactive Digital Storytelling (IDS) in education, teachers considered it as important while students gave it lesser importance. Majority of the users reportedly preferred historic fidelity over artistic liberty in the IDS content [21]. Users and experts alike appreciated the character of the eternal soldier and the overall presentation. The change in historic values and social value associations over time was perceived by the users.

5 - Augmented Tour Through the Refugi 307 Bomb Shelter in Barcelona, Spain [23]. This project was implemented within the Refugi 307 bomb shelter in Barcelona, which was built during the Spanish civil war. It is meant to augment the guided tour experience provided by the Barcelona History Museum.

Designer Intention: School children visiting the underground bomb shelter were taken on a guided tour and presented with context-specific projections of events from the time of the Spanish civil war. Hand-held digital projectors with videos and images arranged in a predetermined sequence were given to one member in each group. As the group passed through various rooms in the bomb shelter, children were told stories of the Spanish civil war and relevant multimedia was projected onto the walls. These ranged from a video of a plane dropping bombs shown at the entry of the shelter to an explanation of how a room, such as the infirmary, was used and how the furniture in it was arranged. The application explicitly attempted to engage emotional and critical thinking of the children in order to improve the contextual understanding of the historical events.

User Perception: Children were observed as they tried to visualise and even physically position themselves to understand the living situation within the bomb shelter during the war. For example, a child crouched under one of the benches in the shelter and commented that it would have been too small to fit them. Observations of the children and later interactions with them acknowledged a strong emotional impact. Children stated that they felt like they were travelling through time and also that they felt sad having seen drawings by other children from the 1930s s (during the Spanish civil war). A child from an initial test group drew the picture of children from war-torn Syria in 2011 as a response to their visit. Value associations that were perceived in this case study include the emotional impact and the collective memory shared by the community. A direct effort was made to highlight the social values and the historic values apart from many wartime experiences from recent memory.

6 - Serious Historical Video Game - Czechoslovakia 38-89 [25, 26]. This project covers the design process and user evaluation of a serious war game based on a semi-fictionalized retelling of World War II events during the German occupation of erstwhile Czechoslovakia. Subsequent iterations of the game have also been created based on the findings from the version discussed here.

Designer Intention: The game lets the user take control of a central character who is the grandson/granddaughter of J. Jelinek, a Czechoslovakian national, who was arrested after the assassination of Reinhard Heydrich, "Reichsprotektor" of the Nazi-occupied Czech Territories. This character is looking to uncover the truth surrounding their grandfather's arrest and comes across multiple people who share their experiences and memories from the time. The creators wanted to explore the potential of a historically accurate and serious wargame as an educational tool. They created multiple fictional characters based on accurate testimonies from the survivors of World War II.

User Perception: User feedback on an educational version showed a lot of positive response in terms of learning of the history, from school students and teachers. The game helped students appreciate how people survived the war and how the nation navigated through its tumultuous military and political history [25]. The main (public) version of this game which was released online received comments from various people who expressed appreciation for the handling of the topic through multiple 'eyewitness testimonies' that showed the injustices and loss faced by the people at the time. Online dialogue surrounding the game showed how people reflected on contemporary political discourse in relation to the historic narratives presented in the game. There were some notable negative reactions to the minority perspectives shown in the game as some users perceived them as foreign or unworthy of being included in to their idea of the national history. The public version of this game titled "Attentat 1942" has gained international attention [13]. Value associations that were perceived in this case study include historic, social, cultural and symbolic values.

Summary of Cases: All cases show instances of intentional CH value inclusion by the designers and points of value appreciation by the users. They were successful in generating emotional responses from the users beyond the mere communication of historic information. The impact of the narrative delivered various values of the communities from the past and facilitated dialogues within their contemporary contexts. National and regional identity, opposition to disliked regimes and struggles at the personal and communal levels were conveyed alongside political, administrative and military discourses of their time. Changes in socio-cultural values and in some cases how little has changed over time could be realized through these experiences. What might otherwise have been limited by brief explanations or illustrations attached to sites and artefacts were turned into evocative narratives. This attempt to go one step beyond a traditional 'descriptive' presentation of information is what elevates the design of these IDN projects.

4   Identifying the Communication Features Facilitating Appreciation of CH Values

The analysis covers six different styles of interactive narratives. We covered projects that featured a story based on a central character [25], piecemeal narratives built from historical records [17], a thematic narrative built on disparate museum objects [1], a slice of life experience in a virtual reconstruction [19], a chronologically structured retelling of the events surrounding the heritage property [21] and an experiential exploration of the site with narratives projected on its wall [23]. Table 3 presents the summary of the findings from the six IDN projects selected for analysis. We attribute the four features listed below as instrumental to the effective communication of CH values in IDNs.

1. **Narrative** structure was used to highlight the **significance** of certain values as seen in traditional narratives.
2. The projects featured **multiple perspectives** and varying values from disparate groups, especially the *community perspective*.
3. **Facilitating** and sometimes initiating an extended **dialogue** about the content of the narrative on digital platforms were supported.
4. The recreations of the original **contexts** in which the heritage properties or events would have existed *over the years* were appraised.

Table 3. CH Values conveyed in the Case Studies and the features of communication that enabled the value appreciation (Abbreviations: Narrative Significance - (NS), Multiperspectivity - (MP), Dialogue Facilitation - (DF), Contextualization - (CO))

Case Study	CH Values	Features
Personalized mobile guide for	1. Socio-cultural values- Reflection on the role of women by comparing ancient history to life today	NS, MP
Archaeological Museum of	2. Historic values- Appreciation of the historic artefacts in the museum	NS, CO
Tripolis, Greece [1]	3. Empathy, Identity- Understanding perspectives of different users on the same information	DF
Audio narratives for a historic site	1. Surviving war - Understanding wartime life of people as compared to normalcy	NS, CO
of a World War 1 camp in the	2. Administrative and Political history- Understanding the consequences of the war	NS, MP
Alps, Italy [17]	3. Fear, Uncertainty, Loss- Experiencing the difficulties of front-line officers and soldiers	CO, NS
	4. Appreciation of military strategy- Being in a trench and participating in warfare	CO, MP
ArkaeVision Archeo VR	1. Religious values - Understanding ancient religious practices and rituals	NS
experience - Paestum archaeologi,	2. Appreciation and wonder for the art and architecture - Paestum temples Architecture recreated	Technological fidelity + CO
-cal site, Italy [19]	3. Socio-cultural values - Understanding the roles of members of society in comparison to contemporary practices (Priestess vs. Priest)	NS, CO
	4. Historic value - Appreciating the myth of Hera	NS
Interactive website for the White Bastion Fortress	1. Administrative and Political history- Understanding how and why the White Bastion fortress developed into what it is today	NS, MP
Bosnia and Herzegovina	2. Pride, Fear- Struggles in the life of a soldier through multiple eras	CO
[20–22]	3. Military history- Understanding the techniques and implements of offense and defense	CO, MP
	4. Social development- Understanding how the region developed and what influenced it	NS, MP
Augmented tour through	1. Surviving war- Understanding wartime life of people as compared to normalcy	NS, CO
the Refugi 307	2. Togetherness- Communal identity	CO, DF
bomb shelter in	3. Loss and Injustice- Facing wartime horrors	CO, MP
Barcelona, Spain [23]	4. Military and Political history- Understanding the consequences of the war	NS, CO
	5. Solidarity with refugees- Empathy towards those suffering from war	DF, CO
Serious historical video game -	1. Surviving war- Understanding wartime life of people as compared to normalcy	NS, CO
Czechoslovakia	2. Inclusiveness- Understanding fate of minorities	MP
38–89 [25, 26]	3. Loss and Injustice- Facing wartime horrors	CO, NS
	4. National and Regional Pride	CO, DF
	5. Military and Political history- Understanding the consequences of the war	NS

Specific CH values were delivered to the user by a combination of communication techniques or features. Each feature and its inclusion in an IDN comes with its own advantages, nuances and caveats. The satisfactory integration of these and other aspects in the design of an IDN such as the UI/UX format, research requirements of the communicator(s) or the objectives of the organization(s) that fund/host the digital communication application can be a demanding task. At this juncture, an exploratory discussion on what these features are and how each feature can be included in the design of an IDN is warranted.

1. **Narrative Significance (NS)** of values in presentation - A narrative that highlights the various qualities of CH value associations presents a holistic view to the user. IDN projects discussed here presented contents by highlighting certain values in their core structure. A heritage property such as a church, mosque, temple or a similar place of worship attached to an existing religion may be aesthetically pleasing but the discussion surrounding it could give prominence to the religious values. The designers of the projects we studied, deliberately chose certain CH values as the core of their narrative. The struggles of the people and the community were the basis for 3 out of 6 narratives. The CH values which took centre stage were appreciated by users in all cases as evidenced by the user feedback. For example, users responded to the narratives about the role of women in antiquity by reflecting on the contemporary status of women in the case of artefacts in Tripolis museum. The socio-cultural values communicated by the narrative significance delivered the expected impact in this case with some users commenting that this understanding must be taught in schools [1]. The act of walking into the virtual reconstruction of a historic temple to be greeted by a priestess who then proceeds, to guide the user through experiencing the rituals within the temple was described as much more impactful by the users. Some users expressed a curiosity to learn more about ancient life and religion due to the narrative significance of religious values [19]. Presenting the cultural heritage values in relation to contrasting values of its time or comparable contemporary values of today is an effective method of communicating heritage information and its associated values. Choosing a narrative significance that encourages comparisons to personal values or contemporary communal values can increase the impact of the CH value appreciation. The ideal narrative would be able to present the significance of certain value associations in a new light.

2. **Multiperspectivity (MP)** in the narrative - There can be multiple perspectives and values surrounding a heritage property and these are likely to change over time. If a project shows coverage of a range of perspectives, then it is likely to generate an appreciation for the associated heritage values in the user. These diverse perspectives are authentically represented by faithfully recreating them in the narrative. Credible perspectives that are under-represented in the 'mainstream' or popular discourse would lead to a lasting impact on the user due to their novelty. Some narratives are very focused on certain values and strongly highlight a singular perspective, such as in the case of refugees living in a bomb shelter during the Spanish civil war [23].

This is not detrimental to value appreciation but it might not give the complete picture of the heritage property. Some relevant information and inherent values are lost in the communication. Some projects cover heritage properties that are not directly associated to any living culture, which leads to not having a community perspective, as it can be seen in the case study of the Hera Temple experience [19]. This also causes projects to not have many different perspectives to present. Making the user a 'protagonist' of the experience can be seen in the case of the narrative covering the WWII memories [25]. This setting was then used to deliver multiple and contradicting perspectives to the user. Other cases have the user taking on the role of an observer or listener that reflects upon the context provided by the narratives and the site. User feedback in every case has shown that users appreciated the opportunity to understand multiple authentic perspectives. Many responses showed the extent of the emotional impact and enhanced understanding of the CH values shared in the applications. Some users reacted negatively to perspectives that they did not personally agree with as in the case of users who did not consider it necessary to include minority perspectives in the historic experiences of WWII era Czechoslovakia [25]. Such reactions are a clear sign of effective communication of the CH values shared through a multi-perspective approach.

3. **Dialogue Facilitation (DF)** for CH values of user-interest - Understanding user perspectives towards the heritage and its associated meanings is a valuable asset for any designer. An evolved understanding of user perspectives is reflected in the content design based on the target audience expectations. Exploration of user and expert opinions sometimes uncovered new value associations that were previously overlooked by the designers. All projects obtained and assessed user and expert feedback after its implementation. Only one case included in-depth expert discussions prior to or during the design of the application which initiated dialogue in the public sphere. Designers of Czechoslovakia 38-89 reported that "dissenting opinion and critique" was generated by their narratives since they chose to include topics that "still resonate in the Czech public sphere and continue to influence the political scene". This is another clear impact of effective communication of CH values [26]. It is also worth noting that facilitating dialogue among users after the narrative experience can bolster the understanding and appreciation of CH values in users. In the case of the Tripolis Museum project, a digital platform was provided to users where they could interact with each other and share opinions about the application. This led to CH values being discussed and re-shared in social media which furthered the self-reflection and appreciation of those values by users [1]. Initiating dialogue as part of the narrative and facilitating it through application design helps foster better appreciation and further propagation of the values. Facilitation of dialogue with both users and experts at the early design stage of an IDN is therefore beneficial to the impact of the values shared.

4. **Contextualization (CO)** of heritage to highlight appropriate CH values - Contextualization is the use of design elements or narrative devices to communicate the ground reality of a heritage property in its time or within its cultural context. An empty battlefield with a memorial wall cannot adequately share the horrors and realities of the battle and the long-lasting consequences of a protracted war. The ruins of a temple or a collection of artefacts with detailed descriptions cannot help a visitor fully appreciate the purpose of the space/artefact at the time of its active use. Contextualization adds the missing details by recreating the use of the space/artefact in the narrative. Contextualizing heritage values using the site or the storytelling delivered a deeper understanding and a stronger emotional impact. This is evident in all cases as users were able to appreciate how the values reflected in the people's actions at the time and its tangible manifestations in history. The context provided by the site and/or the narrative encouraged self-reflection and provided users with an accurate basis for understanding the heritage as seen from the user responses. The project covering the history of the White Bastion fortress explains why certain decisions were made by the lords and how it impacted the regular soldier who guarded the fortress. Some parts of multimedia presentation go on to convey its impacts on the people in the region. Users were able to appreciate the necessity of a fort and were also able to see as to what happened when it was not well-maintained. Being able to explore different 3D models showing the fort architecture from various eras of its existence enhanced the user appreciation of military history [20]. Contextualization is effective but can be tricky to implement. In the Arkaevision VR experience, the technological fidelity of the virtual Hera temple contributed to the contextualization apart from the narrative features.

In essence, contextualization enhances the understanding of the heritage and increases the value appreciation of the user. Creating an IDN environment that places the heritage in an appropriate setting for its time and culture contextualizes CH.

Our approach to the searching and analysis of CHComm projects resulted in a pattern-finding process that uncovered the aforementioned features. The four features discussed here stood out as the common elements in the effective communication of CH values. Inculcating these four features into a design philosophy can generate a process for developing an ideal IDN that includes CH values and helps propagate them. A graphic representing this is shown in Fig. 1. Not every CHComm project needs to use all of these features but taking cues from the ideas discussed here can improve the implementation of any IDN. Conserving authentic CH values and communicating them with fidelity to future generations is an invaluable responsibility of heritage experts, designers and related professionals.

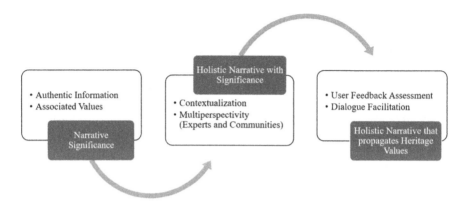

Fig. 1. Process for developing an ideal narrative that includes and propagates cultural heritage values

5   Conclusion

Digital applications for the communication of cultural heritage have effectively employed interactive digital narratives to create emotional experiences. Using a narrative structure that highlights significant cultural heritage values in relation to contemporary personal or community values through comparisons and contrasts is a reliable approach to effectively communicate cultural heritage values. Authentic perspectives that are not always in line with the mainstream or accepted narratives but nevertheless reflect community perceptions help with conserving and propagating cultural heritage values. Dialogue facilitation between users, experts and designers prior to, during and post the design of an application improves the quality of the cultural heritage value appreciation. Contextualizing the narratives in their appropriate cultural and temporal settings enhances user understanding. Evocative experiences have been shown to improve learning and retention in educational settings while also driving user engagement in comparatively 'casual' environments. An ideal IDN would integrate all the four features uncovered in our analysis. Further research is needed to craft a design framework that helps interested designers develop IDNs which takes relevant cultural heritage values into account and aids their propagation.

Acknowledgements. This research is part of the PhD programme Tech4Culture: Technology Driven Sciences at the Universitá di Torino, Italy. This project has received funding from the EU Horizon 2020 research and innovation programme under the Marie Skłodowska-Curie, grant agreement No 754511.

References

1. Antoniou, A., et al.: Bringing a peripheral, traditional venue to the digital era with targeted narratives. Digital Appl. Archaeol. Cultural Heritage **14**, e00111 (2019). https://doi.org/10.1016/j.daach.2019.e00111

2. Australia ICOMOS: Understanding and assessing cultural significance. Technical report, ICOMOS, November 2013
3. Bekele, M.K., Town, C., Pierdicca, R., Frontoni, E., Malinverni, E.V.A.S.: A survey of augmented, virtual, and mixed reality. ACM J. Comput. Cultural Heritage **11**(2) (2018)
4. van Blerk, J.: Federation of European Storytelling FEST Survey on Storytelling in Heritage Contexts. Technical report, Federation of European Storytelling (2019)
5. Duval, M., Smith, B., Hœrlé, S., Bovet, L., Khumalo, N., Bhengu, L.: Towards a holistic approach to heritage values: a multidisciplinary and cosmopolitan approach. Int. J. Heritage Stud. **25**(12), 1279–1301 (2019). https://doi.org/10.1080/13527258.2019.1590449
6. Fredheim, L.H., Khalaf, M.: The significance of values: heritage value typologies re-examined. Int. J. Heritage Stud. **22**(6), 466–481 (2016). https://doi.org/10.1080/13527258.2016.1171247
7. Getty Conservation Institute: Assessing the Values of Cultural Heritage. Technical report, Getty Conservation Institute, Los Angeles (2002). https://doi.org/10.2979/aft.2003.50.2.66
8. Gottlieb, H., Szelag, M.: Engaging Spaces Interpretation, Design and Digital Strategies Engaging Spaces Interpretation, Design and. NODEM 2014 Conference & Expo (2014)
9. Goud, S., Lombardo, V.: Assessment of digital environments for cultural heritage communication. In: Proceedings ofAVI2CH 2020: Workshop on Advanced Visual Interfaces and Interactions in Cultural Heritage (AVI2CH 2020). Association for Computing Machinery, Island of Ischia, Italy (2020)
10. ICOMOS: international charter for the conservation and restoration of monuments and sites (the Venice charter 1964). Tech. rep., International Council on Monuments and Sites, Venice (1964). https://www.icomos.org/charters/venice_e.pdf
11. ICOMOS: The Nara Document on Authenticity. Technical report, ICOMOS (1994). http://whc.unesco.org/uploads/events/documents/event-833-3.pdf
12. ICOMOS International Scientific Committee on Interpretation and Presentation: ICOMOS Charter for the Interpretation and Presentation of Cultural Heritage Sites. Technical report, ICOMOS (2008). https://doi.org/10.1017/S0940739108080417
13. Yarwood, J.: The academics behind 'Attentat 1942' are using games to explore Czech history - The Washington Post (2020). https://www.washingtonpost.com/video-games/2020/07/06/can-video-games-tactfully-handle-nazism-its-aftermath-these-czech-historians-say-yes/
14. Kader, S.A.: Traditional means of communication and modern mass media in Egypt on JSTOR. Ekistics **53**(318/319), 224–230 (1986). https://www.jstor.org/stable/43621982
15. Konstantakis, M., Caridakis, G.: Adding culture to UX: UX research methodologies and applications in cultural heritage. J. Comput. Cult. Heritage **13**(1), 1–17 (2020). https://doi.org/10.1145/3354002
16. Kuflik, T., et al.: A visitor's guide in an active museum: presentations, communications, and reflection. J. Comput. Cult. Heritage **3**(3), 1–25 (2011). https://doi.org/10.1145/1921614.1921618
17. Marshall, M.T., et al.: Audio-based narratives for the trenches of World War I: intertwining stories, places and interaction for an evocative experience. Int. J. Hum. Comput. Stud. **85**, 27–39 (2016). https://doi.org/10.1016/j.ijhcs.2015.08.001

18. McIntyre-Tamwoy, S.: Places people value: social significance and cultural exchange in post-invasion Australia. After Captain Cook: The Archaeology of the Recent Indigenous Past in Australia, pp. 171–189 (2004)
19. Pagano, A., Palombini, A., Bozzelli, G., Nino, M.D., Cerato, I., Ricciardi, S.: Arkae-Vision VR game: user experience research between real and virtual paestum. Appl. Sci. **10**(9), 1–38 (2020). https://doi.org/10.3390/app10093182
20. Rizvić, S., Okanović, V., Prazina, I., Sadžak, A.: 4D Virtual reconstruction of white bastion fortress. In: 2016 Eurographics Workshop on Graphics and Cultural Heritage, GCH 2016, pp. 79–82. Eurographics Association (2016). https://doi.org/10.2312/gch.20161387
21. Rizvic, S., Boskovic, D., Okanovic, V., Sljivo, S., Zukic, M.: Interactive digital storytelling: bringing cultural heritage in a classroom. J. Comput. Educ. **6**(2) 6(2), 143–166 (2019)
22. Rizvic, S., et al.: Guidelines for interactive digital storytelling presentations of cultural heritage. In: 2017 9th International Conference on Virtual Worlds and Games for Serious Applications, VS-Games 2017 - Proceedings, pp. 253–259 (2017). https://doi.org/10.1109/VS-GAMES.2017.8056610
23. Schaper, M.M., Santos, M., Malinverni, L., Zerbini Berro, J., Pares, N.: Learning about the past through situatedness, embodied exploration and digital augmentation of cultural heritage sites. Int. J. Hum. Comput. Stud. **114**, 36–50 (2018). https://doi.org/10.1016/j.ijhcs.2018.01.003
24. Singh, M.: Culture, communication and change in an indian village : a sociological study. Ph.D. thesis, Jawaharlal Nehru University (1997). http://hdl.handle.net/10603/17101, http://shodhganga.inflibnet.ac.in:8080/jspui/handle/10603/17101
25. Šisler, V.: Contested memories of war in czechoslovakia 38–89: assassination: designing a serious game on contemporary history. Int. J. Comput. Game Res. **16**(2) (2016). http://gamestudies.org/1602/articles/sisler
26. Šisler, V.: Critical war game development: lessons learned from attentat 1942. In: Hammond, P., Pötzsch, H. (eds.) War Games: Memory, Militarism and the Subject of Play, chap. 11, pp. 201–222. Bloomsbury Academic, New York (2019). https://www.bloomsbury.com/uk/war-games-9781501351167/
27. Stephenson, J.: The cultural values model: an integrated approach to values in landscapes. Landsc. Urban Plan. **84**(2), 127–139 (2008). https://doi.org/10.1016/j.landurbplan.2007.07.003

Writing with (Digital) Scissors: Designing a Text Editing Tool for Assisted Storytelling Using Crowd-Generated Content

Paulo Bala[1,2(✉)], Stuart James[3], Alessio Del Bue[3],
and Valentina Nisi[1,2]

[1] ITI-LARSyS, Lisbon, Portugal
paulo.bala@iti.larsys.pt
[2] IST, Universidade de Lisboa, Lisbon, Portugal
valentina.nisi@tecnico.ulisboa.pt
[3] Visual Geometry and Modelling (VGM) Lab & Pattern Analysis and Computer
Vision (PAVIS), Istituto Italiano di Tecnologia, Genova, Italy
{stuart.james,Alessio.DelBue}@iit.it

Abstract. Digital Storytelling can exploit numerous technologies and
sources of information to support the creation, refinement and enhancement of a narrative. Research on text editing tools has created novel
interactions that support authors in different stages of the creative process, such as the inclusion of crowd-generated content for writing. While
these interactions have the potential to change workflows, integration
of these in a way that is useful and matches users' needs is unclear. In
order to investigate the space of Assisted Storytelling, we designed and
conducted a study to analyze how users write and edit a story about
Cultural Heritage using an auxiliary source like Wikipedia. Through a
diffractive analysis of stories, creative processes, and social and cultural
contexts, we reflect and derive implications for design. These were applied
to develop an AI-supported text editing tool using crowd-sourced content
from Wikipedia and Wikidata.

Keywords: Digital storytelling · Text editing · Artificial intelligence ·
Crowd-sourced content · Knowledge graphs

1 Introduction

As Artificial Intelligence (AI) technologies evolve and get entangled with our lives
[14,18,32], decisions on how these technologies support us are made by those with
the knowledge on how to develop them (e.g., engineers); most end users struggle
to understand how AI supports them and have no influence on the design of such
digital tools. Considering the field of Creative Support Tools (CST) [9,15,34,37],
recent work have explored more human-centred approaches to the design of these
tools. For example, Han et al. [22] leverage the experience of knowledge workers

M. Vosmeer and L. Holloway-Attaway (Eds.): ICIDS 2022, LNCS 13762, pp. 139–158, 2022.
https://doi.org/10.1007/978-3-031-22298-6_9

(such as researchers) in designing software that works across their different work activities (e.g., active reading, sensemaking, writing). Lately, HCI research has included AI in human-centred approach. Recent work [24] has shifted focus on AI to empower the creative process, leveraging the "non human" qualities as a collaborative partner to humans. In this paper, our research question investigates how AI can support casual authors in storytelling activities.

Acknowledging the broad scope of CST [9,15,34,37] and possibilities of AI integration [24], we restrict the scope of exploration for this work. Firstly, we consider storytelling to be a skill developed over time, in which all users are proficient (but at different levels). Secondly, we consider writing as a foundational base for storytelling. Interfaces for text editing became a fruitful research topic as computers became mainstream and remain relevant in the present, as they impact millions of lives daily [21]. Finally, we constrain the context of the problem space (as done by other similar work [6,17]), to reflect on personal writing of memories and experiences of Cultural Heritage, enriched through searched or recommended content. Such restrictions create a setting where we can identify useful AI and retrieval features needed to support the task of storytelling and the creative process.

Our work is focused on exploring the design space of Assisted Storytelling according to a human-centred approach, and therefore the article is structured following research through design [44]. We set up a co-design workshop (described in Sect. 3), where five participants (including two researchers) were asked to write a story about their Cultural Heritage and later editorialize it, using Wikipedia to add additional information and media to the story. Afterwards, participants presented the created artefact and discussed the story and activity within the group. Given the speculative nature of the activity and the critical making nature of the artefacts, we used a diffractive analysis as inspired by recent work in Human-Computer Interaction (HCI) [12,14,23,30,40]. Based on Barad's diffraction as a metaphor for inquiry [2], the analysis (in Sect. 4) focuses on differences; rather than striving for consensus, diffraction values the individual identity, the conflicts and the absences as a design material. Based on internal discussions, we highlight refinements to the methodology and implications for design. As such, this paper's contribution to authoring interactive narratives relies on the insights for developing tools with Assisted Storytelling, especially tools using crowd-sourced content from Wikipedia and Wikidata. Additionally, we contribute with the design and implementation (in Sect. 5) of an artefact system, a text editing tool with AI support, using the metaphor of digital scissors to create interactive elements of text that support writing and reading.

2 Related Work

Creative industries (such as design, film, entertainment, and others) have fostered the development of novel tools that stimulate creativity and support creative processes [34]. Palani et al. [34] have created a value framework for Creativity Support Tools (CST) based on creative practitioners' experience, including values such as integration within the workflow, emotional connection and User Interface and Experience (UI/UX).

One such example in the CST landscape [15] are text editors tools, which have been a popular research topic since early HCI, and one of the cornerstones that made computing mainstream, as millions of users incorporated it into their work and personal lives [21]. In second wave HCI, digital tools were in particular studied for workplace use [4]; as such, these tools were designed to be efficient and generalizable to various contexts and activities [38]. Third wave HCI [4] refocuses on the user's experience and desire, questioning how the user wants to use the tool. In addition, advancement in technology creates space for customization of interfaces [20]; therefore, tools become partners, not only being manipulable but responsive and supportive to the user's workflow [20]. Through a media archaeology analysis of reading and writing interfaces, Emerson [13] exemplifies this with "readingwriting", a practice of writing through the network, in which the algorithm is "constantly reading our writing and writing our reading" by influencing the user. While the text editing tools used in our daily lives may have not changed dramatically in form, recent research has re-centered interest on work with specific communities of users (to better suit their needs) and on integration of novel and complex interactions (to increase the creativity and expression of their writing). At times there is an intersection of both, with specific set of users (such as interactive narrative designers) requiring complex interactions (such as branching) [19].

On specific communities of users, Han et al. [22] queried patent workers and scientists on their practices, highlighting their need to manage multiple documents while searching, collecting, annotating, organizing, writing and reviewing. This led to the creation of *Passages*, where snippets of text (including relevant metadata such as origin or comments) can be detached from the original documents and fluidly move through the above activities. This work extended *Textlets* [21], in which text selections are treated as persistent interactive items; based on the Instrumental Interaction model [3] and inspired by interviews with legal professionals, textlets turn concepts (such as the selected text) into objects, that can be manipulated by instruments (commands) or meta-instruments (commands that act on instruments). This approach has also been extended to digital ink with *Style-Blocks+Ink* [39]. Structured note-taking (sketchnoting, self-tracking, or bullet journaling) is a (mostly hand-drawn) practice where pride in craftsmanship leads to a perceived increase in the value of the created artefacts. Romat et al. [39] support this practice digitally by treating digital ink as structured data in the form of interactive blocks, susceptible to change by instruments. Finally, Chen et al. [8] interviewed data professionals and identified a lack of connection between text and data, which can lead to writing errors. In their *CrossData* prototype, text-data connections are established automatically, and treated as objects. Using natural language as you write, these connections can be queried to retrieve data (a value for a participant), compute values (mean value) or identify mistakes (assessing the validity of a statement if the value has changed).

Text editing tools can also support the creative process by using crowd-generated content to spark or enhance writing. Using the semantic relationships of structured data from Wikidata, Metilli1 et al. [31] made a semi-automatic tool to make narratives from a sequence of events. Tools can also empower users to create these semantic relationships. *Grannotate* [27] is a semi-automatic annotation tool for transcripts, that identifies entities and the relationship between them, creating knowledge graphs. These knowledge graphs can then be used to make prompts about the original text.

Advances in AI, such as language models like OpenAI's GPT-3 [5], have given more agency for digital tools to act as co-authors. Crowd-generated content can also be aligned to language models to generate text that is not only fluent but also encodes factual knowledge that was not part of the original training data [29]. A common approach to this co-authorship with language models [6,11,17,43] is to structure the interaction as a dialogue between the author and the AI, where the AI responds to a text prompt by the user. New tools are emerging with even more complex interactions. For example, Chung et al.'s *TaleBrush* [10] is an ideation tool using line sketching of a character's story arch and a pretrained GPT-based language model to create short stories. Zhang et al.'s *Storydrawer* [26] uses natural language processing of a child's spoken narrative, extracts relevant entities and retrieves sketches from a dataset, creating a new drawing based on the child's story.

While work on Human-AI collaboration can lead to novel interaction, researchers still struggle with understanding how to make it useful and desirable for users. Mina et al. [26] compiled a dataset of interactions between 63 writers with four instances of language models, varied writing tasks and varied prompts. Authors defend that analysis of large datasets such as this can help understand if language models are adding new ideas (or extending the user's ideas) or help create better suggestions for interactive writing. Other existing work analyses these co-authoring relationships using specific writing content such as novels [6] or science writing [17].

The above works showcase the potential for text editing tools in Assisted Storytelling, especially considering reification (converting concepts into objects) from the Instrumental Interaction model [3]. Written text can be fragmented and acted upon through commands; crowd-generated content (from Wikipedia or Wikidata) can also be considered as objects (with metadata about its connections to other objects). Digital scissors are, therefore, instruments that can be used to construct new structures by acting on objects. How can users use digital scissors to write?

3   Co-design Workshop on Assisted Storytelling

Addressing the Assisted Storytelling design space, we designed a co-design study to engage casual storytellers who have not been trained to work/design with AI or classical storytelling, such as play or screen writing, fiction or journalism. The workshop engaged participants in writing a story artifact related to Cultural Heritage (CH) and subsequently editorialise it with the support of Wikipedia. The prompt of Cultural Heritage worked well as a starting point for a storytelling activity as it evokes personal memories and experiences for the participant. Furthermore, both tangible (e.g., monuments, buildings) and intangible elements (e.g., customs, traditions) are preserved and curated in digital archives such as Wikipedia or Wikidata [7], and therefore pliable for AI. The workshop was designed to explore how storytellers find information (crowd-generated structured information from Wikipedia or Wikidata) and incorporate that information into their storytelling practice.

3.1   Method

The process outlined for this workshop is indebted to multiple existing techniques and strategies such as cultural probes [16], traditional design studio critique [41] structured as focus groups and autoethnography [35]. Similarly, the "Magic Machines" workshop [1] uses multiple techniques to create speculative non-functioning physical artifacts about a prompted topic that are discussed with a group; the value of this method is not on the ingenuity of the artifact itself, but in the reflection of the prompted topic. In our method, while the activity of writing and editorializing will inform the design and development of an AI-driven authoring prototype, the story artifacts themselves are imbued with tensions related to the participant's connection to Cultural Heritage (CH) and its representation in digital archives. The workshop was structured in the following stages:

1. ***Recruitment & Prompt:*** Some days before the session, recruited participants were asked to think of a memory or experience with a connection to CH; this could be expressed as a sketched outline of the story if they wished.
2. ***Writing:*** In the first 20 min, participants were asked to revise or compose their story draft without any external influence or support (e.g., searching online), in their digital/analogical medium of choice, highlighting the story elements that they would wish to clarify (e.g., checking the name of a location, or adding multimedia content).
3. ***Editing:*** For 40 min, participants were asked to edit their story, searching Wikipedia for elements to include. When no desired content could be found, they could describe the missing info via text or sketches.
4. ***Description:*** For around 5 min per participant, each participant presented their story to the group, projected on a public screen. Participants used this time to recount the story, reflecting on what they wrote, how they complemented it with Wikipedia, and on their experience of the workshop activity.
5. ***Group Discussion:*** For around 5 min per participant, researchers and other participants are free to ask questions to the presenting participant. Sample questions included:
   - "In the *Writing* stage, what were the main difficulties in thinking or writing?"
   - "Was there information (that could be added to the story) that you decided to not add? Why?"
   - "Did you think if the information was reliable? Was there information that you decided to not add because of this?"

- "What was your strategy to adding content to your story? In searching for things to add to the story, did you start with one topic (like a town) and branch out? Did you search for specific content? Where you more interested in pictures? How much did you change the text you found?"
- "Some of you learned new things that you did not expect when browsing Wikipedia to support their story (e.g. crusades); how did this influence your experience? Was it enjoyable? Was it frustrating to diverge topic?"
- "If you started by looking at the Wikipedia information first, how would this affect the tone and structure of your story?"

3.2 Participants

Based on the goal and theme of the workshop, participants were recruited to ensure diversity of relationships to cultural heritage. The workshop includes a total of 5 people (recruited through convenience sampling), 2 females and 3 males, between 25 and 50 years of age. Some personal information (e.g., nationality) is disclosed below as it contextualizes the stories created. Four of the five participants are currently in a status of migration, living in a host country; this inclusion criteria was intentional as we wanted participants who would actively reflect about cultural heritage and identity, as migrants (living in a host country) do daily. All participants were asked to consent to the use of their story material for research purposes[1], including the sharing of the story material itself (see Fig. 1). Participants were anonymized by substituting their names with letters and numbers (P1, P2, etc.) and any reference to identifiable personal data was erased or blurred in the reproduction of the stories.

Two of the authors of the paper participated in the workshop. They are both foreign to the local culture; a British citizen living in Italy (P1) and an Italian long-term resident in Portugal (P5). The reason for their participation is two-fold. Firstly, diffractive analysis [40] often requires for researchers to be involved through first-person methods like autoethnography, as researchers must live the data to understand the diffraction and be able to design from it. Secondly, as a co-design workshop, researchers must be included to support participants in any knowledge gap and to direct the workshop (e.g., eliciting dialogue in the group discussion). The remaining participants are students attending a Portuguese university: a local Portuguese PhD student (P2), a visiting Dutch masters student (P3), and a Chinese PhD student (P4).

3.3 Analysis

The workshop involved three researchers as facilitators. Since two of these participated in the workshop, the third researcher observed and took notes of the activity. The *Description* and *Group Discussion* phases were audio recorded, and later transcribed. Researcher notes, transcriptions, and the five created story artifacts were compiled and analyzed through a diffractive stance [14,23,30,40],

---

[1] https://paulobala.github.io/ICIDS2022/.

highlighting differences and gaps among the participants' subjects, structure, methods of storytelling, use of Wikipedia as support and social and cultural contexts. Insights result from internal discussions between all authors.

Fig. 1. Excerpt of P4's story. Stories can be consulted in the online supplementary material.

4 Diffractive Reflections on the Participants Storytelling Process

In this section, we present the researchers' reflections, based on the diffractive analysis [12, 23, 30, 40] of the data (story artefacts, researcher notes and transcribed recordings) from the workshop.

4.1 Participant 1 (P1)

P1's Story - P1, of British nationality, who has been living in Genoa (Italy, Genova in Italian) for five years, wrote about his experience and the changes the city has undergone. After mentioning the confusion between GenOva (in Italy) and GenEva (in Switzerland), P1 wrote about the Lantern, the iconic lighthouse monument of the city, which also stands as an image of Genoa. While consulting Wikipedia, to his surprise, P1 finds out that it was the second tallest lighthouse in Europe. Due to the topology of Genoa, whether by the sea or in the mountains, you can always see the Lantern. P1 mentioned you can always get lost in the contorted street of Genoa - but he could not find good pictures to exemplify this. Further details emerged from P1's story like the lack of parks and the comparison between the architecture at the ground and higher levels. Reflecting on his time there, P1 mentions that it takes time to identify the city's hidden beauty and its historical significance.

P1's Storytelling Style & Process. In summary, this story tells the personal experience of a foreigner becoming accustomed to their new surroundings, including factual and anecdotal facts about the city's heritage. P1 used Wikipedia to find details and often learned new information about the city. P1 was satisfied with the search performance, mentioning that he found everything he was looking for, including most of the pictures, except the ones about the convoluted streets of Genoa. P1's story was anchored to tangible and officially recognized elements of heritage, which might have helped in finding content from Wikipedia (except for the more personal view of the streets of Genoa). The story was plainly formatted, as it met the participant's needs. There was no mention of specific formatting needs, or quality of visuals from external sources; this contrasts with other participants who disliked the linear formatting and were frustrated with the lack and quality of images. Unlike some participants, P1 did not compare his cultural identity to the host country; his story was firmly on the geolocalized heritage of the city.

4.2 Participant 2 (P2)

P2's Story. P2, born and living in Portugal, wrote a story about internal migration, recalling Alcáçovas, her family's hometown in Alentejo. Her mother and grandparents experienced a strong cultural dislocation when moving from a village to the capital city, and this is something that still permeates the younger descendants of that family. Through recounting a summer trip to Alcáçovas with her grandmother and brother, P2 writes a story of contrasts: the village culture versus the city culture and the past versus the present. On the latter, P2 described how urban renewal of transport lines affected her hometown, and complemented her story with information about old and new train stations. Throughout the story, P2 inserts information about her cultural heritage like Chocalhos (a Portuguese cattle bell that is now used in folk music, which she found out is recognized by UNESCO as an intangible cultural heritage) and the Treaty of Alcáçovas (a precursor to the Treaty of Tordesillas that split newly discovered lands in south America, between the Portuguese and the Spanish conquerors).

P2's Storytelling Style & Process. While structured as a free flow of memories, P2's story is linear in nature, using the topic of contrasts as a thread. When asked directly, P2 did not articulate any specific need in supporting the free-flowing storytelling style, but some reflections on the process emerged. P2 used Wikipedia to add facts and images but found it hard to find relevant content. In one case, she was disappointed that she couldn't find a Wikipedia entry for her hometown (regardless of the language of the entry). In another instance, while searching for internal migration, she could find the places where people left and moved to, but could not quantify how many people it affected; she wished there was more of a human factor to the information present in Wikipedia. P2 started writing in a text editor tool, but when adding images and other facts from Wikipedia moved to a digital whiteboard as she wanted to emphasize the images. While narratively linear, the structure started to gain a waterfall aesthetic, as arrows were used to connect text and images, drawing relational meaning. P2 expressed a desire to add their images to further connect to the text.

4.3   Participant 3 (P3)

P3's Story. P3, of Dutch nationality and who has only been living in Portugal for three months, chose to write his story comparing the gastronomic cultures of both countries, accentuating their differences. For example, while people in the Netherlands have more economic power, they rarely eat out and view "food as nothing more than sustenance"; Portuguese, on the other hand, frequently and lengthily spend their time in restaurants, enjoying food with friends and family. The rest of the story identifies several traditional foods in Portugal, and questions if the Mediterranean diet is still maintained in Portugal. P3 complemented this line of reasoning with information from Wikipedia, and linked it back to the type of foods common in Northern European countries.

P3's Storytelling Style & Process. Similar to P2, P3's story uses contrasts or comparison as a guiding motif to his structure. P3 mentioned that he usually writes at the same time as he searches, using parallel windows. When questioned about the process of writing for this activity, P3 answered "I'm always interested in the background, of how things are the way they are. This is hard to find in Wikipedia. All the information is fairly general, lots of fact ridden, but not written like a history book, where they explain how this affects that: how there is this event and then there is that event, this kind of explanation, there is no link - so I couldn't really figure out why, why this is so different?". This highlights his need for causal relationships between information. P3 was also frustrated about reaching dead-ends in his process of searching. In particular, the Wikipedia page for the Mediterranean diet mentioned it being a paradox (eating more red meat but by less prone to cardiovascular diseases), but he could not investigate further, leaving his questions unanswered.

4.4   Participant 4 (P4)

P4's Story. P4, of Chinese nationality, has lived in Portugal for six months and wrote a story exploring a cultural connection between Portugal and China. The Pastel de Nata (custard tart), also called Pastel de Belém, is famous worldwide, especially in countries with historical ties to Portugal such as China. In writing, P4 tries to understand how exactly Belém, a mandatory stop for Chinese tourists, is connected to the pastry. Switching between Chinese and English versions of Wikipedia, he is unable to understand why, but complements the story with information about the colonial nature of the Age of Discoveries and the architectural styles of monuments such as Tower of Belém and Monument of the Discoveries.

P4's Storytelling Style & Process. P4's story is structured as a mystery story with a question that guides the story and the search process in Wikipedia, even though he cannot answer the question by the end. P4 laments the lack of transparency about the sources and the information he is retrieving (yet this is the nature of Wikipedia information as a crowd-generated source). The trustworthiness, but mostly the provenance of the information, is something only this participant has brought attention to. P4 also expressed a desire to use his images since they would better express his story and he was concerned with copyright issues (as he was unaware that Wikipedia images are public domain). Finally, P4 also expressed cognitive overload from the activity as he had to deal with several languages at a time; while he wrote in English, he searched the English and Chinese Wikipedia entries that had Portuguese names. Moreover, by going back to the Chinese Wikipedia, he feels he is defeating the intent of his story, which is to double-check and reference the information he gathered from the Chinese sources with information from other sources, finding an answer to his question.

4.5   Participant 5 (P5)

P5's Story. P5, of Italian nationality, who has lived in Portugal for ten years, previously sketched her story about the sea culture of Italy and Portugal. The story revolves around some self-reflections about migration, and the comparison of the two cultures, highlighting differences and similarities. The size of the two bodies of water, the Mediterranean Sea and the Atlantic Ocean, impacted how the different cultures explored the world. As such, P5 searched for and complemented the story with artefacts such as nautical maps from different cultures.

P5's Storytelling Style & Process. Since P5 had a drafted story, this activity mostly consisted of editing: adjusting words, looking for synonyms, cutting and adding some information and images. While looking up facts on Wikipedia, P5 finds very interesting new threads of information that work as a rabbit hole - where she gets curiously lost - the Portuguese discoveries and the nautical maps representing the limits of their knowledge. P5 tries and fails to complement the story with very specific images (convivial situations in Portugal and in Italy, like family gatherings at Christmas), so P5 uses maps to highlight the differences between the Mediterranean sea and the Atlantic Ocean. After spending some time looking for geographies and maps of the world, P5 manifested interest in adding a branch or an aside to the story to write about the evolution of cartography. Overall, P5 found pleasure in getting lost in the information search, following branching of curiosities and details.

4.6 Findings

After analysing and discussing the data among the researchers, we highlight findings along two main categories: i) Reflections to the methodology used in the workshop, and ii) Insights for the design of the AI assisted authoring tool.

Reflections on Methodology.

Timing Issues - While the allotted *Writing & Editing* phases were correctly timed, the *Presentation & Group Discussion* phases were rushed for participants. Further iterations should account for more time for discussion of the artefacts and the writing process, as these were useful in determining the needs and desires of participants. Furthermore, its important to consider that taking individual time to reflect on each participant, makes this method hard to scale to larger groups.

Prompt - After receiving the prompt, participants asked questions about what to write and in which style. A clear brief or prompt for the story is helpful to get people started right away, but allocating some time to discuss the prompt in the group is also needed, as we can not anticipate how clear the brief would be for all participants.

Group Discussion - When the participants presented, they tended to talk about the story rather than the process. After, during the *group discussion*, the group was not very articulated. The facilitators were needed to step in and ask several questions to clarify and expand on their process, but the timing did not allow for probing deeper, although the answers seemed to converge. Incorporating the facilitators as participants helped as they had first hand experience of the activity and its difficulties, eliciting conversation within the group.

Alternative Tools - Participant wrote the stories and edited it on their own laptops. While logistically easier to use the computer, a paper version of the study, as suggested by participants, could add some tangible and fun dimensions to it. Operating the editorializing as a paper collage with scissors and glue might invite more sharing and group reflections.

Limitations - A limitation of our work is the small number of participants and the inclusion of researchers as participants due to the exploratory nature in terms of both data and methodology. Future studies should capture a more heterogeneous set of participants' needs in regard to the use of "digital scissors". Furthermore, while the inclusion of researchers as participants is useful for contrast in our initial design exploration in "living" with the data, future iterations should focus on the inclusion of participants with different levels of writing experience and cultural connections.

Insights for Design

Access to Information - Using Wikipedia as an auxiliary source was frustrating for participants due to the lack of information and images. Participants would have liked access to more precise information, more variety and better quality of images than what they actually got. Crowd-sourced content, while large in scope, does not guarantee complete coverage or the highest quality. For digital tools leveraging on services as Wikipedia or AI, its important to manage user's expectations. This follows existing insights on using design strategies to deal with failures and breakdowns [18], creating a space for users to adopt a more understanding stance towards technology and its imperfections. A possible avenue to explore is to promote contributions to the crow-sourced content. Participants were keen on adding their own images, and were often knowledgeable about the information they were searching for, so AI could support a symbiotic relationship between the authoring tools and the information services.

Trust and Traceability - While only one participant highlighted concerns about transparency and trust towards the sources of information, trust is a common issues for many storytellers, from journalists, to historical, fiction and biography writers alike. Trust is also relevant regarding crowd-sourced content. Kuznetsov et al. [25] experimented with visual trust indicators for Wikipedia; while these can increase trust about the content, they can also have an opposite effect as it exposes the vetting process behind the content. When using user-generated content to complement narratives, its background information is important; its equally important that the use of auxiliary sources is transparent to future readers. Therefore, AI supported digital tools should keep track of the information provenance as well as if and how it has been manipulated. This insight resonates with previous work on provenance [22], highlighting the need to consider text (or fragments of it) as objects, capable of having metadata to track origin and manipulation.

Embracing Connections among Cultures - Writing about CH often involves connecting, referencing, comparing and deriving meaning from more than your own heritage. It may also involve thinking about cultural identity at a supranational or subnational level (e.g., P2 searching for specific details about the family's hometown). In our study, several participant make use of comparisons to structure their story; this entails supporting comparison and connections across cultures and languages. Searching for a topic from one viewpoint, does not acknowledge the existence of "information borders". Ochigame and Ye [33] mapped Google search results based on multiple geolocations, languages and user profiles; these results showed that search algorithms use cultural assumptions, establishing cultural "filter bubbles". Crowd-sourced content is also susceptible to this, since its likely that the users from a certain culture are the contributors and consumers. AI Assisted digital tools could foster reflection on cultural connections by exposing users to different language entries; our participants did this naturally by switching Wikipedia entries.

Story Structure and Genre - Structuring information in linear, non linear, hierarchical and rhizomatic structures is part of the authors' craft and choices on how to better support their story. The genre of a story can affect its structure, as well as the process of writing. P5's story is structured as a mystery solving quest answering a main question and therefore, exploring different (successful or unsuccessful) avenues when searching. P2's story, adopts a free-flowing reminiscence style about biographical content. P5's story follows the participant discovering new information from auxiliary sources and expressing desire to have a branching narrative. In these cases, the structure and genre of the story is deeply shaped by the process of writing. Assisted storytelling tools could support diverse genres and structures by focusing on the stages of writing. For example, Elicit[2] is an AI research assistant that uses GPT-3 language model and a database of 175 million papers to answer user's research question with key takeaways from abstracts; the workflow for this tool is based on the building blocks of research (e.g., search, summarization, classification).

Story Context - As participants write their stories on cultural heritage, the content is often grounded on some existing physical locations, including images such as monuments or maps to give the reader a sense of context. While previous insights have been focused on supporting the process of writing, one can also think about supporting the process of reading. Assisted Storytelling can leverage existing external services to contextualize a story, offering additional content for the reader. For example, maps can be used to represent entities mentioned in the story and to connect to other cultural heritage sites in those area.

From the diffractive analysis, discussions often delve into "what is not there". On stories about CH, the social and cultural context is needed for readers to better understand the stories. Assisted Storytelling with crowd-sourced content can create these connections for the writer or reader. Furthermore, it can create spaces to critically reflect on why information is not present or not included in a story. For example, some stories identified monuments about the Portuguese discoveries in a positive tone, while the negative effects of colonialism are not presented.

5   Design and Implementation

Starting from basic text editing needs (e.g. formatting, layout, images) and the insights gathered in the workshop, we designed and implemented a minimum viable prototype. While this prototype might not support every insight found at the moment, it can be used for further studies with participants.

---

[2] https://elicit.org/.

The prototype was built using Vue[3], a javascript framework for user interfaces, and a TipTap[4], a rich text WYSIWYG editor and wrapper for Prose Mirror[5]. TipTap treats content as customizable nodes, separating data from presentation; therefore, nodes can be acted upon whether its visually (e.g., formatting such as underlining or more complex user interface elements like pop-ups indicating provenance) or internally (e.g., transforming into another node or keeping track of changes to the data of a node). With TipTap, we can define a structure to the document, supporting saving and loading without losing internal information about the nodes. Making text as nodes allows to treat it with digital scissors, cutting parts and assembling it in a new structure.

Similar to how P3 uses parallel windows for writing, our prototype (see Figs. 2, 3, 4 and 5) uses resizable parallel panels matching the different stages of the writing and editing process. A left panel corresponds to the main text editor, where the user can write and transform nodes. In this panel, we support base editing functions like formatting commands (e.g., bold, italic) and structural commands (e.g., headings, lists, dividers, quotes), as well as history commands (undo/redo) A right panel has multiple views that assist in storytelling:

- **Preview** - Corresponds to how readers would view the story. Nodes can have different behaviour depending on whether they are in a writing or reading panel. This allows for future exploration in how information is shown to a reader. For example, hovering a node can display the original text (see Fig. 4) or show CH sites connected to a physical location.
- **Manual Search** - With multiple sources of information and various modalities (images, text), we need ways of effectively accessing this information within the prototype. In its most straightforward format, this can be a simple keyword-based retrieval (as was used in the co-design workshop). As this is the most ubiquitous approach, it makes sense to include it as the first step to finding relevant content. The co-design workshop focused on Wikipedia alone as a resource, and as participants noted, this provides only one level of granularity. While a general search across the internet can help to resolve this, the integrity of the information is uncontrolled. We, therefore, opt for a two-level approach provided by Wikidata, where Wikidata can satisfy the connectivity of information and the ability to see relevant and similar items. Found content is treated as a node and can be dragged to the main editor window for further editing, keeping track of provenance and changes to content. We expect this mode to be used more in a *writing* phase, where users actively look for content to kickstart the creative process.

---

[3] https://vuejs.org/.
[4] https://tiptap.dev/.
[5] https://prosemirror.net/.

- **Automatic Search** - We assist in editorializing stories in two ways:
  - *Keyword spotting*: Machine learning approaches for language, Natural Language Processing (NLP), has progressed significantly in recent years, especially for the task of Named Entity Recognition (NER) or keyword spotting [28]. Therefore, it is now possible to use State-of-the-Art approaches for other tasks, such as storytelling. For example, using a NER can access both Wikipedia and Wikidata [36], running continuously over the full text as the user writes or edits the story. Therefore, we can present related content that the user can explore and incorporate into their story by dragging it to the main editor.
  - *Context & Connectivity*: Based on the connections that are added to the story by NER or manual search while writing, it can create a virtual subset of Wikidata. As this subset of relevant nodes increases, a contextual search is possible as highly interconnected nodes can have increased relevance. Such an approach can be similar to a simple clustering on Knowledge Graphs, where the more common connections are, the more likely they are relevant. As Wikidata also provides multiple languages, this can be a way to access alternative perspectives (if the user knows the language).
- **Visual Search** - Wikidata commonly offers one image per entity, therefore, leaning itself to visual search. In contrast, to perform an image search on Wikipedia, each document would need to be parsed, the images extracted and encoded into a descriptor [42], which would significantly increase the number of images resulting in a less accurate search. Therefore, one solution is to build a representation for each entity in Wikidata; users can then query by the image when they want a similar image. As this process can be expensive, this can also incorporate filters provided by NER and the relevant virtual subset of nodes.

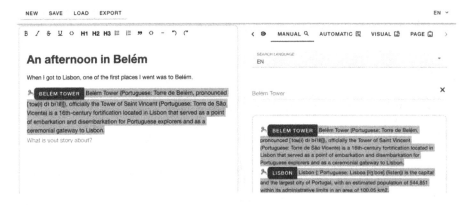

Fig. 2. Prototype tool with Assisted Storytelling – a user manually searches for a topic, and drags the node (content) to the main editor on the left.

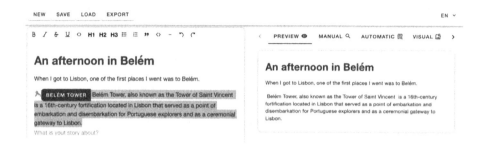

Fig. 3. Prototype tool with Assisted Storytelling – a user rewrites the found node and previews how readers would see it.

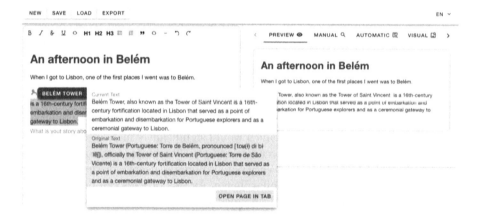

Fig. 4. Prototype tool with Assisted Storytelling – a user can track origin and manipulation by selecting nodes.

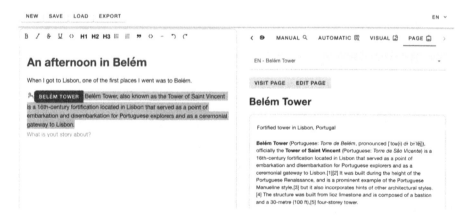

Fig. 5. Prototype tool with Assisted Storytelling – a user can consult more information on a node and compare it in different languages.

6   Conclusion and Future Work

While advances in AI can lead to new ways to empower users, recent work suggests that we should recenter this as how do users want to be empowered by AI? In this paper, we explore how AI can be used for Assisted Storytelling by taking a human-centred approach. Restricting this scope to Cultural Heritage allows us to (1) engage participants in a personal (and sometimes controversial) topic and (2) engage AI in a topic with abundant data, but that is often too complex or nuanced to be understood. Based on a co-design workshop where participants wrote and reused crowd-generated content, we reflect on how AI can be designed to assist writing/editing and the problems and opportunities of using crowd-generated content. We designed and implemented a digital tool leveraging the concept of digital scissors to assist in different stages of the creative process.

Future work will involve a formal evaluation with users to better understand and refine how AI can empower users in writing, as pointed out by previous work [6,17,26]. Future work will also involve further refinements to the prototype, taking advantage of crow-generated content to identify connections (or lack of connections) in what users write and taking advantage of nodes to create more complex interactive narratives (that include casual authors in determining how they should work). Aligning AI and crow-generated content allows recasting the creative process as "readingwriting" [13], where a user can influence and be influenced in a collaborative partnership with digital tools.

Acknowledgements. This research was supported by MEMEX (MEMories and EXperiences for inclusive digital storytelling) project funded by the European Union's Horizon 2020 research and innovation program under grant agreement No 870743, and by LARSyS (Project UIDB/50009/2020).

References

1. Andersen, K., Wakkary, R.: The magic machine workshops: making personal design knowledge. In: Proceedings of the 2019 CHI Conference on Human Factors in Computing Systems, pp. 1–13 (2019)
2. Barad, K.M.: Meeting the Universe Halfway: Quantum Physics and the Entanglement of Matter and Meaning. Duke University Press, Durham (2007)
3. Beaudouin-Lafon, M.: Instrumental interaction: an interaction model for designing post-WIMP user interfaces. In: Proceedings of the SIGCHI Conference on Human Factors in Computing Systems - CHI 2000, pp. 446–453. ACM Press, The Hague (2000). https://doi.org/10.1145/332040.332473
4. Bødker, S.: When second wave HCI meets third wave challenges. In: Proceedings of the 4th Nordic Conference on Human-Computer Interaction Changing Roles - NordiCHI 2006, pp. 1–8. ACM Press, Oslo (2006). https://doi.org/10.1145/1182475.1182476
5. Brown, T.B., et al.: Language models are few-shot learners (2020)
6. Calderwood, A., Qiu, V., Gero, K., Chilton, L.B.: How novelists use generative language models: an exploratory user study. In: HAI-GEN+user2agentIUI (2020)

7. Cameron, F.: The future of digital data, heritage and curation in a more-than human world. Routledge, Abingdon, Oxon, New York, NY (2021)

8. Chen, Z., Xia, H.: CrossData: leveraging text-data connections for authoring data documents. In: CHI Conference on Human Factors in Computing Systems, pp. 1–15. ACM, New Orleans, April 2022. https://doi.org/10.1145/3491102.3517485

9. Chung, J.J.Y., He, S., Adar, E.: The intersection of users, roles, interactions, and technologies in creativity support tools. In: Designing Interactive Systems Conference 2021, pp. 1817–1833. ACM, Virtual Event, June 2021. https://doi.org/10.1145/3461778.3462050

10. Chung, J.J.Y., Kim, W., Yoo, K.M., Lee, H., Adar, E., Chang, M.: TaleBrush: visual sketching of story generation with pretrained language models. In: CHI Conference on Human Factors in Computing Systems Extended Abstracts, pp. 1–4. ACM, New Orleans, April 2022. https://doi.org/10.1145/3491101.3519873

11. Clark, E., Ross, A.S., Tan, C., Ji, Y., Smith, N.A.: Creative writing with a machine in the loop: case studies on slogans and stories. In: 23rd International Conference on Intelligent User Interfaces, pp. 329–340. ACM, Tokyo Japan, March 2018. https://doi.org/10.1145/3172944.3172983

12. Devendorf, L., Andersen, K., Kelliher, A.: Making design memoirs: understanding and honoring difficult experiences. In: Proceedings of the 2020 CHI Conference on Human Factors in Computing Systems, pp. 1–12. ACM, Honolulu, April 2020. https://doi.org/10.1145/3313831.3376345

13. Emerson, L.: Reading writing interfaces: from the digital to the bookbound. No. 44 in Electronic Mediations, University of Minnesota Press, Minneapolis (2014)

14. Frauenberger, C.: Entanglement HCI the next wave? ACM Trans. Comput.-Hum. Interact. 27(1), 1–27 (2020). https://doi.org/10.1145/3364998

15. Frich, J., MacDonald Vermeulen, L., Remy, C., Biskjaer, M.M., Dalsgaard, P.: Mapping the landscape of creativity support tools in HCI. In: Proceedings of the 2019 CHI Conference on Human Factors in Computing Systems, pp. 1–18. ACM, Glasgow, May 2019. https://doi.org/10.1145/3290605.3300619

16. Gaver, B., Dunne, T., Pacenti, E.: Design: cultural probes. Interactions 6(1), 21–29 (1999). https://doi.org/10.1145/291224.291235

17. Gero, K.I., Liu, V., Chilton, L.: Sparks: inspiration for science writing using language models. In: Designing Interactive Systems Conference, pp. 1002–1019. ACM, Virtual Event, June 2022. https://doi.org/10.1145/3532106.3533533

18. Giaccardi, E., Speed, C., Redström, J., Ben Allouch, S., Shklovski, I., Smith, R.C.: AI and the conditions of design: towards a new set of design ideals, Bilbao, Spain, June 2022. https://doi.org/10.21606/drs.2022.1078. https://dl.designresearchsociety.org/drs-conference-papers/drs2022/editorials/27

19. Green, D., Hargood, C., Charles, F.: Contemporary issues in interactive storytelling authoring systems. In: Rouse, R., Koenitz, H., Haahr, M. (eds.) ICIDS 2018. LNCS, vol. 11318, pp. 501–513. Springer, Cham (2018). https://doi.org/10.1007/978-3-030-04028-4_59

20. Grudin, J.: From tool to partner: The evolution of human-computer interaction. Synthesis Lectures on Human-Centered Interaction 10(1), i–183 (2017)

21. Han, H.L., Renom, M.A., Mackay, W.E., Beaudouin-Lafon, M.: Textlets: supporting constraints and consistency in text documents. In: Proceedings of the 2020 CHI Conference on Human Factors in Computing Systems, pp. 1–13. ACM, Honolulu, April 2020. https://doi.org/10.1145/3313831.3376804

22. Han, H.L., Yu, J., Bournet, R., Ciorascu, A., Mackay, W.E., Beaudouin-Lafon, M.: Passages: interacting with text across documents. In: CHI Conference on Human

Factors in Computing Systems, pp. 1–17. ACM, New Orleans, April 2022. https://doi.org/10.1145/3491102.3502052

23. Homewood, S., Hedemyr, M., Fagerberg Ranten, M., Kozel, S.: Tracing conceptions of the body in HCI: from user to more-than-human. In: Proceedings of the 2021 CHI Conference on Human Factors in Computing Systems, pp. 1–12. ACM, Yokohama, May 2021. https://doi.org/10.1145/3411764.3445656

24. Hwang, A.H.C.: Too late to be creative? AI-empowered tools in creative processes. In: CHI Conference on Human Factors in Computing Systems Extended Abstracts, pp. 1–9. ACM, New Orleans, April 2022. https://doi.org/10.1145/3491101.3503549

25. Kuznetsov, A., Novotny, M., Klein, J., Saez-Trumper, D., Kittur, A.: Templates and Trust-o-meters: towards a widely deployable indicator of trust in Wikipedia. In: CHI Conference on Human Factors in Computing Systems, pp. 1–17. ACM, New Orleans, April 2022. https://doi.org/10.1145/3491102.3517523

26. Lee, M., Liang, P., Yang, Q.: CoAuthor: designing a human-AI collaborative writing dataset for exploring language model capabilities. In: CHI Conference on Human Factors in Computing Systems, pp. 1–19. ACM, New Orleans, April 2022. https://doi.org/10.1145/3491102.3502030

27. Lee, Y., Chung, J.J.Y., Kim, T.S., Song, J.Y., Kim, J.: Promptiverse: scalable generation of scaffolding prompts through human-AI hybrid knowledge graph annotation. In: CHI Conference on Human Factors in Computing Systems, pp. 1–18. ACM, New Orleans, April 2022. https://doi.org/10.1145/3491102.3502087

28. Li, J., Sun, A., Han, J., Li, C.: A survey on deep learning for named entity recognition. IEEE Trans. Knowl. Data Eng. **34**(1), 50–70 (2022). https://doi.org/10.1109/TKDE.2020.2981314

29. Logan, R., Liu, N.F., Peters, M.E., Gardner, M., Singh, S.: Barack's wife hillary: using knowledge graphs for fact-aware language modeling. In: Proceedings of the 57th Annual Meeting of the Association for Computational Linguistics, pp. 5962–5971. Association for Computational Linguistics, Florence, (2019). https://doi.org/10.18653/v1/P19-1598. https://www.aclweb.org/anthology/P19-1598

30. Lupton, D., Watson, A.: Towards more-than-human digital data studies: developing research-creation methods. Qual. Res., 146879412093923, July 2020. https://doi.org/10.1177/1468794120939235. http://journals.sagepub.com/doi/10.1177/1468794120939235

31. Metilli, D., Bartalesi, V., Meghini, C.: A Wikidata-based tool for building and visualising narratives. Int. J. Digit. Libr. **20**(4), 417–432 (2019). https://doi.org/10.1007/s00799-019-00266-3

32. Nicenboim, I., Giaccardi, E., Redström, J.: From explanations to shared understandings of AI. Bilbao, Spain, June 2022. https://doi.org/10.21606/drs.2022.773. https://dl.designresearchsociety.org/drs-conference-papers/drs2022/researchpapers/293

33. Ochigame, R., Ye, K.: Search Atlas: visualizing divergent search results across geopolitical borders. In: Designing Interactive Systems Conference 2021, pp. 1970–1983. ACM, Virtual Event, June 2021. https://doi.org/10.1145/3461778.3462032

34. Palani, S., Ledo, D., Fitzmaurice, G., Anderson, F.: "I don't want to feel like I'm working in a 1960s factory": the practitioner perspective on creativity support tool adoption. In: CHI Conference on Human Factors in Computing Systems, pp. 1–18. ACM, New Orleans, April 2022. https://doi.org/10.1145/3491102.3501933

35. Rapp, A.: Autoethnography in human-computer interaction: theory and practice. In: Filimowicz, M., Tzankova, V. (eds.) New Directions in Third Wave Human-Computer Interaction: Volume 2 - Methodologies. HIS, pp. 25–42. Springer, Cham (2018). https://doi.org/10.1007/978-3-319-73374-6_3

36. Ravi, M.P.K., Singh, K., Mulang, I.O., Shekarpour, S., Hoffart, J., Lehmann, J.: Cholan: a modular approach for neural entity linking on wikipedia and wikidata. In: Proceedings of the 16th Conference of the European Chapter of the Association for Computational Linguistics: Main Volume, pp. 504–514 (2021)
37. Remy, C., MacDonald Vermeulen, L., Frich, J., Biskjaer, M.M., Dalsgaard, P.: Evaluating creativity support tools in HCI research. In: Proceedings of the 2020 ACM Designing Interactive Systems Conference, pp. 457–476. ACM, Eindhoven, July 2020. https://doi.org/10.1145/3357236.3395474
38. Rogers, Y.: HCI theory: classical, modern, and contemporary. Synth. Lect. Hum.-Centered Inf. **5**(2), 1–129 (2012). https://doi.org/10.2200/S00418ED1V01Y201205HCI014. http://www.morganclaypool.com/doi/abs/10.2200/S00418ED1V01Y201205HCI014
39. Romat, H., Marquardt, N., Hinckley, K., Henry Riche, N.: Style Blink: exploring digital inking of structured information via handcrafted styling as a first-class object. In: CHI Conference on Human Factors in Computing Systems, pp. 1–14. ACM, New Orleans, April 2022. https://doi.org/10.1145/3491102.3501988
40. Sanches, P., Howell, N., Tsaknaki, V., Jenkins, T., Helms, K.: Diffraction-in-action: designerly explorations of agential realism through lived data. In: CHI Conference on Human Factors in Computing Systems, pp. 1–18. ACM, New Orleans, April 2022. https://doi.org/10.1145/3491102.3502029
41. Schön, D.A.: The reflective practitioner: how professionals think in action. Ashgate, Farnham (2013)
42. Yang, M., et al.: Dolg: single-stage image retrieval with deep orthogonal fusion of local and global features. In: Proceedings of the IEEE/CVF International Conference on Computer Vision (ICCV), pp. 11772–11781, October 2021
43. Yuan, A., Coenen, A., Reif, E., Ippolito, D.: Wordcraft: story writing with large language models. In: 27th International Conference on Intelligent User Interfaces, pp. 841–852. ACM, Helsinki, March 2022. https://doi.org/10.1145/3490099.3511105
44. Zimmerman, J., Forlizzi, J.: Research through design in HCI. In: Olson, J.S., Kellogg, W.A. (eds.) Ways of Knowing in HCI, pp. 167–189. Springer, New York (2014). https://doi.org/10.1007/978-1-4939-0378-8_8

Planner Systems for Historical Justice? A Case Study of a People's History of Lebanon

Fabiola Hanna(✉) ⓘ

The New School, New York, NY 10003, USA
hannaf@newschool.edu

Abstract. This paper examines *We Are History: A People's History of Lebanon* as a case study for pursuing historical justice in post-war contexts. The planner not only satisfies three existing desires—co-creation, polyvocality, and pushing against a singular truth—but also poses the question of the beneficiary of these narratives and digital projects.

Keywords: Planner · Historical justice · Speculative truths · Lebanon

1 Historical Justice in Digital Media Projects

From Jean-François Lyotard's early proposition to counter grand narratives [1], to Saidiya Hartman's call for "Critical Fabulation" to fill the gaps in historical archives in the context of marginalized histories [2], to Tonia Sutherland's and Michelle Caswell's calls to disrupt the white supremacist power structures in libraries and archives [3, 4], to John Brown Childs' offering of transcommunality as a framework for redressing past violence and finding ways to live in difference [5], the field of historical justice is brimming with frameworks to address past violence.

In digital media projects—whether in the field of interactive documentary (known as idocs), in digital activist projects from the NGO world, in digital social art practice, or in the digital art world—the attempts of individual artists and collectives to redress past violence are characteristically motivated by three main desires: (1) to present minoritized histories in a mode of co-creation, (2) to make room for diverse and divergent perspectives in the same digital space (sometimes conceptualized as polyvocality and sometimes as pluralism), and (3) to push against the norms of narrative, thereby making space for speculation, for questioning a singular truth, and for countering inherited values and assumptions in History with a capital H.

In this article, I turn to the field of narrative intelligence for a framework that would not only satisfy these three desires but also advance the goals of historical justice. I first identify narrative intelligence projects as important precedents that inform this thread. I then introduce the work-in-progress project titled *We Are History: A People's History of Lebanon*, briefly summarizing the background and specifics of Lebanese history. I analyze three aspects of *We Are History*: its open archive, its planner system, and its goal of reconfiguring a narrative space as a conversation space. I conclude with a theory of Dialogue Aesthetics.

M. Vosmeer and L. Holloway-Attaway (Eds.): ICIDS 2022, LNCS 13762, pp. 159–170, 2022.
https://doi.org/10.1007/978-3-031-22298-6_10

2 Early Influential Projects

Although much of the work in Narrative Intelligence uses fictional worlds, I turn to two projects that use non-fictional contexts as places in which their stories unfold or that inform their initial state of the world and that engage with the three existing desires outlined above—co-creation, polyvocality, and pushing against a singular truth.

The first, *Living Liberia Fabric*, was developed in 2008 by D. Fox Harrell while at MIT's Imagination, Computation and Expression Lab [6]. Commissioned by the Truth and Reconciliation Commission of Liberia, the project builds on testimonies collected in various cities and villages throughout the country, including people's reflections on the present situation after the country's 17-year civil war. As the infrastructure to the interface he designed for this project, Harrell used the GRIOT system, which he had previously developed as part of his dissertation. The GRIOT system, which was based on traditional African oratory systems, automatically composed poetry in the form of call and response [7]. Additionally, the interface features the visual component of a traditional "African" fabric, whose diamond shapes open up into videos of recorded testimonies. Harrell's use of the GRIOT system to combine different videos enabled a wide range of stories to be remixed based on the user's interaction with the videos. In addition to the technical achievement of the project, it is significant that it was one of the first to use real-world first-person testimonies in an agential human-machine space, thereby automatically engaging with people's lived histories. Through this work, Harrell proposed a Cultural Computing approach that took into consideration the specificities of language, cultural concepts and practices, and heritage [8]. For the purposes of my discussion here, I am limiting my description of this project as it strove to and achieved all three of the previously mentioned goals: it was polyvocal, it did not stick to one version of events, and it tried as much as possible to adhere to a process of co-creation within the confines of the Liberian government's structure.

Another major piece of work I have included in this genealogy is *Terminal Time* by The Recombinant Historical Apparatus, consisting of Michael Mateas, Steffi Domike, and Paul Vanouse, developed in 2000 [9]. In this project, whose subject is the last 1,000 years of history, the world is non-fictional but is made of the collective's description of events such as the Crusades, the invention of Bakelite, etc. The history-telling involves the audience's participation as measured by an applause meter that registers their answers to multiple-choice questions posed by the project. The audience is invited to interact with the project twice, the first time they are free to respond in whatever extemporaneous way they are moved to, and the second they are encouraged to shape the emerging narrative based on the knowledge they now have of the system. This project aims to point out both the various kinds of biases inherent to these histories, as well as the ultimate conclusion that any history is constructed. Here again, limiting my analysis to this project to the three aforementioned goals: it is co-creative, as the agent— the authors and the audience— end up composing the narratives; it is polyvocal in the sense that many viewpoints are included in the system itself; and it lends itself to questioning the singular truth of History.

In addition to both of these projects, several other narrative intelligence projects follow an unconventional path of using non-fictional contexts. These projects include Jamie Carbonell's POLITICS [10], which engaged in the simulation of perspectives and biases one might hold in reaction to political events, and Warren Sack's SpinDoctor [11], which looked at ideological point of view in news stories.

3 We Are History: A People's History of Lebanon

3.1 Description

As an artist and humanist with training in computer science, I have developed a transdisciplinary interactive digital project that threads together individual testimonies about the contested histories of Lebanon into a complex roundtable of collective perspectives and experiences. Titled *We Are History: A People's History of Lebanon*, my project consists of two modules: an archive of recorded memories of daily life in Lebanon from 1943 to the present, and a software system that includes a translation of the transcripts of the contents of the archive and a planner that automatically generates constructed conversations about those remembered events (Fig. 1).

Fig. 1. A screenshot of the interface to *We Are History: A People's History of Lebanon*.

The goal of *We Are History* is to imagine what conversations about the contested past in Lebanon could look like and propose an experiment forward for accountability with the ultimate goal of discussing the past to look towards the future.

3.2 Context of Conversations About History in Lebanon

The context of postwar Lebanon has been extensively studied and its effects examined, including memory studies, socio-economic conditions, sectarian feelings, political deadlock, development, and peacebuilding, etc. [12–18]. Noticeably absent is the widespread phenomenon of Lebanese people's inability to have conversations about their shared pasts. The reasons that conversations about the war have been difficult for survivors of war who are living together in Lebanon can be attributed to many causes. Some scholars have argued that there are currently about a hundred active political parties in Lebanon, which on the one hand creates a democratic arena but on the other complicates the possibility of conversation because of the sheer number of different perspectives [19]. Others have contrasted the case of Lebanon to the South African or Liberian post-war conditions. Whereas in those histories, the amnesties were followed by truth and reconciliation commissions, the amnesty in Lebanon was not followed by any other mediation/moderation, precluding the possibility for people to digest what had happened during the war [16, 20, 21]. Yet others have maintained that, at the end of the war, the warlords who had pushed their followers to fight each other then placed themselves in parliamentary or cabinet seats, and not only promoted their own versions of what had happened but also worked against implementing a truth and reconciliation commission (TRC) or any effort to reconcile versions different from their own [16]. Finally, there are those who have also stressed the importance of the absence of a universally accepted history textbook for use in schools [22–24]. One of the articles in the Taef Accord was to establish a new history curriculum in which all involved parties felt equally represented [25]. However, this has proven difficult; every few years, a committee submits a revised and stripped-down version of a history curriculum, only to be rejected for nonsensical reasons. Further complicating the issue, it should be mentioned that this problem predated the civil war, a vestigial remnant of the colonial period.

Memory studies scholar Lucia Volk's review [26] of two recent books on Lebanese memory of the war [27, 28] concludes in the following way:

> "Efforts by civil society actors and institutions dedicated to preserving and debating memories of war are invaluable, as are the analytical efforts of social scientists with outsider perspectives. Researchers can make important contributions to ongoing dialogues about Lebanon's past, present and future by looking at memories as *both symbols and acts* that create new realities and determine futures." (emphasis in original, 298)

This paper takes Volk's call to "look [...] at memories as both symbols and acts" seriously, and quite literally. As I show below, these memories are first treated symbolically, in the treatment of the transcripts of memories in a database. In addition, when they are to be pulled out and tied together through artificial connections, these transcripts of memory are treated as actions towards conversations.

3.3 Description of Planner System

In this paper, I focus on the planner system, however the earlier steps of inviting interlocutors, the interview process, the questions, etc., played an important role in shaping the project. The oral histories that I recorded between June and September 2010 and which I use to construct artificial conversations go through several translations from beginning to end. These oral histories start with a physical interview which is translated into the medium of video (with audio) via recording, the spoken word in the video is then transcribed, translated from Arabic (mostly) into English (this translation is literal or the most conventional use of the word), and the final translation that takes place is one that takes the form of JSON into the initial facts of the world. The planner is built on Warren Sack's JavaScript translation of James Meehan's dissertation project TALESPIN.

This initial set of interviews, which informed the design of the software system, were based on a specific event, the siege of the city of Zahle in 1981 by the Syrian Army. The specific event was chosen in the pre-interview sessions by my interlocutors who volunteered to participate in the project, knowing that these initial interviews would

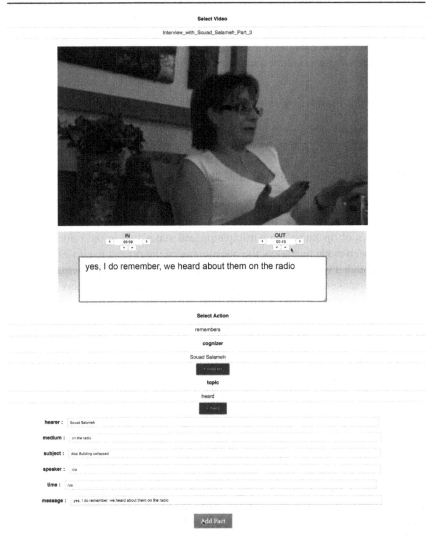

Fig. 2. Screenshot of the transcriber and translator interface. As the transcriber writes each sentence, they also add the data that will compose the JSON database.

shape how the software was written for the project and that this specific event would be one of many across the country that would be covered. The focus of the questions was on memories of daily life during this event, centered, for example, around how people managed to buy food, how they slept, where they lived, what memories stood out to them, what they told their kids, how they remember the siege ending and what they did after that, etc.

This set of interviews was translated into English and transcribed into JSON. I include a screenshot of the interface I developed for the translation and transcription of subsequent interviews (Fig. 2).

In *We Are History*, the planner outputs a constructed conversation from this database of initial facts. The actions from the planner inform an automatic video editor, which is web-based page that with the plan, obtains the input and output times of the sentences used in the conversation, cuts the video according to those times, and displays the video in the front-end user site as an interface with a three-dimensional roundtable.

3.4 Discussion of Planner System in Relation to Historical Justice

In this section, I describe how the planner advances the three main desires in engaging with contested pasts: co-creation, an un-fixed truth, and polyvocality.

Co-creation. CO-Creation or a sharing of authorship is a participatory method where an artist or mediamaker opens up the parameters of engagement with a work to a larger group of people, whether a specific community or an audience, with the explicit goal of striving for more democratic forms of authorship. Sandra Gaudenzi has formulated various "Degrees of openness" in participation and states that in the i-docs world, no attempts have been made that allow the questioning of the project itself [29]. Gaudenzi writes that although it would not be correct to talk about one kind of participation –given that some i-docs makers ask for content itself or co-authoring, while others open up the possibility of co-producing, and yet others make space for co-initiating content– there is not yet an i-doc that involves the subject or the user in the form of the documentary itself.

One form of participation in *We Are History* is my invitation for contributions. Although I set the parameters for participation in that I made the authorial decisions of recording the interviews, using video as the medium, formulated the questions, giving the interviewees a limited set of options for deciding whether they liked the camera placement, the background, etc., I here want to turn my reader's attention to how the planner system moves beyond this limited understanding of co-creation. I will show how the choices I made in how the interview transcripts were translated into code made way for a different understanding of co-creation.

In our early attempts to translate my video monologues into an initial state of the world for the planner, I chose to make my interviewees into characters who existed in the planner's world, and treated their memories as beliefs. For example, in the planner's world, Emile Khalaf's memory of witnessing the approach of a Syrian Army tank to the entrance to Zahle at the beginning of the siege, would have been translated as a belief of Khalaf's location at the entrance of Zahle. The problem with this setup was that the planner could generate a plan that included Emile Khalaf moving in that initial world, but that did not happen; this did not meet my goals of generating imagined conversations. I eventually realized that translating the testimonies by using the interviewees as characters in a planner's world would be imposing new narratives on my interviewees' testimonies, so I started experimenting with different kinds of initial states of the world.

I settled on using these testimonies as memories in a world, rather than as beliefs. For example, Emile Khalaf's memory above would in this case be translated as remembering being there instead of being located there in the planner's world. This was more satisfactory because it acknowledged the medium these testimonies existed within; I had conducted interviews and these testimonies were memories. This decision also allowed me to write methods about different kinds of dialogue that would interweave these memories. For example, a dialogue could be generated by using Emile Khalaf's memory of being at the entrance with Victor Maalouf's memory of being the paramedic who attended the confrontation, the link being that they were both present at the same scene. Another potential dialogue would be Emile Khalaf's memory of being there and Josephine Lteif hearing rumors from passers-by about that confrontation. So the planner now connected testimonies in a dialogue according to the method of how people heard of events or how they experienced them. Our task as author came to define what a possible dialogue could be, rather than defining possible actions for these characters to take within the planner's world.

In this sense, our interlocutors' very words shape how they would be used in the project. While this alone can be likened to other kinds of authorial decision-making, because the database consisted of an open archive, meaning that my interviewees could contribute new video testimony, they could actively shape the project's outcomes in a more radical sense of sharing authorship. However, if the contributions included hate-speech, they would never appear in the constructed conversations, but one could search for hate speech in order to find it. In the next section, I further expand on this idea of an open archive in relation to speculative ways of knowing.

Speculative Truths in an Ever-Evolving Archive. Because the subject matter of *We Are History* is history, and because a history is never complete, it made sense to build an initial state of the world that is also incomplete, and that continually solicits new material. Even if the initial state of the world included a large number of memories, the history would still be incomplete.

In the field of planning however, this was something that has been established since the 90s with Philp Agre and David Chapman's "Theory of Activity" in Pengi [30] with the addition and use of sensors to modify the initial state of the world.

Elsewhere, I have developed a listening framework to analyze the different kinds of ways the system would respond to new material that would be put into an initial state of the world [31]. Instead of trying to come up with all possible user scenarios from the outset, a participatory project that uses listening as a framework would base interaction on what people contribute as they contribute. The initial state of the world would therefore be an incomplete model, one where facts are continually added based on the input of users.

This listening framework depends on two kinds of listening: a listening as a relinquishing of a pre-determined view, and a listening as a metaphor for an indicator for change. In *We Are History*, the framework is used in this project in the following two ways: (1) *We Are History*'s initial state of the world changes as a new testimony is added into its archive, and; (2) *We Are History*'s interface invites the user to generate multiple and changing constructed conversations, themselves a result of the multiple plans output by the planner system.

In the case of *We Are History*, the planner system's changeable initial state of the world and its changeable output of constructed conversations are two ways that reflect the use of a listening framework. This brings me to media and communication's scholar Lisbeth Lipari's term for this: "listening otherwise" [32]. For Lipari, in engaging with difficult stories or perhaps stories that offer different perspectives: "It is [...] a listening otherwise that suspends the willfulness of self- and foreknowledge in order to receive the singularities if the alterity of the other." For this "listening otherwise" to work online, or more broadly in what Warren Sack has called the "computational condition" [33], I argue that it is important for the employed structures, systems, and processes to reflect this specific kind of participation. In other words, in addition to placing "different or everyday voices" side-by-side, it is equally critical for these different perspectives to exist in a space where the medium, whether the recording, the software, the interface and its design, is attentive to what these differences are. In the next section, I describe how *We Are History* also extends an understanding of polyvocality that is attentive to the relationships in the plurality.

Polyvocality. *We Are History* also adopts a polyvocal stance, not least in its placing of multiple videos and perspectives, but also in its treatment of the individual memories in their collective space.

Given that I am working with video of memories from people's lived experiences, my transcripts provided the initial facts of the world. I did not want to generate stories from people's memories, rather I wanted to imagine what conversations would be possible with these individual memories. I rewrote the facts of the world as characters who remembered certain facts about events they experienced. In another sense, a transcript is translated into the database as a memory. Let us look again at Chiraz Chebib's transcript translated into the database of initial facts, where she relays what she heard the night the Absi building collapsed:

```
{"remembers": {"cognizer": "Chiraz Chebib",
               "topic": {"heard": {"hearer": "Chiraz Chebib",
                                   "medium": "across the street",
                                   "subject": "Absi Building",
                                   "speaker": "so much shelling",
                                   "time": "at night",
                                   "message": "at night we had
                                   heard that something collapsed
                                   but because there was so much
                                   shelling, we couldn't tell, we
                                   couldn't tell the differ-
                                   ence"}}}},
```

This is one "Fact" that resides in the initial state of the world. The last part that starts with "message" is the transcript from Chiraz's interview. the other items in that item shape the transcript by framing it as Chiraz remembers hearing. This decision comes from Sack's translation of TALE-SPIN [34], as he chose to use Charles Fillmore's theory of frame semantics. Fillmore developed a theory and then a project called FrameNet that applies this theory into a whole database. In their own words: "the meanings of most words can best be understood on the basis of a semantic frame, a description of a type of event, relation, or entity and the participants in it. For example, the concept of cooking typically involves a person doing the cooking (Cook), the food that is to be cooked (Food), something to hold the food while cooking (Container) and a source of heat (Heating_instrument)." In the case of Chiraz's example, the frame I used for "to hear" comes from the concept of hearsay. Here is the annotation of that frame (Table 1):

Table 1. FrameNet's annotation of hear v.[35]

Frame element	Core type
Hearer	Core
Medium	Peripheral
Message	Core
Period_of_iterations	Extra-Thematic
Speaker	Peripheral
Time	Peripheral
Topic	Core

This frame defines how the transcript is translated. The transcript itself fits under "message" and the other fields such as hearer, medium, speaker, time and topic (replaced by topic to avoid confusion with the other frame used in that item, remember, which has cognizer and topic as frame elements) are filled out with the relevant information. Notice, however, that I decided to leave out the element "period of iterations" as it is extra-thematic and I did not think it was needed for the project in its current iteration.

This whole translation of that transcript into an item in the facts of the initial state of the world would then be used by the planner to fill a task such as when finding a memory of someone who remembers something based on how they heard an event. For example, in looking to construct a conversation that makes connections between transcripts based on how people remember a specific event, such as the Absi building collapsing, the planner searches for all possible items that fits that request.

The act of remembering is added into the world as a fact that Chiraz remembered the night the building collapsed. This would help with connecting people's memories based on topic, on how they remembered, what they remembered, who they remembered and when they remembered it. The specific translation work for each individual testimony shapes how it is used in the collective. In this manner, each testimony maintains its particular position but affects and is affected by the collective.

4 A Theory of Dialogue Aesthetics

Inspecting the concept of dialogue and its function within the field of historical justice, I have noted a problematic pattern across many of these digital projects: individual stories which, while they may be presented together, require the reader to make connections among them instead of that work being part of the digital dialogue project design. In my research to date, I have found that interlocutors' voices are almost always presented as monologues. I posit three reasons for this phenomenon: (1) interfaces to archives that deal with silenced histories inherit language from the form of both testimonial evidence and talking heads in documentary, (2) they are informed by colonial archival practices, and (3) they are limited by technical difficulties. As an antidote, I propose that this unacknowledged ideology—communicated by the form itself, and therefore compromising the goals for the projects in the first place—could be addressed by encouraging a concept of dialogue that leverages the metaphors of speaking, listening, and being heard in presenting these stories in a digital medium.

The idea is to stitch individual monologues into larger conversations in order to show ties and differences in how we remember. I think this combination, of both individual recordings and machine-stitched montages, work against the impression that individual experiences are personal and isolated cases. I hope to show overlapping memories that reveal commonalities and differences in wider systemic environments.

While it cannot replace the long-standing need for a history textbook in Lebanon, I have designed *We Are History* to be used by students and teachers in history classrooms as a step towards much-needed "impossible conversations" via these algorithmically generated dialogues. The narrative intelligence system I have written automatically edits multiple versions of imagined conversations based on the words participants use in their video oral histories. From contributed memory to database and then to constructed conversation, the transcripts are dissected by the transcribers and translators, so that each section is meaningful and can stand alone as an excerpt. These sections are stitched together and they can dynamically change as listeners add their own memories to the archive.

5 Conclusion

I have presented a case study for how planners could be used in pursuing historical justice through the three elements of co-creation, a multiplicity of truths, and polyvocality. *We Are History: A People's History of Lebanon* offers a case study for building speculative and fictional conversations from non-fictional memories. Ultimately, no pursuit for historical justice can be accomplished without the question: who benefits from these projects? My hope is for this project to be used in classrooms in Lebanon as a pedagogical tool and a way forward in search of dialogue about the contested past.

References

1. Lyotard, J.F.: The Postmodern Condition: A Report On Knowledge. University of Minnesota Press, Minneapolis (1984)
2. Hartman, S.: Venus in Two Acts. Small Axe. **12**, 1–14 (2008)
3. Sutherland, T.: Archival Amnesty: In Search of Black American Transitional and Restorative Justice. J. Crit. Libr. Inf. Stud. 1 (2017). https://doi.org/10.24242/jclis.v1i2.42
4. Caswell, M.: Urgent archives: enacting liberatory memory work. Routledge (2021). https://doi.org/10.4324/9781003001355
5. Brown-Childs, J.: Transcommunality: From The Politics Of Conversion to the Ethics of Respect. Temple University Press, Philadelphia (2003)
6. Living Liberia Fabric l Imagination, Computation, and Expression Laboratory, http://groups.csail.mit.edu/icelab/content/living-liberia-fabric, last accessed 30 July 2022
7. Harrell, D.F.: Cultural Roots for Computing: The Case of African Diasporic Orature and Computational Narrative in the GRIOT System. 12
8. Harrell, D.F., et al.: A cultural computing approach to interactive narrative: the case of the living liberia fabric. In: 2010 AAAI Fall Symposium Series (2010)
9. Mateas, M., Domike, S., Vanouse, P.: Terminal time: an ideologically-biased history machine. In: AISB Quarterly, Special Issue on Creativity in the Arts and Sciences, p. 102 (1999)
10. Carbonell, J.G.: POLITICS: Automated ideological reasoning. Cogn. Sci. **2**, 27–51 (1978). https://doi.org/10.1016/S0364-0213(78)80060-3
11. Sack, W.: Actor-role analysis: ideology, point of view, and the news (1994)
12. Dagher, C.H.: Bring Down the Walls: Lebanon's Post-War Challenge. Palgrave Macmillan, Basingstoke (2002)
13. Hanf, T., Salam, N. (eds.): Lebanon in Limbo: Postwar Society and State in an Uncertain Regional Environment. Nomos Publishers, Baden-Baden (2003)
14. Schwerna, T.: Lebanon: A Model of Consociational Conflict. Peter Lang GmbH, Internationaler Verlag der Wissenschaften, Frankfurt am Main; New York (2010)
15. Westmoreland, M.R.: Crisis of Representation: Experimental Documentary in Postwar Lebanon. University of Texas, Austin, Tex (2008)
16. Haugbolle, S.: War and memory in Lebanon. Cambridge University Press, New York (2010)
17. El-Husseini, R.: Pax Syriana: Elite Politics in Postwar Lebanon. Syracuse University Press, Syracuse, New York (2012)
18. Larkin, C.: Memory and conflict in Lebanon: remembering and forgetting the past. Routledge, London; New York (2012)
19. Messarra, A.: Partis et Forces Politiques au Liban: Engagement et Stratégie de Paix et de Démocratisation pour Demain. Librairie Orientale, Beirut (1996)
20. Volk, L.: When memory repeats itself: the politics of heritage in post civil war lebanon. IJMES Int. J. Middle East Stud. **40**, 291–314 (2008)
21. Khalaf, S.: Lebanon Adrift: From Battleground to Playground. Saqi Books, London (2012)
22. Frayha, N.: Education and Social Cohesion in Lebanon. Prospects **33**, 12 (2003)
23. Medawar, E.: Lebanese Historical Memory and the Perception of National Identity through School Textbooks. Presented at the Beirut December 15 (2007)
24. Jaquemet, I.: Fighting Amnesia: Ways to Uncover the Truth about Lebanon's Missing. Int. J. Transitional Justice. **3**, 69–90 (2008). https://doi.org/10.1093/ijtj/ijn019
25. Taif Accords l UN Peacemaker, https://peacemaker.un.org/lebanon-taifaccords89, last accessed 30 July 2022
26. Volk, L.: Memory politics in lebanon a generation after the civil war. Middle East J. Cult. Commun. **10**, 293–298 (2017). https://doi.org/10.1163/18739865-01002013

27. Hermez, S.: War Is Coming: Between Past and Future Violence in Lebanon. University of Pennsylvania Press, Philadelphia (2017)
28. Saade, B.: Hizbullah and the Politics of Remembrance: Writing the Lebanese Nation. Cambridge University Press, New York (2016)
29. Gaudenzi, S.: Strategies of Participation: The Who, What and When of Collaborative Documentaries. In: Nash, K., Hight, C., Summerhayes, C. (eds.) New Documentary Ecologies, pp. 129–148. Palgrave Macmillan UK, London (2014). https://doi.org/10.1057/9781137310491_9
30. Agre, P., Chapman, D.: Pengi: An Implementation of a Theory of Activity. AAAi-87 Proc. 268–272 (1987)
31. Hanna, F.: Software and Dialogue Aesthetics in Post-Civil War Lebanon, https://escholarship.org/uc/item/64q649j0 (2019)
32. Lipari, L.: Listening Otherwise: The Voice of Ethics. Int. J. List. **23**, 44–59 (2009)
33. Sack, W.: The Software Arts. MIT Press, Cambirdge, MA (2019)
34. Sack, W.: A Machine to Tell Stories: From Propp to Software Studies. Temps Mod
35. FrameNet, https://framenet.icsi.berkeley.edu/fndrupal/, last accessed 20 April 2019

Embodied Locative Storytelling of African American Histories

Candice Butts$^{(\boxtimes)}$ ⓘ and Michael Nitsche ⓘ

Georgia Institute of Technology, Atlanta, GA 30332, USA
{cbutts3,michael.nitsche}@gatech.edu

Abstract. This project examines the value of custom-built wearable interfaces for historic reenactment. It uses new media to explore mourning culture, African American identity, and female-led gender roles within the context of Oakland Cemetery, a historic cemetery in Atlanta, GA. Tangible interfaces and site-specific storytelling combine to support a tour on site. Multiple tangible interfaces were integrated into a historic dress and various props to offer novel expressive means to tour guides and engaging activities for visitors. This combination of narrative and performative interaction design aimed to provide cultural framing and emphasize African American histories embedded in the cemetery. The project was evaluated with tour guides (n = 7) and site visitors (n = 11). Key findings confirm narrative effectiveness through empathy, values for playful engagement, emphasis on user interaction in the narration, and close integration of digital technology to the site.

Keywords: Locative storytelling · Tangible interaction · African American history · Embodied reenactment

1 Introduction

Founded in 1850 in Atlanta, GA, Oakland Cemetery is a complicated site reflecting histories of the Deep South. It presents a "physical manifestation" [1] of the city's history with racism, reflecting African American history, particularly in the decades after the Civil War. Today, Oakland is a protected park featuring educational programs about its past – including these injustices. Oakland also provides opportunities to explore female-led cultural practices, especially in the realm of death culture, racial policies, and gender roles from the Victorian era [2]. With one-hundred-seventy-two years of problematic history to uncover, which best practices could the cemetery use to tell these stories?

This project combines locative storytelling and tangible media to re-tell these histories. It examines custom-built wearable interfaces for historic reenactment and new means of audience engagement combining performance and narrative elements. This design should help interpreters and audiences explore difficult topics in an empathetic and non-alienating way. This paper covers research through design to build multiple

Supplementary Information The online version contains supplementary material available at https://doi.org/10.1007/978-3-031-22298-6_11.

historical digital interfaces, their implementation, and evaluation with experts and park visitors. The argument first outlines the problem area and historical context, then examples of related work are covered, and finally a cultural probe clarifies key design criteria. These criteria informed design and implementation processes. The resulting project evaluation will answer the original challenges.

1.1 Problem Area: History of the Site

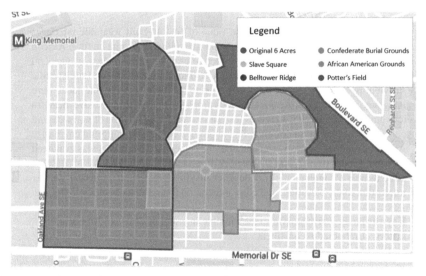

Fig. 1. Map of Oakland Cemetery. Enslaved individuals were disinterred from Slave Square and moved to plots in the African American Grounds and Potter's Field.

By April 1877, Oakland Cemetery served as Atlanta's only public burial grounds [3]. The cemetery expanded several acres north and east since 1865, yet citizens demanded additional plots. In response, the Atlanta City Council voted to clear and sale the northeastern corner of the original six acres [4] (Fig. 1). But the sale cost more than material goods, for the corner was not empty. The area is known as Slave Square and served as burial grounds for African Americans. Half of those interred in Slave Square were children [5]. That did not affect the vote. On April 2, 1877, the city of Atlanta proceeded to disinter bodies and bones of enslaved and free African American persons to re-sell the grounds [3]. All were moved to Potter's Field adjacent to the newer, segregated African American Grounds. Individuals who lacked European-style markers and headboards were placed in a mass grave [5]. The disinterment timing was not coincidental but echoed a backroom deal made in Washington, DC in January 1877 [6]. The Tilden-Hayes Agreement, called the "Great Betrayal" by African Americans, removed military protection for the fledgling Freedmen population and symbolically marked an end to Reconstruction, with lasting consequences [6]. In Oakland, Black Atlantans remained legally segregated to the rear of the cemetery until 1963 [7].

These policies were officially made by men, yet Southern White women were instrumental to the change from Reconstruction to Southern Redemption [2]. Women were the main administers of memorial culture. They established Confederate Memorial Day, an annual ritual to reverence those who fought to maintain the antebellum status-quo [8] and their power to mold perceptions of death and memory influenced policies which extend into the present [9].

Prominent markers of Southern Redemption remain as political and contested statements to this day. In the wake of George Floyd's murder, several Confederate monuments within Oakland were vandalized [10]. The granite obelisk erected by the Atlanta Ladies' Memorial Association (LMA) and the marble lion dedicated by the Daughters of the Confederacy became frequent targets of protest. In response, Oakland moved the lion to a local museum [11]. However, the obelisk's size prevented a similar solution. Rather than ignore this history, Oakland seeks to illuminate the past through educational programming. These efforts include *African American Voices*, a cell phone audio tour [12], and *Remembrance as Resistance*, a multimedia installation honoring hundreds of unmarked African American graves [13]. Our project seeks to help Oakland tell these stories with novel technology and engage participants in these histories on-site. Its narrative design aims to present experiences and question underlying injustices that are embedded in Oakland by combining site-specific storytelling with tangible media.

1.2 Related Work

Locative storytelling pre-dates digital media but has found new forms with Augmented Reality [14], through hypertext and marker-based technologies [15, 16], and educational Interactive Narratives [17]. But using digital technologies on location does not automatically support the place-qualities of the site. It can distract or even de-personalize [18]. That is why Millard et al. call for a "Loco-Narrative Harmony" that avoids focus on technology "where attention is balanced between story and place, and each is designed to enhance the experience of the other" [19]. Our project aimed for such a balanced integration of tangible media into locative storytelling, where stories become embodied in objects – as "object stories" [20]– as well as spaces.

Dow et al. [21] prototyped a drama-based audio tour at Oakland. Visitors equipped with GPS devices explore actor-voiced narrations of cemetery residents. Oakland incorporated the project's storytelling and direct interaction design, implementing these elements into their *African American Voices* phone tour [5]. The GPS technology was not adapted.

Häkkilä et al. [22] connected digital and physical components to create interactive memorials in a cemetery setting. Using RFID cards, their prototype displays changing information about the deceased on gravestones, including photographs, family trees, or social media content. Users saw some value in the concept for reflection and memorialization but argued that the gravesite was not the appropriate location for the display. Novel cemetery designs should follow interfaces which "[belong] to the graveyard context" [22].

Relying on direct interactions between the performer and participants, Demetriou et al. [23] focused on garments as the locus for memorialization. Garment and performer are transformed into interfaces "of social exchange" where participants can share their narratives and build one's "personal heritage" [23]. The garment was reworked into a sound-based interactive installation. When participants pinned notes onto the reworked garment, a microcontroller was activated to play audio narrations of archived letters. The role of sound and garment in the interactive design, and concepts of recording stories to generate personal heritage, stood out.

The garment as active controller was further explored by Isbister and Abe [24]. Live Action Roleplay (LARP) inspired designers to immerse users physically and emotionally in the play process through interactive costumes. Play-interaction centers on role-specific movements. Game wearables were embedded with Android mobile devices, Adafruit mini IOIO boards, and connected via Bluetooth. Resulting play-movements placed audience members into the narrative, building social and emotional connection between participants and toward the narrative [24]. It builds on collaborative storytelling to support immersion.

Site-specific histories have a long tradition in interactive narratives. Within that tradition, tangible technologies have found their own role in memory culture. This is supported by designs for hybrid objects as well as wearables. Role-play and "object stories" offer new opportunities but their successful on-site implementation must avoid de-humanization and respect cultural conditions and practices. These factors drove the approach of the Oakland project.

1.3 Approach

Issues of identity and social standing are etched onto the landscape of Oakland Cemetery and memory culture. Rather than fully embrace Anglo-American traditions, Reconstruction-era Black women melded Anglo and African traditions and used personal mourning customs to uphold cultural values [25]. To highlight these traditions, this project built upon African American symbols and practices for an interactive narrative design. Another key element is participation in constructing personal and shared memory. Hands-on participation provides opportunities for memorable learning encounters [26]. Oakland's more popular events, such as *Sunday in the Park* and *Capturing the Spirit of Oakland*, utilize interpreters to reenact and directly engage with audiences [4, 27, 28]. Within this context of shared events, our project aimed to support two interconnected groups: first, help tour guides and reenactors at Oakland provide means of audience engagement and second, support visitors with engaging educational tools.

Research unfolded first through a cultural probe launched among experts of the field. Results were analyzed and informed the ideation phase. This led to design piloting and iterative designs. The final design was implemented and a concluding (IRB approved) user study with experts and visitors was conducted.

1.4 Cultural Probe

To better understand the needs of guides/interpreters, a survey-based cultural probe was created and distributed to field experts. This project "pursu[es] experimental design" [29]. Its targeted four areas: needs in heritage education, motivation, place-ness (e.g., emotional or sensory attachments), and visitor engagement. Probes contained questionnaires, drawing activities, and thought experiments for "responsive" [29] expert feedback. The seven-question probes were distributed to five experts, of which three returned the material.

One core desire centered on revealing the reality of African American history to audiences and facilitating cultural heritage work that can "help African Americans find their voice" (P#2). Experts' motivations for their work connected to cultural and personal identity. This includes promotion of self-identity by finding commonality with, and building empathy for, marginalized groups (see also [30]). Turning to the site, qualities of "place-ness" related to sensory details and accompanying emotions were key. Avoiding "flashy" displays (P#3) help visitors reflect on the information provided. For example, P#2 mentioned the *Legacy Museum*, in Alabama, which memorialized lynching victims by displaying "the names of men women and children suspended from above" (P#2). Visitor engagement was seen as best realized through storytelling and performance. Props, narrative, and dialogue were noted to increase audience participation. "[A]udience feedback and interaction lets [experts] know if [they are] connecting with the audience," lighten tense moods, and build camaraderie between participants (P#2). Playful interactions bring guests into the conversation and respect their "repository of knowledge" (P#1).

This expert feedback related to data on visitor preferences collected for an updated Oakland master plan, which revealed the value of special events such as tours and annual programming, that attract over 70% of Oakland's visitors [31]. "Informed tour volunteers," "stories of the past and history," and "feeling the history" motivated guests to visit again [31].

Four key design goals emerged from expert feedback:

- Build audience empathy through storytelling.
- Bring enjoyment through playful elements.
- Use direct audience interaction to actuate the project.
- Build immersion with props and space.

The effectiveness of the final design in meeting these criteria are discussed in Sect. 3.3 of this paper.

2 Oakland Project Design

Oakland Cemetery presents numerous design limitations. As a cultural heritage site and active cemetery, Oakland's historical character must be supported, e.g. by avoiding disruptive or damaging additions to the site. Guidelines maintain that signs should be "minimally invasive" and "be added selectively and discretely" [31]. Preservation must also be balanced with increased visitor volume and a variety of changing educational opportunities. New educational technology can be deployed but must conform to site limitations. These site-specific conditions informed the design space as much as the historic-cultural context.

Victorian era mourning was most frequently displayed through clothing and jewelry. Consequently, the design turned to textile and related tangibles. Neither would require additional signage or markers but suit existent practices. Tangible props allow a "feeling of history" through immersive interaction and embodied storytelling on site [31]. Thus, the project emerged in two main parts: a localized narrative tour, specifically designed to focus on the African American history at Oakland, and a range of wearable media that supported each station of this localized story through embodied interaction.

2.1   Locative Narrative Design

The developed tour mirrors the scope of several educational Oakland tours dedicated to the site's racial history and to influential women, such as the *Black Magnolias* [32] tour, which explores African American women interred at Oakland. Like *Black Magnolias*, the new tour was structured as a walking exploration of the cemetery but included new resources: tangible media to enhance the in-situ narrative elements and engage audiences.

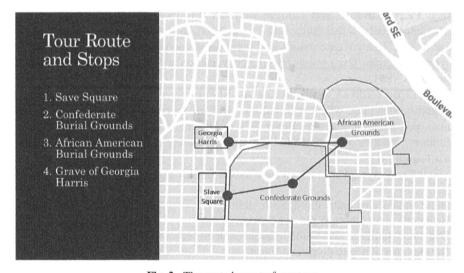

Fig. 2. The route loops to four stops.

Four key sites within Oakland feature in this customized tour: 1) Slave Square, 2) Confederate Grounds Monuments, 3) African American Burial Grounds, and 4) Georgia Harris's Gravesite (Fig. 2). The interpreter leads the tour in character and costume, playing the role of an African American woman living at the end of Reconstruction. Following a Victorian tradition, the interpreter/guide sets out to adorn the grave of a loved-one and has invited friends (site visitors) to participate. Originally buried in Slave Square, this (fictional) loved-one was forcefully disinterred in 1877 and our story follows that journey. Tour stops create a loop from Slave Square, through the Confederate Grounds, to the African American Grounds, and finally ending a few yards from Slave Square at the grave of Georgia Harris. Each stop along the path embodies a micro-narrative representing different challenges posed throughout Oakland's history. They are supported by the guide's dress, its embedded circuitry, and interactive props (necklace, memory badge). Their operation and narrative integration are outlined below.

2.2 Designing the Dress

As the site prohibited installation of new technologies or markers, the focus shifted to wearable interfaces. This included the design of a historic mourning dress for the tour guide.

Numerous projects utilize wearables for enhanced expression, whether this is in dance [33], fashion [34], or education [35, 36]. Garments augmented with interactive media can lead to new practices and tools [36, 37], and support countless project-specific eTextiles. To deliver the targeted embodied storytelling of African American histories at Oakland, the main wearable was designed as traditional Victorian-era mourning dress. The tour's narrative is set immediately after Reconstruction and the gown is based on late 19th century bustle era designs [38] (Fig. 3). The additional space within the collapsible bustle proved useful for hiding technology. The dress was made of contrasting fabrics, a fashionable choice in that era, and reflected mourning styles by shunning decorative trim [39]. It incorporates dark gray, which signified the transitional state of half-mourning, where grieving women could acceptably wear more fashionable hair and clothing, and attend lively social events [39].

A collapsible bustle was created to support the skirt (pattern by, [40]). Pockets attached to each hip housed Arduino boards and batteries. The costume was made from cotton and a petticoat smoothed over protrusions created by the technology. A supportive corset carried the additional weight of bustle, skirt, apron, and added technology.

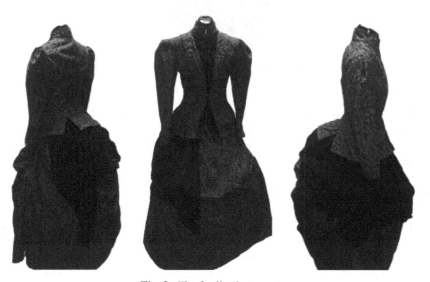

Fig. 3. The finalized garment.

2.3 Designing the Props and Narrative Integration

The dress served as a focal point for the re-enactment but each node included specific tangible interactions reaching from accentuation on the dress itself to props used by visitors during the event. The locative narrative unfolds as the tour guide and visitors traverse the cemetery engaging prepared tangible interfaces with site-prevalent themes at four key moments. In preparation for each tour, visitors receive a small bag of items that they will utilize during this journey.

Fig. 4. Guide assembling beads. Button chatelaine belt for audio tour hang from waistband.

Stop #1 Slave Square. The first narrative node is situated at Slave Square, whose original layout is no longer visible. Thus, the theme of "invisibility" shaped the interaction and narrative. Archaeological studies of pre- and post-war African American sites reveal the ubiquitous presence of small colorful beads (the majority, blue) used for female personal adornment [41]. These beads, which were sometimes left with the deceased, traditionally signify womanhood, and the color blue signifies hope and protection for Black Americans. To reveal the history of Slave Square to visitors, the project builds on these traditions and the tour guide will highlight the story of the beads. We created a modular necklace that, when assembled, forms a complete piece (Fig. 4). Visitors are asked to present the necklace pieces received at the tour start and the audience helps to produce a shared artefact worn by the guide. When the necklace is assembled, an integrated circuit closes to transform pendants from black (unlit), a symbol of mourning, to blue (lit LEDs), a symbol of protection and hope (Fig. 5). Circuited pendants were shaped from modeling clay and plastic to contain an LED with positive and negative wires attached at the ends to a magnetized snap. Pendants snap together with magnets securing this connection and daisy-chain the circuit to the next strand. The device is powered by batteries housed within a secondary necklace worn by the guide. The necklace is completed with wooden, analog beads.

Fig. 5. Fully assembled beads have turn from black to blue (lit LEDs).

Stop #2 Confederate Grounds. After stepping away from Slave Square, the tour passes through the Confederate Grounds. The second node is located at the Confederate Obelisk, where themes center on the role of Southern White women in changes to Oakland Cemetery. The guide conveys the obelisk' story, which was established to represent Confederate "patriotism" which continued to "burn with unquenchable fervor" [42] within the Atlanta Ladies Memorial Association (ALMA). In erecting these memorials women "provided the platform from which ex-Confederate men could lament their defeat" [43] and uphold "a shared commitment to white supremacy" [44].

The interactive portion is an audio tour modeled after the *African American Voices* tour. However, the guide rather than the visitor, is in control and can shape and add to the soundscape. The speaker and controlling Arduino are hidden in the costume and activated with buttons disguised as a chatelaine belt (Fig. 4). White Southerners produced volumes lauding a sanitized view of antebellum society. From these sources three passages were selected for this project. First, a March 1866 LMA letter to "the press and ladies of the South" (cited in [8]) called for annual observances of Confederate Memorial Day. Second, an 1875 proclamation from Atlanta mayor, C.C. Hammock, beaconed Atlanta residents to "kneel at [the] illustrious shrines" of the Confederate dead [45]. Third, a poem written by a secretary for an Alabama branch of the LMA and inscribed on the Confederate monument located on Capitol Hill in Montgomery, AL [46].

Stop #3 African American Burial Grounds. Here, the guide brings attention to the difference between African American and Anglo-American decorative practices. While most of the cemetery is covered with stone and iron monuments, the African American section is open, with irregularly dotted markers and monuments [25]. The different memorial styles illustrate different cultural origins, one primarily West African, and the other primarily Western European. These traditions hold in common an emphasis on nature and color symbolism in mourning. These are the main themes of the third stop.

Jewelry was an essential accessory to the wardrobe of a woman in mourning, signaling stories of memorialization through symbolism [47]. Visitors are provided another jewelry item: Brooches with floral motifs serve as interactive props for this node (Fig. 6). Each contain a neodymium magnet, and within the costume bodice is a neodymium-backed button. When the magnets attract, the button activates a string of LED lights stitched into the skirt in a floral pattern, accentuating the nature theme (Fig. 7).

Fig. 6. Brooch worn to activate skirt with rose inlay.

Fig. 7. Illuminated skirt with floral pattern.

Stop #4 Georgia Harris Gravesite. The concluding stop is the historic grave of Georgia Harris. Harris, who was formerly enslaved, worked for the Boyd family for 27 years and laid to rest in 1920 [32]. Like many Black women Harris sought employment in one of few avenues open to her, domestic service for a White family [48]. We have very little information on Georgia Harris' life or relationship with the Boyd family, but the rear of the headstone refers to Harris as "mammy". In the role of "mammy" Black female domestic servants might work round-the-clock tending to the needs of the white family, even more so if she were a live-in employee [43]. Oakland was racially segregated in 1920 but the Boyd family petitioned Atlanta Mayor James L. Key (and the owners of neighboring plots) for permission to bury Harris in their family plot [4]. Whether these actions reflect Harris' final wishes remains unclear. The question surrounding Georgia's final wishes and the absence of her voice are the catalyst for the final narrative enactment.

Mourning ribbons and arm bands served as mourning signifiers in America since colonial days. These items served as less formal options for individuals wishing to forego the rigors of traditional mourning dress or seeking more economical options [49]. Before the tour begins, visitors are presented with black mourning ribbons to wear throughout the experience (Fig. 8). At the last stop, their ribbon is revealed to be a recording and playback device. Visitors are invited to record reflections on Harris and the location, to contemplate through deliberate action. The goal is to create a closing dialogue between the visitor, the object, and the location. These personal reflections are then collected and can be re-used as a contemporary perspective to the location, its history, and its challenges.

Fig. 8. Mourning ribbons with inserted sound board modules created for the tour.

The narrative is designed to be enacted first with a focus on objects that center on the tour guide. Visitors are handed artifacts, but they are initially unaware of the meaning, while the dress is an immediate historic reference. However, assembling the necklace, activating the brooches, listening to audio, all deliver key themes drawn from the context and location at hand and shift activity outwards. The final node invites visitors to deliver an own reflection, their own voice to the questions that the location poses. By utilizing spatial, auditory, and visual interactions visitors are encouraged to make meaning from narrative and performative interactions with objects, space, and context. The experience offers unique features absent from existent guided or audio tours. We conducted an on-site study of the interfaces to test the efficacy of these designs.

3   Evaluation

A user study assessed whether the narrative design achieved the four central goals: 1) build audience empathy; 2) bring enjoyment through playful elements; 3) successfully use direct audience interaction; and 4) build immersion using props and space. The study was IRB approved and conducted on site at Oakland cemetery.

3.1 Study Design

At the start of the study, participants were introduced to the project and invited to give written consent. Then, they participated in the tour, which lasted about 45 min. After the tour, a questionnaire about the experience was completed followed by a six-question interview. The entire process lasted approximately 1½ h.

Participants were recruited through word of mouth, the network of collaborators at Oakland Cemetery, and digital outreach. Study participants were recruited based on their classification to fit in one of the two target audiences: either expert (individuals with proficiency in cultural heritage fields) or visitor. Participants were encouraged, but not required to, complete the questionnaire or exit interview.

The questionnaire instrument combines elements from three studies focused on cultural heritage and useability. Forrest [50] provides a quantitative model for analyzing visitor experiences within learning environments. Their questions were alternate-reverse coded questions using a seven-point Likert scale. The instruments of Kirchberg and Trundles [51] focus on emotional and physical response analysis within museum spaces. This project used Kirchberg/Trundles [51] to analyze emotional connections in role-play-based experiences by building on Isbister/Abe [24]. Finally, the System Useability Survey (SUS) [52] was included for the expert population to directly analyze the usefulness of our interface for expert use. Concluding the data collection, participants provided demographic data and participated in an exit interview. All studies were conducted in person, at Oakland Cemetery. Walking from the main gate to Slave Square, and then to the remaining three stops is approximately 0.4 mile. The route is paved and accessible by wheelchair and vehicle. Anyone, age 18 and older, was welcome to participate. Minors were excluded due to potentially disturbing subject matters focused on death and racism. The project was conducted in English.

Data collected included field notes, photographs, audio reflections recorded by participants, concluding interview audio recordings, and questionnaires.

3.2 Study Results

Demographics. Twenty-one individuals participated overall. Of those, eighteen participants successfully completed the survey. Seven participants self-identified as "experts", eleven were classified as "visitors." Fifteen of eighteen participants were female, three male. All had some post-secondary education, two thirds had a Master's, Doctorate, or Professional degree.

Scoring. Scores are tallied for the mean and standard deviation for each question (n = 11 visitors (v); n = 7 experts (e)). An overall favorability rating for each section was taken from the average of the combined mean scores and divided by the highest possible favorable rating of seven (7). Unless otherwise noted, the scores from experts and non-experts are compiled as a unit, and not separated. Data will be first broken down for each narrative node and then in relation to the overall narrative tour. To avoid bias in the questionnaire, questionnaires combined negative questions with positive ones. Data was adjusted when overall values (like acceptance) were calculated.

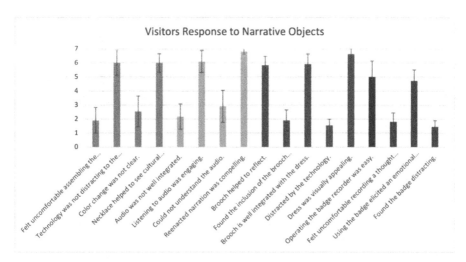

Fig. 9. Visitors' Responses to Narrative Objects (with standard deviation).

Stop #1 Slave Square: Necklace. Four questions about stop #1 resulted in a favorability rating of 83.93% (with negative questions adjusted). Individuals rated: (1) their level of discomfort, (2) technology integration, (3) lack of visual impact of the necklace, and (4) establishing cultural connection. Few participants (visitors = 1.9; experts = 1.4) were uncomfortable engaging with the prop, which was clearly not seen as distracting (v = 6; e = 5.1). The color change was not always immediately detected (v = 2.5; e = 2.1) but it worked to stimulate cultural connections (v = 6; e = 5.8). The necklace was praised by participants for visual storytelling, hands-on learning, and frequently cited as a memorable artefact. The main theme of making suppressed history "visible" was alluded to in interviews: "I thought it was awesome…. I've never seen anything like that. I didn't know about the blue being a protector… You put it together as you were talking about it, so it was like [a] revealing" (Expert C1). The necklace became part of the interpreter/guide own history providing a deeper connection to African American traditions. "The necklace…was a surprise, something I had not thought of and would not have associated with Oakland. But I think it's a way to get people involved to have things they can touch and feel" (Expert D2).

Stop #2 Confederate Grounds: Audio. The audio part for the Confederate grounds focused on the "Southern Women" theme. It received an overall rating of 82.94% (with negative questions adjusted). Participants rated: (1) audio integration into the tour and cemetery setting, (2) audio engagement, (3) understanding the audio, (4) engagement between the audio and reenactor. The audio was seen as overall well integrated. Participants rated the interaction between the audio and reenactor as extremely favorable (v = 6.8; e = 5.5) as well as engaging (v = 6; e = 5.8) and most had no problems understanding

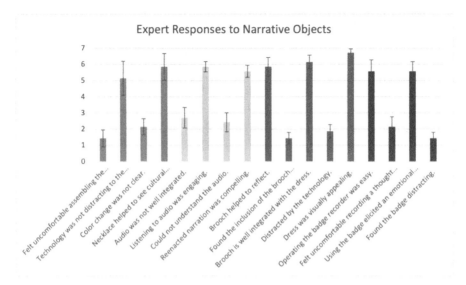

Fig. 10. Experts' Responses to Narrative Objects (with standard deviation).

the audio (v = 2.9; e = 2.4). Most participants were able to hear the prepared sound files, but background noise (vehicles, wind, other visitors) was disruptive. Participants were favorable "to hear [people from the past] in their own words" and described this portion as "really powerful… When you're literally hearing them talk about their [Confederate] markers" (Visitor G3). In one expert interview, a possible disconnect was noted. The interpreter/guide is African American, thus hearing Lost Cause appeals emanating from her dress was noted as "weird." Additional audio, primarily from the viewpoint of the presenter's character could be added to counter this effect.

Stop #3 African American Burial Grounds: Brooch. The third stop centered on the brooch and "nature" motif. Questions assessed: (1) help to reflect through brooch interaction; (2) possible confusion of brooch use; (3) integration of brooch and dress; and (4) distraction through the technology. Gown aesthetics were highly rated at 95.14%. The brooch artefact and lights did not distract from the tour (v = 1.5; e = 1.8), nor was it confusing (v = 1.9; e = 1.4). The brooch interaction did help in reflection (v = 5.8; e = 5.8) with an even higher rating of successful integration (v = 5.9; e = 6.1). There was a slight variance between experts and non-experts in the interviews, as experts were more likely to grasp the connection between the artifact, mourning culture, and nature.

Stop #4 Georgia Harris Gravesite: Memorial Ribbon. The final narrative node centered on the case of Georgia Harris and used the voice recording memorial badge. Participants rated: (1) ease to operate voice recorder; (2) discomfort level recording a thought; (3) the elicited emotional response; and (4) possible distraction through this technology. Average responses provided a score of 81.742% favorability (with negative questions adjusted). Ease in operating the recording module was clearly higher among experts than visitors (v = 5; e = 5.5). Approximately one-third of the participants were unable to successfully record or playback a statement. Experts expressed higher discomfort recording (v = 1.8; e = 2.1) but expressed higher emotional response (v = 4.7; e = 5.5). Still, the personalize nature of this interaction was appreciated, as one expert lauded, "provocative statements that are personal...I'm thinking I should incorporate more...emotional responses, 'cause[sic] that's what they'll remember...[I]f they felt something they'll remember that" (Expert D2).

Overall Assessment. The comprehensive assessment contained nine questions focusing on engagement and immersion, inclusion, mastery, and the value of technology. We used negative as well as positive questions but adjusted them for the analysis.

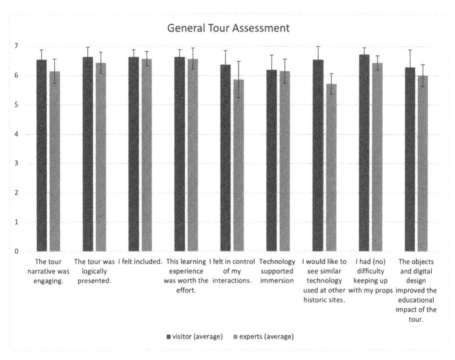

Fig. 11. General assessment results (visitor and experts with standard deviation).

When adjusted for the reverse coded questions, ratings were favorable with a general score of 90.8% with experts rating lower (88.6%) than visitors (92.9%). Notable differences were in ease of keeping up (v = 6.7; e = 6.4) and wish to see the technology at other sides (v = 6.5; e = 5.7). Both groups found the digital tour logical (v = 6.3; e = 6.4), immersive (v = 6.1; e = 6.1), and the narrative engaging (v = 6.5; e = 6.1). As participants, they felt in control (v = 6.3; e = 5.8) and included (v = 6.6; e = 6.5). The overall highest ratings were for worth of the effort (v = 6.6; e = 6.5).

Emotions. Emotion assessment questions were taken from the Exit Survey developed by Kirchberg/Trundles [45]. Following their system, we wanted to know if the tour moved participants emotionally (Fig. 11). The emotion survey is alternating-reverse scored on a Likert scale of 1 to 7. Participants were generally pleased (v = 6.5; e = 6.4). The lowest scored Items include fear (v = 1.7; e = 1.5) and laughter (v = 2.6; e = 3). Higher rated emotions and responses include surprise (v = 5; e = 5) happiness (v = 3.5; e = 4.4), and sadness (v = 4.7; e = 5). But the highest ratings were in reflection and participants clearly noted that the project made them think (v = 6.8; e = 6.5). Notably, anger felt by experts (2.85) diverged from the visitors (4.6). This difference could reflect an expert's tendency to emotionally detach from the information they study and present (which was noted by Expert D2's interview).

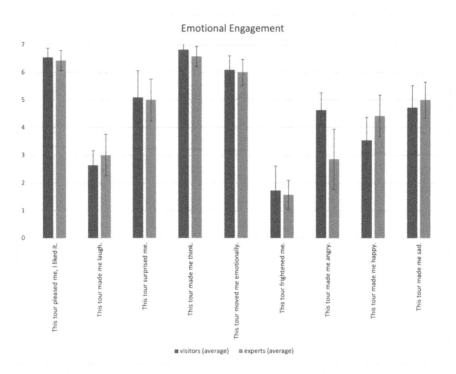

Fig. 12. Emotional engagement values (visitor and experts with standard deviation).

SUS Scores. Seven self-identified experts provided an average SUS score of 76.1, above the standard SUS mean of 68 [53] (Fig. 13). Question phrasing was adjusted slightly from the core SUS survey since experts were not provided the opportunity to wear and operate the garment directly. This was not possible under Covid restrictions. However, the survey conformed to the 10-question, five-point Likert scale rule. The system was rated: want to use system frequently (3.5), too complex (1.8), ease of use (4), need support to operate (2.4), integration of parts (4.2), quick to learn (4.1), cumbersome (1.7), confidence to use (3.5), and need to learn a lot to operate (1.8).

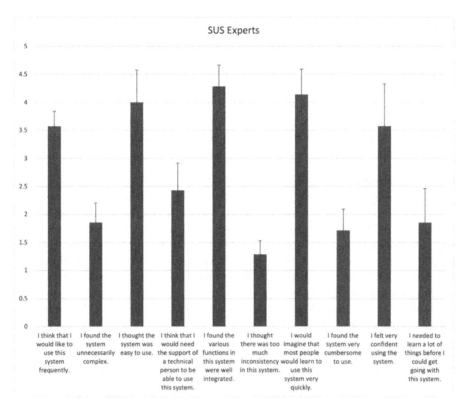

Fig. 13. Individual SUS results, experts only (with standard deviation).

3.3 Discussion

Assembling the individual data points: Did the study support or contradict the stated goals of the Oakland project?

Goal 1: Empathy-building stories. Interactive props were integrated to support the story and themes, bringing historical facts to life. This worked for all Tangible User Interfaces (TUI) of the project. The high values of the overall assessment questionnaire (Fig. 11) and the emotional engagement questionnaire (Fig. 12) support this for the overall experience. Emotional attachment might have initially been triggered by the dress, but response to narrative objects (Fig. 9 and 10) increased further projection and supported empathy through the narrative. Participants expressed an immediate interest in the interpreter upon seeing her in costume but interacting with personalized items such as the necklace and brooch developed this further. Our field observations showed that tour participants familiar with one another were more likely to place themselves within the narrative using statements like: "If I was alive back then…" or "What would I wear?" Although unfamiliar participants were less likely to interact directly with one another during the tour, they were open to conversation and responded during the exit group interview. Narrative and TUI design managed to engage audiences in a complex emotional response, which was expected given the complicated nature of the material.

Goal 2: Provide enjoyment through playfulness. Interfaces served as physical narrative anchors, they helped to "capture [participants'] attention" (Visitor H1). *Ease of interaction* rated high among participants (v = 6.6; e = 6.4), indicating that technology did not overburden participants, a possible problem of technology integration. High positive emotional *engagement* is displayed in general appreciation for the tour (v = 6.5; e = 6.1). The only value higher was in *critical thinking* (v = 6.8; e = 6.5). Enjoyment, here, manifests as a mindful engagement with the locative narrative and its themes. The experience was not light-hearted, as the strong emotional responses overall show, but it was accessible and enjoyable to experts and visitors alike.

Goal 3: Use direct audience interaction. Our design integrated visitor and tour guide interaction through shared prop handling along a spatialized story tour (this worked in all trials). The use of new interactive tools makes this tour unlike any walking tour currently offered by Oakland. Expert feedback highlighted the value in incorporating props, and first-person storytelling supported by tangible. During trials, audiences were engaged, eagerly awaiting the next reveal. We never encountered lack of participation as visitors were willing to contribute, provide own input, and familiarize themselves with each prop. Participants felt *engaged* (v = 6.5; e = 6.1) and believed the experience was *worthwhile* (v = 6.6; e = 6.5). Both, the individual TUI and the overarching variation appealed to participants.

Goal 4: Incorporate immersion through props and space. No additions were made to the cemetery itself. Oakland remained the stage for teaching and the new technology did not cause any noticeable detachment [18]. The successful *integration* of our TUI was the highest rating point in the SUS feedback from the experts (4.28/5) and participants reported feeling *included* (v = 6.6; e = 6.5) and *immersed* (v = 6.1; e = 6.1). We did not track any distancing effects between space and narrative design. Our narrative design took great effort to honor the geography, architecture, and natural setting of Oakland and illustrate the historical realities of the site. The combination of interactive props with specific sites proved to be highly effective.

The overall feedback clearly supported our four goals. The engagement might shift between different interfaces, from the encounter of the dress to the participatory activities centering on the props, ending with the individual sound recordings. Orchestrating engagement was part of the project's ultimately successful design and narrative unfolding.

4   Outlook

The project met its main goals but there are more ways to support and develop this work. We aim to expand the interaction to 20 or more participants, the size of many school classes, without leaving individuals out of the interaction or becoming too repetitive. This scaling up might lead to new design challenges for individual props. In terms of narrative re-focusing, participants expressed desire for more information on the African American Grounds, which could be integrated through additional stops at these grounds. Various technical optimizations would be useful, for the memory ribbons well as the dress. To increase comfort and ensure easier access to embedded technology, the dress should be optimized. For example, a lighter skirt is possible using different LEDs fixtures. Finally, we consider using the mourning ribbons and user-generated reflections for an installation at a gallery space within Oakland. The ribbons can record, store, and play back voice recordings. Thus, we can re-use recordings in an audio exhibition. This would allow a gradually growing spoken-word archive, a continuing reflection about and on the site.

References

1. Flowers, B.: Race, space, and architecture in Oakland cemetery. Scapes 6: Public Works **6**, 42–51 (2007)
2. Janney, C.E.: Burying the Dead But Not the Past: Ladies' Memorial Associations and the Lost Cause. Univ of North Carolina Press (2008)
3. Thomas, B.C.: Race relations in Atlanta, from 1877 through 1890, as seen in a critical analysis of the Atlanta City council proceedings and other related works. https://radar.auctr.edu/island ora/object/cau.td%3A1966_thomas_bettye_c/ (1966)
4. Davis, R., Davis, H.: Atlanta's Oakland Cemetery: An Illustrated History and Guide. University of Georgia Press (2012)
5. Henderson, D.L.: Imagining slave square: resurrecting history through cemetery research and interpretation. In: van Balgooy, M.A., Bunch, L.G., III. (eds.) Interpreting African American History and Culture at Museums and Historic Sites, pp. 106–111. Rowman & Littlefield Publishers, Blue Ridge Summit, UNITED STATES (2014)
6. Jones, S.A., Freedman, E.: Presidents and Black America : a documentary history. CQ Press, Los Angeles, Calif (2012)
7. Henderson, D.L., Van Beck, S.: Illuminating the History of Slave Square – Oakland Cemetery (2019). https://oaklandcemetery.com/illuminating-the-history-of-slave-square/. Accessed 14 Jul 2022
8. Collier, M.W.: Biographies of Representative Women of the South. Atlanta (1920)
9. Cody, M.: Monuments and Memories: Examination of Atlanta's Civil War Monuments. https://www.proquest.com/docview/2615045659/abstract/8AA371C059674D6 DPQ/1 (2021)
10. Abusaid, S.: Confederate statues vandalized in Oakland Cemetery, cops say. https://www. ajc.com/news/crime--law/confederate-monuments-vandalized-oakland-cemetery-cops-say/ f3s4KoXNqCQJlvCgZvpndP/ (2020)
11. Historic Oakland Foundation: The Removal of the Lion of Atlanta from Oakland Cemetery – Oakland Cemetery (2021). https://oaklandcemetery.com/the-removal-of-the-lion-of-atlanta-from-oakland-cemetery/. Accessed 14 Jul 2022
12. Historic Oakland Foundation: Self-Guided Tour – Oakland Cemetery (n.d.). https://oaklan dcemetery.com/self-guided-tour/. Accessed 14 Jul 2022
13. Minniefield, C.: Remembrance as Resistance (n.d.). https://fluxprojects.org/productions/rem embrance-as-resistance-preserving-black-narratives/. Accessed 14 Jul 2022
14. Hameed, A., Klungre, Ø.S., Perkis, A., Bolme, G., Brownridge, A.: User evaluation of a storytelling application assisting visitors in protected nature areas. In: Mitchell, A., Vosmeer, M. (eds.) ICIDS 2021. LNCS, vol. 13138, pp. 349–359. Springer, Cham (2021). https://doi. org/10.1007/978-3-030-92300-6_34
15. Farman, J.: The Mobile Story: Narrative Practices with Locative Technologies. Routledge (2013)

16. Hargood, C., Weal, M.J., Millard, D.E.: The storyplaces platform: building a web-based locative hypertext system. In: Proceedings of the 29th on Hypertext and Social Media. pp. 128–135. Association for Computing Machinery, New York, NY, USA (2018). https://doi.org/10.1145/3209542.3209559

17. Rouse, R.: Someone else's story: an ethical approach to interactive narrative design for cultural heritage. In: Cardona-Rivera, R.E., Sullivan, A., Young, R.M. (eds.) ICIDS 2019. LNCS, vol. 11869, pp. 47–60. Springer, Cham (2019). https://doi.org/10.1007/978-3-030-33894-7_6

18. de Souza e Silva, A., Sheller, M. (eds.): Mobility and Locative Media. Routledge (2014). https://doi.org/10.4324/9781315772226

19. Millard, D.E., Packer, H., Howard, Y., Hargood, C.: The balance of attention: the challenges of creating locative cultural storytelling experiences. J. Comput. Cult. Herit. **13**(4), 1–24 (2020). https://doi.org/10.1145/3404195

20. Tanenbaum, T.J., Tanenbaum, K., Antle, A.: The Reading Glove: designing interactions for object-based tangible storytelling. In: Proceedings of the 1st Augmented Human International Conference. pp. 1–9. Association for Computing Machinery, New York, NY, USA (2010). https://doi.org/10.1145/1785455.1785474

21. Dow, S., Lee, J., Oezbek, C., MacIntyre, B., Bolter, J.D., Gandy, M.: Exploring spatial narratives and mixed reality experiences in Oakland Cemetery. In: Proceedings of the 2005 ACM SIGCHI International Conference on Advances in computer entertainment technology. pp. 51–60. Association for Computing Machinery, New York, NY, USA (2005). https://doi.org/10.1145/1178477.1178484

22. Häkkilä, J., Colley, A., Kalving, M.: Designing an interactive gravestone display. In: Proceedings of the 8th ACM International Symposium on Pervasive Displays, pp. 1–7. Association for Computing Machinery, New York, NY, USA (2019). https://doi.org/10.1145/3321335.3324952

23. Demetriou, P., Pappas, O., Kampylis, S.: Love Letters – Wearing Stories Told: A performance-technology provocation for interactive storytelling. Body, Space Technol. **16**, 13 & 3 (2017). https://doi.org/10.16995/bst.3

24. Isbister, K., Abe, K.: Costumes as Game Controllers: An Exploration of Wearables to Suit Social Play. In: Proceedings of the Ninth International Conference on Tangible, Embedded, and Embodied Interaction, pp. 691–696. Association for Computing Machinery, New York, NY, USA (2015). https://doi.org/10.1145/2677199.2688813

25. Henderson, D.L.: What lies beneath: reading the cultural landscape of graveyard and burial grounds in African-American history and Literature (2008)

26. Kanhadilok, P., Watts, M.: Adult play-learning: observing informal family education at a science museum. Studies Educ. Adults **46**, 23–41 (2014). https://doi.org/10.1080/02660830.2014.11661655

27. Major, D.: Behind the Scenes: Sunday in the Park at Oakland Cemetery (2019). https://oaklandcemetery.com/behind-the-scenes-sunday-in-the-park-at-oakland-cemetery/

28. Capturing the Spirit of Oakland Halloween Tours (n.d.). https://oaklandcemetery.com/event/capturing-the-spirit-of-oakland-halloween-tours/

29. Gaver, B., Dunne, T., Pacenti, E.: Design: cultural probes. Interactions **6**, 21–29 (1999). https://doi.org/10.1145/291224.291235

30. Andrews, R., McGlynn, C., Mycock, A.: Students' attitudes towards history: does self-identity matter? Educ. Res. **51**, 365–377 (2009). https://doi.org/10.1080/00131880903156948

31. Historic Oakland Foundation, Stantec: Oakland Alive: Oakland Cemetery Master Plan Update. Historic Oakland Foundation (2018)

32. Historic Oakland Foundation: Black Magnolias: African American Women in Atlanta's History, (n.d.)

33. Honauer, M., Wilde, D., Hornecker, E.: Overcoming reserve – supporting professional appropriation of interactive costumes. In: Proceedings of the 2020 ACM Designing Interactive Systems Conference. pp. 2189–2200. Association for Computing Machinery, New York, NY, USA (2020)

34. Du, J., Markopoulos, P., Wang, Q., Toeters, M., Gong, T.: ShapeTex: implementing shape-changing structures in fabric for wearable actuation. In: Proceedings of the Twelfth International Conference on Tangible, Embedded, and Embodied Interaction. pp. 166–176. Association for Computing Machinery, New York, NY, USA (2018). https://doi.org/10.1145/317 3225.3173245

35. Zeagler, C., et al.: YOU BETTA WERK: using wearable technology performance driven inclusive transdisciplinary collaboration to facilitate authentic learning. In: Proceedings of the Fifteenth International Conference on Tangible, Embedded, and Embodied Interaction. pp. 1–12. Association for Computing Machinery, New York, NY, USA (2021). https://doi.org/10.1145/3430524.3440622

36. Peppler, K.: A Review of E-Textiles in Education and Society. Handbook of Research on the Societal Impact of Digital Media, 23 p. (2016). https://doi.org/10.4018/978-1-4666-8310-5.ch011

37. Perner-Wilson, H., Buechley, L., Satomi, M.: Handcrafting textile interfaces from a kit-of-no-parts. In: Proceedings of the fifth international conference on Tangible, embedded, and embodied interaction. pp. 61–68. Association for Computing Machinery, New York, NY, USA (2010). https://doi.org/10.1145/1935701.1935715

38. Cramer-Reichelderfer, A.: Fall of the American Dressmaker 1880–1920. https://corescholar.libraries.wright.edu/etd_all/2085 (2019)

39. Bedikian, S.A.: The death of mourning: from victorian crepe to the little black dress. Omega (Westport) **57**, 35–52 (2008). https://doi.org/10.2190/OM.57.1.c

40. Stowell, L.: V346: How to Make a Victorian Bustle – Pattern and Instructions. https://blog.americanduchess.com/2013/01/v346-how-to-make-victorian-bustle.html. Accessed 14 Jul 2022

41. Stine, L.F., Cabak, M.A., Groover, M.D.: Blue beads as African-American cultural symbols. Hist Arch. **30**, 49–75 (1996). https://doi.org/10.1007/BF03374221

42. Memorial Day: https://gahistoricnewspapers.galileo.usg.edu/lccn/sn90052045/1874-05-06/ed-1/seq-4/#date1=04%2F01%2F1874&nottext=&date2=06%2F01%2F1874&words=Cemetery+Oakland&searchType=advanced&sequence=0&index=0&proxdistance=5&rows=12&ortext=&proxtext=oakland+cemetery&andtext=&page=1 (1874)

43. Janney-Lucas, C.E.: If not for the ladies: Ladies' Memorial Associations and the making of the lost cause. https://www.proquest.com/docview/305380909/abstract/712D661E7F034DD1PQ/1 (2005)

44. Black, W.: Untangling the Lost Cause myth from the American story will be hard – The Washington Post. https://www.washingtonpost.com/news/made-by-history/wp/2017/08/25/untangling-the-lost-cause-myth-from-the-american-story-will-be-hard/ (2017)

45. Hammock, C.C.: Proclamation. http://ajc.newspapers.com/image/?clipping_id=54125382&fcfToken=eyJhbGciOiJIUzI1NiIsInR5cCI6IkpXVCJ9.eyJmcmVlLXZpZXctaWQiOjI2ODI0ODg3LCJpYXQiOjE2NTc3OTI4MzMsImV4cCI6MTY1Nzg3OTIzM30.ZLzcexIlPlTScY9kHiCFEqlXquMqFtu7_lX4x__pUfs (1875)

46. Ockenden, I.M.P.: The Confederate monument on Capitol Hill, Montgomery, Alabama, 1861–1900. [Montgomery, Ala.?] Published by the Ladies Memorial Association (1900)

47. Lutz, D.: Death becomes her: a century of mourning attire. Vic. Lit. Cult. **44**, 217–222 (2016)

48. Hunter, T.W.: To Joy My Freedom: Southern Black Womens Lives and Labors After the Civil War. Harvard University Press (1998)

49. Swink, R.C.: Gender and division of labor associated with dying, burial, and mourning in early America. Fairmount Folio: J. Hist. **19**, 14–25 (2019)

50. Forrest, R.: Design factors in the museum visitor experience. https://espace.library.uq.edu.au/view/UQ:348658 (2015)
51. Kirchberg, V., Tröndle, M.: The museum experience: mapping the experience of fine art. Curator: The Museum J. **58**(2), 169–193 (2015). https://doi.org/10.1111/cura.12106
52. Brooke, J.: SUS: a "quick and dirty" usability scale. In: Usability Evaluation In Industry, pp. 189–194. CRC Press (1996)
53. Klug, B.: An overview of the system usability scale in library website and system usability testing. Weave: J. Libr. User Experience **1**, 36–37 (2017). https://doi.org/10.3998/weave.12535642.0001.602

Towards a Decolonial Framework for IDN

Cláudia Silva[1]([✉]) [ID], María Cecilia Reyes[2] [ID], and Hartmut Koenitz[3] [ID]

[1] ITI-LARSyS, IST (University of Lisbon), Lisboa, Portugal
claudiasilva01@tecnico.ulisboa.pt
[2] Vilniaus Universiteto, Vilnius, Lithuania
mariaceciliareyesr@gmail.com
[3] Södertörn University, Huddinge, Sweden
hartmut.koenitz@sh.se

Abstract. This paper discusses the application of decolonial thinking to Interactive Digital Narrative (IDN) with the goal of creating a decolonial framework. We provide motivation for this endeavor, and report on a workshop we conducted called *Time for Repositioning*, aiming to start a decolonizing process in the EU COST Action INDCOR (Interactive Narrative Design for Complexity Representations). Then, we analyze several exemplar IDN works which embody decolonial thinking. Finally, we offer some concrete steps for scholars to decolonialize their work which also provide the foundation of our ongoing work towards a more developed decolonial framework.

Keywords: Interactive digital narratives (IDN) · IDN analysis · IDN education · IDN practice · Decolonial theory · Decolonial framework for IDN

1 Introduction

Interactive Digital Narrative (IDN) exists within societal contexts, which means that both individual works and categorial conceptions are influenced by these contexts. In the last two decades, we have become increasingly aware of the influence hegemonical structures defined by patriarchy, coloniality and intersectional forms of repression have on many aspects of life. When it comes to mediated expressions, such oppressive structures influence the creation of works and the thinking about them. In this initial paper, we want to raise awareness of the issue and lay the foundations for a more fully developed decolonialization framework for IDN. An important step in this direction is the application of decolonial theory, a perspective which has been applied to several areas, ranging from communication studies [1], big data studies [2], to narrative-focused video games and game design in general [3], digital humanities [4] to AI [5] and general computation [6]. In this paper, we discuss the need for a decolonial framework for IDN, report on activities within the EU COST network INDCOR and present relevant use cases. We end the paper with an agenda for our continuing efforts to create a decolonial framework for IDN.

The starting point of this reflection is the insight that there are IDN artefacts which repeat stereotypes and narrative structures that perpetuate inequality and discrimination. Furthermore, there is the danger that such IDN can become the model for successful

IDNs, a phenomenon already consolidated in videogames and movies. For a long while, protagonists have been portrayed predominantly as white cisgender heterosexual men, a "White Savior," while women and non-White people were either not represented at all, relegated to a supporting role, objectified as victims needing saving or associated with negative connotations (e.g., Sinti and Roma with stealing or African American men with violent behavior) [7, 8]. Aside of such overt examples of the problem, there are also many more opaque ways of influence, e.g., by applying supposedly universal Eurocentric models in the design of narrative structures (cf. [9, 10]). Such stereotypical depictions still exist in a considerable number of video games, as Meghna Jayanth recently pointed out in a keynote for Digra (Digital Games Research Association) India [11], building on earlier work by scholars such as Kishonna L. Gray [12], Souvik Mukherjee [13] and Aaron Trammel [14]. "Gamergate" [15], a misogynist campaign against women in games, has recently demonstrated how deeply rooted such thoughts are in parts of the video games community.

Certainly, both scholars and designers in several areas related to IDN, including video games and XR, have begun to address the problem, in part as a reaction to gamergate. Consequently, efforts are in place to understand the structural issues behind oppressive representations in the artifacts themselves, but also in regard to the game community at large, and the workforce in the game industry [16]. Indeed, "Woke Gaming" [17] has been proposed as a particular practice of resistance. Conversely, while Black and female characters are increasingly added, the dominating representation in narrative-focused video games and other forms of IDN remains male and White, and focused on the Global North, as a look at the current list of bestselling games in the US shows (see below) [18]. Indeed, the only overtly non-Eurocentric game on the list aside from fantasy locations (Monster Hunter: Rise) is still set in the Global North, in the Asian part.

1. Elden Ring
2. LEGO Star Wars: The Skywalker Saga
3. Pokemon Legends: Arceus
4. Horizon Forbidden West
5. MLB The Show 22
6. Call of Duty: Vanguard
7. Gran Turismo 7
8. Kirby and the Forgotten Land
9. Mario Kart 8
10. Madden NFL 22
11. Nintendo Switch Sports
12. Minecraft
13. FIFA 22
14. Marvel's Spider-Man: Miles Morales
15. Monster Hunter: Rise
16. Animal Crossing: New Horizons
17. Super Smash Bros. Ultimate
18. Mario Party Superstars
19. Call of Duty: Black Ops: Cold War
20. Dying Light 2: Stay Human [18]

The problem which manifests here is that efforts which can be summarized under the label of 'diversity, equity, and inclusion (DEI)' do not address the deeper roots of exclusion, inequality, and historical power injustices. As Kavita Bhanot explains, the concept of diversity requires an "assumed neutral point from which 'others' are 'diverse' [which is taken as] straight, male, middle-classness" [19] and thus again makes whiteness and masculinity the dominant aspect. Similarly, John P. Hopkins alerts us to the limits of "inclusivity" by pointing out that such a move overlooks and fails to address the prior, centuries-long systematic exclusion [20]. Very often, the inclusion of marginalized communities without a decolonial approach ends with the re-marginalization of these individuals within the so-called "inclusive group". For example, if we turn the protagonist into a person of color, but if we do not address the problem of the underlying narrative structure and adhere to the highly problematic so-called "monomyth," [10] using Campbell's [21] concept of a universal hero's journey, we have done little more than window dressing. For these reasons, we emphasize the need for decolonial thinking, which is actively critical and acknowledges the historical roots of present issues while creating room for healing. Decolonization goes further than what has happened so far in the space of IDN research and design and related areas; an extensive "reckoning" which would be "reparative of the 'European' itself," [21] helping to understand Europe also from the position of those who have been racialized as non-European.

On this basis, we need to rethink our scholarly and creative practice as a community, become aware of the problematic influences of coloniality and start addressing them, which is why we conclude our paper with a series of questions-suggestions that might help scholars critically interrogate their own practice. The perspective of Ngũgĩ wa Thiong'o, as explained in [22], when we ask: *What IDNs, for whom, for what?*

2   Decolonial Thinking Workshop

The COST Action INDCOR is an EU funded network concerned with the use of Interactive Narrative Design for Complexity Representations. In this context, a decolonial perspective is a crucial epistemological endeavor. In order to convey wide-ranging and often global issues with IDN, we must have a keen awareness of the limitations of a Eurocentric view, and we need to ask ourselves whether and how it is possible to overcome such a restrictive perspective when we are a group of European researchers funded by the EU.

On May 5th, 2022, the authors held a decolonial hybrid workshop entitled *Time for Repositioning*. The event started with a brief explanation of decolonial theories, with the following premise: to understand how we can convey complex societal issues of the 21st century, we need first to decolonize our thinking and practices of producing knowledge in general and especially IDNs. This brief oral exposition was followed by a group activity in which all participants had to play a lay decolonial role-playing game called *Living Colors*. The game was developed by a group of Brazilian researchers and students about racism toward devotees of Afro-Brazilian religion. The activity was led by a Game Master, professor Eliane Bettocchi, who also led the development of *Living Colors*. Playing *Living Colors* was a disorienting and discomforting experience for some attendees. In part, this discomfort came from the fact that many workshop participants were unaware of the context of the depicted Afro-Brazilian religion and clueless about what Orisha means. The game master, an Afro Brazilian woman, did not explain this context to the workshop attendees. This was a conscious decision, as the intention of the workshop was to expose the participants to a non-Eurocentric experience. Some attendees were also confused about the meaning of "decolonial." How was the game we were playing connected to decoloniality? A further activity during the workshop was to report on the reflection of an IDN work scaffolded by a questionnaire which had been distributed along with supporting materials prior to the event. This activity led to insightful discussions about colonialist content and structure in the respective works, helped by commentary from Eliane Bettocchi.

By organizing this event, we, as a network, realized that many researchers are not aware of how coloniality shapes the social fabric and contributes to the perpetuation of problematic social and political perspectives. This aspect affects our world view, how we relate to others, but also how we approach and conduct research and the practice of creating and critiquing IDNs.

By drawing on the notion of "postcolonial computing" [6], we adopt the idea that decolonial thinking offers a conceptual tool to generate different questions and different ways of looking at the world, enabling us as creators, narrators, researchers to reread, rewrite, and reimagine the scripts of our existence, as well as our narratives. Following this rationale, we may ask: How can the COST network of researchers challenge colonialist narratives? More concretely, how can we, for example, escape the temptation of the problematic so-called "monomyth," [11, 12]. In this sense, the central concept to understanding decolonial thinking is coloniality, "which is what survives colonialism" [24].

"Coloniality names the continuity of established patterns of power between coloniser and colonised, and the contemporary remnants of these relationships and how that power shapes our understanding of culture, labour, intersubjectivity and knowledge production: what Quijano refers to as the coloniality of power". [5]

Usually, when people hear of "decolonization" they tend to think about the end of some colonial rules in the 20th century and thus about decolonial territorialization, or the dissolution of colonial relations. Decolonization, in the way we argue in this paper, has the role of "structural decolonization" which "seeks to undo colonial mechanisms of power, economics, language, culture and thinking that shapes contemporary life: interrogating the provenance and legitimacy of dominant forms of knowledge, values, norms, and assumptions" [5]. This understanding of decolonial thinking offers a framework to help deconstruct the societal complex issues of our world and can be applied to IDN research, education, and production. To expand on the latter point, in the next section, we will describe use cases of decolonial thinking in the design of IDN artifacts.

3   Applying Decolonial Thinking in IDN Design: Use Cases

In this section, we present three representative IDN artefacts produced from a decolonial thinking perspective in recent years. We have selected these works as they clearly state their position regarding historical and societal problems as a result of colonization, such as racism, occupation, and displacement of native communities, from different angles. On the one hand, the following IDNs were designed and developed by the individuals and communities who have suffered the direct effects of colonization and its impact on current society. On the other hand, each artwork displays an interactive narrative design incorporating decoloniality through its assets, structure, and mode of interaction.

We have selected these three use cases as they have already been the matter of discussion within the IDN community, showing the increasing interest of our community towards decolonial IDN design, production, and transformative impact. The first case was central to the Decolonial Workshop presented in this study, while the other two cases were part of ICIDS 2020 Art Exhibition. Although the mechanics and themes of these IDNs are very different, they share a common trait: casting the interactor in the role of the marginalized community that is represented.

3.1   Case 1. Living Colors: A Game About Afro-Identity

Authored by the Interactive Stories Research Group and Decolonial Collective, led by professor Eliane Bettocchi [3, 25], this IDN is a game for change with the mission of generating a deep transformational experience on its interactors around racism and the erasing of Brazil's African-Diasporic heritage[1]. *Living Colors* uses "online analog role-playing to present the practical and direct consequences of everyday racism, provoking a sensation of discomfort that will open the space necessary for the manifestation of an Orisha, deities of Yoruba origin revered in Candomblé, an African diasporic religion from Brazil. The Afro-Identity and Afro-Resistance goals of the IDN result in a call to action for activism in the Brazilian society.

It is worth noting, as argued by Bettocchi, that *Living Colors: A Game about AfroIdentity* also stands against hegemonic narrative structures, offering "a symbolic alternative to the Judeo-Christian and Greco-Latin imaginaries of character, hero and identity" [3]. By basing its symbolism on African-Diasporic religiosity, the authors safeguard symbols and practices from oblivion while also exposing ethnocentrism. Figure 1 shows the features of one of the "Laroyé", one of the Orishas of the game.

---

[1] *Living Colors* can be played at: https://historias.interativas.nom.br/coresvivasgame/

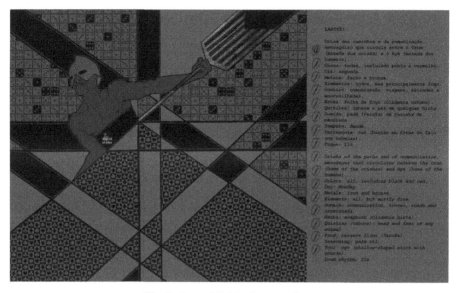

Fig. 1. Laroyé Orisha features sheet

3.2   Case 2. When the Rivers Were Trails

When Rivers Were Trails[2] is a 2D point-and-click adventure game set in the 1890's that portrays the story of an Anishinaabeg displaced from their traditional territory in Minnesota. This IDN displays the impact of colonization in the U.S.A, and the struggles of native nations during the forced displacement produced by land allotment. In this IDN, interactors play the role of an Anishinaabe person from Fond du Lac displaced from their land in Minnesota. The interactive text-based adventure makes the interactor travel from one place to the other on historically accurate maps that "emphasize the reservation lines and railroads of the time while de-emphasizing state names" [26] as shown in Fig. 2.

---

[2] *When Rivers were trails* can be played at https://indianlandtenure.itch.io/whenrivers-were-trails

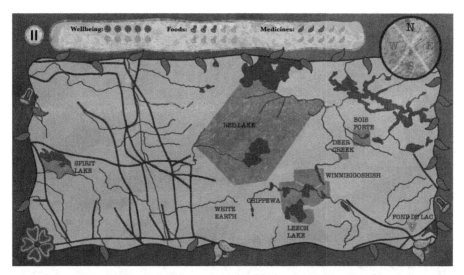

Fig. 2. Map Interface signaling Native Nations' lands

In *Placing stories, stories of place: writing When Rivers Were Trails* [26], Elizabeth LaPenseé, one of the directors of the game, describes the writing and development process of *When Rivers Were Trails* and the challenges of self-determined Indigenous representations in game writing. These challenges transcend the creative process, to deal with intellectual property issues and funding-related constrains. Such issues highlight the intersectional depth of coloniality in what it means to produce an IDN.

The content and modalities of interaction of the IDN itself can and should reflect the decolonial effort. This purpose begins with the development team's working modalities, extending to the IDN and, finally, the interactor experience. The sovereignty, therefore, is not treated just as a concept or content; it becomes a work frame for the creators and the playground for interactors to make decisions and see the world from an indigenous perspective.

3.3 Case 3. Holy Fire

Holy Fire[3] "depicts the suicidal, self-immolation protests by Tibetans against Chinese communist rule of Tibet" [27]. It was first presented at ICIDS 2020 Art Exhibition with the extreme precaution of not displaying any information that could lead to the identity of the pseudonymous author, Abraham Falcon. This web-based IDN, created with Bitsy, uses simple pixel-art aesthetics and limited interaction to convey an emotionally uncomfortable subject. Despite the apparent simplicity of the aesthetics, the author notes that complex mechanics and complicated controls add difficulty to the game [25], as shown in Fig. 3.

---

[3] *Holy Fire* can be played at https://abrahamfalcon.itch.io/holy-fire

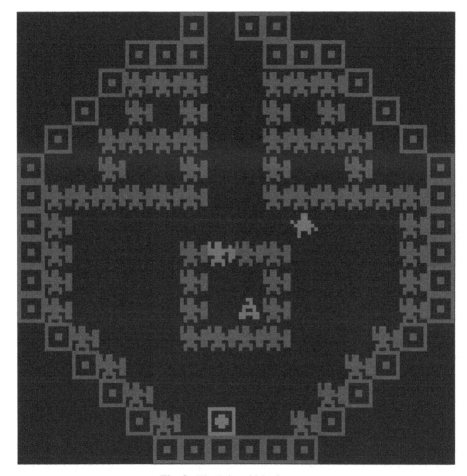

Fig. 3. The Injured Monk room.

The interaction of this IDN is inherently strenuous as interactors need to make hundreds of repetitive moves to finish the story, by playing the role of a Tibetan monk. The author describes that the player is forced to complete ritualistic movement patterns that are inspired by Tibetan Buddhist motifs. These complex and repetitive movements that can irritate represent simultaneously the struggle of a monk trying to improve the conditions of his people, without success, leading the player to the difficult choice of self-immolate in a public manifestation.

4   Towards a Decolonial Framework

The IDN works presented above show the importance of decolonial thinking during design, production, and distribution stages. The three use cases spotlight issues of historically oppressed communities in South America, North America, and Asia, giving the interactor a role in which they can perceive the world from the protagonists' perspectives, feel empathy and even discomfort, with the goal of conveying narratives of those who have been oppressed. Even more transformative, the oppressed are not only taken as subjects in the narrative or simply *given* a voice. Instead, the oppressed are the ones who have an active role in relating their own narratives, histories, oppressions, and thus claim their right for justice, recognition, and a self-determined way of living. This is the particular importance of games like *Living Colors*, a "game by Black people for Black people" [3], or *When Rivers Were Trails* [26], a game for middle-school students developed by indigenous people.

Decolonial thinking permeates the whole authoring process: from attention to the question of whose perspective is being conveyed, who it relates to, who is producing it, how it is designed and built, and which modes of interaction are offered. In addition, the question of the target audience, who will interact with the artifact, and the choice of distribution platforms are also decided from a decolonial approach.

While we certainly need to produce more decolonial IDN artifacts, it is also necessary that IDN researchers approach their academic activities from a decolonial perspective. This (re)positioning calls for researchers to learn from sources and pundits in the Global South, and include them in research, a practice that combats the hegemonic power of the English language. Furthermore, all aspects of narrative – structure, content, perspective, visual depiction, etc., should be scrutinized with the aim to avoid reinforcement of negative stereotypes and prejudices and instead deconstruct exotification and appropriation of cultural heritage. In particular, colonial stereotypes, such as, explorers from the North going to the South to save the poor and fragile, need to be avoided which is a particular challenge for games like *In 90 days* [28] intended to train aid workers.

Education is another important area for decolonial thinking. What is true for scholarly work and for IDN practice also holds for education. This means it is equally our task to educate our students in detecting, challenging, and overcoming colonialities.

With these goals in mind, and as a result of the *Time for Repositioning* workshop, we outline here three areas in which decolonial thinking can be applied by questioning our own scholarly activities. These areas are: (1) Research, (2) Networking, and (3) IDN Design. In Table 1, we propose a series of questions that can lead to best practices in applying decolonial thinking in the IDN community.

Table 1. Decolonial framework for the IDN community

Research	Networking	IDN Design
Who we cite	How we empathize	How we fantasize
Where we study	How we include	How we design
How we problematize	How we share	How we convey
How we theorize	How we co-create	How we engage
How we pass on knowledge	Who gets to speak	Who are the protagonists

To elaborate further on the questions in the Table 1, we built upon the work of [5], who propose three views related to the decolonial knowledge landscape:

– **A de-centering view**: decolonization seeks to reject an imitation of the West in all aspects of life, calling for the assertion of unique identities and a re-centering of knowledge on approaches that restore global histories, problems and solutions. Applying this view to IDNs means for instance replacing the English language as the unassailable medium of IDNs. It also means diversifying protagonists in narratives, and problematizing societal issues from a non-Eurocentric perspective.

– **An additive-inclusive view**: a view that continues using existing knowledge, but in ways that recognizes explicitly the value of new ways of creating knowledge and how it can genuinely flourish, avoiding ideas of universalism in thinking and instead advocating for localization and pluriversalism [27].

– **An engagement view**: this perspective calls for more critical views of scholarly activity. A way to implement it is to examine academic practices from the margins, to place the needs of marginalized populations at the center of the design (who we include in our narratives and IDN productions, from which standpoint, who we cite in our research and why) and research process, and to ask where knowledge comes from - who is included and left out, in whose interest is scholarly work applied and who is silenced.

As part of this effort, we also propose for researchers to clearly identify their own background by means of a Self-Disclosure Statement. We are inspired in this regard by work in the related discipline of Human Computer Interaction (HCI). In a paper on Intersectional HCI [30], the authors suggest HCI scholars should include a "Researcher Self-Disclosure" in their works to "practice" intersectional values, which is coherent with our argument of not theorizing decoloniality but overall applying this thinking in multiple ways, not only in the practice of creating, consuming, and producing IDNs, but also generating scientific knowledge about it. Similarly, feminist HCI methodology [31] reminds scholars to do the same type of disclosure of researcher's position in the world. Therefore, for this paper to practice decolonial thinking, and not just describe or introduce them academically, we aim to self-disclose our own positionality and provide this information below.

4.1 Researchers Positionality/Self Disclosure Statement

To include reflexivity in this paper, acknowledging that research is shaped by positionality – the social and political context of the researcher, and also in accordance with the feminist practice [31] of consciously assessing one's relationship to one's research, we discuss how the positionality of the authors may have given birth to this work.

INDCOR is a European network and is thus comprised of mostly White European researchers, a historical and societal position marked by privilege as a result of colonial exploitation of places in the Americas, Africa, and Asia. However, the authors of this paper, members of INDCOR, reflect a mix of different identities marked by experiences in former colonies dealing with coloniality and that of a colonizer. The first author is a Black female cisgender heterosexual, born and raised in South America, living in the Global North for the last 16 years. The second author is a female cisgender heterosexual Person of Color, born and raised in South America, and living in Europe for the last seven years. The third author is a White male, cisgender heterosexual, born, raised, and living in the Global North.

As such, authors' experiences are different regarding voice and cultural geography. Despite of this, while the unique position of marginalized/underrepresented identities of the first two authors within the network, gave us the perspective to start advocating for a decolonial perspective in IDNs and start developing this framework, our collective experience as privileged academics living in the Global North awarded us access and funding to conduct the workshop described in this paper.

5   Conclusion

In this paper, we have introduced our project of applying decolonial thinking to IDN research, education, and production. We reported on a workshop we conducted, discussed IDN works embodying decolonial thinking and introduced some concrete steps, which we hope will be adopted by the community to overcome existing colonialities.

In addition, we like to point out that our decision to develop a decolonial framework within INDCOR is not only theoretical but is tied to several epistemological practices such as inviting and sponsoring African and South Americans speakers to academic events as well as additional efforts – for example a walking tour in Lisbon focused on the colonial past and slavery history of the city[4] – aimed at decolonizing our knowledge in regards to the cultural heritage of European cities. We will continue to work on a more fully developed framework and invite other scholars to join us in this effort.

Acknowledgments. The authors acknowledge the support of the EU COST Association in the form of the COST Action 18230 INDCOR (Interactive Narrative Design for Complexity Representations). https://indcor.eu.

References

1. Moyo, L., Mutsvairo, B.: Can the subaltern think? The decolonial turn in communication research in Africa. In: Mutsvairo, B. (ed.) The Palgrave Handbook of Media and Communication Research in Africa, pp. 19–40. Springer, Cham (2018). https://doi.org/10.1007/978-3-319-70443-2_2
2. Couldry, N., Mejias, U.A.: Data colonialism: Rethinking big data's relation to the contemporary subject. Television New Media **20**(4), 336349 (2019)
3. Bettocchi, E., Klimick, C., Perani, L.: Can the subaltern game design? an exploratory study about creating a decolonial ludology framework through ludonarratives. Cep **36036**, 330 (2020)
4. Risam, R.: Decolonizing the digital humanities in theory and practice. In: The Routledge companion to media studies and digital humanities, pp. 78–86. Routledge (2018)
5. Mohamed, S., Png, M.T., Isaac, W.: Decolonial ai: decolonial theory as sociotechnical foresight in artificial intelligence. Philos. Technol. **33**(4), 659–684 (2020)
6. Philip, K., Irani, L., Dourish, P.: Postcolonial computing: a tactical survey. Sci. Technol. Human Values **37**(1), 3–29 (2012)

---

[4] https://africanlisbontour.com

7. Wilson, K.B.: Selling the White Savior Narrative: The Help, Theatrical Previews, and US Movie Audiences. Mobilized Identities: Mediated Subjectivity and Cultural Crisis in the Neoliberal Era, pp. 22–41 (2013)
8. Hoffman, D.M.: White savior or local hero?: conflicting narratives of help in haiti. Georgetown J. Int. Aff. **23**(1), 99–104 (2022)
9. Jennings, P.: Narrative structures for new media. Leonardo **29**, 345–350 (1996)
10. Koenitz, H., Di Pastena, A., Jansen, D., de Lint, B., Moss, A.: The myth of 'universal' narrative models. In: Rouse, R., Koenitz, H., Haahr, M. (eds.) ICIDS 2018. LNCS, vol. 11318, pp. 107–120. Springer, Cham (2018). https://doi.org/10.1007/978-3-030-04028-4_8
11. Jayanth, M.: White Protagonism and Imperial Pleasures in Game Design #DIGRA21. https://medium.com/@betterthemask/white-protagonism-and-imperialpleasures-in-game-design-digra21-a4bdb3f5583c (2021)
12. Gray, K.L.: Deviant bodies, stigmatized identities, and racist acts: examining the experiences of African-American gamers in Xbox Live. New Rev. Hypermedia Multimedia **18**, 261–276 (2012). https://doi.org/10.1080/13614568.2012.746740
13. Mukherjee, S.: Playing subaltern: video games and postcolonialism. Games Cult. **13**, 504–520 (2018). https://doi.org/10.1177/1555412015627258
14. Trammell, A.: Decolonizing play. Crit. Stud. Media Commun. **39**, 239–246 (2022). https://doi.org/10.1080/15295036.2022.2080844
15. Quinn, Z.: Crash override: How gamergate (nearly) destroyed my life, and how we can win the fight against online hate. PublicAffairs (2017)
16. Gray, K.L., Leonard, D.J.: Woke Gaming: Digital Challenges to Oppression and Social Injustice. University of Washington Press (2018)
17. Peckham, E.: Confronting racial bias in video games. https://techcrunch.com/2020/06/21/confronting-racial-bias-in-video-games/. Accessed 13 Oct 2022
18. IDG: MultiVersus Debuted as the Best-Selling Game in the US Last Month. https://nordic.ign.com/elden-ring/59311/news/multiversus-debuted-as-the-best-selling-game-in-the-us-last-month. Accessed 13 Oct 2022 (2022)
19. Banhot, K.: Decolonise, not Diversify. Media Diversified. Retrieved 21 Sep 2022. https://mediadiversified.org/2015/12/30/is-diversity-is-only-for-white-people/ (2015)
20. Hopkins, J.P.: Indigenous education reform: a decolonizing approach. In: Indigenous philosophies of education around the world, pp. 129–147. Routledge (2018)
21. Campbell, J.: The Hero with a Thousand Faces. Harper & Row (1949)
22. Gopal, P.: On decolonisation and the university. Textual Pract. **35**(6), 873–899 (2021)
23. Wa Thiong'o, N.: Decolonising the mind: The politics of language in African literature. East African Publishers (1992)
24. Quijano, A.: Coloniality of power and Eurocentrism in Latin Americas. Int. Sociol. **15**(2), 215–232 (2000)
25. Bettocchi, E., Klimick, C., Perani, L.: Ludopoética e didática ludonarrativa para ensino e criação de jogos decoloniais. In: O lúdico em redes: reflexões e práticas no Ensino de Ciências da Natureza [recurso eletrônico]/Joaquim Fernando Mendes da Silva (Org.). Porto Alegre, RS: Editora Fi (2021)
26. LaPenseé, E.: Placing stories, stories of place: writing when rivers were trails. In Reyes, M.C., Pope, J. (eds.) Texts of Discomfort: Interactive Storytelling Art (2021)
27. Falcon, A.: Creating discomforts: game design and personal reflections on authoring Holy Fire. In: Reyes, M.C., Pope, J. (eds.) Texts of Discomfort: Interactive Storytelling Art (2021)

28. In 90 Days: https://kayaconnect.org/course/info.php?id=3149. Accessed 13 Oct 2022
29. Mignolo, W.: Local Histories/Global Designs: Coloniality, Subaltern Knowledges, and Border Thinking. Princeton University Press (2012)
30. Schlesinger, A., Edwards, W.K., Grinter, R.E.: Intersectional HCI: Engaging identity through gender, race, and class. In: Proceedings of the 2017 CHI Conference on Human Factors in Computing Systems, pp. 54125427 (2017)
31. Bardzell, S., Bardzell, J.: Towards a feminist HCI methodology: social science, feminism, and HCI. In: Proceedings of the SIGCHI Conference on Human Factors in Computing Systems, pp. 675–684 (2011)

Applying Black Feminist Technopractice in Digital Storytelling at Cultural Sites

Brandy Pettijohn[✉]

Georgia Institute of Technology, Atlanta, GA, USA
bpettijohn3@gatech.edu

Abstract. We have been habituated to a type of story about Black American experience, and this habituation – the idea that we know a story before we encounter it – can influence how we embark on creating digital narratives for Black cultural and historic sites. The promise of digital media is that we might be able to tell fuller and richer stories; however, technical affordances can place the story in service of technology instead of the story being guided along by technology. Therefore, the ethical dilemma is how can a project, where agency and meaning-making are central concepts for success, be created for a topic that designers actually know little about? Cultural sensitivities need to be considered for digitally mediated cultural and historic environments and unintentional harm to both the story and the people who will come in contact with it can occur if adjustments are not made throughout the design process. These sensitivities will inevitably affect the scope of agency and meaning-making because the variables within the story are more fixed. While technological affordances can help remediate story habituation, in order to avoid some of the pitfalls of harmful storytelling, makers should consider theoretical frameworks to guide their practice. This essay proposes Black Feminist Techhnopractice as a theoretical framework to guide methods in creating interactive narratives for Black cultural sites. Black feminist technopractice is a theoretical framework that guides practices and essentially combines Black feminist design (researchers) and Black technoculture (participants) into a technopractice.

Keywords: Cultural narratives · Black feminist technopractice · Agency

1 Introduction

It's the 1960s and a well-dressed, visibly humble Black man wants to eat lunch. He attempts to eat at a local restaurant where he is rebuked by an increasingly aggressive and even violent white crowd led by a segregationist owner. Communal outrage ensues that eventually brings about a charismatic leader, or maybe said well-dressed and visibly humble man is led to become one himself. Eventually, this leader and his followers' actions bring about legal and ethical change. The once hostile white staff and owner recede into the periphery of the story. Eventually, said well-dressed and visibly humble Black man is able to enter the formerly hostile environment to enjoy a sandwich and maybe even a milkshake. Racism is fixed, hooray!

© The Author(s), under exclusive license to Springer Nature Switzerland AG 2022
M. Vosmeer and L. Holloway-Attaway (Eds.): ICIDS 2022, LNCS 13762, pp. 206–213, 2022.
https://doi.org/10.1007/978-3-031-22298-6_13

This is a basic storyline that permeates storytelling about the Civil Rights Movement of the 1960s. The historical tropes surrounding the Civil Rights Movement allow people to think that they know the story, even before encountering the specifics of the story. Some of us who have a stake in knowing more about the Civil Rights Movement understand that this frame of storytelling is trite and seldom tells the whole story and that this type of storytelling has disappeared the work of women, queer, and ordinary working-class people from history. This narrative also foregrounds the importance of visualizing physical violence against Black people as integral to the storytelling process. Furthermore, this storytelling tells incomplete endings that eliminate the complexities of the outcomes of these actions. What if we learned that the well-dressed, humble Black man was not one but several young men *and* women? What if these people were part of a larger system of organizations that had been part of a multi-year, multi-faceted set of organized desegregation activities? What if that group of people was approached by the attorney general of the United States and encouraged to continue said actions? What if they never wanted to eat at the restaurant at all? What if the hostile owner became governor?

The stories that we are used to consuming about Black Americans in general, and the Civil Rights Movement specifically, lead makers towards habituation of storytelling praxis. Answering these questions complicates what we think we know about history, but more importantly, it gives practitioners the opportunity to use the affordances of digital media in a manner that disrupts the habituation in order to tell fuller and richer stories.

This paper is guided by my own experience of doing historical research for an interactive digital narrative project on a pivotal anti-segregation action that is a part of Civil Rights history much like the one described above. The project that I worked on is a site-specific augmented reality storytelling project, meaning it is situated on or very close to the actual site where Civil Rights protests took place. The stated goal of the project is to highlight the protesters over the segregationist who was famous and powerful. My role in the group was to conduct historical research to find out more information about a core group of three protesters. I came to learn that the design team, who had been diligently working on the technological aspects of the site for a year, knew very little about the people and the mitigating factors around the events that they were designed for. The problem is that if there is only knowledge of basic history, more than likely, a basic story is what will be told. As I saw it, this was an ethical challenge. How do you create a project where agency and meaning-making are central concepts for success, for a topic that you know little about? What assumptions are created when making digital and physical spaces and how reliant are designers on their own habituations versus that of the actual history or the desires of the audience?

It is assumed that designers have an understanding of the technological affordances and rules of interactive narrative that guide their making practice; however, these practices may or may not be tied to non-fiction environments. By only having marginal information about the story, the power dynamic then places most of the focus on technological affordances, which puts the story in service of the technology instead of the technology servicing the story. This becomes especially problematic because there will always be cultural sensitivities that need to be considered when making Black cultural sites and by not making these adjustments can cause unintentional harm to both the story and the people who will come in contact with it. These sensitivities will inevitably affect the scope of agency and meaning-making because the variables within the story, such as time and place of activity, amount of people, outcomes, and mood are fixed. To avoid some of the pitfalls of harmful storytelling, makers should consider theoretical frameworks to guide their practice. This essay proposes Black Feminist Techhnopractices as a theoretical framework to guide methods in creating interactive narratives for non-fiction productions.

2   Black Feminist Technopractice

Black feminist technopractice is rooted in the frameworks of Black feminist thought (BFT). BFT honors the standpoints of the lived experience of marginalized people as an intellectual starting point [2, 5, 6, 9]. Scholars of BFT confront institutional oppression by bringing the stories of marginalized groups to the center, deploying an ethic of care and the politics of pleasure into their projects. Black feminist frameworks seek to increase the understanding and knowledge of both researchers and participants by decreasing the distance that institutional power plays in the relationship between the two. Black feminist technopractice is a theoretical framework that guides practices and essentially combines Black feminist design (researchers) and Black technoculture (participants) into a *technopractice*.

Black feminist design is most evident in feminist and participatory design practice, where scholars such as Christina Harrington and Sasha Constanza-Chock position design as an opportunity to correct power dynamics between design and participants [3, 4]. This type of making engages both the desires and agency of people who can affect stories and how they are told. Scholars Andre Brock and Catherine Knight Steele expound on Black technoculture as existing communication structures that inform technological uses [1, 9]. Andre Brock specifically discusses the libidinal economies inherent in this Black technoculture - these are communication patterns that can help illuminate desires and engagement practices among Black people in digitally mediated spaces. In order to create culturally specific and sensitive environments, these elements need to be deployed together to reduce harm and help create an environment that inspires true meaning-making.

Contextualizing this for the project that I worked on, means thinking about possibly telling a story about Civil Rights history without white people.t This may seem inconceivable; however, it can be done using a Black feminist frame of oppositional gaze [5] which disrupts power dynamics, particularly in visual storytelling. With a Black feminist technoscience perspective in the construction of Black cultural sites we would ask, how much physical and story space should whiteness take up when the focus is supposed to be on African Americans? This leads to a centering question where designers should also ask whose meaning-making are we working toward. It must be said that focusing on whites, even if they are positioned as "bad actors" in the story, still centralizes them within the narratives versus solely on the actions of the activists and their work.

People's attention spaces are shorter than ever, which means as makers of these sites we have just a short amount of time to connect to an audience. Immersion is also an important factor in these environments. This means that designers should make the most of the liberatory aspects of the story and the space available rather than the binaries of good and bad actors. Centering on the activists' experience can have a more focused and pleasurable effect on the audience. Pleasure as an ethic is an anti-oppression counter-narrative tactic that has been building among Black feminist scholars over the past decade with the goals of moving discourse away from pathology, grief, and suffering towards examining joy and pleasure in spite of oppression. The rubric that I use for pleasure comes from Joan Morgan's discussion of Black feminist pleasure as being desire, agency, and engagement [6]. When we think of the possibilities of cultural and site-specific environments, these elements can inform the types of possibilities for meaning-making and immersion at a site. Reframing a project with the desires, agency, and engagement of the people who will come in contact with the story is what it means to leverage technoculture.

3   Historic Research

In order to get a scope of information about the Civil Rights activities at the site, I searched for information about the scope of the environment around the story, which was the South in the mid-1960s. As could be expected, there was a lot of information on aspects of the Civil Rights Movement, namely Freedom Rides, desegregation campaigns from restaurants, hotels, and swimming pools, and a looming election. Once I identified the institution the activists were a part of, I found artifacts from people outside of the core group at the institution that guided me to materials and information that was important to fill up some of the gaps of information that we did not know. In the archives, I found correspondence between secretaries at different organizations that talked about magazine articles that I had not previously identified. I also found audio recordings of lectures by professors who empathized with Black activists. These recordings were affirming the activities by students and other activists during the exact time period where the Civil Rights actions were taking place. While I tried, I was unable to connect with the actual participants or their families due to the deaths of the core participants. However, I was able to find first-person accounts, including memoirs, and a final thesis paper from one of the key participants. Oral histories from activists that were not in the core group of activists but had previously targeted the segregationist years prior added context to why the particular restaurant was a target. By taking the time and doing more digging, I was able to come up with more audio, video, and photographic archival materials that could be used at the site or other platforms that could enrich the digital narrative about the action, the city, and people involved.

Ultimately, research led me to findings that would impact both the physical and the augmented space. First, it illuminated that the activist activity was the work of four men and not three. The physical site had been created to be a commemorative space to honor three men with three physical markers – the lack of in-depth research erased one of the main participants from the space. Depending on the date of the protest, because there were several, there were larger groups of participants ranging from the core four to at least ten. In the augmented space, adding more people changes how the space is designed and feels. When standing in an augmented space surrounded by a violent mob, how does it change a participant's perspective to see ten Black people versus four? Using Black feminist technopractice, culling these seemingly disparate pieces from the archive might have eliminated the need to center violence or the mob at all. In general, these findings could change the narrative that had already been landscaped in augmented reality. In the case of our project, the story and augmentation had already been tied to the binary Black vs. white. My interventions added context to the story in the form of short videos that could be augmented into the site as people entered the main project space, or engaged in other digital platforms. While these videos are not dynamic in the way participants encounter and maneuver around augmented scapes, they do immersively ground participants to the physical space and are meant to act as an invitation. Engaging in Black feminist technopractice means understanding core elements of history and thinking of different ways to break our habituations of storytelling to implement them into the environment to tell a fuller story.

Based on the historical findings, implementing Black feminist technopractice could help the designers ask what and where are the critical points of interest, and what narrative is being centered, and why. In the project that I worked on the perspective of the activists was said to be privileged; however, the mob was hyper-present in the space. By having participants of the site view the activities of a violent segregationist and negotiate their feelings about being among the mob centers creates a point of meaning towards the mob and their activities. While the site says they want to privilege the work and voices of the activists, the apparent habituations within the experience actually have all the points of meaning-making at the intersections of the binary that puts the violence on the same level of importance as the activism.

4   Agency

Agency has been presented as one of the most important aspects of interactive narratives and digital storytelling. In *Hamlet on the Holodeck*, Janet Murray states that "agency is the satisfying power to take meaningful action and see the results of our decisions and choices" [8]. Likewise, Tannenbaum and Tannenbaum (2010) note that agency is a "commitment to meaning," both of these discussions are primarily about games [10] but the ideas about agency are foundational to the approach of digital narratives. Even though the experience that was being created was a non-fictional story, the logic of games was present and while on the surface these aspects of agency do not predict a harmful environment, they create a power dynamic where the desires of the designers and game-making praxis are privileged. Without knowledge of the story beyond its habituated state then what can be created is false agency.

False agency in a digital narrative is dangerous at Black cultural sites, because it is full of choices that no one would make, and creates no extended meaning outside of what people feel like they already know about the story. When false agency is present, participants can switch out of the story, because they no longer have a stake in learning about it, and into a game-player mode who is interested in the affordances of technology; i.e. whether or not they can push avatars around, confront antagonists, or move objects. The participants then become immersed in the technology and have no stake in the digital narrative - and this would be fine if we were not talking about relevant events in US history. Without relevant cultural knowledge or knowledge of the story and environment, I do not know how agency via meaning-making is successfully rendered without leveraging the technopractices of the story and audience that you are designing for. This meaning-making in digital spaces can be fleshed out through the Black feminist technopractice by truly connecting to the desires of the participants [11]. The desires of participants are not hidden. By finding ways to engage with the potential of desire via Black feminist technopractice addresses lopsided power dynamics between technology, story, and participating audience.

One of the prominent claims of scholars of Black technoculture is that the internet is a space where various ways of worldmaking and meaning are constructed [1, 9]. There are meaningful cues that can be found by doing analysis of Black technoculture that can foretell what the culture of the audience (or audiences) privileges when engaging in digital environments. If agency is connected to meaning-making, then being able to connect to some essence of what is showing up can help designers either connect with resonate themes or steer clear of issues that are relevant in online activities. An example of the way agency is enacted in cultural politics and meaning-making is changing online can be seen in the ways people are starting to shift in the wake of incessant videos of Black people being killed by police.

4.1 Cultural Shifts Impact on Agency

Over the last decade, social media has been flooded with videos of Black people being body slammed, beaten, shot, and killed by police. These visuals become commodified as they move from social media into news media, through Hollywood's television and movie productions, and then bounce back into virtual, augmented, and mixed-reality productions. During this period, Black people on social media have seen the sharing of these videos as both important as an element of witnessing; as a way to cultivate an environment where justice might be served as well as a cultural honoring of life. This type of content hit its crescendo in 2020 with the video footage of the murder of George Floyd where no one could escape hearing his cries or seeing him die. Black people were traumatized by this witnessing.

The libidinal economy of shared expressions of pain and exhaustion [1] within the social media feeds started to spread with people (both academically and spiritually) asking if they actually needed to see the footage, while others asked for people to stop sharing it altogether. In the years since Floyd's murder, more police shootings have been caught on dashcam footage, and they are being shared, but anecdotally, I've noticed more calls for these videos not to be shared. Sentiment analysis would need to be done to see the actual change of habits among social media users over time, but what seems clear is the feeling of "importance" around these videos is waning. This marks a new era of a refusal to participate in digitally mediated deaths of Black people and new practices of witnessing and activism around the deaths of Black people among social media participants are starting to be created.

What this means for digital storytelling and Black cultural interactive environments, of course, is a shift in the ways people want to experience Black cultural experiences and how they make meaning within these environments. The agency of social media participants is inherent in the refusal. For our project, a newer member of our team, a young

Black man, asked for a trigger warning at the beginning of the site experience. If we look closely, what is being witnessed in various media environments is an expressed desire to shift away from being visually inundated by pain, suffering, and trauma. Therefore, when we have sites that are dedicated to the Black experience they do not have to always be painful nor do they have violence in them. Black technopractice, again leveraging the design with the technoculture, means that many decisions about what is important need to be constructed that not just breaks habitual modes of storytelling but also keeps the emotional well-being of potential audience members in mind.

5 Conclusion

In the digital narrative that I worked on, the real ending to the story is that the antagonist was able to make money off of signed ax handles that were used as weapons against Black people, he made hundreds of thousands of dollars off the sale of the property, and eventually he became governor. Needless to say this is not exactly a satisfying end and thus most of these details are left out of the narrative. In Murray's article "Did It Make You Cry?" she notes that "we want the characters, events, and settings to fit together in a way that intrigues us... We want to care about the fate of the individual characters and see the events in the imaginary world as fitting our deeper sense of how life is" [7]. Unfortunately, there are many messy endings when it comes to the Civil Rights Movement, and it is an uncomfortable truth that it did not solve or end racism. I suspect and understand that the creators of digital narratives like the one that I am working on are hesitant to engage in a story's ending that is less than desirable. However, this is where the affordances of digital media along with the theoretical grounding of Black feminist technopractice to help bring satisfaction, curiosity, and pleasure back into storytelling at Black cultural sites.

My work is grounded in Black feminism, which privileges the stories of the marginalized. If I had it my way, there would have been far less whiteness at our historic site. There would be more speculative conversations based on artifacts that were found in my research among the Black people to whom the project was focused and of the people and organizations that surrounded it. There would definitely be more points of the digital narrative where the sole purpose would be to disrupt the ways we have come to learn about Civil Rights history. All of these histories are messy, but that is precisely the opportunity that digital media has to offer in digital narratives. Designers need to trust the audiences to make meaning out of a story that has less habituated points across it. Having people walk away from historical experiences thinking that "the good guys won" allows people to think that racism as something that only happened in the past and it ended when Black people and white people could sit next to each other at a lunch counter. These are false and dangerous narratives that serve no one. Using Black feminist technopractice allows participants to use their curiosity to explore characters' trajectories, learn about the institutions that informed their activism, and bring them to the current moment without traumatization or habituation.

References

1. Brock, A.: Distributed Blackness: African American Cybercultures. New York University Press (2020)
2. Collins, H.P.: Black feminist thought: Knowledge, consciousness, and the politics of empowerment. Routledge (2002)
3. Costanza-Chock, S.: Design Justice: Community-Led Practices to Build the Worlds we Need. The MIT Press, Massachusetts (2020)
4. Edwards, E.R.: Charisma and the Fictions of Black Leadership. University of Minnesota Press (2012)
5. Harrington, C., Erete, S., Piper, A.M.: Deconstructing community-based collaborative design. In: Proceedings of the ACM on Human-Computer Interaction, 3(CSCW), pp. 1–25 (2019)
6. Hooks, B.: Black Looks: Race and Representation. South End Press, Massachusetts (1992)
7. Morgan, J.: Why we get off: moving towards a black feminist politics of pleasure. The Black Scholar **45**(4), 36–46 (2015)
8. Murray, J.: Did it make you cry? creating dramatic agency in immersive environments. In: Subsol, G. (ed.) ICVS 2005. LNCS, vol. 3805, pp. 83–94. Springer, Heidelberg (2005). https://doi.org/10.1007/11590361_10
9. Murray, J.H.: Hamlet on the Holodeck: The Future of Narrative in Cyberspace. The MIT Press (2016)
10. Steele, C.K.: Digital Black feminism. New York University Press (2021)
11. Tanenbaum, K., Theresa, J.T.: Agency as commitment to meaning: communicative competence in games. Dig. Creativity **21**(1), 11–17 (2010)
12. Wardrip-Fruin, N., Mateas, M., Dow, S., Sali, S.: Agency Reconsidered. In: DiGRA - Proceedings of the 2009 DiGRA International Conference: Breaking New Ground: Innovation in Games, Play, Practice and Theory. Brunel University (2009)

Interactive Narrative Design

Dramatic Situations for Emergent Narrative System Authorship

Jonathan Lessard[(✉)] ⓘD and Samuel Paré-Chouinard

Concordia University, Montréal, Québec, Canada
jonathan.lessard@concordia.ca

Abstract. When designing and developing an emergent narrative system, one finds themselves in the difficult situation of working with low-level mechanisms while aspiring for high-level, longer-term emergent outcomes. To make things worse, the desired output is not even a concrete artifact but an ambiguous mental construct: something recognized as a story by a human. We think that dramatic situations, as conceptualized by Georges Polti, can act as a useful in-between heuristic: they are objective enough to inform the design of low-level operations, but abstract enough so as not to overdetermine the output.

We have embedded 18 dramatic situations in the possibility space of our emergent narrative system and have documented three emergent stories through a constrained process. We find that identifying a dramatic situation prompts the construction of a story as it incites tracing its causes and finding out its outcome. Observing the behavior of the involved parties significantly contributes to their characterization. As dramatic situations are relatively rare in a character's life and typically have high stakes, they are likely to be noteworthy.

A potential issue is the discernable recurrence of some dramatic situation emergent patterns which might negatively impact players' interest, a common problem of procedural generation. We hypothesize that this issue might be alleviated by the unique situatedness of players and their characters in the world as they encounter these patterns, creating special conditions of relevance.

Keywords: Emergent narrative · Dramatic situations · Authoring · Tellability · Retellings

1 Authoring Heuristics for Emergent Narrative Systems

The notion of emergent narrative is not new to interactive storytelling researchers, and it is now gaining traction in the general public (see Gordon 2020, for example). Yet it remains an open design problem. While there are examples of digital games recognized for their emergent narrative potential, they are relatively rare and heterogeneous. For the would-be designer of an emergent narrative game, there are still no basic templates to follow and very few general design guidelines available. Where does the design of an emergent narrative system (ENS) even begin?

M. Vosmeer and L. Holloway-Attaway (Eds.): ICIDS 2022, LNCS 13762, pp. 217–228, 2022.
https://doi.org/10.1007/978-3-031-22298-6_14

According to James Ryan, a common approach hinges on the hope for "stories to emerge bottom-up from the behavior of autonomous characters in a simulated story-world" (2015). In other words, the authoring does not actually happen at the narrative level, but at the much lower level of world modeling and computational simulation. The question is then: what can inform the design of low-level mechanisms in order to maximize the chances of seeing "good stories" emerge once everything has been put together? Are we bound to time-consuming, expensive trial and error? A key problem with this form of second-order authoring is well summed up by early emergent narrative (EN) theorist Ruth Aylett: "one of the risks of emergent narrative is that it may not emerge" (1999). How can we avoid this?

Louchart et al. (2008) frame emergent narrative systems (ENS) as "story landscapes" in which peaks would represent states of "dramatic intensity" connected by more relaxed and open-ended valleys. As they navigate the possibility space, players end up ascending these hills which culminate in some narrative climax. They note, however, that this metaphor is mostly useful to conceptualize the problem space and "provides no obvious authoring solutions because the author creates this story landscape only indirectly". If we want to make sure some memorable moments emerge out of interacting with my ENS, how do we go about concretely authoring for those peaks? What are "rules of thumb" that EN authors can follow to improve the likelihood of interesting stories emerging from their system?

Tarn Adams, designer of *Dwarf Fortress* (CITE)—a game often lauded for its emergent narrative potential—recommends considering potential player stories first, and then proceed to deduct the low-level components that would be required for their emergence (2019). He warns: "if you don't think about player stories in advance, you might find yourself getting invested in trivial matters[.]" He gives as an example: "A kobold crept into the workshop and stole Urist's masterpiece scepter. Urist was distraught for days afterward." From this he can identify the need for characters that steal, stealth mechanics, item ownership, item value, character feelings, etc.

The Sims (CITE) games—arguably the most successful emergent narrative game—approach this even more concretely by authoring and embedding virtual story trees in the event-space. Studio creative director Matt Brown gives the example of the player-driven "star-gazing" action which can trigger a sequence of potential desires: own a telescope, use it, discover a new planet, join a science career, and ultimately become an astronaut (CITE). When realized, this chain generates a satisfying narrative: "I gave her a telescope when she was a kid and now, she's an astronaut!".

These precedents certainly point towards the fruitful path of identifying higher-order narratives as targets to inform the design of the lower-level mechanisms that will allow them to emerge. However, the examples are both very domain dependent, one being very "dwarf-fortressy" with its allusions to workshops and masterpiece craftsmanship; and the other very "simsy" with its focus on object ownership and career choice. How can we generalize this approach? Are there types of story-structures that are particularly suited for ENS design? What would be the requirements for such compatibility? What we would need is a mid-level goal: something more abstract than low-level simulation mechanisms, but less specific than an actual story—something that would help bridge the gap between these two poles.

In a discussion on avoiding "boringness" in ENS authoring, Ryan evokes one of his later intuitions:

> While early on I did model (either explicitly or implicitly) some basic Schankian absolute interests (sex, danger, death), it is at a higher level of dynamic interaction between the actions that produce such intrigue that literary themes such as betrayal emerge. […] It is possible to target tried-and-true literary themes like underdog stories, narratives of betrayal, and so forth. Again, this is a matter of sculpting the simulation's narrative possibility space […] to support emergent phenomena that matches these themes (p. 112).

Ryan describes this at work in his latest simulation, *Hennepin*, but does not theorize the idea further. This notion of "literary theme" is compelling because it is more general than an actual story, less idiosyncratic. However, it is also vague and lacks the immediate actionability of "we want stories about thieving kobolds and so we need kobolds that thieve and things to steal". In this paper, we want to pick up on this thread and define a more operational mid-level narrative concept that would help inform ENS design while not committing to overly specific story types.

Our hypothesis is that the notion of dramatic situation, as initially theorized by Georges Polti (1912), could prove to be a fruitful emergent narrative authoring heuristic: a mid-level phenomenon that could bridge the design of low-level mechanics to the desired output of actualized narratives. We will begin by explaining this concept and how we see its relevance to the context of ENS authoring. We will then describe how we have implemented this approach in our own project. The results will be assessed through a retelling approach yielding three documented narratives and their analysis.

2 Dramatic Situations for Emergent Narrative

The dramaturgical notion of "dramatic situations" is usually traced to George Polti's *Les Trente-six Situations Dramatiques* (1912) in which the playwright and theatre theoretician proposed a tentatively exhaustive list as could be extracted from a large range of historical and (then) contemporary works. These encapsulate a set of abstract character roles, their relationships and conflicting aspirations. For example, the first situation described, "the supplication", requires a persecutor, a supplicant, and an "indecisive power". This work has been often cited and is still a common staple of screenwriting manuals and even digital games writing resources (Higgins 2008).

Although this list might suggest a "cookie-cutter" approach to authoring, Polti's ambition was not to provide a static inventory of all possible intrigues, but rather encourage the generation of new ideas. His position was that relying on one's "imagination" (he derides this romantic notion) only leads to the endless rehashing of one's own repertoire of themes. He advocates for a more "scientific" method of voluntary combinations of situations leading to an almost infinite variety of new plots. In a sense, he was an early enthusiast of procedural storytelling. Here we identify features of dramatic situations that support their potential as heuristics for authoring emergent narrative systems.

2.1 Sequence-Independent/Sequence-Productive

Stories are generally understood as meaningful causal sequences of events. The problem with using actual stories as templates for ENS authoring is that they are stifled by dependencies and leave little room for variation and significant emergence. For Oedipus to end up marrying his own mother, he must have been born from a king, there must have been a sinister prophecy, a failed attempt to kill him as baby, adopters keeping him in ignorance of his heritage and the unsuspecting murder of his own father. Now if we wanted to generate stories *like* Oedipus, how would we break away from this specific chain of events?

Szilas et al. (2016) had already noted that "a dramatic situation describes a narrative in a static manner" which can "provide potentialities for interesting developments of the story so far, without explicitly providing a temporal order". In other words, dramatic situations are not sequences but states; they are independent of the specific circumstances that have led to them; and of the consequences that will result from their outcome.

Oedipus showcases at least two of Polti's situations: "Slaying of kin unrecognized" (#19) and "Involuntary crimes of love" (#18). We could generate Oedipus-like stories by implementing one or both of these—that is creating the low-level mechanics that would embed these situations in the simulation's possibility space. For "Slaying of kin unrecognized" we would need notions of kinship, murder, as well as a knowledge model allowing characters to not be always fully aware of kin relationships. This would lead to a wide array of potential stories: siblings separated at birth then killing each other on the battlefield as enemies, or an old woman coming back from a long trip and having a fatal dispute with her unrecognized grandchild.

Of course, these stories are quite different from *Oedipus*, but they retain one of the dramatic features that make this story poignant. And, of course, that the stories be different is exactly the point of the whole process. We want emergent narrative systems to surprise us. If we really wanted exactly *Oedipus*, we could just adapt it as is. Let's note, however, that the salt of Oedipus' story is the succession of these two particular dramatic situations, one leading to the other, and in the process refreshing and renewing each other in their interaction. This is how Polti saw the generative efficacy of his situations: in their modularity and great potential for combinations, interactions, enfolding, etc. It is through the process of their actualization in concrete contexts that dramatic situations give rise to stories: specific sequences of events.

In short: dramatic situations allow for emergence by being independent from specific sequences of events upstream and downstream; however, they are generative of such recognizable story sequences through their actualization.

2.2 Character-Independent/Character-Productive

Many narratives hinge on the psychology of characters to make sense and seem plausible. Swiper, the fox villain of *Dora the Explorer*, is a kleptomaniac; this fact explains and justifies that in every circumstance, he will attempt to steal something. That's just how he is. This characterization constitutes a dependency for these stories. Polti, who is concerned with stage drama, sees things differently: "a unique process creates at the same time the episodes, or actions of the characters, and the characters themselves, because they are on the stage only what they do" (p. 206, my translation). In other words, "character" does not necessarily precede a dramatic situation (and so is not a strong requirement) but can instead be its product. In his existentialist theorization of theatre, Sartre also proposed a "theater of situations" (1976). He argued that a psychology-driven theater is deterministic and void of liberty: characters act because of what they are and therefore nothing is at stake since everything is already played out. To this, he opposes:

> [B]ut if it's true that man is free in a given situation and that in and through that situation he chooses what he will be, then what we have to show in the theater are simple and human situations and free individuals in these situations choosing what they will be. [...] The most moving thing the theater can show is a character creating himself the moment of choice, of the free decision which commits him to a moral code and a whole way of life (p. 4).

Can someone be said to be courageous before ever facing a dangerous situation? Beyond philosophical considerations, this is useful for emergent narratives. Dramatic situations can accommodate a very wide range of potential characters, thus affording a large number of variations. The actors of a "slaying of kin unrecognized" can be young, old, smart, dumb, attractive, jealous, vengeful, ambitious, introverted, etc. as long as they are kin, don't know they are kin, and that one of them kills the other. Perhaps the killer was already known to be violent, but we can also find out that they "had that in them" by witnessing their chosen course of action when faced with the dramatic situation. Perhaps this is the salt of this specific story: who knew they had that in them? They had never hurt a fly before that moment! This is particularly valuable in a medium (digital games) that does not always shine at conveying subtle psychological internal states, but can deliver a good visual spectacle: "show, don't tell".

This approach is not necessarily incompatible with a character personality model. Our project, for example, does have a "trait" system that will influence the behavior of characters. However, we can choose whether some traits are "innate" while some are acquired depending on the course of action chosen by the character when faced with a specific situation. This means that once a precedent has been established, chances of repeated behavior are increased.

An additional bonus of dramatic situations' character independence is they can therefore easily connect to the player-character. In traditional interactive storytelling, we need to ensure the player-character enacts the key beats of the story; this is what Fernandez-Vara calls "restoration of behavior" (2009). If dramatic situations are part of the possibility space, player-characters will eventually stumble in them and, in the process, genuinely participate in the generation of their own story.

In sum, dramatic situations do not require prior characterization and are therefore compatible with a wide range of potential characters (allowing for emergence and player-involvement); as they face the situation, however, these characters acquire characterization for the observers.

2.3 Tellable and Eventful

Let's reiterate that our goal is to maximize the likelihood of interesting, story-like sequences emerging amongst what James Ryan calls "the morass of data that [the game's] simulation produces" (2015, p. 7). The field of narratology conceptualizes this as the "tellability" of a story, it's "noteworthiness", "narratability", "reportability", or "it's point" (Baroni 2004). When zooming in on the proceedings that constitute story, we can also evoke notion of "eventfulness": when does an event become an *Event*? (Hühn 2013) What's the qualitative difference between closing a door, and closing a door definitely when leaving a long-term relationship? The latter, which Hühn designates as "type II events", makes a tellable story.

What evidence do we have that embedding dramatic situations in our ENS' possibility space might increase the likelihood of "type II events" occurring? The first argument is the empirical one defended by Polti (who predates narratology): these situations appear in a large number of classical and popular narratives. This prevalence in successful works suggests a participation in their interestingness. How many plays, novels, and films hinge on "crime pursued by vengeance", for example?

Theories on eventfulness also tends to support that these situations are likely to constitute "type II events". For example, Hühn (2013) cites Schmid's five properties that modulate eventfulness: unpredictability (deviation from expectations), effect (consequences), irreversibility, non-iterativity (singularity) and relevance. *Oedipus'* "slaying of kin, unrecognized", for example, checks all these boxes. These situations are called "dramatic" for a reason, they capture moments of high-stake tensions. It seems reasonable that within a specific story, a dramatic situation is likely to constitute a "tellable" moment. At the very least, it seems better than nothing; or, as *Dwarf Fortress* designer Tarn Adams phrases: "[adding] a tangle of mechanics, throwing everything in a jar and shaking it and hoping a story comes out" (2019).

Having strong reasons to believe in their potential, we set out to experiment with dramatic situations as authoring heuristics for our emergent narrative system.

3   Implementation and Documentation Methodology

The local context of this research is the development of an actual game focusing on emergent storytelling. We already had a framework generating a geography, as well as a basic social simulation. The problem of "interestingness" arose when it became obvious that the foundational simulated actions of character sustenance, mobility, and reproduction rarely amounted to anything very "tellable". The question was then: how can we spice things up.

We set out to implement the conditions of possibility for as many of Polti's 36 dramatic situations as possible. These situations are not scripted in or planned for. We only made sure that in the natural course of the simulation, these states are reachable. For example, a married person can still fall in love with another person. If this love is reciprocated, they become lovers (#25 – adultery). If one of the matrimonial partners of the duo discovers this, they may opt to challenge their rival in a duel, which can turn out to be fatal (#15 –murderous adultery). It might happen that the rivals were siblings (#14 – Rivalry of kin) and that a third sibling decides to avenge this death (#4 – Vengeance of kin upon kin). Although our system is not yet "Polti Complete", close to 50% of the dramatic situations can possibly occur in one form or another.

Our objective at this stage is to document whether actualizations of these dramatic situations in the system indeed present our predicted features of being sequence and character productive, and, more generally, contribute to generating "tellable" events.

To do this, we have put the system to a "player retelling test". These retellings are accounts of noteworthy events having occurred during a player's engagement with a game. Eladhari (2018) have argued that the existence of such retellings constitute evidence of the emergent story potential of the games they are derived from. In this case, they speak of retellings occurring spontaneously "in the wild". Kreminski *et al.* however have also used them as part of an active research protocol, requesting testers to produce such retellings after engaging with specific games (2019).

As our project is still in development and not ready for general user tests, we have opted that one of the team members (familiar with the system) would proceed to search for stories and produce retellings. We added a time constraint to the process to get a better sense of the general prevalence and "discoverability" of such stories. We also wanted to focus on a single type of dramatic situation in order to assess whether they could show the kind of variability we are looking for in their actualization, as well as their potential interplay with other situations.

The researcher launched the game, generated and new world and let the simulation run for ~100 years of in-game time (2–3 min). He then had 10 min to identify a cluster of events that he considered "tellable" and that included a character pleading their cause to another (instances of the "supplication" dramatic situation). This was done through a mode of our interface which allows the interactive exploration of all important entities and events that have occurred in the world: the chronicles (Anon ref). At this point, the researcher could take his time to produce a textual narrative, checking facts and details in the game's chronicles as needed (but sticking to the identified plot). The researcher had full liberty in the telling of the story but could not derogate from the simulated facts. At most, he could suggest personal interpretations to fill-in for underdefined events or character motivations.

The process was done three times in a row, all in the same world, at the same time period. These three narratives are reported in the next section and act in themselves as evidence of the potential output of the system. Each is followed by an analysis addressing mainly our three criteria. The results are discussed as a whole in the subsequent section.

4   Emergent Stories

4.1   Valentel Lanuit, Rowdy Drunkard and Master Manipulator

At 63 years old, Valentel Lanuit, powerful leader of the Tristecourant clan, already had a long history of throwing magnificent feasts generally ending in drunken fighting. It was business as usual when, amidst her 278 guests, she suddenly attacked Elandre Lanuit, a peaceful 19 years old gatherer.

This time, Valentel went too far and killed the poor young woman. In her drunken stupor, Valentel could still sense trouble as more than ten relatives of Elandre immediately swore vengeance for this gratuitous act of violence. She fled to the nearby Black Clump region to find refuge with the Elès clan leader Virgilde Spendipersona. There would surely be some solidarity between fellow clan leaders.

What Valentel did not know, however, was that Elandre (the victim) was Virgilde's step-sister and that she herself had also sworn vengeance for Valentel's heinous deed. We can understand Valentel's oversight as in her youth, Virgilde had been adopted no less than two times after the successive demise of her parents, then foster parents. She had, through this process, accumulated up to 34 siblings and step-siblings.

Convincing Virgilde to grant her asylum would definitely be an uphill struggle. Yet, Valentel was not only a wild party animal that doubled with a formidable fighter (a dangerous combination), she also had an extremely smooth tongue. No one knows exactly what was said behind closed doors but Valentel got her way and became a regular (if not respected) member of the Elès clan. Many think Virgilde's judgment had been altered by her recent encounter with a swarm of dangerous insects.

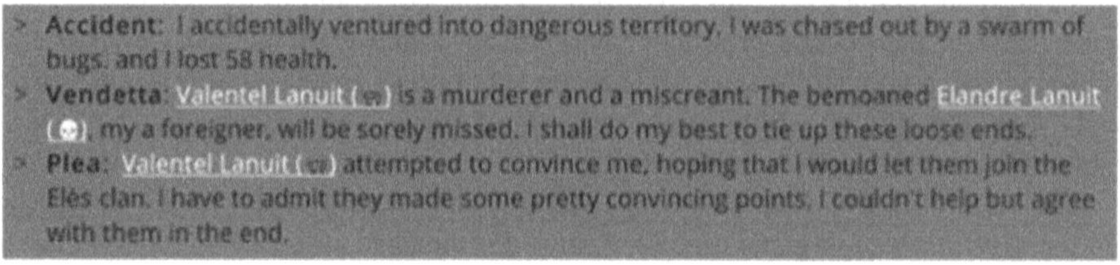

> **Accident:** I accidentally ventured into dangerous territory. I was chased out by a swarm of bugs, and I lost 58 health.
> **Vendetta:** Valentel Lanuit ( ) is a murderer and a miscreant. The bemoaned Elandre Lanuit ( ) my a foreigner, will be sorely missed. I shall do my best to tie up these loose ends.
> **Plea:** Valentel Lanuit ( ) attempted to convince me, hoping that I would let them join the Elès clan. I have to admit they made some pretty convincing points. I couldn't help but agree with them in the end.

Fig. 1. Excerpt from Virgilde Spendipersona's Chronicle

Analysis

In this narrative, the "supplication" situation is made noteworthy by the fact that the authority invoked has itself a desire of vengeance against the supplicant. The story then trumps expectations as the supplicant still gets what she wants in spite of aggravating circumstances. The reasons remain somewhat of a mystery to which the recent accident with a swarm of bugs (see Fig. 1) might offer some explanation (even as an illusory correlation).

Other contextual details help understand Valentel's strange choice of seeking refuge with her victim's step-sister. Here we discover Virgilde has a ridiculous number of siblings. This feature is itself interesting in its unusualness and warrants curiosity for an explanation. The chief's multiple adoptions point towards a proto-story in itself.

In terms of sequence, the supplication situation finds its explanatory causes both in Valentel's transgressive behavior, and in Virgilde's tumultuous childhood. Its surprising outcome concludes the narrative arc. In terms of characters, we discover that Valentel can be very convincing and that maybe Virgilde is a bit of a pushover.

4.2   Ocith Leverre, Who Could not Live up to His MOTHEr's Reputation

Paulance Leverre had a difficult childhood; food was scarce and her family was always on the move, looking for a better place. After having to beg strangers to survive, she eventually resorted to stealing at age 16. This was a revelation to her: she was a natural. The payoff was much higher than anything else, and there seemed to be no consequences.

She not only continued living almost solely on theft, but could even support a family doing so.

When she turned 30, she gave birth to her third child, Ocith Leverre. From his youngest age (and I really mean that) he was fascinated by his mother's profession, wanting very strongly to emulate her. We do not know whether Paulance encouraged this or not but he was obviously not ready for this line of work when at the age of two he attempted to steal food from Nieu Bettertime—his own father. Contrarily to his wife, Nieu had always been an honest gatherer, having never stolen even a radish in his life. Presumably, he was completely unaware of Paulance' profession as he was outraged by his young son's behavior and asked the clan leader to exile him (Fig. 2).

> **StealFood:** I was in a really bad situation and I stole 3,4 foods from Nieu Bettertime (⚬).
> **Exile:** I was banished from the clan because I was caught stealing. Tough, but fair. I shouldn't have done it...
> **Plea:** I pleaded my case to Andram Hardwater (⚬) in an official capacity to spare me from being deported from my social group. Paulance Leverre (⚬) was a tiger in there, but they were shot down mercilessly. I will always be thankful to them for trying.
> **Migrate:** I migrated alone to Vocpa. I was desperate.
> **ClanJoin:** I joined the Del Cacciatore clan.

Fig. 2. Excerpt from Ocith Leverre's chronicles

Horrified by this turn of events, Paulance made a moving plea to spare her child, but to no avail. Ocith was exiled to a faraway land where he survived a few years stealing (and getting caught every time) before being exiled again and eaten in the wilderness by a signa (a nightmarish predator of the world of Vitento).

Analysis

Polti's description of the "Supplication" dramatic situation suggests the presence of a third party: the intercessor. In this story, we have the moving display of a mother interceding for her child. Even though the official authority figure is the clan chief, the sequence suggests the real target is the child's father. This is ultimately a family drama that also fits the description of "#4 – vengeance taken for kin upon kin".

To make sense of this supplication situation, we question the supplicant's behavior: why did they steal from their father? In the process, we can constitute a sequence: the mother was a professional thief, possibly showing the example to her son. On the contrary, the father is an honest, hard-working man. This is the stage of the drama: the child's action possibly revelated that he had been kept in ignorance for years.

This situation certainly produces an interesting set of characters. What kind of man would request that a two-year old (his own son!) be exiled? And, of course, why (and how) would a young toddler steal from his father?

4.3 Noëlalis Froidmerde, She Who Lives by the Sword...

In the year 125, the Sentre chiefdom decided to raid a rich but poorly defended village of the small neighboring Chesieur chiefdom. In what was to be called "The Cowardly

Campaign of Marite", 43 warriors met 5 defenders and, unsurprisingly, prevailed. There was very little fighting as the Chesieur quickly capitulated.

The only casualty was Clémenté Froidmerde, chief of Chesieur, who, in spite of her honorable age, was always keen to go first to battle. According to Chesais cultural tradition, the succession was to go to the chiefdom's most influential member who then was, according to general opinion, Jest Risquejeune.

Now, Noëlalis Froidmerde, the late chief's daughter, would have none of this. She considered herself to be the rightful heir. She challenged Jest to a duel and regrettably killed him. She soon realized that this brash act generated much resentment amongst her clan and decided it would be safer to leave rather than wake up with a sword in her chest. She supplicated Cornelew Cutlot, leader of the nearby Francianas, to welcome her in spite of her deeds, which he did.

This would not save her for long, however. Charlonin Frappejoli, one of the attackers of the "Cowardly Campaign" was apparently in a completionist mood. He tracked her down to her new home of Leman to finish the job. She died so unpopular that only her one-year-old son attended the funeral. Ironically, her assassin–who would also die later that year–was sent off by no less than 36 people.

Analysis
In this story the supplication itself is not very noteworthy, but its uncomplicated nature sets the stage for the "caught up by fate" punchline. It would seem Noëlalis got away easily from the mess she made herself. Yet, she will die that same year—not from the hand of those who had sworn vengeance against her (and whom she successfully evaded)—but from some random warrior from a raid that seemed to have taken place a while ago in a different place (#7 – Falling prey to cruelty/misfortune). And to add insult to injury, we discover that she died a complete pariah, while her assassin was apparently the most popular guy in town. This sad fate is exacerbated by what we know of her grand (but illegitimate) ambitions to become chief.

Concretely, Noëlalis' supplication story articulates a sequence beginning (at least) at the raid which caused her chief's death, and ends with her own death. In the process are revealed her ambitious and hubristic nature (#30 – Ambition; #8 – Revolt).

This narrative provides some bonus pleasure from the generated names. The raid that initiates the events certainly deserves its title of "cowardly campaign". And, considering how she ended, we can also say Noëlalis lived up to her surname.

5   Discussion

The deliberate nature of the story search doesn't allow us to conclude on whether actual players would easily and frequently discover stories while engaging with the game. It remains that these sequences of events were indeed generated by the system and as such represent evidence of its potential. The readers will judge for themselves how interesting (or not) these retellings are, but we can still make some general observations on the contribution of embedding dramatic situations in the possibility space of the system.

Assessing Dramatic Situations
In all these stories the identification of a dramatic situation allowed reconstructing a story:

how did things lead to this point and what is the outcome? In the process, characters are revealed both by their contribution to the advent of the situation and their action towards its resolution. The stories also show that the same dramatic situation can play out in very different ways depending on the context, and so doesn't constitute a repeated story script. This generativity is amplified by the combinatorial potential of the dramatic situation. In the second story, for example, the supplication is made even more poignant by the fact that its outcome also amounts to "vengeance of kin upon kin".

If these stories have some claims at being tellable, the broader context of an emergent narrative system changes the perspective. Exiling one's two-year old son is definitely an *event* in the lifetime of a person, or within the scope of a specific narrative. However, in the simulation of a full world over hundreds of years, it might turn out to be more common than expected. Being very familiar with our system, we know, for example, that the first story's point of departure, the drunken feast gratuitous murder leading to a spiral of vendettas, is relatively common (and probably too common).

As players become aware of such recurrent emergent patterns, such stories might become less tellable as they lose in unpredictability. However, factors of relevance might counterbalance this. Vengeance of kin upon kin might not be entirely unusual in this world in general but still be very salient when the player-character, or one of their relatives, is implicated. As a comparison, a last-minute equalizing goal may not be an extreme oddity in football, but it remains a very exciting event when you care about the outcome of a match. Further research will be needed to test this hypothesis.

Beyond Polti

We have used Polti's list of dramatic situations because they are convenient and inspirational but it should not be limitative. In practice, one should consider the genre of fiction they are engaging in, the peculiarities of the world they are modeling, and consider the kind of situations that are likely to be interesting and relevant in the context. Film scholar Higgins, for example, notes that action movies are often built on dramatic situations, but have their own repertoire of particularly spectacular, time-sensitive ones such as the chase and the standoff (2008). A useful, medium-specific source of inspiration is reading actual player retellings, which provides rich information as to what players of existing games have found worthy of narrating. Situations drawn from *The Sims* (Maxis) retellings, for example, often belong to a rather "comedic situation" spectrum, such as "unlikely lovers", "guests extending their welcome", "small accident, big consequences", etc.

Rather than strictly formalizing and listing these situations, we suggest to embrace their heuristic value and consider them as an intermediary authoring goal. Before engaging in actual scripting, one can first attempt to define and describe a set of relevant dramatic situations for their system, drawing inspiration for existing ones if need be. This step would in itself constitute an opportunity for the authors and team to discuss the sorts of intrigues they hope to generate with their system—a moment of prototyping before committing to specific designs and implementations.

6 Conclusion

Considering the current scarcity of models and resources to specifically inform the design and authoring of emergent narrative games, we have found dramatic situations to be a valuable heuristic to help increase the amount of "storyable" content generated by our system. Although we have relied on Polti's canonical list, we think the notion can be generalized to suit a variety of project situations. The idea is to capture a state of the fiction that orchestrates a tension between various roles that can afford multiple backstories and resolutions. Further work will allow us to confirm whether this "tellability" potential is accessible to general players, and whether it will hold under the stress of sustained engagement with the system.

References

Adams, T.: Emergent narrative in dwarf fortress. In: Short, T.X., Adams, T. (eds.) Procedural Storytelling in Game Design. A K Peters/CRC Press (2019)

Baroni, R.: Tellability. https://www.lhn.uni-hamburg.de/node/30.html (2014)

Compton, K.: Getting Started with Generators. In: Short, T.X. and Adams, T. (eds.) Procedural Storytelling in Game Design. A K Peters/CRC Press (2019)

Eladhari, M.P.: Re-tellings: the fourth layer of narrative as an instrument for critique. In: International Conference on Interactive Digital Storytelling, pp. 65–78. Springer (2018)

Fernández-Vara, C.: The Tribulations of Adventure Games: Integrating Story into Simulation Through Performance (2009)

Gordon, L.: Procedural storytelling is exploding the possibilities of video game narratives (2020). https://www.theverge.com/2021/11/30/22807568/procedural-storytelling-video-games-dwarf-fortress-wildermyth-blaseball. Last accessed 6 Jun 2022

Higgins, S.: Suspenseful situations: melodramatic narrative and the contemporary action film. Cine. J. **47**, 74–96 (2008)

Hühn, P.: Event and eventfulness. https://www.lhn.uni-hamburg.de/node/39.html (2013)

Kreminski, M., Samuel, B., Melcer, E., Wardrip-Fruin, N.: Evaluating AI-based games through retellings. In: Proceedings of the AAAI Conference on Artificial Intelligence and Interactive Digital Entertainment, vol. 15, pp. 45–51 (2019)

Louchart, S., Swartjes, I., Kriegel, M., Aylett, R.: Purposeful authoring for emergent narrative. In: Spierling, U., Szilas, N. (eds.) ICIDS 2008. LNCS, vol. 5334, pp. 273–284. Springer, Heidelberg (2008). https://doi.org/10.1007/978-3-540-89454-4_35

Polti, G.: Les Trente-six Situations dramatiques. Mercure de France, Paris (1912)

Ryan, J.: Curating simulated storyworlds. https://escholarship.org/uc/item/1340j5h2 (2018)

Ryan, J.O., Mateas, M., Wardrip-Fruin, N.: Open design challenges for interactive emergent narrative. In: Schoenau-Fog, H., Bruni, L.E., Louchart, S., Baceviciute, S. (eds.) ICIDS 2015. LNCS, vol. 9445, pp. 14–26. Springer, Cham (2015). https://doi.org/10.1007/978-3-319-270 36-4_2

Sartre, J.P.: Sartre on Theater. Pantheon Books, New York (1976)

Szilas, N., Estupiñán, S., Richle, U.: Qualifying and quantifying interestingness in dramatic situations. In: Nack, F., Gordon, A.S. (eds.) ICIDS 2016. LNCS, vol. 10045, pp. 336–347. Springer, Cham (2016). https://doi.org/10.1007/978-3-319-48279-8_30

"It's Fun not to Know": The Role of Uncertainty in Text-Based Online Collaborative Storytelling

Alex Mitchell[1]([⊠]) [iD], Dennis Ang[1] [iD], and Shao Han Tan[2]

[1] National University of Singapore, Singapore, Singapore
alexm@nus.edu.sg
[2] Curious Chimeras, Singapore, Singapore

Abstract. Computer-mediated communication platforms provide new ways for people to tell stories together, while at the same time introducing new challenges. In this paper we explore how people coordinate process, content, and direction during text-based online collaborative storytelling. In our study, six pairs of participants were asked to tell a story together using two variations of a chatroom-like system. Both conditions provided direct text-based interaction visible to the audience, whereas one condition also included a "backchannel" interface for private communication that was not visible to the audience. The system also provided basic workspace awareness in the form of persistent story text, coloured based on contributor, and a typing activity indicator. Even with just a partial understanding of the content and direction of the story, most participants felt they were able to successfully tell a story together. In fact, some participants preferred the uncertainty associated with limited communication, seeing this as encouraging creativity. This suggests guidelines for designing collaborative tools, which tend to emphasize shared understanding, may need to take into consideration the role of uncertainty in creative activities such as collaborative storytelling.

Keywords: Collaborative storytelling · Improvisation · Backchannel communication · Awareness · Coordination · Uncertainty · Creative collaboration

1 Introduction

Computer-mediated communication has long been used by people to tell stories together. Groups such as the Plaintext Players and the Hamnet Players have made use of MUDs (multi-user dungeons), IRC (Internet Relay Chat), and Second Life for improvisational storytelling [1–4]. Twitter and Facebook have also been used to create improvisational stories in the form of networked improvisations or "netprov" [5, 6]. There have been a number of platforms explicitly designed for online collaborative storytelling, such as *Sleep is Death* [7] and *Storium* [8]. People also tell stories online in less formal settings, such as on social media or using instant messaging systems [9].

A key component in the process of improvisational collaborative storytelling is coordinating the movement towards cognitive consensus, or the development of a shared mental model [10]. As Magerko argues, "Body language, domain-specific cues, and

M. Vosmeer and L. Holloway-Attaway (Eds.): ICIDS 2022, LNCS 13762, pp. 229–248, 2022.
https://doi.org/10.1007/978-3-031-22298-6_15

verbal commands all contribute to the collaborative process [...] Any model of improvisation needs to address how communication to others in the group is used for coordination" [11]. Unlike face-to-face improvisational storytelling, online storytelling is potentially both constrained by the limitations of online media and allows for new forms of communication and coordination. This raises the question of how people use computer-mediated communication to negotiate and coordinate cognitive convergence during online storytelling, and how collaborative storytelling tools can support this.

To explore this question, we focused on an extremely constrained situation, text-only chat, and observed how people coordinate and communicate while telling a story together. Participants were asked to use a text-based communication system to tell a story together in front of a hypothetical online audience. In one condition they only had a public communication channel, and in the second condition they had an additional private backchannel. The system also supported simple workspace awareness: persistent story text, coloured based on contributor, and a typing activity indicator. The two conditions served as stimuli, creating differing contexts to enable us to investigate and probe the ways that people handle these contexts, with and without a backchannel. As such, it is important to note that the focus was not on directly comparing the two conditions, but instead on exploring how participants managed these contexts.

Even with limited channels of communication, and although they claimed to have only a partial understanding of the story content and direction, most participants still felt able to successfully tell a story. In fact, some felt the uncertainty involved was beneficial, with one participant claiming "it's fun not to know" where the story is going. This suggests traditional guidelines for designing shared workspaces, which emphasize workspace awareness and development of a shared mental model, may need to account for the role of uncertainty in real-time online creative collaboration such as collaborative storytelling.

2 Related Work

We begin by summarizing theories of collaboration and coordination in face-to-face improvisational storytelling, and work investigating support for online computer-mediated collaborative writing and collaborative storytelling.

2.1 Improvisation and Coordination

Sawyer [12, 13] characterizes improvisational group creativity as a situation in which "interaction between performers is immediate, durationally constrained to the moment of creation, and is mediated by musical or verbal signs", where "the group has no intention of generating something that will remain after their performance is done" [14]. Each performer proposes possible future content or structure, what he refers to as an "indexical entailment" after Silverstein [15]. Accepted proposals become part of the "emergent" - the cumulative set of indexical presuppositions that have resulted from the interactions up to that moment. Future proposals are constrained by the genre of the performance, other participants in the performance, and the set of previous entailments already accepted into the emergent. Tension exists between maintaining coherence with the emergent and demonstrating some degree of innovation. We are interested in how this tension is impacted by, and impacts, the use of computer-mediated communication as the medium for storytelling.

Research into collaborative storytelling in improv theatre has explored how actors develop a shared mental model of their performance [11]. A mental model is "any underlying assumptions held by an improviser" [10], whereas a shared mental model is the set of mental models where improvisors "think about a phenomenon in a similar manner" [16, quoted in [10]]. Developing a shared mental model inevitably involves misunderstanding and miscommunication, what Fuller and Magerko [10] refer to as cognitive divergence, followed by cognitive convergence, eventually leading to cognitive consensus and a shared mental model of the developing story. Cognitive divergence takes many forms, including disagreements about content, the intended future direction of the story, and the process being used to tell the story. Interestingly, this suggests the process of divergence, convergence and consensus is an essential part of improvisation. Again, we are interested in how computer-mediation impacts and is impacted by this process, and how tools can better support this.

2.2 Computer-Mediated Collaborative Storytelling

Research into computer-mediated synchronous collaborative writing [17, 18] has focused on shared representations and tools for awareness and the use of a shared workspace to support the writing process, with some focus on collaborative storytelling [19, 20]. More recent work examines changes resulting from easily accessible collaborative writing tools such as Google Docs [18, 21]. A key concept is workspace awareness [22, 23], which allows individual collaborators to know what others are doing within a shared workspace, and how an individual's actions relate to their current and planned contributions. Important differences between these situations and what we are examining are the potential presence of an audience during collaboration, and the relative importance of the process, rather than the outcome, of the collaboration.

Another key concept is the provision of an informal, private "backchannel" that parallels a more public "main channel" of communication [24–27]. Work on backchannel communication generally explores private communication between group members in non-performative situations, or between audience members during a performance. Exploring the use of a backchannel by performers in the context of improvisation, *AntWriter* [28] contains a scrolling window where participants enter story fragments to indicate their intended actions, providing time for participants to coordinate before performing. Observations [29] suggest that while participants make use of the ability to share upcoming actions to coordinate their actions, there is a tension between the time needed to plan, and the immediate response needed during improvisation.

3 Research Problem

Previous work on designing and evaluating computer-mediated tools to support collaborative writing emphasizes the need to provide awareness, a shared workspace, and backchannel communication to enable coordination. However, work on face-to-face collaborative storytelling suggests tensions not usually found in non-storytelling contexts: between coherence and innovation, divergence and consensus, and planning and immediate response. These tensions make it is unclear how traditional approaches to supporting collaborative work apply to computer-mediated collaborative storytelling.

This motivates our research question: how do people use communication channels provided by computer-mediated platforms to coordinate during online collaborative storytelling? We aim to understand the specific design requirements for supporting coordination in real-time computer-mediated creative collaboration such as storytelling.

4   Method

We investigated this question through an exploratory, qualitative observational study of people using two versions of a simple online collaborative storytelling tool: one without and one with backchannel communication. 12 participants (6 pairs) took part in the study. The study was structured using a "within-subjects" approach, with each pair using both versions of the system, counterbalanced to account for potential order effects. This approach was chosen so we could ask comparative questions, exploring how the participants felt about the use of the backchannel during storytelling.

4.1   Materials

The tool was implemented in JavaScript and node.js. Each participant interacted with the system through the Chrome browser on a MacBook Pro connected to a wireless network. Information was relayed between the participants through a central communications server, also implemented in node.js running under Ubuntu 14.04.

The tool provides two views of the ongoing story. In version 1 (see Fig. 1), the storyteller's view shows the ongoing story (A), and the audience's view (B) shows the story as seen by the audience. Participants can type new text to be shown to the audience (C). This text is simultaneously added to both views on both participants' screens when the "enter" key is pressed. The system also provides simple awareness features. Story text is colour-coded to show who wrote the text and is persistent and scrollable. When one participant is typing in the public text entry field, "X is typing..." (D), where X is the name of the participant, is shown just above the text entry field on the other participant's interface. Audience members have a simplified interface only showing the audience view (B). For our study, both the storyteller's and audience's views were shown side-by-side on each participant's screen (see Fig. 1). In version 2 (see Fig. 2), in addition to the above features, backchannel communication (E) was provided in the form of text typed by participants and then shown to other participants in a manner visually distinct from the story text (F), and not shown to the audience.

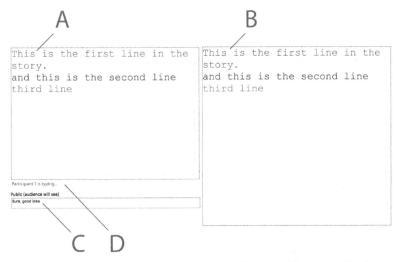

Fig. 1. Version 1 of the storytelling system, with only public communication.

The system was deliberately designed to provide minimal workspace awareness tools [22]. The coloured text provides awareness related to the past, in terms of what has been written and by whom. The "X is typing…" indicator provides awareness related to the present, specifically whether the other participant is currently preparing an entry to add to the story. These tools were provided in both versions, as we wanted to focus specifically on the impact of providing explicit backchannel communication in the form of the private text field.

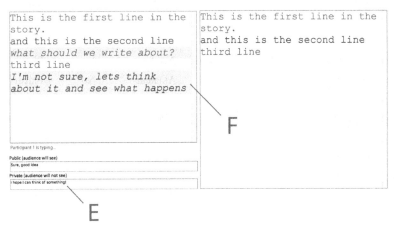

Fig. 2. Version 2 of the storytelling system, with backchannel communication. (Color figure online)

4.2 Protocol

Participants were selected using convenience sampling, with the requirement that they have experience with some form of collaborative storytelling, such as improv theatre or tabletop roleplaying games. Although some participants self-reported "no" to collaborative storytelling experience, all reported having roleplaying experience. Participants were briefed on the study and asked to fill out a demographic questionnaire (see Table 1 for details). They were then introduced to the storytelling system, and any questions about the interface were answered. This was done together to ensure participants received the same briefing.

Participants were then taken to separate rooms and asked to work with their partner to tell a story. They were told the story is for an online audience, represented by the "audience" view in the storytelling tool. Although there was no actual audience, the intention was the implied presence of the audience would emphasize the fact that utterances by the participants are immediately consumed and therefore cannot be edited or retracted, providing time pressure and a need to keep the storytelling process going. To be clear, there was no deception involved here: participants were explicitly asked to imagine there was an audience, to help constrain their use of the "public" text entry field to utterances that they wanted the "audience" to see.

Table 1. Background of participants.

ID	Gender	Age	Rel'ship	Self-reported storytelling experience		
				Individual	Collab	Roleplay
G1P1[1]	Female	28	Couple	None	Yes	Player
G1P2	Male	26		Amateur	Yes	Player/GM[2]
G2P1	Male	35	None	None	No	Player
G2P2	Male	28		Theatre	Yes	Player
G3P1	Female	30	Friends	Amateur	Yes	Player
G3P2	Female	30		Amateur	No	Player
G4P1	Male	32	Worked together	Poet, improv	Yes	Player
G4P2	Male	47		Writer	Yes	Player/GM
G5P1	Male	31	None	Amateur	No	Player/GM
G5P2	Female	33		Amateur	Yes	Player/GM
G6P1	Female	26	None	Amateur	No	Player
G6P2	Male	24		Filmmaker	Yes	Player/GM

---

[1] Participants will be referred to as "GXPY", where X is the group number (1–6), and Y is the participant number (1 or 2). Here, for example, G1P1 refers to group 1, participant 1.

[2] GM refers to the role of "game master", the person who moderates a tabletop role-playing game session.

To start the story, each participant was given a prompt. Participants were told they could optionally make use of this prompt to help them get started. The prompts were randomized separately and were generally not the same for the two participants, although this was not enforced. These prompts were designed to be generic, and to suggest possible story directions. Participants were not shown their partner's prompt.

Participants had 10 minutes to tell the story. They received a 5-minute and 2-minute warning and told to stop once the time was up. Each participant was then separately asked questions related to their understanding of the story, communication, awareness, and use of the tool.

Once both participants completed their interviews, the process was repeated for the second storytelling session, this time using the other version of the system. For groups 1, 3 and 5, participants used version 1 followed by version 2. For groups 2, 4 and 6, the order was reversed.

After both storytelling sessions and individual interviews, participants were brought together and asked questions about the overall storytelling process. Follow-up questions were asked regarding any issues that arose during the individual interviews.

4.3 Data Collection and Analysis

Video recordings were made of all on-screen actions for both participants. Audio was recorded during the storytelling sessions, the individual interviews, and the combined interview. Three researchers engaged in transcription and open and axial coding of the recordings of the storytelling sessions and interviews, then came together to group these codes thematically, resulting in the categories described below. While we generally took a grounded theory approach [30], we also looked for instances of cognitive divergence and convergence, and paid attention to how the participants worked to coordinate. This approach is in line with the position that the use of existing theories is not at odds with grounded theory, as long as researchers exercise reflexivity [31]. Given our focus, we deliberately chose to limit our analysis to process, rather than story quality or audience experience.

5 Results

We observed participants develop several ways of coordinating and negotiating the *process* they would follow during the storytelling session, and the *content* and *direction* of their story, both without and with the presence of the backchannel. We also found that, while most groups claimed not to completely understand the content and direction of the story, they did not see this as a problem, and in some cases felt this contributed to the storytelling process.

5.1 Implicit Coordination Without the Backchannel

Several groups made use of the story text itself to coordinate the content and future direction of their stories, and in some cases also the process for storytelling.

Negotiating Content and Direction Through the Story Text. In group 2, participants had access to the backchannel during the first session but didn't use it. Despite this, they managed to move the story forward by negotiating both the content and direction of the story through the story text. Both participants received abstract prompts that, while different, were not necessarily incompatible. G2P1 received: "something has dropped from your pocket", whereas G2P2 received: "you have been looking into a reflective surface". While these prompts did not immediately suggest any connection, the participants, without ever explicitly sharing these prompts, were able to gradually incorporate both concepts.

G2P1 began by writing short fragments that mentioned his prompt (see Fig. 3, blue text), whereas G2P2 initially went along with G2P1's contributions, and later brought in his own prompt. Immediately after entering this, G2P2 scrolled up to look at the earlier text and his prompt. G2P2 did this several times, clearly attempting to determine how to combine the various fragments into a more coherent story.

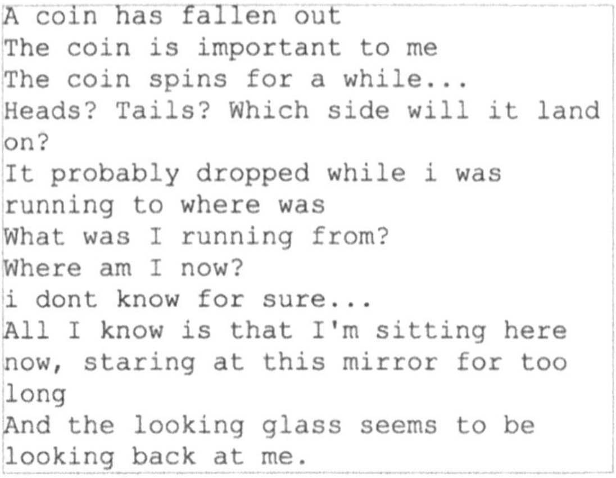

```
A coin has fallen out
The coin is important to me
The coin spins for a while...
Heads? Tails? Which side will it land
on?
It probably dropped while i was
running to where was
What was I running from?
Where am I now?
i dont know for sure...
All I know is that I'm sitting here
now, staring at this mirror for too
long
And the looking glass seems to be
looking back at me.
```

Fig. 3. Negotiating to incorporate 2 unrelated prompts. (Color figure online)

Following this, G2P1 picked up the "mirror" theme, responding with a question. The next few lines related to the mirror, until G2P2 combined the two prompts, asking "I wonder which side the coin landed on [...] perhaps that's the side of the mirror I'm now waiting in" (see Fig. 4). This tied together both the coin that G2P1 had introduced as the result of the "something dropped" prompt, and the mirror introduced by G2P2.

Both participants continued to make connections, taking turns to introduce short sentences that referred to both concepts (see Fig. 5). Again, G2P2 tended to scroll back up, reintroducing the "running" concept from earlier and using this to bring the story to a climax, ending with "There's something behind me", which was supported by G2P1's brief but effective "Look."

The gradual convergence of the participants' contributions suggests an implicit negotiation was taking place, not through the backchannel but through the story text, both in terms of the ongoing contributions and the persistent record of contributions.

```
I wonder which side the coin landed
on...
Perhaps that's the side of the mirror
I'm now waiting in
What does the mirror say about how the
coin landed?
Only that it's the other side
Should I turn around?
press on
look deeper into the mirror
It flipped
The coin? The mirror? I can't quite
figure it out anymore.
I was running...
maybe they are the same thing? How can
you be sure that there is a mirror? or
the coin?
```

Fig. 4. G2P2 (red text) connecting the two threads of the story. (Color figure online)

```
I was running...
maybe they are the same thing? How
can you be sure that there is a
mirror? or the coin?
where are you running to? or where
are you running from?
I know because I can feel it.
There
There is something inside my pocket.
Can you feel it?
It's hard, flat... I'm not sure if I
want to check though.
Then don't look. Focus on the mirror.
There's something behind me.
Look.
```

Fig. 5. Making connections and bringing the story to a close.

Negotiating Content, Direction and Process Through the Story Text. Group 5 was also able to develop a turn-taking protocol, despite not having a backchannel during the first session. The prompts in the first session were the same, something the participants were unaware of as they are not shown each other's prompts. Initially, both participants riffed directly off the prompt. Here they were typing simultaneously. After a few lines, both participants began paying attention to each other's contributions and shifted to a turn-taking protocol. As with group 2, negotiation of content and direction was happening within the story text. This suggests that the story text itself supports coordination.

G5P1's initial contribution responded to the prompt (see Fig. 6, blue text). G5P2 also responded to this, introducing a "bizarre world" theme in response to the second half of the prompt: "What has staggered you so?". G5P1 picked up on this, providing examples of how the world was "breaking apart". Here, there was no direct connection between the contributions, as both partners were making parallel contributions along the "bizarre world" theme. G5P1 wrote "Escalators breaking down…"; simultaneously, G5P2 was typing "All he wanted was to pick up that $10 bill on the ground, and suddenly it had".

```
Starting prompt:
Careful now! You stagger back, nearly
falling, but catch yourself in time.
(What has staggered you so?)

He catches himself from falling, his
hair afly
This reaaaallllly wasn't what he had
intended.
He didn't understand, how did this
situation turn into this... bizarre
world?!
Things were breaking apart just by his
sheer proximity
Escalators breaking down...
```

Public (audience will see)
All he wanted was to pick up that $10 bill on the ground, and suddenly it had

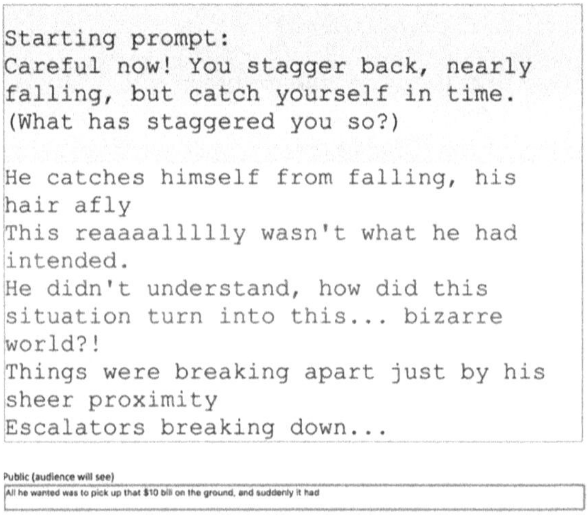

Fig. 6. Group 5 starting to converge (G5P1 in blue, G5P2 in red). (Color figure online)

However, rather than sending this text, G5P2 deleted this line, and instead typed "Pigeons attacking…", a line structurally similar to G5P1's contribution, further building on the theme. This was sent simultaneously with G5P1's "Wedding decorations catching fire…", which appeared first in the text (see Fig. 7).

From here onwards, contributions quickly converged on the concept of a pigeon wedding, with each building on this idea. As G5P2 explained:

> For me I guess that's what I was trying to do, […] is there some way that he can pick up from that, and then we bounce off again, or if he didn't react to that then ok so what did he come up with like open ended sort of stuff that I can pick up on so I guess that was the main sort of communication processes, to make it like back and forth. (I1, 00:07:10)[3]

This "back-and-forth" led to an implicit understanding of where the story was going and how the story was being told, without any explicit communication, much like verbal improv storytelling. A similar process was seen for group 2 during their second story, and for group 4 during both stories.

---

[3] I1 and I2 denotes individual interview 1 and 2 respectively for a given participant, and F denotes final interview involving both participants.

```
sheer proximity
Escalators breaking down...
Wedding decorations catching fire...
Pigeons attacking...
Wait, wedding decorations?
He swore 5 years ago he would never get
married
He doesn't recall breaking mirrors or
crossing any black cats...
But here he is now
At the altar
With a pigeon bride.
She looks resplendent in her gown
it really complements her beautiful red
eyes
P2 is typing...
```

Public (audience will see)
```
Flowers adorning her feathers around her neck
```

Fig. 7. Converging on a common platform without explicit coordination.

5.2 Use of the Backchannel for Coordination

These observations suggest that without using the backchannel, groups coordinated process, content and direction using the implicit communication provided by the story text. However, when breakdown was too great to overcome through implicit coordination, and the backchannel was available, groups made use of the backchannel to overcome breakdown.

Breakdown and Backchannel for Coordination and Support. In group 3's first session, the backchannel was unavailable. Unlike other groups, these participants failed to coordinate using the story text, with G3P1 dominating and G3P2 only making two contributions. There was no visible connection between their contributions, suggesting a failure to reach any cognitive consensus. It is worth considering why this happened.

From the start, G3P2 struggled to keep up with G3P1's contributions. Clearly the two participants were working independently. As G3P2 explained:

> I wasn't really paying attention to hers. Cause, I'll get distracted, [...] And I'm like trying to think about how to make it connect but I was like, but I won't be typing anything because she types faster than me! (I1, 0:00:15)

G3P2 was overwhelmed by the rate at which G3P1 was contributing to the story, making it difficult for her to focus on her own contributions.

When asked, G3P1 admitted she hadn't realized G3P2's contributions were not showing up, assuming G3P2 was adding to the story although she couldn't see her text:

> I saw her, that she was typing, but because it wasn't coming up on the screen, [...] by that point I had already written so much so I just said I will finish my piece and it's just a one piece that's separate from hers. (I1, 00:08:33)

Here G3P1 gave up on collaborating and focused on her own story. Similarly, there was a point where G3P2 decided to ignore her partner and write her own, separate story. At the 5-min point, G3P2 was still editing her first contribution (see Fig. 8). As she said, "I haven't even typed anything, I haven't even entered anything! I'm think I'm going to completely ignore what she's writing" (I1, 00:06:01). The lack of backchannel led to a complete breakdown in coordination, with no means available for negotiation or repair.

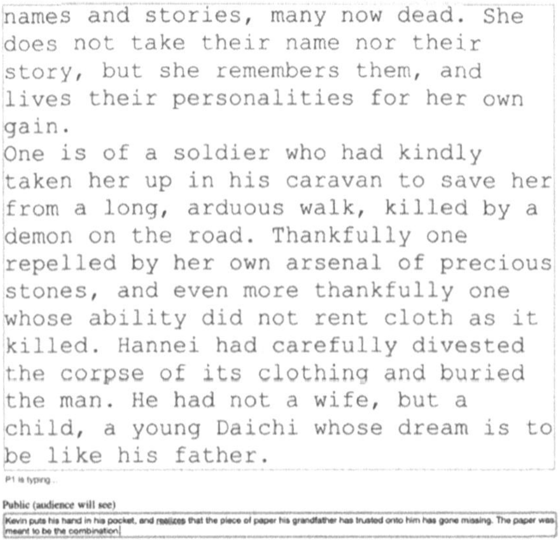

```
names and stories, many now dead. She
does not take their name nor their
story, but she remembers them, and
lives their personalities for her own
gain.
One is of a soldier who had kindly
taken her up in his caravan to save her
from a long, arduous walk, killed by a
demon on the road. Thankfully one
repelled by her own arsenal of precious
stones, and even more thankfully one
whose ability did not rent cloth as it
killed. Hannei had carefully divested
the corpse of its clothing and buried
the man. He had not a wife, but a
child, a young Daichi whose dream is to
be like his father.
P1 is typing
```

Public (audience will see)
Kevin puts his hand in his pocket, and realizes that the piece of paper his grandfather has trusted onto him has gone missing. The paper was meant to be the combination

Fig. 8. G3P1 dominates (blue text), while G3P2 spends a lot of time editing (text entry field). (Color figure online)

In contrast, in the second session the participants immediately made use of the backchannel to establish a turn-taking protocol. They each provided many support responses as they went. The style of contributions also changed, with G3P1 slowing down and both participants thinking about how their contributions will build off each other's text. In the first 2 min of the session, the participants only typed in the backchannel (see Fig. 9). They shared their prompts and decided to use turn-taking. The backchannel allowed them to negotiate the process, content, and direction of their story.

Use of the backchannel continued as they began writing the story. They continuously provided support responses and encouragement (see Fig. 10) and suggested where to take the story. Unlike the first story, the participants connected their prompts and worked together on a coherent story. Although G3P2 continued to spend a lot of time editing, she could do this without the pressure she felt during the first session, as she knew G3P1 would wait for her. They were also able to signal their intent using the backchannel and provide encouragement when they felt their partner needed support.

For group 3, the backchannel was essential for the success of their collaboration. Without any means of direct communication, they were unable to coordinate, whereas when the backchannel was provided, they used it to coordinate both the content and the process of their collaboration. Interestingly, in this group the participants were close

```
threaten or beg. (What is this place?
Where are you trying to go?)

███████, let us do one sentence each and
exchange.
yea, i was also thinking that
i have food related promt
Do you want to do a zombie apocalypse?
Haha I have a gate prompt.
THOU SHALL NOT PASS.
Let us be Kevin.
UNLESS YOU EAT THIS CHICKEN
Hahahahahahaha
The chicken tests if you are a zombie.
Coz zombies only eat BRAAAAAAINS
```

Public (audience will see)

Safety is so close and yet so far, Kevin thinks with a sinking feeling, watching people ahead of him in the queue stopped, one by one

Private (audience will not see)

Fig. 9. Negotiating for both content and process.

```
POOR KEVIN.
Kevin's stomach churns as he stares at
this chicken. His face slightly green.
Hahahaha go on!
He takes a tiny bite. His eye suddenly
beam, "This.... this is actually
delicious!"
omg what did he eat
it must be a durian in chicken form
The guard's eyes widen, and then
squints. "Oh?" he says, slowly, backing
away from Kevin. Two more guards join
him, their batons and guns out.
oh no kevin
"Guys, we got a zombie here!" he
shouts, radio-ing for back up.
You activated the trap card!!
```

Fig. 10. Backchannel support responses and encouragement.

friends, and had taken part in tabletop role-playing game sessions together. Despite this, they still struggled to tell a story together in the absence of the direct communication provided by the backchannel.

Using the Backchannel for Support and Repair. Other groups used the backchannel for support and repair, although not to the extent of group 3. In the second session, group 5 used the backchannel to set the tone of the story ("full on horror"), to determine the turn-taking protocol, and to decide the story would be a continuation of their first story (see Fig. 11). For the next 5 minutes, they worked without using the backchannel, following a loose turn-taking protocol.

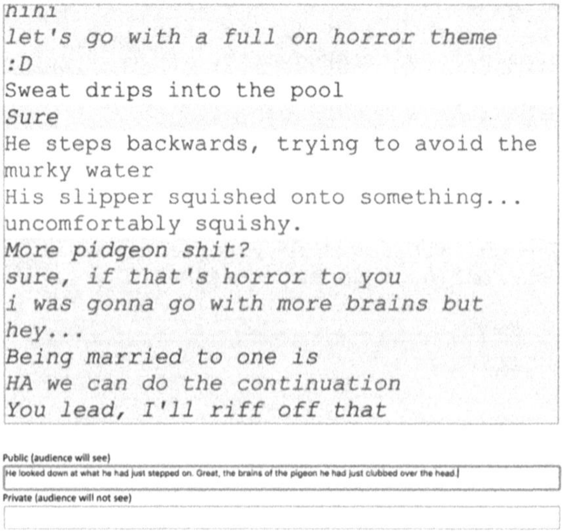

```
nini
let's go with a full on horror theme
:D
Sweat drips into the pool
Sure
He steps backwards, trying to avoid the
murky water
His slipper squished onto something...
uncomfortably squishy.
More pidgeon shit?
sure, if that's horror to you
i was gonna go with more brains but
hey...
Being married to one is
HA we can do the continuation
You lead, I'll riff off that
```

Public (audience will see)

He looked down at what he had just stepped on. Great, the brains of the pigeon he had just clubbed over the head.

Private (audience will not see)

Fig. 11. Determining the tone, protocol, and continuation of previous story.

Although the "pigeon" theme from the first story had re-emerged, the story was veering into comic rather than horror territory. At this point, G5P2 used the backchannel to ask: "what happened to the horror" (see Fig. 12). In response, G5P1 added a line stating the main character's trousers are torn, which G5P2 followed up on in the backchannel, suggesting "maybe he can turn into a pigeon too". G5P1 responded both in the story ("He falls by a tree clutching his leg, pain searing"), and in the backchannel ("Exactomondo"). G5P2 supported this, suggesting "or maybe pigeons start developing a taste for blood", followed by a support response ("great!!") to encourage the direction G5P1 was taking.

As G5P2 explained, here the backchannel enabled them to quickly get back on track:

> We started off with horror, then it kind of went a little bit off and that's why I said, "hey we're going to do horror right?" then he brought it back he did bring it back so that worked out. (I2, 00:11:12)

Here, the backchannel is being used to correct what one participant saw as a straying from the direction they had set, and the other participant responded. As with group 3, the backchannel was being used for support and confirmation.

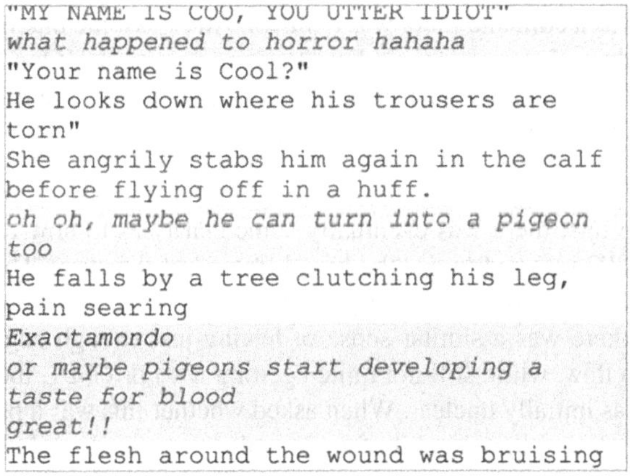

```
"MY NAME IS COO, YOU UTTER IDIOT"
what happened to horror hahaha
"Your name is Cool?"
He looks down where his trousers are
torn"
She angrily stabs him again in the calf
before flying off in a huff.
oh oh, maybe he can turn into a pigeon
too
He falls by a tree clutching his leg,
pain searing
Exactamondo
or maybe pigeons start developing a
taste for blood
great!!
The flesh around the wound was bruising
```

Fig. 12. Using the private backchannel to bring the story back in line.

5.3 Varying Degrees of Cognitive Consensus

One issue arising from these observations is the varying degrees to which the participants could be said to have developed a shared mental model of the story. Despite this, apart from the first session for group 3, the participants were able to move the story forward and maintain some coherence, often without the backchannel. This suggests that an approximation of cognitive consensus is enough for collaborative storytelling.

Importance of a Common Starting Point: Group 3 experienced difficulty during the first session, with one participant completely dominating. Interestingly, in the second session they built on ideas from the first story to ground the second story. During their initial backchannel communication, they decided on their roles. As G3P1 said, "we can try and prompt each other, like I'll be the guard, you be Kevin" (F: 00:02:37). Building on G3P2's character from the first session gave them a common starting point and enabling the collaboration to proceed.

However, as G3P1 explained, this still allowed for uncertainty: "Because she was Kevin, but I didn't know what her prompt was except it was related to food and I didn't really tell her what my prompt was because I didn't really think it was necessary" (I2: 00:03:46). Similarly, G3P2 did not have a complete understanding of the story or its direction: "Not quite, because we would change it, because I wrote something and then she added a twist, and I'd be like ok it went this direction, how would I continue from there" (I2: 00:47:23). Despite this, the group appeared to have enough cognitive consensus to move the story forward, without the breakdown seen in session 1.

Understanding "The Broad Frame" of the Story. For group 2, although both sessions went smoothly, participants admitted they were not clear about story content or direction. When asked if he knew where the second story was going, G2P1 said: "Not really, actually the stronger player in this part is basically the other player, because I'm just reacting, I'm trying to push to the end, to push towards a resolution" (I2, 00:05:00). Similarly, G2P2 initially had trouble determining what was happening in the first story, and struggled to link G2P1's contributions with his own:

I knew there was a coin and there was a mirror. And I assume that his prompt has something to do with a coin, so in a broad way in my mind, [I] kind of wanted to link them together about the sides and falling, so that's the broad frame that I was working with. (I1, 00:09:44)

G2P2 struggled to reach some form of cognitive consensus from which to build the story. Despite this, there was eventually some clarity as to how to move the story forward, what G2P2 referred to as "the broad frame" of the story. This seems to have been enough to allow collaboration to proceed.

For group 6 there was a similar sense of having just enough cognitive consensus for the process to flow, while still not quite "getting it". For G6P1, the direction in the second session was initially unclear. When asked whether this was a problem, she said: "no, it's fun to not know, there's a bit of anxiety also that you don't know, and then you realize that it's not so bad that you don't know" (I2: 00:20:13). This tension between knowing and not knowing is something G6P2 also mentioned:

I found myself being more comfortable in that space of [...] knowing and not knowing at the same time. I knew what I wanted to do but at the same time I had to confirm based on what the other person was going to do, and from there come to a sort of compromise. (I2: 00:04:56)

There was a transition from the need to develop at least some degree of cognitive consensus to the idea that uncertainty and reduced communication can be productive.

Deliberately Retaining Some Uncertainty. This interest in maintaining uncertainty was clearest with group 4. In both sessions the participants could collaborate, despite repeatedly admitting that neither had any idea where the story was going.[4] For the second session they never came to a consensus as to what the story was about or where it was going, but they nevertheless were able to proceed. In fact, G4P1 felt this lack of understanding contributed to the success of the session:

[The] fact that there is some distance between me and [G4P2], in terms of we don't see what the other person's expression is, allows me to have my own take on the story while having [G4P2] input stuff. (I2: 00:16:47)

Similarly, comparing the first session (without backchannel) with the second session (with), G1P2 felt the backchannel might lead to one person dominating:

If we were given the chance to do a private chat, I feel that one person would dominate the other with their [ideas] and just have their story and other would just follow [...] we will follow one storyline, whereas in the first [session] we were both just shooting guns everywhere and having our own storyline (F, 00:14:54)

This suggests G1P2 was concerned too much awareness of where the other person was taking the story might inhibit free exploration of ideas. Likewise, G1P1 felt there

---

[4] It is worth noting that this pair knew each other professionally and were both practicing storytellers: G4P1 works in improv theatre and spoken word poetry, and G4P2 is a published author. This likely contributed to the ease with which they coordinated their storytelling.

should be some preliminary communication to set up an initial shared mental model, but this should stop once basic parameters were established:

> If we want to have a coherent storyline that the audience can enjoy, probably the first minute or two we don't talk to the audience we just set up our own parameters of the storyline, and then in order to have a refreshing, impromptu story, take away the [backchannel] and then we do our own shenanigan things within the set parameters so at least we do not veer too far away and the audience will be able to appreciate it. (F, 00:31:30)

There is an interesting desire here to maintain uncertainty, which some of participants felt would contribute to the quality of both the experience and the resulting story. It was only in group 3, where the uncertainty interfered with the process of telling the story, that the backchannel was seen as necessary and uncertainty as an obstacle.

6 Discussion

Even with limited or no backchannel communication, participants generally felt able to successfully work together to tell a story. For some groups, minimizing direct communication and leaving gaps in their shared understanding seemed to be an important part of the creative process. This suggests that, even in the absence of a clear shared mental model, if participants had a rough idea of the story direction and what their partner thought the story was about, collaboration could proceed. Only with a large amount of divergence, as with group 3, did the process break down.

We can connect our observations to Saywer's [13] notion of the "emergent", the cumulative set of constraints put in place by the contributions made by the participants. In our context, the "emergent" is explicitly represented by the concrete trace of participants' contributions (the text in the scrollable chat window). This captures what has been "said" in the story but does not include the intentions behind those utterances. For most of the groups, the combination of the "emergent" and each participant's individual understanding of what this suggested regarding the future direction of the story seemed to be sufficient for them to form new contributions, even if they didn't ever completely understand what the other participant had in mind. For group 3, however, it was only when they could set some initial parameters in the second session that they were able to move the story forward. They still didn't come to a complete cognitive consensus, but it was enough for them to proceed with the storytelling task.

For some groups this lack of complete cognitive consensus, coupled with limited communication, seemed to be an important part of creative collaboration. This aligns with Sawyer's [13] description of improvisational performances as experiencing a tension between maintaining coherence with the emergent and demonstrating some degree of innovation. It was only when the balance shifted too far towards innovation, with very little coherence, that the lack of cognitive consensus became irreconcilable. This also mirror Magerko et al.'s [11] description of the process of cognitive divergence and cognitive convergence. By deliberately limiting their communication and avoiding sharing too much about their prompts, participants made it more likely they would repeatedly experience the cognitive divergence/cognitive convergence cycle, perhaps using this to manage the tension between coherence with the emergent and innovation.

This need to balance coherence and innovation suggests that online collaborative storytelling tools should provide flexibility for how much, and when, information is shared between participants, rather than providing as much shared information as possible, all the time. When it is possible to move forward with limited information and implicit coordination, it may be better to minimize the information being shared. When participants feel that there is a breakdown, as we saw with group 3, it should be possible to switch to more explicit modes of communication to repair the breakdown and move the storytelling process forward. How this movement between a richer and a deliberately more impoverished mode of communication is initiated, and who controls this (the participants, the system, or some combination of the two), is not clear. This suggests interesting areas for further research.

7 Conclusion

The results of our study suggest that minimal workspace awareness features, a shared representation of the story so far, and a simple backchannel may provide enough awareness and communication to enable some degree of coordination of process, content, and direction. Most participants felt they could tell their story even without achieving a clear shared mental model, suggesting that with some degree of cognitive consensus, participants could continue to contribute. Most important was having either implicit or explicit agreement about the process. In fact, some participants found lack of a clear shared mental model and limited communication channels were productive for creativity. This suggests designers of collaborative storytelling tools should acknowledge the importance of the ongoing process of cognitive divergence and convergence, rather than focusing on support for reaching and maintaining cognitive consensus.

Although we explored text-based collaborative storytelling, there are other, similar contexts, such as storytelling in group chat and social media, where our observations may also be relevant. Future work could extend our observations to wider contexts, to help inform the design of tools for supporting a range of forms of creative collaboration. It would also be worth exploring the impact of the backchannel not just on coordination, but also on story quality and the audience experience.

Acknowledgements. This research was funded under the National University of Singapore Humanities and Social Sciences Seed Fund grant "Communication Strategies in Real-time Computer-Mediated Creative Collaboration".

References

1. Hadley, B.: Social media as theatre stage: aesthetics, affordances and interactivities. In: Hadley, B. (ed.) Theatre, Social Media, and Meaning Making, pp. 53–112. Springer, Cham (2017). https://doi.org/10.1007/978-3-319-54882-1_3

2. Jamieson, H.V., Smith, V.: UpStage: an online tool for real-time storytelling. In: Pan, Z., Cheok, A.D., Müller, W., Iurgel, I., Petta, P., Urban, B. (eds.) Transactions on Edutainment X. LNCS, vol. 7775, pp. 146–160. Springer, Heidelberg (2013). https://doi.org/10.1007/978-3-642-37919-2_8

3. Sant, T.: Theatrical performance on the Internet: how far have we come since Hamnet? Int. J. Perform. Arts Digit. Media **9**, 247–259 (2013)

4. Danet, B., Bechar-Israeli, T., Cividalli, A., Rosenbaum-Tamari, Y.: Curtain time 20: 00 GMT: experiments with virtual theater on internet relay chat. J. Comput.-Mediat. Commun. **1**, JCMC125 (1995)

5. Marino, M., Wittig, R.: Netprov: elements of an emerging form. Dichtung Digit. **42** (2012)

6. Wittig, R.: Literature and Netprov in social media: a travesty, or, in defense of pretension. In: The Bloomsbury Handbook of Electronic Literature. Bloomsbury Academic (2017)

7. Rohrer, J.: Sleep is Death [computer software] (2010)

8. Protagonist Labs: Storium [online platform] (2019)

9. Page, R.E.: Stories and Social Media: Identities and Interaction. Routledge, Oxford (2013)

10. Fuller, D., Magerko, B.: Shared mental models in improvisational theatre. In: Proceedings of the 8th ACM Conference on Creativity and Cognition, pp. 269–278. ACM Press, New York (2011). https://doi.org/10.1145/1822309.1822324

11. Magerko, B., et al.: An empirical study of cognition and theatrical improvisation. In: Proceeding of the Seventh ACM Conference on Creativity and Cognition - C&C 2009, p. 117. ACM (2009). https://doi.org/10.1145/1640233.1640253

12. Sawyer, R.K.: Creativity as mediated action: a comparison of improvisational performance and product creativity. Mind Cult. Act. **2**, 172–191 (1995)

13. Sawyer, R.K.: Group creativity: musical performance and collaboration. Psychol. Music **34**, 148–165 (2006)

14. Sawyer, R.K.: Group Creativity: Music, Theater, Collaboration. Psychology Press, Hove (2014)

15. Silverstein, M.: Metapragmatic discourse and metapragmatic function. In: Reflexive Language, pp. 33–58 (2010). https://doi.org/10.1017/cbo9780511621031.004

16. Levesque, L.L., Wilson, J.M., Wholey, D.R.: Cognitive divergence and shared mental models in software development project teams. J. Organiz. Behav.: Int. J. Ind. Occup. Organiz. Psychol. Behav. **22**, 135–144 (2001)

17. Baecker, R.M., Nastos, D., Posner, I.R., Mawby, K.L.: The user-centered iterative design of collaborative writing software. In: Proceedings of the SIGCHI Conference on Human Factors in Computing Systems - CHI 1993, pp. 399–405. ACM Press, New York (1993). https://doi.org/10.1145/169059.169312

18. Wang, D.: How people write together now: exploring and supporting today's computer-supported collaborative writing. In: Proceedings of the 19th ACM Conference on Computer Supported Cooperative Work and Social Computing Companion - CSCW 2016 Companion, pp. 175–179. ACM (2016). https://doi.org/10.1145/2818052.2874352

19. Mitchell, A., Posner, I., Baecker, R.: Learning to write together using groupware. In: CHI 1995: Proceedings of the SIGCHI Conference on Human Factors in Computing Systems, pp. 288–295. ACM Press/Addison-Wesley Publishing Co., New York (1995). https://doi.org/10.1145/223904.223941

20. Cheng, J., Kang, L., Cosley, D.: Storeys: designing collaborative storytelling interfaces. In: CHI 2013 Extended Abstracts on Human Factors in Computing Systems, pp. 3031–3034 (2013)

21. Boellstorff, T., Nardi, B., Pearce, C., Taylor, T.L.: Words with friends: writing collaboratively online. Interactions **20**, 58–61 (2013). https://doi.org/10.1145/2501987

22. Gutwin, C., Greenberg, S.: A descriptive framework of workspace awareness for real-time groupware. Comput. Supp. Coop. Work (CSCW) **11**, 411–446 (2002)

23. Greenberg, S., Gutwin, C.: Implications of we-awareness to the design of distributed groupware tools. Comput. Supp. Coop. Work (CSCW) **25**(4–5), 279–293 (2016). https://doi.org/10.1007/s10606-016-9244-y
24. Kellogg, W.A., et al.: Leveraging digital backchannels to enhance user experience in electronically mediated communication. In: Proceedings of the 2006 20th Anniversary Conference on Computer Supported Cooperative Work, pp. 451–454 (2006)
25. Harry, D., Green, J., Donath, J.: Backchan. nl: integrating backchannels in physical space. In: Proceedings of the SIGCHI Conference on Human Factors in Computing Systems, pp. 1361–1370 (2009)
26. McCarthy, J.F., Boyd, D.M.: Digital backchannels in shared physical spaces: experiences at an academic conference. In: CHI 2005 Extended Abstracts on Human Factors in Computing Systems, pp. 1641–1644. ACM (2005). https://doi.org/10.1145/1056808.1056986
27. McCarthy, J.F., et al.: Digital backchannels in shared physical spaces: attention, intention and contention. In: Proceedings of the 2004 ACM Conference on Computer Supported Cooperative Work, pp. 550–553. ACM (2004)
28. Mitchell, A., Yew, J., Wyse, L., Ang, D., Thattai, P.: The AntWriter improvisational writing system: visualizing and coordinating upcoming actions. In: Nunes, N., Oakley, I., Nisi, V. (eds.) ICIDS 2017. LNCS, vol. 10690, pp. 336–340. Springer, Cham (2017). https://doi.org/10.1007/978-3-319-71027-3_38
29. Mitchell, A., Yew, J., Thattai, P., Loh, B., Ang, D., Wyse, L.: The temporal window: explicit representation of future actions in improvisational performances. In: Proceedings of the 2017 ACM SIGCHI Conference on Creativity and Cognition - C&C 2017, pp. 28–38. ACM, New York (2017). https://doi.org/10.1145/3059454.3059470
30. Glaser, B.G., Strauss, A.L.: The Discovery of Grounded Theory: Strategies for Qualitative Research. Aldine Publishing, London (1967)
31. McGhee, G., Marland, G.R., Atkinson, J.: Grounded theory research: literature reviewing and reflexivity. J. Adv. Nurs. **60**, 334–342 (2007)

What Inspires Retellings - A Study
of the Game Genshin Impact

Miranda Greting$^{(\boxtimes)}$ ⓘ, Xiehui Mao$^{(\boxtimes)}$ ⓘ, and Mirjam Palosaari Eladhari$^{(\boxtimes)}$ ⓘ

Stockholm University, Stockholm, Sweden
miranda.greting@gmail.com, maoxiehui@outlook.com, mirjam@dsv.su.se
http://www.su.se

Abstract. This paper presents a study of retellings about Genshin
Impact, exploring how the game's narrative design inspires players to
create fiction and art based on the game's universe. A questionnaire
sent to players rendered 1606 replies. Based on the findings in this corpus, eight players and creators of retellings were interviewed in-depth.
Among our findings were that players were most inspired by the characters, detailed worldbuilding, and regional cultures in the game world.
Their motivation to create was often spurred by the gaps and ambiguities in the detailed narrative design, wanting to "fill in the gaps" and,
through their creation of fiction, further explore the intricacies of the
game's narrative elements.

Keywords: Retellings · Fanworks · Fanfiction · Fanart · Narrative
design · Video games · Genshin impact

1 Introduction

The action role-playing game *Genshin Impact* (GI) [12] has, between its release
in 2020 and May of 2022, inspired players to create a multitude of art and fiction
based on the game. Much of this material constitutes retellings - e.g., instances
where players use their play experiences to create art and narratives that are
directly inspired by a game [6]. GI gameplay consists of exploring the open-world
Teyvat, consisting of seven different nations. On *Archive Of Our Own*, an archive
hosting fanworks such as fanfiction and fanart, the number of works amounts to
more than seventy thousand, placing GI fifth on the list of Video Games with
the most fanworks on the website [1]. The study of retellings can inform us about
which aspects of a game narrative are especially meaningful to players.

The work reported here builds upon an earlier study reported in the thesis work by Greting and Mao that studied various aspects of game experience
and retellings based on GI [10]. In this paper, however, we specifically focus on
exploring which aspects of the narrative design of GI inspire retellings in the
form of fanfiction and fanart, asking: *What about Genshin Impact engages and
inspires players enough to not only play it but create their own artistic works
related to the game world?*

M. Vosmeer and L. Holloway-Attaway (Eds.): ICIDS 2022, LNCS 13762, pp. 249–269, 2022.
https://doi.org/10.1007/978-3-031-22298-6_16

The study was done in multiple steps, starting with a questionnaire asking players of GI about their retellings. The questionnaire rendered 1606 replies, detailing aspects of the game and personal recounts of retellers' experiences. Based on this information (detailed in Sect. 3.1), eight players who had indicated their willingness to discuss their artistic endeavors were selected for in-depth interviews. The interviews were semi-structured, allowing players to expand on their sources of inspiration. Questions asked were informed by previous studies [4,6,15,18] and examination of the corpus from the questionnaire. In the interviews, players added more information and depth to their reasoning, and gave illustrative examples from their artistic practice.

2   Background

2.1   Retellings and Fandom

Retellings in relation to games can further be defined as stories constructed out of game play experience, creating a narrative that exists separately from the narrative play in a game [20, 405]. Eladhari [6] describes retellings as artifacts co-created by players and the games they are based on. Examples of game retellings include communicative retellings, e.g., discussing game experiences, simultaneous retellings, such as live-streaming while playing, recorded system output, e.g., gameplay recordings, and retellings with artistic or authorial intent, such as art or stories based on a game, including fanfiction and fanart [6].

Eladhari explains that studying these narrative artifacts could enable a deeper understanding of player experiences and serve as an instrument for critique of narrative systems [6]. Kreminski et al. study the creation of written retellings based on AI-based games, building on Eladhari's work [6], and conclude that: "From this perspective, players are already making use of games as storytelling partners-and, in some cases, seeking out games with the specific intent of using them to support story construction" [15].

In order to differentiate between retellings and fanworks, we offer the following distinctions: Fanworks are, or contain, retellings when their narration is based on play experience. Fanworks are often combinations of retellings and imagination, where creators imagine and add additional material to their works that was not part of the source material. A retelling does not have to be a fanwork, since retelling is not necessarily tied to being a fan of something. A fanwork, however, can be a retelling entirely if it contains no added imaginative aspects. Fanworks are seldom devoid of retelling aspects, as their nature is to build upon the source material.

Fandoms are fan communities consisting of people who like the same media, who gather in social spaces to discuss, share experiences, create art, and write stories based on different media [18]. Hence, fandoms are built largely around retellings and fanworks. Fanworks are not limited to video games. Instead, they can be any form of creative work based on any media, commonly movies, tv-shows, books, or video games [18].

Common types of fanworks include fanfiction and fanart, where fans create art or stories based on, e.g., the characters, scenery, or plot of an already existing media [11]. They can be set in the same world of the media it is based on, or have an entirely different setting, only keeping the characters and sometimes giving them new roles. The latter is called an Alternate Universe (AU) [18]. In fanfiction, it is common to fill in perceived gaps in the source material by, e.g., exploring character relationships, the past or future, or extending scenes (ibid). The source material provides limitations that can be both a framework and a challenge: A framework by having something to build on, e.g., defined characters and setting, and a challenge in constructing a compelling narrative or image by creating along with or against the source material [18].

2.2 Fanwork Popularity Across Different Games

On the archive for transformative fanworks *Archive Of Our Own (AO3)*, fanworks are published for different media. Fanfiction is most common, less frequent are, e.g., fanart, audio-recorded fanfiction, and fanmade music or video [2]. It can not be known how many of the fanworks are retellings according to the distinction between the terms offered in Sect. 2.1. However, considering the intertwined relationship between them, it is likely that a large number contain retelling aspects. The number of GI retellings created since its release in 2020 (see Fig. 1) indicates that GI lends itself well to fanwork creation, one of the reasons GI was chosen for this study.

Video Game	Year of Release	Amount of Fanworks(25th January)	Amount of Fanworks(25th February)	Amount of Fanworks(25th March)	Amount of Fanworks(5nd May)	Total Increase (January - May) 100 days
Genshin Impact (Video Game)	2020	55 411	60 530	64 415	70 692	15 281
Harry Potter - All Media Types	1997*	340 562	346 635	350 678	356 661	16 099
Star Wars - All Media Types	1977*	182 101	185 866	188 314	191 885	9 784
Minecraft (Video Game)	2009	87 110	91 690	95 419	94 844	7744
Final Fantasy Series	1987*	80 283	81 930	83 332	85 141	4 858
Dragon Age - All Media Types	2009	74 161	74 564	75 070	75 637	1 476

Fig. 1. Fanwork popularity on AO3 across different video games.

AO3 was launched in November 2009, marking the year fanworks started being published on the website [16]. Games marked with "*" were launched earlier than this. Data in Fig. 1 shows the total number of fanworks for GI and the five most popular video game fandoms on AO3 between January 25th and May 5th, based on public statistics on AO3's website [1]. Harry Potter and Star Wars have video games and are thereby part of the video game category, even though they are more known from books or movies. Only the five most popular video game fandoms are listed on AO3. The rest are sorted in alphabetical order. Genshin Impact has a comparatively fast growth rate in its amount of fanworks. Up until January 25th, it had 55,411 fanworks published on AO3. Between January 25th and May 5th in 2022, a total of 100 d, GI increased with 15,281 fanworks. In the same period, the number of Harry Potter fanworks increased by 16,099, Star Wars by 9,784, Minecraft by 7,744, Final Fantasy by 4,858, and Dragon Age by 1,476. By comparing this data group, the growth rate of GI fanworks is second only to that of Harry Potter. When splitting the data into more detail, the average daily increase in Harry Potter fanworks is 161, while Star Wars increases by 98, Minecraft by 77, Final Fantasy by 49, and Dragon Age by 15. GI has an average daily increase of 153 works.

On May 5th, 2022, the difference in the total amount of creative works between Dragon Age and Genshin Impact was less than 5,000. Documentation of these numbers is available in [10]. At the time of writing, in mid-July 2022, GI has 80 728 fanworks, exceeding that of Dragon Age. (The statistics in Fig. 1 and Fig. 2 are not representative of fanworks on other sites or forums, where data may look different).

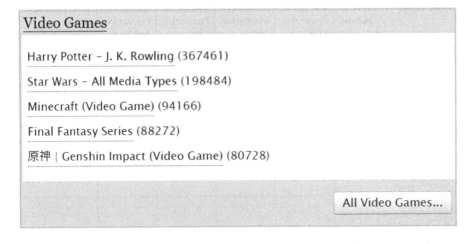

Fig. 2. Statistics from AO3's website - 14 July 2022.

2.3   Genshin Impact

Genshin Impact (GI) is an open world Action Role-playing Game (ARPG). The narrative focuses on the Traveler, who travels between worlds with their twin. The player can choose one of the twins as the protagonist. In Teyvat, they are separated, and the Traveler journeys through the unfamiliar world in search of their lost sibling. Several people they meet along the way are acquirable as playable characters, each with different personalities and unique abilities. The game world Teyvat consists of seven different nations with rich individual cultures and mythology, all inspired by regions in real life. The three currently released regions, Mondstadt, Liyue, and Inazuma, are inspired by Germany and northern Europe, China, and Japan. The game has an elemental-based combat system, where each playable character has skills tied to one out of seven elements: pyro (fire), hydro (water), cryo (ice), anemo (wind), geo (earth), electro (lightning), and dendro (nature). The seven nations are also linked to their own element.

The player can control a team with a maximum of four characters, switching between them to use different abilities. Part of the gameplay is to build different teams, since characters' contrasting elemental and combat skills interact differently with each other [12]. GI also supports multiplayer (Co-Op), allowing players to visit each other's game worlds. However, the upper limit is four people, the max number of characters in a team. Co-Op can allow friends to play together and for people to find new friends in GI [12]. Due to the inability to discuss in-game content with more people than ones in Co-Op, the game community exists mainly outside of the game. Many players use social media to discuss, share, or create content. HoYoverse also encourages fanworks through their own game forum HoYoLab [13].

By depicting cultures to an extent rooted in real life, the game world in GI is an environment for cultural immersion. Video games can provide situations that allow players to learn the culture of a new language through engagement in playing [17]. A study by Dede and Barab [4] detailed how immersion in digital environments can enhance education. Social media or video games can shift learning from passive acquisition of others peoples' knowledge, to an active learning experience involving creativity, critique, and collaboration [4].

The narrative in GI is conveyed through different types of quests and fragmented storytelling. Archon Quests are equivalent to main quests in other Open World games, detailing Traveler's journey through the regions of Teyvat. World Quests, equivalent to side quests, are unlocked by talking to NPCs. They give more depth to the game world, its history, and the people in it. Story Quests focus on individual playable characters, where players get to learn their backstories and personalities better [12]. Some quests are time-limited, often related to in-game regional festivals inspired by real life. Other types of quests are less related to the story and, therefore, not explained in detail.

A significant part of Genshin's storytelling is done outside of quests, through fragmented stories and lore found in item descriptions or while exploring, for the player to discover and make their own connections as to where they fit into the

Genshin universe [12]. Most quests, events, and fragmented stories are connected in different ways, with each form of narration containing pieces of a larger story. The full picture is rarely given, and gaps between questlines, dialogue, and story fragments are left to the player's imagination.

Relationships between characters in GI are shown and given depth by the interactions and the dialogue in the game, text that the players themselves cannot change. Character profiles for each playable character also have a section describing their thoughts about other characters they know (Fig. 3). Scattered information in item descriptions and written records throughout the game world can provide more detail. Close relationships between playable characters, especially romantic partnerships, are not spelled out explicitly within the game. "Pairings" between characters are established out-game, within fandom and fanworks, where players create character pairings according to their imagination, filling in blank spaces between the characters' connections. Neither in-game relationships nor interpreted pairings are limited to gender-normative or hetero-normative portrayals.

Fig. 3. A character profile in GI.

Retellings inspired by Genshin Impact are created in many forms, such as writing, art, animation, videos, live-streams, and music. Fanfiction and fanart are the focus of this paper. A multitude of retellings can be found on social media. Representative examples of fanfiction, fanart, and a podcast are included between pages 5–8 in the thesis work this study builds on [10], including a poem in form of a letter from one character to another, and a re-drawn meme of GI characters portrayed as the role they play in team-builds the creator uses most.

For a more detailed description of the game pertinent to this study, we refer to [10] and to play the game itself [12].

3   The Study

Given the detailed game world and the vast amount of retellings, we took care to approach the area openly to allow us to find data we may not have expected. In the following sections, we present the multi-step journey that the body of work led us to in order to examine what aspects of GI specifically inspire a vast body of retellings. The process of the study is illustrated in Fig. 4.

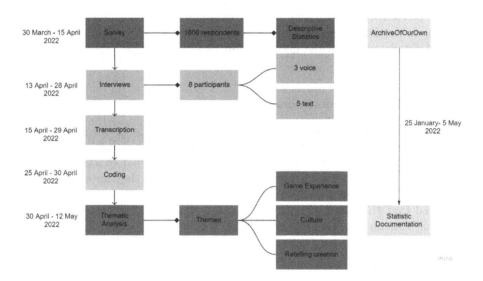

Fig. 4. Data collection and analysis process.

The increase in fanworks on AO3 was documented during this study. A sample of statistics from AO3 was taken once each month between January and March 2022, and on the 100th day since the starting date. This process can be seen in [10], along with all the data samples from AO3.

3.1   The Questionnaire

In order to get information about how players of GI are inspired to create retellings, a questionnaire was published on social media. We asked about how different aspects of in-game elements and cultural representations affected players' creative spark.

The questionnaire was web-based and created using Google Forms [9]. The first section of the questionnaire contained information about the study and its authors, followed by a few demographic questions. A section regarding written retellings was reached if participants answered 'Yes' to creating GI fanfiction. Another section is about hypothetical retellings, regarding other types of creations related to Genshin Impact, reached if answering 'No' to creating fanfiction. If answering 'Yes' to creating GI fanfiction or fanart, it continued to a section 'Interviews', asking if respondents would want to be interviewed, providing contact information to the first authors of this study, and the option for respondents to leave their contact information to be reached out to in an attempt to schedule interviews. The last section, reached by everyone regardless of answers, contained general questions about Genshin Impact.

A pilot-test of the questionnaire was conducted, and subsequent changes and clarifications were made according to feedback. The questionnaire was then posted to HoYoLAB [13], and later to different character forums on Reddit [19] due to not having reached enough potential interview participants. A total of 1606 people answered the questionnaire. A full copy of the questionnaire is available in [10].

3.2   Results from Questionnaire

The questionnaire contained two types of questions, single-choice (select most applicable option) and multiple-choice (select all that apply). Single-choice questions are represented as pie charts and multiple-choice as bar charts.

Twelve (12) percent of the respondents reported that they do write fan fiction about GI. Of these, when asked about their main focus when writing, 58% answered that they focused on backstory and character development, 64% on plot, and 76% on relationships (see Fig. 5).

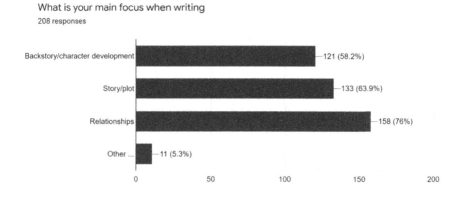

Fig. 5. Players' responses regarding own writing focus.

When asked what in GI attracts them most, 87% of 1,606 participants chose character(s), while plot (59%), art style (58%), and mechanics (54%) have similar numbers, and background music attracts 45% (see Fig. 6). Regarding what makes them like a character, 96% of 208 fanfiction writers answered personality, 76% appearance, 68% backstory, and 35% characters' combat mechanics (see Fig. 7). A large part of respondents write about same-sex relationships, 61% between women, 59% between men, and 53% write about relationships between opposite-sex characters. 45% of creators describe friendship rather than romance, 44% write non-sexual intimacy, 18% poly relationships, and six (6) percent depict other forms of love or intimacy (see Fig. 8).

What do you think attracts you the most in Genshin Impact?
1,606 responses

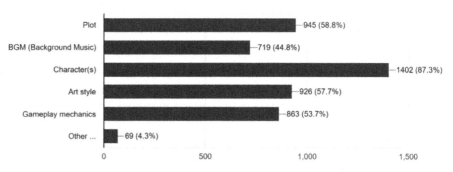

Fig. 6. Player responses on what attracts them in GI.

What makes you like a character?
208 responses

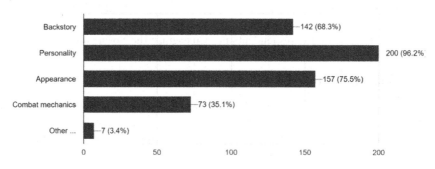

Fig. 7. Player responses on what makes them like a character.

Regarding which region players recognize their culture in most, 28% of 1595 participants responded Mondstadt, 17% Liyue, 4% Inazuma, 20% in regions not yet released, and 31% in none or currently none. When asked which region

What kind of love or intimacy do you like to describe in your writing?
207 responses

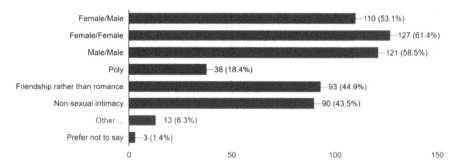

Fig. 8. Kinds of love or intimacy respondents focus on.

inspired their retellings most, 36% of the fanfiction writers answered Liyue, 27% Inazuma, and another 27% Mondstadt. Four (4) percent were most inspired by currently unreleased regions, and six (6) percent answered None (See Fig. 9).

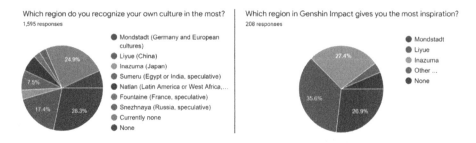

Fig. 9. Region respondents most recognize their own culture in.

3.3 The Interviews

The answers gathered through the questionnaire helped us focus our study further. An interview guide was created, see [10], preparing questions centered around three themes; retellings, immersion, and represented regional cultures.

Participants. Potential participants from the respondents of the questionnaire were approached for interviews. The selection was based on the respondents' individual properties, aiming to get as much information pertinent to the research question as possible. Eight people were interviewed. Five are fanfiction writers, two are fanart creators, and one creates both. One participant who creates fanart also analyzes the lore and history of GI through a podcast and discussion posts. Three participants are from Asia, three from North America, and two from Europe, while 75% of them belong to different Asian cultures.

The Questions Asked in the Interviews. The questions (see Fig. 10) in the interviews are those that rendered the data related to retelling inspiration. The full interview script is available at [10].

Interview Questions
What are the fanfictions you write, or the artworks you draw about?
Is there anything specific in Genshin that inspired you to make them? What?
What is your main reason for writing or drawing?
What in the game makes you feel the most immersed, almost like you are actually part of the Genshin universe? - Is this something that has impacted your creations?
How are the characters you write about or draw impacted by the characters you play/have on your team in Genshin? (Do you write about or draw the same characters you play as?)
Do you get most attached to a character by e.g. playing as them, meeting them in story quests, learning about them through character biographies? (Or inspired by social media and other people who also like them?)
What makes a story important to you? Is there anything specific that makes certain quest lines, character stories or events matter more to you?
Are things that happen in-game while playing also inspiration for your stories or artworks?
Which region (or regions) are you most inspired by when writing or drawing? Why?
Are there any cultures you were not as familiar with before but have been inspired to learn more about by playing Genshin? - Is this something you use when making retellings?
Do character's culture or backstory also make an impact on your writing or drawing?
Are you familiar with the virtual festivals in the game and their corresponding real life festivals? (e.g. Lantern rite or Inazuma's summer festival). If so, have these been inspiration for your writing or drawing? How?

Fig. 10. Interview questions related to retelling inspiration

Procedure and Documentation. A consent form was created, available in [10], and sent out to interview participants when scheduling, to be signed before the interview started. The initial aim was to interview ten people, later lowered to eight due to time limitations.

All interviews were conducted through Discord [5]; three were through voice chat, and five were through text. Voice interviews were recorded using OBS Studio [14] to transcribe after. Text interviews were already a written record on their own. Voice recordings were listened through and transcribed into a Google Docs [8] document, and text interviews were transferred from Discord to another Google Docs [8] document as well. The full transcripts, consisting of 102 pages, are available via [10].

Analysis Procedure. A thematic analysis was conducted to present and analyze the interviews by identifying, analyzing, and compiling codes into themes. The thematization was done inductively to avoid being limited to predetermined themes. A semantic approach was used, basing the codes on the explicit or surface meanings of what respondents had said [3].

The coding was done by identifying the parts of the transcribed interviews that overlapped with the research question, summarizing each into a shorter code in a comment in Google Docs, which marked the referred section. This way, there was an overview of all codes while having them connected to the source material to be able to relate them to the entirety of what was said. The codes were then gone over again, identifying potential themes. Codes were sorted into a table, resulting in three themes; Game Experience, Culture, and Retelling Creation. All codes were examined iteratively to see if respondents expressed similar opinions or experiences. Patterns that formed between codes from different respondents were combined into one, and codes unrelated to the research question were discarded.

3.4   Ethical Aspects

In order to protect participants' privacy, data from the questionnaire and interviews were entirely anonymized so that nothing could be linked back to individual respondents. The only exception is examples of retellings, where credit is given to creators (who were asked for permission and gave their consent), along with links to the post where wanted. To avoid misrepresentation of participants' responses in the interviews, the study was sent to the interview participants before finalizing the text [10] to examine whether their responses were portrayed accurately, and subsequent changes were made where necessary.

Data analysis was made as objectively as possible to operate with scientific integrity. The thematic analysis was done semantically, results build explicitly on what respondents said rather than the authors' interpretations. All data were analyzed and reviewed by both first authors of this paper to avoid biases, assumptions, or personal preferences as far as possible.

3.5   Making Sense of What Was Said in the Interviews

The full table of codes can be found in [10]. For this paper, focusing on what inspires retellings in GI, we offer the subset of the thematization in Fig. 11.

Inspiration			Research	Creative Focus
Character narrative	**Worldbuilding**	**Gameplay**	Reads up on culture and lore to build the world more accurately	Exploring characters and relationships further than the game has
Detailed characters. Even NPC's depicted with own lives, goals & relationships, looped back to as game progresses	Different regions inspire stories of different kinds	Characters' gameplay animations, element and combat skills		Explores inner workings of the game world, character interpretations, and connections to real-life inspiration sources
Character's culture or backstory	'Hidden' lore fill out fanfictions; includes details untold in main story	Using a team of favorite characters or ones with related backstories	Looks up fashion trends in region-corresponding cultures in search of casual clothing to simplify character outfits	
Interesting found family dynamics	Comparison between festivals and their real-life inspirations spark ideas that Genshin has not covered	Takes in-game reference pictures in case they will be drawn	Goes around region for better idea of what it looks like when writing	Memorializes in-game moments (especially co-op) in a drawing or post
Relation between characters (not limited to main character); interactions, indirect connections or related backstories				Creates original characters with backstories set in Genshin universe
Genshin gives an outline, but enough is up for interpretation to spark experimentation with "what if's"	Implied connection between character and places they have not been to in-game		Not reading up on a character's backstory can lead to stereotypical portrayal	Romances or comedies. Especially characters pining
	Inspired by places they loved; incorporates region-specific details and locations			Sees parallels between book and Genshin characters - writes AUs
Dissatisfied with the depth of a character's story; re-wrote it				Exploring human psychology and really digging into emotions
Similarity between characters can be opportunity to bring them together, and they might learn from each other				Stories they want to see do not exist, have to create their own to read
				Uncommon favorite pairings, writes for friends to understand them

Fig. 11. Retelling creation codes.

Results Anchored in Participant Responses. As this paper has a limited length, we do not expand on all aspects of the data gathered, albeit interesting. Here, we describe what we learned from the participants' descriptions of their practice of creating retellings and fanworks, particularly fanfiction and fanart. These results were summed up in the categories inspiration, characters in retellings, research, and creative focus.

Inspiration. The major inspirational factors in Genshin are detailed individual characters, dynamics and interactions between characters, worldbuilding, narrative, regional differences, and cultural representations. These aspects are detailed enough to spark interest, yet open-ended enough to leave room for players' interpretations. One participant summed up these factors as follows:

> "There's a structure and a history to this world, and these characters, like every character you get has some- has a lot of stuff going on in their life, and some intrinsic motivations that are really interesting. So I find that if a world is- even if it's very deeply realized, if it's too open-ended, I don't get that creatively inspired, but if it's too closed off, then there's nowhere for me to kind of insert my questions that become my creative pursuits. Genshin just has the right amount of hooks and intrigue that I think energizes people like me and creators to insert their own interpretation of what we're given".

Another participant similarly highlighted: "I like the character interactions a lot. Also the fact that they gave me an outline, but there's just enough they're missing in each character that I can experiment". They mentioned an important factor being that characters "get to interact with each other and it plays on more interesting dynamics than just you [player/main character] and the character".

As for character pairings, several mentioned bringing together characters with shared traits or loose connections, one example being:

> "I think what I like about pairings a lot is when you have two characters that share a certain trait, or they share a liking for something. [...] then the cultural part comes after that, and they might learn new things from each other".

The scenery and worldbuilding inspired many respondents. One participant described how the in-game lore "alone makes me want to worldbuild by myself, building off existing foundations". They mentioned that for them, the fragmented information in item descriptions or scattered texts "do the most for sparking ideas - it's because they're little morsels of information that you can speculate freely". Most participants also include in-game locations and lore references in retellings where relevant.

Several creators take inspiration from gameplay. One mentioned "When I do write about games, I always like to include little hints at the gameplay itself. For example [...] Venti's element energy, I would try to lean a bit towards his skills and how he works in the game". Another respondent similarly said "I've written a lot about memorable enemies/battles I've gotten into (like the time Xiao beat the primo geovishap with 150 hp and everyone else in the party down...) and I really like using actual map locations when it's applicable".

Research. Most participants look up more information about their favorite characters, and mythology or cultural aspects relevant to them. Two participants mentioned that their reason for looking up more information was to construct the story world more accurately and to avoid stereotypes. One of them highlighted: *"I read up extensively about something so i can build the world as accurately as possible and see if there isn't a way i can slip this all in for extra realism".* Another mentioned, *"I always look up backstories before I start writing a story, [...] I think if people don't look at backstories, that's how the stereotypical portrayals come from".* This relates to another participant's response from the audience's point of view:

> *"they're giving us this cool, complex setting and characters, I tend to like it more when they keep that complexity in fanworks. I know it's always kind of easy to like, reduce them to tropes or something, [...] but I find that doesn't hold my attention as much as when people take all of these details into account".*

Creative Focus. Regarding what types of retellings are created, the interviewed fanfiction writers answered that they write stories exploring characters and relationships further than the game has. Most focus on romance. For example, one writes romantic comedies, and another explores characters' underlying emotions and their inner worlds. One who writes AUs related to books they have read mentions that:

> *"Whenever I read books after I started playing Genshin I started thinking "what if x character was this character instead and y character did this". Kind of like AUs that I wanted to read but couldn't find anywhere. Like "I want x content so I'll do it myself".*

Another focuses on family dynamics, where a character with a tragic past is taken in by other characters, or exploring character constellations who are not related but have formed familial bonds within the game. Regarding art, one also focuses on romantic pairings. Another makes art for their favorite characters' in-game birthdays, and creates original characters inspired by game lore. A third memorializes in-game moments, especially in co-op, through art, and co-hosts a podcast exploring different aspects of GI, including game design and cultural context.

4 Discussion

Artistic and authorial retellings in relation to video games is a relatively unexplored area of study, but one that can be meaningful for, e.g., developers, designers, and player communities. Of significance for GI is the narrative structure, in this study specifically characters and worldbuilding. The study of GI shows how characters and detailed inter-character relationships can not only make them important to the person playing, but motivate players to further explore characters through writing, or recreate them through art. For all interview respondents, their main inspiration is from character attachment and narratives related to them. This is rooted in character design, interactions and connections between characters, along with associations between character narrative and worldbuilding. Individual characters and the dynamics between them are then further explored in retellings and fanworks.

Characters. Of note here is the roundness of the characters; all playable characters have intricate personalities and stories, many more so than the main character.[1] Several NPCs also have major recurring roles, portrayed with lives and pasts of their own. Of potential significance to game designers is if characters and the game world as a whole, feel complete independently of the main character. Expressed by interview respondents was how characters, especially NPCs, do not exist just to further the main character's story, but as their own people with individual goals and struggles. The intricacy and appeal of characters reflect in how some retellings include the Traveler, sometimes as a protagonist, other times as a side character, while other retellings are from other characters' points of view, not including the Traveler at all. The same holds true for relationships: ambiguous and multifaceted, not just between the main character and characters they interact with, but between playable and non-playable characters alike. The questionnaire results showed that romantic relationships are portrayed most in retellings, same-sex relationships slightly more so than opposite-sex ones, followed by friendships, then non-sexual intimacy. Among interview respondents, relationship dynamics were romantic relationships, friendships, familial ties, or family of choice. Same-sex relationships being more common than opposite-sex ones indicates that room for interpretation in GI's narrative can allow people to see themselves in characters, or interpret them as they like, and confirms that fandom provides freedom for character and relationship interpretation.

Characters' richness of detail supports retelling creation in how details can be referred to in art or stories. When depicting character pairings, the creator can have small details be noticed by other characters, which can create intimacy between them. It can also add a second layer of recognition for retelling readers, who might have noticed these details from the game. If not, they can learn about characters from retellings, which could, in turn, impact their attachment to them. This can be important in both fandom and marketing contexts. Social media can have further reach than a game and its marketing on its own. Fan creations can reach people who have not heard of a game, and potentially inspire someone to play, or join a new fandom. This can form a continuous cycle causing both player bases and fandoms to grow.

Worldbuilding. GI's worldbuilding is very intricate, where threads of stories about the present and history of the game world are non-linearly experienced through quests and open-world exploration. The narrative content of these

---

[1] The concept of roundness comes from Forester's description of 'round' characters as rich and complex in comparison to 'flat' one-dimensional characters [7].

threads can be unrelated or out of order, but always linked to something in the game world to challenge the player to slot details into an overlapping narrative. This room for players to figure out connections and gaps between story threads was found to inspire creative works, especially since they can build on existing foundations and add their own interpretation, e.g., to relationships, backstories, and lore. One interview respondent exemplified this by being inspired by characters' implied connection to places they have never been to in-game, e.g., between Kaeya, who lives in Mondstadt, and The Chasm in Liyue, and imagining the history behind it. The character Xiao's voice line of not hesitating to put Zhongli before the Traveler if they should fall on opposing sides also made them curious about their history beyond what is shown in-game. Particularly important for game designers are these gaps; not necessarily non-linearity, but how intricacy combined with missing details provide a space for players to develop curiosity about characters, gameworld, and related stories.

Below (in Fig. 12) are examples of how narrative gaps can inspire retellings based on GI:

Examples of narrative gaps	Application in retellings
Vague connection/similarity between characters - e.g. mentioned letter exchange, or love for music	Connection can be reason for characters to meet, and to further explore their relationship
Implied (unexplained/not shown) connection between characters and locations	Exploring the reason why or depicting the past in a retelling
Murals/ancient tablets with history about the ruins they're found in	Piece together - or stepstone for expansion of - regional history in retellings
Artifact (strength-enhancing material) or weapon descriptions with stories of their origin	Referencing these details in retellings to flesh out character backstories or worldbuilding
Books/Diaries/Notes with fragmented information or stories	Connecting fragmented details to characters or other Genshin lore
Unexplained connection between characters and items/objects	Hypothesize how an item/object came into a character's possession (cause-and-effect)
Character's past - e.g.having lost someone important to them	Exploring who this person was to them, showing them dealing with grief/rewriting a happier future
In-game dialogue or textual records from enemies	Exploring enemies' point of view rather than main character's in retellings
Characters' level up materials (often a flower or gemstone)	Exploring the significance of these materials to the character - e.g. flower language

Fig. 12. How narrative gaps in GI can be applied in retellings

GI's worldbuilding is rooted in represented cultures based on real life, where each character and location reflects their regional culture. For some interview participants, these cultures were an inspiration in themselves. For the other interview respondents, culture was not an individual focus. However, they noted that characters are so intrinsically rooted in their regional cultures that these two notions, "culture" and "character", became inseparable when they reasoned about their creation.

Colorism was pointed out by several respondents, in how characters are portrayed as white or with lighter skin colors than majorities of the culture they are inspired by. How to respectfully portray cultures is something that requires the attention of developers and designers. Portrayed cultures make their way into retellings, often as characters' cultural backgrounds, locations, lore, and other in-game cultural elements. Whether creators look up more information regarding corresponding cultures or rely solely on the content in the game varied among respondents. The accuracy of retellings thereby depends on accurate portrayal in the source material, as inaccuracies would rely on players' knowledge to identify them as such and change them in creative works. It can then have further negative consequences when players bring misconceptions from the game into fandoms, potentially harming people from the cultures that are misrepresented.

Retellings. Relevant to both retellings and fanworks is Eladhari's [6] description of retellings as an instrument for critique, by indicating how different aspects of a game are received by players [6]. Frequent subjects of retellings or aspects explored in-depth, may have left a deeper impression on the player. Where the source material is often changed in favor of imagination could be aspects that did not make much of an impact, or left an unsatisfactory one. The former can indicate highlights of the game, while the latter could potentially signify where the narrative lacks depth and inform developers of what might need more attention.

Several respondents brought up the advantage of having the outline the game narrative provides to base fanworks on. Less introduction is required since the authors, and likely the audience, are already familiar with the game. Hence characters or settings do not have to be imagined from scratch. This matches Stein and Busse's [18] reasoning that part of the appeal of fan creation is creating along with the framework that the source material provides. The source material can provide a challenge to create stories that complement, or diverge, from it but remain close enough for, e.g., characters to be believable [18].

Kreminski et al. [15] further detail how players can use games as storytelling partners. This was found to be true in this study as well, with players telling their own stories or creating art centered around characters and different aspects from the game. One respondent also mentioned creating original characters based on in-game lore, with backstories set in the Genshin universe. Kreminski et al. mentioned how players, in some cases, seek out games with the intent of using them to support story construction. This, however, was found to be the opposite for all the people interviewed. Instead, they started playing after seeing GI content on social media, or having friends that play who recommended it. Their creation of retellings was a response to playing the game, a result of character attachment and inspiration from the narrative and game design. This, however, does not mean that games cannot be sought out to support story construction, just that for people interviewed in this study, it was not the case.

Limitations. Fanfiction and fanart were selected as the focus of this paper to have a limited scope. However, this may render the study findings inapplicable to all types of retellings without further study.

Only eight people were interviewed due to time limitations. The length of the interviews became a trade-off for the amount of data collected. Few interviews along with under-representation especially of Middle Eastern and African cultures may have impacted the results. This study would benefit from more data and varied perspectives, especially cultural ones.

Regarding the data from AO3, only the top 5 titles with the most fanworks were compared, the ones publicly listed on AO3. This was also due to time limitations; a more extensive analysis would involve going through an alphabetical list of video games to compile them in order of popularity.

The questionnaire was not formatted with the intention of performing statistical tests. This became a drawback as inferential statistics could not be used to study significant correlations between questions. Time limitation became another drawback as open-ended questions retained too varied answers to analyze them all.

Future Research. The generalizability of this work would have to be further studied to determine how far these results apply to games and retellings other than GI, fanfiction, and fanart. Particular characteristics of a game that inspire retelling creation is an area of future study as well.

Regarding GI, an area of study is cultural representation, with perspectives from people belonging to cultures portrayed in GI. How accurate representation or misrepresentation in the source material impacts retellings and fandoms, is a relevant area both regarding video games and the creative industry as a whole.

Studies can be made of retellings as a form of promotion for a game, as they are easily spread on social media, with the potential to reach across fandoms and communities. Encouraging fanworks could spread knowledge of the game from the perspective of someone who loved aspects enough to create fanworks of them. Content analysis of retellings could lead to insights about aspects most often referenced in retellings, indicating what is impactful for players.

5 Conclusion

Our study of the retellings created about the game Genshin Impact (GI), shows that what inspires retellings the most are the characters and the connections between them. GI gives the characters vitality and unique charisma through appearances, background stories, and individual characteristics, partly conveyed through fragmented narrative with gaps. The cultures and lore are also inspirations for many, delving deep into different real-life cultures and creating connections between them. How to respectfully portray cultures is, however, something that requires the attention of developers, especially since portrayed cultures also make their way into retellings. It can have negative consequences if players bring misconceptions from the game into fandoms, potentially being harmful to people from the cultures that are misrepresented. The room for players to figure out connections and gaps between story threads was found to inspire creative works, especially since they can build on existing foundations and add their own interpretation, e.g., to relationships, backstories, and lore. Particularly important for game designers are these gaps; how intricacy combined with missing details provide a space for players to develop curiosity about characters, gameworld, and related stories. Given the number of fanworks created about GI, it is likely that its narrative design has contributed to the inspiration for retellings. This narrative design not only gives enough textual background but also reserves enough space to give the creator's imagination room to play.

In summary, we learned that an intricate web of narration and depiction of a fictional world with gaps and ambiguities - can entice an avalanche of artistic and authorial creativity.

Acknowledgements. We would like to thank all interview participants and everyone who answered the questionnaire for dedicating their time and giving valuable and more extensive responses than expected. We also thank professor Hartmut Koenitz for valuable feedback and insights that helped improve the paper. Additionally, we express our gratitude to the reviewers who gave helpful feedback.

References

1. ArchiveofOurOwn: Fandoms (2009). https://archiveofourown.org/media. Accessed 10 July 2022
2. ArchiveofOurOwn: Terms of service (2009). https://archiveofourown.org/tos. Accessed 13 Oct 2022
3. Braun, V., Clarke, V.: Using thematic analysis in psychology. Qual. Res. Psychol. **3**(2), 77–101 (2006)
4. Dede, C., Barab, S.: Emerging technologies for learning science: a time of rapid advances. J. Sci. Educ. Technol. **18**(4), 301–304 (2009)
5. Discord Inc: Discord v136607. [Computer Software] (2015). https://discord.com
6. Eladhari, M.P.: Re-tellings: the fourth layer of narrative as an instrument for critique. In: Rouse, R., Koenitz, H., Haahr, M. (eds.) ICIDS 2018. LNCS, vol. 11318, pp. 65–78. Springer, Cham (2018). https://doi.org/10.1007/978-3-030-04028-4_5
7. Forster, E.M.: Aspects of the Novel. Arnold (1927)
8. Google: Google Docs (live version spring 2022). [Web Application] (2006). https://www.google.com/docs/about/
9. Google: Google Forms (live version spring 2022). [Web Application] (2008). https://www.google.com/forms/about/
10. Greting, M., Mao, X.: Travelers in another world: How game experience in genshin impact inspires retellings. Stockholm University (2022). https://gameresearch.blogs.dsv.su.se/game-related-ba-and-ma-theses-from-dsv/travelers-in-another-world/
11. Hellekson, K., Busse, K., et al.: Fan fiction and fan communities in the age of the internet: new essays. McFarland (2006)

12. HoYoverse: Genshin impact [Video Game] (2020). https://genshin.hoyoverse.com/en/game. Accessed 24 June 2022
13. Hoyoverse: Hoyolab (2021). https://www.hoyolab.com/. Accessed 24 June 2022
14. Hugh "Jim" Bailey: OBS Studio v27.2.4. [Computer Software] (2012). https://obsproject.com/
15. Kreminski, M., Samuel, B., Melcer, E., Wardrip-Fruin, N.: Evaluating ai-based games through retellings. In: Proceedings of the AAAI Conference on Artificial Intelligence and Interactive Digital Entertainment, vol. 15, pp. 45–51 (2019)
16. OrganizationforTransformativeWorks: Announcing open beta (2009). https://www.transformativeworks.org/announcing-open-beta/. Accessed 14 July 2022
17. Soyoof, A.: Video game and culture: a case study of efl student players' views on their acquisition of cultural knowledge and sensitivity. Int. J. Pedagogies Learn. **13**(2), 91–102 (2018)
18. Stein, L., Busse, K.: Limit play: fan authorship between source text, intertext, and context. Pop. Commun. **7**(4), 192–207 (2009)
19. Steve, H., Aaron, S., Alexis, O.: Reddit (2005). https://www.reddit.com/. Accessed 24 April 2022
20. Zimmermann, E., Salen Tekinbas, K.: Rules of Play: Game Design Fundamentals. MIT Press, Cambridge (2004)

Supporting Spatial Thinking in Augmented Reality Narrative: A Field Study

Abbey Singh[1]([✉]) [ID], Matthew Peachey[1] [ID], Ramanpreet Kaur[1],
Peter Haltner[1] [ID], Shannon Frederick[1], Mohammed Alnusayri[1],
David Choco Manco[2], Colton Morris[2], Shannon Brownlee[2] [ID],
Joseph Malloch[1] [ID], and Derek Reilly[1] [ID]

[1] Graphics and Experential Media Lab, Dalhousie University, Halifax, NS, Canada
{Abbey.Singh,peacheym,rm216536,Peter.Haltner,shannon.frederick,mh625076,
Joseph.malloch}@dal.ca, reilly@cs.dal.ca
[2] Fountain School of Performing Arts, Dalhousie University, Halifax, NS, Canada
{david.chocomanco,cl255185,Shannon.Brownlee}@dal.ca
http://gem.cs.dal.ca ,
https://www.dal.ca/faculty/arts/school-of-performing-arts.html

Abstract. Immersive augmented reality (AR) is an exciting medium for locative narrative. Immersive AR experiences are largely custom-made and site-specific, however: we lack generic tools that help authors consider interactions between physical layout, viewer perspective, and story progression, for specific sites or for locations unknown to the author. In this paper we evaluate Story CreatAR, a tool that incorporates spatial analysis techniques used in architecture, planning, and social sciences to help authors construct and deploy immersive AR narratives. We worked with three authors over several months, moving from script writing and story graph creation to deployment using the tool. We conduct a thematic analysis of each author's actions, comments, generated artifacts, and interview responses. Authors faced a steep learning curve, sometimes misinterpreting spatial properties, and found it difficult to consider multi-site deployment. Despite these challenges, Story CreatAR helped authors consider the impact of layout on their stories in ways their scripts and graphs did not, and authors identified several additional areas for spatial analysis support, suggesting that tools like Story CreatAR are a promising direction for producing immersive AR narratives. Reflecting on author experiences, we identify a number of features that such tools should provide.

Keywords: Space syntax · Storytelling · Proxemics · Story CreatAR · Augmented reality

1 Introduction

In this paper, we consider how authors write and deploy locative and immersive augmented reality (AR) narratives using *Story CreatAR* [1], an authoring tool

M. Vosmeer and L. Holloway-Attaway (Eds.): ICIDS 2022, LNCS 13762, pp. 270–291, 2022.
https://doi.org/10.1007/978-3-031-22298-6_17

that uses spatial analysis to *dynamically* place story elements (e.g., characters, audio, objects, and events) in *locative narratives.* We define *immersive AR* as AR facilitated by spatially aware head-worn AR devices (e.g., Magic Leap One [2], Microsoft HoloLens [3]), and *locative narrative* as narratives that incorporate physical environments and navigation into the story. We use *spatial analysis* to refer to space syntax (specifically isovist [4] and convex analysis techniques [5, 6]), proxemics [7], and F-formation theory [8]. Using Story CreatAR, authors specify generic spatial rules and constraints using these techniques, which can be tested in VR using the Oculus Quest 2 [9], and deployed to specific environments in AR using the Microsoft HoloLens 2 [3].

Prior work has contributed a range of tools and guidelines to support AR/VR content creators [10–15] and locative media content creators [16–19]. However, platforms and guidelines for AR/VR content and locative storytelling on handheld devices do not help authors consider how story progression is impacted by viewer perspective, embodied interactions, and the unfolding of the environment through movement. These are compelling aspects of immersive locative AR made possible using head-worn AR devices.

We evaluated Story CreatAR with three authors, who each developed a unique, site-agnostic, immersive AR story that satisfies author-defined spatial constraints. We worked closely with each author to examine how they think about and manage spatial considerations for their story. Each author first created their story script, then created a graph-based representation of a section of the story. Next, the author used Story CreatAR to block out sections of their story.

Our rationale for following these phases is as follows. Scripts are suited to providing rich story detail in a linear format, but cannot easily represent a nonlinear or interactive story [20]. Graph representations can better show nonlinearity, interactivity, high level structure, and spatial relationships in a narrative [21]. Therefore, we expected graphs to ease the translation of a script to AR using Story CreatAR. The author-driven phase explores differences between how authors use Story CreatAR to translate their story using their graph or script. While many authors will use both a script and a graph (or flow-chart, decision matrix, etc.) when authoring interactive narratives, considering each in isolation allows us to closely consider the strengths and weaknesses of each when authoring and deploying immersive locative AR narratives. The developer-driven phase explores how a person with expertise in the spatial analysis techniques employed by Story CreatAR and the technical aspects of content production in AR/VR would use Story CreatAR to interpret an author's work using their script or story graph. We include this phase to model a content production workflow that would involve collaborators with different expertise. This allows us to compare the output generated by authors on their own vs. as part of a team, which helps us consider how the tool might support different workflows.

In this study we ask the following questions:

– What spatial attributes do authors represent using a graph or script that they are unable to apply in Story CreatAR? What are authors missing in their script or graph that would be required for a locative AR story?
– What spatial rules do authors use in Story CreatAR, how often do they use them, and do their rules achieve their desired effects?

2 Background

2.1 Spatial Analysis

In this section we summarize quantitative spatial analysis techniques used in Story CreatAR. Other important attributes of a space (lighting, materials, uses of space, etc.) not directly managed by Story CreatAR are not covered here.

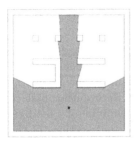  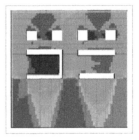

Fig. 1. Left: a point with high openness (high isovist area relative to other points). Middle: a point with high visual complexity (we see a "spiky" isovist, such that the point is visible from many vantage points). Right: visual integration of all points in the building (in aggregate): red shows most connectivity and blue shows least. Note that the alcove area with low visual integration also has low openness and low visual complexity.

Space Syntax. Space syntax [5, 22] is a family of spatial analysis techniques typically applied to urban spaces and buildings–to understand how an area's spatial characteristics influence movement patterns, how spaces are used, and the visibility and accessibility of resources in the space. We present a brief overview here; further details can be found elsewhere [23]. Story CreatAR uses depthMapX [24] and AFPlan [25] to perform space syntax analyses on a floorplan. DepthMapX performs *isovist analysis*, a subset of space syntax analysis involving *isovists*. An isovist may be understood as the space illuminated by shining a flashlight 360 degrees around a point. Story CreatAR uses three characteristics derived from an isovist, shown in Figure 1. *Openness* [4] is the magnitude of the visible area about a point. *Visual complexity* is calculated using the perimeter of the isovist and [4] is a measure of how much you can see from one location. *Visual integration* is an isovist-based measure of the connectedness of a point, in terms of the average number of isovist intersections needed to "reach" the point from any other point: by viewing visual integration values for all points in a space simultaneously, we get an approximation of how "central" different regions are relative to the space as a whole (see Figure 1). These attributes can be combined: for example, high visual complexity and low openness denote a "spiky" isovist, a point visible from disconnected vantage points throughout the space. Story CreatAR uses AFPlan to conduct *convex analysis*, a subset of space syntax analysis which identifies convex regions (e.g., rooms), their dimensions, and their entrance points. Convex analysis generates a convex map, which contains the minimum amount of *convex spaces* to cover the entire environment. A *convex space* refers to an enclosed region where any two points within the region can see each other. Convex analysis allows Story CreatAR to support rules that constrain placement of multiple story elements to the same room or adjoining rooms, for example. Authors may choose to select one or more floorplans provided by Story CreatAR, or they may upload their own. After conducting space syntax analysis on the floorplan(s) Story CreatAR uses them to demonstrate how author rules for content placement and story events could be manifested in each space.

F-formations. F-formations [8] refer to how people arrange themselves to interact with each other in co-located spaces. Kendon et al. [26] describe when f-formations (e.g., L-shaped) occur. They have been used to support fluid interaction between people [27], and to simulate realistic behaviors for avatars in VR [28–30]. F-formations are used in Story CreatAR to arrange avatars in conversation.

Proxemics. Proxemics [7,31–36] is an area of study that describes the impact of relative distance and orientation on relationships between people and devices. Llobera et al. [37] suggest that a viewer's stimulation increases as the distance between themselves and objects in VR decreases. Story CreatAR uses the ProxemicUI tookit [36] to define proxemic (distance and orientation) triggers between the viewer and avatars in conversation. For example, coming within 3 feet of a conversation (proxemic distance trigger) might cause the avatars in the conversation to turn toward the viewer, address them, and adapt the f-formation to include them.

Table 1. Comparing locative media tools to Story CreatAR.

	StoryPlaces	Mscape	Hargood et al.	Story CreatAR
Easy Remapping	✓	✓	✓	✓
Separation of Logic	✓	✓	✓	✓
Extensible Rules		✓		✓
Use of Spatial Analysis			✓	✓

2.2 Locative Media Tools

Locative media has been explored extensively in human-computer interaction (HCI) and new media research [16,38–42]. While some platforms supporting the creation of locative media have been presented in the literature [21,43,44] or made available by practitioners [45,46], we still know relatively little about how to best support such narratives [19,47]. For example, tools often lack support for managing unpredictable user movement and understanding the impact of the setting [48].

In Table 1 we compare Story CreatAR to locative narrative tools in the literature, specifically StoryPlaces [21], Mscape [44], and a location-adaptive system proposed by Hargood et al. [49].

StoryPlaces [21] is a generic web-based authoring system for locative narratives. StoryPlaces uses *sculptural hypertext*: every node is linked by default and these links are filtered out by conditions (logical, locative, and time-based). StoryCreatAR supports locative narrative creation with the same kinds of conditions. StoryPlaces is designed specifically for outdoor experiences, has limited support for using the viewer's proximity and orientation for story progression, and anticipates a web-based interface on a handheld device.

Hargood et al. [49] propose an approach for a rule-based system that uses generic space types (e.g., road, park, noisy) to dynamically map locative narratives to different environments. They envision site-adaptive locative tools that separate the narrative structure and the locative design, find local candidate locations that match requirements set by the authors, and then map story content to suitable locations. Story CreatAR realizes some aspects of this proposal, specifically using author-specified spatial rules to map story elements to suitable locations in an environment.

Mscape [44] is a site-specific authoring tool that provides an interface for non-technical users with extensible rules, the ability to specify events and conditions, to represent user knowledge, to use different media, and to iteratively test rules using a visual representation of the story on site. Story CreatAR provides similar features applied to site-adaptive, immersive AR.

Guidelines for Authoring Locative Media. Longford [16] identifies key design considerations when considering environments: how someone feels in the space, the impact of time, the rules/policies of the space, and the presence of others. According to Packer et al. [19] authors must balance deal breakers (e.g., effort to reach location) and aesthetics (e.g., mapping narrative components to the environment), and make pragmatic decisions (e.g., bottlenecks may force passage). Nisi et al. [50] recommend visual markers to compensate for tracking inaccuracies and enhance understanding, and note that physical features (e.g., walls) can have more influence on user decisions than digital features. Bala et al. [51] find that lighting and audio are effective in directing attention in immersive (VR) stories. Azuma [17] considers three approaches for locative AR experiences: augmentations to improve an interesting environment, re-purpose an environment to fit your story, or retell the stories of an environment.

Many see VR/AR as heirs to or interlocutors with cinema [52–54]. Since cinema considers viewer position and perspective, and content positioning to be important within a setting, AR inherits that importance. Barba [14] defined five scales based on physical movements and interactions within a space that roughly correspond to cuts in cinema: figural, vista, panoramic, environmental and global.

Benford et al. [12] note that maintaining a coherent continuous trajectory for the viewer can be most challenging at key story transitions, or when shifting between a virtual and physical focus. Struck [11] and Dooley [10] also find viewers need time to situate themselves and acclimatize to new spaces as they move through a story.

While there are guidelines and tools in the literature for locative narrative and AR content independently, few consider immersive locative AR narratives specifically, and we lack authoring tool support focusing on viewer perspective, position, and trajectory in relation to the structure of space and events tied to that space.

2.3 Spatial Analysis and AR/VR

The spatial characteristics of buildings and rooms impact a player's experience and satisfaction in mixed reality [55]. For example, in a study by Shin et al. [56] players in AR experienced higher presence and engagement in larger rooms. Seung-Kwan Choi et al. [57] show that mutual visibility–an isovist-based spatial attribute–can be used to place important objects for game levels in optimal locations. Adventure AR and ScavengAR [58] are examples of building-scale AR games that place game elements using space syntax attributes. Recent work [59–63] has considered techniques for adapting AR/VR content dynamically based on spatial properties. While these works show promise of using spatial analysis for content and event placement in AR/VR, they do not consider how to support authors in doing so themselves.

3 Story CreatAR Workflow and Features

This is the first evaluation of Story CreatAR from the author's perspective. Story CreatAR is described in detail elsewhere [1]: here we focus on the authoring workflow and details that are most relevant to our findings.

3.1 Workflow

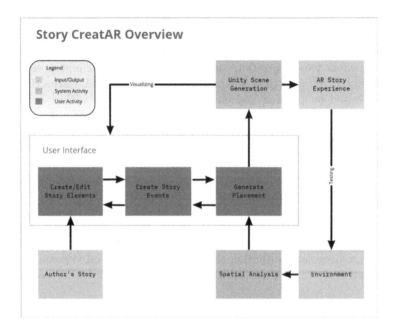

Fig. 2. Overview of the Story CreatAR workflow.

The Story CreatAR workflow is represented in Figure 2 and described as follows.

1. An author creates a draft of their story outside Story CreatAR.
2. Using the Story CreatAR interface through Unity [64], an author adds and edits story elements (avatars, 3D sounds including character audio and narration, objects) and creates story events (conversations, avatar traversals, timer-based events).
3. The author specifies spatial rules for placing story elements, which can be tested by generating placement based on one or more floorplans.
4. If satisfied or curious with the placement, the author can generate a Unity scene, which provides a rich 3D preview.
5. The author can adjust story content in Story CreatAR or make manual changes to the scene before deploying the story.
6. The author can test the deployed story remotely in VR or on-site in AR.
7. This process can be repeated until the author is satisfied with their final output.

3.2   Features

Story Content. Authors are provided with life-like avatars from the *Rocketbox Avatars* [65], spatialized sounds, and 3D objects to compose their narrative. These can be grouped for organization or to apply rules to all group members, where one story element can be part of 0-to-many groups.

Event Mechanics. Using the interface, authors can create *conversation nodes* by specifying the type of conversation (intimate, personal, social), formation (e.g., avatars form a circle), and avatars that may be present. Authors can also specify two types of dialogue: avatars talking to each other or to the player. Conversations can be triggered based on player proximity, elapsed time, or completion of another event.

Story CreatAR also supports avatar traversal and timer events. Timer events can be used to add timestamps for other story events. Traversal events describe where an avatar can move. Both events have preconditions, which start the event only after other event(s) have started/completed.

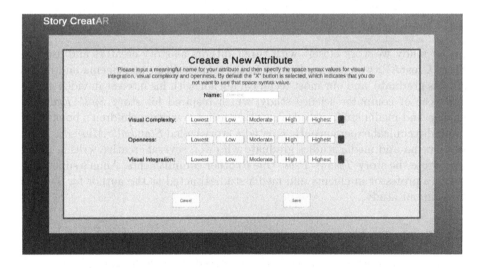

Fig. 3. Authors can create a new attribute in Story CreatAR

Placement Rules. Authors specify spatial rules known as *attributes* to map story elements to different locations. *Rooms* are one type of attribute created by specifying a unique name and size (small, medium, or large). The other type of attribute uses isovist-based space syntax properties: openness, visual complexity, and visual integration. Story CreatAR combines these into several more understandable 'high-level attributes', each consisting of a meaningful name, and ranges of each space syntax property, with the option for authors to create their own, as shown in Figure 3. Based on the attributes and their priorities, an example placement of story elements is displayed, as seen in Figure 4.

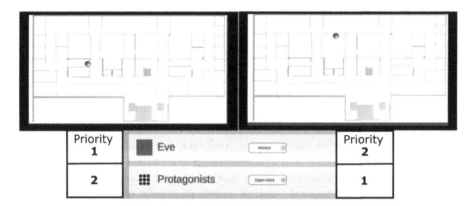

Fig. 4. Left: Eve placed with "Hidden" as highest priority. Right: Eve placed with "Open Area" as highest priority.

4   Methodology

4.1   Population

In our study we work closely with three authors as story creators and users of Story CreatAR; we use pseudonyms in this paper. *Ryan* is a cinema and media studies graduate, and our most technical author with his interest in video games and year of computer science study, which inspired his story *Spill*. *Eric* is a cinema and media studies student with experience writing children's books, but limited technical experience. He created a story called *Standville Museum*. *Anna* is a cinema and media studies graduate who won several creative writing prizes and wrote the story *Tyson's Peak*. Due to other commitments, Anna's supervisor *Amy* (a professor in cinema and media studies) acted as the author for Tyson's Peak in our study.

4.2   Study Design

In this study, three film studies students worked through different phases, summarized in Table 2. Ryan, Eric, and Amy provided informed consent to participate in the study. Due to COVID-19, sessions were recorded and held virtually through Microsoft Teams [66]. During the sessions authors were asked to "think aloud", and a facilitator would probe for more details as necessary. We concluded phases with a semi-structured interview where the author reflected on the phase.

Phase 1: Creating a Story Script. We met with the authors weekly over four months as they wrote their story scripts. We introduced spatial analysis concepts, walked through Story CreatAR and its ongoing revisions, discussed related work in new media and HCI, discussed the feasibility of story ideas the

Table 2. Breakdown and summaries of the three creation phases

Research Phase	Summary	Sequence	Duration
Script Creation	Author creates story script	Related topics (e.g., spatial analysis concepts) were introduced, Story CreatAR features were demoed, and feasibility of story ideas were discussed	16 sessions over 4 months
Graph Creation	Author uses part of story script to create graph in Miro (graphing tool)	Explain Miro features, show developer example, author creates graph, interview questions, and author adjusts graph	6-7 sessions per author (avg. 50 min. each)
Author using Story CreatAR	Author implements story in Story CreatAR using graph and script	Overview of Story CreatAR features, author implements story, and interview questions	4 sessions per author (avg. 1 hour each)

authors had, and shared other stories implemented using Story CreatAR. More details of this process can be found in another paper [1].

These discussions influenced the stories. In *Spill* the player is at a tea-party, where interactions and eavesdropping with party-goers affect the course of the story. In *Standville Museum* the player visits a museum with his son, Max, when Max is kidnapped by a demonic figure. The player follows clues to recover his son, where his choices lead to vastly different endings. In *Tyson's Peak* the player must solve a murder mystery by eavesdropping on eight friends trapped in a snowed-in cabin.

Phase 2: Creating a Story Graph. We introduced the Miro online whiteboard [67] tool and some of its features in the first session, and showed an example graph of "The Three Little Pigs" children's story. In The Three Little Pigs example there was a story start and end node, story events as nodes, transitions between events as arrows, and frames as physical locations.

In the following sessions authors created a graph for a section of their story. We prompted the authors to consider how the graph can indicate aspects of the story that most directly translated to Story CreatAR features: how to represent positions, room descriptions, proximity triggers, formations of avatars, etc. A segment of Eric's graph is shown in Figure 5.

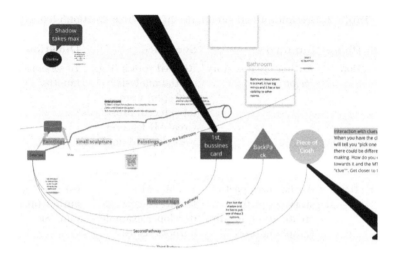

Fig. 5. A segment of the graph for Standville Museum created in the graph creation phase

Phase 3: Authors using Story CreatAR Interface. After creating the graph, the authors used Story CreatAR directly to implement a part of their story in four one-hour sessions. In the first session, the developers showed assets acquired for their stories (e.g., tables, museum paintings, and others) and provided the author with a brief review of features in Story CreatAR. In the remaining sessions, the authors worked on implementing their story. The last session ended with a half-hour interview, during which authors discussed the pros and cons of using a script vs. using a graph to produce content and rules for Story CreatAR, and limitations of the tool.

4.3   Data Collection and Analysis

All sessions were video recorded, and artefacts from story creation (scripts, graphs in Miro, Story CreatAR logs and output) were retained.

Affinity Diagramming Sessions. We conducted *deductive* thematic analysis similar to Braun and Clarke [68]. We began by familiarizing ourselves with the data, creating initial codes and improving the codes after looking at the data, and then we coded the videos. Our initial codes included *confusion, giving up, asking developer, making mistakes*, and *changing mind*. However, we added codes for *developer suggestion, technical confusion, author missing details from the graph, author suggestion, author likes something*, and *changing task without finishing current task*. Two researchers were assigned to code each video until the inter-rater reliability (IRR) was greater than 0.7, in which case the videos were divided between the researchers. We calculated the IRR based on coder agreement [69]: count of matching researcher codes (same code over similar times) over total

Fig. 6. Left: the implementation of Standville Museum in VR, showing the security room. Due to COVID-19, we tested our stories primarily in VR, but on-site AR is the target deployment medium. Right: part of the story rendered in AR. In this case virtual walls are rendered because AR could not be tested in the target deployment site, which was closed to all access.

unique codes. While coding for uncertainty, researchers also noted interesting observations. We also did an *inductive* thematic analysis similar to Braun and Clarke's procedure [68]: familiarizing all but one researcher with the data, noting aspects of the video we found interesting, and creating categories during an affinity diagram session on these annotations.

Six researchers created the affinity diagram. First, we moved the annotations for a subset of the sessions to Miro and divided them equally amongst the researchers. Then, we silently read and moved annotations to form groups. This step continued until we were no longer moving annotations. Then, we verbally settled any differences in opinion between the researchers and labelled annotation clusters as categories. From our initial 247 annotations, we created six categories and 36 sub-categories.

Next, one researcher added the annotations for the remaining videos. As the researcher added annotations, they created sub-categories, increasing the total sub-categories to 74 for 1087 unique annotations. Collaboratively, we reviewed these new categories/sub-categories during an hour-long session, and carefully considered certain categories individually. Some sub-categories were renamed and repositioned, and some were added. This resulted in seven top-level and 93 sub-categories. See Table 3 for a summary of the themes in the graph and interface approaches.

Table 3. Summary of affinity diagram themes for graph and interface approaches.

Theme	Summary	Code Coverage
Space and Placement	- Spatial analysis, position, and room considerations. - Spatial analysis learning curve experienced by authors.	23%
Graph Creation Process and Experience	- Authors process, use of graphing tool, and insights. - Authors creating graph from their script and missing story details.	20%
Events	- Authors use of formations, movement, and event triggers and preconditions. - Difficulty of determining event relationships	14%
Story CreatAR	- Authors experience with the user interface and the generated 3D Unity Scene	19%
Story Graphs	- Visual appearance of story elements in graph - Difficulty with story element representation	19%
Conversations	- Formation of avatars in conversation - Proxemic trigger of a conversation	5%

5   Results

5.1   Events

Timed Events. Authors describe challenges with coordinating event timing and other events, as Amy demonstrates, "You don't know how big the space is, so you don't know how long it takes for the avatar to get to a room". It is less of an issue in film than AR due to the ability for cuts, which could explain why the authors seemed to lack timing details.

Triggers and Group Formations. Authors were able to understand and use proxemic rules in Story CreatAR. However, Ryan and Eric had difficulty quantifying the proxemic distance. For example, Eric says, "I know how close it is, but I don't know how to explain it". Most references to orientation rules were focused on "looking at" story elements (at a player, object, or avatar).

While not supported in the interface, all authors described distance proxemic triggers between the player and rooms, the ability to use multiple triggers (using an "OR"), a trigger based on cardinal direction (North/East/South/West), and Amy wanted an always true trigger. There is also interest in interactions between the player and the walls/rooms/windows.

Authors used, understood, and liked group F-formations. While the circle formation in Story CreatAR was acceptable, authors desired other F-formations like ones that interact with the environment (e.g., props), semi-circles, or custom arrangements. Ryan and Amy chose the distance between avatars in a F-formation based on character relationships.

5.2 Space and Placement

Spatial Analysis Learning Curve. The authors had difficulty understanding space syntax, which may be due to unexpected results of the higher-level attributes in the interface, the difference between the full complement of space syntax attributes and the ones available in the interface, or the unknown value of using space syntax attributes for stories.

Part of the difficulty for authors was that the space syntax characteristics used in Story CreatAR do not account for furniture. Amy's and Ryan's translation of openness, visual integration, and visual complexity based on the term alone is not entirely correct, but it still drove their use of the attribute. Amy reasoned, "Visual complexity may be thinking of metaphor: forest has high visual complexity and field has low visual complexity" and Ryan interprets openness as "assuming limited amount of things around it". Sometimes the author tried to understand extreme cases of the space syntax characteristic or the relationship between them. The understanding may also have been incorrectly built through singular testing of the placement in the interface. Interestingly, the high-level attributes, which were designed to provide more familiar, identifiable spatial properties (e.g., hidden region) were subject to the same misinterpretations as the low-level space syntax characteristics.

Rooms. The authors describe rooms in terms of size categorically (small/medium/ large) or precise measurements, relativity to other rooms or room features (doors/ windows), and visibility to other rooms. Amy experimented with rooms for different floorplans in Story CreatAR. There was evidence that thinking in terms of room attributes is not apparent for authors (e.g., Ryan felt room size was not necessary for storytelling).

The authors also consider the number of doors per room to connect spaces and windows due to light access. Ryan and Amy would specify the hallway as the largest room with the most doors, which could be a way of trying to squeeze specificity out of the tool. Ryan and Eric use doors as a reference point in their story. The authors also described general ways to specify room shape (e.g., long/thin, square/round, spikey/complex). In addition, the authors indicate different room properties would have different priorities.

Positioning. Both Ryan and Amy show a translation from their story script to the default attributes. The use of space syntax had some unexpected use cases and challenges. Unanticipated uses of space syntax include defining where to play an off-screen voice, and having placement correlate to types of characters. For example, Ryan assigns attributes based on character personality (e.g., Bultilda is confident so she is in an open, easy to find area). It was challenging for authors to maintain flexible placement, as shown by authors desire to maneuver objects to appropriate locations manually. Eric felt nervous when adjusting placement rules: "I had like a mini heart attack". Amy iterated on creating a new attribute, reapplying rules, and making modifications based on the placement shown on the map.

We observed a tension between creating meaningful labels for story content and using the high-level attributes. Ryan created a new attribute in an unintended way: to create labels for story aspects not supported by the tool. His labels were used to indicate object containment relationships, interactive events unsupported by the event model logic, and desired placement not supported by space syntax attributes. For example, Ryan creates an attribute with no space syntax attributes called central doorway and shares, "so my hope is that'll [the attribute] just assign it to there [the story element], but I don't think it'll show it here [placement map]".

6   Discussion

6.1   Spatial Analysis Insights

Authors had positive and negative experiences with the spatial rules. Amy appreciated the degree of "accident" caused by the use of automatic room selection. When switching between floorplans, she comments "Oh I like that much better. Perfect actually, I love that, so I like the way the system has just clustered them". Eric commented that Story CreatAR could support story creation due to the flexibility in adding content, despite worrying about how to represent player self-conversations. Conversely, Ryan found the process more difficult than anticipated and doubted Story CreatAR's suitability for implementing highly interactive stories. In this section we discuss several key ways in which Story CreatAR can be improved: addressing the spatial analysis learning curve, helping authors consider multi-site deployments, and supporting more spatial relationships.

Need to Address Spatial Analysis Learning Curve. The literature [56–60] shows several examples of tools designed and used by researchers that use spatial analysis techniques, but they do not support end-users in learning and effectively using those concepts. Moreover, other applications of on-the-fly spatial analysis [61–63] are not appropriate for locative AR due to continuity issues (e.g., an avatar directed to move to a room far from the player, but that content is not generated) involved in building-scale narratives.

In our evaluation, we find a need to help authors overcome the spatial analysis learning curve. Authors had difficulty understanding spatial attributes in the interface and were subject to misinterpreting their meaning. Even with relatively basic proxemic relationships, authors were subject to the same misinterpretations. We expected the small number of attributes available in Story CreatAR (openness, visual complexity, and visual integration) would be effectively used and combined once grasped. Instead, authors more often experimented with each attribute to see if they could achieve an effect they wanted, rather than deliberately choosing and combining attributes based on their comprehension of them. These results are in line with Raford [70], who interviews space syntax experts who warn that space syntax terminology without appropriate technical knowledge is difficult to understand and use.

There are a number of ways to improve space syntax comprehension: presenting different layouts simultaneously, clear descriptions and examples, immersive walkthroughs, and demonstration-based rule creation. Story CreatAR currently supports viewing attributes for story elements across multiple floorplans non-simultaneously, and our authors often did not switch between floorplans when testing their rules. It is also currently possible to deploy and test in VR, but the steps required should be minimized in the interface.

Ryan's and Eric's actions and comments suggest a programming by demonstration interface. When asked how manual manipulations of position on the map could be extended to involve the attributes, Ryan says, "it could actually make it easier to add the attributes because then when you click and drag and you place it [story element] somewhere, you can be like okay generally this is the kind of location I want it to be". When Eric created his graph, he placed objects where they would appear in physical space to demonstrate types of locations objects would be in and their relativity to one another. In this way, authors do not require specific knowledge of the spatial rules, but can instead specify rules based on visual inspection of the layout. Spatial analysis can still be used in the background to remap story content to appropriate locations.

Helping Authors Consider Multi-Site Deployments. For locative narratives, it can be very useful if a tool allows an author to remap story content to multiple locations [21,49], but it is challenging to write content that works in different sites [48]. The inability to specify precisely where story content goes in a site-agnostic experience results in a lack of control that can be challenging for authors.

There were numerous instances of authors indicating the desire for manual control or precise specifications concerning placement. Ryan suggests manual movements, "it would be nicer if you could see more obvious use of the mini-map (click and move objects on the 2D model even if it is a small grid)". Authors also desire specifying precise measurements for rooms. In addition, Eric was worried he would "destroy things" by pressing "reapply rules", which indicates they considered the precise object placements and not the generic rules the sample placement on the visible floorplan was one manifestation of. Amy indicates that thinking of placement flexibly does not come naturally to authors, "If I were just writing a screenplay for fun, that was never gonna be passed on to anyone I actually would design the space, like I would map it. However, with Story CreatAR in mind and that amazing flexibility that it has to be adapted to different spaces, I wouldn't [do manual placement]".

Showing multiple floorplans simultaneously may help authors to consider spatial rules more abstractly. Authors may also want to specify general features likely to be available in a building (e.g., front entrance, stairs) or features specific to the space where the story is meant to be experienced (e.g., theatre stage, balcony, vestibule). Not having any information about how a space is used can produce a negative result. For example, Amy liked the placement of objects in a room that she did not know was a bathroom. In future, Story CreatAR may expose ways for authors or site administrators to exclude certain rooms.

Additional Spatial Analysis Support. The space syntax attributes currently provided in Story CreatAR cannot manifest some of the desired spatial constraints we found in the graphs, scripts, and/or suggestions made while using Story CreatAR. More work is required to determine a parsimonious set of space syntax attributes to make available for use when creating spatial rules. For example, the isovist property of minimum radial length might be useful for placing objects along walls, and isovist intersections can be used to determine mutual visibility [71].

In addition to isovist-based attributes, Story CreatAR should support more convex-based properties. Story CreatAR already uses AFPlan to conduct automatic convex analysis to identify corners of rooms, which can be used to compare relative room size and detect whether a player/NPC/object is inside/outside or entering/leaving a room. A justified connectivity graph could be generated using convex analysis, representing how many rooms need to be traversed to move between two points, as a room-level complement to the visual integration attribute, giving measure of proximity between rooms, and establishing a room's overall accessibility. Agent-based spatial analysis can be added to identify areas of predicted low/high traffic, an attribute our authors suggested. Room dimensions and accessibility can be helpful in determining event timings that involve avatar or viewer movement through spaces. Currently, Story CreatAR uses ProxemicUI for basic relative position and orientation between two entities and circular f-formation placements, but the toolkit allows more varied and complex proxemics relationships and formations to be specified. The "entities" available for use in these rules could be expanded to include room elements (e.g. a doorway) and story objects (e.g. a painting).

Providing attributes like those mentioned provides expressiveness approaching what the authors indicated in their materials and comments. For example, a hallway could be a room with high centrality (determined using the connectivity graph), a rectangular shape, and several doorways (using convex analysis). A rule could place an avatar at one end of the hallway, and it could interact differently as a viewer approaches. Finally, the mechanics of combining and prioritizing spatial rules should also be clear to authors using the tool, as should the impact this will have on the resulting story configurations.

6.2 Limitations

We investigated with three authors, allowing us to explore narrative development in depth over a long period of time. The small sample means our findings may be impacted by high variability, low reliability, and a skewed representation of potential users. Our future work will engage with a wider range of authors with different levels of experience and with different backgrounds. Our authors were influenced by our research focus–on the use and effects of spatial rules for immersive AR narratives–while writing their stories and moving through the authoring phases. Consequently, authors potentially considered rules relating to spatial attributes (e.g., openness, traffic), inter-room relationships, and intra-room relationships precisely because these were discussed with them, even though they were not always available in Story CreatAR. Furthermore, authors were in contact with Story CreatAR designers throughout these phases. We expect that users using Story CreatAR or a similar tool would not have access to this level of support. Additionally, since our authors did not use Story CreatAR over a long period of time, it would be interesting to see how an author's experience changes over time. Would authors still remember decisions they made or would they want to change previous decisions? For example, an author may have previously created an attribute with a specific name and associated space syntax values, but does the author still find this meaningful to use for their story? Finally, while this in-depth qualitative study provided rich data on supporting spatial thinking when authoring immersive AR narratives, studying additional authors with different story ideas would help to establish common graphing approaches, spatial rules, and interface preferences.

7 Conclusion

In this paper, we investigated how three authors of locative AR narratives use spatial rules and how effective those rules are while using Story CreatAR, a tool that allows authors to specify placement rules that are used for remapping story content to different locations. Authors worked in distinct phases: creating a story script, creating a story graph, and using the Story CreatAR tool. We find authors experienced difficulty using the available spatial analysis techniques effectively, often misinterpreting the meaning of specific spatial rules and misunderstanding the sample placement of the rules. Authors also had difficulty thinking abstractly about relationships between their story elements and physical environments. Nonetheless, our authors defined complex spatial rules during story creation that were cross-checked and refined when using Story CreatAR, and they desired more sophisticated spatial analysis support in the tool. Our findings inform future directions for Story CreatAR, but are also valuable for any tool that wishes to make spatial analysis techniques comprehensible and actionable to creators like authors, game designers, and developers of other forms of locative experience. To help these content creators we recommend designing interfaces that promote comprehension of spatial properties as and where they are used, reinforce flexible notions of location and position by visually representing multiple deployment sites and/or multiple applications of a set of spatial rules to the same site, and provide rule composition support that allows authors to both apply basic rules and define more complex rules as needed.

Acknowledgements. We thank the story authors for their ongoing collaboration. This research was funded by NSERC and Snap Inc.

References

1. Singh, A.: Story creatar: a toolkit for spatially-adaptive augmented reality storytelling. In: 2021 IEEE Virtual Reality and 3D User Interfaces (VR), pp. 713–722, Los Alamitos, CA, USA. IEEE Computer Society, Apr (2021)
2. Magic leap. https://www.magicleap.com/en-us/magic-leap-1. Accessed 12 Jan 2022
3. Microsoft. Microsoft hololens: mixed reality technology for business. https://www.microsoft.com/en-us/hololens. Accessed 12 Jan 2022
4. Dzebic, V.: Isovist analysis as a tool for capturing responses towards the built environment (1970)
5. Bafna, S.: Space syntax: a brief introduction to its logic and analytical techniques - sonit bafna (2003)
6. Peponis, J., Wineman, J., Rashid, M., Kim, S., Bafna, S.: On the description of shape and spatial configuration inside buildings: convex partitions and their local properties. Environ. Plann. B. Plann. Des. **24**(5), 761–781 (1997)
7. Edward, T.: Hall. The hidden dimension, Peter Smith Pub (1992)
8. Tong, L., Serna, A., Pageaud, S., George, S., Tabard, A.: Its not how you stand, its how you move. In: Proceedings of the 18th International Conference on Human-Computer Interaction with Mobile Devices and Services (2016)
9. Quest, O.: 2: our most advanced new all-in-one VR headset (2021)
10. Dooley, K.: Storytelling with virtual reality in 360-degrees: a new screen grammar. Stud. Australas. Cinema **11**, 1–11 (2017)
11. Struck, G., Böse, R., Spierling, U.: Trying to get trapped in the past - exploring the illusion of presence in virtual drama
12. Benford, S., Giannachi, G., Koleva, B., Rodden, T.: From interaction to trajectories: designing coherent journeys through user experiences, pp. 709–718. Association for Computing Machinery, New York, NY, USA (2009)
13. Cardona-Rivera, R.E., Zagal, J.P., Debus, M.S.: GFI: a formal approach to narrative design and game research. In: Bosser, A.-G., Millard, D.E., Hargood, C. (eds.) ICIDS 2020. LNCS, vol. 12497, pp. 133–148. Springer, Cham (2020). https://doi.org/10.1007/978-3-030-62516-0_13
14. Barba, E.: Toward a language of mixed reality in the continuity style. Convergence Int. J. Res. into New Media Technol. **20**, 41–54 (2013)
15. Krauss, V., Boden, A., Oppermann, L., Reiners, R.: Current Practices, Challenges, and Design Implications for Collaborative AR/VR Application Development. Association for Computing Machinery, New York, NY, USA (2021)

16. Longford, M.: Territory as interface: design for mobile experiences
17. Azuma, R.: Location-based mixed and augmented reality storytelling. Fundamentals of Wearable Computers and Augmented Reality, 278–295 (2015)
18. Hargood, C., Charles, F., Millard, D.: Intelligent generative locative hyperstructure. 238–241 (2018)
19. Packer, H.S., Hargood, C., Howard, Y., Papadopoulos, P., Millard, D.E.: Developing a writer's toolkit for interactive locative storytelling
20. Dooley, K.: Scripting the virtual: formats and development paths for recent Australian narrative 360-degree virtual reality projects. J. Screenwriting **9**, 175–189 (2018)
21. Hargood, C., Weal, M.J., Millard, D.E.: The storyplaces platform: building a web-based locative hypertext system. In: Proceedings of the 29th on Hypertext and Social Media (2018)
22. Al-Sayed, K., Turner, A., Hillier, B., Iida, S., Penn, A.: Space syntax methodology. Bartlett School of Architecture, UCL, London, England, 4th edition (2014)
23. Space syntax. https://www.spacesyntax.online/. Accessed 12 Jan 2022
24. SpaceGroupUCL. depthmapx. https://github.com/SpaceGroupUCL/depthmapX (2021)
25. Cansik. cansik/architectural-floor-plan: afplan is an architectural floor plan analysis and recognition system to create extended plans for building services
26. Burgoon, J.K., Kendon, A.: Conducting interaction: patterns of behavior in focused encounters. Contemp. Sociol. **21**(2), 256 (1992)
27. Marquardt, N., Hinckley, K., Greenberg, S.: Cross-device interaction via micromobility and f-formations. In: Proceedings of the 25th Annual ACM Symposium on User Interface Software and Technology - UIST 12 (2012)
28. Ben Salem University of Plymouth, Ben Salem, University of Plymouth, Nic Earle University of Plymouth, Nic Earle, Contributor MetricsExpand All Ben Salem University of Plymouth Publication Years 2000 2000Publication counts1Available for Download1Citation count24Downloads (cumulative)1, and Ben Salem University of Plymouth Publication Years2000 2000Publication counts1Available for Download1Citation count24Downloads (cumulative)1. Designing a non-verbal language for expressive avatars (2000)
29. Kang Hoon Lee Seoul National University, Kang Hoon Lee, Seoul National University, Seoul National UniversityView Profile, Myung Geol Choi Seoul National University, Myung Geol Choi, Qyoun Hong Seoul National University, Qyoun Hong, Jehee Lee Seoul National University, Jehee Lee, et al. Group behavior from video: a data-driven approach to crowd simulation (2007)
30. Pedica, C., Vilhjálmsson H.H.: Spontaneous avatar behavior for human territoriality. Intelligent Virtual Agents Lecture Notes in Computer Science, pp. 344–357 (2009)
31. Greenberg, S., Hornbæk, K., Quigley, A., Reiterer, H., Rädle, R.: Proxemics in human-computer interaction (2014)
32. Annett, M., Grossman, T., Wigdor, D., Fitzmaurice, G.: Medusa: a proximity-aware multi-touch tabletop. In: Proceedings of the 24th Annual ACM Symposium on User Interface Software and Technology, UIST '11, page 337–346, New York, NY, USA. Association for Computing Machinery (2011)
33. Marquardt, N., Diaz-Marino, R., Boring, S., Greenberg, S.: The proximity toolkit: prototyping proxemic interactions in ubiquitous computing ecologies. In: Proceedings of the 24th Annual ACM Symposium on User Interface Software and Technology, UIST '11, pp. 315–326, New York, NY, USA. Association for Computing Machinery (2011)

34. Ballendat, T., Marquardt, N., Greenberg, S.: Proxemic interaction: designing for a proximity and orientation-aware environment. In: ACM International Conference on Interactive Tabletops and Surfaces, ITS '10, page 121–130, New York, NY, USA. Association for Computing Machinery (2010)
35. Greenberg, S., Marquardt, N., Ballendat, T., Diaz-Marino, R., Wang, M.: Proxemic interactions: the new ubicomp?, Jan 2011
36. Alnusayri, M., Hu, G., Alghamdi, E., Reilly, D.: Proxemicui. In: Proceedings of the 8th ACM SIGCHI Symposium on Engineering Interactive Computing Systems - EICS 16, 2016
37. Joan Llobera Universitat de Barcelona, Joan Llobera, Universitat de Barcelona, Bernhard Spanlang Universitat de Barcelona, Bernhard Spanlang, Giulio Ruffini Starlab Barcelona, Giulio Ruffini, Starlab Barcelona, Mel Slater ICREA-Universitat de Barcelona, Mel Slater, et al. Proxemics with multiple dynamic characters in an immersive virtual environment, Oct 2010
38. Gampe, J.: Interactive narration within audio augmented realities. In: Iurgel, I.A., Zagalo, N., Petta, P. (eds.) ICIDS 2009. LNCS, vol. 5915, pp. 298–303. Springer, Heidelberg (2009). https://doi.org/10.1007/978-3-642-10643-9_34
39. Holappa, J., Heikkinen, T., Roininen, E.: Martians from outer Space-experimenting with location-aware cooperative multiplayer gaming on public displays (2013)
40. Centieiro, P., Romão, T., Dias, A.E.: A location-based multiplayer mobile game to encourage pro-environmental behaviours (2011)
41. Ardito, C., Buono, P., Costabile, M., Lanzilotti, R., Pederson, T.: Mobile games to foster the learning of history at archaeological sites, pp. 81–86, 10 (2007)
42. Zeffiro, A.: A location of one's own: a genealogy of locative media. Convergence Int. J. Res. into New Media Technol. 18, 249–266 (2012)
43. Know your bristol (2013)
44. Stenton, S.P., et al.: Mediascapes: context-aware multimedia experiences. IEEE Multimedia 14(3), 98–105 (2007)
45. Treasuremapper (2011)
46. Lar - locative augmented reality unity3D tooolkit, May (2020)
47. Millard, D.E., Hargood, C.: Tiree tales: a co-operative inquiry into the poetics of location-based narrative. In: Proceedings of the 28th ACM Conference on Hypertext and Social Media, HT '17, pp. 15–24, New York, NY, USA. Association for Computing Machinery (2017)
48. Tiago, J., Jacob, P.N., Coelho, N.F.: Issues in the development of location-based games. Int. J. Comput. Games Technol. (2011)
49. Hargood, C., Charles, F., Millard, D.E.: Intelligent generative locative hyperstructure. In: Proceedings of the 29th on Hypertext and Social Media, HT '18, pp. 238–241, New York, NY, USA. Association for Computing Machinery (2018)
50. Valentina Nisi, Enrico Costanza, and Mara Dionisio. Placing location-based narratives in context through a narrator and visual markers. Interacting with Computers, 2016
51. Bala, P., Dionisio, M., Nisi, V., Nunes, N.: IVRUX: a tool for analyzing immersive narratives in virtual reality, pp. 3–11 (2016)
52. Barba, E.: Toward a language of mixed reality in the continuity style. Convergence 20(1), 41–54 (2014)
53. Rose, M.: The immersive turn: hype and hope in the emergence of virtual reality as a nonfiction platform. Stud. Doc. Film 12(2), 132–149 (2018)
54. Elsaesser, T.: Pushing the contradictions of the digital: 'virtual reality' and 'interactive narrative' as oxymorons between narrative and gaming. New Rev. of Film Television Stud. 12(3), 295–311 (2014)

55. Abawi, D.F., Reinhold, S., Dörner, R.: A toolkit for authoring non-linear storytelling environments using mixed reality. In: TIDSE (2004)
56. Shin, J., Kim, H., Parker, C., Kim, H., Oh, S., Woo, W.: Is any room really ok? the effect of room size and furniture on presence, narrative engagement, and usability during a space-adaptive augmented reality game. In: 2019 IEEE International Symposium on Mixed and Augmented Reality (ISMAR), pp. 135–144 (2019)
57. Choi, S.-K., Kim, D.-II., Kim, Y.-O.: A study on the placement of game objects using space syntax. J. Korea Game Soc. **12**(5), 43–56 (2012)
58. Reilly, D., et al.: Using space syntax to enable walkable AR experiences. In: 2020 IEEE International Symposium on Mixed and Augmented Reality Adjunct (ISMAR-Adjunct) (2020)
59. Gal, R., Shapira, L., Ofek, E., Kohli, P.: Flare: fast layout for augmented reality applications. In: Mixed and Augmented Reality (ISMAR), 2014 IEEE International Symposium on. IEEE, September 2014
60. Kán, P., Kaufmann, H.: Automatic furniture arrangement using greedy cost minimization. In: 2018 IEEE Conference on Virtual Reality and 3D User Interfaces (VR), pp. 491–498 (2018)
61. Marwecki, S., Baudisch, P.: Scenograph: fitting real-walking VR experiences into various tracking volumes. In: Proceedings of the 31st Annual ACM Symposium on User Interface Software and Technology, UIST '18, pp. 511–520. Association for Computing Machinery, New York, NY, USA (2018)
62. Cheng, L.-P., Ofek, E., Holz, C., Wilson, A.D.: VRoamer: generating on-the-fly VR experiences while walking inside large, unknown real-world building environments. In: 2019 IEEE Conference on Virtual Reality and 3D User Interfaces (VR), pp. 359–366 (2019)
63. Yang, J., Holz, C., Ofek, E., Wilson, A.: Dreamwalker: substituting real-world walking experiences with a virtual reality. In: User Interface Software and Technology (UIST) 2019. ACM, October (2019)
64. Unity Technologies
65. Microsoft. Microsoft rocketbox avatar library. https://github.com/microsoft/Microsoft-Rocketbox (2020)
66. Microsoft teams
67. An online whiteboard and visual collaboration platform for teamwork: Miro
68. Virginia Braun and Victoria Clarke. Thematic analysis., pp. 57–71 (2012)
69. Hallgren, K.: Computing inter-rater reliability for observational data: an overview and tutorial. Tutorials Quantit. Methods Psychol. **8**, 23–34 (2012)
70. Social and technical challenges to the use of space syntax methodologies as
71. Benedikt, M.: To take hold of space: isovists and isovist fields (1979)

Select the Unexpected: A Statistical Heuristic for Story Sifting

Max Kreminski[1,3]([✉]), Melanie Dickinson[2], Noah Wardrip-Fruin[3], and Michael Mateas[3]

[1] Santa Clara University, Santa Clara, USA
mkreminski@scu.edu
[2] Santa Cruz, USA
[3] University of California, Santa Cruz, USA
{nwardrip,mmateas}@ucsc.edu

Abstract. Story sifting techniques, which aim to excavate potentially compelling microstories from vast chronicles of storyworld events, present a promising solution to the challenges of interactive emergent narrative. However, current sifting techniques (which rely on large numbers of hand-specified *story sifting patterns* to identify compelling microstories) are limited by their inability to determine which of many sifting pattern matches are likely to be the most interesting to a human interactor. We present a higher-level *story sifting heuristic* that addresses this problem by identifying sifting pattern matches that are especially *unlikely* from a statistical perspective, and illustrate how this heuristic leads to the surfacing of more interesting microstories.

Keywords: Story sifting · Sifting heuristics · Statistical methods

1 Introduction

Story sifting techniques [19,27] are a family of computational methods (generally employed as part of a larger generative or interactive storytelling pipeline) that aim to automatically identify and extract potentially storyful information from a vast chronicle of narrative events, often generated by a *storyworld simulation* containing a large number of autonomous characters. Sifting techniques have been employed in several contexts, including in podcast generation [27, ch. 12], computationally engaged improvisational theater [31], social simulation [11,35], and mixed-initiative co-creative [21] storytelling [12,14,30]. Moreover, sifting techniques are sometimes used by players of interactive emergent narrative games in the process of constructing *retellings* [6] of their play experiences [16], and sifting has been pitched as a potential solution [28] to several key challenges of emergent narrative [15,22,36] broadly construed.

Most current approaches to story sifting make use of many hand-authored *story sifting patterns* to identify potentially compelling nuggets of narrative content. A sifter that has more of these patterns at its disposal is able to recognize

---

M. Dickinson—Independent

M. Vosmeer and L. Holloway-Attaway (Eds.): ICIDS 2022, LNCS 13762, pp. 292–308, 2022.
https://doi.org/10.1007/978-3-031-22298-6_18

a wider variety of potentially interesting emergent story patterns, and consequently is better able to respond to the unexpected outcomes of storyworld simulation, so past research in story sifting has aimed to make these patterns easy to author in large numbers.

However, once a sifter is equipped with a wide range of sifting patterns, a new problem emerges: the difficulty of determining, from among many matches against many sifting patterns, which matches are the most worthwhile to surface to the player. Since even a single pattern may yield hundreds or thousands of matches when executed against a chronicle of thousands of simulation events, the mere knowledge that a sifting pattern found a match isn't necessarily enough to determine whether this match is likely to be particularly interesting from a human's perspective.

Beyond low-level sifting patterns, past work on story sifting [27, p. 237] has also raised the idea of higher-level *sifting heuristics* that encode a sense of what makes for narratively interesting material in a more generic way. If we had such a heuristic, it might prove useful in selecting the most interesting sifting pattern matches—but the specifics of how to implement sifting heuristics have not yet been seriously investigated.

In this paper, we present a candidate sifting heuristic that uses statistical methods to identify which of many sifting pattern matches are most likely to be interesting from a human's perspective. We call this heuristic the SELECT THE UNEXPECTED heuristic, or simply STU. Intuitively, this heuristic is based on the narrative quality of *unexpectedness*: sequences of events are more likely to be perceived as storyful, and thus to be considered *tellable* as stories [1], if they somehow deviate from expectations. We operationalize unexpectedness by searching for matches against a sifting pattern that are particularly *unusual* relative to other matches against the same sifting pattern. We evaluate our approach by comparing our heuristic's judgments of microstory interestingness to those of human raters (with favorable results); by highlighting several cherry-picked examples of microstories that our heuristic surfaced within the output of a bare-bones test simulation; and by illustrating how our heuristic can obtain results similar to a canonically successful example of story sifting (Ryan's arson-revenge example) with more generic sifting patterns than those employed in Ryan's work. Both data and code for this paper is publicly available online.[1]

2   Background

2.1   Story Sifting

Story sifting as an approach was originally proposed by Ryan under the name "story recognition" [28] and later defined further under the updated name "story sifting" [27]. Ryan's dissertation work also introduced Sheldon [27, ch. 12], a simple autonomous story sifter that makes use of sifting patterns specified as

---

[1] https://github.com/mkremins/statistical-sifting.

blocks of code in the Python programming language. Prior to Ryan, sifting-like techniques were employed in a few different contexts: Cardona-Rivera and Young's work on symbolic plan recognition in narrative domains [3] bears some substantial similarities to pattern-based story sifting, as does Osborn et al.'s work on applying regular expressions to sequences of game states in a social simulation game [25] and Elson's work on using logical patterns to conduct analogy search between plot structures [7]. "Story trees" in *The Sims 2* were also used in a sifting-like fashion [2,23]. However, it is Ryan's work that gave the "curationist emergent narrative" tradition a distinct name and identity for the first time.

Since Ryan's early work, a number of other approaches to authoring story sifting patterns have been introduced [19], including declarative specification of sifting patterns using domain-specific logic programming languages like Felt [13] and Winnow [10], as well as example-based [18] and visual [8] tools to assist users in authoring these declarative sifting patterns.

Relatively little work on story sifting has been done outside the pattern-based paradigm to date. One recent exception to this rule—Arc Sift [20]—performs story sifting via dynamic time warping, aiming to find stories that match specific character fortune arcs drawn by a user without the use of sifting patterns. However, the dominant approach to story sifting still relies heavily on sifting patterns to locate sites of potential narrative interest.

2.2   Toward Sifting Heuristics

The sifting patterns that are used in existing story sifters tend to be fairly low-level, concrete specifications of emergent story patterns that make for good narrative material. Patterns at this level, however, do not necessarily capture more generic notions of what makes for a good story, for instance those that have been set out in cognitive narratology research. This raises the question of how a more generic sense of narrativity [29] or tellability [1] could be encoded into the machine, such that sifters can leverage this information to better understand the player-perceived story—for instance by using tellability to gauge which of many viable sifting pattern matches are most likely to be important to the player-perceived narrative. In the story sifting literature, encodings of abstract narrativity or tellability are called *sifting heuristics* [27, p. 237].

Sifting heuristics may attempt to operationalize constructs from cognitive narratology, including story *interestingness* as defined by Schank [33] and *event salience* [9] (a proxy for story *memorability*) as operationalized in Indexter [4]. An operationalization of *surprise*—which is often treated as a key component of interestingness, and which may be detectable via statistical approaches such as anomaly detection—could also prove useful in sifting heuristics.

Sifting heuristics might also be learned from data on how users interact with existing interactive story sifters, for instance the *Bad News* "wizard console" or the Legends Viewer interface for exploring *Dwarf Fortress* worlds. Samuel et al. have recently conducted an analysis of interaction trace data with the *Bad News* wizard console [32], revealing that certain sets of wizard console commands are often executed together. Recurring patterns of interaction with these lower-level sifting interfaces could potentially be abstracted into high-level sifting heuristics, since a human user's sense of what information is needed to identify a compelling narrative throughline for a whole *Bad News* play session (for instance) could be expected to serve as a good proxy for the information that a computational system would need to make similar determinations.

The sifting heuristic we present in this paper is based on (a relatively naïve interpretation of) a cognitive-narratological construct—namely that of surprise. However, we hope that future work will explore other approaches to sifting heuristic development as well.

3   Pattern-Based Story Sifting

Our story sifting heuristic (which we discuss further in Sect. 4) extends the pattern-based approach to story sifting, particularly the flavor of this approach in which patterns are specified as logic programs (as in the Felt and Winnow story sifting languages). Before discussing the details of our heuristic, we will first briefly recap how pattern-based sifting works in Felt.

Here is an example Felt sifting pattern:

```
(eventSequence ?harm ?scheme ?arson)
[?harm tag harm] [?harm actor ?revengeTarget] [?harm target ?arsonist]
[?scheme eventType hatchRevengeScheme] [?scheme actor ?arsonist]
[?scheme target ?revengeTarget]
[?arson eventType setFire] [?arson actor ?arsonist]
[?arson target ?revengeTarget] [?arson victim ?victim]
```

This pattern, based on the **arson-revenge** pattern discussed by Ryan [27, p. 671–674] and Kreminski et al. [10,19], aims to match an ordered sequence of three events—?harm, ?scheme, and ?arson—with arbitrarily many other events interspersed between. The first of these events, ?harm, represents a character (the eventual ?revengeTarget) doing something that harms another character (the eventual ?arsonist). The second event, ?scheme, represents the ?arsonist resolving to avenge the harm in some way. Finally, the third event, ?arson, represents the ?arsonist getting their revenge by burning down a building owned by the ?revengeTarget—potentially harming a third character, the ?victim, in the process.

Identifiers in the pattern that begin with the question mark character (such as ?scheme and ?arsonist) represent *logic variables*: "roles" that are bound to concrete values, such as character or event IDs, in the process of pattern execution. A match against this sifting pattern consists of a set of bindings for all of these logic variables that satisfies the pattern's constraints.

Constraints, meanwhile, are specified in terms of [square-bracketed] and (parenthesized) expressions. An expression of the form [e a v] represents an assertion that the entity with ID e has an attribute named a whose value is v; generally speaking, e is always a logic variable, while a is usually a literal string (the name of a particular attribute) and `v` can be a literal string or another logic variable depending on context. An expression of the form ⟨ruleName args...⟩, on the other hand, represents an assertion that the inference rule named `ruleName` holds true for the given `args`. Inference rules are Datalog rules [5], written in the DataScript [26] dialect of Datalog. The `eventSequence` rule in our example `arson-revenge` sifting pattern is one such rule; it holds true if each of its arguments is the ID of an event entity and the events these IDs point to are chronologically ordered from left to right.

Executing a sifting pattern returns a list of all valid matches against this pattern that are possible based on the events that have transpired in the storyworld so far. Depending on the pattern and on how long the storyworld has been allowed to evolve, a single Felt sifting pattern may return anywhere between a handful of matches and tens of thousands. (Even larger numbers of matches against a single pattern are theoretically possible, but because Felt runs in browser JavaScript, it generally bogs down when the number of candidate matches is any larger than this.) It is at this point that the need to select the most interesting matches becomes evident—and it is at this point that our sifting heuristic is deployed.

4   Our Heuristic: Prefer Matches with Unusual Properties

Once we have identified many matches against a single sifting pattern, how do we determine which matches are most unusual? Our approach is based on the generation and comparison of a *property signature* [18,24] for each match: a set of simple statements about the plot events captured in this match and how they are related to one another.

In evaluating a single match against a particular sifting pattern, we first generate a list of properties that hold true for this match. For each of the match's properties, we then determine how frequently this property appears in all matches against the same sifting pattern—i.e., the property's *likelihood* of appearing in a match against this sifting pattern. We then average together the likelihood scores of each of a match's properties to determine an overall likelihood score for the match as a whole. A pseudocode definition of our heuristic is given in Algorithm 1.

We employ several distinct *property generation strategies* to discover potentially interesting details about each sifting pattern match. These property generation strategies are based on, but not limited to, those used in Synthesifter [18]. Specifically, for each match, we generate the following properties:

- One **event type property** indicating the event type of each event in the matched event sequence. An event type is a string that uniquely identifies a particular type of action that a character in the simulation can perform.
- Zero or more **event tag properties** indicating the tags of each event in the matched event sequence. A tag is a string that indicates an event has a particular characteristic; for instance, events that relate to an (actual or potential)

Input: pattern: a story sifting pattern
Output: matches: a list of pattern matches with associated likelihood scores
matches ← GetAllMatches(pattern);
propertyCounts ← {};
foreach *match* ∈ *matches* **do**
    match.properties ← GenerateProperties(match);
    foreach *property* ⊢ *match.properties* **do**
        prevCount ← propertyCounts[property] *or* 0;
        propertyCounts[property] ← prevCount + 1;
    end
end
propertyLikelihoods ← {};
foreach *property* ∈ *Keys(propertyCounts)* **do**
    propertyLikelihoods[property] ← propertyCounts[property] / —matches—;
end
foreach *match* ∈ *matches* **do**
    match.likelihood ← Average(Map(λ.prop → propertyLikelihoods[prop],
    match.properties));
end
return matches

Algorithm 1: The STU story sifting heuristic. The likelihood score of a match against a given sifting pattern is the average likelihood score of that match's properties in the context of that pattern. Matches with lower likelihood scores are more surprising and therefore preferable to surface.

romantic relationship between two characters may be tagged `romantic`, while events that represent a character attempting to take an action but failing may be tagged `failure`.

- One **character trait property** for each matched character that has a notable trait. In the simple test simulation that we used for our evaluation, these traits include `friendly`, `unfriendly`, `romantic`, and `secretlyFamous` (with the last of these being especially uncommon).
- One **character relationship property** for each pair of matched characters that are connected by a particular kind of dyadic relationship. In our test simulation, these relationships include `viewsAsFriend`, `viewsAsEnemy`, `onesidedFriendship`, `onesidedEnmity`, `mutualFriendship`, `mutualEnmity`, `attractedTo`, `onesidedAttraction`, `mutualAttraction`, and `childhoodFriends`. (As with character traits, the last of these is especially uncommon.) Each of these relationships is defined by a DataScript inference rule, so new forms of potentially interesting dyadic character relationships can be added to the property generation process relatively easily: for instance, the `mutual` and `onesided` relationships are defined in terms of other, more basic unidirectional relationships.
- One **same-character property** for each pair of matched characters that are actually the same character. For instance, if a sifting pattern contains two distinct character roles for the `?arsonist` and `?victim` characters in

an `arson-revenge` sequence, these roles are unlikely to be played by the same character—but the possibility of both roles being played by the same character is not completely excluded (for instance, if the arsonist accidentally dies in the fire that they set). Consequently, if the same character ends up cast in both of these roles within a particular sifting pattern match, we generate a same-character property to mark this occurrence.

For instance, suppose we are generating properties for the following sequence of events—a match against a `romanticFailureThenSuccess` sifting pattern, in which a single protagonist character experiences two romantic rejections followed by a romantic success. Here's the sifting pattern:

```
(eventSequence ?e1 ?e2 ?e3)
[?e1 actor ?protag] [?e1 tag failure] [?e1 tag romantic]
[?e2 actor ?protag] [?e2 tag failure] [?e2 tag romantic]
[?e3 actor ?protag] [?e3 tag success] [?e3 tag romantic]
[?e1 target ?c1] [?e2 target ?c2] [?e3 target ?c3]
```

And here's an example match, in which the character Alex is bound to the `?protag` logic variable, while Brian and Cara take on the roles of the other characters (`?c1` through `?c3`):

1. Alex flirts with Brian and is rejected
2. Alex flirts with Cara and is rejected
3. Alex successfully asks Brian out on a date

As part of property generation, beyond examining the events themselves, we also query for the traits and relationships of the characters involved. This query tells us that the character Cara has the `friendly` trait, and the character Brian has the `viewsAsFriend` relationship toward Cara. This event sequence therefore yields the following set of properties:

- `eventHasType_e1_flirtWith_rejected`
- `eventHasType_e2_flirtWith_rejected`
- `eventHasType_e3_askOut_accepted`
- `eventHasTag_e1_romantic`
- `eventHasTag_e1_failure`
- `eventHasTag_e2_romantic`
- `eventHasTag_e2_failure`
- `eventHasTag_e3_romantic`
- `eventHasTag_e3_success`
- `eventHasTag_e3_major`
- `charHasTrait_c2_friendly`
- `charsAreRelated_viewsAsFriend_c1_c2`
- `charsAreRelated_viewsAsFriend_c3_c2`
- `sameChar_c1_c3`
- `sameChar_c3_c1`

This list of properties aims to capture the potentially interesting features of this pattern match—a set of assertions that are true about this match, and that might or might not be true for other matches against the same pattern. Some properties might hold for all or almost all matches against a particular pattern: for instance, by definition, every event included in a romanticFailureThenSuccess pattern match will always have the romantic tag, so the eventHasTag_e1_romantic property will hold for every match against this pattern. However, some properties are likely to be less common: for instance, since the romanticFailureThenSuccess sifting pattern doesn't specify that the first and last targets of attempted romantic interaction (?c1 and ?c3 respectively) need to be the same character, the sameChar_c1_c3 property is likely to occur fairly infrequently. Thus we return to the key idea behind our heuristic: **we can define the likelihood of a particular sifting pattern match in terms of the context-specific likelihoods of its various properties.**

5 Evaluation

We evaluate our approach in three ways. First, to determine whether our heuristic's judgments of story interestingness agree with those of human raters, we apply our heuristic to a small test simulation and five Felt sifting patterns designed to sift the output of this simulation. Using data drawn from a single run of this simulation and sifting process, raters are asked to perform blind comparisons between heuristic-preferred and randomly selected matches against these sifting patterns. Second, we highlight several cherry-picked examples of microstories surfaced by our heuristic (as applied to our test simulation and test sifting patterns) that we find particularly compelling. Third, we briefly illustrate how our heuristic is capable of obtaining results similar to Ryan's arson-revenge example—a canonical example of story sifting success—even with more generic sifting patterns than those Ryan employed.

5.1 Comparison with Random Baseline

In order to compare heuristic-preferred with randomly selected sifting pattern matches, we first ran our test simulation once to generate a chronicle of 1000 events. Our test simulation contains 24 possible action types for characters to perform and a cast of 20 characters. At the start of a simulation run, characters are randomly initialized with traits and dyadic relationships. Then, on each timestep, we randomly select a single actor character, a single target character, and a single type of action to perform between them. Actions are chosen probabilistically depending on the traits and relationships of the characters involved; for instance, a character who is attractedTo another character is more likely to perform an action that is tagged romantic toward them.

After running the simulation, we then executed five Felt sifting patterns against the resulting chronicle to collect all possible matches for each pattern.

Once the matches were collected, we applied our heuristic to the complete set of matches for each pattern and calculated a likelihood score for each match.

The five sifting patterns with which we tested include:

- `romanticFailureThenSuccess` (previously introduced in Sect. 4): A character experiences two romantic rejections followed by a romantic success.
- `establishFriendship`: A character performs a friendly gesture toward another character, and this friendliness is subsequently reciprocated.
- `revengeAlliance`: A character performs actions that harm two other characters; these two harmed characters have a friendly interaction; and one of the harmed characters subsequently takes revenge on the character who harmed them.
- `statusReversal`: A character performs two low-status actions toward a second character, followed by a high-status action toward that same character.
- `cantCatchABreak`: A character is harmed three times in succession by other characters' actions, with the last of these harms being major.

Based on a single run of the simulation and sifter, we collected 15 pairs of microstories: three pairs of matches for each of our five sifting patterns. Each pair of matches contained one of the three top-scoring matches for a particular sifting pattern according to our heuristic (i.e., one of the three *least likely* matches for the pattern in question) and one randomly selected match for the same pattern. We chose to compare heuristic-selected matches against random matches because random selection of matches to surface is part of current practice in story sifting (and thus a realistic baseline for comparison), and because random selection is essentially a "zero knowledge" heuristic for match selection (under which the system makes no attempt to discern which matches are most interesting).

We then presented these pairs of matches to three human raters, with each rater reviewing all 15 pairs. For each pair of matches, raters were asked to indicate which match was more interesting, resulting in a total of 45 pairwise interestingness judgments across all raters. To minimize ordering effects, pairs were presented in a randomized order from one rater to the next, and the order of matches within the pair (i.e., whether the heuristic-preferred or randomly selected match was presented first) was also randomized. Raters therefore had no way of knowing which matches were selected by the heuristic and which were selected randomly.

Altogether, across our three raters, we found that raters agreed with our heuristic's judgments of story interestingness in 38 of 45 cases. In other words, raters selected the heuristic-preferred match as the more interesting microstory 84.44% of the time. A breakdown of heuristic/rater agreement across each of the five sifting patterns is given in Table 1.

It is worth noting that this evaluation context represents something like a worst-case scenario for the presentation of sifted microstories. Unlike in interactive emergent narrative gameplay, raters were not given access to the underlying test simulation or any broader context for the microstories we presented, so their knowledge of what kinds of events are particularly common or uncommon

Table 1. Heuristic/rater agreement on microstory interestingness, both per sifting pattern and overall. The "# Agreements" column shows the total number of cases in which a human rater agreed with the heuristic's pairwise interestingness judgment between two microstories, while the "% Agreement" column shows how often a rater's assessment agreed with the heuristic's as a percentage of total cases.

Sifting pattern	# Agreements	% Agreement
establishFriendship	7/9	77.78%
romanticFailureThenSuccess	7/9	77.78%
revengeAlliance	7/9	77.78%
statusReversal	8/9	88.89%
cantCatchABreak	9/9	100.00%
Overall	38/45	84.44%

in the simulation was limited. Additionally, microstories were presented to the raters in a bare-bones text format that required significant mental work to interpret as a story—see Fig. 1 for an example. Finally, two of our sifting patterns (establishFriendship and revengeAlliance) returned very small numbers of matches in our test run of the simulation (13 and 12 matches respectively). This limited the amount of training data to which our heuristic had access in attempting to determine per-property likelihoods for matches against these patterns, and limited the extent to which we might expect noticeable differentiation between heuristic-preferred and randomly selected matches for these patterns (since the heuristic only had around a dozen matches to select from in each case). Nevertheless, agreement between human-rated and heuristic-based judgments of story interestingness remained high. Consequently, we expect that agreement between our heuristic's judgment of story interestingness and that of human interactors will at worst remain the same and at best substantially increase in contexts more similar to typical interactive emergent narrative gameplay.

Which romanticFailureThenSuccess story is more interesting?

Story 1: Isla flirtWith_rejected Quinn. Isla flirtWith_rejected Sarah. Isla flirtWith_accepted Mira. *(Isla is romantic. Quinn is unfriendly. Mira is romantic. Mira viewsAsEnemy Sarah. Mira attractedTo Sarah.)*

Story 2: Mira askOut_rejected Peng. Mira askOut_rejected Peng. Mira flirtWith_accepted Riva. *(Mira is romantic. Peng is unfriendly. Riva is unfriendly. Riva viewsAsFriend Peng. Riva attractedTo Peng.)*

Fig. 1. Example comparison between a pair of microstories, as presented to raters.

5.2 Cherry-Picked Successes

During testing, we found several of the emergent microstories surfaced by our heuristic to be particularly compelling. One of these was a match against the romanticFailureThenSuccess pattern, discovered during early testing when only this pattern was active. The character Oswald asked the character Lexi out on a date and was turned down. Oswald then flirted with another character, Victor, and was turned down again. But when Oswald asked Lexi out a second time, Lexi accepted. Intriguingly, though neither Lexi nor Victor felt much of anything toward Oswald, they both viewed one another as enemies and were attracted to one another—suggesting that Lexi's acceptance of Oswald's second invitation was motivated more by complex feelings of jealousy toward Victor than by any actual interest in Oswald.

Another exemplary microstory was a match against the statusReversal pattern, surfaced as the top heuristic-preferred match on the very first run of the simulation with this sifting pattern enabled. The character Quinn first felt condescended to by the character Isla, but shortly thereafter deferred to Isla's expertise on a career-related topic. Much later, presumably after Quinn had risen to a much greater level of prominence within Isla's social circle, Quinn ended up shunning Isla from this circle. Tragically, the initially higher-status Isla had viewed the initially lower-status Quinn as both a friend and a potential love interest—but Quinn did not reciprocate these feelings, and Isla's attempts to support Quinn ultimately brought Isla nothing but suffering.

More generally, we found examples of all of the following unlikely occurrences in matches that were surfaced by our heuristic:

- **Globally uncommon event types.** For instance, characters in our test simulation rarely physically attack one another even when there exists conflict between them, so microstories involving physical violence stand out as unusual. (In simulations where physical violence is the predominant means of conflict resolution, microstories involving peaceful resolutions to conflict might be highlighted instead.)
- **Pattern-specific uncommon event types.** For instance, even globally common event types (such as visiting a graveyard) may occur very rarely in particular narrative contexts (such as a romance microstory), so a romance microstory in which the initial meet-cute took place in a graveyard stands out as unusual.
- **Characters more related than necessary.** For instance, romantic rivals do not necessarily have to be related in any other way, so a microstory involving two romantic rivals who were also childhood friends stands out as unusual.
- **Characters related in unexpected or apparently contradictory ways.** For instance, romantic affection is generally correlated with platonic affection, so a microstory in which two characters who view one another as enemies become involved in a romantic relationship stands out as unusual.
- **Characters acting against type.** For instance, characters with the friendly trait in our test simulation tend to behave in consistently friendly

ways, so a microstory in which a friendly character performs several mean actions stands out as unusual.

Unexpected occurrences like these are often featured in player-constructed retellings of their gameplay experiences in interactive emergent narrative games, and they may serve as especially fertile jumping-off points for *extrapolative narrativization* [17]: the process by which players who are writing retellings of their gameplay experiences invent additional details (often involving character motives) that are consistent with simulation events, but go beyond the level of detail that the simulation actually models. For instance, in the cherry-picked story of Oswald, Lexi and Victor, the character motivations *implied* by the characters' actions are much more complicated than the motivations actually modeled in the simulation engine—but the story still "works" on an intuitive level because of the reader's capacity for extrapolation.

5.3   Generalizing Arson-Revenge

Perhaps the strongest argument for our heuristic is that it could successfully identify the canonical arson-revenge microstory from Ryan's dissertation [27, p. 637–638] as especially notable, even if it was only given a more generic sifting pattern for revenge stories that do not necessarily involve arson. Ryan's arson-revenge microstory involves a farmhand (Roy Champ) who is bullied by the farm's owner (Julius Eckert) and decides to enact a revenge scheme against him, specifically by burning down his farmhouse. However, in the process, Champ himself is trapped in the burning building and ends up dying, while Eckert (who was away for the weekend) is physically unharmed. Ryan discovered this instance using a sifting pattern that was specifically tailored to search for stories of arson being used as a means of revenge.

Using our heuristic, this microstory would stand out as unusual among all kinds of sifted revenge stories for two key reasons. First, because arson is a rare event both globally (since characters rarely commit arson in general) and contextually (since most revenge schemes are enacted by means other than arson), the mere presence of a `set-fire` action in a match against a generic revenge story sifting pattern would tend to make this match less likely from a statistical perspective. Second, since the avenger and victim roles in this microstory are played by the same character (even though a revenge sequence does not necessarily *have* any victims, and victims would usually be assumed to be characters other than the avenger), this microstory would stand out as an exemplary case of the involved characters being *more related than necessary*. In summary, our heuristic would generate two statistically unusual properties for this match—`eventHasType_e3_set-fire` and `sameChar_avenger_victim`—then detect these properties (and particularly their simultaneous presence in a single match) as statistically unusual. Consequently, our heuristic would lead to the discovery and surfacing of this match—even in the absence of a sifting pattern specific to arson-revenge stories—as long as a more generic sifting pattern for revenge stories of any kind was available.

6 Discussion

6.1 Considerations for Sifting Heuristic Design

Our use of pattern-based sifting as a foundation atop which to implement higher-level sifting heuristics is essentially a solution to a narrative-specific form of the *frame problem* [34]: the difficulty of determining what context is relevant when trying to determine whether a given event is worth mentioning in a story. Interestingly, though past work on story sifting has generally emphasized the importance of giving sifters access to many highly concrete story sifting patterns [19], we found that the presence of our heuristic substantially improves the leverage of more abstract sifting patterns, since more generic patterns tend to match more microstories within the same chronicle of events, giving statistical heuristics more training data on which to base their judgments of microstory interestingness and more options to choose between when selecting microstories to surface. This result suggests that, in two-layer approaches to sifting like ours (which use both patterns and heuristics), the role of patterns is different than in single-layer approaches to sifting (which make use of patterns alone): instead of attempting to capture only tellable sequences of events, patterns should be written to capture event sequences that have narrative structure without regard to tellability, and tellability judgments should be left to heuristics.

The heuristic we describe here offers a form of built-in explainability as to why a particular sifting pattern match has been surfaced over others. Since not just matches themselves but also the individual *properties* of each match are given their own likelihood scores, it is possible to sort all of a given match's properties by their likelihood and directly present the specific properties that are judged as especially unlikely in order to explain why this match was judged as unusual or worth surfacing. Depending on the context in which story sifting is deployed, this form of explanation may help to mitigate the *Tale-Spin effect* [37] (in which human interactors fail to appreciate the complexity of an AI system due to the opacity of its outputs) in interactive emergent narrative games that make use of story sifting. Alternatively, if sifting is deployed in the context of mixed-initiative co-creative storytelling (as it sometimes has been in the past), explanation generation may help to enrich co-creative interaction in the ways envisioned by Zhu et al. [38] in their exploration of explainable AI for designers.

6.2 Limitations and Future Work

One limitation of our heuristic is its poor handling of *correlated unlikelihoods*. For instance, if there exists a rare `kickPuppy` action that most characters never perform, and a character with a rare `villain` trait that causes them to perform the `kickPuppy` action whenever possible, the overall prevalence of sifting pattern matches containing `kickPuppy` actions will be very low overall—as will the overall prevalence of matches involving a `villain` character. But when a match contains a `villain` character who performs a `kickPuppy` action, both the presence of the individually unlikely character trait and the individually unlikely event type will cause the heuristic to rate this match as very unlikely overall—even though this particular rare action is performed very frequently by characters with this particular rare trait. Since our heuristic only considers whether a particular property of a sifting pattern match is common or uncommon among all other matches against the same pattern, it has no way of determining that puppy-kicking is to be expected from villains, and consequently to treat a match that contains both of these correlated unlikelihoods as a relatively likely microstory overall. This remains an issue for future work.

In the future, we also expect that it will be valuable to explore additional property generation strategies beyond those presented here. One set of potentially valuable property generation strategies, which we made no attempt to implement in the initial version of our heuristic, involves pairwise relationships between events themselves. For instance, in a simulation that performs what Ryan terms "causal bookkeeping" [27, p. 162–163], causal relationships between events captured in the same sifting pattern match could be surfaced as properties. Similarly, the amount of time elapsed between events in a matched event sequence could be used for property generation as well: narrative interest can be derived from the fact that a pair of matched events occurred very close together, or very far apart, in time.

Finally, we note that because the comparison-against-random-baseline portion of our evaluation made use of only three human raters, the results of this comparison remain somewhat tentative: although all raters agreed with our heuristic's interestingness judgments in a clear majority of cases, it remains possible that the raters were all outliers in this regard. Future studies could provide stronger evidence for the success of our heuristic by applying a similar study design to a substantially larger number of raters.

7   Conclusion

We present the STU sifting heuristic, which is (to the best of our knowledge) the first high-level story sifting heuristic that can be used to automatically evaluate microstory interestingness in a story sifting context. Agreement between our heuristic's judgments of interestingness and those of human raters is high, and our approach can easily be generalized to other simulation engines besides the simple one with which we conducted our initial testing. We believe that the two-layer approach to story sifting presented here (in which sifting patterns are used in conjunction with sifting heuristics) represents a substantial advance over single-layer approaches to sifting that make use of patterns alone, and we look forward to the development of additional sifting heuristics that can further improve on this approach.

Acknowledgements. Max Kreminski conducted part of this research while in residence at Stochastic Labs.

References

1. Baroni, R.: Tellability. In: Hühn, P., Meister, J.C., Pier, J., Schmid, W. (eds.) The Living Handbook of Narratology. Hamburg University, 18 Apr 2014 edn. (2014). https://www-archiv.fdm.uni-hamburg.de/lhn/node/30.html
2. Brown, M.: The power of projection and mass hallucination: practical AI in the sims 2 and beyond. Invited talk at AIIDE 2006 (2006)
3. Cardona-Rivera, R., Young, R.: Symbolic plan recognition in interactive narrative environments. In: Proceedings of the AAAI Conference on Artificial Intelligence and Interactive Digital Entertainment, vol. 11 (2015)
4. Cardona-Rivera, R.E., Cassell, K.B., Ware, S.G., Young, R.M.: Indexter: a computational model of the event-indexing situation model for characterizing narratives. In: Proceedings of the 3rd Workshop on Computational Models of Narrative, pp. 34–43 (2012)
5. Ceri, S., Gottlob, G., Tanca, L.: What you always wanted to know about Datalog (and never dared to ask). IEEE Trans. Knowl. Data Eng. **1**(1), 146–166 (1989)
6. Eladhari, M.P.: Re-Tellings: the fourth layer of narrative as an instrument for critique. In: Rouse, R., Koenitz, H., Haahr, M. (eds.) ICIDS 2018. LNCS, vol. 11318, pp. 65–78. Springer, Cham (2018). https://doi.org/10.1007/978-3-030-04028-4_5
7. Elson, D.K.: Detecting story analogies from annotations of time, action and agency. In: Proceedings of the LREC 2012 Workshop on Computational Models of Narrative, pp. 91–99 (2012)
8. Johnson-Bey, S., Mateas, M.: Centrifuge: a visual tool for authoring sifting patterns for character-based simulationist story worlds. In: Joint Proceedings of the AIIDE 2021 Workshops (in press) (2021)
9. Kives, C., Ware, S., Baker, L.: Evaluating the pairwise event salience hypothesis in Indexter. In: Proceedings of the AAAI Conference on Artificial Intelligence and Interactive Digital Entertainment, vol. 11, pp. 30–36 (2015)
10. Kreminski, M., Dickinson, M., Mateas, M.: Winnow: a domain-specific language for incremental story sifting. In: Proceedings of the AAAI Conference on Artificial Intelligence and Interactive Digital Entertainment, vol. 17, pp. 156–163 (2021)
11. Kreminski, M., Dickinson, M., Mateas, M., Wardrip-Fruin, N.: Why are we like this?: exploring writing mechanics for an AI-augmented storytelling game. In: Proceedings of the 2020 Conference of the Electronic Literature Organization (2020)
12. Kreminski, M., Dickinson, M., Mateas, M., Wardrip-Fruin, N.: Why are we like this?: the AI architecture of a co-creative storytelling game. In: International Conference on the Foundations of Digital Games (2020)
13. Kreminski, M., Dickinson, M., Wardrip-Fruin, N.: Felt: a simple story sifter. In: International Conference on Interactive Digital Storytelling, pp. 267–281. Springer (2019)
14. Kreminski, M., Dickinson, M., Wardrip-Fruin, N., Mateas, M.: Loose ends: a mixed-initiative creative interface for playful storytelling. In: Proceedings of the AAAI Conference on Artificial Intelligence and Interactive Digital Entertainment, vol. 18 (2022)
15. Kreminski, M., Mateas, M.: A coauthorship-centric history of interactive emergent narrative. In: Mitchell, A., Vosmeer, M. (eds.) ICIDS 2021. LNCS, vol. 13138, pp. 222–235. Springer, Cham (2021). https://doi.org/10.1007/978-3-030-92300-6_21
16. Kreminski, M., Mateas, M.: Toward narrative instruments. In: Mitchell, A., Vosmeer, M. (eds.) ICIDS 2021. LNCS, vol. 13138, pp. 499–508. Springer, Cham (2021). https://doi.org/10.1007/978-3-030-92300-6_50

17. Kreminski, M., Samuel, B., Melcer, E., Wardrip-Fruin, N.: Evaluating AI-based games through retellings. In: Proceedings of the AAAI Conference on Artificial Intelligence and Interactive Digital Entertainment, vol. 15, pp. 45–51 (2019)
18. Kreminski, M., Wardrip-Fruin, N., Mateas, M.: Toward example-driven program synthesis of story sifting patterns. In: Joint Proceedings of the AIIDE 2020 Workshops (2020)
19. Kreminski, M., Dickinson, M., Wardrip-Fruin, N.: Felt: a simple story sifter. In: Cardona-Rivera, R.E., Sullivan, A., Young, R.M. (eds.) ICIDS 2019. LNCS, vol. 11869, pp. 267–281. Springer, Cham (2019). https://doi.org/10.1007/978-3-030-33894-7_27
20. Leong, W., Porteous, J., Thangarajah, J.: Automated sifting of stories from simulated storyworlds. In: Raedt, L.D. (ed.) In: Proceedings of the Thirty-First International Joint Conference on Artificial Intelligence, IJCAI-22, pp. 4950–4956. International Joint Conferences on Artificial Intelligence Organization (2022). https://doi.org/10.24963/ijcai.2022/686
21. Liapis, A., Yannakakis, G.N., Alexopoulos, C., Lopes, P.: Can computers foster human users' creativity? theory and praxis of mixed-initiative co-creativity. Digit. Cult. Edu. **8**(2), 136–153 (2016)
22. Louchart, S., Truesdale, J., Suttie, N., Aylett, R.: Emergent narrative: past, present and future of an interactive storytelling approach. In: Interactive Digital Narrative, pp. 185–199. Routledge (2015)
23. Nelson, M.J.: Emergent narrative in the sims 2 (2006). https://www.kmjn.org/notes/sims2_ai.html
24. Odena, A., Sutton, C.: Learning to represent programs with property signatures. In: International Conference on Learning Representations (ICLR) (2020)
25. Osborn, J., Samuel, B., Mateas, M., Wardrip-Fruin, N.: Playspecs: regular expressions for game play traces. In: Proceedings of the AAAI Conference on Artificial Intelligence and Interactive Digital Entertainment, vol. 11 (2015)
26. Prokopov, N.: DataScript (2014). https://github.com/tonsky/datascript
27. Ryan, J.: Curating Simulated Storyworlds, Ph. D. thesis, University of California, Santa Cruz (2018)
28. Ryan, J.O., Mateas, M., Wardrip-Fruin, N.: Open design challenges for interactive emergent narrative. In: Schoenau-Fog, H., Bruni, L.E., Louchart, S., Baceviciute, S. (eds.) ICIDS 2015. LNCS, vol. 9445, pp. 14–26. Springer, Cham (2015). https://doi.org/10.1007/978-3-319-27036-4_2
29. Ryan, M.L.: The modes of narrativity and their visual metaphors. Style **26**(3), 368–387 (1992)
30. Samuel, B., Mateas, M., Wardrip-Fruin, N.: The design of *writing buddy*: a mixed-initiative approach towards computational story collaboration. In: Nack, F., Gordon, A.S. (eds.) ICIDS 2016. LNCS, vol. 10045, pp. 388–396. Springer, Cham (2016). https://doi.org/10.1007/978-3-319-48279-8_34
31. Samuel, B., Ryan, J., Summerville, A.J., Mateas, M., Wardrip-Fruin, N.: *Bad News*: an experiment in computationally assisted performance. In: Nack, F., Gordon, A.S. (eds.) ICIDS 2016. LNCS, vol. 10045, pp. 108–120. Springer, Cham (2016). https://doi.org/10.1007/978-3-319-48279-8_10
32. Samuel, B., Summerville, A., Ryan, J., England, L.: A quantified analysis of *bad news* for story sifting interfaces. In: Mitchell, A., Vosmeer, M. (eds.) ICIDS 2021. LNCS, vol. 13138, pp. 142–156. Springer, Cham (2021). https://doi.org/10.1007/978-3-030-92300-6_13
33. Schank, R.C.: Interestingness: controlling inferences. Artif. Intell. **12**(3), 273–297 (1979)

34. Shanahan, M.: The frame problem. In: Zalta, E.N. (ed.) The Stanford Encyclopedia of Philosophy. Metaphysics Research Lab, Stanford University, Spring 2016 edn. (2016). https://plato.stanford.edu/archives/spr2016/entries/frame-problem/
35. Summerville, A., Samuel, B.: Kismet: a small social simulation language. In: Joint Workshops of the International Conference on Computational Creativity (2020)
36. Walsh, R.: Emergent narrative in interactive media. Narrative **19**(1), 72–85 (2011)
37. Wardrip-Fruin, N.: Expressive Processing: Digital Fictions, Computer Games, and Software Studies, chap. MIT Press, The Tale-Spin Effect (2009)
38. Zhu, J., Liapis, A., Risi, S., Bidarra, R., Youngblood, G.M.: Explainable AI for designers: a human-centered perspective on mixed-initiative co-creation. In: 2018 IEEE Conference on Computational Intelligence and Games (CIG). IEEE (2018)

An Investigation on the Usability
of Socio-cultural Features
for the Authoring Support During
the Development of Interactive Discourse
Environments (IDE)

Djordan Papilaya$^{(\boxtimes)}$ and Frank Nack

Informatics Institute, University of Amsterdam, Science Park 904,
1098 XH Amsterdam, Netherlands
djpapilaya@gmail.com, nack@uva.nl

Abstract. Though there have been significant developments in authoring tools for interactive narratives as well as a growing number of models
explaining narrative meaning production, there is still a lack of understanding around what type of authoring support is required that can
facilitate authors to handle the complex environment they develop by
maintaining a high content and experience quality. In this paper, we
present an investigation that aims to establish relations between individual information needs and navigation behaviour, which can be used
as patterns to support authors in the design and development of interaction processes for Interactive Discourse Environments (IDE). A prototype of an argumentative discourse environment has been developed,
in which participants can explore information resources in various media
representations and complexity levels to gain better insights on climate
change. The navigation behaviour has been tracked, and qualitative
interviews have been performed to gain deeper insights in the relation
between personal information needs, resource preferences and investigation behaviour. The findings of the analysis show that socio-cultural
attributes can be identified that correlate to certain navigation patterns.
We also show how those patterns can be made available as content and
engine consistency checking devices in an IDE authoring environment.

Keywords: Interactive digital narrative · Interactive discourse
environment · Interactive digital narrative engine · Authoring process ·
Support features

1 Introduction

Human interaction is a crucial element within an interactive digital narrative
(IDN). Koenitz et al. [17] argue that IDNs are interactive environments, which
dissolves the division between the creator and interactors of a story. Only through

M. Vosmeer and L. Holloway-Attaway (Eds.): ICIDS 2022, LNCS 13762, pp. 309–328, 2022.
https://doi.org/10.1007/978-3-031-22298-6_19

the interplay between the provided material and the means of interaction by the creator and the actual interaction with this IDN environment by the audience, the actual story product emerges [16]. The authoring of such complex and hence rich event and asset structures combined with the access engine and related maintenance structures is a complex process because the creator not only has to follow his or her own hermeneutic intentions towards the provided IDN but also has to anticipate both the level of agency and differences in the belief system and knowledge structures of the potential audience. This is in particular problematic as in an IDN no actual linear narrative, as know in film or literature, is designed and implemented but rather the means for different instantiations of a prototypical narrative.

Agency is the amount of freedom and control users have within a story, which is something an author can significantly influence [22, 24]. One contributor to agency is the interactors belief system. Human beliefs are based on the socio-cultural environment people grow up in and are shaped by different ideological systems, such as economics, politics or religion. These aspects of human beliefs significantly impact the way humans make choices [11]. For an author, it is thus crucial to understand why potential audiences make individual choices and how these affect the narrative within an IDN, so that those insights (often based on assumptions) can be designed and implemented. Currently, authors base their narratives on intrinsic assumptions and beliefs and adapt the narrative based on the various assumed user beliefs [17]. Yet, the authors intentions are intrinsically hidden in the overall composition and cannot be traced easily. Providing the author with more insights about the actual argumentative or experiential system state could help support their validation of the story space under development, which could increase the accessibility by the potential audience. Existing authoring tools are currently limited, if not incapable, of providing these insights [30, 31].

This study focuses on identifying socio-cultural parameters support to help an author with the authoring process. We focus on a sub field of IDN, namely an Interactive Discourse Environment (IDE). This field collect applications such as interactive documentaries [1] or opinion journalism in form of large exploratory information pieces[1] The essential element of an IDE is an argumentation engine that facilitates the comparison of various views on a particular complex problem so that the interactor can gain deeper insights and thus can develop an informed personal view on the problem.

2 Related Work

2.1 Agency

According to Moore [22], agency refers to having control over actions that lead to particular consequences. He distinguishes between the feeling of agency (FOA)

---

[1] https://docubase.mit.edu/project/fort-mcmoney,
    https://docubase.mit.edu/project/last-hijack-interactive,
    https://amirahanafi.com/post/155352117400/a-dictionary-of-the-revolution-2017.

and the judgement of agency (JOA). FOA is a lower-level concept that assesses the subjective feeling of agency before an event occurs. JOA is a higher-level concept related to the actual number of perceived agency during an event.

Murray [23] understands and IDN as a participatory medium and in this context established agency as one of three key concepts an IDN has to support (the other two are immersion and transformation). For her agency provides the means to take meaningful action and see the feedback in form of effects or consequences resulting from the choices made. Murray merges here two properties of and IDN – the procedural and the participatory. Agency covers the engagement of the participant to a world that responds to this engagement in an expressive and coherent way. The practice of narrative agency is the challenging point of authorship. In her opinion, an author should be seen as a choreographer who supplies the context, the feel for what will be performed. The interactor, on the other hand, takes the role of a protagonist, explorer, or builder, who makes use of the provided media and interaction means to improvise a particular performance within the digital story system.

According to Harrell and Zhu [8], more agency will not automatically lead to better IDN experiences. Users could feel overwhelmed with too much agency, while little agency could lead to a less enjoyable and tedious experience. Therefore, IDN authors should balance the amount of agency such that the experience is still comfortable for the user.

Agency is also relevant within the field of Human Computer Interaction (HCI). It mainly handles the design and use of interfaces but also addresses issues such as cognitive perception, mono- and multimedia communication, single and multimodality [18,36].

2.2   Belief Systems

A belief system is a set of structured norms in a particular context. Belief systems can establish belief chains, but they could also be independent of each other. [35]. One particular belief system is the political belief system. According to Dawson [5], such a belief system is a set of personal values, instrumental beliefs, and political attitudes bound together by static and dynamic constraints. Sartori [29] described a political ideology not as a particular belief but more as part of the political belief system. He states that not all political belief systems are ideological. In his view, ideology can be seen as a system of several beliefs held in common by multiple people. According to Everett et al. [6], left-right or liberal-conservative dimensions are often used to express political ideologies. The left-right dimension is used to determine voting behaviour, while in society, liberal-conservative dimensions are generally used to identify political ideology. There is more evidence that liberals and conservatives think and perceive differently in recent years, making this dimension even more suitable to identify political ideology [12,33].

2.3 Discourse Psychology

Discourse psychology established process models in form of coherent network of interrelated propositions that reflect the explicit information within a narrative, and the inferences that establish how the particular content is interrelated to different forms of knowledge, i.e. situated, partial, domain, and procedural (skill) knowledge [13,25,34,39]. The establish models, for example, show that narrative receivers monitor situational dimensions, update the mental model when dimensional changes occur, and hence arrange events around these dimensions in their episodic memory. Rich et al. [27] show that agents, objects, and abstract concepts are entities that prominently contribute to narrative structure. Trabasso et al. [34] point out that narrative events are connected via causal temporal and spatial relationships that are hierarchically organised goal episodes. Magliano et al. [21] argue that the multi-dimensionality of mental models might be equally important across media. However, it seems that time is more important in conveying shifts between narrative events than space, no matter what medium is used. Moreover, findings indicate that perceptual and cognitive processes that operate during narrative understanding can be diverted into frontend and backend processes. Front-end processes address the moment-to-moment information processing, whereas back-end processes address the building and maintenance of mental models and experiences. As different media still require special affordances with respect to information distribution (i.e. use of conventions) as well as the receiver's comprehension literacy, it has been suggested that there are transsymbolic (i.e. universal and operational across media) and symbolic-specific process (i.e. unique to a particular medium), where front-end processes affect the information that feeds back-end processes [19,20]. Along those lines develops work in cognitive narratology [10,38], which addresses the conceptualisation of mental representations of time, space and cause-effect and the elements of narrative that enable authors and audiences to construct these, such as schemas and frames. They address the mental relations between audience and the narrator and character, for example via point of view, dialogue, description of action and body language and conveyance of emotion. Empirical studies on these cognitive processes have been conducted by [3,26].

2.4 Authoring and Tools

As outlined in [7], there are essentially a maximum of 9 canonical processes an author passes during production, namely namely premeditation, asset creation, annotation, package, query, construct message, organise, publish, distribute. Those need to be integrated in an IDN authoring tool. Within IDN, several authoring tools already exist that help authors create their narratives. Keonitz [15], Kritromili et al. [14] and Shibolet et al. [30] already provide an excellent overview on existing tools. Shibolet et al. [30], analysed various authoring tools for IDNs and defined an authoring tool as digital software, where the tool should be an independent and comprehensive workspace and simplify the authoring process. For the classification of authoring tools, the authors focused on affordances rather than functionality. However, most of the outlined tools still suffer from limitations [31]. The problem is that complex technical aspects form the essential limitation of such tools, as story ideas do not fit within the engine that renders the story. This limits authors in their creativity and restricts them to change parts of the story at a later stage. These current limitations of the authoring process create for the authors a barrier that is often addressed by simplifying the authoring process. In the study of Cheong et al. [4], PRISM has been developed to create a framework for authoring interactive narratives. In their study, the authors developed a hybrid framework that allows authors to create narratives without significant computer programming knowledge. In their program, authors create narratives by using branching graphs and AI planning to generate stories automatically. Another authoring tool used is the Advanced Stories and Presentation System (ASAPS) [15]. This tool allows authors to create interactive narratives easily to be used by people who are less familiar with IDN. By combining so-called "building-blocks", stories can be created without limiting the author's creativity. This structure is a bottom-up structure, where authors have to think about the essential elements of their story and add IDN elements to their narrative. Research conducted by Harteveld et al. [9] explores the authoring platform Mad Science, used within educational experiences, and identifies what lessons they could learn from this platform. This platform provided users with a way to create their virtual theatre with scientific game-like scenarios. In their evaluation, the researchers indicated that users tend to create scenarios from scratch instead of using existing scenarios or confirming whether or not their idea has already been pursued. The researchers believe that manipulating the creation process and guiding users by making their scenarios could help users create better experiences in this authoring tool. The closest authoring environment for IDEs is the one used in Vox Populi [1], which integrates Toulmin's persuasive argument model into the construction process of persuasive argument generation, which is utilised in a video documentary generator.

3 Approach

The context of this work is the endeavour of ARDIN[2] and the EU COST action INDCOR[3] to develop an open source IDN authoring sandbox that facilitates creator and authoring-tool collaboration. The authoring environment is based on Koenitz' SPP model [16]. The work presented here contributes to the system level (content collection and presentation/analysis engine design). The development of the authoring environment applies the research through design methodology [28,37]. The outlined work is part of the pre-design phase, which focuses on problem analysis. This work is a basic behavioural study rather than an IDN usability study.

The following investigation focuses on gaining a better understanding on how interactors access and navigate an IDE, of which they know the covered domain

---

[2] https://ardin.online/.
[3] https://indcor.eu/.

(Climate Change) but have to learn over time through interaction about the overall structure with respect to levels of complexity regarding content organisation, media types and interaction means (hermeneutic circle).

Climate change was chosen to have a familiar and relevant topic for all the participants and to provide an incentive to actually explore the space. The aim is to identify behavioural pattern that can be linked to hermeneutic parameters so that resulting meta-data structures and processing algorithms can be integrated into an authoring environment to support the design and building of interactor analysis tools as well as the interaction engine.

3.1   Prototype

The prototype was developed as an argumentative discourse environment (see Fig. 1. Within this environment, interactors can explore information on climate change in various media representations and on different complexity levels.

For this discourse space (see Fig. 1 A), 135 resources were selected (an example of text and video are represented in Fig. 1 B and C). To have variation in media types, 45 audio, video, and text items were chosen by 3 researchers (each researcher collected 15 media units of each type). The researchers agreed before on complexity levels (low, middle, high) and applied those to content (number of arguments, diversity of argument structure, abstract level of explanations, number of explanations) and media (length, media aesthetics, style, syntax). In addition each media item was classified based on its political spectrum between conservatism and progressiveness (see Table 1). The researchers collected 5 items per media type collectively (overcome collection biases) and then 10 individually. They collaboratively annotated the material according to the classification and arranged them in consensus into the discourse space, which formed a grid, where the far left resources represent the most progressive, while the far right items represent the most conservative view. Vertically, the top resources were simpler in structure, while the bottom resources were classified as complex. However, the interface did not portray this distribution towards the participants.

Table 1. The distribution of resources for political ideology and complexity. Clustered per media type. Noted as absolute values and between brackets the relative values (value between 0.00 and 1.00)

	All resources (135)	Audio (45)	Video (45)	Text (45)
Progressive	73 (.54)	30 (.67)	21 (.47)	22 (.49)
Middle	25 (.19)	0 (.00)	9 (0.20)	16 (.36)
Conservative	37 (.27)	15 (.33)	15 (.033)	7 (.16)
	All resources (135)	Audio (45)	Video (45)	Text (45)
Simple	47 (.35)	18 (.40)	14 (.31)	15 (.33)
Medium	54 (.40)	21 (.47)	18 (.40)	15 (.33)
Complex	34 (.25)	6 (.13)	13 (.29)	15 (.33)

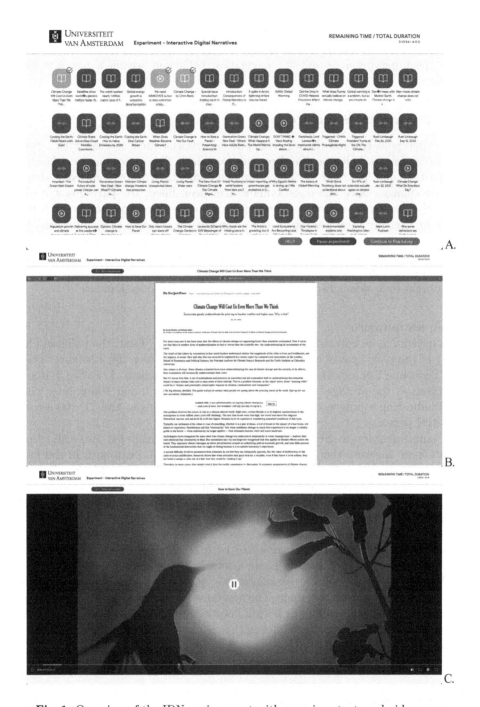

Fig. 1. Overview of the IDN environment with overview, text, and video page

The environment was designed so that all behaviour (clicks and navigation direction) can be monitored. The interactions and visited resources of each inter-actor were stored in an associated relational DB. Moreover, a participant's total time spent per resource and the navigation behaviour within a resource was collected.

3.2 Experiment Structure

The experiment covered three parts. The experiment circle started with a pre-questionnaire (see below section Pre-questionnaire). This questionnaire asked for the participants' political ideology, combined with their prior knowledge about climate change. Once the questionnaire had been filled, the participant could enter the discourse environment. Participants were asked to interact with the space in any way they wanted in the given time constraint (4 h) but with the aim to increase their understanding of the topic. At the point that a participant decided to terminate the experiment, a post-questionnaire appeared. This ques-tionnaire was intended to obtain the participant's justification for their choices and obtain their demographics (see below section Post-questionnaire).

Pre-questionnaire

This questionnaire covered three categories of questions. First, the political ide-ology of the participants was determined. We applied Everett's 12-items Social and Economic Conservatism Scale (SECS) [6]. The 12 scores of the SECS items are taken as the average. A final score ranges between 0 and 100 points, with 0–30 indicating a progressive person, 31–70 a centre person, and 71–100 a con-servative person.

Complementary to SECS, the questionnaire also included two validation questions to measure the participant's actual political background. In the first question, participants had to rank Dutch political parties according to whether they identified themselves with this party. This ranking led to an indication of which political spectrum participants identified themselves with. For the second validation question, participants had to answer which political party they had voted for in the 2020 Dutch National elections. Answering both of these ques-tions was optional, and participants had been informed that all collected data would be anonymised. All participants answered those questions.

Finally, the questionnaire contained two questions about the participant's prior awareness on climate change. The first question intended to identify how far the participant considers him or herself knowledgeable on the topic. The second question measured how much information a participant consumes in general about climate change. Both questions had to be answered with a 6-point Likert scale, where zero indicated no or none and five indicated expert or very much.

Post-questionnaire

This questionnaire was used to ask open-ended qualitative questions about the participant's behaviour during the use of the prototype. The questions were about why participants made choices with respect to media use and complexity levels) and whether they felt influenced by their political background. The questionnaire ended with a demographics investigation, addressing age, sex, and education.

Participants

This experiment select participants based on age, education, and political spectrum. The participants were assigned to two age groups of 18–30 years and 31–60 years. Within these age groups, two groups were created of people with a Master's degree or higher and people with a Bachelor's, Dutch HBO degree, or lower. Within these four subgroups, the aim was to have an equal distribution over the political spectrum. The participants have been sampled based on convenience and snowball sampling.

Experiment Setup

The experiment was conducted online without any guidance from an observatory researcher. Participants received a personalised invitation via email, which contained access information. Qualtrics[4] was used as the environment for this questionnaire.

An introduction before the actual start provided details on the experiment process, rules, and information on privacy issues. After completing the pre-questionnaire, participants could navigate to the discourse space[5] with a personalised generated link by the questionnaire[6].

Within the discourse space, each participant had a maximum of four hours for exploration. There was a possibility to pause and continue at a later stage in time.

After completion, participants were linked to the post-questionnaire. All questions, resources and information were provided in English. Every participant obtained a €5 Bol.com voucher as a reward for participating in the experiment.

4   Results

This section presents the analysis, subdivided into a general analysis, political analysis, resource media type analysis, and complexity analysis.

All data, including data sheets, raw database data, the source code for the discourse space, and high resolution images of the Figures, are available through Github[7]

---

[4] https://qualtrics.com/.

[5] https://idn-experiment.nl.

[6] As the questionnaire and discourse systems were separate items, the links was necessary to ensure that the questionnaire data could be connected to the prototype data.

[7] https://github.com/djordanpapilaya/interactive-discourse-environment-dataset, https://github.com/djordanpapilaya/interactive-discourse-environment-sourcecode.

4.1   Participant Demographics

For this study, in total, 18 participants have been registered. Due to incorrect entries, the actual participant population is 14 (n = 14). Table 2 gives an overview of the participant distribution over the different demographic facets.

Table 2. Participant demographics

	18–30 years	31–60 years	Low/middle educated	High educated	Progressive	Centre	Conservative
18–30 years	10[a]	x	9[b]	1	2	8	0
31–60 years	x	4	3	1	1	3	0
Low/middle educated	9	3	12[c]	x	2	10	0
High educated	1	1	x	2	1	1	0
Progressive	2	1	2	1	3[d]	x	x
Centre	8	3	10	1	x	11[e]	x
Conservative	0	0	0	0	x	x	0

[a] P11, P16 – P21, P23, P24, P26
[b] P10 – P12, P15 – P24, P26
[c] P10, P15 – P24, P26
[d] P10, P11, P19
[e] P12, P15 – P18, P20 – P24, P26

4.2   Data Analysis Methods

The data has been quantitatively filtered and clustered based on the political spectrum, media type and complexity. A statistical mean has been used to calculate the average of all three clusters for all participants. Moreover, repetitive use of items has been collected. By doing so, a list of frequencies was created per category. With these frequencies, it could be observed how long a participant interacted with a particular category.

The qualitative data has been analysed using inductive coding [32]. In three rounds, the open-ended questions were analysed and diverged into a simplified code set. These separate codes then have been compared with the interaction patterns.

4.3   General Analysis

The first analysis addresses data that includes interaction patterns and user behaviour within the discourse space.

Participants spent an average of 01:28:59 h in the environment (min 0:16:51 h, max 3:16:51 h).On average, participants viewed 17 resources during the experiment and spent an average of 05:22 min on each. Participants accessed progressive resources (0.61), followed by conservative (0.21), and finally middle resources (0.18). For the type of media, participants preferred video resources (0.62), followed by text (0.26) and audio (0.12). Finally, participants accessed predominantly simple resources (0.61) compared to medium (0.23) and complex resources (0.16). Table 3 provides a full time overview per media type. Duration values lower than 10 s were removed from the data set because the assumption is that, in this case, participants only previewed a resource and did not perceived its content.

Table 3. Time consumption per media type

	Video	Text	Audio
Min. time	0:00:10	0:00:13	0:00:10
Max. time	0:37:15	0:13:44	0:43:34
Avg. time	0:05:18	0:03:10	0:09:03

In general, participants increased their complexity levels over time when selecting resources.

The prior awareness on climate change for people with a BSc or lower was on average 2,5 (on a scale from 0–5), while participants with a MSc or higher it was 4 (on a scale from 0–5). An informal investigation of the main investigator after the experiment indicated that the awareness level of the participants increased.

4.4 Political Analysis

This analysis has been done based on the political backgrounds of the user groups and their interactions with the discourse space environment. Graphs were extracted representing the interaction paths for every participant. In order to compare these graphs, data was arranged into a scatter plot per user (see Fig. 2, where 1 corresponds with progressive, 0 with middle, and -1 with conservative). For example, P15's starting position was progressive, and the last resource was a progressive item (see Fig. 2).

These political background clusters were further divided into graphs where participants showed similar behaviour. The distribution was based on how many times participants switched between the different types of political resources. This distribution resulted in four clusters (see Table 4).

This analysis shows that participants with a centre or progressive political orientation tend to switch frequently between resources. Political centre participants (groups M1 and M2) tend to switch more compared to progressive participants (P1, P2), but the M1/ M2 groups also spent less investigation time per item. Also, they start with progressive resources (n = 11) while exploring middle or conservative resources later. The majority of them end with a progressive resource (n = 7).

Most progressive participants (groups P1 and P2) also start with progressive articles (n = 2), followed by switching to middle or conservative resources. Moreover, most progressive participants tend to end with a progressive resource (n = 2).

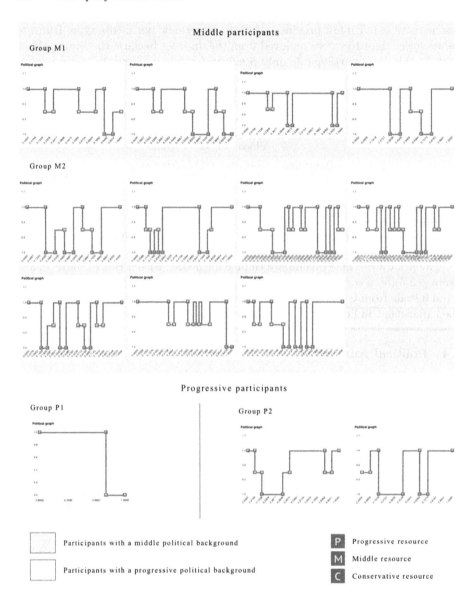

Fig. 2. All interaction paths graphs for the visited resources in a complete session

Table 4. Political background clusters

Group ID	Description	n
M1	Centre participants who switched two times or less between progressive/ middle.	4
M2	Centre participants who switched multiple times between progressive/ middle and conservative resources.	7
P1	Progressive participant(s) who stayed progressive/ middle.	1
P2	Progressive participants who switched two times or less between progressive/ middle	2

4.5   Resource Media Type Analysis

Participants could choose between video, audio, or text resources. The access patterns again have been analysed based on scatter plots, where 1 indicates video, 0 indicates audio, and -1 represents audio. Clusters were made based on demographics, education and age.

The data analysis shows that video is the dominant medium among the participants (see also Sect. 4.3). While filtering on age it can be seen that the 31–60 years group consumes more video than the 18–30 years group and also starts and ends mostly with a video. In contrast, most of the younger participants start with a text resource (n = 8) and end with a video resource (n = 9).

When analysing education demographics, no difference can be observed in video consumption. However, participants with a higher education degree seem to use video as the entry point for their exploration, whereas participants with a lower degree seem to approach the space firstly with a text. Common for both groups is that the last media item used is a video.

When looking at individual media use, it can be observed that audio, even though the least used media source, is processed for the longest period (i.e. three times longer than an individual spends on a text and nearly double the time than for a video).

4.6   Complexity Analysis

The analysis is again based on scatter plot comparison and clustering of the plots. 1 indicated a complex resource, 0 a medium resource, and -1 a simple resource. These plots were clustered based on the demographic data of education, age and the individual awareness level.

In both the education and the age cluster, participants start with simple resources and finish with more complex resources. Moreover, in both clusters, participants switched between all three levels of complexity. However, the amount of time spent on more complex resources was higher among participants with a higher educational degree.

4.7   Qualitative Open-Ended Questions Analysis

The questions have been selected to shed light on why participants chose a specific starting point, whether or not they think their political background had an influence on their interactions, and if they their prior awareness and related knowledge influenced them.

Participants of the centre political group mainly chose their interactions because of personal interest and their interest in a resource. Moreover, participants stated that since climate change is an umbrella term, they were influenced to look at specific areas of climate change that were familiar to them. P22 answered the first question with *"In no way at all"* and the second with *"Looking for similarities in my own experience and topics shown."*. All members of this cluster stated that their political background did not influence their interactions. This is a dominant behaviour in this group independent of age and education level.

Progressive participants also stated that they made choices based on their interests and personal media preferences. The clear difference to the center group is that strategically they approach the start-point differently, as they aim for an interesting resource. For example, P11 stated, *"The first resources that I came across and sounded interesting."*. In addition they show a clear awareness of their political background and how this can influence their navigation behaviour. This use of reflection could indicate, and the behaviour patterns support this view, that members of this cluster try to avoid selecting articles centered on their view but rather select variations (bias avoidance). They stated that they select resources that were out of their belief sphere.

4.8   Combination Analysis

For the final analysis, a combination has been made between the media types and the complexity levels. This analysis aimed to identify if certain media types were preferable with certain complexity levels. In order to perform this analysis, heatmaps have been generated, where the entire interaction path with the selected media type was displayed on the x-axis, and colours indicated which level of complexity a resource represented. All heatmaps were combined and clustered based on education and age demographics. The heatmaps can be found in Fig. 3.

The findings show that participants tend to start with more simple resources and then lean towards increasing complexity. Particularly while looking at media types, it can be observed that this is the case for video and text. Audio is complicated to be evaluated as only a few participants used it (see Sect. 4.3. Moreover, age and education seem to have no influence on this behaviour pattern.

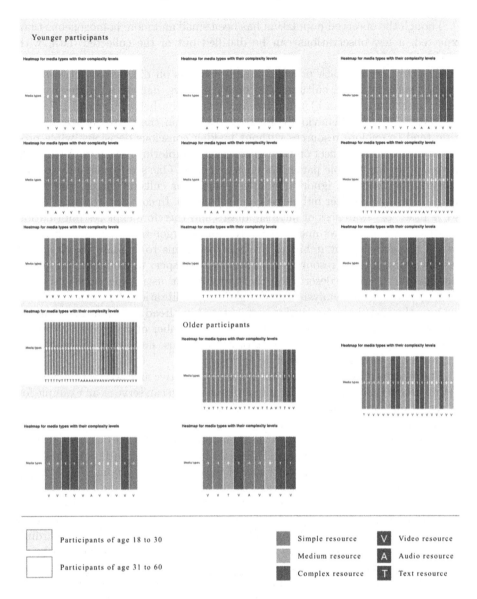

Fig. 3. The interaction path graphs for combination of media types and complexity grouped by age

5 Discussion

The main goal of this study was to identify features that can be utilised in an authoring system to support authors of IDEs during the system design and development process.

Though the observed population has been small and more homogeneous than expected, a few observations can be distilled out of the collected data, with caution though.

Even though the data provides mainly insights on differences between two tenets regarding social, cultural, and political views, namely a progressive and center spectrum, we can identify different interaction behaviours and reflective verification of those behaviours. Participants within the centre political spectrum tend to explore resources without making conscious decisions, while progressive participants reflect on their choices while exploring resources. As a result there are two identifiable pattern of choice making. One strategy mainly follows idiosyncratic interests, ignoring political, social, or cultural biases, and hence can be compared to filter bubble behaviour (see [2]). In contrast, the other strategy is based on awareness of intrinsic biases and therefore explores information with contradicting views and perspectives on a larger scale. For an authoring system this means that it has to provide the means to support the design of various approaches for resource exploration with respect to modelling templates (metadata for resource description and templates for user, experience and event models) and related analysis functionalities (i.e. libraries of functions). From our investigation some descriptive parameters can already be identified, namely complexity levels (low, middle, high), content (number of arguments, diversity of argument structure, abstract level of explanations, number of explanations) and media (length, media aesthetics, style, syntax).

The described linking of quantitative and qualitative analysis tools in our test setting in combination with its actual implementation can serve as an example for an algorithmic approach towards interaction analysis with resulting material recommendation or presentation. However, we could show that similar behaviours show comparable pattern but differ in their temporal duration (i.e. time thresholds to introduce bias challenges). Threshold handling is an authoring challenge that further investigation, in particular if different belief systems, such as religious or economic, need to be integrated.

The outlined approach towards meta-data support can also applied during the authoring process for detecting completeness of resource with respect to levels of complexity as well as media coverage and their distribution regarding diversity. Our results show that video is the most dominant media type being consumed among all identified user groups. This finding is not astonishing, as for example video is constantly increasing its relevance as a news medium (see YouTube or TikTok). We could also show that particular media types (i.e. audio) seem to be preferred for particular types of argument constellations. Here we are in line with findings in the literature (see Sect. 2.3). From an authoring system point of view it is possible to check on placement, number and quality of media resources in the system (i.e. the protostory knowledge graph for placement, or on media features like time and complexity level in relation to user preferences). A system could observe the length of a resources and provide the author with an alert if it is potentially too long for the aimed for context. Yet, the resource analysis on completeness or diversity requires that the author has to provide a vision or intent about the aims of the planned environment, as the basis for a comparison with respect to consistency and aimed or opinion diversity. The interplay between the intent and the actual design of the system needs further investigation.

Regarding the overall structural approach of an IDE, we showed that there are particular navigation patterns, mainly linear, circular, or forking. Considering those patterns an authoring system can identify for a single argument or over a larger argument line if sufficient alternated resources are available and that those argument lines can be fully established (i.e. identifying isolated argument resources or non-finished argument lines). For the design and implementation phase of the system this is an authoring challenge as neither the material nor the resources explicitly establish a final text that can be analysed. Thus, a simulation process needs to be provided that can perform the analysis of the established parameters. What this additional layer of complexity means with respect to the usability of the authoring tool in the context of real world production processes needs to be investigated.

As we merely used user awareness as an indicator to monitor impact of use, we cannot state how the representation of domain knowledge as part of the user model can influence the interaction design in the engine. Yet, it seems that the awareness parameter in its simplicity is already good enough to be used in the engine design to detect progress or regression. This is a minor finding, as the whole domain of system validation is a field of study in itself (see for example work of the COST INDCOR working group 3[8]).

With the created experimental framework work we provided a base that could be reused for other IDE experiments that follow the research through design methodology. The overall design of joining quantitative and qualitative investigations is working. However, we faced several issues with respect to actual experimental setup. To avoid those validation lowering aspects, researchers have to ensure that the user group is well defined for the tasks to be performed, the resources are valid, the population is large enough (which is a challenge as the measuring methods are different – see statistical max numbers versus theoretical saturation), and language aspects are addressed. Though our experiment showed shortcomings in some of those aspects (only representation of 2 political view, material still biased, differences between population language and resource language) the overall test framework (see Sect. 3) can be considered a first step towards standardised IDE evaluation.

6 Conclusion and Future Work

This study aimed to gain insights on authoring system support for authors during the process of interactive discourse environments design and development.

Overall we consider this research a step towards better system support of authors during the design implementation and maintenance of large digital discourse spaces. It can be concluded that the combination of interaction patterns

---

[8] https://indcor.eu/working-groups/wg3-evaluation/.

and user data on socio-cultural parameters can be integrated in the design and development process to facilitate modelling (user, event, knowledge) and interaction processes (engine building) checking. It is challenging to determine socio-cultural groups based on the interaction patterns entirely, but insights about political decisions, media types and complexity levels could be derived. The findings have to be taken with caution , though, as the test population has been small and rather heterogeneous and hence make statements about opinionated navigation critical.

In addition we provide with this work a basic contribution towards a framework for experimental research on IDEs. We are aware that the framework is rooted in the approach of research by design but it seems to us that the presented test environment and the related quantitative and qualitative methods can also be applied in other research methodologies. The test engine as well as the related evaluation methods are available for the community and we look forward to see how they develop over time. We will use the suggested approach in our ongoing research that focuses on authoring tools for IDEs in the domain of opinionated journalism.

Acknowledgement. The work presented in this paper is supported by the EU COST Action 18230 – Interactive Narrative Design for Complexity Representation (INDCOR). The authors also wish to thank Hartmut Koenitz and Lissa Holloway-Attaway for helping in the revision process.

References

1. Bocconi, S.: Vox Populi : generating video documentaries from semantically annotated media repositories, Ph. D. thesis, Mathematics and Computer Science (2006). https://doi.org/10.6100/IR615072
2. Bozdag, E.: Bias in algorithmic filtering and personalization. Ethics Inf. Technol. **15**(3), 209–227 (2013)
3. Bruni, L.E., Baceviciute, S., Arief, M.: Narrative cognition in interactive Systems: suspense-Surprise and the P300 ERP component. In: Mitchell, A., Fernández-Vara, C., Thue, D. (eds.) ICIDS 2014. LNCS, vol. 8832, pp. 164–175. Springer, Cham (2014). https://doi.org/10.1007/978-3-319-12337-0_17
4. Cheong, Y.-G., Kim, Y.-J., Min, W.-H., Shim, E.-S., Kim, J.-Y.: PRISM: a framework for authoring interactive narratives. In: Spierling, U., Szilas, N. (eds.) ICIDS 2008. LNCS, vol. 5334, pp. 297–308. Springer, Heidelberg (2008). https://doi.org/10.1007/978-3-540-89454-4_37
5. Dawson, P.A.: The formation and structure of political belief systems. Polit. Behav. **1**(2), 99–122 (1979)
6. Everett, J.A.: The 12 item social and economic conservatism scale (secs). PLoS ONE **8**(12), e82131 (2013)
7. Hardman, L., Obrenović, Ž, Nack, F., Kerhervé, B., Piersol, K.: Canonical processes of semantically annotated media production. Multimedia Syst. **14**(6), 327–340 (2008)
8. Harrell, D.F., Zhu, J.: Agency play: dimensions of agency for interactive narrative design. In: AAAI spring symposium: Intelligent narrative technologies II, pp. 44–52 (2009)

9. Harteveld, C., et al.: Design of playful authoring tools for social and behavioral science. In: Proceedings of the 22nd International Conference on Intelligent User Interfaces Companion, pp. 157–160 (2017)
10. Herman, D.: Storytelling and the sciences of mind. MIT press (2013)
11. Jameson, A., et al.: Choice architecture for human-computer interaction. Found. Trends Hum-Comput. Interact. **7**(1–2), 1–235 (2014)
12. Jost, J.T., Glaser, J., Kruglanski, A.W., Sulloway, F.J.: Political conservatism as motivated social cognition. Psychol. Bull. **129**(3), 339 (2003)
13. Kintsch, W.: The role of knowledge in discourse comprehension: a construction-integration model. Psychol. Rev. **95**(2), 163 (1988)
14. Kitromili, S., Jordan, J., Millard, D.E.: What is hypertext authoring? In: Proceedings of the 30th ACM Conference on Hypertext and Social Media, pp. 55–59 (2019)
15. Koenitz, H.: Extensible tools for practical experiments in IDN: the advanced stories authoring and presentation system. In: Si, M., Thue, D., André, E., Lester, J.C., Tanenbaum, T.J., Zammitto, V. (eds.) ICIDS 2011. LNCS, vol. 7069, pp. 79–84. Springer, Heidelberg (2011). https://doi.org/10.1007/978-3-642-25289-1_9
16. Koenitz, H.: Towards a specific theory of interactive digital narrative. In: Interactive digital narrative, pp. 91–105. Routledge (2015)
17. Koenitz, H., Ferri, G., Haahr, M., Sezen, D., Sezen, T.İ.: Interactive digital narrative: history, theory and practice. Routledge (2015)
18. Limerick, H., Coyle, D., Moore, J.W.: The experience of agency in human-computer interactions: a review. Front. Hum. Neurosci. **8**, 643 (2014)
19. Loschky, L.C., Larson, A.M., Smith, T.J., Magliano, J.P.: The scene perception and event comprehension theory (SPECT) applied to visual narratives. Topics Cogn. Sci. **12**(1), 311–351 (2020)
20. Magliano, J.P., Clinton, J.A., O'Brien, E.J., Rapp, D.N.: Detecting differences between adapted narratives: Implication of order of modality on exposure. In: Empirical Comics Research, pp. 284–304. Routledge (2018)
21. Magliano, J.P., Loschky, L.C., Clinton, J.A., Larson, A.M.: Is reading the same as viewing. Unraveling the behavioral, neurobiological and genetic components of reading comprehension, pp. 78–90 (2013)
22. Moore, J.W.: What is the sense of agency and why does it matter? Front. Psychol. **7**, 1272 (2016)
23. Murray, J.H.: Research into interactive digital narrative: a kaleidoscopic view. In: Rouse, R., Koenitz, H., Haahr, M. (eds.) ICIDS 2018. LNCS, vol. 11318, pp. 3–17. Springer, Cham (2018). https://doi.org/10.1007/978-3-030-04028-4_1
24. Murray, J.H., Murray, J.H.: Hamlet on the holodeck: the future of narrative in cyberspace. MIT press (2017)
25. Özyürek, A., Trabasso, T.: Evaluation during the understanding of narratives. Discourse Process. **23**(3), 305–335 (1997)
26. Pope, J.: Further on down the digital road: narrative design and reading pleasure in five new media writing prize narratives. Convergence **26**(1), 35–54 (2020)
27. Rich, S.S., Taylor, H.A.: Not all narrative shifts function equally. Mem. Cogn. **28**(7), 1257–1266 (2000)
28. Roggema, R.: Research by design: Proposition for a methodological approach. Urban sci. **1**(1), 2 (2016)
29. Sartori, G.: Politics, ideology, and belief systems. American polit. Sci. Rev. **63**(2), 398–411 (1969)

30. Shibolet, Y., Knoller, N., Koenitz, H.: A framework for classifying and describing authoring tools for interactive digital narrative. In: Rouse, R., Koenitz, H., Haahr, M. (eds.) ICIDS 2018. LNCS, vol. 11318, pp. 523–533. Springer, Cham (2018). https://doi.org/10.1007/978-3-030-04028-4_61

31. Spierling, U., Szilas, N.: Authoring issues beyond tools. In: Iurgel, I.A., Zagalo, N., Petta, P. (eds.) ICIDS 2009. LNCS, vol. 5915, pp. 50–61. Springer, Heidelberg (2009). https://doi.org/10.1007/978-3-642-10643-9_9

32. Thomas, D.R.: A general inductive approach for analyzing qualitative evaluation data. American J. Eval. 27(2), 237–246 (2006)

33. Thórisdóttir, H., Jost, J.T.: Motivated closed-mindedness mediates the effect of threat on political conservatism. Polit. Psychol. 32(5), 785–811 (2011)

34. Trabasso, T., Van den Broek, P., Suh, S.Y.: Logical necessity and transitivity of causal relations in stories. Discourse Process. 12(1), 1–25 (1989)

35. Usó-Doménech, J.L., Nescolarde-Selva, J.: What are belief systems? Found. Sci. 21(1), 147–152 (2016)

36. Wilde, A.G., Bruegger, P., Hirsbrunner, B.: An overview of human-computer interaction patterns in pervasive systems. In: 2010 International Conference on User Science and Engineering (i-USEr), pp. 145–150. IEEE (2010)

37. Zimmerman, J., Stolterman, E., Forlizzi, J.: An analysis and critique of research through design: towards a formalization of a research approach. In: proceedings of the 8th ACM conference on designing interactive systems, pp. 310–319 (2010)

38. Zunshine, L.: Why we read fiction: theory of mind and the novel. Ohio State University Press (2006)

39. Zwaan, R.A., Radvansky, G.A.: Situation models in language comprehension and memory. Psychol. Bull. 123(2), 162 (1998)

When Information, Narrative, and Interactivity Join Forces: Designing and Co-designing Interactive Digital Narratives for Complex Issues

Pratama Wirya Atmaja[1][✉] and Sugiarto[2]

[1] Department of Informatics, University of Pembangunan Nasional "Veteran" Jawa Timur, Surabaya, Indonesia
pratama_wirya.fik@upnjatim.ac.id
[2] Department of Data Science, University of Pembangunan Nasional "Veteran" Jawa Timur, Surabaya, Indonesia
sugiarto.if@upnjatim.ac.id

Abstract. The world is inherently and tremendously complex, yet many people are not well-equipped to deal with complex issues such as sustainability. Consequently, the issues must be communicated appropriately to the public. Narratives are effective for complex issue communication (CIC), especially when delivered through interactive digital narratives (IDNs). However, no design methodology is currently available for IDNs for CIC, especially one that balances the IDNs' information, narrative, and interactivity aspects. Thus, through a literature review, we propose two design methodologies: the first facilitates a comprehensive requirement gathering and design process, and the second restructures the first to enable co-design between interdisciplinary experts, each handling one of the aspects. The co-design methodology's complex systems foundation unites the experts and eases their communication. We close this paper with a discussion of new design concepts in the methodologies, including analyzing the audience's learning process as a hierarchy of atomic hermeneutic cycles and using a syuzhet to restructure the narrative according to the hierarchy.

Keywords: Interactive digital narratives · Complex issue communication · Design methodology · Co-design · Complex systems

1 Introduction

The 21st century has seen climate change and many other "wicked problems," i.e., issues so complex that their solutions seem nonexistent [1–3]. They urgently call for a holistic mindset and solutions involving all aspects of our society [3, 4]. Since understanding or even caring for complex issues can be challenging, the issues must be communicated effectively to the public to raise awareness, combat disinformation, and trigger positive actions [2, 5]. Successful complex issue communication (CIC) depends on various factors, including using narratives to engage and inform [5, 6].

© The Author(s), under exclusive license to Springer Nature Switzerland AG 2022
M. Vosmeer and L. Holloway-Attaway (Eds.): ICIDS 2022, LNCS 13762, pp. 329–351, 2022.
https://doi.org/10.1007/978-3-031-22298-6_20

Due to their link to complexity theory [7, 8], narratives can communicate the intricate spatiotemporality of the world [6, 9], thus helping unravel complex issues. Unique among narrative media for CIC, interactive digital narratives (IDNs) enable active exploration of complex issues and their solutions [10–13], which greatly scaffolds comprehension [14] and triggers positive actions [15, 16]. Many IDNs for CIC are available nowadays [17–19], yet the systematic process of designing one is still elusive. Moreover, most of the current IDNs for CIC lack informational value [18], specific narrative elements, e.g., distinct characters [20], or issue-relevant interactive mechanics [18]. Indeed, how to create IDNs for CIC with balanced aspects of information, narrative, and interactivity is also unclear. Given the increased interest in IDNs for CIC [21], researching this matter has become urgent.

This research, therefore, proposes two design methodologies for IDNs for CIC. The first facilitates a comprehensive requirement gathering and design workflow. Based on the first, the second one balances the information, narrative, and interactivity aspects of IDNs for CIC through co-design between interdisciplinary experts of the aspects. We ground the methodologies on a literature review of IDN elements, available design methodologies from games, and complex systems. With such capabilities, the methodologies will support the design and production of high-quality IDNs for CIC as aimed by COST Action INDCOR[1].

2 State of the Art in IDNs for CIC

Narratives can help make sense of complex and deeply uncertain issues by providing spatiotemporal explanations of the world and how to change it [6, 9]. These explanations are highly compatible with complexity theory due to highlighting causality, temporal progression, and multiple outcome possibilities [7]. Carefully-constructed narratives can also effectively persuade, even more so if congruent with the audience's culture or ideology [22, 23]. Indeed, narratives can evoke empathy through relatable aspects of the story, such as characters [24], including anthropomorphized non-human ones [23]. In particular, hero characters can be powerfully persuasive [25, 26]. However, the overall persuasion effect is not always long-lasting [27], nor does it always lead to substantial behavioral changes [28], suggesting that telling stories alone is not enough.

Over the years, government entities and academia have endeavored to create short videos [29], art installations [30], and other "serious" narrative media for CIC. On the other hand, emotionally-charged complex issues, e.g., climate disaster, have attracted filmmakers and authors, with products like *The Day After Tomorrow* [31] and *The Windup Girl* [28] entering public consciousness and academic discussions. The main strength of such entertainment narratives is their high narrative quality, which can lessen the audience's resistance to their messages [32]. However, they also tend to be less accurate or informative in portraying the issues [31]. We can conclude that narratives for CIC comprise at least two aspects: *information* and *narrative*. The first aspect fills the audience's "information deficit," whereas the second one fills their "narrative deficit" [6].

Meanwhile, IDN is a relatively new yet potent medium for CIC due to possessing a third aspect: *interactivity*. Mainly, it allows for exploring various perspectives, details,

---

[1] https://indcor.eu.

and causal relations in the narrative, deepening and personalizing the audience's understanding [10–13]. Features such as continuous feedback and replay further support the exploration and increase learning gain [21]. Compared to more passive ones, such active learning processes can more effectively trigger positive behaviors and actions [15, 16]. Indeed, if carefully designed and put in a narrative context, interactivity mechanics can express ideas and deliver highly persuasive rhetorics [33].

The existing IDNs for CIC, mainly games and gamification, have already covered a wide range of topics, e.g., climate change and research ethics, application domains, e.g., climate change mitigation practices, and target audiences, e.g., tertiary students and farming stakeholders [12, 18, 19]. Besides pure IDNs, some digital-analog hybrids have also been invented [17], including interactive theaters [34] and tangible narrative systems [35]. A lively landscape aside, the productions of these interactive narratives have been sporadic, although one action is trying to unite the actors. Operating under the EU-based COST agency, INDCOR represents a concentrated, interdisciplinary endeavor for the proliferation of IDNs for CIC, to which robust design approaches are vital [21]. However, a quick review of the IDN literature reveals a dearth of design methodologies, posing a significant challenge to the endeavor.

3   Designing IDNs for CIC

3.1   Design Elements of IDNs

Generally, a narrative comprises a *story* and a *discourse*, i.e., the story presentation [36]. We can further split the story into (1) a *story world* consisting of *settings*, *entities*, i.e., characters and objects, and *internal logic* [37], and (2) a *plot*, i.e., the chronological sequence of *events* in the story world. The interactive nature of IDNs necessitates dynamic narrative components, i.e., a *protostory*, which can instantiate a different narrative each time [38]. The most common dynamic component is a dynamic plot comprising branching or emergent events [13, 38], although IDNs can also dynamize the story world [39] and the discourse [40].

Technically, an "event" is anything involving specific entities in a particular setting and time [36], which may be very mundane, such as a character walking around. To ensure that the IDN always produces engaging narratives, the designer can employ *narrative vectors*, i.e., "plot points" or significant events [38]. A vector network exhibits a specific structure, such as a branching one [41], and rules for vector progressions consider various variables and activities, e.g., gathered clues and combat sessions [38, 41].

A narrative component is either hand-crafted, e.g., a narrative vector, or *procedural* [38]. The latter can directly control the plot, e.g., the "drama manager" artificial intelligence in *Façade* [42], or make the story world come alive, e.g., a physics engine and character movement mechanics [38]. In practice, hand-crafted and procedural components often work together, as exemplified by *Façade*'s combination of the drama manager and manually-designed "narrative beats" [42].

Through a *user interface* (UI), the audience observes and manipulates the narrative progression [13, 38]. The degree of control given to the audience, e.g., choosing an action to trigger an event vs. controlling a character to cause gradual changes in the story world [43], determines the space of possible narratives, limiting the observation of causality [13]. Thus, a high degree of interactivity afforded by procedural components, as in *Façade,* strongly supports CIC [21]. In such a setting, unexpected yet exciting events emerge from interactions between story world components, significantly widening the narrative possibility space [44]. Since some emergent events may deviate from the designer's aims, narrative vectors and rules act as their "limiter" [38]. If done right, this "selective interactivity" delivers meaning most effectively [33].

Meanwhile, the discourse shapes the audience's experience by presenting the ongoing story in a particular manner regarding, e.g., the textual and audiovisual *assets* of event scenes [38], the audience's *point of view* [45], and the *order of presented events*, e.g., going backward in time with "flashbacks" [46]. Regarding the latter, *fabula* is another name for the actual chronological plot, whereas the presented one is known formally as *syuzhet* [46]. A syuzhet's composition aims to tell the story optimally [47], primarily through controlling information flow to aid the audience's comprehension [46], such as relating to multiple perspectives in the narrative, which can be confusing [25]. IDNs also afford *dynamic syuzhets*, through which the audience explores the fabula at will [40].

Other than the syuzhet, available narrative comprehension tools are *cues*, such as changes in camera focus [47], and non-diegetic *learning supports*, such as short documentary videos on the issue [48]. *Metal Gear Solid*, a prominent game series with narratives on complex issues, strengthens its messages by showing such videos at appropriate times during narrative scenes [49]. Indeed, learning supports should appear timely and non-intrusively in the discourse to maintain engagement [50].

3.2 In Search of a Design Methodology for IDNs for CIC

We can gather valuable insights on the methodology from games, one of the most prominent IDN formats. In particular, narrative-driven educational games heavily intersect with IDNs for CIC since CIC is strongly educational [51]. First and foremost, games of all kinds heavily favor *iterative* methodologies [52–54], often broken down into *phases* [52, 54, 55]. The design process typically consists of two or more phases, starting with a *general design* and ending with a *detailed* one ready to be implemented [52, 54, 55]. Game design activities and their sequence vary considerably in the literature [52]. Regardless, designing a narrative often precedes designing game mechanics, i.e., procedural components [53–58]. Designing the *presentation* of narrative and gameplay, such as cutscenes and dialogue texts, may follow as the third activity [55, 58]. A recent IDN course, which taught the sequence of narrative writing, interaction design, and environment and scenery design with some success, has proven the sequence's relevance to IDNs [59].

A dedicated phase for gathering requirements, crucial in game development [60], can take place before the design process [53–55]. *Educational requirements*, such as learning goals and situations, precede others in educational games [53–55, 57]. Next, the appropriate *target players* can be specified, with their attributes including their age range [54, 56], genre preferences [28], education level [55], and degree of appreciation or tolerance of narrative complexity [8]. Together, those attributes influence the *narrative genre*, e.g., mystery [61], the *genre of game mechanics*, e.g., point-and-click [53, 56], and the intended *aesthetics* or *experience* [62]. The latter may consider the *story arc*, e.g., the "Hero's Journey" [63], or the *emotional arc*, e.g., rise-fall-rise [64], to ensure an engaging narrative progression. Meanwhile, the *technological requirements*, such as the platform and operating system [54], may consider the target players' technological proficiency [56], the learning situation, e.g., at a science center [55], and the game genre, e.g., smartphones and tablets are appropriate for scene-based narrative games [54].

Incorporating an *overarching narrative* between the requirements and the design phase has been strongly suggested [50, 53, 54]. It outlines the actual narrative and guides the design of the whole game [53, 54]. Although not part of the end product, the overarching narrative is routinely updated to reflect the game's latest design [53, 54]. Thus, it is typically included in the design iteration.

Two other essential design activities, possibly following the presentation design [59], concern UI and *user experience* (UX). The UX activity, known technically as *micro UX*, aims to improve the system according to its user-related requirements, i.e., *macro UX* [65]. Previous research has identified various UX dimensions in IDNs, including "narrative understanding" and "learning" [66]. Similarly, a crucial part of an educational game's UX is the player's learning process [67]. One way to maximize the process's quality is through the *skill chain*, which games and gameful design use to structure skills hierarchically [68–70]. Analyzing the skill chain of existing game mechanics allows for composing a sequence of gameplay activities most optimal for learning skills inherent in the mechanics [68].

Each node in a skill chain is an atomic *game loop* of acting in a specific context, receiving feedback on the action, and reflecting on the feedback to improve future actions [68, 69]. Such circular processes are also known as *hermeneutic cycles* [13, 71], which in IDNs capture the audience's attempts at understanding the instantiated narratives and the IDN system behind them. Although the cycles are typically discussed as high-level entities in the literature, dividing them into many low-level "atoms" seems possible. For example, such an atomic cycle may concern what turns a character hostile. During one or several playthroughs, the audience can interact with the character until they "exhaust" the cycle and gain complete knowledge of the hostility.

3.3 Terminology of the Proposed Design Methodology

Before we present our design methodology proposal, we will define some technical terms to avoid ambiguity. To distinguish instantiated narratives from narrative possibilities in the IDN, we will call the latter a protonarrative. We may also use the prefix "proto" for any element of the protonarrative, such as its protosyuzhet, to distinguish it from the corresponding one in an instantiated narrative.

3.4 Proposal of a Design Methodology for IDNs for CIC

Figure 1 shows the diagram of the design methodology, consisting of 11 activities. Its three phases are *requirements*, *general design*, and *detailed design*, a time-tested standard in software development [72]. Thus, integrating the framework into an IDN development process should be straightforward. We base every activity, including the first, on Subsects. 3.1 and 3.2. Although the first activity deals with educational requirements, we name it "informational requirements" to avoid misassociation with formal education.

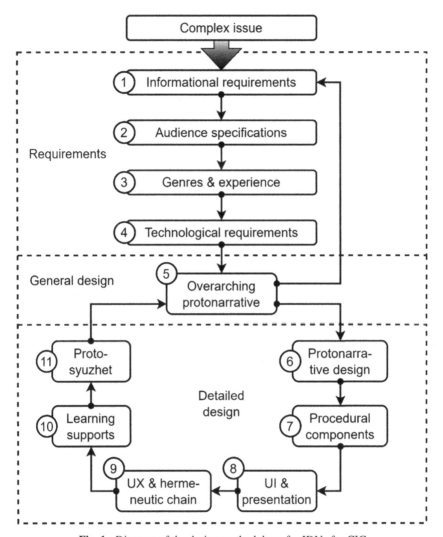

Fig. 1. Diagram of the design methodology for IDNs for CIC

Due to its function as a summary of the IDN, the overarching protonarrative is the general design phase's sole occupant. Following Blakesley's work [53], the main design iteration starts with the overarching protonarrative, details the IDN content, and then revisits the overarching protonarrative. Going back to the requirement phase, as per de Lope et al. [54], is possible; however, it should seldom occur since not being thorough with requirements carries significant risk [60].

The overarching protonarrative's first version chalks out some key story world components and narrative vectors. Rules for chronological vector progressions, world components involved in each vector and their attributes, and any interactivity or procedural processes within each vector are specified briefly. Afterward, the first detailed design activity, *protonarrative design*, commences. The designer fleshes out the key world components and narrative vectors and potentially adds new ones. More specifically, "fleshing out" means detailing the world components' attributes and specifying each vector's subvectors, i.e., minor subevents. Additionally, the designer describes the possible sequences and outcomes of interactive and procedural activities in each vector, giving clear pictures of how they will play out.

The following activity handles the required procedural components. For example, characters may need a real-time movement mechanic throughout an adventure storyline. Some other mechanics, such as combat, may be available only in select narrative vectors. Overall, this activity resembles designing game mechanics, only that every mechanic is "tightly coupled" with the protonarrative. Consequently, the mechanics' elements, e.g., entities and rules [73], should strictly represent those of the protonarrative, e.g., entities and internal logic.

How the audience observes and manipulates the story comes up next. Each narrative vector should have associated assets for its presentation, which may double as procedural components. For example, a "cutscene" can comprise a static image or a combination of 3D scenery and models, the latter also used by the movement mechanic. Meanwhile, the UI manages the control scheme, event presentation, and extra information, e.g., inventory window.

At this point, the designer has worked on actual IDN content, and the remaining three activities optimize the content's quality. First, the designer analyzes the UX afforded by the content, including the audience's learning process quality. To that end, the designer composes a hermeneutic chain (i.e., the equivalent of a skill chain) consisting of atomic hermeneutic cycles. Like a game loop [68], each cycle represents a piece of knowledge or skill regarding a specific part of the IDN. The hierarchy of the cycles should ensure optimal comprehension and emotional experience throughout any instantiated narrative.

Afterward, the designer identifies which hermeneutic cycles the audience may experience difficulties with, for which the designer prepares learning supports. They can improve existing elements, such as a visual cue added to a scene, or exist as separate, non-diegetic parts, such as short videos on the issue. The last activity is appropriately structuring narrative vectors per the hermeneutic chain. It necessitates (1) composing a *protosyuzhet* that references the vectors non-chronologically or (2) directly modifying the vectors' arrangement to be non-chronological. The separate learning supports can also appear as needed in narrative vectors or between them.

As one design iteration ends, the overarching protonarrative is revisited and updated. If the current protosyuzhet or narrative vector arrangement is non-chronological, this new version of the overarching protonarrative should reflect it. Another iteration may then follow, aiming to improve the IDN's quality or add new elements required by the last iteration.

3.5   Application Example of the Design Methodology

We will discuss designing a hypothetical IDN with the methodology. The IDN communicates the issue of global warming, with the learning goals being "understanding the melting of ice caps and the efforts to combat them." The target audience is teenagers and young adults in secondary education or higher who regularly consume popular media with moderate complexity, such as *Marvel Cinematic Universe* films[2]. Accordingly, we choose mystery-comedy as the narrative genre and simulation as the interactivity genre. Mobile platforms are appropriate for the IDN, especially since we do not specify any learning situation.

Figure 2 shows the IDN's network of branching narrative vectors. It starts with a group of protagonists learning about global warming and ice caps. Armed with the knowledge of imminent catastrophe, they try to convince the public, the government, and the private sector to combat global warming. Based on the three parties' attitudes toward the matter, Earth's ice caps may melt completely or be preserved. Even if the worse one happens, the parties' attitudes may save human civilization from destruction.

As seen in Fig. 3, we split the "Convincing" vector into three subvectors with no particular order. In each, the audience controls the protagonists in simulation gameplay, which comprises designing informational media (e.g., PSA flyers), distributing it to the public, and other activities. Humorous characters (e.g., citizens with bizarre behaviors), visuals, and dialogue texts entertain the audience while imparting valuable knowledge.

We can develop Fig. 4's hermeneutic chain by analyzing the audience's learning process. It becomes clear that the audience should first understand and feel the emotional impact of the disaster caused by the ice caps' disappearance. It prompts us to move the "Ice caps disappear" vector to the beginning. The new vector network in Fig. 5 is thus non-chronological: the protonarrative first "fast-forwards" to a bleak future with no ice caps, then "rewinds" to the start of the protagonists' mission. Indeed, giving the "big picture" up front supports audience comprehension and engagement [70].

Glancing over the hermeneutic chain also reveals potential difficulties in understanding how to convince the parties. To anticipate them, we can insert learning supports into the simulation gameplay, e.g., a short video on public communication.

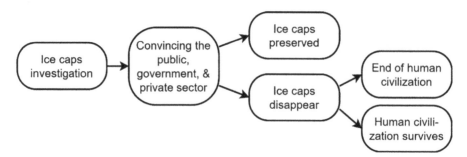

Fig. 2. The narrative vector network of the example IDN

4   Co-designing Balanced IDNs for CIC

4.1   Problems with Current IDNs for CIC and Their Solution

Notwithstanding their positive results [19], many CIC games suffer an imbalance between their three aspects. Serious CIC games have seldomly employed narratives

---

[2] https://www.marvel.com/movies.

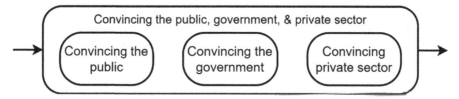

Fig. 3. Subvectors of the "Convincing" narrative vector

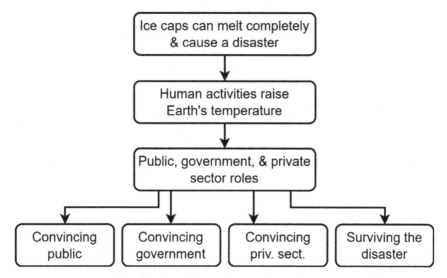

Fig. 4. The example IDN's hermeneutic chain

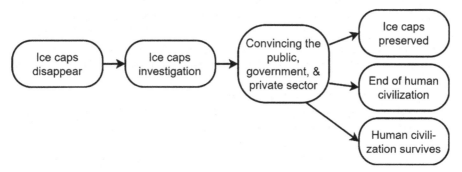

Fig. 5. The rearranged and non-chronological version of the narrative vector network

[18, 19, 74], and the few of them that do often lack crucial narrative elements such as heroes with well-defined motivations, backgrounds, and other attributes [20]. It is unfortunate since (1) hero characters are quite persuasive [25, 26], (2) the importance of characters with such attributes in educational games has been empirically proven [75], and (3) the attributes powerfully influence causality [76]. On the other hand, although stronger narrative-wise, entertainment CIC games mirror their non-interactive cousins in being less credible or informative [18], the latter due to telling stories disconnected from real life or the player's gameplay actions [18]. Indeed, one enduring fallacy in IDNs is using a narrative as a mere "wrapper" of the interactivity aspect, rendering the narrative disposable [21, 77].

How, then, should we design a balanced IDN for CIC? Again, the existing literature on educational games can guide us. An educational game's aspects, such as gameplay and learning, are typically treated as distinct [50] yet must eventually integrate into a singular game [78]. Thus, frameworks like LM-GM [79], ATMSG [80], NSGM [81], and ATTAC-L [82] allow designing the aspects separately yet also according to each other. Following that perspective, a design methodology for balanced IDNs for CIC should (1) draw clear lines between the aspects, (2) compose every necessary element of each aspect to ensure its quality, and (3) ensure inter-aspect integration through correspondences between elements of different aspects.

The aspects treated as distinct yet integrated also allow *co-design* between interdisciplinary actors, each having expertise in one of the aspects. It is especially relevant to CIC since it requires collaboration between experts on the issue and communication practitioners [83]. Indeed, co-design unites disciplines with different yet overlapping vocabularies, practices, and orders of worth so that they may together solve a complex or wicked issue [84].

4.2   Co-designing Through the Complex Systems Perspective

Figure 6 illustrates how interdisciplinary experts can co-design an IDN for CIC. The overlap between its three aspects concerns *complex systems*. Both hard and soft science fields have regularly analyzed phenomena as complex systems [21] through *agent-based* and *system dynamics* modeling methods [85–87], informing policymakers of all sorts [21, 87]. Narratives and complex systems have also intersected and given birth to "complex narratives," where seemingly inconsequential or coincidental events have surprising and profound consequences [7, 76], entertaining and puzzling the audience [88]. Likewise, scholars and developers of games have long championed the holistic and systems-minded design approach, which considers the complex interactions between the game system and the player [62, 89, 90].

Experts on the three aspects agree on the following complex system principles. Firstly, such a system consists of various entities with *actions*, *rules*, and *internal states* [85, 86]. Their non-linear and multi-causal interactions [14] cause system dynamics that, over time, become a chronological sequence of events [87], which exhibits emergent patterns such as critical transitions [91] and system-wide adaptations [92]. The event sequence is often *non-deterministic* due to *indeterminate variables* in the dynamics [14], representing randomness or difficult-to-predict things like choices based on free will [7, 87]. This non-determinism entails that, for each set of entities, there is a network of *possible events* capable of producing many event sequences [7].

The IDN aspects differ in each's focus on the complex system. The information aspect aims to accurately model the issue as the system, even if a perfect model is impossible [87]. The appropriate level of detail, e.g., whether the aspect models individual characters or only their groups, depends on various factors, including the observer's cognitive needs

[7], e.g., a policymaker may not care about finer details [87]. On the other hand, the narrative aspect eases the observer's understanding of the system [93] through affect-based ways: (1) presenting the system in a multimodal and immersive manner [23, 94] and (2) making the system's entities and events more identifiable [23], thus easier to reconcile with the observer's mental model and past experiences [94]. Lastly, the interactivity aspect manages explorations of the system's non-determinism. It provides UI and interaction mechanics appropriate to the audience's psychomotor skills [95] so that they can modify the system's variables to explore "what-ifs" [96]. Ultimately, these differences imply that the aspects do not conflict and are even quite integrable.

Designing through this systems perspective ensures the dynamism of IDN components and facilitates CIC [7, 8, 21, 76]. Additionally, if done right, the system's events are already narratable, negating the need for an "extrinsic narrative" wrapping around the system dynamics [77].

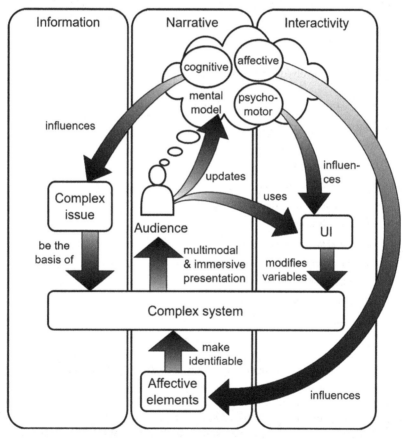

Fig. 6. A model of co-designing an IDN for CIC through the complex systems perspective

4.3   Adjusting the Design Methodology to Facilitate Co-design

We analyze each aspect's involvement in the design methodology's 11 activities, as seen in Table 1. Three activities involve only one or two aspects, necessitating structural changes to the methodology to facilitate co-design.

The information expert, e.g., an educator or a subject expert, should handle the first activity since (1) it is outside the expertise of the narrative and interactivity experts, e.g., a narrative writer and an IDN engineer, and (2) the requirements may come from official sources such as a national curriculum [55]. On the other hand, the second activity needs a joint effort of the three experts, especially if the informational requirements do not specify the target audience. Even if they do, the information expert alone can hardly obtain the audience's complete profile.

In contrast to the first, the third activity excludes the information aspect since an accurate model of the complex issue is genre-less and ignores the observer's emotional experience. The next activity is jointly relevant again: the experts should discuss their experiences with digital technology to decide on the IDN's software and hardware specifications.

Table 1. Involved aspects in each activity in the design methodology

No.	Design activity	Information	Narrative	Interactivity
1	Informational requirements	✓		
2	Audience specifications	✓	✓	✓
3	Genres and experience		✓	✓
4	Technological requirements	✓	✓	✓
5	Overarching protonarrative	✓	✓	✓
6	Protonarrative design	✓	✓	✓
7	Procedural components			✓
8	UI & presentation	✓	✓	✓
9	UX & hermeneutic chain	✓	✓	✓
10	Learning supports	✓	✓	✓
11	Protosyuzhet	✓	✓	✓

Of the seven general and detailed design activities, "procedural components" is handled exclusively by the interactivity aspect. Although the information and narrative experts can outline inter-entity and audience-system interactions, the actual interactivity mechanics fall outside their expertise. On the other hand, even if an activity involves all aspects, their involvement in it may significantly differ. While the information and narrative experts may specify what to present and what system variables the audience manipulates in each narrative vector, they leave out the UI and control scheme entirely. Likewise, while atomic hermeneutic cycles and their hierarchy are relevant to all aspects, UX is meaningless without means of interactions.

4.4 Proposal of a Co-design Methodology for Balanced IDNs for CIC

Figure 7 shows a diagram of the co-design methodology for balanced IDNs for CIC, split into the information, narrative, and interactivity aspects. It starts with gathering informational requirements, handled by the information expert. The requirements may include the learning goals' cognitive, affective, and psychomotor domains, primarily if the expert consults an official source. The next activity below consists of two subactivities: identifying the target audience, which involves all aspects, and specifying the audience's information, narrative, and interactivity-related attributes, each done by the corresponding expert and guided by the learning goals' domains.

Based on the narrative attributes, the narrative expert can specify the narrative genre and narrative experience. Taking the genre, experience, and the audience's interactivity-related attributes as inputs, the interactivity expert formulates the most optimal interactivity genre and experience.

After deciding on the technological requirements, the experts begin designing the IDN. Following the co-design model, every design element, excluding procedural components, is created first by the information expert and gradually enhanced by the other experts. Thus, general and detailed design activities of the same level flow from left to right.

The information expert realizes the complex system as a world and a protofabula, i.e., a chronological network of possible events. The narrative expert then makes the entities and events more identifiable, e.g., humorous or dramatized, while keeping the system's mechanisms intact. The world and protofabula resemble a protonarrative, only less technical. For example, time units in narrative vectors may include game frames, which are meaningless to the information and narrative aspects.

Skipping the procedural components, the information expert specifies the world and event presentations and manipulable system variables. For example, they can decide whether the audience can observe signs of a character's anxiety and whether the protagonist, through audience-controlled actions, can affect the character's attitudes toward them. Next, the narrative expert adds multimodal and immersive elements, such as background music, to the presentation. The interactivity expert concludes the process by fashioning the specifications into implementable designs of UI, control scheme, and presentation assets. This sequence of "initial design, multimodal and immersive enhancement, and technical specifications" also applies to learning supports.

The IDN's hermeneutic chain will undergo this sequence: First, the information expert creates it to optimize the audience's comprehension. Then, the narrative expert enhances it as needed, e.g., by adding new atomic cycles about extra characters in their world. Finally, it matures in the interactivity expert's hands by acquiring new cycles on interactivity mechanics, UI, and psychomotor efforts.

Due to adopting a complex system mindset, the co-design methodology is stricter than the design one in several ways. First, the protofabula should be kept chronological; otherwise, the information expert may struggle to maintain causality in its structure. Since the narrative vectors take the protofabula as an input, the restriction applies to them too. Moreover, it also becomes mandatory for protosyuzhet activities to produce an actual protosyuzhet instead of reorganizing the protofabula or narrative vectors.

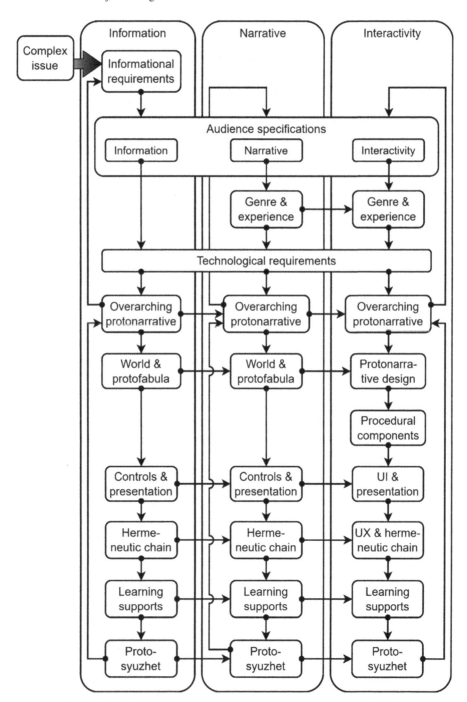

Fig. 7. Diagram of the co-design methodology for balanced IDNs for CIC

4.5 Application Example of the Co-design Methodology

We will take the previous hypothetical IDN and describe its co-design process. The information expert's protofabula and protosyuzhet will resemble Figs. 2, 3, and 5, although their world has no distinct characters, and the events are presented matter-of-factly. The narrative expert will continue the work by creating the protagonists, making other characters more relatable and entertaining, and strengthening the ice caps disappearance's emotional impact through, e.g., camera angles and sad music.

Regarding Fig. 3's subvectors, the information expert will first design how public communication, appealing to the government and influencing the private sector's business plans work in their world, e.g., the rules and involved entities. The narrative expert then takes responsibility for the processes' entertaining elements, such as the humorous citizens. Afterward, the interactivity expert incorporates the other experts' works into the protonarrative design and decides on the simulation gameplay's procedural components, e.g., the mechanic of composing PSA flyers.

Accordingly, the information expert first composes the processes' atomic hermeneutic cycles. Afterward, the narrative expert adds other cycles about their more colorful world, such as the humorous citizens' reactions to PSA flyers. Lastly, extra cycles from the interactivity expert can embody the processes' psychomotor requirements, such as specific button press timings.

4.6 Co-design Workflows and Roles of the Actors

The co-design methodology's two-dimensional structure flexibly facilitates two design workflows. The design team may work vertically by finishing an aspect before moving to the next one. Alternatively, the team may take a horizontal route, which, software engineering-wise, shares the same advantage as the design methodology.

Ideally, each expert becomes the primary designer in their specialty aspect, supported by the other two. For example, the information expert should handle the information aspect while, at the same time, seeking advice from the narrative expert, e.g., on composing a coherent protofabula, and the interactivity expert, e.g., on specifying manipulable variables.

Since there is no limit on how many peers an expert can co-design with, various combinations of experts may emerge. Figure 8 shows an interesting scenario: when the same information expert collaborates with two or more teams of narrative and interactivity experts, producing different IDNs that present the same complex issue. Indeed, there can be a one-to-many relationship between the information expert's design and suitable enhancements by narrative and interactivity experts. For example, other than the simulation gameplay, the hypothetical IDN's public communication process can also implement a *Journey*-like[3] real-time communication-adventure mechanic.

In the scenario, direct communication channels may connect the teams; otherwise, they may indirectly share inputs through the information expert. The opposite scenario is when multiple information experts contribute to the same IDN production pipeline. It can entail the "repurposing" of an IDN (i.e., slight modifications to its protonarrative

---

[3] https://thatgamecompany.com/journey/.

and interactivity components) to communicate various issues, a phenomenon termed "context-agnostic design" in educational games [97].

5 Discussion

We have proposed two design methodologies for IDNs for complex issue communication (CIC). The first is a regular one that suits singular development or research teams in realizing such IDNs with greater precision. Moreover, the methodology and the literature review behind it have shed light on promising design elements. We will first discuss the atomic hermeneutic cycles, which seem to parallel game loops [68] and thus are fit to be structured hierarchically. However:

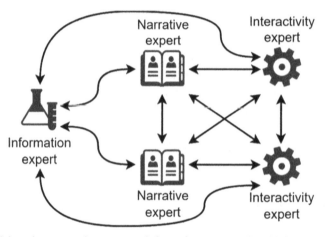

Fig. 8. A collaboration pattern between one information expert and multiple experts of narrative and interactivity. Arrows represent communication channels.

1. Are there practically-relevant differences between game loops and atomic hermeneutic cycles? More specifically, does understanding a narrative process, such as an event transitioning into another, differ somehow from understanding a gameplay one, such as killing an enemy or picking an item? It should not if the principle of "every gameplay event is intrinsically narratable" [77] is true. Yet, we believe the question merits deeper inquiries.
2. Does breaking a hermeneutic cycle down into atomic ones make sense? As we have stated, we believe it does, yet it may also be investigated more thoroughly.
3. Concretely, how should we design atomic hermeneutic cycles and their hierarchy? Is the skill chain method from games and gameful design [68–70] directly transferable to IDNs?

The next elements are non-diegetic learning supports. While their usages in the game industry [49] and educational games [48] have proven their potential for supporting CIC, that potential requires further investigation. Is it relevant to IDNs in general? What kinds of IDNs can tap into it the most? How should we properly design and insert the learning supports into IDNs for CIC?

The last element is the protosyuzhet. There is currently scarce research on using syuzhets in IDNs, especially for rearranging narrative vectors for better comprehension. An IDN should carefully "fast forward" and "rewind" through its branching vector network lest it instantiates narratives that violate causality. Such consideration can lead to dilemmas during the design process. For example, should the designer erase some of the vectors they have created because the hermeneutic chain requires "time jumps" that prevent the vectors from being visited logically? Researching design principles for preventing such wasteful occurrences may be fruitful.

Meanwhile, our second methodology facilitates co-design by restructuring our first methodology into three parallel sections of the information, narrative, and interactivity aspects to ensure their balance in the end product. The methodology is highly novel and relevant to IDNs for CIC due to facilitating interdisciplinary collaboration through a complex system perspective. Although we have tried to ground the methodology on the intersection between complex systems, narratives, and game systems, more research is needed to validate it and its practical relevance. Regarding the latter, co-design techniques such as a design document format and a visual language [55] can support the methodology's applications. Primarily, such techniques should ease modeling a complex issue as a complex system in its three stages: (1) when it is simply informative, (2) when it is informative and emotionally engaging, and (3) when, besides being the previous two, it is also interactable.

As a closing note, we hope our research can contribute significantly to IDNs, not only to its practical, software-engineering side but also to its more theoretical one. Like games, IDNs are inherently interdisciplinary, which comes with many advantages as well as challenges. One such challenge is bridging the humanities and engineering disciplines to realize a rigorous, scientific, yet artistically-rich approach to IDN development [98]. Through this work and future ones, we strive toward that ideal.

References

1. DeFries, R., Nagendra, H.: Ecosystem management as a wicked problem. Science **356**, 265–270 (2017). https://doi.org/10.1126/science.aal1950
2. Janoušková, S., Hák, T., Nečas, V., Moldan, B.: Sustainable development—A poorly communicated concept by mass media. Another challenge for SDGs? Sustainability **11** (2019). https://doi.org/10.3390/su11113181
3. Lehtonen, A., Salonen, A., Cantell, H., Riuttanen, L.: A pedagogy of interconnectedness for encountering climate change as a wicked sustainability problem. J. Clean. Prod. **199**, 860–867 (2018). https://doi.org/10.1016/j.jclepro.2018.07.186
4. Simpson, N.P., et al.: A framework for complex climate change risk assessment. One Earth **4**, 489–501 (2021). https://doi.org/10.1016/j.oneear.2021.03.005
5. Morris, B.S., et al.: Stories vs. facts: triggering emotion and action-taking on climate change. Clim. Change **154**(1–2), 19–36 (2019). https://doi.org/10.1007/s10584-019-02425-6
6. Veland, S., et al.: Narrative matters for sustainability: the transformative role of storytelling in realizing 1.5 °C futures. Curr. Opin. Environ. Sustain. **31**, 41–47 (2018). https://doi.org/10.1016/j.cosust.2017.12.005

7. Simons, J.: Complex narratives. New Rev. Film Telev. Stud. **6**, 111–126 (2008). https://doi.org/10.1080/17400300802098263

8. Bellini, M.: Formal organization and complex responses to video games narratives. In: Proceedings of the ACM on Human-Computer Interaction (2021). https://doi.org/10.1145/3474702

9. Constantino, S.M., Weber, E.U.: Decision-making under the deep uncertainty of climate change: the psychological and political agency of narratives. Curr. Opin. Psychol. **42**, 151–159 (2021). https://doi.org/10.1016/j.copsyc.2021.11.001

10. van Enschot, R., Boogaard, I., Koenitz, H., Roth, C.: The potential of interactive digital narratives. Agency and multiple perspectives in last hijack interactive. In: Cardona-Rivera, R.E., Sullivan, A., Young, R.M. (eds.) ICIDS 2019. LNCS, vol. 11869, pp. 158–169. Springer, Cham (2019). https://doi.org/10.1007/978-3-030-33894-7_17

11. Blokland, E., et al.: Exploring multiple perspectives in citizenship education with a serious game. In: Mitchell, A., Vosmeer, M. (eds.) ICIDS 2021. LNCS, vol. 13138, pp. 293–306. Springer, Cham (2021). https://doi.org/10.1007/978-3-030-92300-6_28

12. Grasse, K.M., Melcer, E.F., Kreminski, M., Junius, N., Ryan, J., Wardrip-Fruin, N.: Academical: a choice-based interactive storytelling game for enhancing moral reasoning, knowledge, and attitudes in responsible conduct of research. In: Bostan, B. (ed.) Games and Narrative: Theory and Practice. ISCEMT, pp. 173–189. Springer, Cham (2022). https://doi.org/10.1007/978-3-030-81538-7_12

13. Knoller, N.: Complexity and the userly text. In: Grishakova, M., Poulaki, M. (eds.) Narrative Complexity: Cognition, Embodiment, Evolution, pp. 98–120. University of Nebraska, Lincoln (2019)

14. Knoller, N., Roth, C., Haak, D.: The complexity analysis matrix. In: Mitchell, A., Vosmeer, M. (eds.) ICIDS 2021. LNCS, vol. 13138, pp. 478–487. Springer, Cham (2021). https://doi.org/10.1007/978-3-030-92300-6_48

15. Creutzig, F., Kapmeier, F.: Engage, don't preach: active learning triggers climate action. Energy Res. Soc. Sci. **70** (2020). https://doi.org/10.1016/j.erss.2020.101779

16. Monroe, M.C., Plate, R.R., Oxarart, A., Bowers, A., Chaves, W.A.: Identifying effective climate change education strategies: a systematic review of the research. Environ. Educ. Res. **25**, 791–812 (2019). https://doi.org/10.1080/13504622.2017.1360842

17. Ferreira, M., Nunes, N., Nisi, V.: Interacting with climate change: a survey of HCI and design projects and their use of transmedia storytelling. In: Mitchell, A., Vosmeer, M. (eds.) ICIDS 2021. LNCS, vol. 13138, pp. 338–348. Springer, Cham (2021). https://doi.org/10.1007/978-3-030-92300-6_33

18. Galeote, D.F., Hamari, J.: Game-based climate change engagement: analyzing the potential of entertainment and serious games. In: Proceedings of the ACM on Human-Computer Interaction (2021). https://doi.org/10.1145/3474653

19. Galeote, D.F., Rajanen, M., Rajanen, D., Legaki, N.-Z., Langley, D.J., Hamari, J.: Gamification for climate change engagement: review of corpus and future agenda. Environ. Res. Lett. **16** (2021). https://doi.org/10.1088/1748-9326/abec05

20. Galeote, D.F., Legaki, N.-Z., Hamari, J.: Avatar identities and climate change action in video games: analysis of mitigation and adaptation practices. In: CHI 2022: CHI Conference on Human Factors in Computing Systems. ACM, New York (2022). https://doi.org/10.1145/3491102.3517438

21. Koenitz, H., Barbara, J., Eladhari, M.P.: Interactive digital narratives (IDN) as representations of complexity: lineage, opportunities and future work. In: Mitchell, A., Vosmeer, M. (eds.) ICIDS 2021. LNCS, vol. 13138, pp. 488–498. Springer, Cham (2021). https://doi.org/10.1007/978-3-030-92300-6_49

22. Crow, D., Jones, M.: Narratives as tools for influencing policy change. Policy Polit. **46**, 217–234 (2018). https://doi.org/10.1332/030557318X15230061022899

23. McCormack, C.M., Martin, J., Williams, K.J.H.: The full story: understanding how films affect environmental change through the lens of narrative persuasion. People Nat. **3**, 1193–1204 (2021). https://doi.org/10.1002/pan3.10259
24. Keen, S.: Narrative empathy. In: Toward a Cognitive Theory of Narrative Acts, pp. 61–94. University of Texas Press (2010). https://doi.org/10.7560/721579-004
25. Fløttum, K., Gjerstad, Ø.: Narratives in climate change discourse. WIREs Clim. Change **8** (2017). https://doi.org/10.1002/wcc.429
26. Raile, E.D., et al.: Narrative risk communication as a lingua franca for environmental hazard preparation. Environ. Commun. **16**, 108–124 (2022). https://doi.org/10.1080/17524032.2021. 1966818
27. Schneider-Mayerson, M., Gustafson, A., Leiserowitz, A., Goldberg, M.H., Rosenthal, S.A., Ballew, M.: Environmental literature as persuasion: an experimental test of the effects of reading climate fiction. Environ. Commun. 1–16 (2020). https://doi.org/10.1080/17524032. 2020.1814377
28. Schneider-Mayerson, M.: The influence of climate fiction: an empirical survey of readers. Environ. Humanit. **10**, 473–500 (2018). https://doi.org/10.1215/22011919-7156848
29. Shriver-Rice, M., Fernandes, J., Johns, L.N., Riopelle, C., Vaughan, H.: Young adults' reactions and engagement with short-form videos on sea level rise. Environ. Commun. **16**, 63–78 (2022). https://doi.org/10.1080/17524032.2021.1963800
30. Bendor, R., Maggs, D., Peake, R., Robinson, J., Williams, S.: The imaginary worlds of sustainability: observations from an interactive art installation. Ecol. Soc. **22** (2017). https://doi. org/10.5751/ES-09240-220217
31. Bilandzic, H., Kalch, A.: Fictional narratives for environmental sustainability communication. In: Weder, F., Krainer, L., Karmasin, M. (eds.) The Sustainability Communication Reader, pp. 123–142. Springer, Wiesbaden (2021). https://doi.org/10.1007/978-3-658-31883-3_8
32. Moyer-Gusé, E., Tchernev, J.M., Walther-Martin, W.: The persuasiveness of a humorous environmental narrative combined with an explicit persuasive appeal. Sci. Commun. **41**, 422–441 (2019). https://doi.org/10.1177/1075547019862553
33. Bogost, I.: Persuasive Games: The Expressive Power of Videogames. The MIT Press (2007). https://doi.org/10.7551/mitpress/5334.001.0001
34. Roth, C.: The 'Angstfabriek' experience: factoring fear into transformative interactive narrative design. In: Cardona-Rivera, R.E., Sullivan, A., Young, R.M. (eds.) ICIDS 2019. LNCS, vol. 11869, pp. 101–114. Springer, Cham (2019). https://doi.org/10.1007/978-3-030-33894-7_11
35. Doherty, S., Snow, S., Jennings, K., Rose, B., Matthews, B., Viller, S.: Vim: a tangible energy story. In: Bosser, A.-G., Millard, D.E., Hargood, C. (eds.) ICIDS 2020. LNCS, vol. 12497, pp. 271–280. Springer, Cham (2020). https://doi.org/10.1007/978-3-030-62516-0_24
36. Kybartas, B., Bidarra, R.: A survey on story generation techniques for authoring computational narratives. IEEE Trans. Comput. Intell. AI Games **9**, 239–253 (2017). https://doi.org/10.1109/ TCIAIG.2016.2546063
37. Schrier, K., Torner, E., Hammer, J.: Worldbuilding in role-playing games. In: Role-Playing Game Studies: Transmedia Foundations, pp. 349–363. Routledge (2018)
38. Koenitz, H.: Towards a specific theory of interactive digital narrative. In: Interactive Digital Narrative: History, Theory and Practice, pp. 91–105. Routledge (2015)
39. Aarseth, E.: A narrative theory of games. In: Foundations of Digital Games 2012, FDG 2012 - Conference Program, pp. 129–133 (2012). https://doi.org/10.1145/2282338.2282365
40. Wood, H.: Dynamic syuzhets: writing and design methods for playable stories. In: Nunes, N., Oakley, I., Nisi, V. (eds.) ICIDS 2017. LNCS, vol. 10690, pp. 24–37. Springer, Cham (2017). https://doi.org/10.1007/978-3-319-71027-3_3

41. Carstensdottir, E., Kleinman, E., El-Nasr, M.S.: Player interaction in narrative games: structure and narrative progression mechanics. In: FDG 2019: Proceedings of the 14th International Conference on the Foundations of Digital Games, pp. 1–9. ACM, New York (2019). https://doi.org/10.1145/3337722.3337730

42. Mateas, M., Stern, A.: Structuring content in the façade interactive drama architecture. In: Proceedings of the First Artificial Intelligence and Interactive Digital Entertainment Conference (AIIDE 2005), pp. 93–98 (2005)

43. Koenitz, H.: What game narrative are we talking about? An ontological mapping of the foundational canon of interactive narrative Forms. Arts 7 (2018). https://doi.org/10.3390/arts7040051

44. Ryan, J.O., Mateas, M., Wardrip-Fruin, N.: Open design challenges for interactive emergent narrative. In: Schoenau-Fog, H., Bruni, L.E., Louchart, S., Baceviciute, S. (eds.) ICIDS 2015. LNCS, vol. 9445, pp. 14–26. Springer, Cham (2015). https://doi.org/10.1007/978-3-319-27036-4_2

45. Diasamidze, I.: Point of view in narrative discourse. Proc. Soc. Behav. Sci. **158**, 160–165 (2014). https://doi.org/10.1016/j.sbspro.2014.12.062

46. McGill, K.M.: The digital lineage of narrative: analyzing interactive fiction to further understand game narrative. In: Bostan, B. (ed.) Games and Narrative: Theory and Practice. ISCEMT, pp. 77–90. Springer, Cham (2022). https://doi.org/10.1007/978-3-030-81538-7_5

47. Cutting, J.E.: Narrative theory and the dynamics of popular movies. Psychon. Bull. Rev. **23**(6), 1713–1743 (2016). https://doi.org/10.3758/s13423-016-1051-4

48. Kuba, R., Rahimi, S., Smith, G., Shute, V., Dai, C.-P.: Using the first principles of instruction and multimedia learning principles to design and develop in-game learning support videos. Educ. Tech. Res. Dev. **69**(2), 1201–1220 (2021). https://doi.org/10.1007/s11423-021-09994-3

49. Stamenković, D., Jaćević, M., Wildfeuer, J.: The persuasive aims of Metal Gear Solid: a discourse theoretical approach to the study of argumentation in video games. Discourse Context Med. **15**, 11–23 (2017). https://doi.org/10.1016/j.dcm.2016.12.002

50. Ke, F.: Designing and integrating purposeful learning in game play: a systematic review. Educ. Tech. Res. Dev. **64**(2), 219–244 (2015). https://doi.org/10.1007/s11423-015-9418-1

51. Wibeck, V.: Enhancing learning, communication and public engagement about climate change – some lessons from recent literature. Environ. Educ. Res. **20**, 387–411 (2014). https://doi.org/10.1080/13504622.2013.812720

52. Osborne O'Hagan, A., Coleman, G., O'Connor, R.V.: Software development processes for games: a systematic literature review. In: Barafort, B., O'Connor, R.V., Poth, A., Messnarz, R. (eds.) EuroSPI 2014. CCIS, vol. 425, pp. 182–193. Springer, Heidelberg (2014). https://doi.org/10.1007/978-3-662-43896-1_16

53. Blakesley, C.C.: The role of narrative in the design of an educational game. In: GLS 9.0 Conference Proceedings, pp. 107–113 (2014)

54. de Lope, R.P., López Arcos, J.R., Medina-Medina, N., Paderewski, P., Gutiérrez-Vela, F.L.: Design methodology for educational games based on graphical notations: designing Urano. Entertain. Comput. **18** (2017). https://doi.org/10.1016/j.entcom.2016.08.005

55. Breien, F.S., Wasson, B.: eLuna: a co-design framework for narrative digital game-based learning that support STEAM. Front. Educ. **6** (2022). https://doi.org/10.3389/feduc.2021.775746

56. Huynh, E., Nyhout, A., Ganea, P., Chevalier, F.: Designing narrative-focused role-playing games for visualization literacy in young children. IEEE Trans. Vis. Comput. Graph. **27**, 924–934 (2021). https://doi.org/10.1109/TVCG.2020.3030464

57. Amresh, A., Clarke, D., Beckwith, D.: GameScapes and SimApps: new techniques for integrating rich narratives with game mechanics. In: Proceedings of the European Conference on Games-Based Learning, pp. 18–25 (2014)

58. de Lope, R.P., Medina-Medina, N., Urbieta, M., Lliteras, A.B., Mora García, A.: A novel UML-based methodology for modeling adventure-based educational games. Entertain. Comput. **38** (2021). https://doi.org/10.1016/j.entcom.2021.100429

59. Fisher, J.A., Samuels, J.T.: A proposed curriculum for an introductory course on interactive digital narratives in virtual reality. In: Mitchell, A., Vosmeer, M. (eds.) ICIDS 2021. LNCS, vol. 13138, pp. 462–477. Springer, Cham (2021). https://doi.org/10.1007/978-3-030-92300-6_47

60. Callele, D., Neufeld, E., Schneider, K.: Requirements engineering and the creative process in the video game industry. In: 13th IEEE International Conference on Requirements Engineering (RE 2005), pp. 240–250. IEEE (2005). https://doi.org/10.1109/RE.2005.58

61. Dickey, M.D.: Murder on Grimm Isle: the impact of game narrative design in an educational game-based learning environment. Br. J. Educ. Technol. **42**, 456–469 (2011). https://doi.org/10.1111/j.1467-8535.2009.01032.x

62. Hunicke, R., Leblanc, M., Zubek, R.: MDA: a formal approach to game design and game research. In: AAAI Workshop - Technical Report (2004)

63. Boyd, R.L., Blackburn, K.G., Pennebaker, J.W.: The narrative arc: revealing core narrative structures through text analysis. Sci. Adv. **6** (2020). https://doi.org/10.1126/sciadv.aba2196

64. Reagan, A.J., Mitchell, L., Kiley, D., Danforth, C.M., Dodds, P.S.: The emotional arcs of stories are dominated by six basic shapes. EPJ Data Sci. **5**(1), 1–12 (2016). https://doi.org/10.1140/epjds/s13688-016-0093-1

65. von Saucken, C., Michailidou, I., Lindemann, U.: How to design experiences: macro UX versus micro UX approach. In: Marcus, A. (ed.) DUXU 2013. LNCS, vol. 8015, pp. 130–139. Springer, Heidelberg (2013). https://doi.org/10.1007/978-3-642-39253-5_15

66. Revi, A.T., Millard, D.E., Middleton, S.E.: A systematic analysis of user experience dimensions for interactive digital narratives. In: Bosser, A.-G., Millard, D.E., Hargood, C. (eds.) ICIDS 2020. LNCS, vol. 12497, pp. 58–74. Springer, Cham (2020). https://doi.org/10.1007/978-3-030-62516-0_5

67. Nagalingam, V., Ibrahim, R.: User experience of educational games: a review of the elements. Proc. Comput. Sci. **72**, 423–433 (2015). https://doi.org/10.1016/j.procs.2015.12.123

68. Horn, B., Cooper, S., Deterding, S.: Adapting cognitive task analysis to elicit the skill chain of a game. In: CHI PLAY 2017 - Proceedings of the Annual Symposium on Computer-Human Interaction in Play, pp. 277–289 (2017). https://doi.org/10.1145/3116595.3116640

69. Deterding, S.: The lens of intrinsic skill atoms: a method for gameful design. Hum.-Comput. Interact. **30**, 294–335 (2015). https://doi.org/10.1080/07370024.2014.993471

70. Miller, J.A., et al.: How do players and developers of citizen science games conceptualize skill chains? Proc. ACM Hum.-Comput. Interact. **5** (2021). https://doi.org/10.1145/3474671

71. Arjoranta, J.: How are games interpreted? Hermeneutics for game studies. Game Stud. **22** (2022)

72. Boehm, B.W.: A spiral model of software development and enhancement. Computer **21**, 61–72 (1988). https://doi.org/10.1109/2.59

73. Adams, E.: Fundamentals of Game Design, 3rd edn. New Riders (2014)

74. Mittal, A., Scholten, L., Kapelan, Z.: A review of serious games for urban water management decisions: current gaps and future research directions. Water Res. **215** (2022). https://doi.org/10.1016/j.watres.2022.118217

75. Breien, F.S., Wasson, B.: Narrative categorization in digital game-based learning: engagement, motivation & learning. Br. J. Educ. Technol. **52**, 91–111 (2021). https://doi.org/10.1111/bjet.13004

76. Varotsis, G.: Complex narrative systems and the minimisation of logical inconsistencies in narrative and dramatic writing. New Writ. **16** (2019). https://doi.org/10.1080/14790726.2018.1510971

77. Cardona-Rivera, R.E., Zagal, J.P., Debus, M.S.: GFI: a formal approach to narrative design and game research. In: Bosser, A.-G., Millard, D.E., Hargood, C. (eds.) ICIDS 2020. LNCS, vol. 12497, pp. 133–148. Springer, Cham (2020). https://doi.org/10.1007/978-3-030-62516-0_13

78. Habgood, J., Ainsworth, S.E.: Motivating children to learn effectively: exploring the value of intrinsic integration in educational games. J. Learn. Sci. **20**, 169–206 (2011). https://doi.org/10.1080/10508406.2010.508029

79. Arnab, S., et al.: Mapping learning and game mechanics for serious games analysis. Br. J. Educ. Technol. **46**, 391–411 (2015). https://doi.org/10.1111/bjet.12113

80. Carvalho, M.B., et al.: An activity theory-based model for serious games analysis and conceptual design. Comput. Educ. **87**, 166–181 (2015). https://doi.org/10.1016/j.compedu.2015.03.023

81. Lim, T., et al.: Narrative Serious Game Mechanics (NSGM) – insights into the narrative-pedagogical mechanism. In: Göbel, S., Wiemeyer, J. (eds.) GameDays 2014. LNCS, vol. 8395, pp. 23–34. Springer, Cham (2014). https://doi.org/10.1007/978-3-319-05972-3_4

82. De Troyer, O., Van Broeckhoven, F., Vlieghe, J.: Linking serious game narratives with pedagogical theories and pedagogical design strategies. J. Comput. High. Educ. **29**(3), 549–573 (2017). https://doi.org/10.1007/s12528-017-9142-4

83. Riedlinger, M., Massarani, L., Joubert, M., Baram-Tsabari, A., Entradas, M., Metcalfe, J.: Telling stories in science communication: case studies of scholar-practitioner collaboration. J. Sci. Commun. **18** (2019). https://doi.org/10.22323/2.18050801

84. Tharchen, T., Garud, R., Henn, R.L.: Design as an interactive boundary object. J. Organ. Des. **9**(1), 1–34 (2020). https://doi.org/10.1186/s41469-020-00085-w

85. Abar, S., Theodoropoulos, G.K., Lemarinier, P., O'Hare, G.M.P.: Agent based modelling and simulation tools: a review of the state-of-art software. Comput. Sci. Rev. **24**, 13–33 (2017). https://doi.org/10.1016/j.cosrev.2017.03.001

86. Ding, Z., Gong, W., Li, S., Wu, Z.: System dynamics versus agent-based modeling: a review of complexity simulation in construction waste management. Sustainability **10** (2018). https://doi.org/10.3390/su10072484

87. Sterman, J.: System dynamics at sixty: the path forward. Syst. Dyn. Rev. **34**, 5–47 (2018). https://doi.org/10.1002/sdr.1601

88. Buckland, W.: Hollywood Puzzle Films. Routledge (2014). https://doi.org/10.4324/9780203106044

89. Koenitz, H., Eladhari, M.P.: The paradigm of game system building. Trans. Digit. Games Res. Assoc. **5**, 65–90 (2021). https://doi.org/10.26503/todigra.v5i3.123

90. Klabbers, J.H.G.: On the architecture of game science. Simul. Gaming **49**, 207–245 (2018). https://doi.org/10.1177/1046878118762534

91. Scheffer, M., Carpenter, S., Foley, J.A., Folke, C., Walker, B.: Catastrophic shifts in ecosystems. Nature **413**, 591–596 (2001). https://doi.org/10.1038/35098000

92. Holland, J.H.: Studying complex adaptive systems. J. Syst. Sci. Complex. **19**, 1–8 (2006). https://doi.org/10.1007/s11424-006-0001-z

93. Bullock, O.M., Shulman, H.C., Huskey, R.: Narratives are persuasive because they are easier to understand: examining processing fluency as a mechanism of narrative persuasion. Front. Commun. **6** (2021). https://doi.org/10.3389/fcomm.2021.719615

94. Bellini, M.: Interactive digital narratives as complex expressive means. Front. Virtual Real. **3** (2022). https://doi.org/10.3389/frvir.2022.854960

95. Gajos, K.Z., Wobbrock, J.O., Weld, D.S.: Automatically generating user interfaces adapted to users' motor and vision capabilities. In: UIST 2007: Proceedings of the 20th annual ACM Symposium on User Interface Software and Technology, pp. 231–240. ACM Press, New York (2007). https://doi.org/10.1145/1294211.1294253

96. Varotsis, G.: Forking-path routines for plot advancement and problem solving in narrative composition and dramatic writing. New Writ. **17**, 428–442 (2020). https://doi.org/10.1080/14790726.2019.1694952

97. Atmaja, P.W., Muttaqin, F., Sugiarto, S.: Facilitating educational contents of different subjects with context-agnostic educational game: a pilot case study. Register: Jurnal Ilmiah Teknologi Sistem Informasi **6**, 53–65 (2020). https://doi.org/10.26594/register.v6i1.1726

98. Engström, H., Berg Marklund, B., Backlund, P., Toftedahl, M.: Game development from a software and creative product perspective: a quantitative literature review approach. Entertain. Comput. **27**, 10–22 (2018). https://doi.org/10.1016/j.entcom.2018.02.008

The Future of the World: From Scientific Account to Interactive Storytelling

Sophie Varone$^{(\boxtimes)}$ (ID) and Nicolas Szilas (ID)

TECFA, FPSE, University of Geneva, Bd du Pont-d'Arve 40, 1211 Genève 4, Switzerland
sophie.varone@etu.unige.ch, nicolas.szilas@unige.ch

Abstract. Starting from the observation that a cognitive distance prevents human beings from taking the measure of the current climate crisis and adopting adequate behaviors, this article asks the question to what extent a narrative approach could help to reduce it. First, it proposes a narratological analysis of some of the scenarios of the future of the world outlined by the scientific community, the Shared Socio-economic Pathways, which leads to the conclusion that, despite the terminology used in the associated commentaries, these scenarios have little narrative value. Continuing with a questioning of the difficulties and implications of the conception of a narrative about the future, it then shows how the approach of anticipation narratives, which consist in envisioning tomorrow on the basis of choices made today, naturally approaches that of interactive narrative. Finally, it argues that transforming the scientific scenario into a fully-fledged narrative cannot be done without adding fictional elements which, if they are coherent and plausible, can only enrich it and sharpen its didactic impact.

Keywords: Anticipation · Future · Narrative · Interactive narrative · Scientific scenarios · Shared Socio-economic Pathways · Degree of narrativity · Climate crisis · Environment · Ecology

1 Introduction

Numerous studies have examined the question of why human beings, now that they are informed and aware of the threat of climate change, show so much resistance to adopting more environmentally friendly behavior. The avenues often evoked to explain this psychological barrier relate in particular to the distance that separates us from the consequences of global warming, whether it be temporal, geographical, socio-cultural, or the uncertain nature of the future [12]. This distance can also be explained by the fact that the information available to understand the ecological crisis, the information conveyed by the scientific community in particular, is not always accessible to a public lacking in expertise. The data from studies carried out by climate scientists or environmental specialists are often transmitted in highly specialized jargon or in a format that may be hard to understand, such as the sixth report of the IPCC[1] and its several thousand

---

[1] Intergovernmental Panel on Climate Change.

© The Author(s), under exclusive license to Springer Nature Switzerland AG 2022
M. Vosmeer and L. Holloway-Attaway (Eds.): ICIDS 2022, LNCS 13762, pp. 352–365, 2022.
https://doi.org/10.1007/978-3-031-22298-6_21

pages.[2] Although attempts to popularize these complex issues are becoming more and more numerous and are aimed at an increasingly varied public (press articles, educational sheets, transition support kits, etc.), the ins and outs of the crisis have not yet penetrated all strata of society, partly because of this lack of clarity.

Reducing this distance may involve "bringing the future mentally closer", to use Markman's expression [12]. This undertaking consists in making tomorrow more tangible, both by thinking about it today and by reducing the degree of complexity with which it is understood by those who hold the scientific keys. This article starts from the hypothesis that interactive storytelling could contribute to this and, after formulating this postulate, it raises the question of what would be the nature of such a narrative as well as its implications on the narratological level.

First, we will look at the way the scientific community tells the future of the world through some of the possible scenarios it proposes. These scenarios will then be analyzed from a narratological point of view in order to evaluate their degree of narrativity, after which the implications linked to the conception of a plausible and believable interactive anticipation narrative will be highlighted.

2   The Scientific Account of the Future of the World

Narratives about the future are no longer the prerogative of literary genres such as science fiction or climate fiction. The rigorous and methodical scientific community itself is infiltrating the sphere of the humanities, or at least borrowing its vocabulary, in order to offer us its own scenarios. The future of the world, as perceived by the so-called hard sciences, takes the form of acronyms that may seem opaque to an uninformed public: RCPs and SSPs, respectively Representative Concentration Pathways and Shared Socioeconomic Pathways in their extended form. Developed by two groups of experts from the climate change research community, these acronyms and their definitions are the result of a process that aims to draw the possible evolution of the world and society by the end of the century on the basis of documented scientific data. This process integrates two types of prospective research leading respectively to two types of scenario. The first one focuses on the atmospheric concentration of the main greenhouse gases and selects five possible climate evolution trajectories between now and the end of the century. These trajectories are summarized in what scientists call Representative Concentration Pathways (RCPs). At the same time, a second group of researchers is more specifically interested in the socio-economic evolution of society and proposes five Shared Socio-economic Pathways (SSPs) [17]. Defined as socio-economic development trajectories based on possible changes in the world [19], the SSPs were developed with a view to providing a common framework for thinking about the analysis of climate change impacts, its possible mitigation and the adaptation of species, the human species in particular. There are also five of them, describing trends in technological, economic, political, and social change that could occur by the end of the century and their potential impact in terms of demographic change (population growth, mortality, fertility, migration, level and type of urbanization) and human development (education, health, equality, social cohesion and participation) [17].

---

[2] See IPCC website, accessed on July 25, 2022. https://www.ipcc.ch/report/ar6/wg2/.

Table 1. Summaries of the five Shared Socio-economic Pathways

SSP1	**Sustainability - Taking the Green Road (Low challenges to mitigation and adaptation)** The world shifts gradually, but pervasively, toward a more sustainable path, emphasizing more inclusive development that respects perceived environmental boundaries. Management of the global commons slowly improves, educational and health investments accelerate the demographic transition, and the emphasis on economic growth shifts toward a broader emphasis on human well-being. Driven by an increasing commitment to achieving development goals, inequality is reduced both across and within countries. Consumption is oriented toward low material growth and lower resource and energy intensity.
SSP2	**Middle of the Road (Medium challenges to mitigation and adaptation)** The world follows a path in which social, economic, and technological trends do not shift markedly from historical patterns. Development and income growth proceeds unevenly, with some countries making relatively good progress while others fall short of expectations. Global and national institutions work toward but make slow progress in achieving sustainable development goals. Environmental systems experience degradation, although there are some improvements and overall the intensity of resource and energy use declines. Global population growth is moderate and levels off in the second half of the century. Income inequality persists or improves only slowly and challenges to reducing vulnerability to societal and environmental changes remain.
SSP3	**Regional Rivalry - A Rocky Road (High challenges to mitigation and adaptation)** A resurgent nationalism, concerns about competitiveness and security, and regional conflicts push countries to increasingly focus on domestic or, at most, regional issues. Policies shift over time to become increasingly oriented toward national and regional security issues. Countries focus on achieving energy and food security goals within their own regions at the expense of broader-based development. Investments in education and technological development decline. Economic development is slow, consumption is material-intensive, and inequalities persist or worsen over time. Population growth is low in industrialized and high in developing countries. A low international priority for addressing environmental concerns leads to strong environmental degradation in some regions.
SSP4	**Inequality - A Road Divided (Low challenges to mitigation, high challenges to adaptation)** Highly unequal investments in human capital, combined with increasing disparities in economic opportunity and political power, lead to increasing inequalities and stratification both across and within countries. Over time, a gap widens between an internationally-connected society that contributes to knowledge- and capital-intensive sectors of the global economy, and a fragmented collection of lower-income, poorly educated societies that work in a labor intensive, low-tech economy. Social cohesion degrades and conflict and unrest become increasingly common. Technology development is high in the high-tech economy and sectors. The globally connected energy sector diversifies, with investments in both carbon-intensive fuels like coal and unconventional oil, but also low-carbon energy sources. Environmental policies focus on local issues around middle and high income areas.

(*continued*)

Table 1. (*continued*)

SSP5	Fossil-fueled Development - Taking the Highway (High challenges to mitigation, low challenges to adaptation)
	This world places increasing faith in competitive markets, innovation and participatory societies to produce rapid technological progress and development of human capital as the path to sustainable development. Global markets are increasingly integrated. There are also strong investments in health, education, and institutions to enhance human and social capital. At the same time, the push for economic and social development is coupled with the exploitation of abundant fossil fuel resources and the adoption of resource and energy intensive lifestyles around the world. All these factors lead to rapid growth of the global economy, while global population peaks and declines in the 21st century. Local environmental problems like air pollution are successfully managed. There is faith in the ability to effectively manage social and ecological systems, including by geo-engineering if necessary.

The SSPs describe societal models in which sustainable development and fossil fuel consumption have varying degrees of importance, different geopolitical situations, different levels of environmental degradation, and different conditions and lifestyles. Their summaries [19] are presented above (Table 1).

3 Shared Socio-economic Pathways, Terminology and Degree of Narrativity

3.1 Terminological Considerations

While modelling the evolution of greenhouse gas emissions and their impact on climate may seem remote from the topics of interest of the humanities and social sciences, modelling societal factors such as the evolution of economic or political paradigms is much less so. This is all the more true when the vocabulary describing them fits so well with that used by specialists in narratology. In the whole literature associated to the Shared Socio-economic Pathways, the word 'Scenario' is indeed used to name them, while 'Narrative' designates their short descriptions [17, 19]. The terms 'pathway', 'scenario' and 'narrative' therefore merit some initial explanation.

As we define 'pathway' as the trajectory followed by an entity in motion, the SSPs seem to inscribe future social and economic changes in a form of 'narrative' that uses the concepts of 'scenario'. The term 'scenario' should be interpreted here in the broad sense of the expected or assumed development of an action over time, a sense very close to that of pathway. The specific meaning given to it by the field of social sciences, i.e. "a strategic and methodical study which uses multiples data to consider various hypotheses and possible decisions" [8],[3] also suits it quite well. Considering each SSP as a 'narrative' invites us however to understand this term in its more widespread cinematic sense.

Starting from a scientific vision of the future of the world, the SSPs are thus presented and discussed using a terminology familiar to narratologists. The question then arises as

---
[3] Our translation.

to the extent to which they possess the characteristics of narrative as understood from a narratological point of view. In other words, we ask ourselves, in the rest of this article, if these SSPs are likely to inspire scenarios of the future of the world in the sense that they are understood in cinema, literature or video games, i.e. scenarios that could take these methodical and plausible forecasts of the future beyond the restricted circles in which they are conceived or for which they are intended, to reach, and perhaps touch, a general public that is too often held back in its projections, especially when these are linked to the environmental crisis. To put it another way, scenarios that could make the consequences of global warming more tangible and generate a reflection on a longer-term future that remains worrying.

3.2   The Degree of Narrativity of the SSPs

Beyond the terminology used to name and define them, can we really consider the 'narratives' of SSPs as fully-fledged narratives? Prince [18] defines a narrative as "the representation (…) of one or more real or fictive events communicated by one, two or several (…) narrators to one, two or several (…) narratees".

Ryan [21] proposes evaluating the degree of narrativity through a framework including eight conditions grouped under four dimensions presented below (Table 2):

Table 2. Ryan's evaluation framework

Spatial dimension	a. Narrative must be about a world populated by individuated existents
Temporal dimension	b. this world must be situated in time and undergo significant transformations c. the transformations must be caused by non-habitual physical events
Mental dimension	d. some of the participants in the events must be intelligent agents who have a mental life and react emotionally to the states of the world e. some of the events must be purposeful actions by these agents
Formal and pragmatic dimension	f. the sequence of events must form a unified causal chain and lead to closure g. the occurrence of at least some of the events must be asserted as fact for the storyworld h. the story must communicate something meaningful to the audience

Evaluating the degree of narrativity of the SSPs through this framework will not lead to an irrefutable conclusion since, in the words of its author, it leaves each one to a fairly wide range of interpretation. However, if we sift through the SSP scenarios on each of these points, a number of problems arise. First, the spatial dimension (a) would be one of the most controversial points. In the commentary associated with this condition, Ryan [21] states that it excludes representations of abstract entities and whole classes of concrete objects, scenarios involving 'humankind', 'reason', 'the state', etc. From our point of view, since the human race is made up of individuated existences and states can be easily personified, the narratives of SSPs partly fulfill this first condition. Only partly, because the interpretation of this notion of individuated existences also depends on the degree of individuality of the entities considered. Concepts such as 'a population', 'an institution', 'a country' or 'an organization' (e.g. TotalEnergies) can indeed be perceived as 'individuated existences', but they are all at different degrees including different levels of concreteness. The temporal dimension is also open to discussion, since while the SSPs are indeed situated in a time frame that extends from the present to the end of the century, the significant transformations mentioned in (b) are not clearly defined. When SSP1, for example, refers to the fact that "the world shifts toward a more sustainable path" or "broader emphasis on human well-being", SSP2 to "the intensity of resource and energy use declines", or SSP3 to "countries (…) focus on domestic or, at most, regional issues", it is difficult to imagine how these significant transformations are actually occurring. While the areas in which they take place, such as development, energy consumption or domestic and foreign policies, are clearly inferred from this kind of formulation, the concrete measures envisaged to make these changes happen are completely elided in the short descriptions of the SSPs. The same type of remark also applies to (c), the unusual physical events causing the significant transformations mentioned in (b). In the context of the climate crisis, we can imagine that these are linked to the damage caused to the environment by the increase in temperature (heat waves, drought, rising water levels, etc.). The consequences of these phenomena, such as the migration of climate refugees, the increase in the population of cities beyond their capacity, a potential water war, etc., are however not mentioned in the SSPs.

The mental dimension, which includes conditions (d) and (e) according to which some of the protagonists are intelligent agents capable of reacting emotionally to events or states of the world which are sometimes deliberately provoked by them, is completely absent from the SSPs. The way in which individuals are emotionally affected by the changes in the world, in other words the psychological impact of the ecological crisis (eco-anxiety, anger, revolt, denial, etc.), does not show up at all in their narratives. Nor do the actions deliberately undertaken by individuals to provoke the events.

Conditions (f), (g) and (h) included in the pragmatic and formal dimension of the framework are less problematic. The fact that some of the events are factual to the world of the story (g) as well as the fact that the story communicates something meaningful to the audience (h) are hardly refutable. On the other hand, condition (f) that the set of events must form a unified causal chain is not at all obvious. The only major cause that produces all the effects represented in the states of the world described in each of the scenarios is the environmental crisis. However, it seems that a number of elements have been overlooked in order to be able to move logically from a cause such as 'the human species is facing a major ecological crisis' to effects such as "resurgent nationalism" or "increasing inequalities and stratification both across and within countries" evoked respectively in SSP 3 and 4.

To conclude this analysis, if we stick to a relatively simple definition, such as the one proposed by Prince [18], it is difficult not to consider the narratives of SSPs as true narratives. Nevertheless, when envisaged through Ryan's [21] more complex evaluation framework, their degree of narrativity remains quite low, even though these scenarios fulfill some of the conditions included in the model.

The question that then arises is how to rewrite these SSPs in such a way as to transform them into a fully-fledged narrative that would be both informative and motivating. In other words, into a narrative that would both retain the scientific relevance on which the SSP scenarios are based and, in so doing, make the narratee's perception of the ecological crisis more accurate and tangible, while at the same time having a sufficiently strong impact to encourage climate action. Avenues for addressing this question may emerge from the interactive narrative discussed in Part 5. Before discussing this topic, the following paragraph raises the question of the nature of the difficulties induced by a narration about the future. As Liveley [10] indeed asks: "By better understanding the ways in which such prospective reading and narrative anticipation works, then, might we better appreciate the subtleties and processes of anticipation in both story worlds and real world scenarios? Could narratological insights into the operations of anticipation offer useful insights into the way we read stories about the future?".

4   Telling the Future, What Difficulties, What Implications?

The process of rewriting the SSPs involves design challenges that, for the most part, are similar to any act of story creation. To put it simply, it is necessary to ask who the protagonists are, in what space-time they evolve, what events to include, what narrative processes to use and what message the narrative delivers and to whom. Each of these questions depends first of all on the nature of the relationship that links the real world to the narrative world. The prospective nature of a narrative about the future, however, induces a mode of narration that differs from that of narratives about the past or the present. This paragraph examines these different questions.

The events narrated in a future story have not yet taken place, so the factual elements are non-existent. The world of the narrative is purely virtual and all the assertions of a future narrative have only an indeterminate truth value at the moment of enunciation. The semantic distinction between fact, negative fact and possibility remains, but these three categories are subject to the 'possibly' operator [11]. From an epistemic point of view, this poses a major problem. Any scenario about the future of the world, even if conceived on the basis of attested scientific data and using methodologically proven models, can only be speculative.

Margolin [11] distinguishes four modalities of future narratives. According to him, the narrative can be in a doxastic register "there will be…", where the speaker believes that what he is recounting will happen; hypothetical, when only the assertion that certain possibilities exist is formulated "it may happen…", optative when he wishes that the events of the narrative will happen "may it happen to you…" or deontic when he imposes obligations on the recipient of his narrative "do this and it will happen…" [11]. The first two modalities are epistemological in nature; they enable certainties or probabilities to be stated. The third and fourth are more ethical in nature. The things we wish to see happen imply a value judgment as to what we consider desirable. Obligation, which belongs to the imperative mode, is related to the philosophy of action, whose link with ethics is undeniable. The SSP project is a scientific one, so it is not surprising that we do not find any formula in the SSPs that is optative or deontic. We can, however, still envisage in the context of a rewriting of these narratives, that they integrate elements that would highlight their underlying values or their ethical implications. When SSP1 mentions, for example, "a broader emphasis on human well-being", we need to be clear about what 'human well-being' means. Even if the issues surrounding the future of the world were to raise profound ethical questions, the SSPs are inscribed in the field of knowledge. More precisely they are anchored in the sphere of what is possible, thus in a hypothetical register, the future being by nature uncertain.

This hypothetical status anchors the different worlds described in the scenarios in the discussion of 'possible worlds' which, from Leibniz through the logicians of the second half of the twentieth century, has finally infiltrated the universe of narratology. From a narratological point of view, in the analysis of Ryan [20] especially, the concepts of Actual World (AW), i.e. the real world, and of Textual Actual World (TAW), i.e. the world formed by the facts presented as actual by the narrative, are central. According to Ryan's [20] principle of 'minimal departure', we reconstruct the world of the narrative in such a way that it is as close as possible to the real world, and this remains true in the case of a narrative about the future until an event shatters our familiar representation of the world.

Moreover, anticipation narratives place their audience in front of a narrative prolepsis, that is to say in front of what Prince [18] defines as "an anachrony going forward with respect to the 'present' moment". It seems then, according to these narratological considerations, that the human mind projects itself into a narrative context concerning the future without getting rid of the filter through which it perceives and interprets the present world, built in part on the way it perceives and interprets its past experience. The cognitive processing of anticipation thus involves a complex interaction between the past, the present and the future [10] essentially built on what is familiar to the narratee.

From this point of view, SSPs are not contradictory to such a cognitive process since they are designed in such a way as to preserve what Ryan [20] calls the identity of the inventory between the present textual world and the actual world, namely the fact that the world of the narrative is composed of the same objects as the real world. This inventory identity is indeed maintained in the scenarios, as they make no mention of specific objects or technologies that do not currently exist in the actual world but would appear in the textual actual world. Expressions such as "there is faith in the ability to effectively manage social and ecological systems, including by geo-engineering if necessary" or "local environmental problems like air pollution are successfully managed", for example in SSP5, only suggest that the inventory of objects is not exactly the same in the two worlds, what we can easily understand in the context of the SSPs. It is indeed impossible to speak about the nature of objects, technologies, geopolitics or some paradigm of a future world without getting lost in conjectures that would instantly render any scientific approach vain.

The question of characters in the case of prospective scenarios, whether they are individuals, governments, groups of governments or organizations, poses the same type of problem. How can we anticipate the events, the conditions of life or the type of relationships that would be experienced by protagonists who have not yet been born or whose nature, boundaries, or even mission or status, would be likely to change?

It seems, therefore, that it is the prospective nature of narratives about the future that condemns them to confine themselves to a known world if they wish to retain their plausibility and verisimilitude. The narrative of a world to come, by nature hypothetical from a scientific point of view, must cling to what is factual in the present world; to break this principle is to assume the metamorphosis of a simple anticipation narrative into a science- or climate-fiction scenario. This point explains, on the one hand, the little room left for the emergence of novelty in the narratives of SSPs, and on the other hand, their highly generalizing character which weakens their narrative nature.

However, in following Ryan's insight that 'Living a narrative prospectively means (…) trying to anticipate possible developments, and experiencing the disappearance of possibilities' (…) but remaining steadily focused on the hatching of the future' [10], departing from scientific methodology to allow creativity to express itself may make sense in a process of rewriting SSPs.

5   From Multiple Scenarios to Interactive Storytelling

Although not directly related to SSPs, numerous video games are based on ecology or environmental crisis. Examples include: *Eco* [4], a game in which players collaborate to create a civilization on a virtual planet; *The Sims4: Eco Lifestyle* [23], where they are encouraged to adopt environmentally friendly behaviors; *Fate of the World* [6], a turn-based strategy game in which users must manage the resources available to an ever-growing population in the context of global warming; *Civilization VI: Gathering Storm* [3], which incorporates natural disasters related to climate change, *The Climate Game* [24], whose goal is to reach 'net zero' by 2050 by answering multiple choice questions, and *Walden a game* [27], which offers to relive the experience of the philosopher Henry David Thoreau when he chose to settle in the woods for more than two years and subsist only on the resources offered by nature. The last one differs from the others in the sense that it is not based on anticipation, since it relates events that took place in the 19th century. However, it is the game that best integrates the narrative dimension, which is at the heart of this article, a fact that is not so surprising since the game is directly inspired by two major works by Thoreau, *Walden: or Life in the Woods* [25] and his *Journal* [26]. All the others, with the exception of *The Climate Game* whose game mechanics follow a question/answer logic, are strategy games, management games or simulation games, genres that certainly include some elements specific to the narrative, but which cannot be assimilated to narrative games. However, the project, which we describe here, which consists in using SSPs to design an interactive narrative would follow an inverted scheme, that is to say a narrative game integrating some management and simulation elements.

To return to the SSPs, the fact that the scientific experts propose from the outset not one but five scenarios, is central to the approach. This set of scenarios is there to signify the presence of different possible futures, and one can thus consider this set as a large multi-linear scenario, which presents several parallel temporal trajectories, in the manner of films such as *Groundhog Day*, *Run Lola Run* or *Smoking/No Smoking*. Multi-linear narratives can be of several types. In the case of the SSP narratives, the five scenarios correspond to five alternative realities, five possible worlds, whose supposed future actualization depends, at least in part, on the actions taken by society. The situation is similar in the films shown as examples above. The creation of an alternative depends on the choices made by certain characters in the story, by branching off from a "mother" variant. These choices are rather implicit in the summarized scenarios that are given to us. For example, scenario SSP4 states: "Environmental policies focus on local issues around middle and high income areas". Faced with such a scenario structure, a transition to interactivity occurs naturally: the choices that make it possible to move from one scenario to another can be taken by the reader-user himself (the player), who becomes, through his participation, "responsible" for the evolution of the projected world. With only five initial scenarios, the material for a new interactive scenario is certainly limited but the addition of interactivity at the level of character choices, as proposed by many video games[4] as well as research on interactive drama [1, 13, 22, 28] seems a relevant way to explore possible futures. The potential benefits of this interactivity are:

- A stronger impact, as we move from passive to active pedagogy and as a higher level of agency, defined by Murray [15] as "the satisfying power to take meaningful action and see the results of our decisions and choices", may indeed increase the perception and awareness of the future consequences of our current choices.
- Simpler content exploration: simply reading the multiple scenarios requires a significant cognitive effort since it requires the reader to compare point by point the differences between scenarios and the causes of those differences.
- A more adequate way than traditional narratives to represent the complexity of our reality [9] insofar as it allows to gather in a single story very different scenarios, sometimes absolutely opposite, which is not so easy in a traditional story.

What is the impact of this interactivity on the nature of the possible worlds generated by the narrative? As discussed above, the possible worlds generated by the SSPs are of a hypothetical type. In the interactive case, the status of the possible world generated by the user's participation may change. One can certainly see this participation simply as a neutral exploration of possible futures. But the action of the user is not neutral, it expresses a global intention, depending on the style of play that the player adopts. For example, we can a priori assume that the user's action is motivated by his desire to do his best to "save the world", to bring global warming under control. From this point of view, "winning the game" means achieving a scenario close to the SSP1, and the possible world generated can be described as optative, according to Margolin's terminology [11]. The opposite case (not winning the game) would be an "anti-optative" world. But the player can adopt a completely different attitude, familiar to role-players: playing a character that is not oneself, stepping outside one's own identity to project oneself into another character, even one that is very far from oneself. For example, a user might decide to play the role of a large oil company and defend the interests of that company. In this case, the possible world is no longer on the optative register but more hypothetical. In all

---

[4] Adventure games, Role-Playing games, life simulators, etc.

cases, the addition of interactivity emotionally enriches the link between the receiver of the scenarios and the possible worlds that are generated during the narrative experience.

We must however conclude this chapter by specifying that if interactivity can potentially improve the reception of SSPs in a significant way, some experiments [5, 7] could not verify the hypotheses according to which it can greatly improve the comprehension of a given situation, the curiosity or the feeling of mastery, and thus of control, of the users. However, these same studies mention the fact that technical problems that occurred during the experimentation process, as well as excessive ergonomic or functional complexity, may have influenced the users in the same way as the interactivity of the tool that was the object of the experimentation. Moreover, the experiment described in McQuiggan et al. [14] suggests that if the learning gain in a narrative-based environment is not superior of that of traditional instructional approaches, it seems to have a significant impact on motivation, especially through a higher level of presence, a fact whose importance should not be overlooked in the context of behavioral changes induced by the climate crisis.

6 Filling the Gaps

Regardless of the underlying technology, interactive storytelling requires a significant amount of content, which the SSPs presented above fall far short of providing. Therefore, "making it interactive" requires filling in the gaps, on several levels.

On the one hand, as mentioned above, five scenarios, i.e. five possible states, do not open up many choices: at most three, in a simple narrative with diverging branches (with no return to the other branches).[5] This limitation can certainly be overcome if we consider that the SSPs are only the tip of the iceberg: the data are very extensive, and refer to numerous scenarios developed by scientists. Moreover, these scenarios are derived from simulation models that can be used (in a simplified way) in the interactive narrative, to provide not discrete but continuous scenarios.

On the other hand, a characteristic of the SSPs noted in Sect. 3 is the lack of concrete characters. Adapting these scripts for the "interactive storytelling" format will therefore require the insertion of characters: character-entities (e.g., a country), characters representing an entity (e.g., a president), or characters in society, whose fate illustrates the globality of society. This is a fairly standard procedure in docu-dramas.

Finally, the actions themselves undertaken by these characters have not necessarily all been documented by scientific studies. The need to create a coherent and engaging narrative may lead the authors of the story to add content to make the whole thing acceptable. The situation is analogous to interactive educational narratives that seek to reproduce a real situation in a credible way (e.g. FearNot! [2] or Nothing For Dinner [16]). These stories are based on real testimonies, which makes them similar to documentaries, but at the same time they have to create situations, which makes them closer to fiction. The fictional elements added should not transform the factual elements, and become counterfactual, but enrich the story in a coherent, plausible way. Too much use of fiction risks becoming manipulative, and can lead to controversy.[6] For the stories of the

---

[5] A 3-choice branching story gives 8 possible endings.

[6] See, for example, the debates around the mini-series *Chernobyl*, released in 2019.

future, it is therefore a question, in the same way, of fleshing out the scientific data, without dissolving them into a purely imaginative science fiction. The symmetry between documentary narratives and scientific narratives of the future is not perfect, however, as explained above, the trajectories traced by the SSPs are not facts, as are historical facts, they are just anticipations in accordance with the scientific knowledge of the moment. A documentary untruth is easy to detect for an expert in the field but a "counterpossibility" is more delicate to detect. As far as the future is concerned, everything is situated in a hypothetical register, and therefore fictional.

7 Conclusion

Through this analysis of the future of the world scenarios delivered by the scientific community via the Shared Socio-economic Pathways, which are qualified as narratives according to the terminology used in the comments that accompany them, this article has attempted to show how their degree of narrativity is, all in all, too weak to consider them as full-fledged narratives. While all the elements of narrative (space, time, characters, transformative events, causal chain and outcome) are present, at least in an underlying or inferred way, the respective descriptions of these scenarios remain too generalized to have an impact similar to that of stories, whatever their nature. Moreover, the prospective nature of all forms of narration about the future places the events described in a register that is only speculative and not factual. This distances us from the scientific approach since the object considered is only hypothetical. These anticipation narratives[7] have however, because of their scientific character, a potential that remains interesting to exploit within the framework of the conception of a real storytelling, notably in an interactive storytelling. Furthermore, the fact that the SSPs present in such an implicit way the choices made today in order to outline five possible futures places the reader in a position where he or she is forced to make multiple inferences from the current world to the world of tomorrow, i.e. in a process of reflection that is itself interactive. As we have seen, using the content of the SSPs in the framework of an interactive narrative would also convey a greater impact as well as a richer exploration, even understanding, of the scientific material transmitted. Such an undertaking would however imply the addition of content that would move away from what science can legitimately affirm today. If these additional fictional elements were to enrich such a narrative in a coherent and plausible way, it could nonetheless contribute to a more generalized awareness of the ecological crisis and reduce the distance that separates us from the consequences of global warming.

References

1. Arinbjarnar, M., Barber, H., Kudenko, D.: A critical review of interactive drama systems. Narrative (2009)

---

[7] Let us keep the term since, despite our conclusion, it is the one used in the reports that concern them.

2. Aylett, R.S., Louchart, S., Dias, J., Paiva, A., Vala, M.: FearNot! – an experiment in emergent narrative. In: Panayiotopoulos, T., Gratch, J., Aylett, R., Ballin, D., Olivier, P., Rist, T. (eds.) IVA 2005. LNCS (LNAI), vol. 3661, pp. 305–316. Springer, Heidelberg (2005). https://doi.org/10.1007/11550617_26
3. Civilization VI: Gathering Storm (2019). https://civilization.com/civilization-6-gathering-storm/
4. Eco (2018). https://play.eco/
5. van Enschot, R., Boogaard, I., Koenitz, H., Roth, C.: The potential of interactive digital narratives. Agency and multiple perspectives in Last Hijack Interactive. In: Cardona-Rivera, R.E., Sullivan, A., Young, R.M. (eds.) ICIDS 2019. LNCS, vol. 11869, pp. 158–169. Springer, Cham (2019). https://doi.org/10.1007/978-3-030-33894-7_17
6. Fate of the World (2011). https://store.steampowered.com/app/80200/Fate_of_the_World/
7. Gapiuk, L., Estupiñán, S., Szilas, N.: Effects of higher interactivity on the interactive narrative experience: an experimental study. In: Cardona-Rivera, R.E., Sullivan, A., Young, R.M. (eds.) ICIDS 2019. LNCS, vol. 11869, pp. 379–388. Springer, Cham (2019). https://doi.org/10.1007/978-3-030-33894-7_40
8. Grawitz, M.: Lexique des sciences sociales, 8th edn. Dalloz, Paris (2004)
9. Koenitz, H.: Representations of complexity – Interactive Digital Narratives Enabling Discourse for the 21st Century. Keynote at Zipscence Conference. Budapest (2018). https://www.slideshare.net/HartmutKoenitz/representations-of-complexity-interactive-digital-narratives-enabling-discourse-for-the-21st-century
10. Liveley, G.: Anticipation and narratology. In: Poli, R. (ed.) Handbook of Anticipation, pp. 1–20. Springer, Cham (2017). https://doi.org/10.1007/978-3-319-31737-3_7-1
11. Margolin, U.: Story modalised, or the grammar of virtuality. In: Pier, J. (ed.) Recent Trends in Narratological Research, pp. 49–61. Presses universitaires François-Rabelais, Tours (2017)
12. Markman, A.: Why People Aren't Motivated to Address Climate Change (2018). https://hbr.org/2018/10/why-people-arent-motivated-to-address-climate-change
13. Mateas, M., Stern, A.: Integrating plot, character and natural language processing in the interactive drama façade. In: Göbel, S., Braun, N., Spierling, U., Dechau, J., Diener, H. (eds.) Proceedings of the Technologies for Interactive Digital Storytelling and Entertainment (TIDSE) Conference, pp. 139–151. Fraunhofer IRB, Darmstadt (2003)
14. McQuiggan, S.W., Rowe, J.P., Lee, S., Lester, J.C.: Story-based learning: the impact of narrative on learning experiences and outcomes. In: Woolf, B.P., Aïmeur, E., Nkambou, R., Lajoie, S. (eds.) ITS 2008. LNCS, vol. 5091, pp. 530–539. Springer, Heidelberg (2008). https://doi.org/10.1007/978-3-540-69132-7_56
15. Murray, J.H.: Hamlet on the Holodeck: The Future of Narrative in Cyberspace. The Free Press, New York (1997)
16. Nothing For Dinner (2014). http://nothingfordinner.org
17. O'Neill, B.C., et al.: The roads ahead: narratives for shared socioeconomic pathways describing world futures in the 21st century. Glob. Environ. Change 42, 169–180 (2017). https://doi.org/10.1016/j.gloenvcha.2015.01.004
18. Prince, G.: A Dictionary of Narratology, Revised edn. University of Nebraska Press, Lincoln (2003)
19. Riahi, K., et al.: The Shared Socioeconomic Pathways and their energy, land use, and greenhouse gas emissions implications: an overview. Glob. Environ. Change 42, 153–168 (2017). https://doi.org/10.1016/j.gloenvcha.2016.05.009
20. Ryan, M.-L.: Possible worlds and accessibility relations: a semantic typology of fiction. Poet. Today 12, 553–576 (1991). https://doi.org/10.2307/1772651
21. Ryan, M.-L.: Toward a definition of narrative. In: Herman, D. (ed.) The Cambridge Companion to Narrative, pp. 22–36. Cambridge University Press, Cambridge (2007). https://doi.org/10.1017/CCOL0521856965.002

22. Szilas, N., Barles, J., Kavakli, M.: An implementation of real-time 3D interactive drama. Comput. Entertain. **5**, 5 (2007). https://doi.org/10.1145/1236224.1236233
23. The Sims4: Eco Lifestyle (2018). https://www.ea.com/games/the-sims/the-sims-4-eco-lifestyle?setLocale=en-us
24. The Climate Game (2022). https://ig.ft.com/climate-game/
25. Thoreau, H.D.: Walden: Or, Life in the Woods. Dover Thrift Editions (1854/1995)
26. Thoreau, H.D.: The Journal, 1837–1861. Orell Füssli, Zürich (2009)
27. Walden, A Game (2017). https://www.waldengame.com/
28. Weyhrauch, P.: Guiding Interactive Drama. Carnegie Mellon University, Pittsburgh (1997)

Intersubjective Pivots in Interactive Digital Narrative Design Learning

Colette Daiute[1]([⊠]) [iD], John T. Murray[2] [iD], Jack Wright[1] [iD], and Terrence Calistro[1] [iD]

[1] Graduate Center, City University of New York, New York, USA
cdaiute@gc.cuny.edu
[2] University of Central Florida, Orlando, USA

Abstract. Interactions between players and designers during IDN authoring are an undervalued source of information about the authoring process. This paper analyzes a corpus of player-author interactions from an online workshop. We classified feedback types and IDN design features, showing player reflections during authoring influenced the peer designer's work. Some types of feedback correlated positively with the overall growth of a design partner's IDN, while other feedback types correlated with story content. When players suggested authoring techniques or other subjective experiences playing through the emerging IDN, their partner's designs expanded structurally (nodes and branches). When players shared negative evaluations, the partner's design did not grow. In comparison, player reflections that were cognitively oriented led to increases in story settings, while player affective expressions led to more character dialogue. Effects include increases in both IDN narrative elements and structure. Some effects correlate with participant gender and native language, although not with race/ethnicity. The study results offer insights about intersubjectivity - what is on novice player-designers' minds as they wrestle with interactive digital narrative authoring. IDN pedagogy can, thus, benefit from designer-player collaboration as students experiment with technical authoring tools, develop and employ relevant vocabulary, and interpret a player's feedback. Additionally, the Authoring-Other Exchange System employed in this study provides a framework and novel measures for future research and pedagogy.

Keywords: Interactive digital narrative design · IDN research methodology · IDN pedagogy · Twine

1 Introduction

Interactions between players and designers during IDN authoring are typically implicit, despite being an important source of information about the authoring process. An IDN artifact is a co-created "...expressive narrative form in digital media implemented as a computational system containing potential narratives and experienced through a participatory process that results in [player] instantiated narratives" [1]. IDN differs from traditional narrative forms in that the designer becomes a narrative architect creating a protostory [1], a digital template with concrete elements for interacting players to

M. Vosmeer and L. Holloway-Attaway (Eds.): ICIDS 2022, LNCS 13762, pp. 366–382, 2022.
https://doi.org/10.1007/978-3-031-22298-6_22

realize potential narratives. Toward that end, IDNs provide players with story elements and options for completing narrative designs in original ways. Authoring tools such as Twine make IDN designing accessible to non-programmers [2], yet knowledge about how novices (such as college students new to IDN authoring) build player participation into their IDN design practice remains scarce [3].

IDN designers must embrace intersubjectivity, or a meeting of minds, with potential players. Novices learn to use Twine's nodes and links expressively, incorporating traditional narrative elements while imagining how players might interpret them and act. Player experience reflections offer information about this intersubjective process of IDN design learning when captured in the think-aloud protocol modified for this line of inquiry [4]. IDN play involves intense cognitive (evaluating and making choices), emotional (role-playing characters in the story), and physical (engaging via a keyboard or game controller) engagement. Therefore, sharing thoughts and feelings while playing can provide valuable insights to the designer. Surfacing player reflection could also motivate design strategies and spark creativity. A practical workshop in a beginning IDN design course is optimal for such inquiry on peer interaction. Sociocultural narrative psychology provides a foundation for this study on intersubjectivity, which is central to interactive digital narrative.

1.1 On Intersubjectivity

Higher order thinking and learning occur in social interaction, mediated by language and other symbol systems [5]. Intersubjectivity was defined in terms of the Zone of Proximal Development (ZPD), where learning occurs via interactions between participants of different knowledge and experience relevant to a challenging intellectual activity and a common goal [5]. The zone metaphor symbolizes what participants share and how they differ, enabling the need and opportunity to create new knowledge. As the quintessential human symbol system, language (including genres like narrative) is the catalytic mechanism for interaction because it embodies culture in flexible and expandable ways.

Scholars have further elaborated the concept of intersubjectivity as a "third space," where social interaction generates new knowledge [6]. Carefully calibrating collaborative partnering has, moreover, shown that matching peers with somewhat similar skills enables fertile exchange and development [7]. Sociocultural similarities and differences offer different kinds of support to the collaborative learning process [8–10]. Finally, according to this sociocultural perspective, narratives orient to actual and imagined audiences and can, thus, be analyzed as speech acts [11, 12], which informs our focus.

We extend this approach by facilitating designer-player interaction and through analyzing designs and player reflections as expressive functions. Inviting pairs of students new to authoring draws on their social language as they adopt digital tools to scaffold each other's learning process.

IDN design seems to inherently require intersubjectivity. Previous related research focuses on managing authors' social interactions in an interactive digital narrative community of collaboration. For example, Rouse provides an example of one such research project, offering guidelines for how to shape and encourage collaboration among larger groups [13]. Kitromili et al. called for additional research on the authoring process itself after reporting on interviews of 20 different digital interactive authors discussing their process [14]. In a prior study on IDN design with player reflection in a physical lab, we found evidence that the amount of sharing positively influenced subsequent designing [4]. The present study takes a major next step by including a relatively large group of college students from a wide range of sociocultural backgrounds. Participants in this learning space bring a range of experiences and knowledge to IDN design learning.

2   Research Questions and Methodology

Our primary research questions were "What types of reflections do novice undergraduate IDN design players communicate with a peer designer?" and "Which kinds of player reflections predict changes in the content and structure of the designs?".

We hypothesized that reading player reflections would influence IDN design measures over time. During the first player reflection turn (P1), players would communicate with someone they did not know (other than from a self-introduction bio). We believed player responses would be sparse and would largely conform to the system prompt to share thoughts and feelings while playing through a partner's IDN. We expected that the types and frequencies of feedback would increase in subsequent player reflection turns (P2, P3). All players offering feedback on player reflection turns (P1, P2, P3) to a partner were also authors in their own design turns (D1, D2, D3, D4), so player reflections indicate learning about authoring tools and observing what kinds of support their partner (and they) seemed to need.

2.1   Data Collection and Database

In this study, college students worked synchronously in real-time in the Authoring-Other Exchange System in Sherlock [15]. The Authoring-Other Exchange System is a special module of Sherlock, a media user research tool created to study reactions to audio-visual stimuli and to collate data and annotations [16, 17]. As previously reported [15], Sherlock records events generated from a modified version of Twine and provides them via the server to each partner. Partners annotate their responses to passages while reading them using a chat interface, which logs the title of the current passage. Sherlock supports participant enrollment (including consent, demographic survey, bio introduction to a partner, scheduling, partner assignment); forwarding the study protocol (outlined in Fig. 1); logging events; administering surveys; and sending the completion certificate. These features supported the real-time exchange of comments with peers and the authoring-other exchange.

2.2   The Authoring-Other Exchange Workshop

Figure 1 charts the nine steps in the 2.5-h participant process, beginning with viewing a basic Twine tutorial, followed by being directed to a participation pane, with the instructions to "[t]hink of a story idea and use the Twine tools you learned to begin designing an IDN." After the initial 15-min authoring session, participants are presented with their partner's design. For this player reflection step, the prompt is "Share with your partner what you are thinking and feeling as you play their emerging design." On the

Fig. 1. Authoring-other exchange for IDN design workshop process

next authoring turn, each participant is prompted to "Consider your player's reflections and continue your IDN design."

This methodology adapts the think-aloud method from cognitive science [18], game studies [19], education [20], and our own prior research [4, 15]. On-screen instructions ask participants to type their reflections to the partner in a player-reflection pane (shown in dark blue in Fig. 2). This platform design provides the player-reflector with access to their partner's design in play mode as they write their comments. The interface gives the designer access to the player's comments as a scrollable chat view during the next authoring phase.

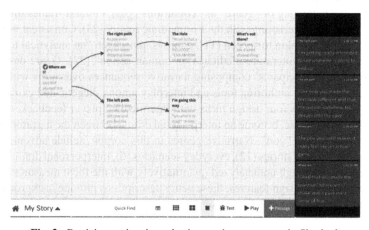

Fig. 2. Participant view in authoring-exchange system in Sherlock

2.3 Participants

From late August through December 2021, 64 individuals in 34 pairs completed the IRB-approved workshop. For this paper, we include data collected from 54 participants. We transferred the data into *Atlas.ti 9* [21] yielding 191 player reflection turn segments (over player reflection turns, P1, P2, P3), which resulted in 1191 expressive units for analysis. IDN design data was available in text form with time stamps and Twine tool codes (e.g. [[...]] and ->) in 240 units over design turns D1, D2, D3, and D4, with 4,000 segmented units (sentences and clauses). Because of our interest in the dimensions of intersubjectivity, information about the participants' sociocultural identifications of gender, race-ethnicity, and language groups are relevant. Sociocultural groups included women[1] (36), men (18), Asian (16), Black (8), White (10), Hispanic (10), Middle Eastern (3), South Asian (7). As an approximation of personal or family immigration, native language is also a sociocultural factor. Because of the large number of native languages participants in this study identified (23), we created language groups for analysis purposes: African, Asian, Austronesian, Balto-Slavic, English, Indo-European, Middle Eastern, Romance, South Asian. After volunteers indicated consent, completed a demographic survey, and selected participation times, we researchers assigned partners based on availability and sociocultural similarity or difference.

2.4 Database

We identified narrative genres in order to describe the types in the corpus. Because IDN designs are protostories for player instantiation [1], and thus not fixed forms, we adopted an understanding of "genre" as "cognitions" [22], cultural frames that authors use to create stories interacting with their immediate reality [23]. Consistent with defining literary objects as akin to speech [11], genre is, moreover, "an analytical tool aimed at understanding how literature meditates on human action" [22]. Genre descriptions were sensitive to participants' composing narrative sequences over turns with varying trajectories enabled by authoring tools and interplay among diegetic and extra-diegetic voices [24, 25]. Across four design turns with intermediate player feedback, a mystery story might, for example, become an interpersonal drama between the narrator "I" interacting with the player "you". Narrative genres in this corpus include adventures (14), mysteries (13), fantasy stories (12), everyday scenarios (6), interpersonal dramas (5), and moral tales (3). Although not analyzed quantitatively with the focal measures of player reflections and IDN design features, these genre descriptions provide background to the focal analysis herein and data for future inquiry.

3   Measures and Analyses

The database is organized and labeled with participant and pair numbers, sociocultural identity factors, player reflection turn (P1, P2, P3), and design turn (D1, D2, D3, D4). Analytic categories described below account for all player experience reflections and IDN design content (literary elements) and structure (tree complexity measure).

3.1 Player Experience Reflection Analysis

Player experience reflections (Player Reflections hereafter) identified the expressive function of each thought unit (sentence or independent clause, phrase, word, verbal

---

[1] The survey included the question "Please state your preferred gender affiliation," most responded "female" or "male"; some responded with pronouns, or "Male" or "Female" and there were no genderqueer or non-binary identifying participants in the study.

emojis such as "lol") participants shared in writing in the player reflection pane, over three 15-min turns playing their partner's IDN. As shown in the player view in Fig. 2, the player's comments appear in the dark blue column, with entries logged by passage and time. Using narrative discourse analysis, the first author developed expressive (speech act) categories to account for reflections in the database. The iterative process for identifying the player reflection categories was as follows: reading through all the player reflection turns several times, reading again to parse the comments into sentences (when possible) or communicative units (such as independent phrases or verbal emojis) in each turn. For example, the following parsing acknowledges two expressive units: "I love that" and "the two were childhood friends." Consistent with speech act theory applied in our prior IDN design research [4, 15] and streamlined to yield the most robust categories, the following account for all the player reflection functions: PRcogint, PRaffect, Eval-Neg, EvalPos, IDNfeature, RepNarr, SuggNarr, SuggProc. Table 1 presents the Player Reflection categories of all the comments offered to the partner over reflection turns.

The eight mutually exclusive categories were applied to ensure they accounted for all the player reflections, were added to the project Manual, and entered into the *Atlas.ti* coding list. After the first author coded the player reflections, she checked the consistency *within* each category by viewing all of its exemplars and changing any that did not fit. Future work could include validating the annotations through inter-annotator agreement, but this study relied on a single annotator.

Table 1. IDN typology of player reflections

Category	Example
Affective statements (PRaffect)	*It's really fun to follow along;* *It gave me a sense of fear* *Hahaha; lol*
Cognitive statements (PRcogint)	*I'm confused;* *I'm getting really interested to see*
Negative evaluations (EvalNeg)	*This isn't interactive*
Positive evaluations (EvalPos)	*This is great!* *Good job so far*
IDN feature mentions (IDNfeature)	*This IS interactive;* *If you click the first choice...* *→*
Repeat partner's narrative sequences (RepNarr)	*... how Doe sounded strange on the call;* *The person somehow fell deeper ito the cave*
Suggestions of new narrative sequences (SuggNarr)	*You should punish their selfishness* *Where is the narrative going to end up?*
Suggestions of authoring strategies (SuggProc)	*Use [[...]] to create a branch* *Add more choices*

3.2 IDN Literary Analysis

The IDN Literary Analysis identified IDN elements and choice node/options. Adapting prior IDN analysis [4, 15, 26], elements include Character, Object, World, and Events added in each of the four design turns. To account for as many narrative features as possible, the analysis identified each character by number in order of appearance in the design process with the author's depiction of that character, such as character description, character action, character dialogue, and character psychological state. This process yielded from 1 to 26 characters (with the character functions); 0 – 26 objects (with object description or object animation), and world elements describing spatial (nature, rooms) and temporal marking. Events were coded when they occurred without a character or object.

Figure 3 shows the application of IDN elements to a first turn by a participant identifying as Hispanic women, whose native language is English.

Fig. 3. Excerpt of IDN element coding applied in Atlas.ti

Figure 3 illustrates the strategy of a non-diegetic character (Char1) directing entry to the story by stating the title ("#Bardon Manor Murder Mystery/") and an initiating action ("a murder has taken place in the bardon manor"). Given our emphasis on the functions of narrative elements and importance of applying categories mutually exclusively to expressive units, we determine the major function of each parsed unit. In the sentence, "#can you find the murderer?", Char2 - "you" - is introduced (Char2Des), then elaborated with a psychological state "find" (Char2Psy), followed by introduction of another character "the murderer" (Char3Psy). As well as other characters and elaborations (Char1Dia), the author of the excerpt in Fig. 3, adds a World setting ("It was a dark and stormy night") and an Event ("At the party, the lights go out").

The second phase of the IDN Literary Analysis was a choice analysis. Adapted from choice poetic theory [27], our analysis focused on the conceptual dimension of options the designer offers after choice nodes. Choice poetics identifies diverse conceptual options from the perspective of the designer in relation to players' expectations as they engage with different options [27]. Our analysis explores choice options as spontaneously generated by our beginning designers to identify how and when these emerge across the design turns. This offers insights about how these beginners integrated the authoring tool and narrative content. Choice dimensions that account for all the choices in this data set include: "Single" dimensions (such as next steps in a journey "left" or "right"; "China" or "Afghanistan"; object selections "apple" or "banana," and so on). "Adventure" dimensions (such as fighting or fleeing; continuing on a quest or retreating); "Socioemotional" dimensions (such as trusting another character or distancing oneself; speaking with another character or not; loving or hating); and moral dilemmas (spending a found dollar on candy or giving it to a homeless man).

3.3 IDN Tree Structure Complexity

The IDN Tree Complexity Metric (TCM) describes the size and shape of a Twine story as it appears on a design screen. The purpose of the TCM is to offer a single quantitative measure of the structural shape of an interactive digital narrative. Sensitivity to current IDN scholarship considering a wide variety of interactive mechanics [28] and the dimensions and scope of overall hand-coded complexity [29, 30] contributed to the development and application of the TCM for this study. TCM was developed through 2500 pairwise comparisons of IDNs, with experts judging which IDN they viewed as more complex [31].

Features scraped from the data export files were used to calculate the following variables of the tree structure at the end of a design turn: number of nodes, number of branches, number of leaves (nodes with no posterior links), number of non-leaf nodes (nodes minus leaves), number of choice nodes (nodes with multiple exit branches), maximum path length (path length is defined as the number of nodes connected to each other reaching from the origin to a leaf), average path length, and recursive branches. Elo ratings, used to rank chess players on ability [32], were calculated for each IDN. A random forest machine learning model was built to predict a complexity metric on tree pictures outside the training sample IDNs ($R^2 = .75$). This model accurately predicts how the features described above affect an expert's opinion on structural complexity and returns a continuous metric.

3.4 Statistical Analyses

Analyses of the player reflections, IDN literary elements, and TCM were transferred to CSV data files for two types of statistical analysis addressing our research questions about patterns of design and reflection over time and the impact of the player reflections on the IDN designs. For patterns of use, change, and group differences (race/ethnicity, gender, native language), we applied Multilevel Generalized Linear Model (MGLM) with a Poisson distribution of the player reflections and IDN elements. We used the textual content at the end of each design turn (D1, D2, D3, D4) and all player reflections made during each play turn (P1, P2, P3). To examine relationships between player reflections, IDN elements, and the TCM, we applied t-tests and Wilcoxon signed-rank hypothesis tests to assess whether a reflection type affected the designer's subsequent activities.

Given the variability in participants' activity across design and player reflection turns, we sampled "active turns" to analyze the feedback-design effect relationships. Although Sherlock automatically advanced and remained in the design and play modes with instructions on the participant view, participants were in control of their messages and activity. Because participants might not have made changes, for whatever reason, to their designs on every turn, we sampled design turns with changes ("active" turns). To determine the influences of player reflections on designs (the major focus of this study), we established the "Design-Play-Design (D-P-D) Unit" using active participation cycles. The D-P-D is, in brief, a unit of interaction between the designer and player, and the core of the intersubjective exchange.

This combination of rigorous qualitative and quantitative measures allowed us to describe processes, products, and relationships across the design, play, and reflection activities in this workshop. The study methodology has the potential for generalization in future research on a larger scale, as discussed in Sect. 6.

4   Results

Because our primary focus is on the nature of player reflections and the impacts of specific reflections on the IDN designs, we present the player reflection analysis first. Then, we present the IDN measures (content and structure), followed by results of the analysis of relationships between the measures to assess for impact.

4.1   The Typology of Player Reflections

The eight categories illustrated in Table 1 accounted for 1191 expressive units shared in three player reflection turns.

As we had hypothesized, players shared thoughts (PRcogint) and feelings (PRaffect) prominently on the first player reflection turn. In addition, players offered other kinds of feedback, such as evaluations of the partner's design (EvalNeg, EvalPos) which we did not specifically prompt for. Not surprisingly, people also used vocabulary related to interactive digital narrative like "interact" or tools like "branches" and "[[…]]".

Table 2 shows that the player reflection process changed over time/turn. A MGLM with Poisson distribution revealed four categories that changed significantly over the player reflection turns: PRaffect, EvalPos, and SuggProc increased, whereas EvalNeg decreased.

Table 2. Player reflection function average additions over play reflection turns

Category	P1	P2	P3	P2–P1	P3–P2
EvalNeg	0.418	0.182	0.155	−0.236	−0.027
EvalPos*	**0.418**	**0.591**	**0.828**	**0.173**	**0.237**
IDNfeature	0.881	0.727	0.828	−0.153	0.100

(continued)

Table 2. (*continued*)

Category	P1	P2	P3	P2–P1	P3–P2
PRaffect*	**1.358**	**1.061**	**2.000**	−0.298	**0.939**
PRcogint	1.701	1.439	1.552	−0.262	0.112
RepNarr	0.731	0.879	0.931	0.147	0.052
SuggNarr	0.448	0.530	0.517	0.083	−0.013
SuggProc*	**0.149**	**0.455**	**0.534**	**0.305**	0.080

*P < .05 on the MGLM with Poisson distribution.

Along with the decrease in negative evaluation, this pattern of change indicates increasing familiarity with the other person (PRaffect, EvalPos), their design and the authoring process (SuggProc).

The analysis revealed significant declines in CharDes and World across gender groups. The decline in the elements was stronger/steeper for women than men. The MGLM with Poisson distribution showed significant time by gender interactions CharDes (OR = .81, p = .004, CI 95% = [.70,.93]). The results also indicated significant declines in CharDes based on participant native language group. The decline in the elements was found to be stronger/steeper for non-English native speakers than for native English speakers. No differences were found for race/ethnicity groups.

These differences show some sensitivity of IDN design learning to sociocultural experience but do not greatly qualify our current focus on the player reflections and interactive digital narrative design across the participants.

5   IDN Design Analysis

Participants also changed the IDN elements in their compositions over design turns. Table 3 presents frequencies of participant uses of the different IDN elements in design turn one and those added in each subsequent design turn.

As illustrated in Table 3, participants added fewer new elements each design turn. Literary elements that decreased significantly include character descriptions (CharDes), events (Events), object descriptions (ObjDes), and world descriptions (World). This makes sense as additions to a story on later design turns require integrating with the settings, characters, events, etc. established in prior turns. And, because interactive digital narrative design involves using authoring tools to organize and link narrative passages, the designer also has structural material to consider and integrate over time. In addition, designers had player reflections between the design turns to read, interpret, and possibly apply.

Another interesting observation of the data shown in Table 3 is the relative increase in character dialogue and character psychological states. When compared to naming/describing characters (CharDes) and depicting actions (CharAct), character dialogue (CharDia) and character psychological states (CharPsy) elaborate characters by bringing them to life with statements of their speech, thoughts and feelings. To explore such

Table 3. IDN literary elements by frequency over the 4 design turns

IDN element categories	Design turn 1	Design turn 2	Design turn 3	Design turn 4
CharAct	185	132	148	92
CharDes*	227	123	149	96
CharDia	174	156	181	133
Events*	88	48	37	23
CharPsy	277	210	292	189
ObjDes*	143	81	71	55
ObjAnim	27	18	30	17
World*	134	66	78	37

$^*P < .001..$

character elaboration, we correlated percentages of the basic and elaborated character expression within all the IDN elements for active D-P-D Units. The analysis showed basic character enactments (CharDes+CharAct) and elaborated character enactments (CharDia + CharPsy) are inversely correlated, r = .64. This shows that although fewer new literary elements and expressions are added overall across turns, when we account for the data relatively (in active D-P-D units as a percentage of all elements), character development increases as other kinds of literary element depictions decrease.

Like character development, the literary quality of options designers presented following choice nodes could increase during an IDN learning workshop. To explore that, Table 4 shows the results of the choice type analysis.

Table 4. Choices by frequency added in each of *Four* design turns.

Choice type	D1	D2	D3	D4
Single dimension	43	26	30	9
Adventure	23	16	18	13
Socioemotional	6	17	11	10
Moral dilemma	7	1	6	1
Totals	*79*	*60*	*65*	*33*

Table 4 indicates an increase in offering the player decisions revolving around socioemotional dynamics, such as trusting a relevant character. In contrast, single dimension choices such as choosing an apple or a banana decrease in frequency. Adventure choices decrease somewhat less dramatically, and moral dilemmas vary across turns. Including choice nodes and options is a hybrid narrative content and structure skill, so these changes are important. We follow this focus on the content with a structural analysis.

5.1 Relationships Between IDN Literary Analysis and the TCM

IDN elements and TCM account for different dimensions of interactive digital narrative. The TCM accounts for authoring tool use manifested in visual representations of a tree structure. IDN elements analysis, on the other hand, accounts for narrative content additions that may be within a single node. Together, the elements and TCM indicate overall complexity of IDN genres and their development, at least for these beginning designers working collaboratively in practice.

Because the IDN elements analysis focused on narrative content rather than structure, we expected the literary elements analysis to complement the structural analysis. Consistent with that expectation, the statistical analysis of active D-P-D Units revealed only one IDN element type, character actions, related positively to distributions in TCM differences (p < .05). Adding nodes is, as we presented above, a major factor in the TCM increase, thus requiring some additional content. Because one way to continue designing over turns was to add passages (nodes), introducing another character or adding action to a previously introduced character might be an obvious way to fill new passages. Given the attention required for using authoring tools that would fit with prior protostory designs, a basic character add might be easy. Also consistent with our expectation that TCM and IDN elements would capture different aspects of IDN design learning is that the following categories were not related to the TCM (for active D-P-D Units): character description, character dialogue, character psychological state, object animation, and world.

5.2 Relationships Between Player Reflections and the TCM

Two types of player reflections in active design-play-design sequences revealed differences in the distributions of the TCM (p < .02). Suggesting Procedures and Processes accounted positively for differences in TCM changes over design turns, and Repeating Narrative Sequences decreased TCM over design turns. Mentions of IDN feature approached significance (p = .06) as well. The most pivotal kind of comment for increasing the tree structure were comments coded as SuggProc, including tool-based suggestions ("use brakets [sic] to con)nect [[]]"); narrative focused suggestions ("it would be great to have another option"); or fluency prompting ("Where does the story go from here?").

It is important to notice that such a focus on technical design tools also occurred with increasing affect expression and positive evaluation, as well as decreasing negative evaluation (as reported above). The overwhelmingly more frequent sharing of affect and cognition indicates that participants followed directions to share their feelings and thoughts on early turns and spontaneously increased attention to specific suggestions of Twine tools or narrative elaborations (but not literal narrative sequences (RepNarr).

To identify potent player reflections, we searched the D-P-D Units for influential reflection types. Table 5 illustrates player and designer interaction in a D-P-D Unit. This D-P-D Unit was located by searching the database for a SuggProc between design turns with IDN elements added and a significant TCM differential.

The example on Table 5 enacts a *Support Strategy Shift* in which the player reflections led to a design change after a few rounds of commenting. On Table 5, we observe a pivot in a final D-P-D Unit by a pair including a woman identifying as a South Asian native English speaker (participant 29) as the designer and a white man identifying as a native Russian speaker as the player (participant 30). Before the interchange presented below, the player tentatively connected to the other "can someone see my messages?", then offered a structural suggestion "use brakets [[]]", and only later demonstrated how to create a choice node *with* the designer's own narrative sequence. Reading this transcript, we can consider that when his negative evaluation and cognitively focused comment on P1 did not spark a design change on D2, he suggested an authoring tool with an illustrative narrative sequence. That progression of gradually increasing affective and technical comments seems to have done the trick.

The structural plus affect comments shifted the designer's single passage narrative to an interactive design. The participant made a qualitative transformation in design turn three when she added three choice nodes, one with choice options including narrative passages and two others marking the place for subsequent elaboration (although she couldn't implement those options in time). In addition to those qualitative changes, this demonstrates a dramatic relation between player reflection and design structure change, with the TCM of 425 at the end of D1, 448 at the end of D2, no change in D3, and 1034 in D4. In summary, this designer's work demonstrated positive results of her and her partner's effortful yet patient interaction in the design process.

The interaction and change by this pair points to the value of bringing people of different sociocultural backgrounds together. In addition to gender and ethnicity, prior engagement with digital games could explain participant choices on the first design turn. The partner whose bio mentioned interest in digital games implemented digital tools early on, while the partner who instead mentioned interest in biology studies began with a relatively fluent narrative.

Relevant to the ebb and flow of design activity over time is that although the behavioral data in this study manifest design and comment processes, we cannot record information about activities during any non-active turns. Because the workshop was online and included limited input, participants could have been taking a brief break, replaying, and/or thinking about next steps. For their material to have been included in this analysis, they would have returned to and completed the workshop.

Another D-P-D Unit by two Hispanic women indicated a pivotal structural change after a relatively terse player reflection combining subjectivity with procedural suggestions. On her first design turn, the designer (identifying as Hispanic native English speaker) created a series of four linked passages setting the scene for two sisters on a mundane trip to a grocery store when a shooting ensues. The author begins with nodes headed "# The beginning of the end" and "#We start at a market and you are with. Your sibling", detailed with Character Actions, Descriptions, Spatial and Temporal Setting elements. She then added another node "#All of a sudden you hear gun shots" elaborated with psychological states ("your sibling is crying", "you are trying to calm her down so they can't hear you…" and ending the turn with "#what do you do?" followed by "choice 1" and "choice 2". On the first player reflection turn the partner (identifying as Hispanic Spanish speaker) comments "This is a very interesting Story. Definitely should continue to work on it and develop more ideas about the 2 choices at the end." This combination of a cognitive reflection with two procedural suggestions and an IDN feature

Table 5. Support strategy shift across a design-play-design (D-P-D) unit.

Design Turn 2 Text (D2)	Literary elements added on turn	Structural note & TCM
There is a girl name Vanessa and a guy named Jackson. They met in college and for Jackson it was love at first sight The two's bond between one another soon evolved into something more and sparks flew Vanessa's bestfriend, Chris, always had a negative feelings towards Jackson and believed he was someone that he was not. As Vanessa and Jackson's relationship grew stronger, Vanessa and Chris's relationship lessened	CharDes (4) CharPsy (6) Event (1) World (1)	Narrative in a single node; TCM − 428
Player Reflection Turn 2 (P2)	**Player Reflection Categories**	
Time offset: 92:36 #Dangerous Love Try writing this [[follow her heart and see where it goes]] In that new slide you can make choices or write an end of the story Time offset: 93:14 #Dangerous Love Same thing you can do for [[focus on school]]	IDNfeature (2) SuggProc (2) RepNarr(1) Shifting from EvalNeg + PRcogint on P1; IDN feature + SuggProc with no RepNarr on P2	
Design Turn 3 Text (D3)	**Literary elements added on turn**	**Structural note & TCM**
Text: Addition after "not" on previous turn: [[Should she believe her best friend]] [[Follow her heart and see where it goes]] [[Focus on school]] # Dangerous Love Fast forward 6 years # Untitled Passage Double-click this passage to edit it # Follow her heart and see where it goes They end up being together and live a long life. Should they… [[Have kids together]] [[Travel the world together]] [[Build a house together]] # Should she believe her best friend She leaves Jackson and is now lonely and sad. Should she… [[Find Jackson in hopes of rekindling their love]] [[Move on and find someone else]] [[Get cats instead]] # Focus on school she graduates college becomes a succesful bussiness women but is lonely and depressed	CharAct (4) CharDes (2) Event (2) ObjDes (1)	Added 2 choice nodes; with 3 options each; added passages in 2 of the options TCM = 1034

mention is the pivot to the designer's second turn where she adds an narratively named choice node "[[which one do you take?]]", followed by other choice nodes "[[left]]" and "[[right]]", as well as new character descriptions (7), character actions (3), character dialogue (5), character psychological states (1), object descriptions (3), an animated object, and physical setting sequences. The TCM changed from 782 to 1062 over the interactive unit.

In addition to accounting for important variability, the D-P-D Unit analysis we introduce in this paper is an indication of intersubjectivity: that is, it links partners' processes and products.

5.3   Relationship Between Player Reflections and IDN Elements

When we focus on the relationships between player reflections and IDN elements, results are consistent with our general hypothesis about the usefulness of providing practice where designers and players have the benefit of explicit shared communication. Some player reflection types uniquely controlled for several D-P-D units. Sharing player cognitions related to expression of world elements (physical and temporal settings) ($p = .02$). Sharing affect related to increases in character dialogue ($p = .054$), mentioning IDN features related to increases in character actions and options of choice nodes ($p = .01$). Two player reflection categories – suggesting procedures ($p = .0017$) and negative evaluating ($p = .005$) related to increases in object animations.

6   Discussion and Implications

Our main finding was that communication between player and designer in this study had a positive impact on beginning IDN design learning. Findings about the specific types of feedback that played a role in stimulating authoring add to our understanding of the IDN design development process. Researchers could investigate whether other demographics have similar results, including K-12 students or even non-students. The role that content type (e.g. genre or specific situations) and the amount and types of instruction and/or guidance play are promising future directions for study.

Operationalizing D-P-D units is relevant to future IDN research, not only about designers and players individually as creators or users, but as interdependent collaborators. Augmenting connection with the "zone of proximal development" concept, our D-P-D unit analysis is a concrete way to embody and define intersubjectivity available in contemporary technologies. Moreover, findings about relationships between specific reflection types and design changes indicate what we refer to as "pivots" during those intersubjective spaces.

In addition to identifying dynamics of intersubjectivity with the player reflection to design connections, results of this study indicate specific kinds of sociocultural factors at play in whether and how those dynamics occur. That women and native language partners adopted some different interaction patterns over time suggests that the intersubjective space is not culturally neutral. Pairs of women's steeper decreases in the basic character and setting descriptions, for example, indicate their orientation to other kinds of IDN developments. Future explorations of such specific as well as more general manifestations of intersubjectivity in IDN are worthwhile.

The Authoring-Other Exchange Workshop can inform pedagogy. Instructors could use this workshop and analysis model with students to examine their own design teaching and learning processes, thereby identifying any need for additional expert guidance. Faculty and students could, for example, notice whether and how the typology presented here helps them focus on their own work to foster intersubjective orientation.

This paper presents findings from analyzing interactions with several coding schemes at the scale of the present study. We described our experience conducting an online workshop with a large number of diverse participants and discuss the findings for researchers studying IDN collaboration. Our next goal is to release the software used for the workshop, making it easier to conduct and study collaborative interactions that represent intersubjective activities.

References

1. Koenitz, H.: Towards a specific theory of interactive digital narrative. In: Koenitz, H., Ferri, G., Haahr, M., Sezen, D., Sezen, T.I. (eds.) Interactive Digital Narrative, pp. 91–105. Routledge
2. Klimas, C.: Twinery: Twine Homepage (2009). https://twinery.org/
3. Dubbelman, T.: Narrative game mechanics. In: Nack, F., Gordon, A.S. (eds.) ICIDS 2016. LNCS, vol. 10045, pp. 39–50. Springer, Cham (2016). https://doi.org/10.1007/978-3-319-48279-8_4
4. Daiute, C., Duncan, R.O., Marchenko, F.: Meta-communication between designers and players of interactive digital narratives. In: Rouse, R., Koenitz, H., Haahr, M. (eds.) ICIDS 2018. LNCS, vol. 11318, pp. 134–142. Springer, Cham (2018). https://doi.org/10.1007/978-3-030-04028-4_10
5. Vygotsky, L.S.: Mind in Society: The Development of Higher Psychological Processes. Harvard University Press (1978)
6. Gutiérrez, K.: Developing sociocritical literacy in the third space. Read. Res. Q. 43(2), 148–164 (2008). https://doi.org/10.1598/RRQ.43.2.3
7. Perret-Clermont, A.-N.: Thinking spaces of the young. In: Perret-Clermont, A.-N., Resnick, L.B., Zittoun, T., Burge, B. (eds.) Joining Society: Social Interaction and Learning in Adolescence and Youth, pp. 3–10. Cambridge University Press, New York (2004)
8. Cohen, E.G.: Designing Groupwork: Strategies for the Heterogenous Classroom. Teachers College Press (2014)
9. Daiute, C., Campbell, C., Cooper, C., Griffin, T., Reddy, M., Tivnan, T.: Young authors' interactions with peers and a teacher: toward a developmentally sensitive sociocultural literacy theory. In: Daiute, C. (ed.) The Development of Literacy Through Social Interaction, pp. 41–66. Jossey Bass Publishers, San Francisco (1993)
10. Lee, C.D.: Toward a framework for culturally responsive design in multimedia computer environments: cultural modeling. Mind Cult. Act. 10(1), 42–61 (2003)
11. Bakhtin, M.M.: Speech genres and other late essays. In: Emerson, C., Holquist, M. (eds.). Trans. Vern W. McGee. University of Texas Press (1986)
12. Daiute, C.: Narrative Inquiry: A Dynamic Approach. Sage Publications (2013)
13. Rouse, R.: Someone else's story: an ethical approach to interactive narrative design for cultural heritage. In: Cardona-Rivera, R.E., Sullivan, A., Young, R.M. (eds.) ICIDS 2019. LNCS, vol. 11869, pp. 47–60. Springer, Cham (2019). https://doi.org/10.1007/978-3-030-33894-7_6
14. Kitromili, S., Jordan, J., Millard, D.E.: What authors think about hypertext authoring. In: Proceedings of the 31st ACM Conference on Hypertext and Social Media, pp. 9–16. ACM, Virtual Event (2020). https://doi.org/10.1145/3372923.3404798
15. Daiute, C., Cox, D., Murray, J.T.: Imagining the other for interactive digital narrative design learning in real time in Sherlock. In: Mitchell, A., Vosmeer, M. (eds.) ICIDS 2021. LNCS, vol. 13138, pp. 454–461. Springer, Cham (2021). https://doi.org/10.1007/978-3-030-92300-6_46
16. Murray, J., Mateas, M., Wardrip-Fruin, N.: Proposal for analyzing player emotions in an interactive narrative using story intention graphs. In: Proceedings of the 2017 International Conference on the Foundations of Digital Games (2017)

17. Murray, J.T.: Telltale Hearts: Encoding Cinematic Choice-Based Adventure Games (2018). https://escholarship.org/uc/item/1n02n02z
18. Ericsson, K.A., Simon, H.A.: Protocol Analysis: Verbal Reports as Data. MIT (1984)
19. Knoll, T.: The think-aloud protocol. In: Drachen, A., Mirza-Babaei, P., Nacke, L. (eds.) Games User Research. Oxford University Press (2018)
20. Siddiq, F., Sherer, R.: Revealing the processes of 'students' interaction with a novel collaborative problem-solving task: an in-depth analysis of think-aloud protocols. Comput. Hum. Behav. **76**(Nov), 509–525 (2017)
21. Atlas.ti. Scientific Software Development GmbH
22. Bemong, N., Borghart, P.: Bakhtin's theory of the literary chronotope: reflection, applications, perspectives. In: Bemong, N., Borghart, P., De Dobbeleer, M., Demoen, K., De Temmerman, K., Keunen, B., (eds.) 'Bakhtin's Theory of the Literary Chronotope: Reflections, Applications, Perspectives, pp. 1–16. Academia Press, Ghent (2010)
23. Bakhtin, M.M.: Forms of time and of the chronotope in the novel: notes toward a historical poetics. In: Holquist, M., Bakhtin, M.M. (eds.) The Dialogic Imagination: Four Essays, pp. 84–258. University of Texas Press (1990)
24. Barbara, J., Haahr, M.: Who am I that acts? The use of voice in virtual reality interactive narratives. In: Mitchell, A., Vosmeer, M. (eds.) ICIDS 2021. LNCS, vol. 13138, pp. 3–12. Springer, Cham (2021). https://doi.org/10.1007/978-3-030-92300-6_1
25. Sagae, K., et al.: A data-driven approach for classification of subjectivity in personal narratives. In: Finlayson, M.A., Fisseni, B., Lowe, Meister, J.C. (eds.) Workshop on Computational Models of Narrative, pp. 198–213. OpenAccess Series in Informatics. Dagstuhl Publishing (2013)
26. Arseth, E.: A narrative theory of games. In: FDG 2012. ACM (2012). 978-1-4503-1333-9/12/05
27. Mawhorter, P., Mateas, M., Wardrip-Fruin, N.: Generating relaxed, obvious, and dilemma choices with Dunyazad. In: AAAI Conference on Artificial Intelligence and Interactive Digital Entertainment, pp. 58–64 (2015)
28. Kreminski, M., Wardrip-Fruin, N.: Sketching a map of the Storylets design space. In: Rouse, R., Koenitz, H., Haahr, M. (eds.) ICIDS 2018. LNCS, vol. 11318, pp. 160–164. Springer, Cham (2018). https://doi.org/10.1007/978-3-030-04028-4_14
29. Knoller, N., Roth, C., Haak, D: A Complexity Analysis Matrix for Narrative Userly Texts (2021). https://doi.org/10.13140/RG.2.2.16551.68004
30. Yoon, S, Goh, S.-E., Yang, Z. : Toward a learning progression of complex systems understanding. Complicity: Int. J. Complex. Educ.**16**(1) (2019). https://doi.org/10.29173/cmplct 29340
31. Wright, J.J.: IDN tree complexity. MS Thesis, School for Professional Studies, Graduate Center, City University of New York (2022). https://rpubs.com/JackJWright/902090
32. Elo, A.E.: The Rating of Chessplayers, Past and Present. Arco Pub, Tomar (1978)

Integrating Brechtian Concepts in the Design of a Tangible Narrative: The Case of "The Non-myth of the Noble Red"

Daniel Echeverri[(⊠)] [iD]

Department of Visual Computing, Faculty of Informatics, Masaryk University, Brno, Czech Republic
Daniel.Echeverri@mail.muni.cz

Abstract. Extending previous research on tangible narratives, this paper introduces a new design case - *The Non-myth of the Noble Red*. The preliminary work for building the case draws from and tests against a typology that characterises the tangible artefacts with narrative meaning and a narrative architecture for tangible narratives. The paper exemplifies how *The Non-myth of the Noble Red* integrates concepts from Brechtian theatre and presents its technical considerations. It concludes with the importance of emphasising the critical discourse of the narrative and that examining alternative storytelling methods allows the author to approach concepts that are rarely considered in conventional interactive media.

Keywords: Tangible Narratives · Interactive storytelling · Tangible interaction · Epic Theatre · *The Non-myth of the Noble Red*

1 Introduction

Interactive media that combines physical manipulation of objects, interactivity and narrative are commonly known as tangible narratives [7]. On the one hand, they contain a plot and present a world that individuals and objects populate. On the other hand, its computational components subtly support unfolding the narrative in the background [7, 10]. Combining these aspects brings interesting opportunities to design experiences that integrate concepts from other practices to inform how people interact and how the narrative's message can be brought forward. This paper introduces *The Non-myth of the Noble Red*. This tangible narrative uses a series of computationally enhanced cardboard puppets which allow the user to interact with a physical environment to unfold the narrative. The paper departs from the discussion presented in [4] while mainly focusing on its narratological and authorial aspects. This design case integrates aspects from the study of tangible interaction and performative arts, notably Bertolt Brecht's *Epic Theatre* [2]. The core purpose of looking at Brecht's work in building this tangible narrative is to bring forward, probe, and exploit gendered roles inherited from prototypical western literature, for instance, the active male or passive female characters [15], or the adventurous hero and the helpless, family-dependent heroine [17], by providing people engaging with the narrative with ways to bend, break, or follow these roles.

© The Author(s), under exclusive license to Springer Nature Switzerland AG 2022
M. Vosmeer and L. Holloway-Attaway (Eds.): ICIDS 2022, LNCS 13762, pp. 383–394, 2022.
https://doi.org/10.1007/978-3-031-22298-6_23

This design case aims to explore alternative approaches to designing and authoring tangible narratives and to study the implications they might have on social dynamics and comprehension during the narrative experience. This paper briefly discusses *Epic Theatre* and its implications for analysing interactive narratives. Then it introduces *The Non-myth of the Noble Red*, discusses its authoring and technological considerations, and compares the design approaches between *Letters to José*, an earlier tangible narrative case, and *The Non-myth of the Noble Red*. Finally concludes with the importance of exploring alternative authoring methods for interactive narratives.

2 *Epic Theatre* and Its Implications for Interactive Narratives

As a counter comment to *Aristotelian* or classic drama, playwright Bertolt Brecht proposed the idea of *Epic Theatre* [2]. Classic drama offers an *illusion* to the audience that develops empathy toward what is narrated. In contrast, *Epic Theatre* is anti-illusionist and self-conscious [2]. According to Brecht, through the *Verfremdung* effect, *V-Effekt*, estrangement, distancing, or the alienation effect, it is possible to eliminate any sense of immersion and "alienate the social gest underlying every incident" [2]. Considering Marxist theories, *Epic Theatre* is associated with the ideas of *social gestus* and *historicisation* [2]. The alienation effect drives the spectators to think about the social repercussions of what is presented, placing in the forefront its social realities and historical aspects [2].

A Brechtian understanding of the study of interactive narratives has been explored before. For instance, Hammond, Pain, and Smith [9], discussing player agency, argued that from a Brechtian approach, while the narrative constrains the players, the experience allows them to reflect outside of it by "reminding them that they are witnessing an artificial representation." Similarly, de Wildt [18] argues that exemplified in the game *Spec Ops: the Line*, the player's identity with their character is disrupted during what can be described as alienating moments: characters asking the player to quit the game or a loading screen that display the number of casualties. De Wildt notes that through those alienating moments, the game challenges the player's ideologies and brings them forward social realities. Dunne [3] describes two forms of alienation in video games: *aesthetic alienation*, for instance, when bugs and glitches are integrated into the story world—and *system alienation*—where the system and its relationship with the game are brought into the narrative itself. While aesthetic alienation reminds the players their engagement with a simulation, system alienation blurs the line between the diegesis of the game and the implications of the players' actions (e.g., tampering with the external files or cheating). Finally, Mitchell [12], considering Shklovsky's concept of *defamiliarisation*, which is closely related to Brecht's alienation effect because both estrange the habitual and familiar [14], suggests a series of techniques that defamiliarise the players and, in a certain way, allows them to see things differently. These techniques refer to removing control from the player, for instance, through cut scenes, breaking the flow of game time, by placing the character in another location after a break, or by blurring the boundaries of the form, for example, by making the experience of the game more like watching a film than a game on itself. While Shklovsky's *defamiliarisation* in interactive narratives can be used to examine how the user is estranged through play, Brecht's alienation can analyse how formal devices are used to bring forward social conflicts and problems [14]. However, it is important to note that alienation is not exclusively a Brechtian outcome but also a tool used in designing interactive narratives. For instance, in *Metal Gear Solid*, a boss character comments on the player's save files. In *Boktai: The Sun is in Your Hand*, by standing in the sunlight, the player can recharge batteries the character can use later on in the game, or in *The Stanley Parable*, where there is always a conflict between what the narrator tells and what the player does [1].

Although the cases described in this section look at the work of Bertolt Brecht as a theoretical lens for the analysis and design of interactive narratives, these experiences are limited to onscreen interaction. This presents an interesting opportunity to consider Brechtian concepts in authoring tangible interactive narratives. Can the alienation effect inform not only the design of the experience and the story but also the design of how people interact with tangible artefacts in the narrative? A Brechtian approach to tangible narratives possibly implies dismissing the idea that the tangible is trying to be something else. In its place, the narrative should instead focus on more socially significant aspects of the story by using the tangible as a whimsical gesture that suggests something without entirely portraying it. That is what *The Non-myth of the Noble Red* intends to explore.

3   The Non-myth of the Noble Red

The Non-myth of the Noble Red (henceforth, *The Non-myth*) is a tangible narrative that conceptually expands upon the theoretical and design learnings reported in the research and design of *Letters to José*, an earlier tangible narrative case [5, 7]. This narrative was presented as three paper-based story worlds that depicted the exchange of letters between two brothers. Each story world was comprised of separate panels that acted as the story's stage and interface. As a stage, they allowed the enactment of various narrative aspects. As an interface, the panels allowed the person to control how the system presented the narrative, for instance, by triggering sound after touching or manipulating an object. The design of *Letters to José* and an empirical study revealed multiple considerations for authoring tangible narratives [6]. Among these is a narrative architecture—which considers several levels of narrative and non-narrative content—and a typology of tangible artefacts for storytelling—which describes artefacts from their position in the narrative, their function, the relationship between action and outcome, and the interaction methods it allows [5]. These considerations have significantly influenced the design and authoring of *The Non-myth*.

The plot of *The Non-myth* is relatively concise: The Villainous Yellow threatens a community. The Noble Red, the descendant of the Hopeless Grey—ruler of the land, is ultimately taken to the villain's lair when the villain asks for a sacrifice to soothe its wrath. As soon as the Heroic Blue learns of this, it chooses to act to save everyone. At this point, the narrative departs from convention and raises many questions in the story that the users/performers must eventually answer: Does the Noble Red want to be saved? Can it protect itself without help from the Heroic Blue, or is the Noble Red really the weakest link in the story? Does the Villainous Yellow want to be a villain? Is the Heroic Blue indeed needed? It is up to the users to answer these questions.

The main conflict in the original myth—the eventual encounter between the maiden, the hero, and the villain—is positioned at the centre of *The Non-myth*, not as the narrative's opening point but rather as its middle. The progression through the plot of *The Non-myth* depends on the choices made by the users. In contrast to the first act, where users advance the narrative episodically and rarely interact with other characters, the second and third acts depend on the choices and actions made together. They have three options for getting to the conflict's resolution: two can choose the same path, take different paths, or none, as the story can catastrophically end with no other paths to choose from. In any case, the narrative does not prescribe an ending; instead, it allows the users to explore the options and mutually decide which conclusion best matches their interpretation of the plot.

3.1   Epic Theatre and *The Non-myth of The Noble Red*

The Non-myth considers principles from Brecht's *Epic Theatre* to explore alternative approaches to authoring interactive digital narratives. Its narrative architecture is grounded on the learnings gained from the design of *Letters to José*, while the story is inspired by U.A. Fanthorpe's poem "Not my best side" [8]. Fanthorpe's poem criticises the myth of Saint George and its depiction in Paolo Uccello's "St. George and the Dragon." Although the myth narrates the typical struggle between good and evil, Fanthorpe's poem critiques conventional gender and mythological roles depicted in Uccello's painting (and the myth itself). In *The Non-myth*, the Dragon, St. George, and the maiden from the original tale were transformed into the Villainous Yellow, the Heroic Blue, and the Noble Red, respectively. The resulting characters preserve some of the few but essential characteristics of the original narrative.

As encouraged by Brecht, many representative aspects of the original myth are questioned through interruptions and inconsistencies [2], breaking the illusion of the narrative and alienating the user. Brecht proposed several ways to accomplish the alienation effect. For example, through fourth wall breaks [2]. In this case, *The Non-myth* always distances the users from their performing character. For instance, at the beginning of the story, once the user chooses a character, the system states:

```
Instead of being noble or heroic, you decided to perform as the
Villainous Yellow.
```

As such, according to the rules of mythology, the Villainous Yellow, a really mean being, lived alone at The High (in the geography of *The Non-myth*, the highest point) inside an empty, dark space.

Other methods included transposing into the third person (through a narrator) and transposing into the past, allowing the character (and audience) to look back [2]. According to Brecht, the latter announces to the audience what already has happened, providing a different general standpoint. *The Non-myth* also uses this method. For instance:

`The Heroic Blue walked closer to the Low` (in the geography of *The Non-myth*, the lowest point) `to better look at the Villainous Yellow. It indeed looked big and menacing from afar.`

The use of stage directions and commentaries out loud are other methods common in *Epic Theatre,* which are also considered in *The Non-myth.* While on the stage, the director provides these directions; in *The Non-myth,* it is the system that does it by addressing the user as *performer*:

`Performer, after a few days, were there enough crops for the Villainous Yellow to eat?`

Some Brechtian methods are combined to reinforce the distancing from the story allowing the creation of prompts where the user considers the implications of their choices. For instance, at the start of the second act—the conflict—the user playing as the *Noble Red*—representing the implicitly feminine character—must decide if the "hero" saves the *Noble Red* or faces the villain by itself. The narrative alienates the users by providing a statement that presents, in Brecht's words, "an expectation that is justified by experience but, in the event, disappointed" [2]. In *The Non-myth,*

First, it presents the users with two hypothetical possibilities, the second one alienated. In other words, *this could have happened, but instead, this happened.*

`The Noble Red was not confident about being saved but confused.`

Then provides two paths, one that answers to the stereotypical attitude,

`After thinking for a while, the Noble Red decided the Heroic Blue should rescue it... after all, it was the Heroic Blue's mythological duty`

While the other breaks said stereotype,

`After thinking things better, the Noble Red decided to take the Villainous Yellow by itself... after all, heroes were a thing of the past.`

Similarly, other texts also alienate the user by driving attention to specific peculiarities of what is narrated. For instance,

`The Villainous Yellow waited inside a cave for its sacrifice to arrive. Surprisingly, both the Noble Red and the Heroic Blue arrived at the same time. In fact, the Villainous Yellow was not expecting a hero to step into its story.`

Although the story is told through audio and resources common to Brechtian theatre, such as placards or projections [2] are not used, others, such as music or spoken voice, play an important role. Auditive notifications tell the start of each act to the users, while music indicates alienating pauses where users are supposed to perform and others to observe.

Brecht also noted that the actor is alienated from the story, arguing that they do not become the characters but *show* them instead, comparing this to how Chinese theatre actors look at their hands [2]. Something similar happens in *The Non-myth* when the users "wear" the puppet in their hands. Coordinating the puppets' movements compels the users to keep attention to how their hands move—with the puppet—in the physical space of the experience. This also relates to Brecht's note on the visibility of the technical aspects behind the story [2]—not only to highlight them but reveal the work of those behind the stage. In *The Non-myth,* these aspects (e.g., the wiring and connectors) are only visible on the back of the puppet, which only its corresponding user can see.

In summary, the authoring of *The Non-myth* uses several Brechtian methods to distance the user from the story. These methods include:

- **Breaking the fourth wall:** It changes the attention of what is depicted in the story to the audience.
- **Transposing:** These provide a different standpoint of the narrative. It usually focuses on the consequences of what is described.
- **Providing commentaries and directions:** They add an external voice to the narrative with remarks about what is being depicted.
- **Highlighting peculiarities of the narrative:** It takes an everyday moment and brings out what makes it unique.
- **Creating musical and auditive pauses:** It breaks an action at crucial moments. It becomes a counterpoint of the action.
- **Making visible technical aspects:** It breaks the illusion of the stage that intends to hide its inner workings.
- **Focusing on movement:** It makes self-observation an act of awareness.

3.2   Artefact and Narrative in the Non-myth of the Noble Red

The user interacts with *The Non-myth* through cardboard puppets worn in the user's hand, comparable to glove puppets (Fig. 1). They are computationally enhanced and use mechanisms that borrow inspiration from traditional Indonesian puppetry, Chinese shadow puppets, and Eastern European marionettes. The Puppets (and the users) can interact with other puppets, spaces, and objects through different sensors. Previous studies have demonstrated that puppets as interfaces: mediate between imagination and the real world [13], promote self-recognition [11], enhance digital/physical interactions [16], increase users' feelings of agency, and make the narrative more expressive and spontaneous [6].

The typology of *artefacts for storytelling* [5] describes tangible narrative artefacts in three qualities: *diegesis, embodiment,* and *function,* as well as the interaction methods that allow the creation of relationships with the physical world (Table 1):

Considering the above, the puppets in *The Non-myth* can be described mainly as *trans-diegetic* because their representation bridges the real world and the story world, *fully embodied* because action and outcome manifest in the same space, and *ontological* because the choices taken by the user can alter the plot.

Fig. 1. The Heroic Blue (Color figure online).

Table 1. Summary of qualities and methods in *the artefacts for storytelling* typology [5].

Diegesis	Embodiment	Function	Interaction Methods
If artefact and representation exist in the space-time of the narrative	The closeness between the action and the outcome of that action	How the actions made through the artefact can influence the story	
Diegetic: Its representation is the same in the storyworld and the real world	Full: It is the means of performance and the space where the outcome manifests	Ontological: Represents possible decisions or consequences. It can change the plot	Space-directed: how a person negotiates and navigates a space by manipulating an object
Transdiegetic: It exists in the storyworld and the real world. It bridges both worlds	Coupled: the result of the performance happens very near	Exploratory: offers changes in the perspective of the narrative. It does not change the plot	Artefact-directed: how the person creates relationships between one or more artefacts
Extradiegetic: It exists in the narrative system but resides outside the storyworld	Non-graspable: the artefact has a relationship with another detached artefact		Body-directed: related to the person's awareness of their bodies

The puppets in the most recent prototype of *The Non-myth* are attached to the user's wrist for support. A battery-powered *ESP32* microcontroller is housed on the wrist of the user and connected to sensors placed across the puppet: two capacitive sensors in the microcontroller housing, a colour sensor on one *leg* of the puppet, an NFC/RFID tag reader on its *hand*, and an accelerometer and gyroscope sensor in its *torso*.

A puppet can interact with objects and other puppets through *artefact-directed* methods like tapping and "touching", thanks to the NFC reader affixed to its hand (Fig. 2). Through *space-directed methods* such as walking and moving, assisted by a matrix of capacitive surfaces spread out on the environment of the storyworld and various coloured shapes positioned on top of these surfaces, the system can also track the puppet's location (Fig. 3).

Body-directed methods are quite important because the puppet is moved through the hand. The users have a rod attached to their thumb to move the puppet's hand while they imitate the gesture of walking by placing their index and middle fingers on the puppet's legs (Fig. 3). The motion sensor, mounted on the puppet's torso, allows the device to monitor movement. Allowing movement increases the naturalness of the experience and expands how the user can engage with various narrative elements. Finally, the user can select "a" or "b"-like options using two capacitive sensors placed on the microcontroller's enclosure (Fig. 4).

Fig. 2. Top view of two puppets interacting with the prototype environment

Fig. 3. The Villainous Yellow (left) and the Heroic Blue (right) puppets interact (Color figure online).

Fig. 4. Making choices through the microcontroller enclosure.

The Non-myth runs on an installation of *NodeRed*, an open-source tool designed for *Internet of Things* systems that allow devices to exchange data (Fig. 5). Each Puppet runs a web server that sends data from and to the sensors to a *NodeRed* flow. Content is provided directly to the user through a *Twine* story, which in the case of *The Non-myth*, is served from within *NodeRed*. The user's mobile phone access the Twine story and delivers it audibly. This way, the users rely on a set of earphones to listen to spoken audio while engaging with the story. Since they do not have to interact with the screen, the users can keep the mobile in their pocket while engaging with the story.

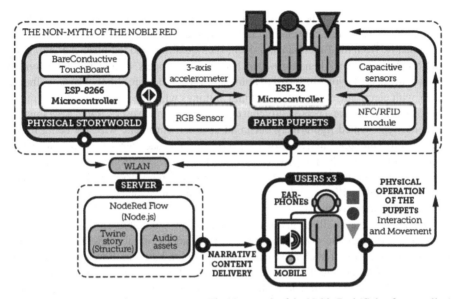

Fig. 5. Map of the technology that supports The Non-myth of the Noble Red (Color figure online)

4 Discussion

Comparatively, while artefacts in *Letters to José* sought to represent the reality of the narrative (e.g., a church or a clinic) and users were expected to interact according to that reality (e.g., driving a car), in *The Non-myth of the Noble Red*, artefacts hint and symbolise a story world that is presented from multiple, synchronous perspectives with rules that differ from reality (e.g., symbolised objects, abstract shapes, and colour codes that point towards more complex ideas). In *Letters to José*, authoring the story was to allow people to enact a character's life. In contrast, in *The Non-myth of the Noble Red*, the authoring is about making visible the social repercussions of rejecting certain roles by relying on methods that seek to keep the user conscious of their actions.

From the perspective of the *artefacts for storytelling* typology, in The *Non-myth of the Noble Red*, *trans-diegetic* artefacts like the Puppets—allow the user to move between the reality of the story world and the real world and have a more prominent role compared to artefacts in *Letters to José*. While in *Letters to José*, most tangible artefacts were either *diegetic*—the same representation in the real world and story world, for instance, Jesús is represented in a movable cardboard avatar—or *extra diegetic*—which only exists in the real world and usually control the way the narrative is expressed, like a switch or a button—in *The Non-myth*, a single puppet assumed multiple diegetic qualities and expressed aspects of the narrative in different ways, always bridging both story and the real world. For instance, the puppet blinks a light to indicate something will happen but also can physically stand over a shape to hint at an imaginary place in the physical environment of the story. This back-and-forth between conceptual spaces is always supported by the audio conveyed to the user. Although the puppets in *The Non-myth* are technically much more complex artefacts compared to the cardboard avatar in *Letters to José*, it is in the artefact's ability to be *trans-diegetic* and *fully embodied* that shortens the distance between interaction and narrative.

Ironically, from the Brechtian approach, such qualities also facilitate estranging the user from the narrative. Alienation occurs because the puppets' design does not intend to represent anything beyond its bipedal, humanoid form. They are simply black cardboard vessels with electronic components that hint at things which the user to express through them. The Puppets have a personality that develops only in the user's mind, a personality that is not represented figuratively but in an abstract, chromatic way. By being *trans-diegetic, fully embodied,* and *ontological (*as the actions made through them can change aspects of the story)*, the puppets' design and the story's environment allow the user to move more consciously between the real world and the story world. This interplay movement limits the illusion offered by traditional narrative methods, bringing forward the real implications of the story.

Considering the qualities given to an artefact in a tangible narrative allows the designer to consider the potential narrative affordances of such artefacts. This way, the designer is aware of such affordances and can plan based on how the artefact tells the story through the multiple connections between diegetic, functional, and embodied qualities and methods. Ultimately, these connections support the user's imagination, motivations, enjoyment, and sense of feeling rewarded, among other phenomena and subjective experiences, when engaging with the story.

5   Conclusions

This paper briefly discussed the implications of *Epic Theatre* in designing interactive narratives. The paper presented *The Non-myth of the Noble Red*, which builds on reported learnings from authoring and designing *Letters to José* [7]. *The Non-myth* incorporates ideas from the study of performative art, particularly Brechtian theatre. This coupling examines performative arts as a source for innovative and unique approaches to creating interactive narratives. The strategy emphasises the exploration of distinct aesthetic approaches to storytelling and the critical discourse of the narrative. The authoring of *The Non-myth* was about making visible, questioning, and challenging assumed roles inherited from prototypical western literature by providing ways to bend, break, or follow them. This was achieved by using authoring methods brought from Bertolt Brecht's *Epic Theatre* to distance the users from the story and facilitate their focus on the social implications of the narrative. A fully working version of *The Non-myth* has yet to be entirely developed, although the paper reports in the latest prototype. Still, the author believes that the ideas and questions raised here can help guide and motivate future efforts to create engaging tangible narratives. Future work will look a finishing a fully working prototype and conducting a study that will look at the impact of Brechtian principles in the narrative, the possible emergent social dynamics during the experience, and draw considerations for the design of tangible narratives.

Acknowledgements. The author thanks the Department of Visual Computing of the Faculty of Informatics at Masaryk University for the resources and support in developing this work. The author also thanks Prof. Huaxin Wei from the School of Design at The Hong Kong Polytechnic

University for her constructive feedback and comments on this paper and Prof. Martina Musilová from the Department of Theatre Studies of the Faculty of Arts at Masaryk University for her thoughtful advice.

References

1. Akay, K., Simsek, C.N.: Design of alienation in video games. In: Lee, N. (ed.) Encyclopedia of Computer Graphics and Games, pp. 1–6. Springer, Cham (2018). https://doi.org/10.1007/978-3-319-08234-9_150-1
2. Brecht, B.: Brecht on Theatre. Bloomsbury Academic, London; New York (2019)
3. Dunne, D.J.: Brechtian alienation in videogames. Press Start 1(1), 79–99 (2014)
4. Echeverri, D.: The non-myth of the noble red: exploring Brechtian principles of storytelling and performance in the authoring of a tangible narrative. In: Proceeding of CC 2022, Venice, Italy, p. 6. ACM Press (2022). https://doi.org/10.1145/3527927.3535207
5. Echeverri, D., Wei, H.: Designing physical artifacts for tangible narratives: lessons learned from letters to José. In: Proceeding of TEI 2021, Salzburg, Austria. ACM Press (2021). https://doi.org/10.1145/3430524.3446070
6. Echeverri, D., Wei, H.: Exploring the experience with tangible interactive narrative: Authoring and evaluation of Letters to José. Entertain. Comput. 44, 100535 (2023). https://doi.org/10.1016/j.entcom.2022.100535
7. Echeverri, D., Wei, H.: Letters to José: a design case for building tangible interactive narratives. In: Bosser, A.-G., Millard, D.E., Hargood, C. (eds.) ICIDS 2020. LNCS, vol. 12497, pp. 15–29. Springer, Cham (2020). https://doi.org/10.1007/978-3-030-62516-0_2
8. Fanthorpe, U.A.: Not my best side. In: Selected Poems, pp. 28–29. Penguin Books, London, UK (1986)
9. Hammond, S., et al.: Player agency in interactive narrative: audience, actor & author. In: Proceedings of the AISB Annual Convention, Newcastle upon Tyne, UK, pp. 386–393. Artificial Societies for Ambient Intelligence (2007)
10. Harley, D., et al.: Towards a framework for tangible narratives. In: Proceedings of TEI 2016, Eindhoven, Netherlands, pp. 62–69. ACM Press (2016). https://doi.org/10.1145/2839462.2839471
11. Mazalek, A., et al.: Recognising self in puppet controlled virtual avatars. In: Proceedings of the 3rd International Conference on Fun and Games - Fun and Games 2010, Leuven, Belgium, pp. 66–73. ACM Press (2010). https://doi.org/10.1145/1823818.1823825
12. Mitchell, A.: Making the familiar unfamiliar: techniques for creating poetic gameplay. In: Proceedings of 1st International Joint Conference of DiGRA and FDG, Dundee, Scotland, UK, p. 16. Digital Games Research Association (2016)
13. Nitsche, M., McBride, P.: A character in your hand: puppetry to inform game controls. In: Proceedings of DiGRA 2018, p. 16 (2018)
14. Pötzsch, H.: Playing Games with shklovsky, brecht, and boal: Ostranenie, V-Effect, and Spect-actors as analytical tools for game studies. Game Studies 17, 2 (2017)
15. Rubegni, E., et al.: Detecting gender stereotypes in children digital storytelling. In: Proceedings of the 18th ACM International Conference on Interaction Design and Children, Boise, ID, USA, pp. 386–393. ACM (2019). https://doi.org/10.1145/3311927.3323156

16. Sakashita, M., et al.: You as a puppet: evaluation of telepresence user interface for puppetry. In: Proceedings of the 30th Annual ACM Symposium on User Interface Software and Technology, Québec City, QC, Canada, pp. 217–228. ACM (2017). https://doi.org/10.1145/3126594.312 6608
17. Toomeos-Orglaan, K.: Gender stereotypes in Cinderella (ATU 510A) and the princess on the Glass Mountain (ATU 530). J. Ethnol. Folkloristics **7**(2), 49–64 (2013)
18. de Wildt, L.: Enstranging play: distinguishing playful subjecthood from governance. In: Proceedings of the Philosophy of Computer Games Conference 2014, Istanbul, Turkey, p. 23 (2014)

Exploring Classical Music Narratives Through Multimodality in AR/VR Experiences

Svetlana Rudenko, Maura McDonnell, Timothy Layden, and Mads Haahr[✉]

School of Computer Science and Statistics, Trinity College, Dublin 2, Ireland
haahrm@tcd.ie

Abstract. Although Music is considered the field of emotions and moods, every composition has a structure: beginning, development, climax and conclusion. In classical music, there are many genres, but each piece always tells a story. Even more, most classical compositions follow the familiar structure of Aristotelian drama. Classical music narrative can take a number of forms: as music analysis on structures of the form (e.g., *Sonata* form with contrasting themes), emotional narrative (usually miniatures dedicated to one mood range, e.g., the genre of Prelude) or a program narrative according to composer's notes (e.g., Berlioz's *Symphonie Fantastique*). Generally speaking, perception of music is multisensory, so when music tells a story, it does so in a multimodal fashion. In this position paper, we present our investigation into visualisation of music narrative based on different forms of music narratives, and then show how visuals developed by cross-modal associations and synaesthesia art can be used to construct music narrative that is interactive. Our ultimate aim is to develop the approach into AR/VR visualisations of classical music with a strong narrative content.

Keywords: Interactive narrative · Music narrative · AR/VR · Synaesthesia art

1 Introduction

The advent of digital technologies is of course the foundation for Interactive Digital Narrative (IDN). The digital representations of more traditional storytelling forms (e.g., text, film, comic books, etc.) have allowed modes of interactivity that the original forms did not support and resulted in new experiences, such as hypertext, interactive cinema and interactive graphic novels [1]. Music plays a considerable supportive role in many IDN works, but it is often given less (or at least, secondary) attention compared to many other interactive narrative elements, such as plot, setting, character, visuals, and of course agency. Generally speaking, perception of music is multisensory [2], so when music tells a story, it does so in a multimodal fashion. This is an important consideration when music is used to support an existing narrative where the story is primarily told through other modalities, but it also means that the use of music as a narrative medium is more complex than it may appear at a first glance.

Fred Everett Maus observed that, "[f]or many listeners, some instrumental music, especially in the tradition from Haydn and Mozart through Brahms, invites comparison

M. Vosmeer and L. Holloway-Attaway (Eds.): ICIDS 2022, LNCS 13762, pp. 395–404, 2022.
https://doi.org/10.1007/978-3-031-22298-6_24

to drama or narrative" [3]. While music is often used in a supportive narrative function, it can also serve as the primary motor in a narrative experience, especially when used in a deliberately multimodal fashion, such as through multisensory design [4]. Music narrative can take several forms: as music analysis on structures of the form (e.g., Sonata form with contrasting themes), emotional narrative (usually miniatures dedicated to one mood range, e.g., the genre of Prelude) or program narrative according to composer's notes (e.g., Berlioz's *Symphonie Fantastique*). For example, the Classical Sonata form has ABA structure: Exposition, Development, Recapitulation, which is similar to the Aristotelian dramatic arc. In short, every composition has a narrative, or even multiple narratives co-existing as different forms.

In this position paper, we are concerned with what technology can offer to classical music and its potential for interactive narratives. The purpose of the paper is to show how music can serve not only as a tool for supporting a narrative that is primarily written in text or visuals (as is typical for most IDN works), but also how it can serve as a primary narrative motor, i.e., where the music is narrative in itself. Our approach is to present and discuss three experimental works – one by other researchers and two of our own – and discuss their potential for interactive narrative content. The works reviewed are primarily AR/VR applications that create visuals for representing narrative content of classical music. Not all the case studies are interactive in the sense that they give the audience authorial control, but they are all dynamic and allow the audience to interact with the content through attention direction and exploration. Some of the works allow interaction by the performer (rather than the audience), which is a mode of interaction not typically supported by IDN works because the author is typically absent during the experience. While the interactions offered by the case studies can be considered somewhat basic, they are nevertheless there, and an important contribution of our paper is to identify and discuss them as first steps in a new form. The purpose of this analysis is help us understand the potential for such music-driven experiences to create future interactive narratives, especially through the visualisation of music narrative structures.

Visual music is of course not a new field. In the context of pop/rock, Pink Floyd pioneered laser visuals in the 1980s, and later, more digitally based genres of music have developed visualisation concepts further. Earlier examples of visualisations inspired by music include Disney's *Fantasia* from 1940 and visuals developed for classical music by Oscar Fischinger [5] and Mary Ellen Bute [6]. The complexity of classical music and sensitive content of intellectual emotion makes visualisation approaches intriguing but raises the question: What approaches to music visualisation are suitable for music narratives, i.e., which approaches engage in a suitable fashion with music plot and dramaturgy and still remain true to musicology? [7].

A promising starting point can be found in recent research on music consciousness and perception [8, p. 271], which has brought to view sensory aspects of imagery and music as a multimodal experience [9]. Synaesthesia Art based on music, in particular, offers interesting insights on interconnection between different sensory modalities [10]. Ramachandran and Hubbard called synaesthesia "a window into perception, thought and language" [11], and Jamie Ward viewed synaesthesia as a "system to understand variations in human perception" [12]. Modelled on synaesthesia art, multisensory AR/VR applications [13] designed for music could bring new opportunities for interactive narrative experiences.

In the following three sections, we present one related work and two of our own experiments in using music visualisation to realise music narrative already present in classical music and discuss how the visualisations can add dynamic and interactive elements and what their future potential are. In the final section, we conclude the paper.

2 Related Work: Dramatic Progression in Holst's *the Planets*

Augmented Reality (AR) and Mixed Reality (MR) technologies have several promising applications in adding to the experience of live music performances at concert venues. For example, they could supply additional information, such as program notes, and music scores, and also help the audience appreciate the performance and its narrative progression. However, AR/MR also allows more creative features, such as art visualisations intended to resonate with the primary music narrative.

First Augmented Reality Classical Concert is an AR/MR experience based on Gustav Holst's "The Planets" Op. 32, developed in 2017 by Marcel Thomas Geraeds, Cristian Vorstius Kruijff and Jeroen de Mooij [14]. The authors created powerful visualisations based on a 1-min extract of Holst's dramatic music and used Microsoft Hololens to show the visualisations floating above the performers in a concert hall. (See Fig. 1.) The extract was from "Mars, the Bringer of War" which is perhaps the most iconic of the seven movements of Holst's orchestral suite. While the suite also contains movements for Venus, Mercury, Jupiter, Saturn, Uranus and Neptune, the Mars movement is particularly impressive. Written shortly before WW1, and taking the form of a march, the movement

Fig. 1. View through Augmented Reality glasses for classical music concert. Screenshot from video "First Augmented Reality Classical Concert."[1]

---

[1] https://vimeo.com/219373289.

evokes the relentless and unstoppable approach of war and impending violence, opening quietly but soon building to a powerful and dramatic climax. The monumental visuals developed by Geraeds et al. aims to tell the "true story" [14] of the composition and add a strong visual aspect to the already awe-inspiring narrative experience of Holst's music.

Through its novel use of AR visuals, *First Augmented Reality Classical Concert* shows the potential of creative visualisations in a concert hall setting and how dramatic narrative elements inherent in the music can be made more easily accessible to an audience through visualisation. The AR viewer bears witness to the red planet turning slowly, suspended ominously above the performing orchestra. As the music progresses towards its dramatic climax, meteors cut across the concert hall, striking the planet and lighting up its already glowing surface. The animation is a 360 degree visualisation, and the audience member can direct their gaze towards particular elements as they like. However, the animation does not respond to this interaction, and the narrative interaction afforded by the work is therefore one of attention direction, rather than any ability to affect the narrative. This absence of narrative agency resonates well with the movement's theme (the unstoppable approach of war), but it is easy to imagine more sophisticated interactivity being possible for similar experiences based on other themes.

3 Experiment #1: Mood Evocation in Brahms' Intermezzo

While the work discussed in Sect. 2 features a narrative progression that is easy to identify, music narrative can also feature considerably less change in musical texture than Holst's composition. This type of music narrative is more akin to depicting a mood or evoking a setting in the mind of the audience. An example of such a piece is Johannes Brahms' Intermezzo No. 2 Op. 117, which we used for our first experiment. Composed in 1892, the three intermezzi were created for solo piano and are considered to express a certain mood, often described as having an autumnal quality. Composer and Brahms biographer Walter Niemann describes the second intermezzo as follows,

> The second piece in this collection [Intermezzi op. 117] in B-flat minor places Man (*Mittelsatz* in D-flat major) amidst the pallid, fleeting, whirling autumn wind. This deeply restless *Hauptsatz*, expressed in far-reaching arpeggio-like figurations, is thematically almost completely elusive; it is only in the coda, through the repetition of the secondary theme, when this ghostly and shadowy piece synthesizes into one of those deeply and intensely soulful, moving lamentations of life that are so characteristic of Brahms' works. [15, our translation, emphasis added].

Niemann's descriptions show that Brahms' intermezzo is clearly mapped by emotional state narrative. It is evocative of a mood, a feeling, a setting or perhaps a state of mind or consciousness, which is itself narrative in nature.

For our first experiment, we took our starting point in Brahms' composition, but rather than focusing merely on a textual musicology description, such as that offered by Niemann, we developed the experiment based on synaesthesia art. Synaesthesia is a benign condition that is characterised by cross-modal perceptions. In addition to perceiving one stimulus, people with synaesthesia may perceive an additional quality to the experience – a colour or smell or feeling. Jamie Ward mentions that the brain of a new-born baby is cross-modal and infants therefore experience synaesthesia: "The senses are intermingled, in which vision may be triggered by hearing as well as sight, and so on" [16, p. 17]. Further into adulthood, nature protects the brain from sensory overload by separating senses into logical functionalities. Music is one of the stimuli that can induce cross-modal perception. An interesting characteristic of synaesthesia is that the multisensory connection is naturally generated as the result of the neurological activity, and there is evidence that the modalities are synchronised and linked even for non-synaesthetes [17]. Hence, while not everyone experiences the cross-modal connections consciously, it appears that artworks that use them resonate deeply also with people who are not synaesthetes [16]. Charles Spence's summarises this as follows:

A growing body of empirical research on the topic of multisensory perception now shows that even non-synaesthetic individuals experience crossmodal correspondences, that is, apparently arbitrary compatibility effects between stimuli in different sensory modalities. [18]

Our first experiment was realized in the form of a prototype smartphone application that produces AR animations to be used by audience members during live performances of Brahms' composition. The visualization constitutes a support for the music narrative in the form of original artwork by artist-synaesthete Timothy Layden, who has sound to colour and shape synaesthesia, which he used for creative inspiration from Brahms' composition while painting Brahms' Intermezzo live during the performance. We performed 3D modelling of Layden's artwork in Blender and presented it in Unity 3D as an animated, dynamic AR visualization prototype app installed on audience members' smartphones and used during live performances of the Intermezzo to offer an additional layer of experience to the mood of the composition. (See Fig. 2.) Similarly to the work reviewed in Sect. 2, our experiment allows individual audience members to have an interactive multisensory experience of a music narrative during a live performance. However, the smartphone platform offers a different type of interaction and has a different reach than a headset. Moving the handset rather than one's head feels different, and while a

Fig. 2. Screenshot of music consciousness narrative with Synaesthesia Art. Synaesthesia Art by Timothy Layden.[2]

---

[2] https://vimeo.com/556654065.

handset is less immersive than a headset, it is more familiar to audience members. Furthermore, the experience is potentially much more widely available due to the ubiquitous presence of the smartphone compared to the Hololens.

4 Experiment #2: Archetypes in Scriabin's Sonata

As discussed in Sect. 1, there are many types of music narrative, and the works presented in Sects. 2 and 3 engaged with dramatic progression and mood/setting evocation, respectively. Another type of music narrative is structural and relates to the sonata form through a system of archetypes of musical texture. Generally, musical texture can be thought of as a matrix of musical composition, created by complex set of elements such as rhythm, melody, and harmony accompaniment. Musical texture is also an inducer of cross-modal associations. Bulat Galeyev has observed that cross-modal associations are "a normal process in musical thinking" [19], and together with audio stimuli, areas of the brain that are responsible for processing visual, tactile and olfactory experiences, become involved in music listening and musical performance. Again, the phenomenon of synaesthesia is helpful to broaden our understanding of how the sound and music can be perceived [19] and also forms the foundation for our second visualisation experiment.

Alexander Scriabin (1872–1915), is a Russian mystic symbolist composer who was influenced by ideas of Schopenhauer, Nietzsche and theosophy. Scriabin's life ambition was to create a multisensory drama *Mysterium* to influence the human psyche and bring humankind to next level of consciousness [20]. Mystic symbolists believed in the idea of "collective creation, the collaborative attempt to create a bridge between artistic form and events in the real world" [21]. Scriabin's late piano compositions are nearly direct sketches for *Mysterium,* and their themes reflect on certain philosophical categories and symbolic energies [21]. Scriabin was a synaesthete and included a colour organ into his symphonic poem *Prometheus* to make the harmony moves more evident [22]. He composed Sonata No. 5 Op. 53 in 1907 and included the following epigraph, which is helpful as a textual guide to the narrative:

I call you to life, O mysterious forces!

Drowned in the obscure depths

Of the creative spirit, timid

Shadows of life, to you I bring audacity [23]

Like the first experiment from Sect. 3, the second experiment produces visuals for classical music narrative via cross-modal associations and music analysis by the performer. However, where the first experiment used a reflection on a mood as the foundation of the music narrative, the second experiment uses the archetypes of musical texture. Our aim with the second experiment is to show how, with help of visuals based on Musicology and Synaesthesia Art, we can unfold the dramaturgy of the music narrative inherent in Scriabin's Piano Sonata No. 5 Op. 53. As mentioned in Sect. 1, the traditional Sonata form is structured in three parts: Exposition (introduction of contrasting themes and concluding section in unstable dominant key), Development (interaction of themes and transformation through different keys) and Recapitulation (conclusion in main key). In Scriabin's Piano Sonata No. 5 Op. 53, the music narrative follows the composer's structural and philosophical plot, and in our experiment, it is complemented by a visualisation, which is based on cross-modal associations of a performer pianist and the creative sensory responses of a synaesthete artist. The intention is for this organic combination to provide the audience with a visual narrative to complement the music narrative structures. As for the first experiment, the underlying assumption is that the music and visualisation combination will encourage multisensory perception and thereby enrich the audience's aesthetic appreciation of music narrative.

The music narrative in Scriabin's composition is more complex than that of Holst's and Brahms' covered in Sects. 2 and 3 Analysing Scriabin's one-movement late sonatas, Susanna Garcia identified six basic archetypes of musical texture: The Notion of Mystical Unity; The Divine Summons: Fanfare Motive; The Eternal Feminine; Motive of Light; Motive of Flight; and Vertiginous dances [24]. Figure 3 shows a map depicting a music analysis based on the archetypes described by Garcia and additional archetypes developed by us to fit the content and the dramaturgy of the music narrative in Scriabin's Piano Sonata No. 5 Op. 53. The image/animation assigned to each archetype reflects on the symbolic content of the composition. Two art images – Delville's cover from the *Prometheus* score and Vrubel's *The Swan Princess* – are used to reflect on the symbolic philosophical narrative of the composition, complemented with sensory art responses by artists-synaesthetes Timothy Layden and Svetlana Rudenko, and animation by Maura McDonnell.

Fig. 3. Music narrative map showing system of archetypes of musical texture and dramaturgy of Scriabin's Sonata No. 5 Op. 53.

The experiment was performed at the International Association of Synaesthetes, Artists, and Scientists (IASAS) held in October 2019 at the Museum of Moscow. (See

Fig. 4.) Animated images, projected on a screen beside the performing pianist, are used to map the archetypes of musical texture of Scriabin's sonata to follow the dramaturgic development of the composition. The visualisations were controlled by a second performer (a visual artist) who used an interactive digital tool to adapt them live to the specific piano performance. Similarly to the works discussed in previous sections, this experiment allows interaction by the audience directing their attention towards elements of interest, rather than by allowing specific narrative control. While this experiment engages with a more complex music narrative than our first experiment, it offers somewhat lower degree of direct audience interaction. This is something we expect to explore further in future experiments with VR technologies. However, the presence of a second (visual artist) performer to adapt the visualisations through an interactive process is a type of performative interaction that does not exist in the other two case studies and is absent from most types of conventional IDNs.

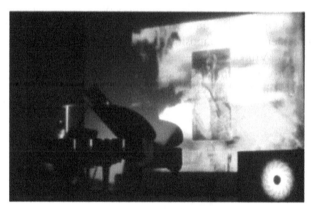

Fig. 4. Photo from concert with visuals reflecting on symbolistic narrative. A. Scriabin. Sonata No. 5, op. 53.[3]

5   Conclusions and Future Work

This paper has explored the use of music visualization of a variety of types of music narrative of a wide range of complexities. We have documented early work in a new category, so many open questions remain. First, the types of music narrative discussed here are merely a small subset of a much wider variety of genres that is ripe for further exploration. While we have focused on classical music, music narrative is more obvious in theatre, ballet and opera. In classical music compositions, music narrative tends to be complex and symbolical and can be challenging unless the composer supplies a written program. While this increases the difficulty of conducting experiments such as those presented in this paper, it also means that there is real potential in the inherent multimodality of AR/VR to guide the audience in their exploration and understanding of

---

[3] https://vimeo.com/337354023.

the music narratives embedded in these complex compositions, as well as the emotional journeys undertaken during the experience of music narrative. Aletta Steynberg writes:

> In Arrival VR, we thought to overcome mere engagement, surpass engrossment, and take the user on a journey of full immersion. Immersion is defined as the engagement of all senses through cognitive processing and natural attention direction. This engagement results in an illusion of embodiment in a non-physical space through the emotional response that influences attention. Player [participant] immersion results in greater emotional connection and internalization of digital narrative. [25]

As mentioned in Sect. 1, perception of music is multisensory [2]. While we have covered AR and projection-based works in this paper, Steynberg's observation that all senses need to be engaged to offer immersion indicates to us that VR seems particularly promising in its ability to emphasise the multisensory experience of music narrative, because it can help increase the immersive qualities of narrative experiences. Additionally, we hope this paper has shown how music can serve not only as a tool for evoking emotion or supporting a narrative in a different medium, but also how it can serve as a primary narrative motor in a new set of experiences, and this is forming the focus for our next experiments in VR.

As discussed in Sect. 1, the works reviewed are relatively basic in the degree of agency offered to the audience: they are limited to attention direction and exploration. However, as discussed in Sect. 5, music narrative has the potential of a performer serving as interactor (perhaps on behalf of the audience), which is a performative mode of interaction not typically offered by IDN works. Nevertheless, most interactive narrative forms give some degree of authorial control to the audience, and an open question relates to how this type of agency could be offered in the context of music narratives. A possible avenue could be to allow audience attention to direct the narrative or visualisation, such as that used in Pia Tikka's film *Obsession* [26].

A particularly important open question concerns the evaluation of audience experience of interactive music narrative works. A suitable methodology should ideally use a combination of quantitative and qualitative methods. For the quantitative part, Likert scale questions should be developed to estimate the audience's degrees of understanding/appreciation of the dramaturgy and music narrative of the work, the self-reported presence/absence of emotional responses, the identification of specific narrative elements (e.g., characters, settings, dramatic progressions), the degree of narrative agency experienced, and finally the audience's overall appreciation of the experience. The qualitative part of the evaluation should focus on a small number of experts (e.g., music educators) and examine their assessment of the suitability of the experiences in different contexts, e.g., for music education in graduate schools.

References

1. Koenitz, H., Ferri, G., Haahr, M., Sezen, D., Sezen, T.I., (eds.) Interactive digital narrative: history, theory and practice. Routledge (2015)

2. Russo, F.: Multisensory processing in music. In: Thaut, M.H., Hodges, D.A., (eds.) The Oxford Handbook of Music and the Brain, Oxford (2019)
3. Maus, F.: Music as Narrative (PhD dissertation, Princeton) (1990)
4. Velasco, C., Obrist, M.: Multisensory experiences: where the senses meet technology. Oxford University Press, Oxford (2020)
5. Lee, C.: Original Creators: Oskar Fischinger, The Father Of Visual Music. Creators (2012). https://creators.vice.com/en_us/article/pgzn97/original-creators-oskar-fischinger-the-father-of-visual-music
6. Gillies, C.: WBUR iLab- Mary Ellen Bute
7. Greckel, W.: Visualisation in the performance of classical music: a new challenge. Q. J. Music Teach. Learn. (1992), Accessed: Feb. 04, 2018. http://www-usr.rider.edu/~vrme/v16n1/volume3/visions/winter6
8. Bailes, F.: Musical imagery and the temporality of consciousness. In: Music and Consciousness, vol. 2, pp. 271–285. Oxford University Press, Oxford (2019)
9. Timmers, R., Gravot, R.: Music as a multimodal experience. Psychomusicology: Music, Mind Brain 26(N2) (2016)
10. Van Campen, C. .: The Hidden Sense. Synesthesia in Art and Science. The MIT Press, Cambridge (2010)
11. Ramachandran, V.S., Hubbard, E.M.: Synaesthesia- a window Into perception, thought and language. J. Conscious. Stud. 8(12), 3–34 (2001)
12. Ward, J.: Synaesthesia as a Model System for Understanding Variation in the Human Mind and Brain. Sussex University (2020). https://files.osf.io/v1/resources/87fuj/providers/osfstorage/5fd1eff80694b7009ef3600e?action=download&direct&version=1
13. Haverkamp, M.: Synesthetic Design: Handbook for a Multi-Sensory Approach. Birkhäuser (2012)
14. Geraeds, M.T., Kruijff, C.V., de Mooij, J,: Augmented Concert (2017). https://www.behance.net/gallery/50955905/Augmented-Concert
15. Niemann, W.: Brahms. Schuster & Loeffler Verlag.; German Language edition (1 Jan. 1920)
16. Ward, J.: The frog who croaked blue: synesthesia and the mixing of the senses. Routledge, London and New York (2008)
17. Bor, D., Rothen, N., Schwartzman, D., Clayton, S., Seth, A.: Adults can be trained to acquire synesthetic experiences. Sci. Rep. 4, (2014). https://www.nature.com/articles/srep07089
18. Parise, C., Spence, C.: Audiovisual crossmodal correspondences and sound symbolism: A study using the implicit association test. Exp. Brain Res. 220(3–4), 319–333 (2012)
19. Galeyev, B.M.: The Nature and Functions of Synesthesia in Music. Leonardo 40(3), 285–288 (2007)
20. Rudenko, S.: Synesthete composer A. Scriabin: Reception History and Archetypal Imagery of Late Piano Miniatures" PhD dissertation (2018). http://digibug.ugr.es
21. Morrison, S.: Scriabin and Theurgy. In: Russian Opera and the Symbolist Movement, p. 184 University of California Press (2002)
22. Gawboy, A.M., Townsend, J.: Scriabin and the possible. Society for Music Theory 18, (2012)
23. Philipp, G., Skrjabin, A.: Ausgewählte Klavierwerke, Leipzig: Edition Peters (1971) Plate E.P. 12588
24. Garcia, S.: Scriabin's Symbolist Plot Archetype in the Late Piano Sonatas. University California Press, vol. 23 (2000)
25. Steynberg, A.J. Using Reverse Interactive Audio Systems (RIAS) to Direct Attention in Virtual Reality Narrative Practices: A Case Study. In: International Conference on Interactive Digital Storytelling, pp. 353–356. Springer, Cham, 2020
26. Tikka, P., Vuori, R., Kaipainen, M.: Narrative logic of enactive cinema: Obsession. Digital Creativity 17(4), 205–212 (2006)

Interactive Storytelling and the Paradox of Democracy

Warren Sack[⊠]

University of California, Santa Cruz, CA 95064, USA
wsack@ucsc.edu

Abstract. Interactive stories have a politics that leans democratic. This politics hinges on the ability of the audience to interrupt and pose a question or ask for an alternative narrative. The history of democratic interactive storytelling in multiple media is briefly outlined. The "paradox of democracy," analogous to the "narrative paradox," is introduced and a challenge for the design of interactive democratic narrative systems – *agency with accountability* -- is presented by shortly examining two implemented systems.

Keywords: Democracy · Narrative paradox · Free speech · Agency · Accountability

1 Introduction

Politics is storytelling. -- US Senator Ted Cruz [1]

In the United States, it is widely recognized by both Republicans and Democrats that storytelling is crucial to politics. On the left, the cognitive scientist George Lakoff [2] is the most visible academic to explain the political importance of framing one's story. The most renowned Republican pollster who crafts stories for the right is Frank Luntz [3]. Freedom of expression is considered to be essential for all participants in a democracy and it is enshrined in the United States Constitution. Yet, allowing any and all stories to be told without regard to truth or honesty poses a problem for democracy. In a recent book, *The Paradox of Democracy: Free Speech, Open Media, and Perilous Persuasion*, media scholars Zac Gershberg and Sean Illing write,

> We call this **the paradox of democracy**: a free and open communication environment that, because of its openness, invites exploitation and subversion from within. [4]

According to them, "throughout history, when new forms of communications arrive—from the disingenuous use of sophistic techniques developed in Athens to the social media–enabled spread of propaganda we see today—they often undermine the practices of democratic politics. The more widely accessible the media of a society, the more susceptible that society is to demagoguery, distraction, and spectacle. We see this

M. Vosmeer and L. Holloway-Attaway (Eds.): ICIDS 2022, LNCS 13762, pp. 405–413, 2022.
https://doi.org/10.1007/978-3-031-22298-6_25

time and again: media continually evolve faster than politics, resulting in recurring patterns of democratic instability." [4] Gershberg and Illing's is the scholar's perspective. In contrast, we argue from a designer's perspective that interactive digital storytelling technologies can be designed for democratic stability, even if the design challenges for doing so are not commonly addressed. We illustrate a design challenge for democratic design – *agency with accountability* -- by shortly reviewing two implemented systems.

2   Interaction and Democratic Surrounds

The introduction of each new medium has engendered the fear that free speech and the power to interrupt will be lost and with it the power to dispute the veracity of the storyteller and to demand alternatives. This fear has spurred innovation. For example, in the early 20th c., Soviet filmmaker Sergei Eisenstein attempted to introduce dialectic—and thus reflective thought—into cinema via the invention of techniques to montage clashing and conflicting clips: "It is art's task to make manifest the contradictions of Being. To form equitable views by stirring up contradictions within the spectator's mind, and to forge accurate intellectual concepts from the dynamic clash of opposing passions" [5].

Later the mass media of film and radio were employed by the Nazis to—as diagnosed by social scientists of the time—hypnotize publics changing them into mobs by depriving them of their ability to think and act as individuals with "democratic personalities." As art and media historian Fred Turner has shown, in order to counteract the Nazi propaganda of mass media, American intellectuals, artists, and government officials "advocated a turn away from single-source mass media and toward multi-image, multi–sound-source media environments" [6] to exercise an individual's abilities of free choice necessary for democratic self-governance. These interactive, multimedia environments of the 1940s and 1950s—Turner calls them "democratic surrounds"—were originally developed in the United States by the refugee artists of the Bauhaus (such as architect Walter Gropius and multimedia artists László Moholy-Nagy and Herbert Bayer) and presaged the digital, interactive environments that came later.

Media ecologist Neil Postman argued that television too (like earlier mass media) undermined the power of literary and conversational interaction and debate so important for democracy [7]. We see the same concerns about contemporary media in the critiques of sociologist Sherry Turkle [8] and others, like Gershberg and Illing.

3   Are Social Media Democratic?

Despite the misgivings of Turkle, Gershberg, Illing and others, it seems, in some ways, as Turner mentions, today's social media environments could be taken to be the fulfillment of the World War II-era vision of a "democratic surround" since all users have the opportunity to also be producers. But the design and the business models employed by social media platforms have worked against their democratic potential. Instead of rational debate and conversation, the social media platforms of today, and the people who post, are incentivized to promote incendiary, polemicizing content and misinformation to increase traffic—the currency of surveillance capitalism [9, 10]; a form of capitalism wherein a business makes money by pulling in users with compelling content, profiling them to determine their likes and dislikes, and then serving them personalized advertising. Without a protocol to circumscribe what is meaningful commentary, interaction on, for example, YouTube frequently materializes the worst nightmares of disfunction projected by the skeptics of democracy—from Plato [11] to Walter Lippmann [12] to today. To reiterate Gershberg and Illing's point, paradoxically providing everyone equal freedom of speech is essential to democracy, yet freedom of speech without accountability fills the public sphere with lies and fake news destructive of democracy.

4   Is Interactive Digital Narrative Democratic?

The politics implicit to IDN is democratic and at odds with the surveillance capitalism of profiling and personalization. This is clear in the concern devoted over the years to user agency, starting with the very first paper presented at the first (2008) incarnation of ICIDS; Andrew Stern, wrote "agency is the primary feature that must be offered players" [13].

The concern in the IDN literature for audience/viewer/player agency continues to the present where other commercial platforms are seen to fall short of the ideal. For example, in their empirical analysis of Netflix's first interactive feature for adults (the 2018 *Bandersnatch* for *The Black Mirror* series), Christian Roth and Hartmut Koenitz conclude that "At the core of the design and enjoyment of Interactive Digital Narratives lies user agency, the power to impact the narrative progression. … However, granting full agency seems not possible with the current Netflix technology and prerecorded material. It is therefore crucial to identify design strategies for offering the audience meaningful choices that use the limited agency this format provides to the best effect" [14]. A subsequent study, by Lobke Kolhoff and Frank Nack, of a larger *Bandersnatch* audience came to similar conclusions: "What we can show is that the basic assumption of all IDN research, namely that people desire agency to alter story paths, is correct" [15].

To surmount the inherent difficulties of contemporary social media platforms, we argue that the important work accomplished by IDN researchers to address the narrative paradox is applicable to addressing the analogous paradox of democracy. The principal difficulty for the democratic design of digital interactive narratives is akin to that of the narrative paradox, the inherent tension between narration and interaction, the tension between the author or performer of a narrative and interactions with the audience, as discussed in the IDN literature (e.g., [16–19]).

5   Institutions of Democracy and the Paradox of System Design

In the terms of classical political theory, the paradox of democracy can be described as the conflict between *isegoria* and *parrhesia* [20]. Both are aspects of free speech but *isegoria* refers to equality of speech and *parrhesia* refers to liberty. *Isegoria* describes the equal right of citizens to speak and act in public. *Parrhesia* describes the right of citizens to say or do whatever they will. Colloquially, liberty/*parrhesia* clashes with equality/*isegoria* when your right to swing your fist meets my nose; when your right to shout drowns out my voice; when your right to tell your story eclipses my opportunity to tell mine. Consequently democratic governments have prohibitions – such as those against slander, libel, and hate speech – that arguably curtail liberty but preserve equality.

The concern in the IDN literature for audience/viewer/player agency employed in solving the narrative paradox needs to be paired with an attention for accountability to address the paradox of democracy. Or, to put it in political terms, a citizen's liberty has to be balanced with a concern for the equality of others so that they too have the same liberty. Thus, in assessing the democratic potential of any given system, we examine both what can be done by a citizen (rights/agency) and the obligations incumbent upon a citizen (responsibility/accountability).

Conventionally, a social science analysis of a social, political or economic system would reduce it to a set of institutions and the rights and responsibilities of the individual; e.g., the constitution, the courts, the executive branch, the legislative branch, etc. According to the Nobel prize winning economist Douglass North, "Institutions are the rules of the game in a society ... They are a guide to human interaction, so that when we wish to greet friends on the street, drive an automobile, buy oranges, borrow money, form a business, bury our dead, or whatever, we know ... how to perform these tasks" [21].

While institutions can be both formal (e.g., the U.S. Constitution) or informal (e.g., how to tell a story to a child), when Gershberg and Illing -- starting at the beginning of their book -- articulate an approach to democracy that eschews an institutional account of democracy in favor of one based on an understanding of the conditions of communication and action available to citizens, they do so because they are predominantly concerned with the weaknesses of formal institutions as an analytical framework. For example, for them, the First Amendment to the United States Constitution engenders and facilitates but does not guarantee free speech in the US. In fact nothing guarantees it indelibly – there are many circumstances in which free speech has been and could be circumscribed. From their perspective the accomplishment of free speech, or democracy more generally, is a precarious one that is emergent from interactions in culture and media. They write, "To see democracy as a culture of free expression is to foreground its susceptibility to endless evolution, even danger" [4].

To understand how institutions "evolve," we need to understand what precedes, follows and surrounds them and thus what is mutually recursively defined with them: social interaction. In social science, it was Harold Garfinkel's book *Studies in Ethnomethodology* [22] that pushed social scientists to think outside the institution and, instead to focus on informal, quotidian, social interaction. From an ethnomethodological perspective social order, like democracy, is produced in and through processes of everyday social interaction. So, even though a formal institution may have a specific authorship and date of authorship (e.g., the Constitutional Convention of 1787), informal institutions are constantly "evolving," constantly being revised on a day-to-day basis.

Starting with Lucy Suchman's 1987 book, *Plans and Situated Actions* [23], ethnomethodology has been widely employed in interaction design, frequently for user needs analysis and user studies of prototyped or completed software systems. It is an empirical science, a form of micro-sociology attendant to the fine-grained details of how work is accomplished in specific settings and how knowledge is situated in those settings. It is not devoted to how things should be – the normative – but rather to the observation of everyday life to see how things are actually accomplished through conversation and action.

The employment of ethnomethodology in the design of technologies has been called "technomethodology" by Graham Button and Paul Dourish [24]. As they point out, the descriptive nature of ethnomethodology is at odds with the necessarily prescriptive agenda of design to make things according to plan. Ethnomethodologists pay attention to the smallest of details of everyday life while designers are compelled to keep the big picture in mind, to be able to see things from top-down, to make sure that the forest doesn't get lost in the trees. This has spawned a paradox: "Ethnomethodology, in attending in particular to the details of everyday action and work practice, has been able to expose an unfortunate paradox in the design of technologies for collaborative activity (or socially-constructed action). This is the *paradox of system design* —that the introduction of technology designed to support 'large-scale' activities while fundamentally transforming the 'small-scale' detail of action can systematically undermine exactly the detailed features of working practice through which the 'large-scale' activity is, in fact, accomplished" [24].

An example of this paradox in action is Facebook which had, in its first mission statement, the goal "to make the world more open and connected" which it has, perhaps, accomplished for some of the world, but while also making some parts of the world more closed and divided. Cases like this motivate ethnomethodology and technomethodology to examine the differences between a formally defined institution (like Facebook, its algorithms, its mission statement, etc.) and the everyday, informal practices, techniques and technologies that animate and change it.

6 Design Challenge: Agency with Accountability

To illustrate how the paradox of democracy was addressed in two example systems, we pay attention to (a) the formal institutions of democracy that inform their respective designs; (b) the points at which their respective designs diverge from the legacy institutions; and (c) the forms of accountability incorporated into their designs. We identify a challenge of *agency with accountability* for democratic system design.

Within ethnomethodology accountability means something very specific. According to Garfinkel, "the activities whereby members produce and manage settings of organized everyday affairs are identical with members' procedures for making those settings 'account-able'" [22]. So accountability is the property of choosing and ordering words and actions to create a stable but contingent production (a system, a situation, a statement, an informal institution, etc.) that can be interrogated and understood according to defined norms or ideals or principles (of rationality, legality, morality, etc.).

Note that in terms of accountability of a software system, this is largely analogous to the current pursuit of explainable artificial intelligence (XAI). For example, if a self-driving car crashes we want to know what it did and why in terms of some set of ideals or principles; we do **not** want to receive an explanation like "it crashed because parameter number 815 million of the neural net had a value of 0.74."

Unlike XAI, agency with accountability needs also to apply, symmetrically, to the human user and entails providing in the system interface principled actions for the user to employ. This is quite unlike what is usually provided in contemporary commercial systems that are driven by personalization algorithms wherein we buy this or watch that because an algorithm put it into our cue and we clicked on it -- not because we made some rational and thus consciously explicable decision to do so. Agency with accountability entails exercising our agency with the system for explicable reasons.

If they are not to be found on commercial platforms, where then are, to cite Roth and Koenitz, the "design strategies for offering the audience meaningful choices"? Democratic design strategies can be found materialized in systems designed for democratic governance and civil society. We shortly present two here: *We Are History: A People's History of Lebanon* [25] and *Peer-to-PCAST* [26].

We Are History was created by Fabiola Hanna for her PhD dissertation at the University of California, Santa Cruz: *Software and Dialogue Aesthetics in Post-Civil War Lebanon.* Employing a set of components familiar to IDN research (a hierarchical task network planner [27], a logic programming language, a language generator [28]) originally developed for a critical update and reimplementation [29] of James Meehan's *TALE-SPIN* system [30], *We Are History* automatically remixes a database of videoed stories from survivors of the Lebanese Civil War (1975–1990). Clips from these interviews are automatically montaged to juxtapose ideologically opposed positions on the Lebanese Civil War.

The *We Are History* system is designed to be an intervention into the institution of secondary education in Lebanon where the Civil War is not taught because – with over one hundred opposing political parties in Lebanon [31] – there is no consensus about the history of the Civil War. The myriad of political parties makes the composition of a textbook on the Civil War impossible. Yet the system database is capacious enough to include stories from all of the opposing parties and the architecture includes a means for viewers to become producers by recording their own story and uploading it into the database. Therefore the system design is made accountable to all parties and, via the montage methods of the system, all of the stories in the database are held to account by being juxtaposed with opposing stories.

Even though there are interesting parallels with previous work presented at ICIDS on the automatic weaving of conversation and narration of testimony (such as David Traum et al.'s work to preserve a Holocaust survivor's interactive storytelling [32]), that previous work aims to allow viewers to pose questions of the primary narrator, but not to present an opposing narrative – for obvious reasons.

The second system, *Peer-to-PCAST* [26] was built with NSF funding (Award #0916292) as an alternative to the official website of the US President's Council of Advisers on Science and Technology (PCAST). The scientific testimony presented to the PCAST is not peer reviewed. *Peer-to-PCAST* was designed to address this oversight by providing a web interface that allows scientific peers to review proffered scientific testimony – even if those peers are not present during the PCAST meeting.

While speakers giving testimony to PCAST, and the scientific advisors of PCAST, are given the floor during the live proceedings of the committee, *Peer-to-PCAST* allows the video of the proceedings to be annotated at any second via a RESTful architecture employing the attributes of the HTML < video > element and code that immediately positions a user in a threaded discussion on a subreddit (of reddit.com) devoted to the recorded testimony. This provides a virtual floor to be yielded to a scientific peer after the proceedings have been recorded and with which the peer can record an objection or provide an alternative.

As a speaker gives testimony to PCAST, *Peer-to-PCAST* dynamically fetches previously published scientific articles by the speaker and those referred to by the speaker. These articles are pulled from scholar.google.com so that they can be read by the viewer; and a citation and social network is drawn linking the speaker to all of their co-authors and publications. The result is a diagram of the speaker's position and standing in the scientific community.

The *Peer-to-PCAST* facilities of peer review of testimony, the background checks of speakers, and the means of annotation differ from all previous instantiations of PCAST. PCAST has been reinstituted in practically every administration since its initiation by President Franklin Roosevelt. Since 1972 there has been an influential legislative context that applies to it: the PCAST and all the other thousand-and-more federal advisory committees operate under the provisions of the FACA, the 1972 Federal Advisory Committee Act [33].

Section 10 of the FACA dictates that all advisory committee meetings are to be open to the public; that notice of the meeting be published in the *Federal Register*; that interested parties be allowed to attend, appear before, or file statements with any advisory committee; that meeting records and minutes be kept; and, that "the records, reports, transcripts, minutes, appendixes, working papers, drafts, studies, agenda, or other documents which were made available to or prepared for or by each advisory committee shall be available for public inspection and copying." *Peer-to-PCAST* provides web-based reinventions of the paper-based faculties dictated by Sect. 10 of the FACA.

We understand the FACA to be the formal institution of democracy that both informs the design of *Peer-to-PCAST* and from which it diverges in multiple ways, including the new forms of accountability supported by the peer-review functionality.

Essentially both *We Are History* and *Peer-to-PCAST* are websites backed by databases of videos. They are both interactive storytelling systems insofar as they afford users the agency to upload, download, stream, interrupt, and comment on the stories/testimony archived in the videos. They are more effective than commercial streaming video platforms for addressing the paradox of democracy because of the various forms of accountability that are incorporated into them.

7 Conclusions

Presented was a short history of the role of interactive storytelling in democratic politics – and the anti-democratic dangers of non-interactive storytelling. Historian Fred Turner has described how the visions of interactive, multimedia installations of the 1940s and 1950s presaged the attempts to develop digital "democratic surrounds" of the 1960s and after. While it may at first appear that contemporary platforms like YouTube and Netflix are democratic in design and thus salutary digital interactive narrative systems, we show this not to be the case. The principal design difficulty for democratic digital interactive narrative systems is the "paradox of democracy," analogous to but not equivalent to the "narrative paradox." We articulate a design challenge – agency with accountability – necessary to address the paradox of democracy and illustrate it with short descriptions of two prototype systems, *We Are History* and *Peer-to-PCAST,* both of which incorporate forms of accountability not present in the institutional forms they are designed to supplement or replace.

References

1. Inskeep, S.: Interview with GOP Senator Ted Cruz: Senator Cruz Among Those Who Will Hear From Trump's Supreme Court Nominee. https://www.npr.org/2020/09/30/918572911/sen-cruz-among-those-who-will-hear-from-trumps-supreme-court-nominee
2. Lakoff, G.: Don't Think of an Elephant!: Know Your Values and Frame the Debate--The Essential Guide for Progressives. Chelsea Green Publishing (2004)
3. Luntz, F.: Words That Work: It's Not What You Say. Hachette Books, It's What People Hear (2007)
4. Gershberg, Z., Illing, S.: The Paradox of Democracy: Free Speech, Open Media, and Perilous Persuasion, pp. 1–4. University of Chicago Press, Chicago, IL (2022)
5. Eisenstein, S.: A dialectic approach to film form. In: Leyda, J., (ed.) Film Form: Essays in Film Theory, p. 46. Harcourt, New York (1949)
6. Turner, F.: The Democratic Surround: Multimedia and American Liberalism from World War II to the Psychedelic Sixties. University of Chicago Press (2013), Kindle locs. 70–78
7. Postman, N.: Amusing Ourselves to Death: Public Discourse in the Age of Show Business. Penguin, New York (1985)
8. Turkle, S.: Reclaiming Conversation: The Power of Talk in a Digital Age. Penguin, New York (2016)
9. Zuboff, S.: The Age of Surveillance Capitalism: The Fight for a Human Future at the New Frontier of Power. PublicAffairs, New York (2019)
10. Jaron, L.: Ten Arguments for Deleting Your Social Media Accounts Right Now. Henry Holt and Co., New York (2018)
11. Reeve, C.D.C.: Plato. The Republic, Hackett (2004)
12. Lippmann, W.: Public Opinion. Free Press (1997)
13. Stern, A.: Embracing the combinatorial explosion: a brief prescription for interactive story R&D. In: Spierling, U., Szilas, N. (eds.) ICIDS 2008. LNCS, vol. 5334, pp. 1–5. Springer, Heidelberg (2008). https://doi.org/10.1007/978-3-540-89454-4_1
14. Roth, C., Koenitz, H.: Bandersnatch, Yea or Nay? reception and user experience of an interactive digital narrative video. In: ACM International Conference on Interactive Experiences for TV and Online Video, 05–07 Jun, Salford (Manchester), United Kingdom, p. 253 (2019)
15. Kolhoff, L., Nack, F.: How relevant Is your choice? In: Cardona-Rivera, R.E., Sullivan, A., Young, R.M. (eds.) ICIDS 2019. LNCS, vol. 11869, pp. 73–85. Springer, Cham (2019). https://doi.org/10.1007/978-3-030-33894-7_9
16. Crawford, C.: Is Interactivity Inimical to Storytelling (1996) http://www.erasmatazz.com/library/the-journal-of-computer/lilan/is-interactivity-inimical.html
17. Aylett, R.: Narrative in virtual environments—towards emergent narrative. In: Mateas, M., Sengers, P., (eds.) Proceedings of the AAAI Fall Symposium on Narrative Intelligence. The AAAI Press (1999)
18. Louchart, S., Aylett, R.: Solving the narrative paradox in Ves—Lessons from RPGs. In: Rist, T., et al. (eds.) Proceedings for the IVA Conference. Springer, Berlin (2003). https://doi.org/10.1007/978-3-540-39396-2_41
19. Roth, C., van Nuenen, T., Koenitz, H.: Ludonarrative Hermeneutics: A Way Out and the Narrative Paradox. In: Rouse, R., Koenitz, H., Haahr, M. (eds.) ICIDS 2018. LNCS, vol. 11318, pp. 93–106. Springer, Cham (2018). https://doi.org/10.1007/978-3-030-04028-4_7

20. Foucault, M.: Discourse and Truth and Parrhesia. In: Fruchaud, H.-P., and Lorenzini, D., (eds.) University of Chicago Press, Chicago (2019)
21. North, D.: Institutions, Institutional Change and Economic Performance. Cambridge University Press (1990), p. 3, 4, and 6
22. Garfinkel, H.: Studies in Ethnomethodology. Polity Press (1991)
23. Suchman, L.: Plans and Situated Actions: The Problem of Human-Machine Communication. Cambridge University Press (1987)
24. Button, G.,   Dourish, P.: Technomethodology: paradoxes and possibilities. In: Proceedings of the Conference on Human Factors in Computing Systems: Common Ground, CHI 1996. Vancouver, BC, Canada, 13–18 April (1996)
25. Hanna, F.: Software and Dialogue Aesthetics in Post-Civil War Lebanon. PhD dissertation, Film Digital Media Department, University of California, Santa Cruz (2019)
26. Deckert, M., Stern, A., Sack, W.: Peer-to-PCAST: What does open video have to do with open government? Information Polity **16**, 225–241 (2011)
27. Nau, D., et al.: SHOP2: An HTN planning system. J. Artifi. Intell. Res. **20**, 379–404 (2003)
28. Sack, W., Hanna, F.: *Spinner* source code talk-through. https://www2.ucsc.edu/softwarearts/
29. Sack, W.: Une machine a raconter des histoires : de Propp aux software studies. In: Les Temps Modernes. Année 68, No. 676, novembre-décembre, pp. 216–243 (2013)
30. Meehan, J.: The Metanovel: Writing Stories by Computer. PhD dissertation, Computer Science Department, Yale University (1976)
31. Messara, A.: Les partis politiques au Liban : une expérience arabe pionnière et en déclin. In: Revue des mondes musulmans et de la Méditerranée. Année, 81–82, pp. 135–151 (1996)
32. Traum, D., et al.: New dimensions in testimony: digitally preserving a holocaust survivor's interactive storytelling. In: Schoenau, H., Bruni, L.E., Louchart, S., Baceviciute, S. (eds.) ICIDS 2015. LNCS, vol. 9445, pp. 269–281. Springer, Cham (2015). https://doi.org/10.1007/978-3-319-27036-4_26
33. US General Services Administration: Federal Advisory Committee Act; https://www.gsa.gov/policy-regulations/policy/federal-advisory-committee-management/legislation-and-regulations/the-federal-advisory-committee-act

RichCast - A Voice-Driven Interactive Digital Narrative Authoring System

Christopher Ferraris[1]([⊠]) and Charlie Hargood[2]

[1] Panivox, Kenilworth, UK
chris.ferraris@panivox.com
[2] Bournemouth University, Poole, UK
chargood@bournemouth.ac.uk

Abstract. We present RichCast a platform for conversational audio Interactive Digital Narrative (IDN). RichCast includes an accessible 'No-code' authoring tool, a community driven library of works, and voice interactive medium for interactive storytelling.

Keywords: Interactive Digital Narrative · Authoring tool · Voice control · Mobile gaming

1 Introduction and Background

Voice recognition technology grows increasingly pervasive. With the launch of Apple Siri in 2010, Microsoft Cortana in 2013, Amazon Echo in 2014 and Google Assistant in 2016, voice as a user interface is becoming increasingly normalised in our day-to-day lives. Where once specific voice commands were required, today's voice recognition systems consist of, 'conversational AI' which can include Automatic Speech Recognition (ASR), Natural Language Processing (NLP) and Text-to-Speech (TTS) and have been used to create, 'emotive speech' systems, where users can interact with AI agents using natural language [2].

Voice and audio as an interactive medium hold great potential for Interactive Digital Narrative (IDN), providing potentially screen, and hands, free interactive story experiences. Some forms of IDN which lend themselves to a reduced reliance on screens, such as locative narrative where the users physical surroundings are critical, stand to benefit from further research in screenless forms of interaction. Beyond this other forms of IDN may benefit from a conversational approach to storytelling where using voice and audio the player/reader can converse with characters and ask questions in natural language as a voice extension to the NLP powered free agency first explored by Façade [9]. There are some examples of emergent technologies to support this, including the bespoke actors of Charisma [12], or the voice controlled experiences of Fabella [16]. In this work we present one of these emerging technologies in the form of a community centric conversational narrative framework RichCast[1].

---

[1] RichCast by Panivox as available here https://www.richcast.com/ as of 20/7/22.

M. Vosmeer and L. Holloway-Attaway (Eds.): ICIDS 2022, LNCS 13762, pp. 414–423, 2022.
https://doi.org/10.1007/978-3-031-22298-6_26

RichCast is more than just a means of voice interaction, its community centric approach means authors and authoring tools are a priority. Authorship and authoring technologies have long been both a critical area for IDN research and one that presents many challenges [4,15]. How 'authoring tool' is defined is a matter for debate [5,14] - but broadly we can refer to applications that are used by authors principally for the creation of IDNs. A range of interface design paradigms can be seen from the classic Hypertext graphs of StorySpace [1], to domain specific languages such as in Inform 7 [11], to faceted approaches as seen in StoryPlaces [7,10]. However, a principle challenge for all authoring tools remains accessibility [4,10,15] and enabling non technical authors to create IDN and work within the medium without the need to hire programmmers. Indeed, much of the success of Twine [8] (arguably one of the more widely used IDN authoring tools) has been attributed to the tools accessibility for non technical creatives [3,13]. The accessibility of our authoring tools not only impacts usability but can influence the resulting works themselves [6] and potentially the entrance of new creative voices in our community [3]. Consequently ways to bring IDN authorship to the author and improving accessibility of our tools can be considered a long standing priority for IDN authoring tool research. It is also to be noted that IDN is not a single form, with games, locative narratives, Hypertext, parser fiction and more all existing under the IDN umbrella - and these different forms demand bespoke authoring tools [10].

In this demo submission we present both RichCast and it's authoring tool.

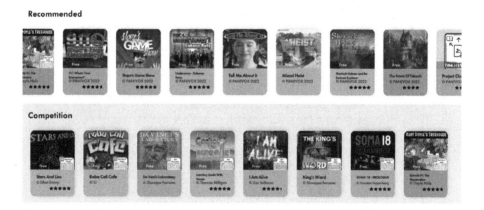

Fig. 1. RichCast supports voice-driven IDN authoring by it's community"

2   RichCast

RichCast's key design features are:

- **Conversational Storytelling** Using conversational AI', the Keywords and Fallback systems and customizable AI Voice Actors

– **'Effortless' IDN authoring** With a design philosophy that aims to make IDN creation 'effortless' for new and advanced creators, through design techniques such a 'No code' audio & visuals and supporting visual clarity via the Junction Tile

2.1 Conversational Storytelling

RichCast brings conversational voice interactive AI with accessible authorship to IDN. Utilising the accessibility of voice-driven technology as a user interface, RichCast aims to support community-created content and encourage anyone to create their own voice-driven interactive experiences, as seen in Fig. 1.

Creating a tool that supports conversational storytelling by anyone, regardless of their IDN or technical experience, is the foundation of RichCast and presents some interesting challenges. With RichCasts's conversational storytelling, players can interact with AI agents using natural language, this can be to ask questions, roleplay conversation, or take actions as seen in an example Sherlock Holmes story in Fig. 3 on the next page. How can we present a relatively complex system in a format that anyone can use to create voice-driven IDNs? To this end, RichCast's design has focused on reducing barriers traditionally associated with using voice in IDN projects, from coding knowledge to the user interface to the production costs associated with voice input and voice acting, so that we can support a wide variety of creators.

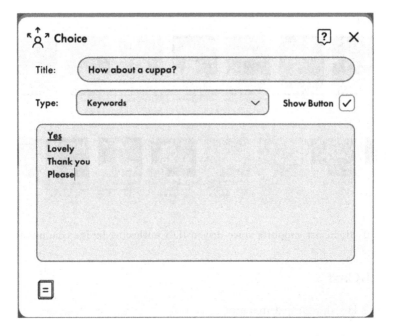

Fig. 2. RichCast's choice tile using keywords to take voice inputs without code.

Watson presents the challenge

The player chooses what to do

Watson introduces a character

The players asks Watson for help

Watson suggests an action

The player agrees and continues

Fig. 3. Example of conversational storytelling, with RichCasts's "Sherlock and the Eminent Explorer". The IDN delivers the scene and setting to the player audibly and visually they can issue instructions, ask questions, and converse with the characters.

Keywords & Fallback System. When a creator wishes to create a response to specific voice input by a user, they use Keywords. Keywords are a re-imagining of 'intent' words used by systems such as Amazon's Alexa system. RichCast developers have not created the speech recognition libraries themselves. Indeed there are many freely accessible APIs such as Google Speech-to-Text, Microsoft Azure and Amazon Transcribe. Panivox have created a best-in-class system to embrace these technologies by enabling a system of accessibility and ease of use.

In order to build a voice-driven interactive experience, IDN creators need to instruct RichCast to respond to a user's words. The Keyword system is part of the 'Choice' tile. The Choice tile, like all of RichCast tiles, follows the 'no code' design philosophy to support creators with no coding knowledge and presents the creator with an easy to navigate window where they can customise how a user's voice input is managed as seen in Fig. 2 at the start of this section.

Within the Choice window, Keywords such as 'Yes' are underlined, indicating they are part of a Keyword group. Keyword groups allow creators to easily see all the associated voice responses associated with a given voice input and allow users to provide a variety of responses. For example, the Keyword, 'Yes' also supports the user voice input of, 'ok', 'confirm', 'sure', 'yup', and 'of course' as seen in Fig. 4.

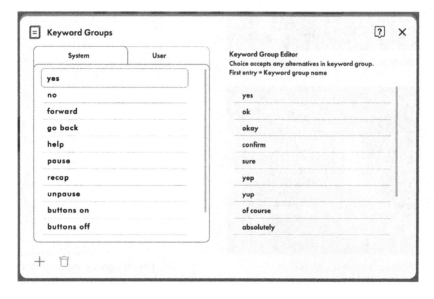

Fig. 4. RichCast's keyword group system grouping varied responses under key actions to aid voice interaction design.

Using voice to interact with a game's cast of characters can create memorable experiences. However, one challenge for IDN creators is to present non-player characters as believable 'living' agents, rather than computer simulations.

The Fallback system supports this goal of presenting characters as living agents by providing creators with the option to customize the automated responses provided by a character in response to unrecognized voice commands as seen in Fig. 5. This form of elegant failure allows the author to creative immersive experiences that feel conversational rather than filled with dead ends.

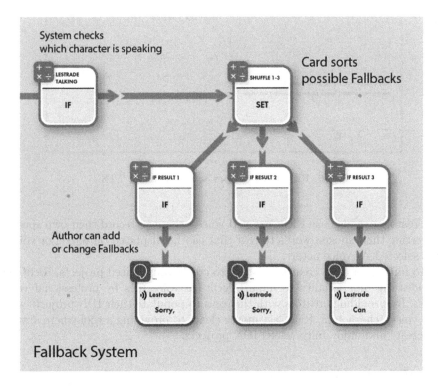

Fig. 5. RichCast's fallback system allowing authors to specify elegant failure.

The Fallback system takes a user's voice input, determines which NPC is being interacted with and then directs the RichCast system to one of a number of responses. The system then uses a 'card shuffle' algorithm to randomize the responses given to the user and minimize the chances of the same response being repeated consecutively. creators can customize their own Fallback responses, either changing the existing texts provided by RichCast or adding their own, as suits the style of experience and character they wish to create.

AI Voice Actors. Learning from other AI voice developers, such as IBM, Apple, Amazon and & Google, has allowed RichCast to deliver over 150 AI voice actors, with a wide variety of backgrounds and personalities, for Creators to use in their IDN Projects. Each AI voice actor's voice can be adjusted for pitch and speed by creators to support there IDN projects as depicted in Fig. 6.

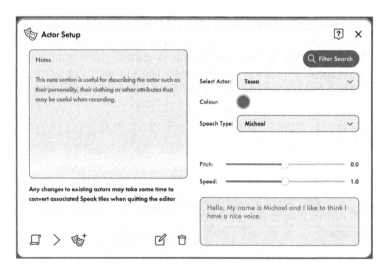

Fig. 6. RichCast's custom actor set up for TTS

Creators can also use RichCast's AI voice system to record their own speech, converting their spoken words to text that can be displayed on screen or voiced by a selected AI voice actor.

To further support creators wishing to create fully voiced projects, RichCast provides the functionality to import recorded voice files by professional voice actors. By providing creators with the tools to populate their IDN projects with fully voiced characters, RichCast moves closer to providing a tool where anyone can create and enjoy fully-voiced IDN projects.

2.2 'Effortless' IDN Authoring

RichCast aims to support IDN authors from all backgrounds. To this end, the system incorporates a number of design techniques in an effort to improve the IDN authoring experience.

Project Structuring. IDN tools make use of Hypertextual graphs in the form of flowcharts to support creators as they structure and create their projects. As a IDN project becomes more complex, its flowcharts can become a complex, intricate network of tiles that can be difficult to understand, even for professional creators.

Flowchart systems permit a value to exit a tile along multiple paths, depending on the condition within the tile. RichCast utilises a binary node system for each tile with, 'one input, one output', where a value passes through a tile if the condition in the tile is true. Visually, logic conditionals are represented as their own discrete tiles, rather than being displayed on connecting path, so that a user only needs to follow and check each title. While this does mean an additional element is introduced into the flowchart system, it does aim to present a clearer representation of what it happening in a project, as shown in Fig. 7.

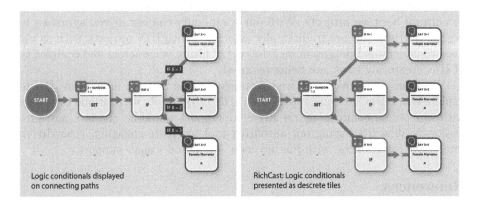

Fig. 7. Improving flowchart readability using binary nodes

Junction Tile. The 'Junction' tile provides users with an 'empty' tile that can be implemented in IDN projects to help them manage the visual representation of their experience. The Junction tile takes any input and connects it to other tiles within the flowchart system as shown in Fig. 8.

When a flowchart diagram represents a complex system, overlapping connections between nodes can create a representation that is 'messy' and hard to read. Using the Junction tile, creators can better manage their flowchart systems, 'untangling' connections between nodes. This cleaner representation of the flowchart supports the creators and their collaborators directly, by improving readability.

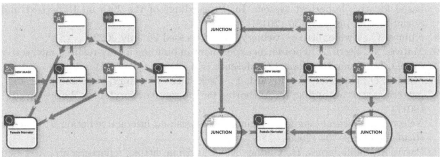

Flowchart with no Junction tiles   RichCast: Using Junction tiles

Fig. 8. RichCast's Juction tiles, circled in red, allow the user to organise the layout of their flowchart (Color figure online)

3 Conclusion

RichCast presents conversational AI technology for IDN creators, to support a wide range of voice-driven IDN projects, from interactive fiction, to quizes, to cultural heritage projects. With our community-content driven approach to design, barriers that are traditionally associated with IDN projects, such as the need to understand programming, the cost of hiring voice actors and complexity of IDN creatoring tools, are being removed.

With our 'Creators Fund' we encourage anyone with an interest in IDN to explore how RichCast can support their IDN projects. As we continue to engage with our online community, we strive to support would-be creators and professionals alike from using our authoring tool to create engaging, voice-driven interactive experiences, with full 'no code' audio and visuals support.

References

1. Bernstein, M.: Storyspace 3. In: Proceedings of the 27th ACM Conference on Hypertext and Social Media, HT 2016, pp. 201–206. Association for Computing Machinery, New York (2016)
2. Charles, F., Pizzi, D., Cavazza, M., Vogt, T., André, E.: Emoemma: emotional speech input for interactive storytelling. In: Proceedings of the 8th International Conference on Autonomous Agents and Multiagent Systems, vol. 2, pp. 1381–1382 (2009)
3. Ellison, C.: Anna anthropy and the twine revolution. The Guardian **10** (2013)
4. Green, D.: Don't Forget to Save! The Impact of User Experience Design on Effectiveness of Authoring Video Game Narratives. Ph.D. thesis (2021)
5. Green, D., Hargood, C., Charles, F.: Define "authoring tool": a survey of interactive narrative authoring tools. In: Authoring for Interactive Storytelling Workshop 2018 (2018)
6. Green, D., Hargood, C., Charles, F.: Use of tools: UX principles for interactive narrative authoring tools. J. Comput. Cult. Herit. (JOCCH) **14**(3), 1–25 (2021)
7. Hargood, C., Weal, M.J., Millard, D.E.: The storyplaces platform: building a web-based locative hypertext system. In: Proceedings of the 29th on Hypertext and Social Media, pp. 128–135 (2018)
8. Klimas, C.: Twine. https://twinery.org/. Accessed 26 July 2022
9. Mateas, M., Stern, A.: Façade: an experiment in building a fully-realized interactive drama. In: Game Developers Conference, vol. 2, pp. 4–8 (2003)
10. Millard, D., Hargood, C., Howard, Y., Packer, H.: The storyplaces authoring tool: pattern centric authoring. In: Authoring for Interactive Storytelling Workshop 2017 (2017)
11. Nelson, G.: Natural language, semantic analysis and interactive fiction. IF Theory Reader **141**, 99–104 (2006)
12. Parry, A., Salili-James, B., Gadney, G.: Charisma. https://charisma.ai/. Accessed 26 June 2022
13. Salter, A.: Interactive narrative. Humanities Commons (2020)
14. Shibolet, Y., Knoller, N., Koenitz, H.: A framework for classifying and describing authoring tools for interactive digital narrative. In: Rouse, R., Koenitz, H., Haahr, M. (eds.) ICIDS 2018. LNCS, vol. 11318, pp. 523–533. Springer, Cham (2018). https://doi.org/10.1007/978-3-030-04028-4_61

15. Spierling, U., Szilas, N.: Authoring issues beyond tools. In: Iurgel, I.A., Zagalo, N., Petta, P. (eds.) ICIDS 2009. LNCS, vol. 5915, pp. 50–61. Springer, Heidelberg (2009). https://doi.org/10.1007/978-3-642-10643-9_9
16. Wanderword: Fabella. https://fabellacreator.com/. Accessed 26 June 2022

Theory, History and Foundations

When You Hear the Chime: Movable Books and the Dramaturgical Functions of Sound in Mixed Reality Interactive Narrative Design

Lissa Holloway-Attaway(✉) and Rebecca Rouse(✉)

University of Skövde, 54128 Skövde, Sweden
{lissa.holloway-attaway,rebecca.rouse}@his.se

Abstract. In this paper we outline the pre-digital histories of recorded and synthe-sized sound, exploring their entanglements with both the literal codex and larger literary imaginary. In particular, we focus on intersections of sound and movable books, offering the rich genealogy of the movable book as a fertile addition to the IDN (interactive digital narrative) family tree, as an example of pre-computational interactive narrative with a long history. Drawing on this intermedial history, along with our own experience designing an MR (mixed reality) movable book, we offer a taxonomy of dramaturgical functions of sound in MR IDN. We demonstrate the use of this taxonomy in analysis of our own work, and suggest opportunities for expanding the taxonomy in support of future speculative research and design imaginaries for IDNs.

Keywords: Sound · Mixed Reality · Interactive Narrative

1 Introduction

In this paper we explore a range of historical and contemporary examples that illus-trate the entanglement of codex and audio in interactive storytelling. Reflecting on our own experience designing an MR (mixed reality) movable book, *Simmer (2019),* that prominently features audio, we draw out a set of seven sonic registers for the designer to consider, defined by their aesthetic quality and material relations, along with their resulting dramaturgical function. The focus of our paper is audio, but not audio alone - rather it is audio in intermedial relation with other elements (digital, physical, or both) and within the codex as a frame. Our aim is to develop a nuanced understanding of audio and embodied, affective interactive storytelling experiences across time and media and to create a model for innovative future design that expands the boundaries and imagination of the IDN discipline.

Our transhistorical perspective stands in opposition to reductive, binary theoreti-cal framing about the so-called passive nature of books and readers as less-than the complexity of digital technologies and their so-called more active users. The geneal-ogy of intermedial audio storytelling we present here is informed by prior research on the long prehistory of the codex structure [1–3], and can serve to complement research

M. Vosmeer and L. Holloway-Attaway (Eds.): ICIDS 2022, LNCS 13762, pp. 427–440, 2022.
https://doi.org/10.1007/978-3-031-22298-6_27

emphasizing the differences between the codex, literary forms, and IDN (Interactive Digital Narrative) [1]. This discussion of movable books and MR audio is also relevant for historicizing and expanding contemporary discussions of presence, audio, VR, and interactive media design which focus on the body in three dimensional space, or in simulated three dimensional space [2–4]. While the history of IDN Is often traced through twentieth century antecedents both technological and analogue, such as Dadaist cut-up poetry [3] or early experiments with computational narrative [4], we find the deeper time of interactive storytelling history to be inspirational and informative for our contemporary IDN practice. We consider the long history of movable books as equally significant in the ancestry of IDN, along with the more commonly cited twentieth century examples.

Movable books are a broader category than the contemporary pop-up book. While the pop-up book primarily relies on the potential energy of the central codex fold to activate three-dimensional paper structures, movable books can include pop-ups as well as many other forms inviting interaction such as rotating volvelles, flaps, transformation views, and enclosures. Enclosures can allow for the incorporation of many interactive paper forms within the codex, such as tunnel books, flip books, maps, puzzles and more. Movable books have a long history that predates printing, and can be traced back to manuscript books such as Matthew Paris' *Itinerary Maps from London to Palestine* (c. 1250). Movable books are an important ancestor for IDN given the ways in which these books upend commonsense notions of reading as a passive practice, and the book as neutral container for information [5, 6]. While paper-based movable books may not be computational, they can be understood as digital, as in, requiring the digits of the hand to facilitate interaction and the meaning-making process [7]. In this paper, however, we focus on MR movable book design, bridging the paper-based movable book form with the computational medium. In particular, we focus on the use of digital audio, both recorded and synthesized sound, and the dramaturgical role of MR audio in the larger experience design.

By MR (mixed reality) we refer to applications that combine both physical and digital elements via a layering aesthetic. This layering can take many forms, for different ends, but does "seek to combine the physical and virtual into an effective hybrid for the sake of the experience. [...] the effect is one that cannot be achieved by the physical or digital alone" [8]. While MR can be achieved by using a range of technologies, the project we discuss here, *Simmer (2019),* makes use of computer- vision image tracking off of paper components of a hand-made movable artist book, facilitating digital audio delivery via smartphone. In this way, *Simmer* bridges the hands-on digitality of the paper-based movable book, with its long heritage, with the touch-screen digitality of the computational medium, to activate a synesthetic tactile-visual-audio MR experience design. While each component of our design comes into meaning through intermedial relation with the others, in this paper we focus in particular on the role of sound, which has been identified in prior IDN research as a key factor in facilitating user engagement within an interactive storytelling environment [9].

2   A History of Intermedial Storytelling with Sound

To better support innovative research in practice in IDN with sound we look back to earlier time periods and technologies, to develop a fuller understanding of the entangled histories that intersect intermedial storytelling with sound. By intermedial, we mean not stand-alone sound storytelling as in audiobooks, which have their own fascinating history as researched by Matthew Rubery [10], but rather intermedial storytelling with sound, as in sound in combination with other visual, tactile, immersive or interactive media. There is a long history of sound amplification for storytelling purposes such as the construction of amphitheaters in antiquity [11]. More contemporary examples include the sound walk, as created by Janet Cardiff. We are more particularly interested in intermedial storytelling examples that bring together both the literal codex itself along with audio and other media as well.

The codex alone can also be understood as indexical to a kind of cognitive audio experience. While we may often think of reading as a silent activity, cognitive research by Ben Alderson-Day [12] and others has shown that some readers listen to their own voices as inner speech in a simulated, cognitive fashion while reading text. There is also the long history of books that instruct in the generation of sound such as Medieval sheet music and prayer books. More than these cognitive or instructional links between books and sound, we are interested in books that themselves produce sound, in hybridized text-image-audio mashup. These examples can be divided into two categories: those that synthesize sound, and those that reproduce recorded sound.

2.1 Synthetic Sound and Automation

The Speaking Picture Book from 1893 provides an interesting example that bridges books that instruct the reader to make sound, with books that themselves produce sound. *The Speaking Picture Book* has a series of levers to pull at the side which activate mechanical sounds of animal noises made from wood and paper card bellows. Short verses about each animal accompany the pictures in this book for children, meaning it is likely the book was also read aloud. This method of using reeds and bellows to synthesize sound dates from earlier experiments in the 1760s-1780s by Wolfgang von Kempelen [13], who is perhaps best known as the inventor of the infamous chess playing turk automaton, which toured Europe for decades but was ultimately revealed as a fake. Von Kempelen's dalliance with the chessplayer overshadowed his many other accomplishments including his life's work, the Speaking Machine. Von Kempelen conceptualized the mechanism of the human voice in a uniquely scientific manner for his time, based on careful observation and concluded that his machine "[...] will yet require not so much effort and work as a common keyboard instrument or pianoforte" [14]. Thus demonstrating the development of skill necessary to 'play' the synthetic voice as instrument, and also indicating this synthetic voice was not 'automatic' by any means. Indeed, von Kempelen's text describes the careful, iterative design process through which he developed the conjunction of bellows-based lung, reed-based glottis, and funnel-shaped oboe bell mouth into a cohesive apparatus, which through skillful operation were capable of synthesizing not only single vowel sounds but also simple words such as mama, papa, and so forth [15].

Von Kempelen's dual interests in synthetic sound and automation are reflective of the long entangled history of the mechanical production of imitative sound with the history of automata. One strand of this history can be traced back to Islamic water powered automata from the 1100s [16] and the later European automata which had their origins in the 14th century "singing towers" or turret clocks with carillons [17]. These church tower clocks are also related to later 14th and 15th century musical clocks, some of which had mechanical organ soundtracks, such as the Lund Cathedral astronomical clock which dates from c. 1420. Examples of musical automation increase throughout the 17th and 18th centuries, with examples such as self-playing spinets manufactured by Langenbucher and Bidermann and musical automata such as The Musician, constructed by Pierre Jacquet-Droz and sons during the second half of the 18th century [18]. By the 19th century automata and cylinder music boxes were mass produced, and hand-cranked musical pipe organs proliferated as well, bringing mechanically produced sound squarely into the realm of popular culture [19]. The turn of the 20th century dancehall organs such as those manufactured by De Schuyt and Mortier can be seen as an apex of this development, during the same time period as the project to capture the human voice through new technologies of sound recording.

The technical and philosophical problems associated with capturing the *human* voice and reproducing and amplifying it are very different from the project to synthesize or mechanically produce animal noises, sound, or music. As Stephen Connor discusses in his cultural history of ventriloquism, the human voice has its own particular grain, it is deeply entangled in notions of personhood and the self, and it is embodied - it literally comes from inside us out into the world, connected to breath, and therefore life itself [20]. At the intersection of synthetic sound and the reproduction of the human voice we find the history of synthetic voice. Von Kempelen's Speaking Machine constitutes an important early mechanical example, and roughly a century and a half after his experiments the notable electronic examples emerge from the mid-1920s and early 1930s from Walter Ruttmann, Rudolph Pfenninger and Oskar Fischinger, all of which predate Homer Dudley's later more well-known 1938 Vodor [21]. Ruttman, Pfenninger, and Fischinger's iterations in synthetic voice research were conducted via optical sound on film, using hand-drawn sound waves to simulate speech [22]. This approach was carried forward in further optical film sound practices, a culminating point of which is the award-winning optical soundtrack to Norman McLaren's 1952 short film, *Neighbours*. While synthetic voice complicates the notion of the voice as a marker of authenticity, troubling even the basic notion of voice as an index of the larynx, the optical sound voice simulations were still indexical in quality — as indices to the human hand, instead of the human larynx. This thread continues today in synthetic speech research that makes use of artificial intelligence approaches made possible by the computational medium [23]. These synthetic voices have many applications today, including the literary, when they are used in text-to-speech programs that make written text accessible to those with visual impairments [24].

2.2 Recorded Sound

The history of recorded sound, while related to the history of sound synthesis, has a distinct path that is even more closely related to text and the literary. From the earliest stages of recorded audio development in the late 19th century, these new technologies were entangled with text and the literary. In a laudatory 1877 editorial letter praising Edison's early version of the phonograph (which functioned via indented paper strips, inspired by his embossing translating telegraph) the invention is discussed in explicitly literary terms: "Will letter writing be a proceeding of the past? Why not, if by simply talking into a mouthpiece our speech is recorded on paper, and our correspondent can by the same paper hear us speak. Are we to have a new kind of books? There is no reason why the orations of our modern Ciceros should not be recorded and detachably bound so that we can run the indented slips through the machine, and in the quiet of our own apartment listen again, and as often as we will, to the eloquent words" [25]. Media historian Jonathan Sterne has discussed this interconnection of speech, writing, sound, text, and presence as a kind of synesthesia: "The names for these machines were all hybrids of one sort or another: phonograph, graphophone, and gramophone suggest a mixture between speech and writing; telephone suggests the throwing of speech; radiotelegraphy and radiotelephony suggest the radiation of waves out from a single point. At the core of all these transformations (alongside the many others) is the isolation, separation, and transformation of the senses themselves" [26].

Even earlier experiments in capturing the human voice were connected to the body, albeit sometimes in disturbing ways. Johnathan Sterne describes the history of Alexander Graham Bell and Clarence Blake's 1874 "ear phonautograph" machine which was used to visualize sound. The ear phonautograph was made from an actual human ear nailed to a wooden frame, with a straw attached to the tympanic membrane, in order to scratch sound visualizations onto a piece of smoked glass [27, 28]. Beside the obvious ick factor with the use of the human ear, which was harvested from a cadaver, Sterne elaborates on the able-ist philosophy behind this research [29]. Blake and Bell wanted to make sound visible to deaf people so that they could learn to speak by imitating the sound wave inscriptions with their own voices. Blake and Bell's motivation was to eliminate linguistic differences, and stamp out deaf culture. Thankfully, it was a failure.

Later recording technology, such as Edison's Phonograph, was successful. As early recording technologies proliferated, mashup approaches that combined elements of both recording technology and sound synthesis were present as well. For example, the Reginaphon was a disc-based music box that combined the form and structure of wax (and later lacquer) disc and cone amplification found in the phonograph with the punch card approach to sound synthesis. The development and take-up of sound technologies did not follow a straight line of evolutionary progress, and indeed not all applications introduced were successful. While early recorded sound was successfully mechanically synched to accompany early film in broad commercial application, as in works by director Alice Guy Blaché such as her film version of the opera *Mignon* from 1906, Edison's attempt at commercializing recorded sound from the 1890s with a talking doll product had been a huge flop. As discussed by Gaby Wood [30] the doll was cumbersome to produce and difficult to maintain.

But what about intermedial reading/audio experiences? Other technologies - technologies of transmission, like radio, provided platforms for experimentation. From the 1920s, one example is the radio photologue as discussed by Katie Day Good [31]. This example of early media convergence brought together multiple new technologies, with audio from the radio programmed as narration to accompany a full page pictorial spread in the *Chicago Daily News*, made possible by rotogravure printing processes, which enabled for better reproduction of photographic images.

Around the same time, in 1917, a series of read-along record sets known as "Bubble Books" were developed for children by inventor Ralph Mayhew [32]. Mayhew's patent describes the way in which some pages of the book are bound together to form pockets for the miniature records that were enclosed, and that the "story or song which is printed and illustrated in the book may be heard at the time the text is read, and while the book is open at the cut illustrating the story or song. The theme is in this way brought to one's attention in various ways at the same time" [33]. Specially produced hand-cranked gramophones were sold for use with the tiny records, which were advertised for use both in the nursery and the classroom. A further innovation on the format from 1925 included cut-and-fold paper dolls of characters from the stories, which included specialized cardboard stands for mounting these figures onto the gramophone, such that they could be made to seem to dance along with the movement of the record [34].

By the late 1940s, with the development of the long playing record, other companies such as Golden Books and Disney began to produce increasingly elaborate read-along book and record sets for children, in which popular stories and animated films were distilled and adapted to a picture book format, designed to be accompanied by recorded narration, sound, and music on a vinyl record. The reading and listening child was cued to turn the page with a sound like a tinkling chime, as instructed by the phrase: "When you hear the chime, it's time to turn the page." By the 1970s and 1980s, these book and record sets transitioned to cassette tape instead of vinyl record. The cassette tape allowed for even longer, less abridged narrations.

2.3 Computational Fusion: Synthesized and Recorded Sound Together

With the development of the computer medium, a technology emerges that is capable of producing both synthesized and recorded sound from a single platform. This too has been incorporated into books themselves through a range of approaches. In the early 2000s two women inventors, Winnie Yip [35] and Debra Kirwan [36], each filed separate patents for differently configured children's book structures that incorporated digital sound, embedded directly into the book. Kirwan's approach was that of a soundboard adjacent to the book, with buttons for the child to press, and even record their own narration. Yip's approach was for sound chips embedded in each page, activated by the child pressing part of the illustration, initiating a circuit contact to play pre-recorded sound.

And today, books, sound, and narrative have become even further entangled in complex configurations such as MR (mixed reality) books that feature IDNs. Mixed reality refers to the overlay of digital information (sound, graphics) on the physical world, in a layering practice [37]. Early examples include the Magic Book [38] project from 2001 in which the reader uses a digital viewfinder to see digital augmentations layered over physical book pages. With the development of mobile MR in the 2010s, the technology has since become more accessible and widely spread. Digital content can be delivered to mobile devices based on GPS location or via computer vision image recognition. Thus MR technology brings the phone to the book, the phone being a technology of voice transmission, and also entangled in the history of the development of sound recording, amplification, and synthesis technologies. However, today the phone is not really a phone at all, but a computer.

3   The Sounds of *Simmer*: Entangled Audio Affect

In our own work *Simmer,* we explore how sound can function dramaturgically in a contemporary MR interactive narrative book. Using the computational medium in a way that combines, remixes and references older technologies and modes of sound and audio delivery, as well as hybrid physical/digital book design, we engage a number of entangled registers for interactors and interactive storytelling. By register, we refer to the vocal register, as discussed by voice performance practitioners and theorists [39, 40]. Given the authors' shared background in theatre and voice training, we reference the range of registers the voice can take on, from intimate to presentational, and use this range to develop a set of categories for a new taxonomy of the dramaturgical functions of audio in MR IDNs (see Fig. 1). Grounding our taxonomy in the vocal allows us to focus on the affective qualities of audio, while also expanding our classification to include synthetic sound. Using our movable book IDN project *Simmer* as a case study for developing our taxonomy allows us to provide a broad, media archaeological perspective to our approach, taking inspiration from beyond the cinematic, which has been the focus of some prior research on functions of sound in IDN [41]. In *Simmer* our MR audio content is intermingled by nature, drawing on both synthetic and recorded sound, a diverse range of storytelling practices including radio play, drama, and the literary. This combination of influences also foregrounds the entangled material transhistories of codex structures and contemporary digital media. By focusing our taxonomy on the dramaturgical [42], we refer to the structure, composition, and material and aesthetic qualities of a work that facilitate interpretation and meaning-making for an interactor across the seven audio registers we identify: **Inner Monologue, Monologue, Direct Address, Dialogue, Diegetic Sound, Ambient Speech,** and **Musical Soundtrack**.

AUDIO REGISTER	AESTHETIC QUALITY	DRAMATURGICAL FUNCTION	MATERIAL RELATIONS in *SIMMER*
Inner Monologue	Intimate	Bringing the interactor close; intimacy; encouraging identification with the speaker; trust; complicity.	The interactor projects self into small interior spaces, peering and peeping into the tunnel book and miniature book, just as interior thoughts are expressed via fragmentary, associative, whispered audio.
Monologue	Narrative	Expository; translating fragmentary information accessed elsewhere into linear cohesion.	Hands-on work by the interactor enables physical transformations that help illustrate the monologue narratives, with the animation of the cocktail flip-book and the thermochromic paint revealing an additional layer on the map.
Direct Address	Metatheatrical	The interactor becomes part of the performance; complicit.	The interactor manipulates paper dolls in a performative manner, as though they are puppets in a toy theatre, enacting Lucinda's relationship with her daughters as per her instructions.
Dialogue	Conversational	Eavesdropping, voyeurism.	The interactor moves their gaze slowly across each panorama panel, in sync with attentive listening to radio play style dialogue on the accordion fold side of the book.
Diegetic Sound	Environmental	Contextualizing; elaborating the environment, time period, or setting.	The interactor collects ephemera in the form of miniature LP records that resonate with the time period, helping to provide verisimilitude and context to the setting of the story.
Ambient Speech	Textural	Activating subconscious or automatic response; creating mood.	Activating the uncanny speech on the paper dolls, the interactor's initial visceral response of repulsion helps lead toward decoding relations between dolls, archival audio, dollhouse surroundings, and story.
Musical Soundtrack	Emotional	Affective support for the narrative development and shifts.	The interactor engages in a cinematic listening practice as the emotionally shifting underscoring of the musical soundtrack shifts from bubbly to troubled moving from left to right across the panorama frame.

Fig. 1. Taxonomy of Dramaturgical Functions of Sound in MR IDNs, with *Simmer* as case study. The first three columns of the taxonomy are general; the fourth column is highly specific to each project due to the nature of MR.

3.1   Resisting Presence Through Affective Audio Design

Our design strategies for *Simmer* are based on the desire to support affective and embodied experiences for MR interactive narratives. As such they combine a number of dramaturgical functions that entangle audio registers with a range of aesthetic and material Intermedial relations. Drawing on affect and new material perspectives exploring computational, human, and more-than-human intra-relationships, we consider design practices that perceive technical and analog relationships as deeply intermingled, co-constitutive, performative, and material in both virtual and physical domains [43–48]. This form of mutual relationship is organic, rhythmic, and emergent, and is driven by curiosity and a desire to discover the world in fragments, distributed across a plane of synesthetic and sensory encounterings. This transhistorical and multisensory approach also helps us to sustain a more expansive speculative perspective for IDNs that goes beyond traditions such as Electronic Literature that separates pre-digital/digital influences and privileges both computational media as interactive and centers the textual.

Our project *Simmer* is an exemplar of this other more expansive perspective on IDNs. *Simmer* is a reimagining of the John Cheever short story "The Swimmer" (1964) and at its core, the work foregrounds the hidden stories and voices of the women in the original text who are silenced by a focus on the narcissistic male protagonist, Ned Merrill. Ned's voice dominates the original short story and the world he tells, *his* world, is revealed through his first-person, biased perspective. As such the primary women in the story (his wife, his four daughters, and his mistress) are only referenced through him. Our aim in *Simmer* was to literally *give voice* to them through the MR design. Using a variety of dramaturgical functions that connect audio to other material and aesthetic relationships, we bring them forward, while resisting the urge to make them whole, or wholly present. Resisting the minimalism associated with the high Modernist mid-century short-story, characterized by Cheever's text, we worked toward inclusion and multiplicity. In *Simmer*, we bring in the noise [44] to the story by augmenting, layering, fragmenting, dispersing, and complicating the material story spaces To express this complexity we then overtly resisted the traditions that connect passive readers to material codex books and active readers to digital forms and remixed them to refute these false binaries.

3.2   Complex Codex Forms and Digital Interfaces

In its material construction, *Simmer* moves between a traditional codex structure and other more deconstructed material and virtual configurations to promote affective resonances meant to actively engage interactors. *Simmer* is first encountered by a user who sees it as a literal codex book, a folded set of pages bound on one side, and even closed tightly with a decorative ribbon. But when the ribbon is removed, the book reveals its codex form as an illusion. It is not a *closed* text, and the book opens instead as a long, linear accordion fold book, or panorama, and it functions to present a re-telling of Ned's story from his perspective. The long, narrow surface of the panorama reflects Ned's long-winded, narcissistic musings, common to the original Cheever short story where his first-person voice dominates. The accompanying audio, that tracks off of the panorama's trigger images through the interactor's mobile phone, is not singular and monolithic. It presents radio-play style dialogue, recalling an earlier media form, and atmospheric background music for context, resonant of 1960s style jazz and the innovative syncopation of Bossa Nova style beats. Combining **dialogue** and a **musical soundtrack** in the audio design, the panorama supports attentive listening, contextual identification and cinematic framing for the interactor. The interactor becomes an eavesdropper and a voyeur on this side of the narrative, overhearing snippets of conversation, party music, and stylized dialogue that over-emphasize Ned's greatness.

There is little to interact with physically on the panorama side, except a series of pictures and the associated trigger images, and so engagement for interactors is relatively subdued. However, they are not entirely static either, if they listen closely while also looking for and using visual cues to interact. The attentiveness of an interactor to both visual and audio material is required to discover the nuance of the narrative, and the storytelling shifts, getting darker in tone as one moves from left to right along the panorama fold out. The panorama requires focus, visually and aurally, but also tactilely if one considers the interaction with the mobile phone to trigger the audio. It offers a slow, introduction and scene-setting for an interactor who may only begin to sense what the story is about through its multiple aesthetic and entangled material affordances.

3.3   Dollhouse: Drawing Connections and Domestic Redistribution

A red thread is also visible on the panorama side, sewn through the book to the other side, making literal connections among characters, locations, and stories on each side. But the thread, a well-known unifying device for storytelling to bring elements together for a reader, is not quite so distinctive and functional in *Simmer*. Here it creates metaphorical connections between linear and non-linear writing forms, but ultimately is somewhat misleading as the book as a whole never fully coheres in form or content. This lack of unity and desire to tell a story clearly is more fully revealed when the accordion book is turned inside-out, transforming it into a much more complex dollhouse structure that the interactor must traverse to collect the story elements. In this more complex movable book form the storytelling world is further deconstructed through the creation of a more domestic, private space, populated by women's voices, outsiders, and musical compositions all distinctly resistant to patriarchal control and social rules and norms. Here a range of dramaturgical functions are introduced, from **inner monologues**, other **monologues,** forms of **direct address**, to **ambient speech** and **diegetic sound**. The red thread draws the two sides of the book together, but also indicates there are two+ sides of this story, only tenuously connected, and then redistributed across many registers to create a materially complex interactive MR experience.

The nonlinear narrative of the domestic house space, which is clearly more Lucinda's, not Ned's world, is pieced together through the reader's exploration of its found objects and by manipulating a variety of traditional pop-up and movable book elements, revealed through a range of physical interactions (touching, listening, opening, reading, breathing on) accompanied by narrative audio fragments that are *attached* to particular objects. Hidden in the objects found in the folds and spaces of the book, the interactor is drawn into hybrid material/virtual encounters to enrich and add depth to the stories. Objects like tunnel books, flip books, record albums, paper dolls with instruction sheets for use, and the map of the Merrill's neighborhood painted over with thermochromic paint, invite the interactor to participate in the story, while listening to its secrets in the discovered audio. They can peep through the tunnel book, for example, with its cover trigger image of a woman's gaping mouth, while learning about/listening to stories of the Merrill's failed marriage via one of Lucinda's inner monologues. Story materials are presented physically and aurally. Interactors can, for example, flip the pages of a tiny book to animate a hand-drawn cocktail glass, filling and refilling it, a silent and pre-digital way to bring objects to life. But by activating the flip book in tandem with the audio track triggered by the image on the cover, they can listen to Lucinda's mother's voice in another spiteful monologue, describing her disgust for Ned and his drunken lineage passed down from his alcoholic father. Each of the objects represents a specific kind of dramaturgical function, and the increased number of hybrid interactions, in comparison to the panorama, offers a more complex interactive MR platform for engagement and storytelling.

3.4   Confessional Monologues

To more fully support the interactor's ability to engage with narrative elements and material objects through hybrid interaction, the dollhouse uses other **monologue** forms that draw on *human* relationships and personal confessions. The monologue, a form of single-voice speech, as the name denotes, is conventionally associated with theater and cinema and is often used as a way of thinking aloud, or connecting one character to another in the form of private confession, or for intimate and extended personal expression. It *spotlights* a particular individual, giving a character the stage, allowing an uninterrupted way to mediate information or to reveal something personally significant to an other, and/or to one's self (such as in the form of a soliloquy). Our audio design contains two kinds of monologues, the **inner monologue**, a private expression, not intended to be spoken aloud or overheard, and the more communicative **monologue** used to find connection or sympathy with others, or to give direct information to the listener, often offering exposition to help translate needed story details for the interactor. Collectively they offer both proximity for the interactor, drawing them into the narrative, while often simultaneously distancing them as they work to translate and process the disturbing information they hear to form a larger narrative picture.

Here, we can hear, for example, Lucinda's voice for the first time in a series of **inner monologues** as she describes her experiences living with a narcissist, in the suburbs, in first-person. Lucinda's inner monologues, triggered by a variety of objects, are semi-whispered, and most reveal her mocking derision and contempt for Ned and for her four daughters, for whom she feels no maternal connection at all. Not a sympathetic victim to an overbearing husband, she appears bitter and resentful of her marriage and of motherhood. Brought closer to this reality, the audio connects the interactor intimately to the necessary story elements, as they piece together her life experiences. But these interior musings also create discomfort for interactors upon hearing her secret, anti-social confessions, including her open disgust for her husband (shared by her Mother) and for all four of her daughters. Collectively her confessional monologues reveal her internal resistance to the social domestic norms dictated by her times.

The **monologue** spoken in the voice of the teenage boy, whom Lucinda gets drunk and sexually assaults to get back at Ned for his own affair, offers a very dark perspective on who Lucinda truly is. The teenager, having no memory of the assault assumes he is the sexual predator, and he apologizes for his sins, begging forgiveness from Lucinda. His pain is deeply evident in his voice, and his naïve misunderstanding of his own victimization, offers an uncomfortable experience for the interactor who should feel disoriented and disgusted by the shocking information he reveals. The read-aloud letter is both material and aural, handwritten and virtually present through the voice. Additionally it is triggered by an image on a fold-out map covered in black patches of thermochromic paint that obscure the background. When touched or breathed on, the patches lighten and reveal fragments of the boy's letter, offering a multisensory experience for the interactor, bringing them into proximity with the fragments of the dark narrative.

3.5   Historical Intermediality and Transformative Change

Simmer draws on a long intermedial transhistory of writing and audio forms and technologies including poetry, recorded and synthesized music, and early audio experiment and works to connect them in a network of representation. The red thread, for example, discovered earlier on the panorama side is found again on the dollhouse part of the book. Used on this side, it is also an interactive narrative device, a way to tell a story through an entangled MR intermedial experience. The red thread when followed from the Panorama, emerges in the dollhouse at Lucinda's writing desk within the hand-sewn binding of a miniature book of poetry. The cover of the miniature book triggers an audio **inner monologue** from Lucinda that begins with a reading of an Emily Dickinson poem, followed by her reflection on it and her own failed life as a poet. Lucinda, tells of her kinship with this secret 19th century storyteller of *other* domestic spaces and connects it to her own secret poetry writing. This transhistorical meta- narrative about writing is another method to deepen the intermedial and interactive narrative threads and to refute the newness of the interactive digital book.

Miniature LPs play musical themes for several of the female characters (Lucinda, her Mother, and even Ned's Mistress). These themes are deconstructed and introspective inversions of the cheery **musical soundtrack** from the pool-party side of the book. The album collection's audio, when activated by each cover image, reveals another kind of transgression through their **diegetic sound** design. The album themes are dark, not cheery and dynamic as with the cool Jazz and chill Bossa Nova musical compositions of the panorama, and they help comprise the atmosphere of the failed domestic space. The diegetic sound comprising the album content is dark and plodding, more synthetic, rather than purely instrumental. Like the woman they represent, the album collection creates an environmental atmosphere of loss, despair, and change derived from betrayal and rejection of social norms.

As Lucinda's experience and those of the others in the dollhouse are revealed, we also learn the devastating impact Ned's narcissism has had on her and the family, especially the daughters. In order to reveal their emptiness, and the negative representation they hold for both of their parents, the audio associated with the girls is depersonalized and mechanical. The four daughters are represented by paper dolls and voiced by restored audio recordings of Thomas Edison's mechanical dolls, a (failed) experiment in technical innovation offering instead simplistic, reified notions of woman, machine, and girlhood. Following instructions from Lucinda documented in a folded written letter one discovers in the living room, a dramaturgical form of **direct address**, the interactor is invited to interact with these daughters, not as people, but as paper dolls, emptied of humanity. Eerie recordings of the Edison nursery rhymes are attached to each daughter as forms of **ambient speech** triggered by their paper doll visual representations and then re-voiced through the young girls whom Edison enlisted to serve as his mechanical content makers. These mechanistic recordings, almost unintelligible, but faintly familiar, offer a stark contrast to the other audio content with their uncanny voices, almost human, but not quite, creating a kind of disturbing textural vocalization denoting absence, rather than presence.

4 Conclusions

In this paper we have outlined the rich histories of recorded and synthesized sound, exploring their entanglements with both the literal codex and larger literary imaginary. In particular, we have focused on intersections of sound and movable books, offering the genealogy of the movable book as a fertile addition to the IDN family tree, as an example of pre-computational interactive narrative with a long history. We have developed a taxonomy of dramaturgical functions of sound in IDN, and provided an in-depth analysis of *Simmer* via this taxonomy. We suggest the taxonomy has uses in the analysis of the functions of audio in other IDNs, beyond our particular case study, and we see an opportunity to further extend the framework beyond the initial seven registers we have presented here, and we encourage others to use it. The implementation of the taxonomy for generative design purposes offers a promising direction for expansion of the IDN discipline into more speculative multisensory design research informed by a broader perspective on pre-digital histories as relevant to the field.

References

1. Koenitz, H., Di Pastena, A., Jansen, D., de Lint, B., Moss, A.: The myth of 'universal' narrative models. In: Rouse, Rebecca, Koenitz, Hartmut, Haahr, Mads (eds.) ICIDS 2018. LNCS, vol. 11318, pp. 107–120. Springer, Cham (2018). https://doi.org/10.1007/978-3-030-04028-4_8
2. Gampe, J.: Interactive narration within audio augmented realities. In: Iurgel, Ido A., Zagalo, Nelson, Petta, Paolo (eds.) ICIDS 2009. LNCS, vol. 5915, pp. 298–303. Springer, Heidelberg (2009). https://doi.org/10.1007/978-3-642-10643-9_34
3. Rettberg, S.: Electronic Literature. Polity Press, Cambridge (2019)
4. Ryan, J.: Grimes' fairy tales: a 1960s story generator. In: Nunes, N. et al. (ed.) Interactive Storytelling. LNCS, vol. 10690, pp. 89–103 (2017). https://doi.org/10.1007/978-3-319-710 27-3_8
5. Reid-Walsh, J.: Interactive Books: Playful Media Before Pop-Ups. Routledge, London and New York (2018)
6. Field, H.: Playing with the Book: Victorian Movable Picture Books and the Child Reader. University of Minnesota Press, Minneapolis (2019)
7. Rouse, R., Holloway-Attaway, L.: Playing at the page: designing to support creative readership practices. J. Interact. Books 1(1) (2021). https://doi.org/10.57579/2022JIB013RR
8. Rouse, R., Engberg, M., Parvin, N., Bolter, J.D.: MRx: an interdisciplinary framework for mixed reality experience design and criticism. Digital Creativity 26(3/4), 175–227, 179 (2015)

9. Sigarchian, H.G., De Meester, B., Salliau, F., De Neve, W., et al.: Hybrid books for inter-active digital storytelling: connecting story entities and emotions to smart environments. In: Schoenau-Fog, H. et al. (eds.) Interactive Storytelling. LNCS, vol. 9445, pp. 105–116. Springer, Heidelberg (2015). https://doi.org/10.1007/978-3-319-27036-4_10
10. Rubery, M. (ed.): Audiobooks, Literature, and Sound Studies. Routledge (2011)
11. Mattern, S.: Sonic archaeologies. In: Bull, M. (ed.) The Routledge Companion to Sound Studies, pp. 222–230. Routledge, London and New York (2019)
12. Alderson-Day, B., Bernini, M., Feryhough, C.: Uncharted features and dynamics of reading: voices, characters, and crossing of experiences. Consciousness Cognition **49**, 98–109 (2017)
13. Von Kempelen, W.: Mechanismus der menschlichen Sprache nebst der Beschreibung seiner sprechenden Maschine. J. C. Degen, Vienna (1791)
14. Brackhane, F., Sproat, R., Trouvain, J. (eds.): Wolfgang von Kempelen: Mechanismus der menschlichen Sprache, p. 513. TUD Press, Dresden (2017)
15. Brackhane, F., Sproat, R., Trouvain, J. (eds.): Wolfgang von Kempelen: Mechanismus der menschlichen Sprache, p. 388. TUD Press, Dresden (2017)
16. Nadarajan, G.: Islamic automation: a reading of Al-Jazari's book of knowledge of inge-nious mechanical devices (1206). In: Grau, O., (ed.) Media Art Histories, pp. 163–178. Cambridge University Press, Cambridge (2007)
17. Truitt, E.R.: Medieval Robots: Mechanism, Magic, Nature, and Art. University of Pennsyl-vania Press, Philadelphia (2015)
18. Peppè, R.: Automata and Mechanical Toys. The Crowood Press, Ramsbury (2002)
19. Blott, M., Manschot, B. (eds.): Museum Guide to the National Museum from Musical Clock to Street Organ. National Museum van Speelklok tot Pierement, Utrecht (2005)
20. Connor, S.: Dumbstruck: A Cultural History of Ventriloquism. Oxford University Press, Oxford (2000)
21. Dudley, H.W.: System for the Artificial Production of Vocal or Other Sounds. US Patent 2,121,142, 21 June 1938
22. Levin, T.Y.: Tones from out of Nowhere: Rudolf Pfenninger and the Archaeology of Synthetic Sound. In: New Media Old Media: A History and Theory Reader, pp. 45–81. Routledge, New York (2006)
23. Luck, M., Aylett, R.: Applying artificial intelligence to virtual reality: intelligent virtual environments. Appl. Artif. Intell. **14**(1), 3–32 (2000)
24. Szarkowska, A.: Text-to-speech audio description: towards wider availability of AD. J. Specialized Transl. **15**, 142–162 (2011)
25. Johnson, E.H.: A wonderful invention-speech capable of indefinite repetition from automatic records. Scientific American, p. 304, 17 November 1877
26. Sterne, J.: The Audible Past: Cultural Origins of Sound Reproduction, p. 50. Duke University Press, Durham and London (2003)
27. Bell, A.G., Blake, C.J.: Letter from Clarence J. Blake to Alexander Graham Bell, August 5. 5 August 1874 Manuscript, Library of Congress (1874). https://www.loc.gov/item/magbell. 29700101/. Accessed 19 July 2021
28. Blake, C.J.: The use of the membrana tympani as a phonautograph. Boston Med. Surg. J. **92**(5), 121–124 (1875)
29. Sterne: pp. 37–41 (2003)
30. Wood, G.: Edison's Eve: A Magical History of the Quest for Mechanical Life. AA Knopf, New York (2002)
31. Good, K.D.: Listening to pictures: converging media histories and the multimedia newspaper. Journalism Stud **18**(6), 691–709 (2017)
32. Mayhew, R.: Book. U.S. Patent 1,236,333, 7 August 1917
33. Mayhew, R.: Book. U.S. Patent 1,236,333, 7 August 1917, Line 17–23

34. Johnson, B.: Cut Out Toy. US Patent 1,544,645, 7 July 1925
35. Yip, W.: Children's Sound Book. US Patent 6,641,170, 4 November 2003
36. Kirwan, D.G.: Interactive Picture Book with Voice Recording Features and Method of Use. US Patent 6,985,693, 10 January 2006
37. Rouse, R., Engberg, M., Parvin, N., Bolter, J.D.: MRX: an interdisciplinary framework for mixed reality experience design and criticism. Digital Creativity **26**(3–4), 175–181 (2015)
38. Billinghurst, M., Kato, H., Poupyrev, I.: The MagicBook: moving seamlessly between reality and virtuality. IEEE Graph. Appl. **21**(3), 6–8 (2001)
39. Rodenburg, P.: The Actor Speaks: Voice and the Performer. Methuen Drama, London (1997)
40. Linklater, K.: Freeing the Natural Voice: Imagery and Art in the Practice of Voice and Language (2006)
41. Berndt, A., Hartmann, K.: The functions of music in interactive media. In: Spierling, Ulrike, Szilas, Nicolas (eds.) ICIDS 2008. LNCS, vol. 5334, pp. 126–131. Springer, Heidelberg (2008). https://doi.org/10.1007/978-3-540-89454-4_19
42. Turner, C., Behrndt, S.: Dramaturgy and Performance, Revised Palgrave MacMillan, London and New York (2016)
43. Barad, K.: Meeting the Universe Halfway: Quantum Physics and the Entanglement of Matter and Meaning. Duke University Press, Durham and London (2007)
44. Parikka, J.: 12. Mapping noise: techniques and tactics of irregularities, interception, and disturbance. In: Media Archaeology, pp. 256–277. University of California Press (2011)
45. Rouse, R.: Woyzeck: augmented reality performance installation Master's project. Master's thesis, Communication and Culture. York University, Canada (2007)
46. Speiginer, G., MacIntyre, B., Bolter, J., Rouzati, H., Lambeth, A., Levy, L., Baird, L., Gandy, M., Sanders, M., Davidson, B., Engberg, M., Clark, R., Mynatt, E.: The evolution of the Argon web framework through its use creating cultural heritage and community–based augmented reality applications. In: Kurosu, Masaaki (ed.) HCI 2015. LNCS, vol. 9171, pp. 112–124. Springer, Cham (2015). https://doi.org/10.1007/978-3-319-21006-3_12
47. Holloway-Attaway, L.: Digital bridges and liquid borders: everyday storytelling and/as Baltic identity. In: Ekstrand, T. (ed.) Art Line: A Baltic Collaboration. Blekinge Museum (2012)
48. Holloway-Attaway, L.: Performing materialities: exploring mixed media reality and *Moby-Dick*. Convergence Int. J. Res. New Media Technol. **20**(1), 55–68 (2014)

Approaches Towards Novel Phenomena. a Reflection on Issues in IDN Research, Teaching and Practice

Hartmut Koenitz[1(✉)] and Mirjam Palosaari Eladhari[2]

[1] Södertörn University, Alfred Nobels allé 7, 141 89 Huddinge, Sweden
hartmut.koenitz@sh.se
[2] Stockholm University, 106 91 Stockholm, Sweden
mirjam@dsv.su.se

Abstract. What happens when scholars approach novel phenomena such as Interactive Digital Narrative (IDN)? How can we be certain that theoretical frameworks, analytical approaches, and vocabulary are adequate,which means that they are able to fully describe the specific characteristics of the novel phenomena? The same goes for approaches in the practice - how can we be sure that the chosen design methods enable the use of the full expressive potential of a novel phenomena? Furthermore, we ask how we can critique and improve categories and approaches? We reflect on how theory and analytical approaches have been produced so far, identify issues with the current practice, consider alternatives and propose a number of measures to improve the situation. Amongst them are increased efforts on the meta-level in terms of theoretical development and reflective works which concern themselves with the further development of the field, iterative approaches towards theory and method, a more critical approach in education, multi-method analysis, and dynamic representations.

Keywords: Novel phenomena · Analytical approaches · Semantic creep · Analytical blur · IDN studies · IDN Design · Multi method analysis

1 Introduction

In 2019, we [28] identified five major challenges affecting research and education in Interactive Digital Narrative (IDN), amongst them the dependency on legacy analytical frameworks (Groundhog Day), the lack of a shared vocabulary (Babylonian Confusion), the missing institutional memory of the field (Amnesia), the absence of established benchmarks (No Yardstick) and the overproduction of uncoordinated and quickly abandoned tools (Sisyphean Tool Production).

This paper is a follow up on this topic, in particular the 'Groundhog Day' question, by asking what it means to approach a novel topic from both a scholarly and professional perspective. We reflect on how theory and analytical approaches

© The Author(s), under exclusive license to Springer Nature Switzerland AG 2022
M. Vosmeer and L. Holloway-Attaway (Eds.): ICIDS 2022, LNCS 13762, pp. 441–454, 2022.
https://doi.org/10.1007/978-3-031-22298-6_28

have been produced so far, identify issues with the current practice and consider alternatives. To exemplify our a perspective, we consider a number of unsolved issues. Finally, we propose ways how scholars and practitioners can address the identified issues. In particular, we advocate for the recognition of both theoretical work and of efforts on a meta-level, which concern themselves with the development of the field.

2   Approaches Toward Novel Phenomena

What are novel phenomena? A working definition could be the following:

> Novel phenomena have characteristics which have not been described previously and which depend on the existence of a configuration or technology not previously available.

This definition distinguishes novel phenomena from those which have already existed, but have escaped detection and classification. We might understand these as newly detected phenomena. Examples of novel phenomena are radio, air travel or IDN, while exoplanets, bacteria and subatomic particles are all phenomena which existed long before they were detected. Novel does not mean that every aspect is entirely new - voice communication certainly existed long before it was transmitted via radio waves, air travel was understood in principle from the observation of birds and interactive forms of narrative existed long before the digital age. The novelty is therefore in an assembly not previously available.

From a scholarly perspective, a phenomenon can be understood as 'novel' long after it ceases to be 'new'. The latter means that the phenomenon has recently appeared, while the former denotes a situation when basic definitions, foundational terms and analytical/methodological approaches are still frequently debated by scholars. The related field of games studies is an example for a prolonged novelty status, as there is no commonly accepted answer to the question what exactly a game is. Indeed, game designer and scholar Paolo Pedercini of Molleindustria has created a satirical definition generator, producing many varieties of game definitions (http://www.gamedefinitions.com), to comment on the situation.

Equally, the field of IDN has novelty status, which has consequences for the scholarly approach towards it. In particular, we should be aware of the limitations imposed by using theory, methods and vocabulary originally developed for different, earlier phenomena. Consequently, we should ask the following questions in regard to IDN:

- What is the context in which theoretical concepts have been developed?
- What associated concepts do we inherit if we use a particular theoretical concept?
- Does the current object of analysis match the original object of analysis of a given analytical perspective?

- Are there specific aspects which are not covered in the original theoretical perspective?
- What is the correct way to distinguish different aspects? Binary (e.g. story/discourse) distinctions are popular, but are they adequate in a given context? Is a multi-dimensional perspective necessary?
- Do existing concepts embed a patriarchal, colonialist or otherwise oppressive perspective?

These questions are not asked often enough. In the next section, we will discuss what happens instead and why.

2.1 Limitations of Existing Approaches

When we analyze IDN as 'texts' (in the sense of 'mediated expression' as used in humanities disciplines) or by applying any other preexisting analytical perspective, we simultaneously - and perhaps unintentionally - define the ontological and epistemological status of IDN. There are number of reasons why scholars might be tempted to do so, for example in order to fit into existing academic discourses or because they want to use methods which are designed to analyze text objects. The problem here is that in doing so, IDN is assumed to posses the same characteristics as the original object of analysis. This is a problematic assumption, which limits analytical insights in three different ways. First, breakthrough insights often require novel frameworks. As a case in point is that Einstein could not understand the relation between time and space through gravitation with the means of Newtonian mechanic and consequently, he had to create the framework of relativity [15]. Secondly, as we have learned from the poststructuralist critique of structuralist perspectives [19], theoretical perspectives are not separate from reality, but instead create reality. Climax in narrative exists because the concept of climax has been created. Thirdly, as we have learned from feminist [6,9,22] and intersectional [13] scholars, established categories and concepts are often based on stereotypical, misogynist and racist perspectives and we are well advised to critically evaluate existing frameworks in this regard.

Abstracting from this discussion, we can identify an 'ideal sequence' of steps which should be followed in order to identify adequate analytical methods:

1. A novel phenomenon is detected
2. Characteristics of the novel phenomenon are identified
3. Existing analytical methods are evaluated whether they can detect and provide insights about these characteristics
4. Existing analytical methods are evaluated in terms of their underlying assumptions to identify potential repressive biases (e.g. racist, misogynist, classist)
5. If the methods show to be productive in step 3, and no problems are detected in step 4, they can be used effectively from now on
6. Else, novel methods for analysis need to be developed

The problem with the direct application of prior analytical perspectives for IDN is that steps two, three, and four are ignored. The question is what changes are necessary in scholarly practice to assure that these steps are no longer ignored. In approaching these questions, we first need to admit that our ideal model is also unrealistic, as existing analytical methods are the only ones initially available for the analysis of novel phenomena. A more realistic view might thus be the following:

1. A novel phenomenon is detected
2. Existing analytical methods are used to analyze the novel phenomenon
3. Existing methods are adapted to cover novel characteristics
4. When limitations of the resulting analytical insights are detected, further adaptations are introduced
5. The results are 'semantic creep' (the meaning of terms becoming increasingly vague) and 'analytical blur' (the extension of analytical lenses to include ever more categories)
[The following step might happen only after considerable time has passed and in some cases is yet to happen]
6. Eventually, a new paradigm of analytical methods and vocabulary is proposed and accepted by the community of scholars in the field

What we describe with our terms 'semantic creep'[1] and 'analytical blur' are problems which lead to the inability to distinguish phenomena from earlier, related ones and the failure to identify specific aspects. In such cases, progress in terms of analytical insights will be severely impeded until novel approaches and specific vocabulary are introduced (Step 6). In addition, potentially problematic underlying assumptions are also not detected.

A case in point for both 'semantic creep' and 'analytical blur' is the concept of paratext, as used in the related field of games studies. Jan Svelch [41] points to considerable issues with adaptation of the concept. In an analysis of over 200 publications, he notes that an expanded understanding (analytical blur) is dominant amongst game studies scholars, creating a conflict with the original meaning of the term (semantic creep) and effectively blinding the field from the more appropriate alternative 'cultural epiphenomena':

[...] it is not Gérard Genette's original definition from 1982, but rather the expanded version proposed by Mia Consalvo in 2007 that is used in 70 percent of the 235 analyzed academic texts written in English and published between 1997 and 2019. [...] In particular, the expanded framework, [...] tends to be too all-encompassing by stripping away the original limitation on authorship of paratextual elements and instead resembles the screen studies term cultural epiphenomena. [41]

Maybe the most prominent example of both 'semantic creep' and 'analytical blur' in regard to IDN is the use of Aristotelian Poetics (cf. [27]). Aristotle's

---

[1] A related perspective exists in psychology with the term "concept creep" [23].

original text has little to say about narrative in general and is instead focused on analyzing a specific form of Athenian drama, the tragedy. To apply Aristotle's framework to anything but a specific variety of classic Greek drama constitutes 'analytical blur,' while the notion of "Aristotelian tension arc" [34] is a particular case of 'semantic creep,' as neither the term 'tension' nor the term 'arc' exist in the original text (in two different English translations [2,3]) and the overall concept of an 'arc' is a later reinterpretation, originating with Gustav Freytag in the 19th century [20].

2.2   Aspects of the Scholarly Profession

Unfortunately, the problems of 'semantic creep' and 'analytical blur' might not be noticed, especially if the novel phenomena are being analyzed within the context of long-established disciplines, e.g. IDN within literary studies. In such a situation, there is little if any motivation to consider the limits of adaptation for pragmatic reasons. A scholar working on IDN in a literary studies context could very easily place themselves outside of that context once they leave established frameworks for literary analysis behind. The consequences for that scholar's career could be considerable in terms of finding suitable venues for publishing as well as competent and understanding evaluators and reviewers. What we are describing here is a severe professional problem for academics, an amalgam of normalized analytical approaches and pragmatic career pressures which impede scientific progress.

The multidisciplinary aspect of IDN research increases the severity of the problem. Scholarly access to fields different from their own is often naïve, meaning that they will apply a limited understanding of the related field in their own work. A case in point is the problematic use of narratological frameworks without proper justification by some artificial intelligence (AI) researchers, a practice, which has been criticized by Gervás et al.:

> Often, the most significant reason behind a particular choice of theory is that AI researchers find it easier to work with models that a previous researcher has already translated to AI jargon and applied in some previous computer program [21]

In addition, one of the authors has previously described [26] several fundamental differences between approaches in the humanities and the sciences in the difference between empirical observation and deduction. In particular, Seymour Chatman is testimony to this difference, when he states that "literary theory [...] should assume that definitions are to be made, not discovered" [12]. Scientific definitions originate in empirical observation, definitions in the humanities are deduced and created by the researchers.

Another important aspect is the lack of an aesthetic-critical perspective in narratological frameworks, while such a perspective is crucial as a success criterion for the evaluation of design-related work such as IDN research. Chatman sees any kind of critical evaluation of individual works as outside the realm of narratology and as a task for literary criticism.

Consequently, AI formalisms derived from narratological frameworks can produce output which might be structurally well-formed, yet "still be boring, haphazard, and trivial" [26]. Consequently, there is a need for an additional layer of "aesthetic evaluation" (ibid) in order to produce compelling IDN works. Ultimately, computer scientists working on IDN are encouraged to re-conceptualize their own position vs. narrative theory. They should no longer act as recipients of theoretical/analytical frameworks created in another discipline, but as scholars who create and further develop narrative theory themselves. Unfortunately, this type of perspective change does not happen often enough, yet some examples exist [11,16,35]. The reason for this overall lack of engagement with theory is two-fold: 1.) a concern of not having the necessary training to engage with theory and 2.) the lack of recognition of such activity in the home discipline of computer science.[2]

The second aspect is a problem also outside of computer science. In many academic disciplines, it is much easier to find recognition for studies using established qualitative or quantitative methods than for the development of novel frameworks and vocabulary. There is a problematic tendency to only see the former as proper academic work and disregard the latter. What is lacking here is the meta-level of evaluation which considers the overall impact of a given work on a field beyond established evaluation methods focused on the immanent coherence of a particular work. The point we are making here is that empirical evaluation should not be preferred over theoretical development. The former can become 'busywork' - technically correct but with little impact when it comes to advancing a field if the latter is not progressing also.

3   Further Examples of Problematic Approaches

Beyond the examples we have already mentioned - semantic creep and analytical blur in the concept of paratext and in regard to Aristotelian poetics, as well as a naïve approach of many AI researchers towards narratological models, many more issues exist which are related to the overarching problem of problematic approaches toward the novel phenomenon of IDN. In the following sections we exemplify the limitations of static representations, discuss the question of 'foreign' evaluation frameworks and reflect on the limitations of mechanical approaches in IDN production.

3.1   Static Representations of Dynamic Artifacts

The question of representation is a foundational but underdeveloped issue of the field. Highly dynamic systems, such as IDN works in the form of narrative-focused games can have thousands of simultaneous players, and works where procedural content generation is used, can produce a large number of different experiences for the interactor. Sophisticated rule system for fictional worlds may

---

[2] A rare positive counter example might be the field of software studies.

allow interactors to add content, and to steer the narrative directions, allowing for individual meaning making.

How can we adequately represent interactive and dynamic artifacts? Or rather: how much of the actual experience are we missing when we represent IDN through non-interactive representations such as journal articles, proceedings papers and student essays? Intuitively, it is clear that the fixed textual form of standard academic publications limit us to a mode of 'telling about the phenomena' we are concerned with, but we are unable to show or demonstrate. In this way, existing publication formats are inadequate to represent the dynamic forms we discuss here. And yet, there has been little if any discussion on this topic, which shows how easily we accept the established output formats of scholarly work, despite their obvious limitations. A related issue pertains to the depiction of interactive experiences in non-interactive formats. Janet Murray's Holodeck metaphor [38] provides a useful backdrop for discussions of advanced IDN formats, yet we must be mindful that the holodeck is a cinematic vision of a highly developed interactive artifacts in several variants of the Star Trek TV series franchise and not a demonstration of an actual implementation.

3.2   Evaluation Methods for Non-interactive Forms

Many evaluation methods exist which were originally developed for non-interactive forms. For example, Busselle and Bilandzic's [8] narrative engagement scale was developed by observing viewers of feature films and television programs. Using such frameworks as well as prior research concerned with immutable forms of narrative in IDN research is problematic, as the specific characteristics of IDN works are not covered by them. Moreover, if we evaluate IDN works with a framework meant for printed texts, then what we really measure is how well the respective interactive artifact performs in the foreign role of printed text. Consequently, applying such analytical perspectives will in all likelihood provide overly negative results, which are essentially 'false negatives', due to an inappropriate framework.

3.3   The Limits of Mechanical Thinking in Design

How can we as scholars and designers, conceptualize, analyze and understand an artifact which is highly procedural and where any particular experience and outcome is unpredictable? In game design, the idea of the artifact as the sum of its parts is still prevalent. Similarly, when it comes to analysis, variants of 'close reading' methods that assume a limited number of possible outcomes are still frequently used. However, these embodiments of mechanical thinking are highly problematic.

If the studied artifact is a zero-sum game, such as Chess or Go, or if it is a branching story with a limited set of outcomes (endings and win conditions), then it is perfectly feasible to describe and study these outcomes as fixed entities or elements. However, if the artifact in question has a high level of dynamism, for example, when the interactors are being afforded means of co-creation, then methods derived from the study of static objects such as print literature are no longer appropriate. In these cases, novel approaches are necessary to make sense of the artifacts themselves, the experience, and the product. It should also be clear that by only looking at the artifact itself, we are missing much of what makes an IDN artifact what it is, as a system made to be experienced and potentially changed and not read or viewed. There are many factors that will shape the experience, the co-created narrative, and individual meanings that emerge from the co-creative realization of the potential of an IDN. Much of what we have said in this section so far is common knowledge, yet mechanistic approaches are still widely used in analysis, teaching, and design. The paradigm shift to a new understanding of "system building", something we have argued for recently [29] is still a work in progress. One of the elements of this shift is to embrace newer models - cybernetics, system theory, chaos theory over Newtonian mechanics. Strangely, even though chaos theory has been commonly established since the 1960s and the other mentioned perspectives are even older, it is not uncommon for both system designers and scholars to fall back to a mechanistic world view. There are several reasons for this state of affairs, including school education systems that seldom feature these newer models in their curricula as well as the perceived complexity of these models. However, an important reason for the continued popularity of mechanical thinking is most likely in the completeness it offers, in the form of complete control over all aspects of design and in the complete analysis of a work. After all, as creators of a fictional world, should we not be able to know all the potential outcomes, and cater for whatever an interactor does, and assure that we give our audience a satisfying experience? Indeed, if we produce zero-sum games, branching stories and use confined rule systems, we can. There are multiple tools that successfully implement a mechanistic model to ensure that complex balances of asymmetric game play in resource based games are balanced (such as the Machinations framework [14]) and to ensure that a narrative does not contain logical fallacies, using STRIPS and systems spanning from STRIPS type planning systems [18]). However, a large portion of narrative-focused games, in particular games with thousands of simultaneous players such as MMORPGs, MOBA's, games using procedural content generation (PCG) and other IDN systems that allow co-authoring will not be predictable. These are phenomena that should be considered as novel and consequently requires novel approaches in both analysis and design.

As we have explained earlier [29], the MDA model [24] is an example for analytical lenses which embed the limitations of a Newtonian world view, in this case that a dynamic resulting from a mechanic is always predictable. Mateas and Stern [36] even argue that In order to understand procedural, dynamic artifacts, is necessary to recreate them. In addition, they argue that the act of building can facilitate the analysis of existing games. This stance is one that resonates with much of the practice in current games education, where prototyping and game making is central. The act of building allows to explore game design spaces. However, this perspective might also be unrealistic, as the time and effort for building is not always available, especially during the course of an educational program. Therefore, Mateas and Stern's approach does not mitigate the need for a conceptual understanding of interactive systems and a paradigm of system building. Fundamentally, the system builder designs for unpredictability. Hence, the scholar making sense of an unpredictable game or IDN needs to cater to this nature of the artifact. We do not yet have the analytical tools to fully understand this kind of artifact and consequently, more work is needed on such frameworks.

4   Measures for Improvement

In this section, we will propose several measures intended to improve the issues we have identified.

4.1   Encourage Meta-Level Scholarly Work

Meta-level reflections are critical components in advancing a field. Such scholarly works comes in the form of introductions of novel theoretical concepts, overview papers, literature review articles and meta-evaluations. A case in point in the related field of game studies is a paper by Law et al. which critically evaluates the widely used Game Experience Questionnaire (GEQ) and discovers considerable issues with it, chiefly the lack of a canonical version which impedes the comparison of results [33]. Without this particular publication, the GEQ in its current problematic form would have been used unquestioned by many more projects. Here we are reminded of the infamous calculation error which ascribed 'superfood' status to spinach and forced generations of children to eat an unloved food. For this reason, we need to continuously question, reflect and investigate, regardless how well established a particular methods, perspective or vocabulary is. In terms of the scholarly discipline this means to make space for theoretical development, meta-level work in academic outlets such as conference proceedings and journal papers. It is equally important to make sure such reflective efforts count for tenure and promotion.

4.2   Iterating on Theory and Method

Once we realize that scholarly tools, such as theory, method and vocabulary need adjustments or might even need to be reinvented to match novel phenomena, we need to start considering ways in which such developments and innovations can happen. A productive perspective would be to consider an approach common in sociology, where the awareness of the need for theoretical innovation is more developed. Grounded Theory and Extended Case Method [7] are frequently used to create theoretical innovation. The underlying idea of grounded theory is to fill gaps in the existing understanding by 'going to the ground', e.g. by means of a field study of previously unaccounted phenomena, using the results to create an improved, grounded, theoretical understanding.

A similar approach would help the field of IDN research and should therefore be encouraged. It would entail a critical reflection of existing analytical approaches to identify gaps and blind spots through observations, autoethnographic methods, interviews and comparisons with related fields. Instead of making the analysis of IDN works conform to frameworks established for different kinds of expressions, we need analytical frameworks that conform to IDN works in such a way that they can be used to analyze the object in question as well as possible.

4.3   Education for Critical Thinking, Not Assimilation

The questions we raise here are also a problem of education when we train students to find a matching theory or a fitting reference but do not train them to critically engage with theory. While students have been encouraged to unmask the intersectional discrimination inherent in many theoretical and analytical concepts, this critical approach should be extended. We also need to teach students to be critical from a purely academic perspective. The question we should train students to ask is whether a concept makes sense in the given context to reduce the unquestioned status of established concepts in academia. Academics should not have dogmas and need to be mindful of the effects of respect for established scholars. An analytical framework, a categorization, an analysis, are not automatically correct, remain useful or provide relevant insights just because a famous scholar has introduced them a while ago. We always need to ask whether something still applies, and we need to be prepared to identify limitation of previous work. Even well-established frameworks could and should be scrutinized. Conversely, we are not calling for baseless criticizing, but for educating students in a critical perspective, which asks basic questions such as whether a particular concept, analytical method, or vocabulary actually match the object of inquiry? As a concrete example, we could discuss with students the question what effect the framing of Façade [37] as a one-act Aristotelian drama has on our perception of the work and what alternative theoretical perspectives might fit.

4.4   Multi-method Analysis

Recently, the authors proposed the method of multi method analysis (MMA) in a jam format [17]. The notion of "jam" originates in music and describes a collaborative form of making music together, and the term has also been used in the context of game development in recent decades. In a 'game jam,' developers of all levels collaborate for a short, fixed period of time to create games together in groups. In an MMA jam, groups of scholars analyze the same artifact, during a fixed amount time, where each group uses different methods of analysis as their lenses. For example, at the DiGRA conference of 2022, around twenty scholars came together for an afternoon to analyze the narrative game *Firewatch* [10]. Five groups analyzed this narrative-focused game over the course of three hours. One group studied the game through a praxiological lens [31], foregrounding the making of the game. Another group analyzed the narrative design of the game using the SPP model [25,30], and a third approached the game by studying it's elements using formal analysis [32]. The fourth group investigated retellings of the game [16], and the fifth studied the games by means of close-play [42]. The MMA jam was concluded with a plenum where all five groups presented their findings. The discussion in the plenum resulted in a multifaceted rich understanding of the artifact, and showed how findings from one method can inform another. An example was the insight that decisions in the development process identified in the praxiology approach helped explain particular player experiences detected in the analysis of the retellings.

Given the diversity of the fields of IDN and game studies, in terms of academic backgrounds, where we use different types of methods for sense making and analysis, a collaborative exercise in this manner can be very informative. The goal of an MMA jam is unifying in that its explicit aim is to understand the IDN artifact including its experience by interactors from different perspective at the same time. In the current context, we suggest that an MMA jam is a valuable method to investigate novel phenomena in two ways. First, to investigate which types of analysis and methodological tools produce useful results and secondly, to understand what kinds of results are obtained by different methods. These insights can help to see what gaps there might be in the understanding of the artifact in question and may help to see if there is indeed an already existing methodological way of approaching it. The results of a jam might also suggest what types of mixed methods could be used and can spur a discussion of how different methods may elevate each other. Finally, the outcome of an MMA jam might also be a clear indication that existing methods fail to capture important aspects, and if this is the case, it can provide the basis for novel approaches.

4.5 Dynamic Representations and Analyses

How can we, as scholars, analyze and represent highly dynamic artifacts, describe them, and think about what meaning and impact they may have on individuals as well as on society and culture? One way to address this problem is by means of new publication formats which provide room for interactive experiences within the publication itself. The announced new Journal of Interactive Narrative Research, co-published by ARDIN and ETC Press, plans to offer such a format and if these plans are realized, would signify a significant step forward. In terms of students' essays an interesting way to overcome textual limitations is the use of Letsplay videos, as proposed by Rene Glas and Jasper van der Vught [42].

When it comes to analytical tools, we position our own work on the SPP framework (system, process, product) [25,30] and on retellings [16] as steps to address the analytical question. SPP understands the IDN artifact as a dynamic system, taking inspiration from Roy Ascott's theory of cybernetic art [4,5]. The next category - process - enables the analysis of a central aspect of IDN, the experience shaped in the constant exchange between system and audience as interactor. Finally, product recognizes different outputs as the result of the process, either in the form of an objective product (recording) or as a subjective product, a retelling. The latter provides a way to examine what comes out of these experiences in terms of what people tell each other about their experiences in the form of retellings [11]. These experiences are unique, and unless interactors tell each other about a specific sequence of events, they will not be known unless for the off-chance that someone would examine a log file. The personal experience can never be known by another unless it is told. It is crucial to understand that interactors do not only tell each other about sequences of events, as in recounting a story. They tell about what they experienced, what was important. In many cases the experiences in a fictional universe motivate interactors to create their own art. Frequently, such examples of fan art, including both images and narrative texts, are published on dedicated Internet forums, or at sites for fan fiction, such as *Archive of Our own* [1]. Studies of these retellings can provide insight of what players found meaningful, and why.

Calculating and visualizing the possibility space is yet another way to understand dynamic artifacts and systems. Summerville [40] has expounded on methodologies for assessing and analyzing generators of procedural content, expanding a concept from Smith and Whiteheads' notion of Expressive Range [39], a method for examining the range of variation of generated content and impact of changed input parameters. Summerville highlights the need for using technologies for visual assessment, for finding examples to highlight when describing a method to others, such as in a research paper, and for ways to assess to what extent a generator has learned a certain design, in particular for machine learned generation systems. Developing methods for these types of assessments and representations are vital for the future of the field, allowing system builders to assess generative systems, that in turn create aspects and elements of artifacts.

5   Conclusion

In this paper, we have considered issues that stem from the field's concern with a novel phenomenon, IDN. Novel in this regard has a double meaning - pertaining to the phenomenon itself, but also to the status of frameworks, analytical perspectives, design approaches and representations. While the former meaning denotes configurations which did not exist previously, the latter meaning is 'unsettled', denoting that debates about the ontological and epistemological status are ongoing. In this context we have discussed limitations of current approaches, but also considered reasons for them in terms of current professional structures for scholars and designers. Finally, we propose a range of measures to improve the situation, amongst them increased efforts on the meta-level in terms of theoretical development and reflective works which concern themselves with the further development of the field, iterative approaches towards theory and method, a more critical approach in education, multi-method analysis, as well as dynamic representations and analyses. We encourage fellow scholars to adapt and extend these measures. Our hope is that this article contributes another step to the development of the field.

References

1. Archive of Our Own: Fandoms (2009). https://archiveofourown.org/media
2. Aristotle, transl. Scholtz, A.: Poetics (2008). http://harvey.binghamton.edu/~clas214/aristotle_poetics.pdf
3. Aristotle, transl. Butcher, S.H.: Poetics (1902). http://classics.mit.edu//Aristotle/poetics.html
4. Ascott, R.: The Construction of Change. Cambridge Opinion (1964)
5. Ascott, R.: The cybernetic stance: my process and purpose. Leonard **1**(2), 105–112 (1968). https://doi.org/10.2307/1571947
6. de Beauvoir, S.: The Second Sex. Cape (1953)
7. Burawoy, M.: The extended case method. Sociol. Theory **16**(1), 4–33 (2016)
8. Busselle, R., Bilandzic, H.: Measuring narrative engagement. Media Psychol. **12**(4), 321–347 (2009). https://doi.org/10.1080/15213260903287259
9. Butler, J.: Gender trouble. Routledge, London, New York
10. Campo Santo: Firewatch (2016)
11. Kleinman, E., Carstensdottir, E., Seif El-Nasr, M.: A model for analyzing diegesis in digital narrative games. In: Cardona-Rivera, R.E., Sullivan, A., Young, R.M. (eds.) ICIDS 2019. LNCS, vol. 11869, pp. 8–21. Springer, Cham (2019). https://doi.org/10.1007/978-3-030-33894-7_2
12. Chatman, S.B.: Story and Discourse: Narrative Structure in Fiction and Film. Cornell University Press, Ithaca (1980)
13. Crenshaw, K.: On Intersectionality. The Essential Writings of Kimberle Crenshaw, New Press (2012)
14. Dormans, J.: Simulating mechanics to study emergence in games, pp. 2–7 (2011)
15. Einstein, A.: Die grundlage der allgemeinen relativitätstheorie **49**(7) (1916)
16. Eladhari, M.P.: Re-Tellings: the fourth layer of narrative as an instrument for critique. In: Rouse, R., Koenitz, H., Haahr, M. (eds.) ICIDS 2018. LNCS, vol. 11318, pp. 65–78. Springer, Cham (2018). https://doi.org/10.1007/978-3-030-04028-4_5
17. Eladhari, P.M., Koentiz, H.: MMAJams - multi-method analysis of games in research and education. In: Proceedings of the 2020 DiGRA International Conference: Play Everywhere, Tampere, Finland (2020)
18. Fikes, R.E., Nilsson, N.J.: Strips: a new approach to the application of theorem proving to problem solving. Artif. Intell. **2**(3–4), 189–208 (1971). https://doi.org/10.1016/0004-3702(71)90010-5
19. Foucault, M.: Power/Knowledge: Selected Interviews and Other Writings, 1972–1977. Knopf Doubleday Publishing Group, New York (1980)
20. Freytag, G.: Die Technik des Dramas (1863)
21. Gervás, P., Lönneker-Rodman, B., Meister, J.C.: Narrative models: narratology meets artificial intelligence. In: International Conference on Language Resources and Evaluation (2006)
22. Haraway, D.J.: A cyborg manifesto: science, technology. and socialist-feminism in the late twentieth century. Social. Rev. **15**, 424–457 (1985)
23. Haslam, N.: Concept creep: psychology's expanding concepts of harm and pathology. Psychol. Inq. **27**(1), 1–17. https://doi.org/10.1080/1047840X.2016.1082418
24. Hunicke, R., LeBlanc, M., Zubek, R.: MDA: A Formal Approach to Game Design and Game Research. AAAI Press, Palo Alto (2004)
25. Koenitz, H.: Towards a specific theory of interactive digital narrative. In: Interactive Digital Narrative: History, Theory and Practice (2015)

26. Koenitz, H.: Interactive storytelling paradigms and representations: a humanities-based perspective. In: Handbook of Digital Games and Entertainment Technologies, pp. 1–15. Springer, Singapore (2016). https://doi.org/10.1007/978-981-4560-52-8_58-1

27. Koenitz, H., Di Pastena, A., Jansen, D., de Lint, B., Moss, A.: The myth of 'Universal' narrative models. In: Rouse, R., Koenitz, H., Haahr, M. (eds.) ICIDS 2018. LNCS, vol. 11318, pp. 107–120. Springer, Cham (2018). https://doi.org/10.1007/978-3-030-04028-4_8

28. Koenitz, H., Eladhari, M.P.: Challenges of IDN research and teaching. In: Cardona-Rivera, R.E., Sullivan, A., Young, R.M. (eds.) ICIDS 2019. LNCS, vol. 11869, pp. 26–39. Springer, Cham (2019). https://doi.org/10.1007/978-3-030-33894-7_4

29. Koenitz, H., Eladhari, M.P.: The paradigm of game system building. Trans. Dig. Games Res. Assoc. **5**(3) (2021). https://doi.org/10.26503/todigra.v5i3.123, http://todigra.org/index.php/todigra/article/view/123

30. Koenitz, H., Eladhari, M.P., Louchart, S., Nack, F.: INDCOR white paper 1: A shared vocabulary for IDN (Interactive Digital Narratives) (2020). https://arxiv.org/abs/2010.10135, _eprint: 2010.10135

31. Kultima, A.: Game design praxiology. Ph.D. thesis, Tampere University, Finland (2018)

32. Lankoski, P., Björk, S.: Formal analysis of gameplay. In: Game Research Methods, pp. 23–35. ETC Press, Pittsburgh (2015)

33. Law, E., Brühlmann, F., Mekler, E.: Systematic review and validation of the game experience questionnaire (geq)-implications for citation and reporting practice. In: CHIPlay 2020 (2018)

34. Mateas, M., Stern, A.: Structuring content in the façade interactive drama architecture. In: Third Artificial Intelligence for Interactive Digital Entertainment Conference (2005). http://www.aaai.org/Papers/AIIDE/2005/AIIDE05-016.pdf

35. Mateas, M.: A preliminary poetics for interactive drama and games. Dig. Creat. **12**(3), 140–152 (2001)

36. Mateas, M., Stern, A.: Build it to understand it: ludology meets narratology in game design space. In: DiGRA 2005 - Proceedings of the 2005 DiGRA International Conference: Changing Views: Worlds in Play, Vancouver, Canada (2005)

37. Mateas, M., Stern, A.: Procedural authorship: a case-study of the interactive drama façade. In: Digital Arts and Culture: Digital Experience: Design, Aesthetics, Practice (DAC 2005), Copenhagen, Denmark (2005)

38. Murray, J.H.: Hamlet on the Holodeck. The Free Press (1997)

39. Smith, G., Whitehead, J.: Analyzing the expressive range of a level generator. In: Proceedings of the 2010 Workshop on Procedural Content Generation in Games, PCGames 2010, Monterey, California. Association for Computing Machinery, New York (2010). https://doi.org/10.1145/1814256.1814260

40. Summerville, A.: Expanding expressive range: evaluation methodologies for procedural content generation. In: Proceedings of the AAAI Conference on Artificial Intelligence and Interactive Digital Entertainment, vol. 14, no. 1 (2018)

41. Švelch, J.: Paratextuality in game studies: a theoretical review and citation analysis. Games Stud. **20**(2), 1–3 (2020)

42. Van Vught, J., Glas, R.: Considering play: from method to analysis. Trans. Dig. Games Res. Assoc. **4**(2) (2018). https://doi.org/10.26503/todigra.v4i2.94

Constructing a Catbox: Story Volume Poetics in *Umineko no Naku Koro ni*

Isaac Karth[1], Nic Junius[1], and Max Kreminski[1,2(✉)]

[1] University of California, Santa Cruz, Santa Cruz, USA
{ikarth,njunius}@ucsc.edu
[2] Santa Clara University, Santa Clara, USA
mkreminski@scu.edu

Abstract. Many interactive digital narrative (IDN) systems are capable of producing numerous distinct *storylines*, which share some common properties but differ from one another in ways that appear contradictory when attempting to treat them as co-canonical. One theory of IDN poetics therefore positions an IDN system as defining a *story volume:* a generating function that produces storylines, and whose meaning lies not just in the storylines themselves but also in the relationships *between* these storylines. However, the discussion of story volumes has until now been entangled with the discussion of choice and emergence, making the scope of this theory's applicability unclear. To advance understanding of the poetics of story volumes, we examine *Umineko no Naku Koro ni*—a heavily metafictional visual novel series with no emergent narrative component and almost no player choice, but in which the characters explicitly understand themselves as existing within a story volume—as a case study of how story volumes can be used to create narrative meaning.

Keywords: Game studies · Narrative design · Story volumes · Interactive digital narrative · Poetics · Theatricality

1 Introduction

Many interactive digital narrative (IDN) systems are capable of producing numerous distinct *storylines*, which share some common properties but differ from one another in ways that appear contradictory when attempting to treat them as co-canonical. One theory of IDN poetics therefore positions an IDN system as defining a *story volume*: a generating function that produces storylines, and whose meaning lies not just in the storylines themselves but also in the relationships *between* these storylines.

The theory of story volumes was originally proposed by Jason Grinblat in the context of interactive emergent narrative. For Grinblat, a story volume is "a family of emergent stories, all of which are begotten by a set of carefully curated system parameters" [16]. However, despite its introduction in the context of emergent storytelling specifically, the theory of story volumes also has a broader

M. Vosmeer and L. Holloway-Attaway (Eds.): ICIDS 2022, LNCS 13762, pp. 455–470, 2022.
https://doi.org/10.1007/978-3-031-22298-6_29

applicability to IDN in general, providing a common terminology for discussing issues related to the experience of difference and repetition across multiple stories generated by a single IDN system. It would therefore be useful to disentangle the discussion of story volumes from the specifics of their use to understand interactive emergent narrative in particular.

To advance a more general understanding of the poetics of story volumes, we examine *Umineko no Naku Koro ni*—a heavily metafictional visual novel series with no emergent narrative component and almost no player choice, but in which the characters explicitly understand themselves as existing within a story volume—as a case study of how story volumes can be used to create narrative meaning. *Umineko* is unusually explicit in its discussion of its own structure, and therefore presents an unusually strong exemplar of story volume poetics in a non-choice-based and non-emergent context. Notably, *Umineko* has also seen little discussion in the English-language academic literature to date,[1] making this paper one of the first descriptions of *Umineko* from a game studies lens.

2   Related Works

Our definition of *story volume* is taken from Grinblat's "Emergent Narratives and Story Volumes" [16], which in turn builds on the sense of the term introduced in a Project Horseshoe group report [12]. The story volumes framework is elaborated further by Grinblat et al. [17], who contrast story volumes with the *protostory* concept from Koenitz's *System, Process, Product* model of IDN [28]: unlike a protostory, a story volume puts its "emphasis on the shape of the Product stories and de-emphasis on any narrative cohesion prescribed by the System" [17]. We elaborate further on the connection between story volumes and *Umineko* in the remainder of this paper.

Umineko involves the repeated diegetic "replaying" of very similar events. There have been many discussions of the role that replaying and rewinding have in games. For instance, Kleinman et al. present a framework for discussing rewind mechanics [27]. In that framework, from our perspective as players, *Umineko* has designer controlled rewind; has either scope 0 or global scope; uses UI and narrative elements in its rewind presentation; has a linear structure at its meta-level; and acknowledges the existence of the rewinding to an unusually metafictional degree, even when compared to many other games that have extra-diegetic acknowledgement of rewinding.[2]

In "Reading Again for the First Time: A Model of Rereading in Interactive Stories," Mitchell and McGee "propose a model of rereading in interactive stories

---

[1] With rare exceptions, such as the occasional undergraduate or MA thesis [21,31]. The previous games in the *When They Cry* media mix (*Higurashi no Naku Koro ni*) have had more attention [1,19,32,39], though that is partially due to the anime adaptation and overall cultural impact rather than the games per se.

[2] From the *characters'* metafictional perspective, the "game board" (as discussed in Sect. 4.1) has designer dominant control, dynamic scope, and an ontologically complicated narrative justification.

in which readers are initially rereading to reach some form of closure" [35]. Separately, Mitchell and Kway discuss replay and rereading in storygames with a rewind mechanic, particularly with the distinction of playing for completeness and playing for closure in the context of *Elsinore* [33]. While *Umineko* continually rewinds to the beginning, the more linear metafictional frame story emphasises reading "in a new way" [33] and presents another form of repeat experience to include in future analyses.

3   What is *Umineko no Naku Koro ni?*

Umineko no Naku Koro ni (lit. *When the Seagulls Cry*) is an independently-developed episodic visual novel by the doujin circle 07th Expansion [13,14]. It consists of eight episodes, beginning with four Question Arcs (each of which depicts an alternative version of the same events) and concluding with four Answer Arcs (which present additional backstory and metafictional discussion between the characters regarding what happened in the question arcs).

Umineko's first episode begins as a realistically-grounded orthodox whodunit murder mystery on an isolated island, portraying itself as a Golden Age detective puzzle novel: the kind of mystery that the reader has a fair chance to solve through examining the clues. In-text it explicitly compares itself to the structure of Agatha Christie's *And Then There Were None* [9].

The initial plot is straightforward. Following years of estrangement from his family, Ushiromiya Battler pays a visit to his outrageously wealthy and occult-obsessed grandfather's private, isolated island of Rokkenjima[3] during a family conference in October 1986. The family's arguments about their future inheritance are abruptly interrupted by ritual murder. While the more superstitious people present attribute the murders to the unseen magical witch Beatrice, most of the family is initially skeptical, unwilling to pass the blame to a presumably nonexistent witch who never appears on-screen. They gradually become less skeptical as the ritual continues, with characters being killed in seemingly impossible locked-room murders. The first episode ends with all of the characters presumed dead and the mystery of the impossible murders unsolved.

So far this mirrors the structure of Agatha Christie's novel, with an extra dash of slasher horror. The story swerves at this point: in an extradiegetic epilogue the characters conclude that the unsolved murders mean that they were in a fantasy novel, with magical murders as the only logical explanation. Battler disagrees, vehemently. At this point the previously unseen Beatrice walks through the fourth wall and appears on-stage, setting up the metafictional debate that drives the remaining episodes: Were the murders somehow committed by a human culprit or was it a witch's magic? Is Beatrice real? Is this mystery or fantasy?

As befitting a game about the ontological status of a particular murder mystery, the mystery genre itself is a major theme and discussed in detail, particularly the sub-genres that focus on solvable puzzles. Authors such as Agatha

---

[3] Which can be read as "Six House Island" in a nod to Ayatsuji Yukito's title conventions (e.g. *The Decagon House Murders* [2]).

Christie, Shimada Souji, and (anachronistically) Ayatsuji Yukito[4] are mentioned by name, as well as the personification of Knox's "Ten Commandments" for detective fiction [22], tying it to both the Western Golden Age [23] detective fiction tradition as well as the parallel Japanese *honkaku* and *shin honkaku* subgenres [11,41].

By borrowing elements of detective fiction, *Umineko* sets up a parallel between what we might term the game of solving a mystery and the game of understanding the story volume. The characters and the player are both trying to understand the same thing: what are the rules that govern this space we find ourselves in?

4   How Does *Umineko* Illuminate Story Volume Poetics?

Umineko's first four episodes—the Question Arcs—depict four alternative storylines drawn from a single story volume: different versions of the Rokkenjima Incident, in which the vast majority of those present on the island are killed in some way. The final four episodes—the Answer Arcs—shift to presenting backstory and conflict between the characters as to which interpretation of the story volume as a whole is most true or valid. The mystery that the characters (and the audience) seek to solve thus gradually shifts from centering on the question of what happened in *one particular storyline* to the question of what common circumstances are consistent with *all* of the depicted storylines: in other words, what parameters define the story volume.

In a metafictional move, in *Umineko* discussing the shape of the story volume is a central part of the plot. This first becomes apparent in the epilogue of episode 1, which initially appears to be a non-diegetic, non-canonical, out-of-character *omake* in the form of a "wrap party," with the characters speculating about how they could do better next time (Fig. 1). But when Battler objects to blithely accepting the magical nature of the murders, the witch Beatrice breaks the fourth wall's fourth wall, walking onto the stage and turning the backstage conversation into part of a larger diegesis.

This meta-diegesis sets the stage for the rest of the games: in a tea room in Purgatory, Battler and Beatrice argue about whether the story is fantasy (and the culprit is a witch) or mystery (and a human somehow committed the impossible murders).

Structurally (in the Carstensdottir et al. sense of the graph structure [7]), *Umineko* consists of a linear sequence of eight episodes. With one major exception, the episodes are linear visual novels, though the player has access to a hypertextual "Tips" menu that enables them to revisit key information about

---

[4] Episode 5:
　「綾辻行人のデビューは来年だ。」
　「魔女のくせに細かいこと気にしますね。」
　Beatrice: "Ayatsuji Yukito doesn't make his debut until next year."
　Erika: "You sure are picky for a witch.".

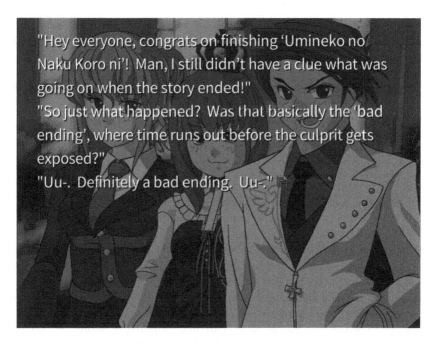

Fig. 1. Characters in the first episode epilogue, discussing the ending of the episode in branching narrative terms.

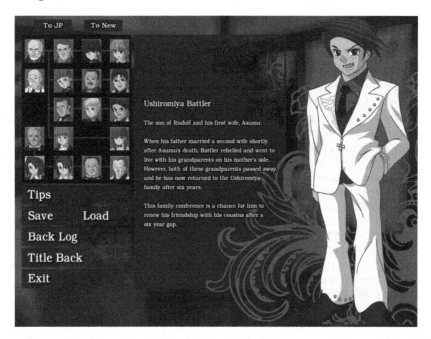

Fig. 2. The game is mostly linear but includes hypertextual information about the characters and clues.

the characters and events of this episode so far (Fig. 2). The final episode contains several opportunities for player choice leading up to a conclusive interactive branching point, which puts the question to the player: is it fantasy magic, or a mystery trick?

This mostly-linear structure that nevertheless is intimately concerned with examining story volumes gives us a unique opportunity to consider story volumes in the absence of emergent and choice-based narrative considerations.

4.1   A Diegetic Story Volume

The degree to which *Umineko* discusses its own structure is somewhat unusual, even within the context of metafictional story volumes.[5] The shape of the story volume is an explicit topic of discussion as the characters try to figure out the rules of the mystery.

Battler and Beatrice refer to the storylines that play out in front of them as games on a game board. The characters on the island are referred to as game pieces, first as a metaphor and then, in a pataphoric move, as the literal pieces in the game Battler and Beatrice are playing (as they grow into the diegetic roles of detective-story reader and author respectively).

The game board that the characters are using emanates, in our terms, a story volume: the game board is a set of rules that express what stories are possible within that story volume.[6] The first four episodes of *Umineko*, therefore, depict a series of storylines drawn from the same story volume, presented as both a repeated in-world tragedy on the game board and a discussion topic in the metafictional debate.

The reason *Umineko* gives for foregrounding the story volume is to get the reader to start thinking about the differences and similarities between storylines. It deploys the metafictional discussion as part of a poetic strategy to encourage the player to look beyond the immediate situation of a single storyline.[7] The games encourage the player to triangulate the mystery from multiple angles, with an explicit goal of inducing the audience to reason out the solutions and their implications while avoiding explicitly stating them within the text.[8]

---

[5] The character roster eventually includes personifications of the author, the reader, fanfic writers, internet commentators, love, marriage, the roles of certainty and miracles in narrative, detective fiction genre conventions, guns, and duct tape.

[6] Episode 5:
「...同じゲーム盤を使う以上、この子に出来ないことは出来ません。......しかし、この子がやらないことはやれます。」
Virgilia: "...Since they're using the same game board, they cannot do anything that this child cannot do. However, they can do things that this child wouldn't do.".

[7] Episode 7 Tea Party:
伝えたいたった一つのことを、いくつものゲームを重ねて語る。
A single message can be conveyed over several games.

[8] In several ways this is reminiscent of the novels described in Borges' "Examen de la obra de Herbert Quain" [6]—Like *The God of the Labyrinth* the reader is left to discover for themselves that a stated solution is wrong, like *April March* the text

The first step of story volume poetics is to convey to the player that there *is* a story volume. Making the metafiction diegetic is a particularly blunt way to do it, though many other games have experimented with other ways to signal this: "Clementine Will Remember This" in *The Walking Dead* [43] implies a story volume extradiagetically, the diegetic time travel [20] in *Majora's Mask* [37] and *Ocarina of Time* [36] uses time loops and contrasts between timelines, *Nine Hours, Nine Persons, Nine Doors* [10] includes a flowchart mapping out the story volume, and repeated resurrections in *Planescape: Torment* [4] make the common videogame dying/respawning cycle diegetic.

4.2   The Cat Box and the Game Board

The game board encompasses the events that happened during two days on Rokkenjima. As the episodes continue, it is revealed that people outside the island do not know the solution to the mystery either. In-game this unsolved mystery is described as a *cat box*, in reference to Schrödinger's cat: just as the cat is at once both alive and dead until the box is opened, without the knowledge of the true ending, any of the storylines might be true.

This is an explicit statement of the poetics of a branching or emergent narrative game, making some of the possible procedural rhetorics [5] more visible. For example, *Umineko* frequently makes use of the multiple storylines to give us multiple perspectives on the characters, in a way that is difficult to do without a story volume. Changing the mutually-exclusive situations that the characters are subjected to expands our insight into their relationships: we can see both how George reacts to the death of his mother Eva, and how Eva reacts to the death of her son.

Rather than being limited to a single version of the character, we can examine all possible versions. This is a useful device for a writer: since we aren't locked in to a single version of events, we can try out different combinations. As the characters become more fleshed out, they transition into actors playing new roles.

Part of the pleasure of playing the game comes from being able to build up a mental model of the characters through seeing them react to multiple variants of the same situation. This anticipation of behavior and the contrast between characters is accelerated in the context of a story volume.

By means of two mutually-exclusive storylines, the first two episodes establish a parallel between Natsuhi and Rosa: how does each character behave when thrust into the role of being the sole responsible adult, trying to protect her daughter as their family is murdered around them? We see how they both define themselves through their role as a mother, their sense of failure in living up to the expectations the patriarchal environment has placed on them, and the tragedy this engenders. Comparing their roles across storylines, we can see themes that would otherwise be less visible.

---

branches backwards in time, like *The Secret Mirror*, the characters find themselves in stories written by others, and like *Statements* several of the stories are deliberately calculated to disappoint the reader.

On the other hand, the opportunity to show the characters from multiple perspectives shows how the story volume can be used to enrich the characters. Rosa's relationship with her daughter Maria is explored across multiple storylines. A pivotal event for them that occurs early in most storylines is when Maria is caught in the hurricane's torrential rain: we see different ways that it could happen and a range of possible outcomes. Was Rosa neglectful, forgetful, abusive, or uninformed? The different configurations of their relationship are reiterated across multiple storylines, allowing the intertwined horror and love to assume new configurations in each. The player's role as they are exposed to different readings and portrayals of recurring events can be likened to that of the dramaturg in theatrical production, who is sometimes tasked with compiling the production history of a play to better understand the decisions made and themes emphasized in previous productions [8].

The general trend in interactive fiction that is centered around discovery is toward what Sedgwick termed *paranoid reading*, focusing on teasing out the "true" meaning from a text [40]. *Umineko*, however, refuses to build up to a singular "true" ending, instead repeatedly emphasizing that every storyline being presented is potentially true, though not equally plausible. Thus, the player is invited to actively engage in *reparative play*, taking parts that "arrive in disrepair" and assembling them into a coherent whole [17]. With the cat box left deliberately unopened, it is ultimately up to the reader to assemble their own preferred interpretation of the events on Rokkenjima, drawing on fragments of potential truth that were presented across many mutually contradictory storylines.

4.3   Probability and the Shape of the Story Volume

One way that *Umineko* encourages reparative play is through its depiction of probability and plausibility. Though the events of each storyline can be seen as true, some events take place in a majority or plurality of possible storylines, while some are rare, taking place only in storylines where multiple unusual circumstances intersect.

As an unrolled[9] story volume, *Umineko* can induce a felt sense of probability in the player by literally controlling how frequently a certain event takes place across the storylines that are presented. Because all of the presented storylines conform to the rules of the story volume, as players we begin to develop a sense of what is and is not probable as we untangle the overdetermined tragedy. This can be used to establish some recurring scenes as highly likely, if not inevitable (e.g., Maria being caught out in the rain, which occurs in all of the Question Arcs) and even to create a sense of dramatic irony: while the characters speculate that Jessica would have been less headstrong and independent if she had been raised in other circumstances, we players know from observing her across multiple storylines that this aspect of her personality is a constant.

---

[9] *Unrolled* in the sense of an unrolled loop in computer science: code that would have been repeated in a loop is instead written sequentially (e.g. [29]).

Simultaneously, through its metafictional elements, *Umineko* is able to *invoke* probability by having characters with greater metafictional awareness discuss it directly: for instance, when Bernkastel (the story volume-traversing Witch of Miracles) states that a particular depicted event is so rare that "there's actually a 2,578,916/2,578,917 chance" against it happening[10]. Because the player has (by this late stage in the game) directly witnessed the fact that some events are more plausible than others across the story volume, an explicit statement about probability from a metafictionally privileged character can thus be used to create the felt sense of a miracle—just as explicit procedural die rolls can be used in games like *Disco Elysium* [45] to make the player feel that they have succeeded or failed against all odds.

From a storyteller's perspective, manipulating the weight of probability as felt by the reader is difficult in the absence of a story volume but highly effective in its presence. In *Umineko*, this becomes even more apparent when we move from considering the vanishing probability of a miracle to the certainty of tragedy.

4.4   Logical Quantifiers

In order to explicitly lay out the rules for fair play in the mystery, *Umineko* introduces a mechanic for stating absolute truth: red text. When a witch makes a statement with red text, it is axiomatically true. This allows the mystery narrative to continue without excessive haggling about descriptive details in the clues, but it also sets up a set of logical constraints on the shape of the story volume: something stated in red text is true of all storylines. If it is stated in red text that the murders were never done with small bombs, then that is true across the entire story volume, closing off previously-perceived possibilities. This applies to *previously encountered* storylines as much as future ones: while we readers might encounter storylines in a particular order, they are notionally parallel, not sequential.

Red text has utility to both the characters, who are debating the rules of the story volume, and the players, who are trying to learn the rules of the story volume. Its appearance primes players to actively participate in the mystery-solving (by giving them footholds on which to base their theories) while also actively directing them to think of the mystery in terms of the story volume and its possible shapes.

As a device, absolute statements can also be deployed for emotional effect: the pacing of a reveal can be timed to crush a character's dreams with the realization that such a thing is categorically impossible. Further, discovering absolutes in the story volume can imbue previously insignificant-seeming details with new narrative weight, provoking players to reinterpret the implications of previously depicted events.

Notably, none of this requires resolving the ambiguities in the text. *Umineko* wants its players to grasp the ambiguity, but not necessarily to resolve it. The text explicitly encourages engagement with what *could have* happened, perhaps

---

[10]   ２５７万８９１７分の２５７万８９１６の確率で．

even more than it encourages players to solve the mystery of what *did* happen—and most often, red text is deployed to rule out a single hypothesized explanation for past events without suggesting any obvious alternative. Thus, absolute statements are used to keep the player in a state of uncertainty, even as the player attempts to uncover the story volume's ultimate truth.

4.5 Storygameness and Story Volumes

Mitchell's work on *storygameness* discusses how the player's understanding of a game as a storygame affects their focus: "as players experience a storygame, they shift focus between the narrative and the playable system" [34]. *Umineko* explicitly engages with the question of whether the story or the system should be the focus of player understanding at several points.

In *Umineko*'s fifth episode, the role of the detective is taken over by Furudo Erika, and her approach is explicitly contrasted with Battler's quest. By this point, Battler is more interested in the message that he believes the rules are intended to communicate. Erika, in contrast, wants to learn the rules in order to reduce the mystery to a logic puzzle and never have to think about it again. In a deliberate construction, neither is right: Battler is unable to comprehend the message without understanding the rules, and Erika is unable to solve the mystery without understanding the message.

This theme continues, and it is extended to the audience: when answers to the mysteries are presented in later episodes, the reveals are structured so that the logic is incomplete without understanding the characters and their motivation in the narrative. Ultimately, *Umineko* is structured so that the narrative is incomprehensible without understanding the rules of the game board, but the rules are incomplete without also understanding the narrative.

The interdependence of system and story in the mystery as a whole is emphasized in other episodes: for example, when in-universe authors appear on stage, writing what is—from their point of view—real-person fan fiction [15,44] about the murders, strictly following the rules of the game board. Or the extended discussion of the role of the author and the reader in the meta-frame story for the meta-world of the game-board in the fifth episode.

In each case, the rules and the narrative coexist: while an author could, in theory, write anything, there is a limit to a reader's suspension of disbelief, particularly when the story needs to conform to the expectations of the mystery genre. Getting the reader to accept a miracle is difficult. This is part of why *Umineko* focuses on probability: as with the die rolls in *Disco Elysium*, the reader needs some mechanism to accept improbable results, even—or especially—good results.

As it turns out, the author *can't* write just anything: they can only write what fits within the story volume.

4.6   PCG Poetics

By treating a story volume as a generating function or ruleset for many different storylines, we also gain the ability to analyze story volume poetics using tools that were originally developed to understand the subjective experience of procedural content generation (PCG).

For example, Karth's category of *repetition* in PCG poetics is a useful lens to use for analyzing story volumes, since the parallel story threads have an aesthetic effect via *repetition* [25]: the similarities help the differences stand out, while also making it more obvious what each storyline has in common. Viewed through this lens, the aesthetic effect of the storylines is linked to the ritual repetition of events. *Umineko* makes this explicit with a literal occult murder ritual, but this repetition aesthetic can be seen more broadly as other elements repeat. When viewed together, parallel instances of the ritual have the feeling of call-and-response, as we anticipate the next seemingly inevitable murder.

In a generative system, an artifact that breaks the pattern draws attention. In a story volume narrative, we read to discover what is different this time: a difference signals that there is more story to be found. We use these landmarks to orient ourselves.

The relationship between the individual instance and the distribution of possibility can communicate something that neither could on their own. We need the story volume to be able to notice differences, and the individual storyline to appreciate why those differences matter. We can only understand the heart of the story when we have a sense of both.

We can think of both generative systems and story volumes as possibility spaces, with each individual storyline a point in this space. This implies that tools for analyzing generative spaces—such as Expressive Range Analysis [30, 42]—can be applied to interactive narratives, and tools for working with interactive narratives can be applied to generative systems.

This is similar to how tabletop roleplaying games and procedural content generators are systems of rules that describe a volume of possible content. As Guzdial et al. argue, viewing tabletop roleplaying games under a PCG lens gives us a way to describe how roleplaying game systems can produce widely varied content that is nevertheless bounded by its possibility space [18]. In contrast, viewed through the lens of a game between the player and the author, the process of "solving" a mystery story revolves around narrowing a space of possible storylines down to a plausible and satisfying explanation.

Umineko is a mystery story, but it is also a commentary on the puzzle-mystery genre. The concept of the "fruitful void" [3] from tabletop roleplaying theory—the unsystematized central theme at the heart of every tabletop roleplaying game—is particularly interesting in this light. In *Umineko*, the solution to the mystery is never explicitly stated.[11] Instead, the reader-player is encouraged to discover the thematic heart of the story by circling but never fully resolv-

---

[11] Indeed, the writer has stated in interviews that one desire was that the solution would not be presented in such a way as to able to be captured in a screenshot [26].

ing the ambiguity. The multiple endings leave it up to the reader to determine: was it mystery, or was it magic?

4.7 Theatricality

This cycle of replaying the same storyline with minor variations conforms to the definition of *theatricality* discussed by Junius et al.: "a property of creative works that repeatedly reinterpret and recontextualize a partially fixed performance over a period of time, in such a way that this continual recontextualization is at least partially exposed to the audience" [24].

Similar to how *Hades* cycles players between the *stage* (a single attempt to escape the underworld) and the *diegetic backstage* (the House of Hades) [24], *Umineko* implements internal theatricality: it has both a stage (the "game board", on which a particular version of the Rokkenjima Incident plays out) and a diegetic backstage (the purgatorial tea room). In both cases, the characters return to the backstage to debrief, where we see them as actors (or playing pieces) rather than characters. In the backstage our collective understanding of the story-volume/play-script increases: diegetically, the actors come to understand their roles better as we players grow our understanding in parallel. Additionally, in both *Umineko* and *Hades*, this performance/reflection loop calls attention to subtle differences between performances, leading the player to pay attention to details that they would have overlooked otherwise.

For Junius et al., theatricality also enables the player to experience the production process, from early rehearsals to opening and finally closing nights. In episode 8, *Umineko* implements this diegetically, presenting a final command performance, with the characters commenting on the skill in staging the mystery gameboard, while a character tries to come to terms with the meaning of the story volume as a whole.

Theatricality, in this sense, is directed to getting you to try new things: the central mechanic of the mystery genre is the player coming up with a theory to explain the mystery; because *Umineko* incorporates this cycle of theatricality, it can diegetically demolish the theories that you formed on previous runs. But the cycle continues, inviting you to form new and better theories. The player's improving skill is invested in acquiring a deeper understanding of the rules of the mystery and the themes of the story volume.

Theater and theatricality can be viewed as a search for novelty and "making the old look new" [38], as described by Zeami Motokiyo in his treatises on Nō theater. Our understanding of the characters and their situations is fueled by this cycle of new looks at old things. Characters who are unsympathetic from one perspective are more understandable from another angle.

For one example: We get some familiarity with Maria's interests in the occult in the first episode, a deeper look at her troubled relationship with her mother in the second episode, and much deeper insight how both of them connect later, all of which is necessary for understanding how the conclusion of the fourth episode could be possible. Each cycle gives us a new perspective on old events.

Understanding can build up through successive episodic cycles, triangulating insights about the story volume that are never explicitly stated in the text.

5   Summing It All Up: The Heart of the Story Volume

Viewing a storyline in the context of its story volume tells us more than either would on their own. The possibility space of a story volume defines an *expressive range* [42] of storylines that meet the story volume's constraints. The meaning of an individual storyline is partially dependent on its positioning within the overall story volume, much as Kreminski et al. [30] argue that individual artifacts from a generator's expressive range derive their meaning in part from where they fall within this expressive range (cf. Sect. 4.6). After observing multiple storylines, the player develops a sense for what is probable, possible, or impossible in the story volume as a whole.

Episode 7 takes advantage of *Umineko*'s metafictional nature to explicitly address this by combining multiple storylines, looking across the entire story volume. This leads to a central theme of *Umineko* as a whole: knowing the facts isn't as important as understanding the heart of the story volume.

The theme of knowing the heart is most explicitly put forward by a character in the seventh episode, Will,[12] an about-to-retire detective who is driven by his care for the people affected by mysteries: "If you want to play the detective, don't neglect the heart,"[13] in his terminology, referencing the importance of understanding the motivation of the culprit when solving the mystery.

While a distant read of the shape of the story volume can give us valuable information, we also need the individual storylines to understand the heart of the story. The shape can't tell us what motivates the characters to make the decisions that create that shape. The statistics of the story volume don't tell us about the emotional impact. We need to experience the storyline for ourselves to feel the emotional impact of Maria being abandoned in the rain.

The importance of understanding the story's heart is perhaps made clearest by the introduction of a new game mechanic in episode 5. Like the red text that is used to make absolute assertions from episode 2 onward, *Umineko*'s Answer Arcs also feature occasional instances of gold text—the exact meaning of which is never made explicit. However, it can be inferred that gold text statements represent conclusions that can only be drawn by someone who understands the story completely, particularly the character motivations that shape the story volume. We can therefore think of *Umineko* as a ritual guide—leading the player to a place from which they, too, can make conclusive statements about the shape of the story volume, speaking from the heart.

---

[12] Willard H. Wright (ウィラード・H・ライト), who is also an oblique reference to the American mystery writer S. S. Van Dine.

[13] 探偵気取るなら、心を忘れるんじゃねェ．

6   Conclusion

By examining *Umineko no Naku Koro ni* from the perspective of story volume poetics, this paper sets out an initial theory of how story volumes can create narrative meaning, independent of player choice and emergence. In particular, we find that distinctive forms of narrative meaning can arise in works of story volume narrative from the presentation of mutually contradictory storylines as equally true; from the player's felt sense of *probability* (i.e., what happens more or less frequently in storylines drawn from the same story volume); and from the existence of *logical quantifiers* (i.e., absolute truths about what is always required to happen, or never capable of happening, in any storyline drawn from the story volume). We also find strong connections between story volume poetics and the conceptual frameworks that have previously been used to make sense of *storygameness* (i.e., the extent to which players understand a game as a storygame); *PCG poetics* (i.e., the aesthetic effects of procedural content generation in games); and *internal theatricality* (i.e., the aesthetic effects of a system-facilitated performance/reflection loop in IDN).

Broadly speaking, this analysis of story volume poetics paves the way for a clearer understanding of any IDN work that encourages replay-with-variation; positions its characters as having awareness of the multiple storylines that might emerge from the system; or makes use of strategic re-presentation of events to achieve aesthetic effects on the player. From a technical perspective, this analysis also begins to suggest a novel, story volume-aware approach to story *generation*: by generating stories that are intended to be experienced as part of a story volume, we can take advantage of story volume poetics to achieve aesthetic effects that conventional forms of narrative might not be able to leverage as easily. We are especially excited to pursue this direction in the future.

Acknowledgements. Max Kreminski conducted part of this research while in residence at Stochastic Labs.

References

1. Andrews, D.K.: Genesis at the shrine: the votive art of an anime pilgrimage. Mechademia **9**, 217–233 (2014). http://www.jstor.org/stable/10.5749/mech.9.2014.0217
2. Yukito, A.: The Decagon House Murders. Pushkin Vertigo, London (2020–2017)
3. Baker, V.: The Fruitful Void (2005). http://lumpley.com/index.php/anyway/thread/119
4. Black Isle Studios: Planescape: Torment (1999)
5. Bogost, I.: Persuasive Games: The Expressive Power of Videogames. MIT Press, Cambridge (2007)
6. Borges, J.L.: Fictions. Calderbook; CB428. Calder Publications, Paris (1998)
7. Carstensdottir, E., Kleinman, E., El-Nasr, M.S.: Player interaction in narrative games: structure and narrative progression mechanics. In: Proceedings of the 14th International Conference on the Foundations of Digital Games. FDG 2019, Association for Computing Machinery, New York (2019). https://doi.org/10.1145/3337722.3337730

8. Chemers, M.: Ghost Light. Sothern Illinois UP (2010)
9. Christie, A.: And Then There Were None. Harper, New York (2011–1939)
10. Chunsoft: Nine Hours, Nine Persons, Nine Doors (2009)
11. Crampton, C.: Honkaku: a century of the Japanese whodunnits keeping readers guessing (2021). https://www.theguardian.com/books/2021/apr/27/honkaku-a-century-of-the-japanese-whodunnits-keeping-readers-guessing
12. Eiserloh, S.A.E., et al.: Group report: generative systems, meaningful cores. In: The Tenth Annual Game Design Think Tank Project Horseshoe 2015 (2015). https://www.projecthorseshoe.com/reports/featured/ph15r3.htm
13. 07th Expansion: Umineko no Naku Koro ni (2008). English release in 2016
14. 07th Expansion: Umineko no Naku Koro ni Chiru (2010). English release in 2017
15. Fathallah, J.: Reading real person fiction as digital fiction: an argument for new perspectives. Convergence **24**(6), 568–586 (2018). https://doi.org/10.1177/1354856516688624
16. Grinblat, J.: Emergent narratives and story volumes. In: Short, T., Adams, T. (eds.) Procedural Generation in Game Design. CRC Press, Hoboken (2017)
17. Grinblat, J., Manning, C., Kreminski, M.: Emergent narrative and reparative play. In: Mitchell, A., Vosmeer, M. (eds.) ICIDS 2021. LNCS, vol. 13138, pp. 208–216. Springer, Cham (2021). https://doi.org/10.1007/978-3-030-92300-6_19
18. Guzdial, M., et al.: Tabletop roleplaying games as procedural content generators. In: International Conference on the Foundations of Digital Games (2020)
19. Hack, B.: Ominous images of youth: worlds, identities, and violence in japanese news media and when they cry. Mechademia: Second Arc **10**, 236–250 (2015). https://www.jstor.org/stable/10.5749/mech.10.2015.0236
20. Hanson, C.: Recursive Temporalities, pp. 135–155. Indiana University Press (2018). http://www.jstor.org/stable/j.ctv176q4.10
21. Hattingh, J.: The intellectual hero's representation in anime: an exploration. Ph.D. thesis, University of Pretoria, Pretoria (2016). http://hdl.handle.net/2263/60363, MA Dissertation
22. Haycraft, H.: Murder for pleasure: the life and times of the detective story. Biblo and Tannen, New York, Newly Enlarged edn, with notes on additions to a cornerstone library and the haycraft-queen definitive library of detective-crime-mystery fiction (1974–1951)
23. Golden age traditions (2005). https://doi.org/10.1093/acref/9780195072396.013.0277, https://www.oxfordreference.com/view/10.1093/acref/9780195072396.001.0001/acref-9780195072396-e-0277
24. Junius, N., Kreminski, M., Mateas, M.: There is no escape: theatricality in Hades. In: The 16th International Conference on the Foundations of Digital Games (FDG) 2021 (2021)
25. Karth, I.: Preliminary poetics of procedural generation in games. Trans. Digit. Games Res. Assoc. **4**(3) (2019). https://doi.org/10.26503/todigra.v4i3.106
26. Keiya: Saishūkōsatsu umineko no naku koro ni chiru: answer to the golden witch Episode 5–8. ASCII Media Works, Tōkyō (2011)
27. Kleinman, E., Carstensdottir, E., El-Nasr, M.S.: Going forward by going back: Redefining rewind mechanics in narrative games. In: Proceedings of the 13th International Conference on the Foundations of Digital Games. FDG 2018. Association for Computing Machinery, New York (2018). https://doi.org/10.1145/3235765.3235773
28. Koenitz, H.: Towards a specific theory of interactive digital narrative. In: Interactive Digital Narrative, pp. 91–105. Routledge, London (2015)

29. Koseki, A., Komastu, H., Fukazawa, Y.: A method for estimating optimal unrolling times for nested loops. In: Proceedings of the 1997 International Symposium on Parallel Architectures, Algorithms and Networks (I-SPAN 1997), pp. 376–382 (1997). https://doi.org/10.1109/ISPAN.1997.645123
30. Kreminski, M., Karth, I., Mateas, M., Wardrip-Fruin, N.: Evaluating mixed-initiative creative interfaces via expressive range coverage analysis. In: 3rd Workshop on Human-AI Co-Creation with Generative Models (2022)
31. Landt, M.: Sentiment analysis as a tool for understanding fiction. Undergraduate course final project report, 2014/LIS590AD, University of Illinois at Urbana-Champaign (2014)
32. Mireault, J.: No slaughter without laughter?: music and genres in Japanese popular media. Ph.D. thesis, McGill University, Montréal, Canada, February 2013. https://escholarship.mcgill.ca/concern/theses/mc87pt98z
33. Mitchell, A., Kway, L.: "How do I restart this thing?" Repeat experience and resistance to closure in rewind storygames. In: Bosser, A.-G., Millard, D.E., Hargood, C. (eds.) ICIDS 2020. LNCS, vol. 12497, pp. 164–177. Springer, Cham (2020). https://doi.org/10.1007/978-3-030-62516-0_15
34. Mitchell, A., Kway, L., Lee, B.J.: Storygameness: understanding repeat experience and the desire for closure in storygames. In: DiGRA 2020-Proceedings of the 2020 DiGRA International Conference. DiGRA (2020)
35. Mitchell, A., McGee, K.: Reading again for the first time: a model of rereading in interactive stories. In: Oyarzun, D., Peinado, F., Young, R.M., Elizalde, A., Méndez, G. (eds.) Interact. Storytelling, pp. 202–213. Springer, Berlin Heidelberg, Berlin, Heidelberg (2012)
36. Nintendo: The Legend of Zelda: Ocarina of Time (1998)
37. Nintendo: The Legend of Zelda: Majora's Mask (2000)
38. Rimer, J.T., Yamazaki, M., et al.: On the Art of the Nō Drama: The Major Treatises of Zeami; Translated by J. Yamazaki Masakazu. Princeton University Press, Thomas Rimer (1984)
39. Ruh, B.: Adapting anime: transnational media between Japan and the United States. Ph.D. thesis, Indiana University, Bloomington, Ind., USA, May 2012. https://hdl.handle.net/2022/15920
40. Sedgwick, E.K.: Paranoid reading and reparative reading, or, you're so paranoid, you probably think this essay is about you. In: Touching Feeling, pp. 123–152. Duke University Press (2003)
41. Silver, M., Herbert, R.: Japan, crime and mystery writing in (2005). https://doi.org/10.1093/acref/9780195072396.013.0348, https://www.oxfordreference.com/view/10.1093/acref/9780195072396.001.0001/acref-9780195072396-e-0348
42. Smith, G., Whitehead, J.: Analyzing the expressive range of a level generator. In: Proceedings of the 2010 Workshop on Procedural Content Generation in Games (2010)
43. Telltale Games: The Walking Dead: Season One (2012)
44. Thomas, B.: Fans behaving badly? Real person fic and the blurring of the boundaries between the public and the private. In: Thomas, B., Round, J. (eds.) Real Lives, Celebrity Stories: Narratives of Ordinary and Extraordinary People Across Media, pp. 171–186, 1 edn. Bloomsbury Academic (2014)
45. ZA/UM: Disco Elysium (2019)

Narrative Mode of the Third Kind

Nicolas Szilas[(✉)] [iD]

TECFA, FPSE, University of Geneva, Bd du Pont-d'Arve 40, CH 1211 Genève 4, Switzerland
nicolas.szilas@unige.ch

Abstract. The boundary between non-interactive and interactive narrative is a central focus in the debates regarding interactive media and narrative. Another boundary is highlighted in this article when interactivity is such that the audience *lives* the story offered to them. To represent this new boundary, we introduced a third narrative mode, in addition to the classic diegetic and mimetic modes, which we term the demiurgic mode of narrative, as it enables the author to make live the narrative events. This third mode clarifies what may be truly specific to highly interactive narrative or drama that many researchers in the field aspire to implement. The specificities of this mode are then further discussed regarding cognitive representations. In particular, representing and transmitting works relying on the demiurgic mode of narrative is particularly difficult, which may explain why this mode is less present in our culture.

Keywords: Mimesis · Diegesis · Demiurge · Demiurgic mode · Interactive narrative · Interactive digital narrative · Interactive drama · Cognitive representation

1 Drawing the Line

The domain of interactive narrative (IN) encompasses all narrative forms in which the audience influences the narrative by making what E. Aarseth denotes "non-trivial effort" [1]. Early researchers in the field of hypertext – an emblematic form of interactive digital narrative (IDN) – revealed that interactivity in the text[1] did not first appear in the digital arena but can be found in much older documents [1, 9], so that drawing the line between non-interactive and interactive narratives is not obvious, and the degree of interactivity or ergodicity varies [1].

In addition to hypertext, video games can offer a high degree of interactivity, particularly in open-world games (e.g. *The Sims, The Legend of Zelda: Breath of the Wild*), and often have a narrative aspect, making IDN an extremely vast domain. In commercial video games, since the *story* itself, understood as "content pane of narrative" [31], as opposed to the *discourse* [8], is often only slightly influenced by the audience's actions, academic researchers have investigated the possibility of generating the story dynamically, according to the user's choices. The user usually acts as one of the characters in the story [7, 11, 28, 33, 38, 42, 46], more deeply influencing the course of the events,

---

[1] We are using here the usual meaning of "text", not the semiotic one.

© The Author(s), under exclusive license to Springer Nature Switzerland AG 2022
M. Vosmeer and L. Holloway-Attaway (Eds.): ICIDS 2022, LNCS 13762, pp. 471–479, 2022.
https://doi.org/10.1007/978-3-031-22298-6_30

the narrative coherence being maintained thanks to Artificial Intelligence driven mechanisms. This creates another dividing line between usual IDN and other more interactive IDNs, sometimes qualified as "highly interactive" [19, 34, 41]. However, what "highly" means in this context remains difficult to define formally. Is it a matter of quantity of choices? In this case, it is difficult to define a threshold. Is it a matter of underlying technology: scripted vs generated? This type of technological criterion, although used in the past (see the early definition of B. Laurel on interactive drama [22]), is also problematic because if one imagines that the same interactive experience is produced with two different systems, one generative, the other scripted, then these two systems would be either highly or not highly interactive, depending on the technology employed, while the user experience is exactly the same.

Is this lack of clear boundaries between types of IN problematic? Ultimately, it may be acceptable that interactivity is considered a continuum in the same way narrative itself is considered a continuum [37]. However, the above-mentioned division related to "highly interactive" narratives evoke a more qualitative and radical change between highly IDN and classical IDN. The notion of freedom is sometimes mentioned in this respect: "The job of an interactive drama system is to subtly guide the experience of the User so that she retains her freedom while fulfilling her destiny" [46]; "the user-controlled character(s) can physically and socially interact with ideally (perceived) total freedom while experiencing a dramatically interesting narrative" [4]. Agency, the "satisfying power to take meaningful action and see the results of our decisions and choices" [29], and, more precisely, global agency [25] is a concept often highlighted regarding highly IN. Interactive drama is also defined according to a reciprocity criterion: "the main character in interactive drama has the same range of actions as other characters" [40], which implies a high level of interaction if nonplayer characters have rich behaviors themselves. Freedom, agency, and reciprocity are criteria that indicate a boundary exists and that differentiate qualitatively different works. However, these criteria are not always easy to differentiate from interactivity.

The thesis of this article is that a fundamental narratological distinction exists between highly INs and other narratives, and that this distinction helps to understand better the complex status of research on interactive drama.

2   Interactive Narrative as Life-Bringing

Our claim is that some forms of IDN, but not all, represent a new mode of narrative. To introduce this new mode, let us first introduce the first two modes, via a narratological analysis.

There are several dichotomies in narratology that distinguish between two ways of representing narrative events: diegesis vs mimesis [15, 20], telling vs showing [20], and narrative vs dramatic. As a prolegomenon of this narratological discussion, let us note that each of these three distinctions is subject to debate, with no clear agreement between theorists. In the scope of this article, we do not revisit those debates, but present, it is hoped, a simpler distinction between these two modes based on how narrative events are presented to the audience in terms of external representation [2]:

- Type I (diegetic): events are represented via the language, whatever the sensorial modality convened by the work (text read, audio narrative, sign language, etc.). In this type, the author tells events, and the audience receives these told events and needs to imagine them: that is, to translate what he or she perceives via words into an internal representation of the events. Note that Type I narratives encompass all text-based narratives, including those describing an event mimetically (e.g. "he stood up, and raised his hand").
- Type II (mimetic): events are represented directly to the audience, usually visually, but not exclusively (see audio drama). The events can be acted (theater), drawn (still image, comic strip, animated film), or recorded (film, audio drama). The author shows the events, and the audience perceives or witnesses the events as they are displayed to them. Regarding cognitive representation, there is an analogical relationship or structural similarity between the external representation of events and their internal representation within the audience's mind, as discussed in the field of mental images [12].

In practice, if novel and pantomime would be two typical exemplars of the types I and II respectively, many works would contain the two types of event representation. Type II narrative usually includes Type I elements via characters' dialogue (the event itself contains language) and filmic techniques (voiceover, inter-titles) [30]. More precisely, a Type I or Type II mode would apply to different components of a given work. For example, in a film where an empty house is explored by the camera while a voiceover narration describes events that happened there in the past, the spatial wandering falls under the Type II mode, while the past events are conveyed in the Type I mode.

We now introduce Type III narratives, in which the audience enacts some events and observes other events as the consequences of these enacted events. In other words, the audience *lives* the events represented in the narrative. This type is not equivalent to living by projection or by identification since the audience is making actual lifelike decisions in a fictional world that responds to these decisions. The author, in this case, is neither telling nor showing, but is allowing the audience to live a fictional life by simulating some lifelike processes. Extrapolating from the "mimesis/mimetic" terms, that emphasize the author's role of mimicking the reality, we named these Type III narratives after the Greek term *demiourgos* (demiurge), known as the great architect of the universe in Plato's texts [48], because the author is creating a universe in which the audience can live. The Type III mode of narrative is, therefore, the demiurgic mode, following the diegetic and mimetic modes. Note that the terminological borrowing from Greek philosophy does not mean that we have any intention to extend the Platonist concept of *demiourgos*. This proposition of a third mode was already made by M.-L. Ryan: "we need to expand the catalog of narrative modalities beyond the diegetic and the dramatic, by adding a phenomenological category tailor-made for games" [36]. While the concept was introduced and discussed only in the concluding paragraph, the demiurgic mode proposed in this article extends M.-L. Ryan's initial concept by defining and characterizing it.

Like the two other modes, the demiurgic mode is not exclusively narrative. Both narrative and non-narrative sequences of events can be read, seen, and lived. Video games are the iconic modern medium able to convey events in the demiurgic mode.

Video games can uniquely convey emotions when the audience feels like living in a fictional world. For example, in some video games, the player can be manipulated and perform a certain action that is reprehensible, and therefore feel some regret regarding this action (see Quantic Dream's games such as *Heavy Rain* or *Beyond: Two Souls*).[2] This emotion of regret, that we could name "demiurgic regret", differs from the feeling of regret that an audience would feel, by empathy, for a character regretting some action within a film—such emotion may be named "empathetic regret". More precisely, even in a video game, as in film, empathetic regret exists [47] but differs from demiurgic regret. This example reveals the demiurgic mode exists in some video games. However, demiurgic narrative, beyond a single emotional moment, is less common, as discussed in the next section. Films displayed on immersive virtual reality are another type of narrative works where the concept of demiurgic mode is relevant: while the story is represented in the mimetic mode, the user action of orienting the gaze is demiurgic, since the author has allowed the user to look everywhere, as in real life.

The three types/modes of narrative are organized in an ordered relationship, from the less-direct to the more-direct mode of communication. The diegetic mode requires language as a cognitive tool to access the fictional world (a.k.a. the diegetic world or diegesis). In contrast, the mimetic mode involves the fictional world being directly perceived by the senses of the audience, who only has to perceive the events taking place. However, there is still a distance with this mode, created by the fourth wall, the separation between the audience and the stage in the theater. Even when this wall is occasionally broken, when the actors in theater ask for the audience's participation, or in an interactive movie – which creates a metaleptic effect – this barrier remains. In the demiurgic mode, the audience is not only witnessing events, or influencing these events occasionally, but also stepping into the fictional world and living in it through the actions they perform. The distance between the narrative and the real world is minimal. As for the Type I and Type II distinction, many works would combine Type II and Type III, making the evaluation of such a distance more difficult. For example, within works that mostly falls into the mimetic mode, the distance vary, between a web series watched on a phone, a film seen in a large screen, a 360° screen or an immersive VR device. In these examples, the user may feel closer to the virtual world because a more immersive device. The user interface to the diegetic world, in particular when it is interactive, has an important real role to play in this distance [13]. But the distinction between the three types goes beyond the interface, because it involves how the audience is able to influence the diegetic world. The VR case is slightly different because, as we described above, it is demiurgic at the level of the gaze. We may conclude that there is a continuum between mimetic and demiurgic, but this would blur the analysis of a work. Rather, we suggest that a proper analysis of a work should consider each component, and analyze, for each of these components, which ones are demiurgic, that is at which level(s) the audience may live his or her action.

It seems that Plato considered the mimetic mode inferior to the diegetic mode [15, 16], since it is dangerous and seductive, and he condemned it accordingly: "[Socrates] pursues the idea that mimesis [...] requires a particularly strong and therefore psychologically dangerous mode of narrative imagination" [16]. Modern critics of video games, regarding

---

[2] https://www.quanticdream.com/en.

the risk of applying violent in-game behaviors to the real world, echo Plato's judgment. This view illustrates that the demiurgic mode follows and extends the mimetic mode on a scale of "directness," with all the accompanying fears of excessive impact.

The characteristics of the three modes of narratives are summarized in Table 1 below, the last column of which is explained in the next section.

Table 1. Three modes/types of narrative, with corresponding characteristics.

Type	Narrative mode	Author act	Audience act	Type of communication	Type of representation
I	Diegetic	Tell	Interpret via language	Language	Linguistic
II	Mimetic	Show	Perceive	Demonstration	Analogical
III	Demiurgic	Bring life	Live	Simulation	Enactive

3 Representational Issues in the Demiurgic Mode

The ultimate goal of interactive drama in terms of agency, freedom, or reciprocity has been often presented as a "holy grail" [17, 27, 32, 45]. Even if a few encouraging works have been released (*Façade* [26], *Nothing For Dinner* [49], *The Unwelcome Proposal* [14]), narrative in the demiurgic mode seems extremely complex to realize. Why is it so complex? Why is this third mode of narrative so underdeveloped? Why was narrative in the demiurgic mode overlooked in the pre-digital area?

To provide some answers to these questions, it should be first noted that narrative in the demiurgic mode does exist outside the digital world, in particular in children's play, as noted by early researchers in the field [22, 29]. Children can build IN scenes together, based on predefined "genres" or narrative settings ("mum and dad," "cops and robbers," "doctor," etc.). Adults lose this ability, but it is found in all forms of roleplay, a domain that has inspired many IDN researchers [3, 24, 39, 44]. Nevertheless, roleplay remains a niche medium.

Our assumption is as follows. As explained above, the higher the narrative type, the more direct the communication with the narrative content. This point implies that the higher the narrative type, the more difficult it is to record traces of the experience and to build a heritage of the works. Language-mediated narratives (diegetic mode) are either oral-based and orally transmitted (or transcribed in books) or directly produced as books. Drama-based narratives are also recorded as books, via written dialogues and blocking. The written transcription of drama reduces the entire narrative experience, but it has proven sufficient to transmit the work and to contribute to the culture of the society that produced it. Regarding the demiurgic mode, the possibility of recording the experience is greatly reduced. The mere recording of an IN interaction is fundamentally different from the work itself, characterized by the IN experience [23]. What needs to be recorded are all the mechanics that drive the interaction, and since this interaction, in the case of child play, mostly happens within human players, what needs to be recorded to reproduce a similar IN experience lies inside human minds. In roleplay, written rules exist, but, similarly, the experience heavily relies on information stored within the human participants (the game master in particular). The transmission of games as part of a culture is possible, however, thanks in part to the coding of the game rules. In the case of narrative, these rules are not easily externalized, and therefore, according to our hypothesis, this explains why demiurgic narrative does not significantly participate in the cultural heritage of a society, at least within written-based societies.

This high difficulty of recording the works is due to the lack of a language to code the narrative interaction with the user. In IDN, because the work occurs on a computer or equivalent, a code exists that enables the computer to manage the interaction, namely the programming code, written in a computing language. The existence of this code does not make IDN works any easier to record and transmit, however: first, because this code is mostly opaque to humans – creating authoring issues; and second, because this code quickly becomes obsolete when programming language, operating systems, and hardware evolve. The IDN artifact that carries the programming code becomes a useless object that barely evokes a possible narrative experience.

These observations suggest the demiurgic mode of narrative highly depends on the issues related to the external representation of the works. As far as hypertext and hyper-media are concerned, graphs are a convenient way to represent interactive works, and, in some cases, they are even used within the work [6], as a map (e.g. *Beyond: Two Souls*[3], *To Be or Not To Be*[4]). Demiurgic works require some forms of procedural narrative content generation, based on internal variables, conditional events, rules, planning algorithms, multi-variable evaluation functions, etc. These interaction mechanics are complex and difficult to represent. Issues of computation (finding the appropriate algorithms), author-ing (finding authorable algorithms, tools, and methodologies), and preservation (ensuring IDN works are transmitted in time) merge into the central issue of representing narrative interaction.

4   Historical Perspective as Conclusion

Since the 1980s, a period when the computer became accessible to the public, both theorists and creators have started thinking that it could afford radically new ways of telling stories. The major characteristic of the computer propounded ever since this period is interactivity. Interactivity enables the audience to become an actor [5], blurs the line between author and reader [10, 21], and gives them some power, etc. The term "interactivity" has been used exaggeratedly in very different situations, and was therefore criticized and replaced by "ergodicity" [1], but conceptually, this term covers the same idea of identifying a radical change as soon as the audience physically modifies the narrative content. The term IDN covers many forms, such as hypertexts, adventure games, interactive fiction, three-dimensional action-adventure games, interactive drama, chatbots, etc., all of which are effectively interactive but rarely carry the revolutionary

---

[3] https://www.quanticdream.com/fr/beyond-two-souls.

[4] https://tinmangames.com.au/games/to-be-or-not-to-be/.

properties claimed to be brought about by interactivity. The concept of the demiurgic narrative mode introduced in this article shifts the boundary and enables people to identify more clearly what may be radically different in some forms of IDN: that is, the ability for the player to live within a narrative world, even without the freedom of real life. This experience goes beyond interpreting a message that describes a story (Type I – telling), or directly perceiving it as a spectator (Type II – showing). In other words, some interactive works would remain under the diegetic or mimetic modes, whereas others would switch to the third mode, the demiurgic mode.

Nevertheless, this general theories of the three narrative types does not pretend to cover all narrative aspects of interactive works. Other viewpoints such as environmental storytelling [18], embedded stories [35, 43], sandbox games that enable users to create their own stories represent alternative ways to approach the relation between narrative and interaction. Several approaches may co-exist in a single game.

Introducing the demiurgic mode solves no technical issues regarding highly interactive narratives and interactive dramas, but places them in a different perspective. The very fact the author is in charge of "making live" the audience, as a demiurge, places him or her in the difficult position of controlling how the work will react to the life-like actions the audience may carry out. This explains why the number of narrative works that manage to achieve this goal remains limited.

Interestingly, this demiurgic ambition echoes the well-known artificial intelligence project to create living machines. However, in the demiurgic mode of narrative, life remains on the side of the human interactor, and the author-created machine generates a narrative environment able to offer this "living interaction."

References

1. Aarseth, E.J.: Cybertext - Perspectives on Ergodic Litterature. The Johns Hopkins University Press, Baltimore and London (1997)
2. Ainsworth, S.: The functions of multiple representations. Comput. Educ. **33**, 2–3 (1999). https://doi.org/10.1016/s0360-1315(99)00029-9
3. Louchart, S., Aylett, R.: Solving the narrative paradox in VEs–lessons from RPGs. In: Rist, Thomas, Aylett, Ruth S., Ballin, Daniel, Rickel, Jeff (eds.) IVA 2003. LNCS (LNAI), vol. 2792, pp. 244–248. Springer, Heidelberg (2003). https://doi.org/10.1007/978-3-540-39396-2_41
4. Barber, H., Kudenko, D.: Generation of adaptive dilemma-based interactive narratives. IEEE Trans. Comput. Intell. AI Games **1**(4), 1–18 (2009)
5. Barboza, P.: Fiction interactive "métarécit" et unités intégratives. In: L'image actée : scénarisations numériques, pp. 99–121. L'Harmattan (2006)
6. Bouchardon, S., Ghitalla, F.: Récit interactif, sens et réflexivité. In: H2PTM'03. Hypertextes et hypermédias. Produits, Outils et Méthodes, pp. 35–46, Paris, France (2003)
7. Balet, O., Subsol, G., Torguet, P. (eds.): ICVS 2001. LNCS, vol. 2197. Springer, Heidelberg (2001). https://doi.org/10.1007/3-540-45420-9
8. Chatman, S.: Story and Discourse: Narrative Structure in Fiction and Film. Cornell University Press, Ithaca (1980)
9. Clément, J.: L'hypertexte de fiction, naissance d'un nouveau genre ? In: Vuillemin, A., Lenoble, M. (eds.) Littérature et informatique. La littérature générée par ordinateur, pp. 63–76. Artois presses université, Arras (1995)

10. Couchot, E., Hillaire, N.: L'Art numérique – comment la technologie vient au monde de l'art. Flammarion, Paris (2003)
11. Crawford, C.: Assumptions underlying the Erasmatron storytelling system. In: Mateas, M., Sengers, P. (eds.) Narrative Intelligence, pp. 189–197. John Benjamins Publishing Company, Amsterdam/Philadelphia (2003)
12. Denis, M.: Représentation imagée et résolution de problèmes. Revue française de pédagogie **60**, 19–29 (2022)
13. Dow, S. et al.: Initial lessons from AR Façade, an interactive augmented reality drama. In: Proceedings of the 2006 ACM SIGCHI International Conference on Advances in Computer Entertainment Technology - ACE 2006, p. 28. ACM Press, Hollywood, California (2006). https://doi.org/10.1145/1178823.1178858
14. Evans, R., Short, E.: Versu — a simulationist storytelling system. IEEE Trans. Comput. Intell. AI Games **6**(2), 113–130 (2014)
15. Genette, G.: Figures II. Editions du Seuil, Paris (1969)
16. Halliwell, S.: Diegesis – Mimesis. In: Meister, J.C. (ed.) Living Handbook of Narratology (2013)
17. Hurel, P.-Y.: Les récits numériques : de nouvelles formes narratives ? In: Ludovia, pp. 1–14 (2013)
18. Jenkins, H.: Game design as narrative architecture. In: N. & P. (Hrsg.) First Person: New Media as Story, Performance, and Game. MIT Press, Cambridge, MA (2012)
19. Kelso, M.T., et al.: Dramatic presence. Presence J. Teleoperators Virtual Environ. **2**(1), 1–15 (1993)
20. Klauk, T., Köppe, T.: Telling vs. Showing. In: Meister, J.C. (ed.) Living Handbook of Narratology (2014)
21. Landow, G.P., Delany, P.: Hypermedia and literary studies: the state of the art. In: Landow, G.P., Delany, P. (eds.) Hypermedia and Literary Studies, pp. 3–50. MIT Press, Cambridge, MA (1991)
22. Laurel, B.: Towards the design of a computer-based interactive fantasy system. Ohio State University (1986)
23. Louchart, S., Aylett, R.: Towards a narrative theory of Virtual Reality. Virtual Reality **7**(1), 2–9 (2003)
24. Magerko, B., et al.: An empirical study of cognition and theatrical improvisation. In: Proceedings of the Seventh ACM Conference on Creativity and Cognition, pp. 117–126. ACM, New York, NY, USA (2009). https://doi.org/10.1145/1640233.1640253
25. Mateas, M., Stern, A.: Build it to understand it : ludology meets narratology in game design space. In: DiGRA Conference, pp. 16–20 (2005)
26. Mateas, M., Stern, A.: Façade. http://games.softpedia.com/get/Freeware-Games/Facade.shtml
27. Mateas, M., Stern, A.: Façade: an experiment in building a fully-realized interactive drama. In: Game Developers Conference (2003)
28. Mateas, M., Stern, A.: Integrating plot, character and natural language processing in the interactive drama Façade. In: Göbel, S. et al. (eds.) Proceedings of the Technologies for Interactive Digital Storytelling and Entertainment (TIDSE) Conference, pp. 139–151. Fraunhofer IRB, Darmstadt (2003)
29. Murray, J.H.: Hamlet on the Holodeck: The Future of Narrative in Cyberspace. Free Press, New York (1997)
30. Nünning, A., Sommer, R.: Diegetic and mimetic narrativity: some further steps towards a narratology of drama. In: Pier, J., Landa, J.Á.G. (eds.) Theorizing Narrativity, vol. 12, pp. 331–354. Walter de Gruyter, Berlin/New York (2008)
31. Prince, G.: Dictionary of Narratology. University of Nebraska Press, Lincoln (1987)

32. Rawlings, J., Andrieu, J.: Player-protagonist motivation in first-person interactive drama. In: Göbel, S. et al. (eds.) Proceedings of the Technologies for Interactive Digital Storytelling and Entertainment (TIDSE) Conference, pp. 31–44. Fraunhofer IRB, Darmstadt (2003)

33. Riedl, M., et al.: Managing interaction between users and agents in a multi-agent storytelling environment. In: Proceedings of the Second International Joint Conference on Autonomous Agents and Multiagent Systems, pp. 741–748. ACM, New York, NY, USA (2003). https://doi.org/10.1145/860575.860694

34. Ryan, M.: Interactive drama: narrativity in a highly interactive environment. Mod. Fiction Stud. **43**(3), 677–707 (1997)

35. Ryan, M.: Possible Worlds, Artificial Intelligence, and Narrative Theory. Indiana University Press, Bloomington (1991)

36. Ryan, M.-L.: Beyond myth and metaphor-the case of narrative in digital media. Game Stud. **1**, 1 (2001)

37. Ryan, M.L.: Toward a definition of narrative. In: Herman, D. (ed.) The Cambridge Companion to Narrative, pp. 22–36. Cambridge University Press, Cambridge, MA (2007). https://doi.org/10.1017/CCOL0521856965.002

38. Smith, S., Bates, J.: Towards a Theory of Narrative for Interactive Fiction - CMU-CS-89-121 (1989)

39. Swartjes, I., Vromen, J.: Emergent story generation: lessons from improvisational theater. In: Intelligent Narrative Technologies. Number FS-07-05 in AAAI Fall Symposium Series (2007)

40. Szilas, N., et al.: An implementation of real-time 3D interactive drama. Comput. Entertain. **5**(1), 5 (2007). https://doi.org/10.1145/1236224.1236233

41. Szilas, N.: IDtension - highly interactive drama. In: Darken, C., Mateas, M. (eds.) Proceedings of the Fourth Artificial Intelligence and Interactive Digital Entertainment Conference. The AAAI Press (2008)

42. Szilas, N.: Interactive drama on computer: beyond linear narrative. In: Mateas, M., Sengers, P. (eds.) Narrative Intelligence - Papers from the 1999 AAAI Fall Symposium - TR FS-99-01, pp. 150–156. AAAI Press, Menlo Park, CA (1999)

43. Szilas, N., Axelrad, M., Richle, U.: Propositions for innovative forms of digital interactive storytelling based on narrative theories and practices. In: Pan, Zhigeng, Cheok, Adrian David, Müller, Wolfgang, Chang, Maiga, Zhang, Mingmin (eds.) Transactions on Edutainment VII. LNCS, vol. 7145, pp. 161–179. Springer, Heidelberg (2012). https://doi.org/10.1007/978-3-642-29050-3_15

44. Szilas, N.: The future of interactive drama. In : Proceedings of the Second Australiasian Conference on Interactive Entertainment (IE 2005), pp. 193–199 (2005)

45. Wardrip-Fruin, N., Harrigan, P.: Cyberdrama. In: Wardrip-Fruin, N., Harrigan, P. (eds.) First Person: New Media as Story, Performance, and Game. MIT Press (2004)

46. Weyhrauch, P.: Guiding Interactive Drama. Carnegie Mellon University (1997)

47. Wulansari, O.D.E., Pirker, J., Kopf, J., Guetl, C.: Video games and their correlation to empathy. In: Auer, M.E., Hortsch, H., Sethakul, P. (eds.) ICL 2019. AISC, vol. 1134, pp. 151–163. Springer, Cham (2020). https://doi.org/10.1007/978-3-030-40274-7_16

48. Zeyl, D., Sattler, B.: Plato's Timaeus. In: Zalta, E.N. (ed.) The Stanford Encyclopedia of Philosophy. Metaphysics Research Lab, Stanford University (2022)

49. Nothing for Dinner. http://nothingfordinner.org. Accessed 2 Apr 2019

Tools and Systems

Locative Authoring: Evaluating the StoryPlaces Authoring Tool

Sofia Kitromili[1]([⊠]), Charlie Hargood[1], David Millard[2], Huiwen Zhao[1], and Jim Pope[1]

[1] Bournemouth University, Bournemouth, UK
{skitromili,chargood,hzhao,jpope}@bournemouth.ac.uk
[2] University of Southampton, Southampton, UK
dem@soton.ac.uk

Abstract. Locative Narrative is a form of Interactive Digital Narrative (IDN) where the readers' location and movement are the main form of interaction. The StoryPlaces platform provides a general toolset for the creation and delivery of these location aware stories. However, while there is existing research on the reader experience with this technology, comparatively little is known about the author experience. We recruited five interactive narrative design students to participate in a usability test of the StoryPlaces pattern-based authoring tool, using observations, interviews, and analysis of their stories to understand their experience. We show that while participants superficially liked the interface of the StoryPlaces authoring tool, they had difficulty understanding the aspects that were less clearly visualised and struggled to test their creations. The patterns enabled them to add complex functionality easily but became a barrier if they wanted to deviate from them. Our findings mostly support Green's five principles of IDN authoring (on the value of visual metaphors and fast track testing), but suggests they need refinement as in application it was important to distinguish between the visualisation of different aspects of the story (location vs. logical structures), and that failure to properly visualise sometimes led to avoidance or displacement of activity rather than a drop in its quality.

Keywords: Interactive digital narratives · Interactive storytelling · Locative storytelling · User experience · Usability test · Authoring tools · Sculptural hypertext

1 Introduction

Storyplaces[1] is a sculptural hypertext tool developed to explore the poetics of locative literature [1, 2]. Storyplaces allows authors to create narratives positioned in a real-world environment which readers read in-situ and must navigate physically via a location aware device (example screen shots in Fig. 1). Authoring stories for locative systems is complex, authors must balance the needs of the story with interaction and agency all aligned with a real-world environment with its own opportunities and challenges [3]. Despite this

---

[1] Storyplaces authoring tool: https://storyplaces.soton.ac.uk/

M. Vosmeer and L. Holloway-Attaway (Eds.): ICIDS 2022, LNCS 13762, pp. 483–498, 2022.
https://doi.org/10.1007/978-3-031-22298-6_31

complexity there is relatively little work exploring the experience of locative authors, and StoryPlaces, like many IDN tools, has an authoring tool lacking any formal User eXperience (UX) evaluation. Such evaluations help us to understand both the efficacy of the tools in supporting authorship and the impact of design paradigms, such as supported forms of interaction. StoryPlaces' particular pattern centric approach to authorship [1] means a formal evaluation can inform us of both the author experience and the impact of the pattern approach.

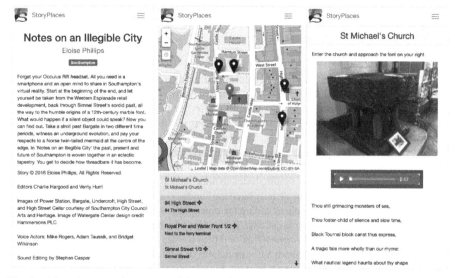

Fig. 1. A locative narrative presented in StoryPlaces where the reader must travel from place to place to explore the story.

The main aim of this paper is therefore to understand how the design of the Story-Places authoring system, and its pattern centric approach, impacts its users' intentions and their workflow. Additionally, Green [4] identified a list of five design principles relevant to IDN tools (Metaphor testing, Fast Track Testing, Structure, Experimentation, and Branching Interfaces) developed through empirical analysis of existing IDN authoring tools [5]. Through the study of StoryPlace's author experience we can extend our understanding of these principles and test them in the context of locative IDN systems.

As such we set out to answer the following questions:

1. What is the user experience of the StoryPlaces authoring tool?
2. What impact does the pattern-based design of StoryPlaces have on this experience?
3. Does the design of the tool impact this experience in line with the principles proposed in Green [4]?

To answer these questions, we undertook a qualitative task-based evaluation with five expert participants of the StoryPlaces authoring tool, using observations, interviews, and artefact analysis to create a picture of the authoring experience.

2 Background

2.1 Locative Narrative and IDN Authoring Tool Research

Locative Narrative (sometimes referred to as location-aware or location-based narrative) concerns storytelling works (and the systems that support them) where the content reflects the readers location, the reader travels to locations to interact with the IDN, and/or the story is designed to be read in the context of a specific location or category of place [3]. They can take a range of forms from intelligent tour guides [6], to cultural heritage installations [7], to mixed reality interactive experiences [8], to interactive locative games [9], and educational location centric experiences [10]. While these works make use of a variety of different technologies on top of the locative narrative, from Spierling's work with augmented reality [8], or Haahr's gameplay approach [9] there are common factors that unite the medium. Readers, typically using mobile devices, travel between locations where GPS, QR codes, or some other location detection allows them to access new content on the device designed to be read, viewed, or played with in place – either for diegetic reference (such as a tour guide specifically discussing the surroundings) or thematic relevance (such as a story designed to be read in a particular atmospheric context). Storyplaces [2] (as studied in this work) represents a significant step towards a generic platform with which to create and deliver a range of locative experiences.

IDN authorship is often supported by a range of tools which help to create content and define logic for the interactive story. The definition of what is an "authoring tool" is a topic of some discussion in the community [11, 12], however broadly speaking applications designed to assist in the creation of IDN works can be considered authoring tools. This includes a range of proprietary and community tools such as the popular Twine [13], Inform 7 [14], Ink [15], and StorySpace [16], as well as academic research prototypes such as ASAPs [17], StoryPlaces [1, 2], IDTension [18], and Deig [19]. There are many others but documenting a full survey of all of them is beyond the scope of this paper. Authoring tools adopt a range of visual paradigms in their design, and while the nodal story graph as seen in Twine [13], StorySpace [16], and others is the most common, we also see domain specific languages such as in Inform 7 [14], and faceted approaches such as in StoryPlaces.

Authoring tools are a critical part of the wider framework of IDN practice and technology [20]. Their accessibility can influence who works in the medium, and their interface and design choices can influence the author [5] and consequently, the resulting works. However, despite this the majority of authoring tools do not present published UX evaluations from which we might learn how they support authors or affect their practice. A majority of tools, including Twine [13], StorySpace [16], ASAPs [17], Ink [15] and many others are only evaluated in the sense of presenting examples of works created in the tools, This is often due to a focus on the "reader experience" over the "author experience" with many works, such as those by Revi [21] and O'Flynn [22] focusing on the reader, and this includes existing evaluations of StoryPlaces [23]. Where author evaluations do exist, they are often limited to informal collaborations with authors [24, 25] that fall short of rigorous evaluation, or limited quantitative studies that do not fully explore the experience [26], or a focus on forms rather than the authoring tools themselves [2]. This is not to say that full rigorous evaluations of the author experience never happen, Engstrom's work with Deig and Poulakos' work with SWB [27] describe detailed studies of the author experience, but these are the exception and only seen for a minority of tools.

There are a number of potential explanations for this issue. Reader experience remains an important part of IDN research, and readers are both easier to recruit and potentially easier to work with [20]. Furthermore, existing established UX methods such as task centric usability studies [28] raise challenges for authoring tool evaluation where representative tasks are hard to identify and even harder to execute within a study. While longitudinal works such as Engstrom's [19] are commendable it is important to remember the need for pragmatic UX methods [28, 29] and relying on high-cost difficult methods for our domain will be an inhibitor to research. As Greenburg and Buxton called for, there is a need for bespoke methods suited to the tools in question way from method-ological dogma [30], and in this paper, we continue to develop our own approaches to pragmatic authoring tool evaluation.

2.2 GREEN's Principles

Green's principles of IDN Authoring Tool UX are based on empirical data gathered from user studies of author response to tools [5] and interfaces [1]. They can be summarised as follows:

- **Metaphor Testing** - Interfaces that use a visual metaphor to represent story structure and connectedness will result in less testing of non-complex stories.
- **Principle of Fast-Track Testing** - Letting users jump to any state of the story enables more rapid and focused testing sessions.
- **Principle of Structure** - Interfaces that use a visual metaphor to represent story structure and connectedness enable idiosyncratic organization and management of an author's own story structure
- **Principle of Experimentation** - Interfaces that use a visual metaphor to represent story structure and connectedness enable easier experimentation of structure and connectedness.
- **Principle of Branching** - Interfaces that use a visual metaphor to represent story structure and connectedness enable easier creation and management of branches.

Greens principles were originally validated with three traditional IDN authoring tools (Quest [31], Inform 7 [14], and articy:draft 3 [32]) as well as the Novella design [33], and our study will extend this to a locative authoring tool as well as seek to gather further evidence on the validity and specifics of these principles.

3 Methodology

We undertook a task-based usability test of the StoryPlaces authoring tool, gathering data through a qualitative observation and interview methodology supported by descriptive quantitative data. The study was approved by Bournemouth University ethics board (Ethics ID: 43208).

Invitations were disseminated via an email advertisement and via word of mouth to game design students with IDN authorship experience. Participants who expressed interest were provided with an information sheet that explained the details of the study, what it hoped to achieve, what data would be collected, and how the data would be used. If participants decided they wanted to take part, they were allocated a 1 h and 45-min slot upon agreement to attend the usability test and follow up interview in Bournemouth University's Talbot Campus.

All participants were provided with a consent form to sign prior to beginning the test. Once consent was granted a fifteen-minute introduction to StoryPlaces was given, and the participants were introduced to their story and task. They were then given an hour to experiment with the tool and continue writing a preprepared part-completed story, an adaptation of the classic Grimm fairy tale *Hansel and Gretel*, which we geolocated within Talbot Woods, a woodland area near Bournemouth University. This approach of having participants finish a preprepared story that is started for them has been used previously with some success [5] and permits an evaluation of an authoring tool without the extended longitudinal effort of the author writing an entire story from scratch while also ensuring the author engages in more than the limited set up activities of a cold start. During the task the first author was present as an observer and made notes on the activity of the participants without intervention except to answer specific questions.

We purposefully sought to recruit participants local to Bournemouth and preferably familiar with certain parts of town for them to be able to attach familiar and feasible locations to their portion of the narrative. We did however provide the participants with a sample of coordinates from various locations and an image library for their use.

Following the usability test, a 30-min semi-structured interview followed in which we inquired about the participants' experience with StoryPlaces. Interview questions were framed in such a way that would enable a collection of information relevant to the participants' overall experience while exposing how StoryPlaces confirmed or refuted the design principles identified by Green [4]. The top-level questions were common across all the interviews (although the conversation was allowed to deviate from these in order to explore the participants' perspective). They included a set of **Introduction** questions to act as an ice-breaker and establish the experience and skillset of the participant, a set of **Experience** questions focused on their way of working with the authoring tool, participants use and mastery of its functions, and their perspective on its positive and negative aspects, finally a set of **Post-Activity** questions exploring their reactions and reflections in terms of the story they had created, interest in further exploring the tool or medium, and any suggestions on changing the tool in the future. The stories that they created were also stored and later analysed to answer specific questions around interactive structure.

We limited ourselves to five participants and focused on in-depth qualitative analysis. Our scale of experiment is relatively small; however, we purposefully took the approach demonstrated by Nielsen and Molich [34], who claimed that an ideal number to conduct individual evaluations for a study such as ours is between three to five people, as greater numbers have proven to be no more effective in showing a system's issues.

Further we focused our study on the experience of authors of using the tool rather than their abilities to use it. As such we sampled our participants to have general IDN experience with authoring tools, rather than ask for explicit knowledge of locative narratives. Their ability to create a "good locative narrative" was less relevant for us at this stage of our work than their ability to express story ideas in the tool and be comfortable enough to interact with the tool in a genuine capacity.

4   Analysis and Findings

A summary of the participant information is shown in Fig. 2. In total we recruited 4 male and 1 female participant, all with previous experience in writing with tools such as Twine (branching hypertext) and Inform 7 (natural language parser based). In the following sections individual participants are identified with P1-5.

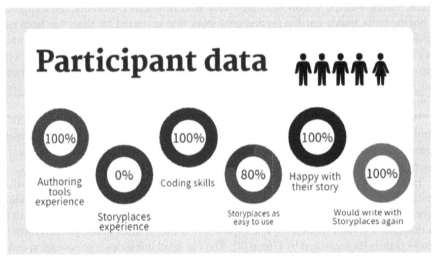

Fig. 2. Basic quantitative participant data

None of the participants had any experience with StoryPlaces but all participants had a basic level of coding skills. This was sufficient for them to grasp the constructs of variables, conditions, and functions within StoryPlaces:

"I have like brief knowledge on like programming or like coding but not like a whole lot, just enough to be able to logically plan how things work." - P1.

All the participants superficially liked the interface and the approach taken by the tool:

"The UI is pretty simple… It's representing concepts and ideas like constraints and variables which is like, in my mind, is quite coding vibe, but it's like making it very user friendly for people who obviously aren't very coding savvy…. It becomes like a visual thing, rather than writing a programming language. It's far more approachable. I am not very good at coding at all, but I understand a lot of concepts." - P5.

4.1 The StoryPlaces User Experience

Our first research question is around the overall user experience of StoryPlaces and to answer this we undertook inductive coding of the interviews, shown in Table 1 (where *No. Participants* reflects the number of people who generated that code at least once). The issues mentioned fell broadly into three high level themes, positive aspects of the tool, negative aspects, and aspects that were felt to be missing.

Table 1. StoryPlaces experience feedback

Themes	Feature	No. Participants
Positive concept	User interface	4
	Ease of use	2
	Browser accessibility	1
	Map	1
Negative concept	Non-intuitive navigation	3
	No Structure or Node Graphs	3
	No run-time testing	2
	No Documentation	2
Missing concept	Amendable content design (fonts, colours)	2
	Run-time testing or compiler	2
	Responsive map on pages	1
	Sorting function on components	1
	Search function on components	1
	Amendable system settings (mode)	1
	Time-consuming navigation	1
	Programming environment	1
	Non-directed pages	1
	Interactive dialogue	1

There were several **Positive Concepts**, and participants were overall pleased with the tools' interface, and happy with what they could achieve in the limited amount of time they were offered:

"The tool is a lot easier to use than I was expecting. With the whole drag and drop functions with the pins and stuff like that, it was very accurate with just the locations which I really enjoyed and the UI (User Interface) and just like the general just interface of it is just nice." - P2.

"Yeah, I think with how it turned out I was quite happy. I mean if I had longer and be able to work a bit more, I probably could have done bit more, but I'm quite glad

with what I ended up with. I basically made it have a branching path essentially, which is kind of neat, different." - P4.

Given the opportunity they would use StoryPlaces again:

"Yeah, I would have to like, have a story in mind that makes sense to use this tool for. Like it'd be really cool if I was doing like a historical thing that was set in, I don't know like the great fire of London and then you went around like London." - P3.

However, some of this positivity may have come from the medium itself – locative storytelling – which was previously unknown to all the participants:

"Being able to just look at the location thing is…. It's like, oh this is where I am, you know… cause it's a fictional narrative based on everything you know. Having like little stories that go along, you know, even if you don't have the visuals of like the squirrel that I had. You might not have that visual, but you have enough material to be able to encourage the world that you're creating… This is unlike anything I've used to create before, which is quite interesting, right?" – P1.

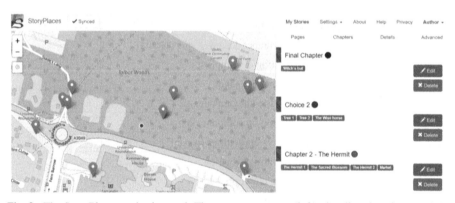

Fig. 3. The StoryPlaces authoring tool. The map component (left) visualises locations, and the chapter tab (right) visualises pages and chapters

Graphical views of the work were a key part of the **Negative Concepts** identified. StoryPlaces has a detailed graphical view of locations within the fiction, and it also shows a partial view of logical structure, but this is only the chapters of the story and the positions of the pages within those chapters (Fig. 3 shows one of the participants stories loaded in the tool – with the graphical map on the left, and semi-graphical representation of chapters on the right). Previous work has shown that these graphical aspects of Storyplaces do make it easier to achieve some tasks than in other tools [35], but these graphical aspects were not always sufficient for our participants. In particular StoryPlaces does not provide graphical visualisation of navigational paths between pages, or the links between rules and constraints that govern those paths (e.g., that a certain variable must be set in order to read this page). Visual graphs were something that most users commented on:

"I would like if I was gonna make like a big project I would need, some sort of visual representation of how the player can get from page to page... because once even with the three [pages] that I made I got really confused on being like go from here to there to here... 'cause if they're similar names [page names] I have to like keep it in my head." – P3.

They also were behind negative comments around navigation, as the information was held in different panes and tabs, and participants were not always clear where to go to find particular elements.

Runtime testing was also identified as a shortcoming. StoryPlaces offers testing by launching a temporary copy of the story in reading mode. This means that to test the story's behaviour authors must read the story from beginning to end (or to the point they want to test) in order to experiment and make adjustments. This can be an arduous process depending on the size of the work and which points are being tested. For example, when looking for unplanned dead ends:

"I think if there's no nodes when it's not the end, I think like a sort of note saying 'there's no nodes here' either you haven't assigned the next node to appear either within the page itself or within the chapter it's in. ... It's really hard to check up on those things, and that's something that I've experienced." – P4.

Most of the **Missing Concepts** theme were around addressing these shortcomings, for example by introducing *run-time testing*, *logical maps*, *sorting and search*. Some of the things requested, such as *interactive dialogue*, are possible in StoryPlaces, but its focus on granular Storylets and a lack of visualisation of conditional structure make dialogs complex to author at any scale. Other additions would be genuinely new to the tool, such as *non-directed pages* (pages that don't show up on the map, so readers have to search for them), *content-design* options to enable different fonts and styles, and a *programming environment* that would enable conditional content within pages.

4.2   The Impact of Patterns on the User Experience

Our second research question is around the impact of the patterns embedded into the StoryPlaces tool. These are **Phases** (a way of scoping that enables for easy episodic structure such as Acts or Chapters – and is called Chapters in the tool), and **Unlocking** (a way of creating navigational paths in sculptural hypertext systems by unlocking new pages as old ones are read). Authors were told about these elements of the tool, but the task did not require them. By looking at their practice we are therefore able to identify whether authors were embracing and understanding those patterns or whether they were resisting or avoiding them. In the remainder of the paper *observation* data is indicated by (O), *interview* data by (I), and *analysis* of the produced stories by (A).

The analysis revealed that all of the authors used the unlocking pattern, and all but one (P3) either used or extended the existing chapter structure. However, while most participants seemed keen to experiment with the tool, many were puzzled as to why their structures failed to respond the way they expected. This was often linked to the unlocking of chapters. It was easy for participants to grasp attaching unlocking constraints on pages

Table 2. Participants in favour of StoryPlaces patterns

Chapters & Unlocking	P1	P2	P3	P4	P5
Were new chapters created? (A)	✓	✗	✗	✗	✓
Were old chapters evoked? (A)	✓	✓	✗	✓	✗
Has the unlocking pattern been used in pages or chapters? (A)	✓	✓	✓	✓	✓

and to chain them together (unlock them one after another) but when those pages were part of a chapter none of the participants thought to replicate those unlocking constraints on the chapter themselves (thus opening up a new stage of the story). When pages are within chapters, both need to be unlocked before a reader can see them.

The interviews also revealed that the structure that the patterns imposed was not always helpful to the users' specific goals and needs.

> *"How do I make this interesting? I'm like, OK, I could possibly test the users on their observation and like how engaged they are without disciplining them... I was thinking like how do I reward those who are observing more and getting like involved with their surroundings ... how can I do this in a way that will help people progress without just giving them the answers and I was just like working that out whilst also having like this quiz thing. Being written out and getting that to work with the system was a bit difficult I guess."* – P1.

This fits the problem of *conceptual misalignment* between the expectations of the author and the affordances of a tool [36, 37], and suggests a general problem with embedding patterns in the interface [38] which gives certain structures a primacy that the author might not share.

4.3   The Storyplaces User Experience Against Green's Principles

As well as the user experience of StoryPlaces it was our intent to test whether our participants use of StoryPlaces reflects the design principles identified by Green in [4]. For each principle we drew on the observations, analysis, and the interviews to understand their behaviour with the tool and compared that behaviour against the predictions made by Green. Tables 2, 3, 4, 5, 6 and 7 show the evidence for this analysis.

Principle of Metaphor testing

Table 3. Green's principle of Metaphor testing

Principle of Metaphor Testing	P1	P2	P3	P4	P5
How many times did they test during authoring? (O)	3	1	4	1	3

All participants tested their story at least once but only two of them during the writing stage of the task. The rest mostly tested at the beginning to see how the existing story worked before they modified it, or at the end to see whether what they did worked as planned.

Green's principle of metaphor testing states that having a visualisation of the story structure will result in less testing. StoryPlaces visualises locations, and some logical structure (chapters), but not any other logical structure (such as branches). In observation we noted that the participants who tested more frequently (P1, P3, P5) were the ones that tended to have more examples of these invisible logical structures.

We suspect that for P2 and P4 being able to visualise how pages were grouped in chapters was sufficient to reduce the amount of testing that they needed to conduct. We also note that the overall level of testing was low, but that this is probably a factor of the limited time participants had to complete their task.

Principle of Fast-track testing

Table 4. Green et al.'s principle of Fast-Track Testing

Principle of Fast-Track Testing	P1	P2	P3	P4	P5
Have they asked for fast-track or current node testing? (I)	✗	✗	✓	✓	✓

The principle of fast-track testing states that letting users to jump to any story state will result in more rapid and focused testing. StoryPlaces does not have this function, and instead only allows stories to be tested from the beginning. Three of the participants asked for this feature (P3, P4, P5), so it was clearly missed. However, there was not a clear correlation between users who asked for the feature, and those that undertook multiple tests (Table 2). This indicates that the response to its absence ranges from perseverance to avoidance, and that in at least one case (P4) the reaction was not to have slower and less focused testing, but rather to simply reduce the amount of testing that was undertaken.

Principle of Structure

Table 5. Green's principle of Structure

Principle of Structure	P1	P2	P3	P4	P5
Have they felt the need to invoke visual graphs for structure organisation? (I)	✓	✗	✓	✗	✓
Did they use an external representation of structure (O)	✓	✗	✗	✗	✓

The principle of structure states that using a visual structure in the tool will allow idiosyncratic organisation by the author. Several of the participants (P1, P3, P5) suggested that visual graphs would be helpful during their creative process, and two of them (P1 and P5) requested a piece of paper and proceeded to use that to draw out and organise their story. This indicates that the principle is correct, but that the lack of visual structure does not necessarily lead to a lack of authorial structure, but rather the displacement of that activity to outside of the tool.

StoryPlaces does have a visualisation of chapters and pages, and colour codes pages to show their membership to different chapters, but this was clearly not sufficient to fulfil this principle. It could be the case that they were simply unfamiliar with this way of organising a story, but most participants directly mentioned graphs and one of the participants (P5) claimed that they use graphs for everything that they do, which implies that it is a desire for a specific kind of representation – one that matches their own mental model of their story.

Principle of Experimentation

Table 6. Green's principle of Experimentation

Principle of Experimentation	P1	P2	P3	P4	P5
Have they created chapters and added pages to them? (A, O)	✓	✗	✗	✗	✓
Did they experiment with advanced features? (O)	✓	✗	✓	✓	✓
Did they reconfigure their structure during the task (O)	✗	✗	✗	✗	✗

All participants were keen to experiment with the tool. Four of the participants wanted to test the advanced constructs on purpose merely to see what they could achieve. Even the participant that did not experiment with these features (P2) expressed that while they were satisfied with the basic functionality, they would invoke the advanced constructs if they really wanted to do something specific. However, this experimentation did not extend to the story or its structures. Only two of the participants created new structural elements (P1 and P5 who both created chapters), and none of the participants reconfigured their structure or tried out alternative arrangements. This supports Green's principle and indicates that the visualisation of logical structure within StoryPlaces is not sufficient.

Principle of Branching

Table 7. Green's principle of Branching

Principle of Branching	P1	P2	P3	P4	P5
Were they confused about the creation of branches? (I)	✗	✗	✗	✗	✗
Have they created branching pages or chapters? (A, O)	✓	✗	✓	✗	✓

The principle of branching states that if there is a visual representation of story structure then it is easier for users to create and manage branches (points of agency and divergence within the story). Participants did not seem to be struggling to create nodes even with the lack of a visual metaphor, and all seemed to have been able to create a set of pages with unlocking behaviour to manage progression. However, while P1, P3, and P5 created explicit branches using the unlocking feature, P2 and P4 did not, and instead stuck to a linear structure, even though in the interview they stated that they were comfortable with how this could be done. P2 and P4 are the same participants that were also reserved in their use of structure (Table 4), so it is unclear whether this is because of the tool, or because of a personal preference for more linear or structurally simple experiences.

5   Conclusion

In this paper we have presented a focused UX study on the experience of authoring with the StoryPlaces locative storytelling tool. We examined the experience of five participants who were skilled working with interactive digital narrative, but novice to the tool, through a task-based evaluation with data gathered through observation and semi-structured interviews. We were aiming to create a picture of the overall user experience, explore how the patterns embedded into the authoring tool impacted on that experience, and to explore whether our findings reflected Green's five design principles (identified in [4]).

On the overall experience: our participants were able to use the tool and praised the clear user interface, especially around locations, but the other aspects of visualisation (the relationship between chapters and pages) were not seen as sufficient with participants calling for a visual representation of the logical structure that lies behind the story. In short, participants understood how to do specific things within the tool but struggled to fully understand their creation as it grew. Testing was also an issue, with StoryPlaces simple launch-from-start approach criticised as increasingly arduous as the story size and complexity grew. Most of the suggestions were based around correcting these shortcomings, but participants also wanted more control over the style and presentation of their story, as well as new functionality such as contextual content, and hidden pages.

Regarding the use of patterns within the tool: our participants were all able to successfully use unlocking to create navigational paths and were also able to use the chapter functionality to pace the story (although there was some confusion over the unlocking of pages, and the unlocking of their parent chapters – both need to be unlocked before a page is visible). However, the use of patterns means that the tool is strongly encouraging the author to use it in a particular way, and in some cases, we saw a clear *conceptual misalignment* between what the tool offered and what the author was trying to do. The effectiveness of the patterns thus rests on their alignment with the author's expectations and needs. When they align they are effective, but when they do not they can actually hinder the author from achieving their goals.

Finally, we looked at whether our analysis followed the five principles set out by Green [4]. The principles are mostly based around the visualisation used in a tool. Applying them to StoryPlaces was thus complicated by the fact that StoryPlaces breaks its visualisation into different parts: a visualisation of the locations (which users found effective) and a partial visualisation of the logical structure in the form of the relationship between chapters and pages (that was less effective). Generally, we found that the principles held, but that we needed to distinguish between these two aspects (for example, participants who leant towards locative structure tested less frequently than those who leant towards a more complex logical structure). The principles all imply that the presence of one design phenomena leads to a given behaviour or experience - however from this study our understanding of this behaviour has become richer. For example, inability to jump to story states in testing does not necessarily lead to slower testing, it can also lead to the avoidance of testing. Similarly, the lack of a visualisation of the logical structure did not always lead to a lack of organisation, but instead to that organisation is redirected and occurring on paper alongside the digital tool. This implies that the principles can as a result of this study, and further studies, be refined to depict a broader set of resulting behaviour.

Our work provides an example evaluation of an authoring tool, specific suggestions for the next generation of locative authoring tools, lessons for integrating patterns into authoring tool interfaces, and a partial validation of Green's five principles. We hope that it will contribute to introducing more user-centric research methods in the understanding and improvement of IDN tools. IDN authoring is both an expert and expensive activity, yet with a relatively small set of users we have uncovered novel and actionable insights that have helped us understand how we can improve StoryPlaces and contributed to our theoretical understanding of authoring tools. We hope to inspire more tool creators to seek out users and authors and test their tools in this managed way. If we improve our tools based on the needs of authors, we can accelerate their evolution, and ultimately allow creative minds to exploit IDN beyond our own expectations.

References

1. Millard, D.E., Hargood, C., Howard, Y., Packer, H.: The StoryPlaces authoring tool: pattern centric authoring. In: Authoring for Interactive Storytelling Workshop, p. 6. Springer International Publishing, Madeira, Portugal (2017)
2. Hargood, C., Weal, M.J., Millard, D.E.: The StoryPlaces platform: building a web-based locative hypertext system. In: Proceedings of the 29th on Hypertext and Social Media, pp. 128–135. Association for Computing Machinery, New York, NY, USA (2018). https://doi.org/10.1145/3209542.3209559
3. Millard, D.E., Hargood, C.: Tiree tales: a co-operative inquiry into the poetics of location-based narrative. In: Proceedings of the 28th ACM Conference on Hypertext and Social Media, pp. 15–24. Association for Computing Machinery, New York, NY, USA (2017). https://doi.org/10.1145/3078714.3078716
4. Green, D.: Don't forget to save! User experience principles for video game narrative authoring tools (2022). https://eprints.bournemouth.ac.uk/36637/
5. Green, D., Hargood, C., Charles, F.: Use of tools: UX principles for interactive narrative authoring tools. J. Comput. Cult. Herit. **14**, 41:1–41:25 (2021). https://doi.org/10.1145/3458769
6. Nisi, V., Wood, A., Davenport, G., Oakley, I.: Hopstory: an interactive, location-based narrative distributed in space and time. In: Technologies for Interactive Digital Storytelling and Entertainment. TIDSE 2004. LNCS, vol. 3105, pp. 132–141. Springer, Berlin, Heidelberg (2004). https://doi.org/10.1007/978-3-540-27797-2_18
7. Dionisio, M., Nisi, V., van Leeuwen, J.P.: The iLand of Madeira location aware multimedia stories. In: Aylett, R., Lim, M.Y., Louchart, S., Petta, P., Riedl, M. (eds.) Interactive Storytelling. ICIDS 2010. LNCS, vol. 6432, pp. 147–152. Springer, Berlin, Heidelberg (2010). https://doi.org/10.1007/978-3-642-16638-9_19

8. Spierling, U., Kampa, A.: Structuring location-aware interactive narratives for mobile augmented reality. In: Mitchell, A., Fernández-Vara, C., Thue, D. (eds.) Interactive Storytelling. ICIDS 2014. LNCS, vol. 8832, pp. 196–203. Springer, Cham (2014). https://doi.org/10.1007/978-3-319-12337-0_20

9. Naliuka, K., Carrigy, T., Paterson, N., Haahr, M.: A Narrative Architecture for Story-Driven Location-Based Mobile Games. In: Luo, X., Cao, Y., Yang, B., Liu, J., Ye, F. (eds.) New Horizons in Web-Based Learning ICWL 2010 Workshops. ICWL 2010. LNCS, vol. 6537, pp. 11–20. Springer, Berlin, Heidelberg (2011). https://doi.org/10.1007/978-3-642-20539-2_2

10. Weal, M.J., Michaelides, D.T., Thompson, M.K., DeRoure, D.C.: The ambient wood journals: replaying the experience. In: Proceedings of the Fourteenth ACM Conference on Hypertext and Hypermedia, August 2003, pp. 20–27 (2003)

11. Green, D., Hargood, C., Charles, F.: Define "Authoring Tool": A Survey of Interactive Narrative Authoring Tools. Presented at the, Dublin, Ireland December 5 (2018)

12. Shibolet, Y., Knoller, N., Koenitz, H.: A framework for classifying and describing authoring tools for interactive digital narrative. In: Rouse, R., Koenitz, H., Haahr, M. (eds.) ICIDS 2018. LNCS, vol. 11318, pp. 523–533. Springer, Cham (2018). https://doi.org/10.1007/978-3-030-04028-4_61

13. Klimas, C.: Twine/An open-source tool for telling interactive, nonlinear stories. https://twinery.org/. Accessed 23 July 2022

14. Nelson, G.: Inform 7. http://inform7.com/. Accessed 23 July 2022

15. Ingold, J., Humfrey, J.: inklewriter. https://www.inklestudios.com/inklewriter/. Accessed 23 July 2022

16. Bernstein, M.: Storyspace. http://www.eastgate.com/storyspace/index.html. Accessed 23 July 2022

17. Koenitz, H.: Extensible tools for practical experiments in IDN: the advanced stories authoring and presentation system. In: Si, M., Thue, D., André, E., Lester, J.C., Tanenbaum, T.J., Zammitto, V. (eds.) Interactive Storytelling. ICIDS 2011. LNCS, vol. 7069, pp. 79–84. Springer, Berlin, Heidelberg (2011).https://doi.org/10.1007/978-3-642-25289-1_9

18. Szilas, N.: IDtension: a narrative engine for Interactive Drama. Presented at the (2003)

19. Engström, H.: I have a different kind of brain—a script-centric approach to interactive narratives in games. Digit. Creat. **30**, 1–22 (2019). https://doi.org/10.1080/14626268.2019.1570942

20. Spierling, U., Szilas, N.: Authoring issues beyond tools. In: Iurgel, I.A., Zagalo, N., Petta, P. (eds.) ICIDS 2009. LNCS, vol. 5915, pp. 50–61. Springer, Heidelberg (2009). https://doi.org/10.1007/978-3-642-10643-9_9

21. Revi, A.T., Millard, D.E., Middleton, S.E.: A systematic analysis of user experience dimensions for interactive digital narratives. In: Bosser, A.-G., Millard, D.E., Hargood, C. (eds.) ICIDS 2020. LNCS, vol. 12497, pp. 58–74. Springer, Cham (2020). https://doi.org/10.1007/978-3-030-62516-0_5

22. O'Flynn, S.: Media Fluid and Media Fluent, E-Literature in the Era of Experience Design. Hyperrhiz: New Media Cultures (2019). https://doi.org/10.20415/hyp/020.int03

23. Millard, D.E., Packer, H., Howard, Y., Hargood, C.: The balance of attention: challenges of creating locative cultural storytelling experiences. J. Comput. Cult. Herit. **13** (2020)

24. Miles, A.P., Jenkins, K.: (Re)Born digital–trans-affirming research, curriculum, and pedagogy: an interactive multimodal story using twine. Vis. Arts Res. **43**, 43–49 (2017). https://doi.org/10.5406/visuartsrese.43.1.0043

25. Szilas, N., Marty, O., Réty, J.-H.: Authoring highly generative interactive drama. In: Balet, O., Subsol, G., Torguet, P. (eds.) ICVS 2003. LNCS, vol. 2897, pp. 37–46. Springer, Heidelberg (2003). https://doi.org/10.1007/978-3-540-40014-1_5

26. Stefnisson, I., Thue, D.: Mimisbrunnur: AI-assisted authoring for interactive storytelling. In: Proceedings of the AAAI Conference on Artificial Intelligence and Interactive Digital Entertainment, vol. 14, pp. 236–242 (2018)

27. Poulakos, S., Kapadia, M., Maiga, G.M., Zünd, F., Gross, M., Sumner, R.W.: Evaluating accessible graphical interfaces for building story worlds. In: Nack, F., Gordon, A.S. (eds.) ICIDS 2016. LNCS, vol. 10045, pp. 184–196. Springer, Cham (2016). https://doi.org/10.1007/978-3-319-48279-8_17

28. Goodman, E., Kuniavsky, M.: Observing the User Experience: A Practitioner's Guide to User Research. Morgan Kaufmann (2012)

29. Medlock, M.C., Wixon, D., Terrano, M., Romero, R.L., Fulton, B.: Using the RITE method to improve products; a definition and a case study, p. 7 (2002)

30. Greenberg, S., Buxton, B.: Usability evaluation considered harmful (some of the time). In: Proceedings of the SIGCHI Conference on Human Factors in Computing Systems, pp. 111–120. Association for Computing Machinery, New York, NY, USA (2008). https://doi.org/10.1145/1357054.1357074

31. Warren, A.: Quest. http://textadventures.co.uk/quest. Accessed 23 July 2022

32. articy:draft 3. https://www.articy.com/en/. Accessed 23 July 2022

33. Green, D., Hargood, C., Charles, F., Jones, A.: Novella: a proposition for game-based storytelling. In: Proceedings of the 7th International Workshop on Narrative and Hypertext hosted at ACM Hypertext and Social Media, Baltimore, USA, 9 July 2018

34. Nielsen, J., Molich, R.: Heuristic evaluation of user interfaces. In: Proceedings of the SIGCHI Conference on Human Factors in Computing Systems, pp. 249–256. Association for Computing Machinery, New York, NY, USA (1990). https://doi.org/10.1145/97243.97281

35. Kitromili, S., Jordan, J., Millard, D.E.: How do writing tools shape interactive stories? In: Rouse, R., Koenitz, H., Haahr, M. (eds.) ICIDS 2018. LNCS, vol. 11318, pp. 514–522. Springer, Cham (2018). https://doi.org/10.1007/978-3-030-04028-4_60

36. Kitromili, S.: Authoring Digital Interactive Narratives (2021). https://eprints.soton.ac.uk/455723/

37. Kitromili, S., Jordan, J., Millard, D.E.: What authors think about hypertext authoring. In: Proceedings of the 31st ACM Conference on Hypertext and Social Media, pp. 9–16. Association for Computing Machinery, New York, NY, USA (2020)

38. Millard, D.E.: Authoring with IDN Structural Patterns. In: Narrative and Hypertext Workshop, p. 5 (2022)

Adventures in TwineSpace: An Augmented Reality Story Format for Twine

PS Berge(✉) ⓘ, Daniel Cox ⓘ, Jack Murray ⓘ, and Anastasia Salter ⓘ

University of Central Florida, Orlando, FL 32816, USA
hello@psberge.com

Abstract. Augmented reality games have moved into the mainstream thanks to headline-catching titles such as *Pokémon GO* (2016) and *Harry Potter Wizards Unite* (2019). However, these games represent only a small portion of what is possible in this space, as demonstrated by emerging independent and serious game efforts in this area. Such development is hindered by the challenges facing individual and casual designers in finding AR tools and accessible engines. By exploring the legacy of casual, "low-friction" AR development and text-game design, we argue previous attempts to integrate narrative engines with augmented reality (e.g. Argon.js + Twine, ARIS) and image recognition (Vuforia, AR.js) have yet to meaningfully center casual development. With this in mind, we present a working prototype called TwineSpace combining popular hypertext authoring tool Twine 2 with open-source augmented reality tools A-Frame and AR.js that opens the possibilities for play within the world of spatial narrative. By combining open-source solutions, we hope this new authoring experience can help improve spatial storytelling for indie game designers, teachers, storytellers, and casual creators alike.

Keywords: Twine · Augmented Reality · Story Format · Prototype

1 Introduction

1.1 Augmented Reality for Casual Creators

Augmented reality (or AR) gaming captured the public imagination in 2016. In what has been called the "summer of *Pokémon Go*", thanks to a moment of global player enthusiasm, upwards of 45 million players engaged with augmented reality at the same time [12, 25]. *Pokémon Go* (2016) trained a wide base of players in a previously obscure genre, creating an incentive for movement and travel as the center of an experience design. This success should have inspired endless imitators in the months and years after 2016, but screen-based augmented reality has grown more slowly. Opportunities for locative play remain limited and tend towards large-scale global productions. *Zombies, Run!* (2012) focuses on movement. *Jurassic World Alive* (2018) brings roaming dinosaurs to the neighborhood. *Minecraft Earth* (2019) offered a short-lived augmented

© The Author(s), under exclusive license to Springer Nature Switzerland AG 2022
M. Vosmeer and L. Holloway-Attaway (Eds.): ICIDS 2022, LNCS 13762, pp. 499–512, 2022.
https://doi.org/10.1007/978-3-031-22298-6_32

world focused on crafting. Such experiences have elements of interactive narrative (particularly through quests and environmental design) but lack depth or complexity in their implementation of story experience.

In this paper, we introduce TwineSpace, a story format for creating interactive digital narrative experiences using the authoring tool Twine designed specifically for casual creators interested in making augmented reality projects [7]. We briefly review how others have attempted similar goals, what success they found, and how each project ultimately ended. We then examine what can be learned from these previous attempts and how TwineSpace builds on these lessons. Finally, we examine the potential for digital storytelling with augmented reality and how TwineSpace helps build toward exciting new prospects for engaging the border between physical and virtual materiality. Ultimately, we argue authoring experiences like TwineSpace might enable new kinds of stories and encourage novice designers to experiment with interactive narrative through augmented reality digital storytelling, offering further potential for exploring the experiential and educational usage of the form.

2   Building Interactive Digital Narratives in AR

Twine has an established legacy among independent, student, and hobby creators. Scholars and designers have described how Twine's ease-of-use has helped marginalized creators build experimental and personal interactive digital narratives [6], and Twine has been pivotal in the classroom for teaching interactive digital narrative design [8]. merritt k notes how the Twine's continued success stems from both the accessibility of the platform, and that "Twine has been the site of an incredible artistic flourishing at the intersections of digital games and fiction: a rebirth of hypertext. People who might never otherwise make a videogame make them with Twine" [9]. There have been several previous efforts to incorporate augmented reality into Twine or similar tools; each attempt was marked with limited success and frequently a lack of long-term support. In this section, we provide a brief overview of these previous projects and libraries.

2.1   Twine and the Geolocation API

In 2015, Shawn Graham documented a process for incorporating location-based play with the SugarCube story format in Twine 2. Using the Geolocation API already available in most web browsers, Graham created a small software library to communicate between the web browser and Twine story to design augmented reality experiences with Twine. As users neared specified coordinates, the game could trigger changes in the passages. Initially developed for a workshop, Graham later documented this approach along with a criteria for building future AR libraries using Twine labeled "low friction" [10]. This criteria included making the creation experience "like a text-editor", making sure "the coding is minimal," and allowing the produced artifacts to be "fairly accessible no matter what device the user has" [10]. While one of the earliest documented attempts to combine AR and text-game design in Twine, Graham's library comes with two major constraints. The first is its reliance on external code: users looking to use the library must manually add the library's code to an existing story in Twine. The second constraint is in its purposefully limited design: Graham's framework was not intended to use the user's camera or visual dynamics. Rather, it was entirely text-based. Building off the Geolocation API in web browsers, the library can only react to near-exact geolocation positions, requiring a user to have these coordinates ready when working on a story.

2.2 The Argon Browser

In 2017, the Augmented Environments Lab (AEL) at Georgia Tech published Argon, an AR-enabled browser application created for mobile devices. Using the image recognition tool Vuforia, this browser allowed designers to create geolocational experiences and use image and marker tracking. The browser supported image tracking and marker-based experiences for spatial narratives without relying on coordinate-driven geolocation. Like with Graham's process [10], AEL also built off the SugarCube story format in Twine [11]. By adding Argon-specific functionality (called macros) for SugarCube, the authors were able to create projects using Twine. Using this approach, demonstrations showcased image tracking to build dynamic spatial interactions such as an AR "magic book" projects to display messages and three-dimensional models when the device's camera detected certain markers [11]. Unfortunately, while documentation on Argon and macros of the SugarCube story format still survive, the mobile browser itself does not, and so these libraries and demonstrations are largely deprecated.

2.3 A-Frame and Twine

In 2018, Ada Rose Cannon published an essay describing a proof-of-concept game combining the virtual and augmented reality web framework A-Frame with the Harlowe story format in Twine [13]. A-Frame is an open-source WebXR framework for building virtual reality and augmented reality experiences in HTML based on JavaScript library Three.js. Unlike other previous solutions, Cannon's approach was to bypass the story format functionality and to write additional code to listen for both story navigation and user interaction events in the browser. In this approach, the JavaScript library jQuery, built into the Harlowe story format, was used to intercept possible user interactions and manipulate how the story was presented to a user by triggering events in the story format as if a user had done them directly. Using A-Frame to create a three-dimensional scene, a user could click on different elements to prompt an on-screen avatar to navigate through the space between them or move between story segments. While highly specific to the solution created by Cannon, the approach to using A-Frame and manipulating how a user perceived a story establishes a strong foundation for additional work using a similar process.

2.4 Proprietary Solutions

There is also a legacy of AR development tools aimed at casual creators (and especially educators) outside of Twine. One of the earliest efforts to inspire independent AR creators using mobile devices was ARIS, a platform for "mobile games, tours and interactive stories" conceived in 2008. Developed by the Field Day research lab at University of

Wisconsin-Madison, ARIS supported multiple spatial configurations, including geolocation, map-based, and Bluetooth beacons. Its proprietary authoring tool was designed around a scene-based framework with additional support for items, inventories, and other adventure game mechanics [14]. ARIS boasted an impressive base of tens of thousands of creators at its height [14]. Despite its current deprecation, ARIS attracted much scholarly attention about the applicability of augmented reality in narrative game spaces in the classroom [15]. A more recent effort includes Niantic's 8th Wall, which launched in 2018. Perhaps the closest commercial solution to a tool for casual creativity, it is built on the open-source framework A-Frame. 8th Wall allows users to create interactive experiences including image tracking, three-dimensional model-viewing, face filters, and interactive scenes. While popular with some audiences, 8th Wall requires users to code scenes directly and additionally requires a monthly service fee for the tool and online deployment [16].

Admittedly, these solutions exist in the shadow of popular, but high-barrier tools for AR creation connected to game engines like Godot, Unity and Unreal. Plugins for these engines often require moderate coding knowledge and fail the "low friction" criteria. These commercial plugins and libraries frequently cost money for both software and additional hardware devices. For example, Unity's in-engine AR solution and numerous asset store plugins for AR are comprehensive, but require preexisting knowledge of a complex game engine, higher coding literacy, and potentially paying expensive licensing fees. Such platforms also forefront models and genres of play outside of interactive digital narratives, and instead focus on games with themes of combat or conquest [8]. While we recognize the ubiquity of these solutions for AR development, we argue there exists an important need for more low-barrier tools for encouraging casual creativity, particularly in the interactive narrative design space. As "tools impact the stories created using them in ways that are not obvious," [17] rethinking our available tools has the potential to reshape how we approach developing AR interactive digital narratives going forward.

3   TwineSpace Overview

Each previous attempt to create a tool for augmented reality projects in Twine has seen success. In particular, the "low friction" criteria established by Graham provides a useful guide for developing new projects. However, each also ended when factors within the design of the projects affected their continued longevity. Users should not have to bypass story format functionality, as was the case with Cannon [13], nor use additional, external code, as was the case with Graham's solution [10]. Creating an entire web browser dedicated to augmented reality projects like Argon has the greatest potential for many use cases [11], but carries with it an issue of projects no longer working when support for the application ends. There are multiple lessons to draw from these previous efforts:

- Proprietary frameworks, especially those linked to university labs and external funding, often struggle to maintain support and longevity.
- Reliance on private libraries and frameworks frequently contribute to shorter project lifespans.

- There remains an interest in creating AR experiences with Twine.

With these lessons in mind, we present our ongoing work to develop TwineSpace, an open-source Twine story format designed specifically for augmented reality experiences [7]. TwineSpace builds from both Graham's work on "low friction" augmented reality, while expanding Cannon's work combining Twine and A-Frame. Our goal with TwineSpace is to bridge two extant casual creator spaces (text-game design and WebXR) while avoiding the pitfalls of previous efforts to build casual AR solutions.

TwineSpace represents a kind of compromise between a dedicated browser and needing to include external code libraries themselves: a new story format specifically designed for augmented reality projects. It builds from previous approaches for creating augmented reality projects in Twine. TwineSpace is a story format based on jQuery, A-Frame, and AR.js (a web library for creating augmented reality projects). Most importantly, it provides a "translator" interface between the text of Twine passages and HTML elements processed by A-Frame.

Instead of asking users to potentially copy and paste code into their stories to enable new functionality, TwineSpace is designed to allow users to create AR experiences from the start. Creators can easily add the story format TwineSpace to Twine by selecting Formats from the story listing, using the Add a New Format tab, and pasting a link from the GitHub repository. TwineSpace incorporates several features akin to other popular story formats such as Harlowe [18] and SugarCube (such as "script" tags for passages) [19], but is based on another story format, Snowman [20]. Our decision to extend the Snowman story format was one of convenience: one of the coauthors of this project (Daniel Cox) designed and maintains the current version of the Snowman story format. Both Graham's work in 2015 and the Vuforia-based mobile browser Argon in 2017 used SugarCube, a popular story format for authors in Twine [21]. TwineSpace, however, is an entirely new story format based on Snowman—following in the well-defined footsteps of other projects based on, such as Trilogue [22] and Botscripten [23]. TwineSpace also takes advantage of the technical details released as part of the Twine Specification repository first published in early 2020 [24].

In this section, we characterize TwineSpace and describe how authors might make use of AR solutions in their projects.

3.1 Macros

Many Twine story formats include named functionality using special syntax or characters. When these appear in the content of a Twine story, the story format packaged with the project performs specific actions such as creating a new variable or changing how content is presented to a user. Following the pattern established by the story format Harlowe, TwineSpace provides macro functionality using parentheses around the use of the macro with a colon after its name. The author can also add additional values associated with the macro after the colon. As TwineSpace is built on A-Frame, this allows users to quickly use macros to represent HTML elements with special meaning to A-Frame such as (box:) to represent the equivalent A-Frame element of <a-box>. At present, TwineSpace supports the macros shown in Table 1.

Table 1. Sample TwineSpace Macros

(box:) (cone:) (ring:) (sphere:) (torus:) (octahedron:) (icosohedron:)	Creates a three-dimensional primitive of the respective type. *No arguments required*
(circle:) (triangle:) (plane:)	Creates a two-dimensional primitive of the respective type. *No arguments required*
(image:) (video:) (curvedimage:)	Displays an image or video on a two-dimensional plane. *Source required*
(text:)	Creates three-dimensional text. *Value required*
(gltf-model:) (obj-model:)	Displays a three-dimensional model in .glTF or .OBJ format. *Online source required*
(videosphere:)	Displays a 360-degree video, projected onto a sphere around the camera. *Source required*

Macros streamline A-Frame's HTML-based entities into a quick shorthand for users. These macros allow creators to quickly 'set the scene' with custom shapes and models. In each case, these macros can be expanded to contain any of the arguments specified in the A-Frame documentation for the given primitive—but these arguments are not required. For example, to creating a videosphere requires a source video URL as an argument, but it does not require any position or rotation information. Carrying over from A-Frame's default placement, TwineSpace will also automatically place new objects at the center of the scene unless given a specific position. In this way, authors can determine how much or how little they want to customize these primitives by adding as few or as many macros as they wish.

A-Frame uses the metaphor of a scene to describe a set of three-dimensional entities. In TwineSpace, this metaphor is extended. Each time a user navigates to a new part of a story, its content is parsed. If specific macros are found, a new A-Frame scene is generated, allowing each part of a story, what Twine calls a passage, to be a separate "scene" for both the creator and user experiencing it.

3.2 Embedding Passages

While macros allow creators to quickly generate and customize individual A-Frame elements within passages, we have also developed a solution for pasting entire A-Frame scenes as HTML directly into Twine. This is handled by a unique macro: *(embed-scene: [name])* where *[name]* is the title of another Twine passage in which the user has placed the complete HTML of an A-Frame scene. Through the *(embed-scene: [name])* macro, a creator can define all the elements for a scene as part of one passage and "embed" it in another. For example, one could include the following macro in a text passage:

```
(embed-scene: "Another")
```

When launched, TwineSpace would find a separate passage titled "Another" and treat its content as A-Frame HTML elements where the macro was embedded:

```
<a-scene>
    <a-entity position="-6 -1 0">
        <a-box position="0 0.2 0" color="#4CC3D9"></a-
box>
    </a-entity>
</a-scene>
```

Our hope is this feature will be useful for both established A-Frame users who want to incorporate Twine into their own projects as well as Twine creators interested in using widely available scene templates in their projects. Users unfamiliar with HTML can still generate simple primitives with macros, but embedded scenes provide a more robust solution for those who want to generate complexity (see Fig. 1).

TwineSpace also features the ability to designate certain passages as containing JavaScript code by adding the tag script to the passage during story editing. These special passages, like scene passages, are not linked to the story but instead are run before the story started, allowing a more advanced user to define additional functionality in multiple places, if wanted. In this way, advanced JavaScript users who wish to change how A-Frame works more directly can do so by adding code into these special passages. While we expect this to be beyond the scope of what most users will require for their projects, it remains a useful solution for advanced users.

4 Re-imagining Casual AR with TwineSpace

Augmented reality projects invite new examinations of the ways in which movement through space and the digital gaze can complicate the borders between physical and digital materiality. At the intersection between narrative gaming in the form of the hypertext authoring tool Twine and existing open source libraries for creating WebXR experiences, A-Frame and AR.js, TwineSpace seeks to encourage greater explorations of space with image tracking, what Hjorth et al. (2020) have called "a mode of hybridized digital wayfaring" [25]. Based on specific user cases, TwineSpace seeks to meet the demands of a "low friction" design for casual creativity while also hoping to open new possibilities for digital storytelling. In this section, we examine the design goals of the project, its known technical limitations, and how TwineSpace and other solutions point toward new approaches in augmented reality digital storytelling.

Fig. 1. A passage in TwineSpace displaying a pre-built A-Frame demo implemented using the script passage function on mobile. The user can move the camera around to view the 3D scenes while interacting with the narrative elements in Twine.

4.1 User Cases

TwineSpace's design started with three user cases based on our previous research. Many of the previous attempts to bridge AR and Twine focused on three-dimensional models, effects, and other mixed media in their demonstrations. Our own solution, we realized, must also afford similar possibilities with media. This led us to the creation of the first user case:

1. *I am a creator. I want to include AR media in my interactive fiction.*
   The inclusion of the *(embed-scene:)* macro allows creators to remix existing A-Frame projects with photospheres, three-dimensional models, and image tracking directly in TwineSpace. Combined with other macros, creators can then add new shapes and models to a project without needing to edit or re-write large amounts of HTML to produce a story in Twine with augmented reality experiences.
   Building from the first user case, the second focused on classroom usage around augmented reality. While TwineSpace is not designed exclusively for classroom contexts, we wanted to make sure the approaches we took matched how Twine was already used in pedagogical spaces as seen in previous scholarship and on platforms like ARIS [15]. Building on this, we developed our second user case:

2. I am a teacher. I want to work with my students to create simple AR experiences in a classroom using Twine.

   With this in mind, we wanted to make sure TwineSpace would be effective for similar educational and industry practices, with an attention to the casual creator across fields. This involved a) maintaining our emphasis on low-friction tools for design, b) focusing on marker-based and image-tracking models rather than geolocational models (which are more conducive to building spatial projects on a single campus), and c) ensuring our tools relied on no paid licensing or libraries. At the same time, TwineSpace provides a tool for rapidly outlining or creating a workable digital mockup (or 'whiteboxing') of larger AR games prior to more fiscally committed development.

   Finally, our last user case emphasized the importance of image-tracking solutions, as demonstrated by Argon and previously discussed AR games which relied on image tracking:
3. I have a mobile device in a specific space. I want to see locative image markers as part of my interactive fiction experience.

   We anticipated the low-barrier and open-source nature of TwineSpace would have potential for educators, but we also hope physical spaces such as libraries and museums as well as indie artists working in installations and interactive fiction creators could use image-tracking solutions in combination with Twine to create spatial narratives. We believe image-tracking to be a more generous solution for narrative AR than geolocational solutions, which often only work at scale and make distribution difficult.

4.2 Technical Limitations

There remain several technical limitations we are aware of for the TwineSpace story format:

- A-Frame relies on WebGL support to display three-dimensional content. Some mobile devices have limited or no WebGL functionality.
- Versions of the Safari web browser found on iPad and iPhone devices have higher default security restrictions than other web browsers. Some users may not be able to access their camera to process image markers or view certain WebGL content. In these cases, using an alternative web browser such as Chrome on the same device will provide access and better process content.
- TwineSpace currently supports very limited communications between authored content and the current A-Frame scene. While it is possible to setup event handlers and more complex interactions (i.e. touch, timers, locomotion controllers, etc.) all of this would need to be added by a creator themselves using JavaScript.
- TwineSpace inherits another limitation of A-Frame: the lack of a meaningful scene-builder. While the default A-Frame scene inspector can be used to modify existing scenes and templates, there is currently no tool to design and build scenes in a visual inspector.

Finally, it is worth noting how A-Frame can be used as a comprehensive WebXR framework capable of supporting both AR and VR projects. Because of this support,

TwineSpace can be used to build VR projects. However, because such projects frequently require specialized hardware or configurations, we excluded such a focus as it was against the "low-friction" and casual creator uses case behind the design of TwineSpace. VR projects are certainly possible in the future with TwineSpace, but were not within the scope of the current project.

4.3 Built on Open Source

Much of the research on previous approaches on tools for using augmented reality in Twine showed solutions built on proprietary code or commercial libraries. In these cases, once support for the tools ended, so too did the ability for any projects using them to run. Understanding this risk, we followed in the patterns established by solutions from Graham [10] and Cannon [13] for using open-source libraries and documenting not only our code, but the processes around them as well. Active investment in any coding project extends their lives beyond their initial publishing, and this is even more true for open-source projects [26]. Building from established open-source libraries with existing documentation and communities gives us the best chance for TwineSpace's longevity in the cases of possible future abandonment or a change in developers in the future [27, 28].

4.4 Making New Space for Casual Augmented Reality Storytelling

By building from existing solutions to create augmented reality experiences, the story format TwineSpace provides a flexible template for combining the best of existing storytelling approaches for both Twine and AR. Relying upon the ubiquity of mobile devices, augmented reality storytelling unlocks new and exciting considerations of how the metaphors of space, movement, and gaze can be rethought as understood through the lens of a user's digital camera. Projects like The Augmented Environments Lab's image-based 'storybook' show how augmented reality can be used with Twine to change the perception of the "physical" page for a reader [11]. Similarly, grave snail games' *Fish & Dagger* (2021) challenges digital stories as presented on screens, asking readers to find hidden messages within the in-game text by 'scanning' the page with their phone, as shown in Fig. 2 [29].

While Twine creators have often found sources of additional interactive content through Bitsy (a casual creator tool for building HTML minigames) [30] and JavaScript [31], AR media offers new possibilities for building additional interactive elements, art, and immersive storytelling. For example, videospheres have proven to be a simple yet effective way to complicate the player's viewing experience with mobile media: placing the player inside a video (and encouraging them to pan around and explore while reading). In TwineSpace, these can be implemented quickly with an existing video and single line of code, as shown in Fig. 3.

The introduction of AR to Twine games recontextualizes spatiality. Creators can orient (or disorient) users by projecting an interpretive, 'haptic' layer onto physical space [32]. This can be done either by mapping these spaces onto real-world spaces (often campuses, landmarks, and natural areas) or by designating locations within a certain proximity of the user, such as in micha cárdenas and the Creative Realities Studios' AR

Fig. 2. grave snail games' *Fish & Dagger* includes an image-tracking AR puzzle [24]. This game served as a model for the narrative possibility of marker-based AR in Twine stories.

Fig. 3. A recent build of TwineSpace showing a videosphere with an interactive Twine passage, optimized for mobile viewing. The videosphere plays looping clips of the underside of a waterfall while the user interacts with the narrative in the textbox at the bottom of the screen.

game *Sin Sol* (2018) [33]. The dynamic possibility of displaying rendered content onto images encourages different kinds of navigation: images might be scattered across a physical space (such as posters or banners in a library or museum) or another kind of paratext (such as a website or book). While Twine games are already about navigating hypertext, our hope is TwineSpace's AR media and marker tracking affordances further enable designers to play with the dual-navigation of space and narrative [12].

5 Conclusion

While TwineSpace still remains in-development, it is informed by a history of AR interventions and offers new possibilities for the accessible development of augmented reality interactive digital narratives. By combining existing open-source libraries and creating a dedicated story format for Twine, we hope TwineSpace can be a springboard for additional bridges between WebAR communities and interactive digital narrative design. As with other projects emerging from ICIDS and casual creator communities, this framework is intended to be adopted, hacked, and reimagined by any user so inclined. We have drawn extensively from previous efforts to engage AR and narrative gaming, and hope that by relying on open-source tools already popular with casual creators (and educators from this community and elsewhere, including electronic literature and digital humanities spaces), TwineSpace might be better positioned to expand ongoing design work and attract newcomers.

While the TwineSpace story format is released and functional [7], our next steps forward involve engaging with the Twine community and WebAR enthusiasts to receive more feedback and extend functionality. At the same time, we are currently building documentation, tutorials, and examples to hopefully make TwineSpace more accessible to those unaccustomed to AR or who have never used a modified story format in Twine before.

While AR continues to be defined by headline-catching, global-scale collection-games, we hope this project emphasizes the important potential for new, low-friction AR game development tools supporting casual creativity. While we recognize TwineSpace is merely a tool, and that bridging hypertext and AR does not imply novel narrative structures, we also recognize the ways previous expansions of Twine's framework have galvanized creators and ushered forth new hypertext [34] and digital art [35]. What kinds of stories might independent designers tell with the affordances of AR media? Perhaps more importantly, how might augmented reality—still largely associated with gigantic, global gaming franchises—be transformed by the possibilities of casual creation? It is our hope that TwineSpace might support these new inquiries as it supports the projects exploring new approaches to interactive digital narrative design, allowing us to envision the next opportunities and challenges at this "milestone moment" in the development of the form [36].

References

1. Bonsignore, E.M., Hansen, D.L., Toups, Z.O., Nacke, L.E., Salter, A., Lutters, W.: Mixed reality games. In: Proceedings of the ACM 2012 conference on Computer Supported Cooperative Work Companion, pp. 7–8. Association for Computing Machinery, New York, NY, USA (2012). https://doi.org/10.1145/2141512.2141517

2. Donald, N., Gillies, M.: Novel dramatic and ludic tensions arising from mixed reality performance as exemplified in better than life. In: Schoenau-Fog, H., Bruni, L.E., Louchart, S., Baceviciute, S. (eds.) ICIDS 2015. LNCS, vol. 9445, pp. 297–308. Springer, Cham (2015). https://doi.org/10.1007/978-3-319-27036-4_28

3. Arenas, L., Zarraonandia, T., Díaz, P., Aedo, I.: A platform for supporting the development of mixed reality environments for educational games. In: Zaphiris, P., Ioannou, A. (eds.) LCT 2015. LNCS, vol. 9192, pp. 537–548. Springer, Cham (2015). https://doi.org/10.1007/978-3-319-20609-7_51

4. Compton, K., Mateas, M.: Casual creators. In: Proceedings of the Sixth International Conference on Computational Creativity, pp. 228–235 (2015)

5. Green, D., Hargood, C., Charles, F.: Contemporary issues in interactive storytelling authoring systems. In: Rouse, R., Koenitz, H., Haahr, M. (eds.) ICIDS 2018. LNCS, vol. 11318, pp. 501–513. Springer, Cham (2018). https://doi.org/10.1007/978-3-030-04028-4_59

6. Anthropy, A.: Rise of the videogame zinesters: how freaks, normals, amateurs, artists, dreamers, drop-outs, queers, housewives, and people like you are taking back an art form. Seven Stories Press (2012)

7. Cox, D., Berge, P., Murray, J., Salter, A.: TwineSpace (2022). https://github.com/videlais/twine-space

8. Barbara, J.: Twine and DooM as authoring tools in teaching IDN DESIGN of LudoNarrative dissonance. In: Bosser, A.-G., Millard, D.E., Hargood, C. (eds.) ICIDS 2020. LNCS, vol. 12497, pp. 120–124. Springer, Cham (2020). https://doi.org/10.1007/978-3-030-62516-0_11

9. Kopas, M. (ed.): Videogames for humans: twine authors in conversation. Instar Books (2015)

10. Graham, S.: Tutorials for Augmented Reality & Archaeology (2021). https://github.com/shawngraham/ar-archaeology/blob/42a93b0a930b17184d4012f10ed800c2887f3bfa/workshop%20materials/Hacking%20Twine%20to%20make%20a%20location-based%20game.md

11. Understanding AR (2022). https://github.com/argonjs/understanding-argon-twine

12. e Silva, A.D.S. and Glover-Rijkse, R. (eds.): Hybrid Play: Crossing Boundaries in Game Design, Player Identities and Play Spaces. Routledge, London (2020). https://doi.org/10.4324/9780367855055

13. Cannon, A.R.: How I built a game in a week. https://medium.com/samsung-internet-dev/how-i-built-a-game-in-a-week-5810b1197686. Accessed 07 Feb 2022

14. Holden, C.L., Gagnon, D.J., Litts, B.K., Smith, G.: ARIS: an open-source platform for widespread mobile augmented reality experimentation. In: Neto, F.M.M. (ed.) Technology Platform Innovations and Forthcoming Trends in Ubiquitous Learning, pp. 19–34. IGI Global, Hershey, PA, USA (2014). https://doi.org/10.4018/978-1-4666-4542-4.ch002

15. Perry, B.: ARIS: a tool to promote language learning through AR gaming. CJ **35**, 333–342 (2018). https://doi.org/10.1558/cj.36318

16. 8th Wall | Pricing and Plans - WebAR, AR, WebVR Developer Tools and SDK. https://www.8thwall.com/pricing. Accessed 21 July 2022

17. Kitromili, S., Jordan, J., Millard, D.E.: How do writing tools shape interactive stories? In: Rouse, R., Koenitz, H., Haahr, M. (eds.) ICIDS 2018. LNCS, vol. 11318, pp. 514–522. Springer, Cham (2018). https://doi.org/10.1007/978-3-030-04028-4_60

18. Hansen, M.: modality/harlowe (2022). https://github.com/modality/harlowe

19. Edwards, T.M.: SugarCube v2 (2022). https://github.com/tmedwards/sugarcube-2

20. Cox, D.: Snowman (2022). https://github.com/videlais/snowman

21. Cox, D.: Static Echoes: Exploring the Life and Closing of the Free Twine Hosting Service, philome.la. Electronic Literature Organization Conference 2020 (2020)

22. Kemenade, P. van: Trialogue (2022). https://github.com/phivk/trialogue

23. Heuser, J.: Botscripten (2022). https://github.com/jakobo/botscripten

24. Twine Specifications (2022). https://github.com/iftechfoundation/twine-specs
25. Hjorth, L., Richardson, I.: Pokémon GO: Mobile media play, place-making, and the digital wayfarer. Mob. Media Commun. **5**, 3–14 (2017). https://doi.org/10.1177/2050157916680015
26. Avelino, G., Constantinou, E., Valente, M.T., Serebrenik, A.: On the abandonment and survival of open source projects: An empirical investigation. In: 2019 ACM/IEEE International Symposium on Empirical Software Engineering and Measurement (ESEM), pp. 1–12. IEEE, Porto de Galinhas, Recife, Brazil (2019). https://doi.org/10.1109/ESEM.2019.8870181
27. Aberdour, M.: Achieving Quality in Open-Source Software. IEEE Softw. **24**, 58–64 (2007). https://doi.org/10.1109/MS.2007.2
28. Kaur, R., Kaur, K.: Insights into developers' abandonment in FLOSS projects. In: Nagar, A.K., Jat, D.S., Marín-Raventós, G., Mishra, D.K. (eds.) Intelligent Sustainable Systems. LNNS, vol. 333, pp. 731–740. Springer, Singapore (2022). https://doi.org/10.1007/978-981-16-6309-3_69
29. Fish & Dagger by grave snail games. https://gravesnail.itch.io/fish-and-dagger. Accessed 27 July 2022
30. The Tower by communistsister. https://communistsister.itch.io/the-tower. Accessed 27 July 2022
31. my father's long, long legs by ztul. https://ztul.itch.io/mflll. Accessed 27 July 2022
32. Pozo, T.: Queer Games After Empathy: Feminism and Haptic Game Design Aesthetics from Consent to Cuteness to the Radically Soft. Game Studies, p. 18 (2018)
33. Sin Sol / No Sun | micha cárdenas. https://michacardenas.sites.ucsc.edu/sin-sol-no-sun/. Accessed 25 Apr 2022
34. Millard, D.E., Hargood, C.: Hypertext as a lens into interactive digital narrative. In: Mitchell, A., Vosmeer, M. (eds.) ICIDS 2021. LNCS, vol. 13138, pp. 509–524. Springer, Cham (2021). https://doi.org/10.1007/978-3-030-92300-6_51
35. Salter, A., Moulthrop, S.: Twining: Critical and Creative Approaches to Hypertext Narratives. Amherst College Press (2021).https://doi.org/10.3998/mpub.12255695
36. Murray, J.H.: Research into interactive digital narrative: a kaleidoscopic view. In: Rouse, R., Koenitz, H., Haahr, M. (eds.) ICIDS 2018. LNCS, vol. 11318, pp. 3–17. Springer, Cham (2018). https://doi.org/10.1007/978-3-030-04028-4_1

Resources for Comparative Analysis of IDN Authoring Tools

Yotam Shibolet[1](✉) [iD] and Vincenzo Lombardo[2] [iD]

[1] Utrecht University, Utrecht, Netherlands
y.shibolet@uu.nl
[2] CIRMA and Department of Informatics, University of Torino, Torino, Italy
vincenzo.lombardo@unito.it

Abstract. Authoring tools are a crucial component in the practice and research of interactive digital narrative design, yet there is no contemporary knowledge base to evaluate and comparatively analyze the great many tools that currently exist. This paper takes on the tasks of constructing a framework for the description and comparison of IDN authoring tools and their defining characteristics and affordances, and of developing this framework into a community resource. We propose a descriptive framework and an online resource meant to facilitate the development of a tool database and curate its properties.

Our framework is composed of 30 tool descriptors, addressing (among other factors) the tools' basic identify, business model, use context, technical information, interface affordances and unique design elements. Values were additionally created to define the answer range for most descriptors and streamline the process of tool-logging via the online form we created. In this paper, we explain and demonstrate our framework and present the online database and examples of the sort of meta-analysis it can generate, testifying to the potential usefulness of our framework to the research and practice community.

Keywords: Authoring tools · Narrative system design · Tool description and comparison · Software studies · Design interface

1 Introduction

Interactive digital narrative (IDN) authoring tools - software that facilitate the creation of IDN works (see our full definition in 3.2) - have long been acknowledged by the research community as highly relevant aspects for the understanding and progression of this discipline. However, in recent years, as the field and the number of tools available within it grew exponentially, we have found ourselves rather lacking an overview of available tools which approaches thoroughness, and similarly lacking a clear framework for describing the main characteristics of different tools and comparing between them across the great many different sub-contexts of IDN design. Building on previous work, in this paper

M. Vosmeer and L. Holloway-Attaway (Eds.): ICIDS 2022, LNCS 13762, pp. 513–528, 2022.
https://doi.org/10.1007/978-3-031-22298-6_33

we present a framework and infrastructure for the logging, description and comparison of authoring tools in the context of IDN research and practice.

We begin by providing some reflection and historical perspective on authoring tools and their past analysis, then turn to explain the scope, aim and perspective of our work and the definition of authoring tools refined in accordance to them. We then present our descriptive framework and discuss its infrastructure and process of iterative development. Finally, we present the web resource for the collection and presentation of our data, in hopes that our tool description project would be utilized and expanded further by the research community.

2   Reflection on Authoring Tools Research

2.1   History and Past Work

Some stepping stones in the early decades of the field: the first authoring tool (arguably) meeting our definition criteria (see Sect. 3.2) is Brown's Eamon (1979) [10], which included a creation kit for adventure games with combat mechanics. The Adventure System (1982) is another candidate. Authoring tools at this point are either customized editors for a specific game interface or basic hypertext systems. Sharples' 1984 thesis [14] on the use of computers for creative writing may be the first academic text that addresses interactive authoring software (despite not distinguishing it from software for linear writing) and presents its own tool prototype. While not specifically connected to narrative, Conklin's analysis of hypermedia authoring and early hypertext systems was pivotal to establishing the field [4]. Bolter and Joyce's work [3] is likely the first academic publication focused exclusively on interactive digital narrative authoring, and the tool they presented - Storyspace - was an influential leap in the design of hypertext tools.

By the late 1990s, the gradually growing number of narrative-oriented tools called for some comparative research. While narrative authoring tools were included in previous reviews of different hypertext systems (e.g. [18]), Mateas' "Oz-centric review" [11] may be the first meta-analysis overview comparing the structure of interactive narrative systems (including both story generation tools and authoring tools). Authoring tool analysis papers from the following decade often focus on a specific aspect or sub-type of tools, such as drama management systems ([1,13] or structural representation [9].

Running from 2009 to 2011, the IRIS EU project was an important landmark in this research: it both presented new tools and tool prototypes (e.g. [16]) and new theoretical reflection on the broader context of interactive authoring and tool use (e.g. [17]).

2.2   Shortage of Meta Analysis

Over the last decade or so, the number of available authoring tools has dramatically proliferated and the scope of their use has vastly extended. This is the case not only for text-based software - once the predominant association for the term authoring tool - but also for authoring tools facilitating the creation of other forms of interactive digital media, most commonly:

- visual novel authoring tools, such as Ren'Py, popular predominantly, but far from exclusively in Japan;
- interactive video tools, such as Korsakow and Klynt;
- game engines such as Unity and Unreal (following in the footsteps of earlier engines like GameMaker Studio and Source).

These tools reached massive popularity, and despite their lack of specific emphasis on narrative design, we view it as undeniable that relevant and resonant narrative works, e.g. "Gone Home" (Fullbright, 2013) and "What Remains of Edith Finch" (Giant Sparrow, 2017) are constantly being designed using powerful and publicly available engines. We therefore hold that it is crucial to consider game engines as relevant authoring tools. The same engines are also often used - alongside other dedicated software tools - for the design of XR media, which is another relevant territory for the authoring of powerful interactive narrative experiences with its own range of design potentialities and constraints. As the amount of available tools continued growing, the amount of academic work dedicated to comparative meta analysis of existing tools lessened (probably unsurprisingly, given the amount of work creating a survey that can be viewed as anywhere near substantial now takes). Over the last decade, most academic work on authoring tools has been dedicated to presenting a brand new tool or tool prototype designed by the authors (most often text-based) - as Koenitz comments, following Jay Bolter, it seems that every researcher nowadays wants to have their own authoring tool [8]. Although the introduction of a new tool is sometimes complemented with a some degree comparative analysis of previously existing tools ([6] is a good example), other tools are discussed in such works predominantly in the context of showcasing what the new tool being presented does differently or uniquely. While many new academic tools appear intriguing and potent, this constant reinvention of the wheel is not necessarily the most productive vein for the development of knowledge within the research field. We believe such work should be complemented by more consolidating efforts, dedicated to accumulation of and reflection on existing knowledge and resources.

Shibolet, Knoller and Koenitz aim to take some initial steps in this direction with their taxonomy and description framework presented in [15]. This paper is primarily focused on a broad overview of over 100 available tools and their division into 9 taxonomic categories, based on the type of end-product (e.g. game; interactive fiction; VR) and degree of self-containment: does the tool generate all the assets it employs for authoring, or alternatively relies on importing external assets such as video segments? In addition to its mapping of the field, this paper ends with a descriptive framework, meant to make any tool included in its taxonomy analyzable across a unified set of clear parameters. This set of descriptors is presented as preliminary, and is not further discussed or precisely defined there. Our early attempts to utilize this framework revealed that, being built around open text parameters, it insufficiently enables the production of consistent results when applied by different researchers. In this paper, we therefore build upon the authors' initial list of descriptors to provide a more refined, narrowed-down and operational framework, which truly facilitates meta-analysis and comparison between authoring tools in addition to clearer descriptions of each individual tool. We created a structured form defining possible values for each descriptor to accommodate this.

3   Aim, Perspective and Definitions

As a result of the shortage of broad analysis discussed above, it is currently quite difficult for both researchers and practitioners to learn which authoring tools are out there, what their common characteristics and differences are, and how to choose the right tool for a given project. We see this lacuna as the main issue that our proposed framework and database infrastructure aim to move towards alleviating.

3.1   Aim and Perspective

Our primary aim is to pave the way towards the creation of a database that would allow researchers and practitioners to inspect an adjustable overview of the field of available tools, as well as examine the main characteristics of any given tool they may be interested in and how those compare to other authoring options. We view this descriptive framework and database as a potentially vital community resource to the study of authoring tools. For IDN practitioners, this can be a way to explore the field of available tools and potentially choose the most fitting tool to work with for a prospective project. For academics, this can be a useful gateway to comfortably access key information on the different available tools, facilitating better tool research and hopefully further meta-analysis and broad insight on the structure and affordances of different types of tools. As an added benefit, by mapping the many characteristics of tools and their intended end-products, this project also provides an interesting snapshot of the IDN field at large.

We take a very broad perspective on the study and description of IDN authoring tools. The craft of interactive narrative design is not encapsulated by the explicit authoring of narrative structures, but also involves other key aspects such as the design of interface (e.g. [2]) and game mechanics (e.g. [5]) that are pivotal to shaping narrative meaning in the end-user's experience. Our approach is additionally influenced by Werning's recent work on game creation tools [19], which views authoring tools as "manipulatable and shareable objects" that "shape the relationship between stakeholders" and "meaningfully frame the purpose they are intended for." The broad perspective that Werning suggests calls for the analysis of tools not only through their interface and structure, but also through the context of their use (e.g. its target audience, ownership, use and publication license, discourse surrounding the tool, its self-presentation, etc.). In accordance, we find it important to analyze authoring tools beyond the often dominant focus of most past work on their formalized design of narrative structures. Our framework aims to address additional aspects and components take central part in shaping the IDN design process - centrally including the tool's interface and its various design affordances, as well as the context of tool use.

Finally, our understanding of the broad field of tools and their relevant qualities is influenced by additional modules that are typically involved in the IDN production process, namely the entities managed by the tool, the media outcomes, and the story engine [12]. While not every tool element can be addressed in full and this broad approach inevitably comes at the expense of discussing particular elements in more depth, our descriptive framework hopes to provide a zoomed-out outline of the relevant aspects of different tools, which could then potentially serve in-depth research of specific tools or tool groupings and their characteristics.

Werning's book also raises pertinent questions regarding the many ways by which tools may shape the design process, the end-product(s), and the (often implicit) understanding of the medium in which the designer is working. In a somewhat similar vein, Koenitz raises three pertinent questions regarding IDN authoring tools [8]: what drives their creation? How should we describe them? How do they shape IDN artefacts? Here we directly tackle the second of these three questions; however, our descriptive framework and database can also hopefully provide resources that could aid in the future studies of the other two.

3.2 Defining Authoring Tools

In line with our perspective on the subject, we define an IDN authoring tool as digital software, which meets the following three criteria:

1. Provides an **independent and comprehensive workspace**, including an IDE and GUI, which allows a prospective author to create an IDN work from start to finish. The tool gears its end products to run on an engine, which is often - though not necessarily - also embedded within the tool's environment.
2. **Simplifies the authoring process**: the tool streamlines the design of the storyworld, the end-user interaction model, and/or the other central narrative elements such as characters and events, in order to make the IDN creative process easier and more effective than design through a general-purpose programming language would be.[1]
3. **Is actively being used** or was actively used in the past to create IDN products - focused on interactive narrative aspects - by a community of practitioners besides the tool's creator(s). Prototypes and in-house tools may also meet this criteria, if they demonstrate clear and explicit potential to be actively used in the future, once or if they are publicly released.

---

[1] An "easier"/"more effective" IDN creative process could mean different things: a workflow that is more directed and integrated, less time-consuming or demanding fewer technical skills; improved accessibility and tangibility of design strategies and representation structures in the tool's UI; improved narrative abstraction/conceptualization in the work environment, and/or making narrative structures and concepts more ready-to-hand.

This definition is meant to pragmatically address the tool's capability to facilitate the creation of interactive narrative works, regardless of whether it was specifically or explicitly meant for narrative authoring. While the lack of narrative-specific elements in a given software may certainly and validly be seen as a flaw or at least an issue, we believe such lack should not disqualify software that fits our criteria and is actively and successfully being used to author IDN products from being considered as an IDN authoring tool and and analyzed in comparison to other such tools. We therefore regard the explicit narrative design emphasis - largely missing, for example, from most widely successful game engines - as one relevant characteristic for the comparison between different types of authoring tools (and potentially their end-products and the understanding of the medium that their use inspires), rather than a necessary defining criterion.

We realize that such 'loose' definition of IDN authoring tools opens the field of discussion to a degree that some would consider problematic. However, we believe that this high inclusivity makes our understanding of authoring tools more effectively responsive to the state-of-the-art, and that the active use criteria keeps it from stretching out beyond the point of productivity. For example, it has been pointed out to us that Microsoft PowerPoint could be understood as an authoring tool under our definition since it technically allows for the authoring of a multi-linear narrative work; However, since nothing in PowerPoint's interface, design affordances or rhetoric directs its users towards any sort of comfortable narrative authoring, the emergence of a community of PowerPoint IDN practitioners remains extremely unlikely; and if such community were to nonetheless emerge, we could then happily include PowerPoint in our broad database, as there would likely a reason for such emergence that makes the software relevant to study in this context - even if only for the purpose of deeming it an unproductive authoring tool and understanding why it is used as such nonetheless.

4   Descriptive Framework

This section outlines our framework for tool description and comparison: We explain the methodology we followed, discuss an overview of the descriptor clusters, and finally present some examples of the value range we defined for various descriptors.

4.1   Methodology and Process

Our research project was conducted within INDCOR, the COST Action dedicated to the research of narrative complexity. We chaired a taskforce on authoring tools analysis within Workgroup 1, dedicated to the research of design and development of IDN systems[2]. We have followed the methodology of a focus group, as outlined in [7], composed of scholars and practitioners with some previous experience in the study of authoring tools. The five taskforce participants

---

[2] https://indcor.eu/working-groups/wg1-design-and-development/.

(in addition to the two coordinators) covered several areas of expertise balancing between the practice of authoring and the study of models, between the production setting and the didactics of writing, between humanistic and technological backgrounds. Our role as coordinators was to initialize and facilitate the discussion, work on a review of the theoretical framework after each meeting and make the results available to the group members, and revise the tool description framework in accordance to group feedback and discussion.

The goal of this qualitative research was to approach inter-subjective consensus on the definition of the authoring tool and on the framework for its description. Our group meetings (7 in total) and the work in-between were dedicated to the following:

Initial Reflections and Discussion. In order to develop a mutually agreed understanding of our subject of inquiry and on how to loosely draw the boundaries of the objects of our research, we discussed our aforementioned definition of an authoring tool and the main categories of descriptive characteristics, resulting in some rounds of revisions.

Iterative Improvement of the Descriptive Framework. Taking the descriptor list sketched out in [15] as a starting point, we gradually refined the descriptors - reducing their number from 38 to 30, re-calibrating, renaming or uniting some, and adding a few new descriptors or new explanations or subquestions for existing ones. After initial theoretical discussions of the descriptor categories, each participant was asked to select 1–2 tools to analyze through our initial framework. We performed an iterative process of refining the framework through this assignment: panelists' output, experience, and insight from each round of analysis was discussed and reflected upon in group meetings; we then adjusted the framework accordingly, adding, removing, rephrasing, or clarifying descriptors as needed; and then asked group members to re-conduct their analysis through the revised version.

Over our first iteration of this process, we could clearly detect some operational gaps for achieving a consistent analysis: in particular, many of the more complex descriptors were too open-ended, causing interpretations of precisely what was required to describe to vary between panelists, who contributed with widely different styles of filling out the free-text rubrics. To alleviate this issue, we decided to develop a set of clear, pre-defined value options for most descriptors (and adjust the descriptors themselves to accommodate this), that would better and more clearly streamline the tool logging process. This value range or answer key became a central part of our project.

To ease the tool-logging process and the collection and analysis of results into a database, we designed a Google form[3] facilitating our descriptive framework and the value range defined for each descriptor. This form - and through it, our value range for various descriptors - was further improved and revised based on panelists' feedback after each iteration.

For our final round of iteration, we ran a workshop with six participants (all IDN researchers interested in the subject) who were not part of our focus group.

---

[3] https://forms.gle/mBVGHH3QB4G52WQw6.

Based on their feedback and the results of their logging effort, we incorporated final adjustments to the prototype descriptive framework. At the end of this phase of the process we had a sample database of 13 authoring tools logged through the latest version of our framework.

Community Resource and Proof of Concept Meta-analysis. We created a web resource to serve as an interim community database, making the full results of the work completed so far accessible, searchable and analyzable and showcasing the ability of our framework to generate meta-analysis and statistics through a proof-of-concept comparative survey.

4.2 Descriptor Listing and Clusters

Our framework includes a total of 30 descriptors, divided into 5 clusters. These clusters are explained below - alongside an example answer key for a descriptor in each cluster - and laid out in Table 1:

A. The 'identity and type' cluster contains key information for initial understanding of the authoring tool and what it generally does. This includes for example the tool's origin and chronology, the end-product it is intended to create, the target audience it is intended for and its ownership model: the "creator's affiliation" can be defined as "company"; "academic"; "artist" or "enthusiast". This cluster primarily aims to provide prospective end-users of our database with an efficient and accessible overview of each tool's defining characteristics.

B. The 'use context' cluster concerns information that addresses the tool's availability, usability (e.g. license type), and documentation resources (e.g. tutorials, publication portal). The 'life status' descriptor (09) addresses the well-known problem of relatively rapid tool obsolescence. Tools can be described as 'alive' (active user community and/or actively updated and moderated), 'in limbo' (no longer qualifies as 'alive' but still publicly available), 'dead' (no longer available/doesn't run on contemporary platforms), or 'prototype' (still prior to full/public release).

C. The 'technical structure' cluster concerns technical information on how the tool is built (e.g. programming language written in) and its technical functionality (e.g. author-facing programming language). 'Self containment' (19) describes whether the tool's work environment is fully self-contained, allows for optional integration of plugins, or requires interoperable import/export to complete the authoring process.

D. The authoring interface cluster describes the salient features of the tool's interface and its organization, for examples its primary focus (characters, events, spaces or links) and a rough assessment of its level of intuitively. The primary authoring action(s) descriptor (21) concerns the most common actions that the author likely performs during the authoring process on the tool. This is built as a multiple-choice checkbox, with options for common actions including 'drag & drop' (working with visual templates, e.g.

Table 1. The 30 descriptors in 5 clusters

A: Identity and type	(01) General description
	(02) Introductory quote
	(03) Creation and ownership
	(04) Year of release
	(05) End-product
	(06) Main target audience(s)
	(07) Interface screenshots
	(08) Creation mode
B: Use context	(09) 'Life' status
	(10) Available works
	(11) Web Resources and docs
	(12) Tool analysis citations
	(13) Tool License
C: Technical structure	(14) Programming language(s)
	(15) Work platform(s)
	(16) Importable formats
	(17) Exportable formats
	(18) Supporting technical resources
	(19) Self-containment
D: Authoring Interface	(20) Primary design focus
	(21) Primary authoring action(s)
	(22) Main interface window(s)
	(23) Designable elements
	(24) Built-in presets
	(25) Authoring difficulty
E: Design Affordances	(26) Narrative specific emphasis
	(27) Procedural authoring
	(28) End-product control interface
	(29) Additional design affordances
	(30) Additional tool-specific parameters

Unity), 'manipulating extendable objects/blocks' (e.g. Twine), 'visual coding', 'abstract coding' (either in a tool-specific or pre-existing programming language), or 'navigating text menus'.

E. The design affordances cluster concerns specific capabilities that shape the emphasis of the authoring process towards a particular IDN end-product. For example, the extent to which the tool underscores the design of narrative-specific elements and the control (or end-user input) interface of the final product. The procedural authoring descriptor (27) concerns the possibilities for procedural AI generation of various design components. This descriptor first asks how primary procedural authoring is to the tool's authoring process ('central'/'optional'/'nonexistent' emphasis). It then presents a multiple choice checkbox for available procedurally-authored elements, which includes 'characters', 'environments', 'objects/items', 'events', and an 'other' option for any potential additional procedural components deemed relevant for IDN authoring using the tool.

4.3   Descriptor Values

A central part of our effort was to create and revise the value list for each descriptor, in the attempt to lay out the different options to describe tools as comprehensively, accurately and clearly as possible. This work on the value list often also intertwined with our revision and re-framing of the descriptors themselves (see Methodology above).

To produce these values, we integrated bottom-up insights provided by the panelists' logging practice about the various features of tools, with top-down conceptual discussions on various aspects of the state-of-the-art tool landscape and the appropriate vocabulary to describe it. Since the full range of values included in our form cannot be laid out in the scope of this paper, here we present the reader with a few examples (in addition to the ones in the section above), representing the different sorts of values we produced, their role within our framework and the work process this involved.

Example 1: Primary Design Focus

- Descriptor explanation: At what level/through what underlying concept is the story primarily conceived?
- Value options:
  - Events (occurrences triggered by preconditions/timelines)
  - Nodes and links (linking between individual segments, e.g. Twine)
  - Space (environment design)
  - Character
  - Dialogue
  - Other...

This descriptor asks for a broad assessment of the authoring modality the tool primarily offers, requiring tool-loggers to pick the option that fits best. Forming the value range here demanded more conceptual, top-down thinking about how to divide the field into categories of narrative-composition modes. This descriptor therefore forms a sort of zoomed-out typology of tools (see Fig. 2b below that reports the statistics for the sample database), determined primarily through group discussion based upon prior knowledge (from narratology, game studies and hypermedia studies). Note that of the five options the group came up with, the tool logging done so far shows that events and dialogue-based tools appear to be rare, while none of the tools logged so far implements the "character" option.

Example 2: Creation Mode

– Descriptor explanation: What ways of authoring work does the tool support?
– Options:
  - Coding/scripting creation mode (e.g. Ren'Py);
  - Visual coding creation mode (e.g. Scratch);
  - Tagging creation mode (e.g. in-out keywords in Korsakow);
  - Spatial creation mode (e.g. Unity);
  - Nodes and links creation mode (e.g. Twine)

This descriptor and its chosen value range aims to complement the one in the above example by inquiring about the general means of authoring work a tool primarily offers. This distinction from primary design focus is important since a tool's range of creation modes is not limited to the primary mode in which the story is conceptualized: for example, game engines like Unity are clearly space-focused, but variably offer additional creation modes. Some engines can actually require authors to spend more time designing the end-product spatial environment via abstract coding; other engines, built around WYSIWYG (what-you-see-is-what-you-get) interface and built-in templates, allow the design work to occur closer to the spatial level and are often more amateur friendly. For this descriptor, as well as some additional descriptors such as "primary authoring actions", we ended up switching from requiring a single selection to allowing multiple choices, since often a given tool does not cleanly fit into one value category. The value range is therefore not quite a typology breaking down the field into distinct tool groups, and more of a tagging system that will mark many tools as hybrids. The categories given as answer options, however, are framed as a closed list (there is no "other" option) presenting the full range of relevant options for current tools based on both our bottom-up prototype logging process and top-down conceptual group discussion.

Value sets for other descriptors are more strictly bottom-up: values for the "designable elements" descriptor, for example, are presented as an open list containing a variety of different options (in this case 17, including video segments, environmental states, camera controls, dialogue etc. etc.), as well as an open "other..." option. This is a crowdsourced listing developed purely through our tool-logging process: new options were added whenever found relevant for a given tool being described. This list is highly extendable, as additional answer options easily can be added to the listing if any further elements are found relevant enough in future logging efforts.

Finally, some of our descriptor values do not fit the categories of above examples: Descriptors such as "general description" and "introductory quote" (both kept for the curative purpose of opening each tool's description with a quick showcase of its unique identity), have to be filled out by open writing. Other descriptors, such as "role of procedural authoring" ("nonexistent", "optional" or "central") or "authoring difficulty" ("easy", "medium" or "hard") require subjective assessment and were given values across a narrow scale of three options to reduce variance. While such subjective assessments provide less empirical value for accurate tool comparison, descriptors with such values were kept in our framework with an eye towards the curation of our online resource, meant to address and describe each tool in a way that is useful also for prospective designers and newcomers to the field. Subjective assessment of dimensions such as difficulty are far from ideal, but were thought of as the best available option to nonetheless provide some sort of perspective on parameters such as how amateur-friendly a given tool is, which can be crucial for the choice of which tools would be fitting to work with.

5   Online Resource and Proof of Concept Meta-Analysis

As mentioned, our final step so far was to develop an online resource[4] in order to showcase the work done so far. This resource, published on the portal of the INDCOR initiative, also facilitates the future logging of further tools, paving the way towards potential utilization of this framework for a larger scale research. Our database is capable of implementing results comfortably from our Google form, and points users towards this form for the prospective logging of additional tools and for providing further feedback on the descriptive framework.

Our web portal additionally contains a tag-cloud feature (see Fig. 1), which allows end-users to search for tools fitting any of the specific answer keys or "tag" terms from our descriptors (e.g. tools written with Python, tools targeting professional IDN authors, tools that enable the design of events, etc.). It is also possible to search for specific tools or attributes in the portal's main page.

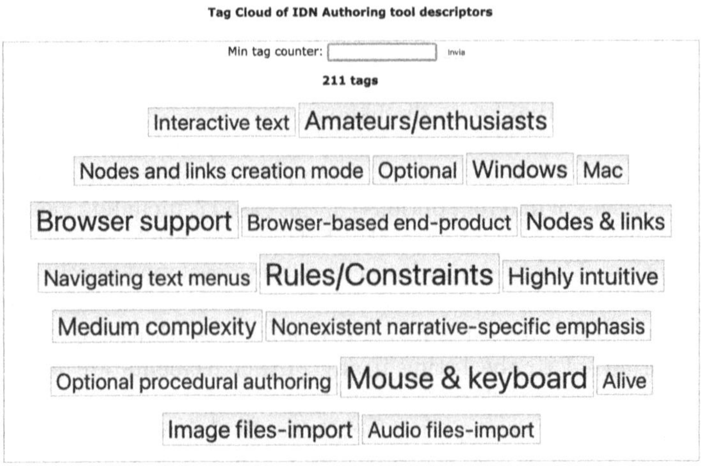

Tag Cloud of IDN Authoring tool descriptors

Min tag counter: [   ] Invia

211 tags

Interactive text   Amateurs/enthusiasts

Nodes and links creation mode   Optional   Windows   Mac

Browser support   Browser-based end-product   Nodes & links

Navigating text menus   Rules/Constraints   Highly intuitive

Medium complexity   Nonexistent narrative-specific emphasis

Optional procedural authoring   Mouse & keyboard   Alive

Image files-import   Audio files-import

Fig. 1. The tag cloud display, limiting tags to those with a minimum frequency of 6.

As it currently stands, this platform forms a proof-of-concept for our framework and serves as inspiration for further contributions. The system currently

---

[4] https://omeka-s.indcor.eu/s/idn-authoring-tools/page/idn-authoring-tools.

displays the metadata for the 13 tools logged and analyzed by the panelists and workshop participants, namely: ASAPS, Bitsy, Construct 3, HypeDyn, Korsakow, Inklewriter, Ren'py, Storygraphia, Storyspace, Texture, Twine, Unity and Unreal Engine. As further proof-of-concept for the sort of information display potentially available on the online resource, we present two sample statistical breakdowns of results collected so far for two of our tool descriptor in Fig. 2. While the number of tools logged so far is insufficient to substantiate any broad conclusions on the field, it demonstrates the sort of data that could be generated given a more statistically significant sample size of tools logged into our database.

Figure 2a, relating to the programming language(s) descriptor, shows that tools were written in a large variety of programming languages: results are divided between Javascript, Python, C, C++, Processing, Ruby and java. By looking at metadata on the other question included in this descriptor, regrading author-facing programming languages (which are actively part of the design process the tool offers), we find that many of these languages are also employed in various ways during the authoring process, alongside tool-specific markup languages. Figure 2b displays our collected data on the primary design focus descriptor, discussed above. It shows that the nodes & links paradigm, resulting in hypertextual narratives, is by far the most common in our sample size survey; while the presence of game engine tools in the survey corresponds with a good amount of space-based design tools as well. The 'event' and 'dialogue' focus applies for 1 tool each, while none of the 13 is focused on character design.

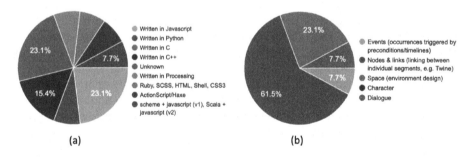

Fig. 2. Two statistical breakdowns from the prototype survey of 13 authoring tools: (a) programming languages in which tools are coded; (b) primary design focus.

6   Conclusion and Future Plans

This paper has reported on a prospective community resource for the classification and analysis of IDN authoring tools. Based on previous work, we have compiled a list of 30 descriptors, grouped into 5 clusters, addressing, respectively, the identity of tools, their use context, the technical infrastructure, tool interface, and significant design affordances. We worked with a focus group of experts to define and refine our set of descriptors and descriptor values, and implemented this work to create an online database allowing access to tool metadata. As the proof of concept survey demonstrated, our descriptive framework and the online resources developed to facilitate it are capable of representing the state-of-the-art of available tools, and of producing various tool comparisons and breakdowns across a multitude of factors alongside individual tool descriptions.

A limitation of our framework, discovered during the workshop we ran, is that the process of logging a tool through our 30 parameters remains, despite our refinement efforts, both somewhat time-consuming (taking around an hour for professional researchers familiar with the tool they are logging) and somewhat challenging for amateurs or newcomers to the field. To ease the logging process, we found it useful to add explanations for parameters and value keys that were judged to cause confusion by either the panelists or the workshop participants. Further efforts to make our framework and logging process more accessible could certainly be productive, though at least some forms of simplifying the framework to alleviate this issue might take away from the quality of data being generated unless this is done accurately and carefully. More broadly, we are certain our framework still has much space to further improvement and refinement, that could make the data it produces more concisely valuable.

In the future, we aim to substantially increase the size of our database via crowdsourced effort. For this we ask the help of the IDN research community: community members are warmly encouraged to access our form and log a tool they are familiar with. Given more tool data, we could be able to gradually grow our database into a portal allowing for more statistically significant and comprehensive meta-analysis of the state-of-the-art. Important curatorial questions regarding this portal - including the dilemma of potential gaps in the assessment of tools by different loggers, a likely weakness of our crowdsourced methodology - will need to be addressed as the database grows, based on the amount and quality of data provided (e.g. how often will assessments of authoring difficulty diverge when a tool is logged by multiple researchers?). We additionally hope that community feedback and discussion on the tool-logging process could help us make our framework more accessible and accurate.

If this potential of our framework is realized, our wish is that the database would also be utilized to aid future research broaching more open-ended and less clearly defined questions on tool characteristics and their impact - thereby further delving into the nuanced relationship between tools, authors, and end-products. We are particularly interested in the question of how a tools' design, structure, and use context may tilt authors towards designing particular types of stories in particular ways. If tools indeed play a significant role in shaping the authors' understanding of the IDN creation practice - and therefore by extension, end-users' experience and understanding of IDN media - the database we envision could generate some highly valuable insight.

Acknowledgements. We are exceedingly grateful to Alex Mitchell, Mattia Bellini, Fanny Bernabe and Noam Knoller, for their active and productive participation in the taskforce and focus group process. Additional help was provided by Hartmut Koenitz, Nicolas Szilas, and Christian Roth. The first author would like to thank Hartmut Koenitz and Noam Knoller also for their supervision of the initial research project that helped shape this framework. Our thanks goes to INDCOR Cost action 18230 and Workgroup 1, in particular, for inspiring this work and hosting the prototype resource and the tag cloud.

References

1. Arinbjarnar, M., Barber, H., Kudenko, D.: A critical review of interactive drama systems. In: AISB 2009 Symposium: AI & Games, Edinburgh, UK. Citeseer (2009)
2. Bizzocchi, J., Ben Lin, M., Tanenbaum, T.: Games, narrative and the design of interface. Int. J. Arts Technol. **4**(4), 460–479 (2011)
3. Bolter, J.D., Joyce, M.: Hypertext and creative writing. In: Proceedings of the ACM Conference on Hypertext, pp. 41–50 (1987)
4. Conklin, J.: Hypertext: an introduction and survey. Computer **20**(09), 17–41 (1987)
5. Dubbelman, T.: Narrative game mechanics. In: International Conference on Interactive Digital Storytelling, pp. 39–50. Springer (2016). https://doi.org/10.1007/978-3-319-48279-8_4
6. Green, D., Hargood, C., Charles, F.: Contemporary issues in interactive storytelling authoring systems. In: International Conference on Interactive Digital Storytelling, pp. 501–513. Springer (2018). https://doi.org/10.1007/978-3-030-04028-4_59
7. Hill, C., Thompson, B., Williams, E.: A guide to conducting consensual qualitative research. Counseling Psychologist - COUNS PSYCHOL **25**, 517–572 (1997). https://doi.org/10.1177/0011000097254001
8. Koenitz, H.: Three questions concerning authoring tools. AIS, ICIDS (2017)
9. Magerko, B.: A comparative analysis of story representations for interactive narrative systems. In: AIIDE, pp. 91–94 (2007)
10. Maher, J.: Eamon, part i. https://www.filfre.net/2011/09/eamon-part-1/
11. Mateas, M.: An Oz-centric review of interactive drama and believable agents. Artif. Intell. Today **1600**(June), 297–306 (1999). 10.1.1.47.9259
12. Pizzo, A., Lombardo, V., Damiano, R.: Interactive Storytelling: A Cross-Media Approach to Writing, Producing and Editing with AI. Routledge (forthcoming)
13. Roberts, D.L., Isbell, C.L.: A survey and qualitative analysis of recent advances in drama management. Int. Trans. Syst. Sci. Appl. **4**(2), 61–75 (2008). http://www.cc.gatech.edu/isbell/papers/itssa08-survey.pdf
14. Sharples, M.: Cognition, computers and creative writing. Annexe Thesis Digitisation Project 2016 Block 5 (1984)
15. Shibolet, Y., Knoller, N., Koenitz, H.: A framework for classifying and describing authoring tools for interactive digital narrative. In: International Conference on Interactive Digital Storytelling, pp. 523–533. Springer (2018). https://doi.org/10.1007/978-3-030-04028-4_61
16. Si, M., Marsella, S.C., Riedl, M.O.: Interactive drama authoring with plot and character: an intelligent system that fosters creativity. In: AAAI Spring Symposium: Creative Intelligent ... (2008). http://www.aaai.org/Papers/Symposia/Spring/2008/SS-08-03/SS08-03-012.pdf
17. Spierling, U., Szilas, N.: Authoring issues beyond tools. In: Joint International Conference on Interactive Digital Storytelling, pp. 50–61. Springer (2009). https://doi.org/10.1007/978-3-642-10643-9_9

18. Theng, Y., Jones, M., Thimbleby, H.: Reducing information overload: a comparative study of hypertext systems. In: IEE Colloquium on Information Overload, pp. 6–1. IET (1995)
19. Werning, S.: Making Games: The Politics and Poetics of Game Creation Tools. MIT Press (2021)

Computational Support for Trope
Analysis of Textual Narratives

Mandar S. Chaudhary[1] and Arnav Jhala[2(✉)]

[1] eBay Inc., 2065 Hamilton Avenue, San Jose, CA 95025, USA
manchaudhary@ebay.com
[2] North Carolina State University, 402 Venture 4, Raleigh, NC 27695, USA
ahjhala@ncsu.edu

Abstract. Narrative tropes are repeated patterns of recognizable communicative elements across stories. Tropes are a set of patterns that aid readers in story comprehension. They are also a reflection of sociocultural norms that are formally or informally present in the particular context for authors and readers. Trope-based analyses are common in media studies but are limited to close readings and individual analyst perspectives. Distant reading of tropes is challenging due to the lack of precise definitions and the variety of forms in which tropes manifest in language, and over space and time within story worlds. This paper presents a trope labeled dataset of scripts, an initial analysis framework, and a system for computational support of trope analysis. For highlighting the challenges of developing computational models, we present a trope prediction algorithm on a movie script dataset based on a model trained with human-annotated tropes from TVTropes.

Keywords: Trope analysis · Distant reading · Text processing

1 Introduction

Narrative analysis in the media studies discipline draws from established methods of close and distant reading in the humanities and social sciences. Close readings are subjective analyses of a small set of pieces, often clustered along a particular dimension. Distant readings provide high-level, often statistical, account of patterns present across a larger set of media artifacts [17]. In this work, we explore computational tools for text processing that could support semi-automated trope analysis. In their current form, these tools support distant analysis and provide insight into the challenges for extending such computational support for closer analysis. We introduce a new dataset of labeled scripts with tropes from the human labeled TVTropes resource. We provide initial naive benchmarks on this dataset for trope prediction based on both bag-of-words and word embedding approaches.

1.1 Tropes in Media Studies

For socio-cultural influence and impact of narrative media, tropes have been commonly used by researchers to present their arguments. Narrative inquiry is a

© The Author(s), under exclusive license to Springer Nature Switzerland AG 2022
M. Vosmeer and L. Holloway-Attaway (Eds.): ICIDS 2022, LNCS 13762, pp. 529–540, 2022.
https://doi.org/10.1007/978-3-031-22298-6_34

research method in education and other social science fields where collected narratives of experiences are coded and analyzed for extracting patterns or tropes [1,8]. Tropes are also commonly used in media studies as a method of analysis in narratology [14]. Paxson [15] utilizes narrative tropes as a method for revisiting deconstructionist narratology that seeks to understand cultural narratives by deconstructing and analyzing the various constituent parts. Barrowman [2] provides a comprehensive analysis of action film over the years through the lens of tropes that have manifested in them over the years. Marling [10] studies how tropes containing mobile phone usage have been utilized in film. Bucciferro [3] analyzes the movie Black Panther through the lens of tropes related to gender and race that this movie breaks. In this case, tropes provide a mechanism for talking about how non-conformity to traditional tropes signals a shift in popular culture about these issues.

1.2   Tropes in Interactive Narrative Research

Closer to home, within the narrative generation and interactive narrative community [11,12] tropes related to relationships between people are leveraged for setting up *expectations for user interaction with underlying plots*. According to a view expressed by Carroll [4], historical writing is to be seen as the historian's narrative interpretation of available data that fills in fictional aspects that fit tropes specific to the historical context drawn from available original sources. Squire [16] utilizes tropes of similarity and familiarity to study narratives related to HIV. Squire suggests that narratives' importance for social change within the context of the stories of HIV can be understood through a systematic analysis of rhetorical tropes embedded within these narratives.

Among few attempts for providing computational support for trope analysis, a notable one is from Gala et al. [6]. They provide a computational model for the analysis of gendered tropes through language processing techniques and show statistically the preponderance of verbs associated with particular genders in the movies from a curated dataset. These prior research efforts across disciplines that utilize trope analysis, when taken together, present us with some interesting gaps and challenges. First, the methods and standards of rigor vary across disciplines. This is reflected in their choice of artifacts for analyses, choice of tropes, definitions of tropes, and tolerance to the degree to which the tropes in their respective works are explicitly present in the artifacts that they are analyzing. Second, tropes identified or analyzed through subjective methods do not have precise definitions. This leads to challenges in scaling these methods for annotation through crowdsourcing due to the potential of low inter-rater agreement. Third, tropes occur at different scales. Some occur at a single sentence level (e.g. *Shout Out*). Others occur across larger spans (e.g. *Chekhov's Gun*). Yet others manifest in character actions (e.g. *Mad Scientist*) or are simply present as character traits (e.g. *Creepy Child*). Finally, there are hundreds of tropes with possible overlaps in terms of their definitions or in the way that they are present in artifacts. The formal relationships between tropes is as yet under-studied.

Assuming the benefits of organizing and communicating research across disciplines related to narrative through tropes, these are all opportunities for further research that would benefit both traditional non-interactive narrative and with appropriate extensions for interactive media.

2   Dataset Introduction and Analysis Framework

2.1   Data Sources

We work with two sources of data: TVTropes[1] for collecting films with trope annotations and the Internet Movie Script Database (IMSDb)[2] for film scripts. TVTropes is a wiki-style crowd sourced database founded in 2004 which has over 15K contributors that annotate tropes for a wide range of media such as anime, video games, films, and television. A user must pass the registration process on TVTropes.org where a moderator reviews the application and upon approval, the user can start contributing to the platform. In addition to labeling media with tropes, they can also propose new tropes by following TVTropes' *Three Rules of Three* guideline which includes a brief concise explanation of the trope, its name and reviewer approval. The trope name has to be reviewed by at least three reviewers followed by discussions with fellow contributors for three days.

TVTropes has 26K annotated tropes on films with an average of 47 tropes per film. A recent study analyzed the gender and age of 256 contributors after extracting tokens related to gender and age in their biographies [6]. The median age of a contributor was 20 with 64% of the contributors being male, 33% female and 3% were bi-gender, genderfluid, non-binary, trans, or agender.

2.2   Data Preparation

In the first step, we collect movies with tropes from TVTropes website using a publicly available tool named tropescraper[3]. The scraper creates a JSON file with a movie's name as the key and the list of tropes as its value. We collect the movie scripts from IMSDb using another publicly available tool named ScreenPy[4]. The movie scripts are collected over several genres such as Action, Comedy, Drama, Romance, Thriller and others. In the next step, we identify movies with tropes and scripts by matching the movie names found by TVTropes website and ScreenPy. We use Levenstein distance, a string-based distance metric to find movies with tropes and scripts and while most of the movie names are mapped using this metric, we have to manually match several movie names by looking up the movie's release year and production crew details. Overall, we gather 717 movies with tropes and scripts. A distribution of movies with tropes and scripts in each genre is shown in Table 1. Note that a movie can belong to

---

[1] https://www.tvtropes.org/.

[2] https://imsdb.com/.

[3] https://github.com/rhgarcia/tropescraper.

[4] https://github.com/drwiner/ScreenPy.

Table 1. Distribution of movies across genres with total movie count in each genre and the movie count with tropes and movie script.

Genre	Total movies	Movies with tropes and scripts
Action	290	263
Drama	579	399
Thriller	373	242
Comedy	347	199
Crime	201	122
Romance	192	102
Adventure	166	72
Sci-Fi	155	90
Horror	149	83
Animation	35	3
War	26	14
Family	39	13
Musical	22	11
Mystery	107	60

Table 2. Distribution of tropes across movies with scripts.

Genre	Mean	Min	Max
Action	180	7	843
Drama	77	1	416
Thriller	99	12	354
Comedy	104	11	338
Crime	248	248	248
Adventure	262	240	284
Sci-Fi	78	20	172
Horror	76	17	144
Animation	11	11	11

more than one genre so the total sum of movies in the *Movies with Tropes and Scripts* column of Table 1 is higher than 717. We also present a distribution of tropes across movies in each genre in Table 2.

The movie scripts in our dataset are stored in JSON format that represents the script as a key-value pair format, where the key is the movie character name and the value is the dialog spoken by the movie character. We parse the JSON files and concatenate all the dialogs from each movie script as a single string object. The string is generated for each movie which is then pre-processed to remove irrelevant words (tokens) before extracting features from movie scripts. Specifically, we

Table 3. Top-5 frequently occurring tropes across 717 movies along with their definition and example.

Trope	Size	Definition	Example
Shout Out	320	Reference to something outside the narrative like a pop culture reference	"And I'm Carmen Sandiego! Guess where I am." – Hellsing Ultimate Abridged
Oh Crap	259	The moment at which a character realizes that something really bad is about to happen	After Simba confidently laughs in the face of danger, he gets this reaction after he hears danger (i.e. the hyenas) laugh back. – Lion King
Chekhov's Gun	245	An insignificant object that later turns out to be important	Harry notices that Quirrell is wearing a purple turban that he was not wearing when they first met and shook hands. The reason for this turban is revealed at the end of the book. – Sorcerer's Stone
Foreshadowing	222	An allusion in the narrative that predicts some later event	In the first episode of the series, camera shows a raven in closeup, then tilts up to Bran practicing archery foreshadowing. – "Winter is Coming" episode Game of Thrones (TV)
Bittersweet Ending	198	Victory came at a harsh price and the heroes cannot fully enjoy the reward of their actions	Poirot has solved the crime and justice has been done. Unfortunately, the only way to achieve justice was for Poirot to kill the murderer, then die of a heart attack. Hastings has lost both his wife and his best friend, and his daughter has gone to Africa. – Curtain by Agatha Christie

apply simple string pre-processing techniques that remove stopwords, punctuation and words with fewer than 3 characters. The processed movie scripts are used to extract features for training prediction models. The target variable in our dataset is generated from the tropes that are annotated by the TVTropes community. As shown in Table 2 the distribution of tropes per genre is very skewed and not every trope has sufficient instances of movie scripts to be useful for training a prediction model. Therefore, we identify top-5 frequently occurring tropes across all the genres and build a binary prediction model for each trope. The top-5 frequently occurring tropes, their sample size, definition and an example of their occurrence in media is shown in Table 3. Note that although we select top-5 frequently occurring tropes, we have an imbalanced class distribution for each trope as even the most frequently occurring trope *Shout Out* has 320 instances which is less than 50% instances in our dataset of 717 movies.

2.3 Feature Extraction

Our dataset consists of text in the form of movie scripts. Extracting features from text includes several different types of Natural Language Processing techniques such as Bag-of-Words (BoW) model such as generating a Term Frequency Inverse Document Frequency (TF-IDF) matrix, word and document embeddings [9,13, 18], as well as more recent transformer architecture based deep neural networks.

Deep learning based approaches require large amounts of data in the order of hundreds of thousands of text documents to capture the information in the form of embeddings. Since our dataset consists of 717 movie scripts, we implement a BoW model and a paragraph embedding model to extract features from movie script. However, movie counts continue to increase every day and future works can benefit from the increasing sample size by experimenting with more complex feature extraction methods using deep learning.

Bag of Words. We extract features from movie scripts dataset using a Bag-of-Words (BoW) model. Specifically, we generate a feature from each token in the movie script string such that the token is weighted in the movie script based on its frequency count across all movie scripts. For example, if the word *alone* occurs in almost all the movie scripts then it is assigned a lower weight since its presence in the movie script is not indicative of a trope being present. To do this, we generate weights for each token by calculating its Term Frequency-Inverse Document Frequency (TF-IDF) score. This score is calculated in two steps, first, the term frequency, tf_i is calculated by measuring the relative frequency of the term, w_i in a given movie script, d. $tf_{i,d}$ measures the importance of w_i within d_i. In the next step, the inverse document frequency idf_i is calculated by measuring the rarity of w_i across all movie scripts. idf_i will be low if w_i is common across movie scripts, thereby indicating the token does not contain predictive information with respect to the target variable. The final TF-IDF score of w_i is the product of tf_i and $idf_{i,d}$. More formally, the equations for calculating the TF-IDF score are shown below,

$$TF - IDF_i = tf_{i,d} \times idf_i \qquad (1)$$

$$tf_{i,d} = \frac{f_{i,d}}{\Sigma_{i' \in d} f_{i',d}} \qquad (2)$$

where $f_{i,d}$ is the raw count of the number of times w_i occurs in movie script d.

$$idf_i = log\left(\frac{1 + N}{1 + df_i}\right) \qquad (3)$$

where N is the total number of movie scripts and df_i is the document frequency which measures number of documents that contain the word w_i. This equation contains a 1 in the denominator to avoid division-by-zero error when w_i is not present in the corpus.

TF-IDF scores can also be generated for bi-grams and tri-grams but with increasing number of words, the size of the feature set increases exponentially and TF-IDF matrix generation might become computationally infeasible. In our experiments, we generated TF-IDF matrix for unigrams and bi-grams, and then selected the top-50 features to train prediction model. Finally, we generate five different datasets, one for each trope mentioned in Table 3. The predictor set is a TF-IDF matrix of the movie script and the target variable is a binary vector which contains 1 if the trope is annotated in the movie and 0 otherwise.

Doc2Vec Paragraph Embeddings. We also implemented feature extraction using the well-known doc2vec paragraph embedding technique [9]. The doc2vec algorithm generates an embedding vector based on the sequence of words in the document. In our experiments we implemented three variants of doc2vec algorithm namely, distributed memory (DM), distributed bag-of-words (DBOW) and a combination of distributed memory and bag-of-words (DM+DBOW).

The DM variant maps each document and every word to a unique vector respectively and trains a single hidden layer neural network with the document vector and word vectors of a given word sequence as the input and the next word in the sequence as the output. The document vector acts as a memory to remember the context of the words and finally a trained document vector is used as features that represent the document. The DBOW variant works similar to the Bag-of-Words model as it ignores the context of words for training the document vector. In this variant, a text sequence is sampled from the document and the neural network is trained to predict a random word in the sequence given the document vector as the input. We trained document vectors by varying the size of embedding vector from 10 to 200 and observed no improvement in performance metrics with embedding size greater than 100. Therefore, in our experiments we generated embedding vectors of size 100 for trope prediction.

3 Experiments

3.1 Trope Prediction Entire Script

We train a gradient boosted decision tree to predict tropes using the TF-IDF vector and document vector of a movie script. As mentioned in Sect. 2.2, the distribution of tropes across movies is skewed with the most frequently occurring trope has less than 50% sample count, we experimented with XGBoost algorithm as it is well-known to deal with imbalanced class distribution. The classification model was trained by splitting the data into train set and test set using the repeated stratified 2-fold cross-validation method to maintain the class distribution.

The predictive performance of the classification model was measured using the Area Under the Receiver Operating Characteristic (AUROC), Average Precision (AP) and Balanced Accuracy. The Balanced Accuracy score is computed by first selecting the threshold for the classifier in the AUROC curve where the difference between the true positive rate and the false positive rate is the highest, and then computing the average recall score corresponding to the threshold for both the classes. The results shown in Table 4 are averaged across 10 repeated runs of stratified 2-fold cross-validation, and the code and dataset are publicly available for future research work[5].

This preliminary study presents interesting results as a binary classifier trained with a small sample size of 198 for the *BittersweetEnding* trope can achieve a average precision (AP) of 0.36 and a maximum AP of 0.6 for *ShoutOut*

---

[5] https://github.com/mandarsc/TropeAnalysis.

Table 4. Performance metrics for the top-5 frequently occurring tropes across 717 movies. A binary classifier is trained for each trope and evaluated using AUROC, AP and Balanced Accuracy. The mean and standard deviation values for each metric are reported from repeated stratified 2-fold cross-validation.

Trope	Method	AUROC	AP	Balanced accuracy
Shout Out	TF-IDF	0.64 ± 0.04	0.59 ± 0.04	0.61 ± 0.04
	DM	0.51 ± 0.06	0.48 ± 0.04	0.55 ± 0.03
	DBOW	0.51 ± 0.06	0.48 ± 0.06	0.54 ± 0.03
	DM+DBOW	0.5 ± 0.05	0.46 ± 0.05	0.54 ± 0.03
Oh Crap	TF-IDF	0.63 ± 0.03	0.53 ± 0.04	0.61 ± 0.03
	DM	0.51 ± 0.04	0.39 ± 0.04	0.54 ± 0.02
	DBOW	0.51 ± 0.07	0.38 ± 0.06	0.55 ± 0.03
	DM+DBOW	0.51 ± 0.04	0.39 ± 0.04	0.55 ± 0.02
Chekhov's Gun	TF-IDF	0.57 ± 0.03	0.56 ± 0.04	0.59 ± 0.03
	DM	0.55 ± 0.04	0.39 ± 0.04	0.57 ± 0.02
	DBOW	0.52 ± 0.08	0.38 ± 0.07	0.55 ± 0.03
	DM+DBOW	0.53 ± 0.05	0.38 ± 0.04	0.55 ± 0.03
Foreshadowing	TF-IDF	0.58 ± 0.04	0.38 ± 0.03	0.56 ± 0.04
	DM	0.5 ± 0.06	0.35 ± 0.04	0.54 ± 0.02
	DBOW	0.48 ± 0.04	0.33 ± 0.04	0.53 ± 0.03
	DM+DBOW	0.49 ± 0.05	0.33 ± 0.04	0.54 ± 0.02
Bittersweet Ending	TF-IDF	0.57 ± 0.04	0.36 ± 0.03	0.56 ± 0.02
	DM	0.5 ± 0.06	0.31 ± 0.04	0.55 ± 0.04
	DBOW	0.49 ± 0.03	0.3 ± 0.03	0.54 ± 0.02
	DM+DBOW	0.51 ± 0.06	0.3 ± 0.06	0.54 ± 0.04

trope. Clearly, we observe an improvement in AP with an increasing sample size. Furthermore, it is interesting to observe that the feature extraction methods that generate document embeddings using the doc2vec algorithm perform much worse compared to the TF-IDF method which suggests that the current sample size is not sufficient to train useful document embeddings. The only existing work which is similar to our study is a deep learning based architecture which predicts trope as a multi-output binary vector using embeddings from words and sentences in movie synopses [5]. Their experiments are conducted on predicting manually selected 95 tropes with mean average precision of 0.187. Although we selected 5 tropes in our experiments, these results present a baseline result for exploring the movie scripts dataset for trope prediction.

3.2 Trope Prediction with Progressive Dialog Sequence

In this experiment, we applied the decision tree model trained in Sect. 3.1 to the sequence of movie dialogues from the script. Specifically, we take all the movie

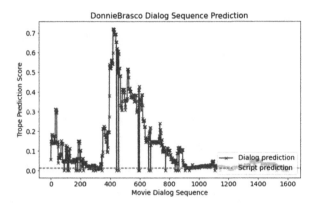

Fig. 1. Trope prediction scores obtained using the dialogs from the script of the movie *Donnie Brasco*. The dialog sequence prediction starts with the first movie dialog and its score from the trained classification model. This process is repeated every time after including the next dialog in the sequence until the entire movie script is treated as a single dialog.

dialogues spoken by the characters at a given point, generate its TF-IDF vector and predict the probability of a trope being present. We begin with the first movie dialogue in the script, then append the next dialogue in sequence and continue until the end of the script. The goal of this experiment is to explore if certain dialogues in the movie have stronger signal that indicate the trope's presence. It is important to note that current annotation methods such as those on TVTropes label an entire movie with certain tropes being present. The crowd-sourced platform does not provide information on the scale at which the trope is present. For instance, a character in a movie will often use exclamation to express the *OhCrap* trope such as *"You have GOT to Be Kidding Me!"* and *"This Cannot Be!"*.

As a use case we consider the *OhCrap* trope and apply the dialog sequence prediction model. Specifically, we consider movies which are labeled with the trope but their movie script score predicted by the gradient boosted decision tree is very low. We study such false negatives to understand if considering dialog-level predictions could indicate the presence of the trope. Figure 1 shows the dialog sequence prediction for the movie *Donnie Brasco* which has a movie script score of 0.012 as indicated by the red dotted line. The blue data points indicate the movie prediction score with the dialogs at a given sequence in time. We observe that certain dialogs in the script of this movie contain strong signals which increases the trope prediction score as high as 0.72. This suggests that movie dialogs contain important text predictive of the trope's presence and can be explored for future research.

We further investigate the dialogs in the movie *Donnie Brasco* and find the dialog whose addition leads to the highest prediction score. The following dialog has been found to increase the prediction score from 0.597 to 0.72.

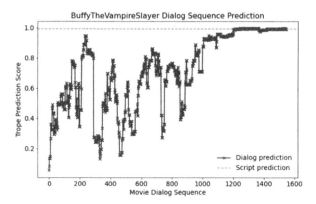

Fig. 2. Trope prediction scores obtained using the dialogs from the script of the movie *Buffy The Vampire Slayer*. The dialog sequence prediction starts with the first movie dialog and its score from the trained classification model. This process is repeated every time after including the next dialog in the sequence until the entire movie script is treated as a single dialog.

"I had no idea you were coming home. I'm supposed to go to the movies tonight with the Grants. She enters the bathroom as he wipes the shaving cream off. He looks up, half his moustache SHAVED OFF. Her face FALL"

The dialog describes a conversation between Donnie and his wife Maggie who enters the bathroom and is disappointed to see Donnie shaved off his moustache. This illustrates a good example of a moment with trope *OhCrap* that Maggie has after seeing Donnie's face. While this is an example, we believe there will be false positives from our method. However, this work presents an interesting benchmark for future research to leverage and focus on discovering tropes at different scales.

The progressive movie dialog prediction of the movie *Donnie Brasco* in Fig. 1 indicates that tropes can be present at a granular scale of a dialog-level. The entire script or synopsis might be too coarse to capture the signals for the *OhCrap* trope. Another interesting example is that of the movie *Buffy The Vampire Slayer* whose dialog sequence prediction is shown in Fig. 2. This presents an example where the prediction score is the highest when almost all the dialogs in the movie script are considered. These two movies indicate the wide difference of the scale at which the trope could be present in movie scripts. Compared to previous works that have focused on predicting tropes from movie synopsis [5, 6], our work not only focuses on trope prediction using fine grained signals such as movie scripts, but it also presents a motivational case for future research to focus on trope scale for better prediction.

4   Limitations and Threats to Validity

As the results of our initial benchmarks suggest, trope analysis is a challenging problem for various reasons. First, there are thousands of tropes that operate across several narrative dimensions such as plot, character, and media-specific idioms. This introduces challenges for computational approaches in terms of the number of possible classes for classification and the amount/quality of gold standard data for training models. Second, tropes are embedded across multiple spatial and temporal scales both within the diegetic world and with references to the extra-diegetic. This introduces challenges in terms of the knowledge representation of models to be able to capture and preserve semantics of content. Finally, trope definitions for popular media are imprecise and their interpretations constantly change with respect to social, cultural, and economic conditions of the audiences in any particular time period. This provides an interesting challenge for computational analysis and human interpretation of the outputs of these systems.

Another limitation for trope analysis is the labeling bias present in TVTropes dataset. Recent work by Garcia et al. [7] on exploring this dataset reported skewed distributions in number of tropes per films with some films having less than 5 annotated tropes while popular films like *James Bond*, *The Avengers* and *Star Wars* having thousands of tropes. Films in the Action and Adventure genre were found to have the highest number of tropes, and the number of annotated tropes per film increases over time. Addressing such bias could be a separate research avenue where researchers can address debiasing trope labeling by genre, year or a combination of other factors.

5   Conclusion

This paper motivates the need for computational support for trope analysis in narrative media, especially for distant reading analysis. We demonstrate an approach that takes an existing dataset of human annotations of tropes for movies and develop computational tools for rich statistical analysis of tropes in movie scripts. Analysis of tropes occurring at the linguistic level allows us to localize trope detection to specific parts of the narrative arc. Initial results are promising and also point to the challenges of precision of trope definitions, scale of occurrence, and the application of more sophisticated language processing algorithms. While this work doesn't directly fall under the interactivity aspect of narrative, integration of trope detection directly within authoring environments like Twine and Inform could be useful for deeper analysis of interactive fiction.

Acknowledgements. The authors would like to thank the reviewers for their insightful comments and feedback. We would also like to thank the TVTropes and IMSDb community for providing a curated dataset of thousands of tropes and scripts. Finally, we would like to thank Dr. Chris Martens.

References

1. Barrett, M.S., Stauffer, S.L.: Narrative inquiry: from story to method. In: Narrative Inquiry in Music Education, pp. 7–17. Springer, Heidelberg (2009). https://doi.org/10.1007/978-1-4020-9862-8_2

2. Barrowman, K.: Origins of the action film: types, tropes, and techniques in early film history. Comp. Action Film, 9–34 (2019)
3. Bucciferro, C.: Representations of gender and race in ryan coogler's film black panther: disrupting hollywood tropes. Crit. Stud. Media Commun. **38**(2), 169–182 (2021)
4. Carroll, N.: Interpretation, history and narrative. Monist **73**(2), 134–166 (1990)
5. Chang, C.H., et al.: Situation and behavior understanding by trope detection on films. In: Proceedings of the Web Conference 2021, pp. 3188–3198 (2021)
6. Gala, D., Khursheed, M.O., Lerner, H., O'Connor, B., Iyyer, M.: Analyzing gender bias within narrative tropes. In: Proceedings of the Fourth Workshop on Natural Language Processing and Computational Social Science, pp. 212–217. Association for Computational Linguistics, Online (2020). https://doi.org/10.18653/v1/2020.nlpcss-1.23. https://www.aclweb.org/anthology/2020.nlpcss-1.23
7. García-Ortega, R.H., Sánchez, P.G., Merelo-Guervós, J.J.: Tropes in films: an initial analysis. arXiv preprint arXiv:2006.05380 (2020)
8. Kock, C.: Narrative tropes: a study of points in plots. Occas. Pap. **1977**, 202–52 (1976)
9. Le, Q., Mikolov, T.: Distributed representations of sentences and documents. In: International Conference on Machine Learning, pp. 1188–1196. PMLR (2014)
10. Marling, W.: Mobile phones as narrative tropes. J. Pop. Film Telev. **36**(1), 38–44 (2008)
11. Mateas, M., Sengers, P.: Narrative Intelligence (Advances in consciousness research, 1381–589X; v. 46). John Benjamins Publishing Company (2003)
12. Mateas, M., Stern, A.: Interaction and narrative. Game Des. Reader Rules Play Anthol. **1**, 642–669 (2006)
13. Mikolov, T., Sutskever, I., Chen, K., Corrado, G.S., Dean, J.: Distributed representations of words and phrases and their compositionality. Adv. Neural Inf. Process. Syst. **26**, 1–9 (2013)
14. Mishler, E.G.: Models of narrative analysis: a typology. J. Narrat. Life Hist. **5**(2), 87–123 (1995)
15. Paxson, J.J.: Revisiting the deconstruction of narratology: master tropes of narrative embedding and symmetry. Style **35**(1), 126–149 (2001)
16. Squire, C.: Narratives, connections and social change. Narrat. Inq. **22**(1), 50–68 (2012)
17. Underwood, T.: A genealogy of distant reading. DHQ: Dig. Human. Q. **11**(2), 1-12 (2017)
18. Vaswani, A., et al.: Attention is all you need. Adv. Neural Inf. Process. Syst. **30**, 1–11 (2017)

Bronco: A Universal Authoring Language for Controllable Text Generation

Jonas P. Knochelmann[1] and Rogelio E. Cardona-Rivera[1,2]($\boxtimes$)

[1] School of Computing, University of Utah, Salt Lake City, UT, USA
[2] The Entertainment Arts and Engineering Program, University of Utah, Salt Lake City, UT, USA
`rogelio@eae.utah.edu`

Abstract. We present Bronco: an in-development authoring language for Turing-complete procedural text generation. Our language emerged from a close examination of existing tools. This analysis led to our desire of supporting users in specifying *yielding grammars*, a formalism we invented that is more expressive than what several popular and available solutions offer. With this formalism as our basis, we detail the qualities of Bronco that expose its power in author-focused ways.

Keywords: Text generation · Authoring tools · Programming language · Grammars

1 Introduction

We presently enjoy a plethora of grammar-based tools for text-generation [6,8,11,16,18,23]. Broadly, these tools share the aim of maximizing *authorial leverage*—i.e., "the power a tool gives an author to define a quality interactive experience in line with their goals, relative to the tool's authorial complexity" [2]. Available tools maximize leverage via different means [10] and each one strikes a different balance between four dimensions of *authorability*: (1) the *technical proficiency* expected of the end user, (2) the *complexity* an end user must contend with to author content, (3) the *clarity* the system offers the end user about the system's state and dynamics during authorship, and (4) the *controllability* the system offers the end user for generating content as they intend.

Despite the cornucopia of tools that explore the design space of authorability, these are effectively powered by context-free grammars (CFGs). We contend that, as a result, the tools in this space mostly explore circumscribed variations on procedural text generation. In view of this gap, we designed Bronco (Fig. 1), a generator that offers greater controllability than existing grammar-based tools.

Bronco affords this controllability by letting users author *yielding grammars*, a novel formalism we have defined that is Turing-complete. Bronco offers a large selection of expressive features that permit precise control in text generation. The language currently supports features useful to our design practice and we

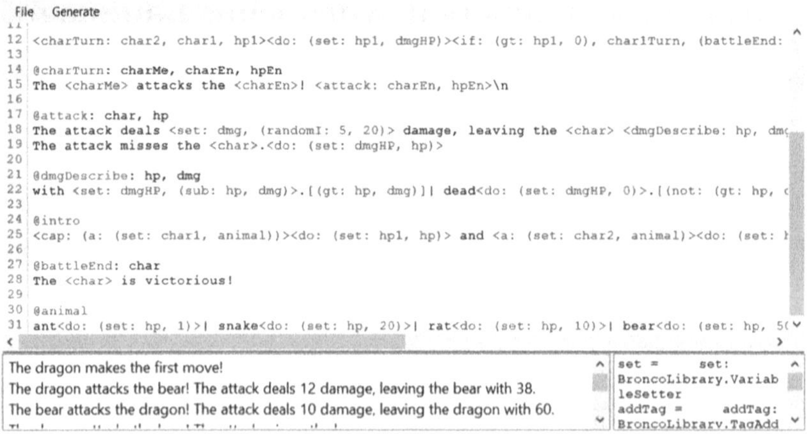

Fig. 1. A screenshot from Bronco IDE with code describing the grammar (top), a sample output (bottom-left) and some debug information (bottom-right).

expect to refine its specification going forward. Although still nascent, we are emboldened by its promise so far.

In this paper, we detail Bronco's design. We focus on its underlying formalism in order to mathematically contrast it against two tools closest to us: Tracery [6] and Expressionist [23]. We also discuss the expressive features the language offers, and present a small case study in our experience writing grammars for both Tracery and Bronco.

2   Literature Review and Background

Bronco is a *universal* text-generation authoring language—a language capable of specifying Turing-complete grammars that can yield finely-controllable templated text; both as a stand-alone tool and as part of a larger system.

Within the design space of authorability, Bronco is Tracery-like in author-focus and Expressionist-like in grammar-specification, but is more flexible than both. To demonstrate how, we rely on the following formalisms and concepts.

2.1   Baseline Formalism: Context Free Grammars

Context-free grammars (CFGs) are a restricted subset of formal grammars notable for being the backbone of many text and story generation systems [1]; they are also a Turing-incomplete formalism [24].

A CFG is a construct that formally describes how to form strings from a (typically finite) set of grammar symbols Σ called an *alphabet*. This formal description is specified as a set of hierarchically-nested rules P called *productions*, which relate a single *non-terminal symbol* (ones in the alphabet that are designated as decomposable) to a finite sequence of *other* grammar symbols;

non-terminal symbols $N \subset \Sigma$ in the sequence can be successively decomposed, whereas *terminal symbols* $T \subset \Sigma$ are elementary tokens.

The set of strings that can be formed from a given CFG is called a *language*. All such strings begin with the distinguished *start symbol* $n_{start} \in N$, which is special in that it never appears in the finite sequence of a production. Formally:

Definition 1 (Context-free Grammar). *A quadruple $G = \langle N, T, P, n_{start} \rangle$. N, T, P, and n_{start} are the non-terminal symbols, terminal symbols, productions, and start symbol as described earlier. An element in $\Sigma = N \cup T$ is called a grammar symbol, and $N \cap T = \varnothing$. We refer to the elements of T and N as* terminals *and* non-terminals, *respectively.*

Each production $p \in P$ is a pair of the form $p \colon X \to \alpha$, where $X \in N$ is the left-hand side and $\alpha \in \Sigma^*$ is totally ordered set of 0-or-more grammar symbols called the right-hand side. *Applying p to substitute the left-hand side for the right-hand side is called a* derivation.

Finally, the start symbol never appears on the right-hand side of a production (i.e. $\forall p \in P \colon n_{start} \not\subseteq \alpha$). The language $\mathcal{L}(G)$ is obtained by starting with n_{start} and recursively deriving symbols $\forall p \in P$ until only terminals remain; this recursive sequence of derivations is a trace *and can be visualized as a* parse tree.

Figures 2 and 3 illustrate an example CFG and a sample trace of it visualized as a parse-tree, respectively.

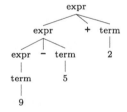

$expr := expr$ **+** $term \mid expr$ **-** $term \mid term$

$term := term$ ***** $factor \mid term$ **/** $factor \mid factor$

$factor := \mathbf{digit} \mid ($ $expr$ $)$

Fig. 2. An example CFG in extended Backus-Naur form for arithmetic expressions. The non-terminals *expr*, *term*, and *factor* help capture precedence and associativity of the operators **+**, **-**, *****, and **/**.

Fig. 3. Parse tree for a trace of the expression 9-5+2 via the CFG in Fig. 2.

2.2 Grammar-Based Procedural Text Generators

CFGs are powerful, but by default are too rigid to support fluid text-based authoring within interactive digital narratives. In fact, despite their marketing as CFG-powered tools, Tracery and Expressionist deal with a formalism more powerful than context-free grammars; namely, *attribute grammars* [21].

Attribute Grammars. An attribute grammar (AG) augments a CFG by supplying two additional constructs: *attributes* and *semantic rules*.

Informally, an attribute can be thought of as a variable in a programming language. Each attribute a can take on a range of values V; for example, a can be an integer number (making $V = \mathbb{I}$), a rational number ($V = \mathbb{R}$), or a string literal ($V = [\text{A-Za-z0-9}]^+$). A semantic rule is what specifies which value in V a given attribute actually takes.

Every grammar symbol $X_i \in \Sigma$ has an associated set of attributes $A(X_i) = \{a_0, \ldots, a_m\}$ ($m \geq 0$) whose values collectively represent what X_i *means*. In turn, every production $p\colon X_0 \to X_1 X_2 \cdots X_n$ ($n \geq 0$) has an associated set of semantic rules R_p that specify how an attribute $X_i.a$ gets its value, for all $a \in A(X_i)$. For example, the CFG from Fig. 2 can be augmented as illustrated in Fig. 4, which defines a *value* attribute for each of the non-terminals. Said *value* is manipulated via the semantic rules next to each production.

$$
\begin{aligned}
expr &:= expr_1 \text{ + } term & \{\ expr.value = expr_1.value + term.value;\ \} \\
&\mid expr_1 \text{ - } term & \{\ expr.value = expr_1.value - term.value;\ \} \\
&\mid term & \{\ expr.value = term.value;\ \} \\
term &:= term_1 \text{ * } factor & \{\ term.value = term_1.value * factor.value;\ \} \\
&\mid term_1 \text{ / } factor & \{\ term.value = term_1.value/factor.value;\ \} \\
&\mid factor & \{\ term.value = factor.value;\ \} \\
factor &:= \mathbf{digit} & \{\ factor.value = \mathsf{valueOf}(\mathbf{digit});\ \} \\
&\mid (\ expr\ ) & \{\ factor.value = expr.value;\ \}
\end{aligned}
$$

Fig. 4. An AG that augments a CFG in extended Backus-Naur form with semantic rules on the right-hand side. As derivations are applied, the *value* of expressions, terms, and factors gets iteratively computed based on the semantic rules.

Every set of attributes $A(X_i)$ can be partitioned into two disjoint subsets: the *inherited attributes* $I(X_i)$ and the *synthesized attributes* $S(X_i)$. Whether $a \in A(X_i)$ belongs to $I(X_i)$ or $S(X_i)$ depends on how its value is determined. If a is determined from attribute values at X_i or within derivations of X_i (i.e. children of X_i in the parse tree), then it is *synthesized*; $a \in S(X_i)$. For example, the parse tree in Fig. 5 contains *only* synthesized attributes. However, if a is determined from attribute values within derivations that *contain* X_i (i.e. parents of X_i in the parse tree), then it is *inherited*; $a \in I(X_i)$.

We require attribute grammars to be *well-formed*, which means that dependencies between attributes must be acyclic. This constrains each attribute in the grammar to be either synthesized or inherited-with-constraints. The inheritance constraints manifest in the semantic rules, which should not introduce a circular dependency between attributes. For a given production $p\colon X_0 \to X_1 X_2 \cdots X_n$ with inherited attribute $X_i.a$ computed by a rule $r \in R_p$, r is constrained to use only: (a) inherited attributes associated with X_0, or (b) attributes associated with $X_1, X_2, \ldots, X_{i-1}$ (symbols to the left of X_i). Formally, an AG is thus:

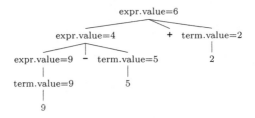

Fig. 5. Parse tree for a trace of the expression 9-5+2 via the AG in Fig. 4. As the trace happens, the *value* of intermediate expressions is recursively computed until the full expression is parsed with a *value* of 6.

Definition 2 (Attribute Grammar). *A triple $AG = \langle G, A, R \rangle$. G is a CFG as in Definition 1, A is a set of* attributes, *and R is a set of* semantic rules.

The set A is obtained from the attributes associated with each symbol X_i in the grammar, and the set R is obtained from the semantic rules associated with each production $p \in P$ of the grammar. Letting $\Sigma = N \cup T \in G$:

$$A = \bigcup_{X_i \in \Sigma}^{G} \{A(X_i)\} \qquad \text{and} \qquad R = \bigcup_{p \in P}^{G} \{R_p\}$$

Each R_p is a set of rules of the form $X_i.a = f(y_1, \dots, y_k), k \geq 0$, such that all the following is true:

(1) either (a) $i = 0$ and $a \in S(X_0)$ or (b) $i > 0$ and $a \in I(X_j), 1 \leq j < i$;
(2) each y in f is an attribute associated with some symbol in production p; and
(3) f is the semantic function—a map from values $y_1, \dots, y_k$ to value $X_i.a$.

Tracery and Expressionist: Attribute Grammar Metalanguages. In view of the preceding formalisms, Tracery and Expressionist are *metalanguages* that facilitate authoring a unique kind of attribute grammar: a probabilistic one [15]. In essence, a probabilistic attribute grammar (pAG) indirectly assigns to each element in $\mathcal{L}(AG)$ some probability of being generated as part of a trace. The probabilities are directly specified as attachments to productions: if a derivation involves a choice between one or more productions to apply for the same non-terminal, a production is chosen based on its assigned probability.

Tracery is Effectively CFG-based. Tracery affords authoring a restricted form of pAG's: the choice between productions for the same non-terminal is done randomly, making individual derivations for the non-terminal equally probable.

The Tracery metalanguage can be written in JSON; the one in Fig. 6 defines an attribute grammar where the terminals are defined by symbols in string quotes (e.g. "light") and non-terminals are defined by symbols within number signs (e.g. #move#). Productions are compactly written as name/value pairs delimited by commas. For example, the line "**path**":["stream", "brook", "path",

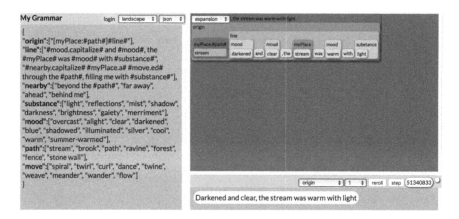

Fig. 6. Tracery's online editor, displaying a JSON-encoded attribute grammar (left) with one inherited attribute (highlighted, right). Productions are delimited by commas, terminals are quoted string literals, and non-terminals are surrounded by the '#' character (for example, #mood# is a non-terminal in the line production).

"ravine", "forest", "fence", "stone wall"] is a specification of 7 productions, i.e. path→"stream", path→"brook", path→"path", and so on. Further, the start symbol is always origin. Finally, the example in Fig. 6 defines an inherited attribute called myPlace, which is generated from selecting a random production (of the 7 applicable) to path. This inherited attribute is then used during the derivation of the line non-terminal, as illustrated in in Fig. 7.

Tracery defines several built-in semantic functions beyond assignment of attribute values; e.g. the Fig. 6 grammar uses the capitalize function to modify the attribute values it obtains. While there are other such functions in the metalanguage, Tracery does not support defining new functions within its grammars.

As a result, attributes in a Tracery-language grammar are limited to taking values only from finite domains (i.e. productions that randomly generate a value from a list) and whenever the same attribute is used across derivations, its value must also be the same. *This makes Tracery-language grammars more compact to specify than traditional CFGs, but still only as expressive as CFGs* [17].

Expressionist is Potentially Turing-Complete. Expressionist affords a finer-degree of control in text generation than Tracery; it requires a user to directly specify the probability distribution between the productions they write. Interestingly, *Expressionist's expressive power depends on whether it is running as a stand-alone authoring tool or as a tool within a host environment capable of generating derivations for grammars written in the metalanguage.*

When running via a stand-alone tool, the Expressionist metalanguage is as expressive as Tracery, albeit with affordances that make its grammars more compact than Tracery's. Formally, all non-terminals $X_i \in N$ in an Expressionist-language grammar have two special attributes: the tagset $\in I(X_i)$ and the tags $\in S(X_i)$. The value of X_i.tags is a string literal set by the author, intended

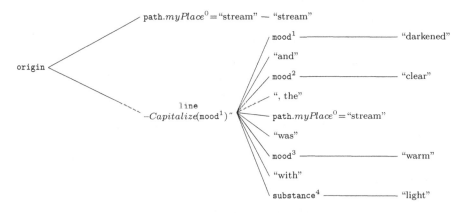

Fig. 7. A parse tree for a trace of the Tracery-language grammar in Fig. 6, read from top to bottom (derivations closer to the top happen earlier). Tracery supports randomly-generated attributes that are inherited elsewhere in the tree (e.g. **path**.*myPlace*, above).

to represent a semantic annotation of interest. The value of X_i.**tagset** is a string literal set by the Expressionist tool during a trace. Every time a production $p: X_0 \rightarrow X_1 X_2 \cdots X_n$ is applied, X_0's **tags** are simply concatenated to the **tagset** of $X_1 X_2 \cdots X_n$.

When running within a host environment (e.g. a game world), Expressionist is *potentially* Turing-complete; it depends on whether the host is (1) capable of parsing X_i.**tags** or X_i.**tagset** as programming instructions for the environment, and (2) the environment itself is Turing-complete. If both conditions are met, Expressionist offers a powerful metalanguage akin to a probabilistic programming language [22]. In this mode, an attribute $X_i.a$'s values are non-deterministically dependent on the host's state, and *vice-versa*. This power comes at the cost of needing to engineer a non-trivial amount of machinery to enable it, which presents a considerable trade-off in its use.

Other Related Text Generators. The remaining tools we discuss in this section are all less expressive than Bronco and/or further afield in their design than either Tracery or Expressionist. However, the ones we mention next have particular features similar to our system. Bronco is like Ink [13,14] – a narrative scripting language for game developers – in that it affords quick access to word-by-word variation. Further, Bronco is like Blabbeur [18] – a CFG-powered language for text generation specifically designed for development in Unity – in that it affords easy and explicit limiting of a sub-structures within the grammar.

Finally, MKULTRA [12] and Dunyazad [20] are project-specific tools for text generation. Notably, they rely on *definite-clause grammars* rather than CFGs (making them Prolog-like in nature). As such, they are as expressive as Bronco. However, they are less focused on offering author-focused features that support a person's authoring experience.

2.3   Problem Statement: The Motivation for Bronco

There remains a gap somewhere beyond Expressionist and Tracery in terms of controllability. On the one hand, Expressionist is potentially-costly to implement while also bound in expressivity by its host environment. On the other hand, Tracery is a more-compact alternative but effectively rigid in generative capability. We are left with a motivating question: might there be an alternative?

Bronco emerged in our pursuit of an answer to that question, and we describe its architecture next.

3   Bronco

3.1   Design Considerations and Qualitative Rationale

We propose to explore greater controllability for procedural text generation via a Turing complete formalism. This aim, combined with our observation of the successes and shortcomings of the tools discussed in the previous section, led us to the following list of requirements we believe our tool must fulfill to push the boundaries of authorability toward greater authorial leverage. Based on our analysis, the tool...

1. *...should be easily integratable with other systems in an existing project.* Text generation is, more often than not, a relatively small part of a project's experience. Thus, we cannot expect practitioners to base their code's architecture around the generator; the tool should ideally work in any architecture.
2. *...should provide many ways to easily limit the output of the generator.* The simplest possible CFG derivation system provides no control at all over the output, and most of the unique features in existing tools provide various ways of limiting the random possibility space.
3. *...should have in built, general-purpose logic.* No matter how many pre-built features a tool comes with, there will always be certain things it is unable to do. A tool's general-purpose logic should support users to program their own functionality, for the cases when pre-built functionality falls short.
4. *...should be easily extensible.* Similar to the previous point, but focused on how the general-purpose logic of the language manifests. Ideally, the tool should support the development of features via its own language or an industry-grade programming language.
5. *...should be accessible to non-programmers.* This requirement is one that many existing tools have tried to fulfill. Because writing makes up such a large portion of creating a text generator, it stands to reason that professional writers should be able to use the tool, not just programmers.
6. *...should be easier to use than implementing a generator from scratch.* Arguably the most important, one that all existing tools have succeeded in. However, it must be carefully counter-balanced with the goal of making it author-focused and easy to use.

With this list of requirements laid out, we may construct an image of what such a tool would look like. In order to be easily integrated and extended upon, we decided our tool should exist at a library level in a language that is commonly used in development, and game development in particular. Further, this library should simultaneously exist as a standalone portion of the code base and have many points where programmers are able to inject external code.

In order that users of the tool have fluent access to limiting the generator's output, general-purpose logic, and that the tool be easily accessible to non-programmers, the generators should be authored via a custom-built, text-based programming language. This language could then be stored in separate files such that non-programmers could edit them without entering the code base. The general-purpose logic and output limiting then could be accessed in a similar way to simple general-purpose programming languages. Having access to a miniaturized general-purpose language within the generator language would also make it easier to access features extended from the base language. The aforementioned library then would be responsible for parsing this language and producing a generator runnable in the implementing language.

To meet the final point, both the language and the library need to be designed with the end-user in mind. For the language, this means a minimal syntax that gives very quick access to the design patterns most commonly used in a text generator. For the library, whatever complexity exists under the hood, a limited set of interactions should be exposed to the end programmer.

We now have a fair idea of what a generative text tool for game development should look like: It should be a library in a popular language that parses a custom-built programming language both of which are designed for usability.

3.2   A Formal View of Bronco

The formalism underlying Bronco is a variant of attribute grammars we're calling *yielding grammars* (YG). Programmable, this system defines *symbols* as objects that provide a function definition for *yield*, which takes zero or more symbols as arguments, must return another symbol. The only other requirement is that successively calling the yield function on the return value of the previous yield will eventually result in a *terminal symbol*, which is a defined as a symbol that yields itself. This process of repeated yielding is called *flattening*.

This formalism is somewhat similar to the Lambda Calculus, in that it is entirely made up of function-like objects [3]. Indeed, it was designed with the hope that it would be used in a functional manner. It differs only in the fact that symbols may not be deterministic, and may have an internal state that can be assessed and modified by other symbols.

This formalism, which was synthesized iteratively during development, has proven invaluable in the construction of Bronco. It benefits both the end-user programming in the language and the developer writings extensions to the language in addition to providing Turing-completeness. For the end-user, it removes the distinction between calling a function and referencing a function, and most of the difficulties that come with a type system: since writing in the language is effectively constructing a tree, users can rely on the flattening algorithm to collapse the tree into a final output text without considering when exactly each branch of the tree is flattened. If a symbol requires a certain type for one of its arguments, for example, the flattening algorithm will flatten that argument's branch until the specified type is reached, throwing an error if it reaches a terminal first. For developers extending Bronco with custom symbols, they can again lean on the flattening algorithm. They are only required to define an evaluation, and that evaluation only needs to provide a symbol that is one step closer to a terminal.

Formally, yielding grammars are defined as follows:

Definition 3 (Yielding Grammar). *An attribute grammar $Y = (G, A, R)$ as defined previously, with the following restrictions:*

Every production $p \in P$ of the grammar, must have the form $x \to y$ or $x : p_0, p_1, ... \to y$ where $x \in N$ and $y, p_0, p_1, ... \in N \cup T$. $p_0, p_1, ...$ are called parameters, *and are treated by R_p as if $(x, p_0, p_1, ...)$ is a single symbol. (e.i. the attributes of $x, p_0, p_1, ...$ are all defined by R_p as well as y's) Within this, all productions must be* inherited.

3.3   Authoring in Bronco

As a piece of software, Bronco is a toolset consisting of a custom-built programming language for authoring procedural text generators, and a highly extensible C# library that can parse the Bronco language, and output the generated text. The library portion of the toolset is largely backend that models the internal grammar. It fronts the parser, as well as a range of objects to be derived, and a way to inject derived objects into the parser. In addition to these, a small authoring tool simply titled "Bronco IDE" has been built to make authoring in Bronco as easy as possible (See Fig. 1).

Bronco is atomically made up of symbols. All data types in Bronco are symbols including, numbers, text, and functions. The language itself has taken heavy inspiration from Markdown and the minimalist syntax of Ink [7,13]. Like Tracery, and Blabbeur, Bronco grammars are defined in terms of random production rules, which are called *bags* [6,18]; a type of symbol. Each bag is made up of a title (denoted '@' followed by the bag's title; e.g. @start), and a number of items (written as normal text separated by newlines or '|'), one of which will be picked at random upon a reference to the bag's title (denoted by the bag's title surrounded by '<>'). In addition to user-defined bags, Bronco comes with a large number of other symbols that can be easily referenced in the same format, and provide other functionality. These predefined symbols can also be easily added to via the C# library, which is the primary method of adding custom functionality to the language. Figure 8 shows basic Bronco syntax.

When defining a bag, you may include arguments that can then be referenced by the bag's item (denoted with ':', followed by arguments separated by ','). Similarly, most of the predefined symbols also take one or more arguments. Arguments can then be added to any symbol reference, which modifies the way

```
@start
My favorite color is <color>
I like the color <color>

@color
red| green| blue| yellow| dark <color>
```

My favorite color is blue

I like the color green

I like the color dark red

Fig. 8. Bronco code that generates a description of a favorite color (left), and sample output (right).

that symbol resolves into text. This lets users of Bronco interact with symbols in a similiar way to how they might interact with functions in a traditional programming language.

With symbols that take arguments, comes general-purpose logic. We are able to support conditional statements for example, as a symbol whose first argument must be a Boolean expression, whose second argument will be included in the output if the first argument resolves to true, and whose third argument will be included otherwise. In a similar manner, we are able to support operators for things like arithmetic and comparisons. Figure 9 showcases the use of arguments and general-purpose logic.

```
@start
My favorite number is <set: favNum, (randomI: 1, 20)>, because it is
<numFact: favNum>!

@numFact: num
<if: (gt: num, 5), `greater than 5`, `less than 6`>
<if: (equal: num, 13), `unlucky`, `isn't unlucky like 13`>
just a good number
```

My favorite number is 7, because it is isn't unlucky like 13!

My favorite number is 15, because it is greater than 5!

My favorite number is 3, because it is just a good number!

Fig. 9. Bronco code that generates a description of a favorite number (left), and sample output (right).

In addition to the features mentioned so far, Bronco gains much expressive power by its inclusion of conditions and weights. A weight is just an easily specifiable constant number that changes the probability of a given item being picked from a bag (a '%' followed by a number, written at the end of a bag item). To dynamically change the probability of items being picked, conditions can be attached to an item (a symbol surrounded by '[]' at the end of a bag item). Conditions can be any symbol that resolves to a number, which is then multiplied by the base weight for a dynamic weight. Since Boolean type symbols are treated as a type of number in Bronco (with a value of 1 for true and 0 for false), items can be effectively enabled or disabled from a bag by entirely customizable logic. Figure 10 shows conditions on bag items.

As a means of storing and relating data more abstractly, symbols in Bronco can have tags attached to them (one or more '#' followed by the identifier, written at the end of a bag item). A tag is a key-value pair consisting of a text-identifier and a number. Tags do not have any implicit function but can be accessed, compared, and manipulated through various predefined symbols in

```
@start
<draw>The <numToValue: value> of <numToSuit: suit>s

@draw
<do: (set: value, (randomI: 1, 13)), (set: suit, (randomI: 0, 4))>

@numToSuit: num
Spade[(equal: num, 0)]| Heart[(equal: num, 1)]| Diamond[(equal: num, 2)]|
Club[(equal: num, 3)]

@numToValue: num
Ace[(equal: num, 1)]| Jack[(equal: num, 11)]| Queen[(equal: num, 12)]|
King[(equal: num, 13)]
<num>[(and: (gt: num, 1),(lt: num, 11))]
```

The 3 of Hearts

The King of Spades

The Queen of Diamonds

Fig. 10. Bronco code that generates a description of a playing card (left), and sample output (right).

Bronco. This allows authors to annotate a large list of words with a theme for example, and then increase the probability of a word being picked if it matches a theme specified in advance. Tags might also be accumulated, during one part of the generation, and then used as a filter in a later part of the generation, ensuring consistency. Figure 11 demonstrates the use of tags for consistent sentences.

```
@start
<do: (set: pro, pronoun)><cap: (their: pro)> favorite color is <set:
favColor, color>. <cap: (they: pro)> <like: pro> it, because it goes so
well with <colorCompliment: favColor>.

@color
red#red| green#green| yellow#yellow| blue#blue| purple#purple|
orange#orange

@colorCompliment: color [(tagOverlap: color, item)]
green#red| red#green| purple#yellow| orange#blue| yellow#purple|
blue#orange

@they: pro [(tagOverlap: pro, item)]
they#they| she#she| he#he

@their: pro [(tagOverlap: pro, item)]
their#they| her#she| his#he

@like: pro [(tagOverlap: pro, item)]
like#they| likes#he| #she

@pronoun
they#they| she#she| he#he
```

Her favorite color is green. She likes it, because it goes so well with red.

His favorite color is yellow. He likes it, because it goes so well with purple.

Their favorite color is purple. They like it, because it goes so well with yellow.

Fig. 11. Bronco code that generates a consistent sentence (left), and sample output (right).

4   Assessment

We will be assessing the performance of Bronco with two distinct methods: Firstly, we will consider the notion of *expressivness* as it applied to Bronco and how it compares to Tracery. The second is similar to that used by Martens and Simmons and their language *Inbox*, where it is directly compared with an existing tool in a similar space [19]. We have chosen to evaluate Bronco with respect to Tracery, because it is the most popular and direct influence for Bronco.

Expressionist, another popular and strong influence, requires its users to write their own expansion engines, which makes it difficult to compare objectively, so we will not be comparing with it.

4.1 Expressiveness

We rely on Felleisen's [9] notion of expressiveness to assess Bronco. Conceptually, we can say that one Turing-complete language is more expressive than another in a particular context, if a local change in the first language would require a global change in the second language in order to achieve the same behavior.

As discussed in Sect. 2.2, Tracery is not strictly context-free but is only capable of referencing branches taken earlier in the expansion by outputting the exact text that branch output. Bronco on the other hand, can reference previous branches by outputting text from any definable function of earlier expansions. Although a great deal of complexity is possible within Tracery's system, in the general case, the number of additional branches needed increases combinatorially with the number of previous branches that need to be taken into account. If branch Q has an outcome dependent on the outcome of an earlier branch P, then Tracery-like systems requires an additional n branches, where n is the number of branches between P and Q. In a Bronco-like system, only 1 extra branch is needed.

As an example, consider a generated story in which a character may or may not find a key at the beginning. At a certain point far into the story, the character can use the key, if they have it, to unlock a door, resulting in a new section of generated story. Though this is certainly possible in Tracery, it would require two entirely separate branches for finding the key or not finding the key up to the point where the key-related part of the story ends. Figure 12 shows a more general example in which branch C will only be taken if A is taken first, and the same thing for D and B. Even if $N_1, N_2, ..., N_n$ are unaffected by the outcome of P, they must be repeated if there is no general way to reference earlier expansions. The increase in size from the first figure to the second is multiplied with every new branch that needs to be considered.

Figure 13 represents the same generator written in Bronco on the left, and Tracery on the right. This example was taken directly from the Tracery website [4]. The figure serves to demonstrate the advantage of a custom-built language for procedural generation by the neatness of the Bronco code when compared with the Tracery code. To put this more quantitatively (admittedly at a very coarse grain of detail), we can count the number of characters that are being used for structural organization versus the number of characters that can actually be output by the generator (this count ignores characters in aesthetic white space and indirect functions like capitalization and variable assignment). For this generator, both versions have 313 characters that can appear in the output, Bronco uses 88 characters for organization (Including the newlines that Bronco

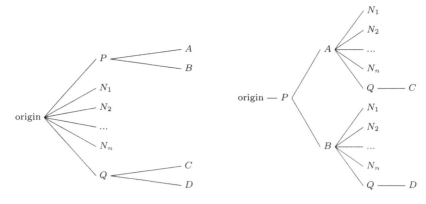

Fig. 12. Trees describing the structure of two grammars, the first without dependendcies between P and Q and the second with dependencies.

```
@start
<do: (set: myPlace, path)><line>

@line
<cap; mood> and <mood>, the <myPlace> was <mood>
with <substance>
<cap; nearby> <a: myPlace> <ed: move> through the
<path>, filling me with <substance>

@nearby
beyond the <path>| far away| ahead| behind me

@substance
light| reflections| mist| shadow| darkness|
brightness| gaiety| merriment

@mood
overcast| alight| clear| darkened| blue|
shadowed| illuminated| silver| cool| warm|
summer-warmed

@path
stream| brook| path| ravine| forest| fence| stone
wall

@move
spiral| twirl| curl| dance| twine| weave|
meander| wander| flow
```

```
{
"origin":
["[myPlace: #path#]#line#"],

"line":
["#mood.capitalize# and #mood#, the #myPlace# was
#mood# with #substance#",
"#nearby.capitalize# #myPlace.a# #move.ed#
through the #path#, filling me with
#substance#"],

"nearby":
["beyond the #path#", "far away", "ahead",
"behind me"],

"substance":
["light", "reflections", "mist", "shadow",
"darkness", "brightness", "gaiety", "merriment"],

"mood":
["overcast", "alight", "clear", "darkened",
"blue", "shadowed", "illuminated", "silver",
"cool", "warm", "summer-warmed"],

"path":
["stream", "brook", "path", "ravine", "forest",
"fence", "stone wall"],

"move":
["spiral", "twirl", "curl", "dance", "twine",
"weave", "meander", "wander", "flow"]
}
```

Fig. 13. The same generator written in Bronco (left), and Tracery (Right)

uses to separate items) and Tracery uses 165. Although it is difficult to conduct this kind of count objectively, these numbers suggest that about twice as much redundant typing is needed to write this generator in Tracery as it is in Bronco. To be sure, writing in JSON has many advantages, such as being relatively understandable by a majority of programmers, and being easily parsed.

Figure 14 and Fig. 11 show two simple generators in Bronco that would be difficult to write in the default version Tracery. The code in Fig. 14 generates

```
@start
<intro><battle>

@battle
The <char1> makes the first move! \n<char1Turn>| The <char2> makes the
first move! \n<char2Turn>

@char1Turn
<charTurn: char1, char2, hp2><do: (set: hp2, dmgHP)><if: (gt: hp2, 0),
char2Turn, (battleEnd: char1)>

@char2Turn
<charTurn: char2, char1, hp1><do: (set: hp1, dmgHP)><if: (gt: hp1, 0),
char1Turn, (battleEnd: char2)>

@charTurn: charMe, charEn, hpEn
The <charMe> attacks the <charEn>! <attack: charEn, hpEn>\n

@attack: char, hp
The attack deals <set: dmg, (randomI: 5, 20)> damage, leaving the <char>
<dmgDescribe: hp, dmg>| The attack misses the <char>.<do: (set: dmgHP,
hp)>

@dmgDescribe: hp, dmg
with <set: dmgHP, (sub: hp, dmg)>.[(gt: hp, dmg)]| dead<do: (set: dmgHP,
0)>.[(not: (gt: hp, dmg))]

@intro
<cap: (a: (set: char1, animal))><do: (set: hp1, hp)> and <a: (set: char2,
animal)><do: (set: hp2, hp)> prepare for battle.\n

@battleEnd: char
The <char> is victorious!

@animal
ant<do: (set: hp, 1)>| snake<do: (set: hp, 20)>| rat<do: (set: hp, 10)>|
bear<do: (set: hp, 50)>| dragon<do: (set: hp, 70)>| emu<do: (set: hp,
30)>| lion<do: (set: hp, 40)>
```

A snake and a rat prepare for battle.
The rat makes the first move!
The rat attacks the snake! The attack deals 17 damage,
leaving the snake with 3.
The snake attacks the rat! The attack misses the rat.
The rat attacks the snake! The attack misses the snake.
The snake attacks the rat! The attack deals 8 damage,
leaving the rat with 2.
The rat attacks the snake! The attack deals 17 damage,
leaving the snake dead.
The rat is victorious!

Fig. 14. Bronco code that generates the description of a battle (left), and sample output (right).

a simple description of a battle that you might see in a roll playing game. It makes use of basic dynamic elements like numeric variables and conditional recursion. The example in Fig. 11 generates two sentences describing a person's favorite color. It is notable for its use of Bronco's tagging system, which let it use consistent pronouns and to track a color's compliment. Although Tracery is fully integrated with JavaScript making it capable of performing any kind of computation, neither of the two examples given could take meaningful advantage of Tracery's in built features.

5   Future Work

One area in need of improvement is the tagging system. It has already proven very useful for communicating abstract connections such as correct pronouns, an area that is difficult in Tracery [5]. However, the way tags currently work makes it difficult to take full advantage of them. Ideally, they should make it effortless for branches to have prerequisites or be mutually exclusive, but this is currently not the case. Their function will need to be re-worked in the future.

Possibly the most obvious weakness in Bronco right now is its syntax. Generally speaking, there are many areas of the syntax that should be easier to write for users than they are. This is no individual issue, but a broad set of problems that need to be addressed for Bronco to meet its goal of ease of use.

A large portion of this research that has not been discussed in this paper is Bronco's integration into a game that contextualizes Bronco's design. In this game, characters are procedurally generated, and procedural text will be used for their in-game conversations. This project demands a nuanced, dynamic, and realistic output. We expect that this game will continue to yield insights for the design of Bronco. Fully explicating how the game and generator designs are mutually constraining and reinforcing will be a third area of our future effort.

6   Conclusion

In this paper, we (to our knowledge, for the first time) formally described two landmark generative text systems: Tracery and Expressionist. We did so in order to distinguish our novel system, Bronco, as a Turing-complete procedural text generator that is computationally more expressive than either of these. In summary, while Tracery/Expressionist are marketed as though they depend on context-free grammars, the formal properties they rely on makes them instead dependent on restricted attribute grammars. Bronco's expressivity stems from our novel yielding grammar formalism, which carefully relaxes the restrictions that Tracery/Expressionist impose on their underlying attribute grammars. This expressivity was necessary for us; in specific, generating text within a dynamic domain that relies on conditional expansions (as discussed earlier) is too onerous to specify in Tracery relative to Bronco.

At the same time, we offer a necessary caveat: our distinction should not be construed as an implied claim of universal superiority. We look to Tracery, Expressionist, and all systems cited herein with profound respect and admiration, and note that Bronco is pragmatically neither better nor worse than any system we have cited; it is simply *different*. The question of *how* it is different requires we be precise, which explains how our discussion centers on Bronco's unique advantages (as opposed to further explicating how prior systems serve as distinct inspiration for our work). The choice of which procedural text generator to use is highly context-specific and it is entirely possible that—in the words of one our anonymous reviewers—Bronco "is likely to be another tool to be thrown on the cornucopia, only to languish in lack of use." While that comment reflects an honest assessment of the difficulties in gaining widespread traction with particular tools, we are hopeful that Bronco pushes procedural text generation into a heretofore under-explored corner of the authorability design space: one that affords Turing-complete controllability.

Acknowledgements. This material is based upon work supported by the National Science Foundation under Grant No. #2046294. We also wish to thank Monthir Ali, Nancy N. Blackburn, Michael Clemens, and the anonymous reviewers who were tremendously helpful with their comments during peer review.

References

1. Black, J.B., Wilensky, R.: An evaluation of story grammars. Cogn. Sci. **3**(3), 213–229 (1979)
2. Chen, S., Nelson, M., Mateas, M.: Evaluating the authorial leverage of drama management. In: Proceedings of the 5th AAAI Conference on Artificial Intelligence and Interactive Digital Entertainment, pp. 136 141 (2009)
3. Church, A.: An unsolvable problem of elementary number theory. Am. J. Math. **58** (1936)
4. Compton, K.: Tracery (2015). https://www.tracery.io/
5. Compton, K.: Practical low effort PCG: tracery and data-oriented PCG authoring. In: Roguelike Celebration (2016)
6. Compton, K., Kybartas, B., Mateas, M.: Tracery: An author-focused generative text tool. In: Proceedings of the 8th International Conference on Interactive Digital Storytelling (2015)
7. Cone, M.: Basic syntax—markdown guide (2022). https://www.markdownguide.org/basic-syntax/
8. Dias, B.: Procedural Storytelling in Game Design, chap. Procedural Descriptions in Voyageur. Taylor and Francis (2019)
9. Felleisen, M.: On the expressive power of programming languages. In: European Symposium on Programming, pp. 134–151. Springer (1990). https://doi.org/10.1007/3-540-52592-0_60
10. Garbe, J.: Increasing Authorial Leverage in Generative Narrative Systems. Ph.D. thesis, University of California, Santa Cruz (2020)
11. Grinblat, J.: Procedurally generating history in 'caves of qud'. In: Game Developers Conference (2018)
12. Horswill, I.: Architectural issues for compositional dialog in games. In: Proceedings of the Workshop on Games and Natural Language Processing at the 10th AAAI Conference on Artificial Intelligence and Interactive Digital Entertainment (2014)
13. Humfrey, J.: Ink: the narrative scripting language behind '80 days' and 'sorcery!'. In: Game Developers Conference (2016)
14. Inkle: Inkle: Ink (2021). https://github.com/inkle/ink/blob/master/Documentation/WritingWithInk.md
15. Jelinek, F., Lafferty, J.D., Mercer, R.L.: Basic methods of probabilistic context free grammars. In: Speech Recognition and Understanding, pp. 345–360. Springer (1992). https://doi.org/10.1007/978-3-642-76626-8_35
16. Johnson, Z.: Beyond the mad lib (but just barely): an oral history of the ways in which kingdom of loathing uses procedural text generation for flavor and humor. In: Roguelike Celebration (2016)
17. Koster, C.H.: Affix grammars for natural languages. In: International Summer School on Attribute Grammars, Applications, and Systems, pp. 469–484. Springer (1991). https://doi.org/10.1007/3-540-54572-7_19
18. Lessard, J., Kybartas, Q.: Blabbeur - an accessible text generation authoring system for unity. In: Proceedings of the 14th International Conference on Interactive Digital Storytelling (2021)
19. Martens, C., Simmons, R.J.: Inbox games: poetics and authoring support. In: International Conference on Interactive Digital Storytelling (2021)
20. Mawhorter, P.A.: Artificial intelligence as a tool for understanding narrative choices. Ph.D. thesis, University of California Santa Cruz (2016)

21. Paakki, J.: Attribute grammar paradigms–a high-level methodology in language implementation. ACM Comput. Surv. (CSUR) **27**(2), 196–255 (1995)
22. Ryan, J., Mateas, M., Wardrip-Fruin, N.: Characters who speak their minds: dialogue generation in talk of the town. In: 12th Artificial Intelligence and Interactive Digital Entertainment Conference (2016)
23. Ryan, J., Seither, E., Mateas, M., Wardrip-Fruin, N.: Expressionist: an authoring tool for in-game text generation. In: International Conference on Interactive Digital Storytelling (2016)
24. Ullman, J., Hopcroft, J.: Introduction to automata theory, languages, and computation, chap. Chapter 4: Context-Free Grammars. Addison-Wesley (1979)

Exploring the Design Space of Social Physics Engines in Games

Shi Johnson-Bey[1]($\boxtimes$), Mark J. Nelson[2], and Michael Mateas[1]

[1] University of California Santa Cruz, Santa Cruz, CA 95060, USA
ismajohn@ucsc.edu
[2] American University, Washington D.C. 20016, USA

Abstract. Social simulation in video games approximates believable social behavior between characters. Game franchises like *Crusader Kings*, *The Sims*, and *Dwarf Fortress* became famous for using social simulation for emergent storytelling. Despite the success of using social simulation as a core aspect of gameplay, there is a seeming lack of publicly available tools for helping game developers create these types of experiences. To help encourage the development of open-source social simulation tools, we further explore the concept of social physics engines—self-contained solutions for modeling dynamic social relationships between non-player characters and players. We propose a design space for constructing social physics systems. It is inspired by rigid-body physics engines and is informed by a design space analysis using commercial and academic social simulation games and systems.

Keywords: Social physics · Social simulation · Emergent narrative

1 Introduction

Character-based social simulation (CBSS) games model dynamic social states comprised of multiple non-player characters (NPCs), players, and their relationships with one another. The simulation's job is to approximate believable social behavior through character interactions that evolve the social state. Social simulations situate characters in social contexts of inter-character and player-character relationships that may include power imbalances, familial ties, romances, friendships, and rivalries. Social simulation games provide players with a playable model of social interaction that affords local and global autonomy [16], as players may plan and observe the immediate and long-term effects of various social interactions.

Social simulation games create opportunities for emergent narratives by relying on the unscripted actions of individual characters to drive the story instead of scripted content. Game franchises like *Crusader Kings*, *The Sims*, and *Dwarf Fortress* became famous for using the emergent nature of CBSS for emergent storytelling. These games have active communities of players who eagerly recount

© The Author(s), under exclusive license to Springer Nature Switzerland AG 2022
M. Vosmeer and L. Holloway-Attaway (Eds.): ICIDS 2022, LNCS 13762, pp. 559–576, 2022.
https://doi.org/10.1007/978-3-031-22298-6_36

their gameplay experiences online[1].[2][3]. Gameplay *retellings* are one of the ways players engage in the narrative generation process [10]. Also, Their retellings are a valuable tool for evaluating the game's AI. They capture more subjective aspects of the player experience that pure playtrace evaluation methods might not capture [14].

Despite CBSS' success in producing interesting and emergent gameplay, there are few publicly available tools for integrating social simulation systems into games. For instance, within Unity's Asset Store of more than 60,000 packages, only four (ranging in price from $25 to $175 per license) offer game makers capabilities to do any social modeling or create socially intelligent characters. This observation is interesting, given that many social simulation systems have been proposed in the academic literature to help game developers. This disconnect could be addressed by developing better nomenclature for the various aspects of social simulation systems and designing custom systems that target popular platforms.

This paper discusses the design space of *social physics engines*, tools for developing social simulation games. The term "social physics" was first proposed by [19] when discussing their work on *Comme il Faut (CiF)* the social simulation engine that powered the game *Prom Week* [18]. In *Prom Week*, the player must choose a series of social interactions to achieve a given character's social goals (become friends with a particular character, be mean to 3 people, start dating someone). The authors likened their social puzzles to physics-based puzzles in games like *Angry Birds* [25]. There is no single method for solving these puzzles; players can use their knowledge of the game rules to devise new solutions.

The purpose of performing a design space analysis is to identify design questions, provide options that address those questions, and provide criteria for assessing and comparing design options [15]. One of our aims here is to more fully develop this framing of interactive social simulation systems as *social physics engines*, drawing an analogy to the traditional physics engines found in many game engines. This analogy is a deliberately opinionated take on the more general concept of computational social simulation, which we explain in more detail in Sect. 3. Here we describe our design space and use it to make clear the significant design considerations when designing social physics for games. Our design space should allow us to better reason about the designs of social simulation systems and discuss their affordances for various end-user experiences and storytelling.

2   Related Work

CBSS has a foothold in both digital entertainment and computational social science. We build on previous efforts to understand social simulation and make it a more accessible tool to game makers and storytellers. This effort is divided

---

[1] *Sims 4* subreddit: https://www.reddit.com/r/Sims4/.
[2] Crusader Kings subreddit: https://www.reddit.com/r/CrusaderKings/.
[3] *Dwarf Fortress* subreddit: https://www.reddit.com/r/dwarffortress/.

between system design, taxonomy building, and tool evaluation. Simulating autonomous characters for interactive and emergent storytelling has been a topic of interest since the late 1990s when Aylett described the challenges of using autonomous agents (characters) for generating narratives [2]. Since then, there has been much work on developing systems for socially intelligent characters in games. We cover a tiny subset of these systems as part of our design-space analysis.

Social physics engines as a concept began with *CiF* [19] and *Prom Week*'s [18] social physics gameplay. Players need to understand the game's social context (how characters feel, their current/past relationships, and their goals) to find strategies for actions to take. *CiF* was succeeded by the *Ensemble Engine* [31], an attempt to take the lessons learned from working with *CiF* and repackage its rule-based AI architecture as a general-purpose tool for social simulation. It was released as a desktop application that helped users create social worlds by defining the current cast of characters, actions, relationship values, and social rules. We discuss other academic social simulation tools throughout the rest of this paper. Please see Table 1 for a list of the systems.

[4] provides a taxonomy of social simulation in games and a shared vocabulary for comparative analysis between different social simulation systems. They are an ideal reference for thinking about design options when designing a social simulation system. Their taxonomy surfaced the following themes: *communication, flow of knowledge, relationships* and *emotions*. Our work complements theirs as we add additional layers to enable people to compare social simulation systems. From a user perspective, many social simulation games can feel like they are doing the same thing, but each approach expresses concepts differently from a developer's perspective.

Finally, recent efforts have looked into challenges encountered while teaching people outside of computational media how to leverage social physics to author custom experiences [8]. As we will discuss, deriving the math and processes that define the social dynamics of a game world is not a trivial task. Much more work must be done to properly teach people the procedural literacy needed to successfully develop experiences that leverage social physics. Evaluating the usability of a given social physics system from the perspective of a particular target audience of designers may raise additional interesting system-design questions.

3   Drawing Inspiration from Physics Engines

We draw inspiration for our social physics engine design space from rigid-body physics engines used in games. We found them helpful when developing design questions for social physics engines because they perform a similar role. Physics engines approximate believable physical interactions between objects in virtual space. They are an almost essential part of all games today and come prepackaged with most game engines. Physics engines alleviate the growing complexity of creating believable physics by supplying reusable libraries that handle common physics concepts such as forces, movement, collisions, and constraints like joints and springs. Physics engines are not concerned with graphical presentation. They only track where objects are and how they interact with other objects.

Popular examples of physics engines are *Bullet*[4], *Box2D*[5], *PhysX*[6], and *Havok*[7]. These physics engines pull from a shared ontology of fundamental physics concepts like velocity, acceleration, force, mass, and friction. They then apply these concepts to 2D or 3D domains and allow users to model *rigid-body dynamics*[8], *soft-body dynamics*[9], and *fluid-dynamics*[10].

Rigid-body physics engines represent the world using three core software abstractions, *bodies*, *constraints*, *forces*, and *dynamics functions* that proceduralize physics mechanics of forces and motion. *Bodies* are the objects that exist in the world. They can have various attributes like position, mass, velocity, acceleration, gravity effects, and collision bounds. *Constraints* represent interconnections between bodies, such as fixed distances, joints, and spring connections. *Forces* like gravity act on bodies to produce movement. Finally, dynamics equations govern how bodies, constraints, and forces interact. With this toolbox, users can represent many physical scenarios. For example, a scene with two cars colliding can be modeled as two rigid bodies moving on intersecting paths with masses and collision bounds. Users can also simulate soft objects, like cloth or plants, using a mesh of bodies interconnected with constraints. Lastly, they can simulate fluid movement, such as flowing water, by treating it as a large collection of tiny bodies. One does not need to be an expert in physics to take advantage of physical behavior. Ideally, all one needs is a general understanding of the underlying concepts.

An interesting aspect of video game physics is its focus on believability over realism. Most games do not have the computational resources to perform high-precision physics simulations involving many parameters. Their goal is to produce plausible physical behavior given the player's knowledge of the game world. Sometimes this involves relaxing the rules of physics to achieve desired gameplay. For instance, it is not realistic for a 5-foot tall, 300-lb plumber to have a vertical jump that is twice their height, but this makes sense in the context of the *Super Mario* series[11]. Game physics is a computational caricature [34] as it exaggerates the most salient components of real-life physics. The rocket-boosted soccer-playing cars of *Rocket League* [23] are not running *NASA*-level rocket simulations, nor are they running hyper-realistic driving simulations like those found in *Forza Horizon 5* [36] or *Gran Turismo 7* [9]. It is running a bespoke kart physics model that relaxes the constraints of realism to support an intuitive yet surreal play experience [6].

---

[4] https://pybullet.org/wordpress/.

[5] https://box2d.org/.

[6] https://developer.nvidia.com/physx-sdk.

[7] https://www.havok.com/.

[8] The simulation of bodies under the influence of external forces with the assumption that all bodies are solid/non-deformable.

[9] The simulation of realistic deformable objects like cloth, hair, and plants.

[10] The realistic simulation of fluids like water and smoke.

[11] Mario stats taken from fan wiki: https://characterprofile.fandom.com/wiki/Mario.

What we want to borrow from physics engines is the clean abstraction of physics concepts into bodies, relationships between those bodies, and dynamics that define how bodies interact. Using a familiar architecture to design and describe social physics engines should help people better conceptualize their role in game development. In the following section, we describe our design layers based on concepts we borrow from physics engines.

4 Sampling Social Simulation Projects

We selected a subset of commercial social simulation games, experimental games, and academic systems to form our design space. We found academic projects by searching *Google Scholar* and various conference venues, and commercial games were chosen based on the complexity of their social mechanics. We chose to focus on games that require social reasoning and feature non-linear, systemic behavior resulting from autonomous characters acting independently of the player. Games like *Animal Crossing: New Horizon* [21], *Stardew Valley* [5], and dating sims were excluded because our understanding is that their relationship models are linear progression systems driven by players presenting gifts to NPCs. This interaction style does not require any social reasoning beyond determining the best gift to give each character. We also excluded commercial games with very little information online to provide insight into their social systems and character AI. We excluded *Crusader Kings III* from direct analysis due to there not being enough information online specifically describing *CKIII's* systems. Instead, we use system descriptions for *Crusader Kings II*, which seems to share much of the same underlying social systems.

We then gained information on underlying social systems using hands-on experience, research publications, *Game Developers Conference* presentations, game architecture deep-dive videos, crowd-sources wikis, and games journalism articles. Some academic projects do not have fully-fledged game experiences and were included for their potential to create interesting gameplay.

We chose the following projects/games as the focus of this design space analysis: *Talk of the Town/Bad News* [27,29,32], *Versu/Blood and Laurels* [11,12], *PsychSim* [24], *Comme il Faut/Prom Week* [18,19,30], *City of Gangsters* [26,35,40], *The Sims 4* [17], *Lyra* [3], *Crusader Kings II* [13,22,38], *Shadow of War* [20], *Kismet* [37], *Dwarf Fortress* [1],and *Gossip* [7]. A short description of each project is given in Table 1.

5 The Design Space

A design space analysis (DSA) places an artifact in the space of possibilities and seeks to explain it was particularly chosen [15]. We borrow the QOC methodology from [15], which has the following parts:

- **Questions**: Identifying key design questions
- **Options**: Providing options to answer design questions

– **Criteria**: Methods to evaluate various options

We apply this DSA method to the various layers for social physics engines (bodies, constraints, dynamics, forces, and collisions) that we adapted from rigid-body physics engines: *character and relationships, social dynamics*, and *social interaction* (see Fig. 1). For each layer, we ask, "how would this be represented?" then, we supply design options based on our selected sample of social simulation games and systems. We do not apply any criteria for evaluating which options are better than others. These criteria are best left to the authors of the final experience and what their social physics engine implementation needs to support. We recommend that designers choose the simplest approach that achieves their goals.

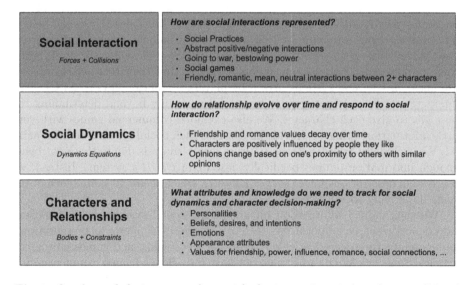

Fig. 1. Our layered design space for social physics engines is based on traditional physics engines in games.

Our design space is divided into three layers. The first layer is characters and relationships. It is concerned with managing what information characters need to know for action selection. The social dynamics layer is concerned with the mathematics and processes operationalizing how character relationships evolve. It is based on the concept of physics dynamics, the study of the movement of physical bodies over time. Finally, the social interaction layer encompasses character decision-making, action definitions, and how actions use social dynamics to evolve the current social state.

There is no particular order to follow when designing a social physics engine. It is OK to start with a guiding social concept like, "scratch my back, and I will scratch yours," then proceed to determine the exact attributes, dynamics, and interactions needed to realize it.

6   Characters and Relationships

All social simulation systems contain characters and relationships. They are essential to modeling social structures and are analogous to bodies and constraints in rigid-body physics. Here we explain what kinds of data are modeled within characters and relationships and provide examples from our selection of projects.

6.1   Characters

Characters can represent individuals (players and non-players), groups, institutions, and concepts. They are similar to the physical bodies modeled in physics engines. Characters have self-contained collections of attributes that represent knowledge characters have about themselves and other characters. Attributes can be simple values like name, age, money, gender, and ethnicity. Character models may also contain more complex structures like personality, emotion, belief, and goal models. NPCs leverage their internal models to decide what social actions to take and how to respond to actions initiated by other characters. We discuss mechanisms for NPC decision-making within the *Social Interaction* section.

Traits and Statuses. Two common abstractions for more complex attribute representations are *tags* and *statuses*. Tags are generally used like static/long-term runtime type information and can modify other aspects of the character's state. For instance, in *Prom Week*, traits represent a character's permanent personality traits like bravery or intelligence that affect the social exchanges in which a character engages. *Crusader Kings II* also uses an extensive set of traits to calculate how characters feel towards one another in the opinion system (covered in the relationship section). Their traits may also evolve into other traits over time. For example, a character with a *playful* trait could develop *deceitful*, *gregarious*, or *lunatic* traits later in life. Statuses serve the same purpose but are temporary modifications to the character's state such as *moodlets*[12] in *The Sims 4* and emotions in *Prom Week* [18].

Personalities. There is no set way to represent a character's personality. Personality is meant to be one of the drivers of character behavior, so it is tightly coupled with the action-selection strategy. *Dwarf Fortress*, models personalities as a collection of character goals (fall in love, rule the world, master a skill, ...), beliefs (power, loyalty, harmony, ...), and relationship facets (greed, anxiety, humor, ...)[13]. *Talk of the Town* relies on the Big 5 Personality model (openness, conscientiousness, extraversion, agreeableness, and neuroticism) for character decision-making and social dynamics. Relationships are then calculated as a function of the compatibility between two characters' personality traits. Finally,

---

[12] https://sims.fandom.com/wiki/List_of_Moodlets_(The_Sims_4)/Life_Status.

[13] https://dwarffortresswiki.org/index.php/DF2014:Personality_trait.

Versu represents character personality as world states that characters wish to make true. Not only do these describe who the characters are, but they also serve as goal states for ranking the utility of potential actions.

Theory of Mind. Theory of mind models track information about what characters think other characters believe. *PsychSim* uses this to enable characters to make decisions based on recursive beliefs of how the other characters will change their beliefs of the first character.

Shared Knowledge. Shared knowledge encompasses all data that is not explicitly part of any single character's model. These are global resources that any character can update and leverage for decision-making. Shared knowledge is where a designer may choose to encode generic social norms. For example, *Prom Week* used a shared global knowledge base that encoded rules for "cultural knowledge" on what is considered cool or lame. A typical example is homework and cafeteria food being considered lame, while skateboards and cell phones are deemed cool [19].

6.2   Relationships

Relationships track objective facts, subjective feelings, and shared understanding of characters' various social connections. Azad and Martens give an extensive explanation of relationships in social simulations [4]. Here we give a brief overview and suggestions for abstractions to use when representing character relationships.

Relationships are the other core component of social simulation, after characters. They are analogous to constraints in physics engines because they connect one character to another. Relationships are best represented as a graph data structure where the characters are the nodes and relationships are the edges that connect characters. Relationship graphs may be undirected or directed. Undirected relationships have information that is mutual between characters. For example, if two characters work for the same company, they both consider the other a coworker and thus can share a single connection in the relationship graph. However, sometimes characters may have differing opinions of each other. Undirected graphs are suitable for representing power imbalances or cases where perhaps one character feels a strong romantic attraction to another, but their love is unrequited.

Like attributes on characters, relationships can have an arbitrary amount of complexity depending on the associated data. Modeling a character family tree like in *Talk of the Town*, *The Sims 4*, and *Dwarf Fortress* can be accomplished by creating a directed graph where each relationship has a tag indicating the type of connection (parent, sibling, uncle, grandparent, ancestor, in-law). Relationships can also hold valence values representing abstract feelings like friendship, romance, opinion, and salience. This convention is most common among the projects we selected. *Talk of the Town* and *The Sims 4* represent relationships as a combination of two scalar values that track friendship and romantic affinity.

Moreover, *Crusader Kings II* was praised for its Opinion System [38] that leverages character traits and past social exchanges between characters to calculate a single value that represents how much a character respects another. The opinion system is at the core of how characters make decisions regarding the player. Characters with a higher opinion of the player are less likely to betray them and align with another kingdom. Opinions are not mutual values, so one character can respect another that does not respect them.

Event Histories. Designers may choose to utilize recorded events that have transpired between characters. *City of Gangsters* uses event histories directly in their relationship model. NPC attitudes are a sum of the valence buffs for each event associated with a relationship. NPCs factor in their interactions with the player and interactions the player has had with other NPCs into their relationship's score. So, if an NPC learns that the player took a transgressive action against one of the NPCs family members, they will be less likely to trade goods with them or offer favors.

In *Shadow of War*, Orcs can recall specific events such as the player retreating from a battle, killing the player, or the player humiliating the orc following a defeat. They use these events for cueing voice clips to get an emotional rise out of the player. We are unsure if these events factor directly into the *Nemesis System*.

7   Social Dynamics

Social dynamics are the math and processes that operationalize changes to the social state. The critical design question for this section is, "how do characters calculate how they feel about each other?". Developing the social dynamics for a system requires designers to express abstract sociological theories in code. This concept is the most challenging part to explain because most games do not publish their exact algorithms for character relationships.

We start with an example from *Gossip* [7], by Chris Crawford (see Fig. 2). In it, characters (including the player) call one another and display facial expressions to communicate their opinion of someone else. Characters then change their internal opinions based on whom they are talking to and whom they are talking about. They are influenced positively by people they like and negatively by people they do not like. By the end of the game, the player's goal is to have the most characters like them. Figure 3 shows two equations for how character attitudes evolve based on gossip that a character hears from another. These equations define the social dynamics of the world. Relationships (character attitudes toward each other) are a function of how much they like the person speaking, the opinion given by the speaker, and their opinion of the subject of conversation.

Fig. 2. Screenshots of *Gossip*. (Left) The main game screen showing two characters talking on the phone. Dan is telling the player that Liz likes them. (Right) The pause menu that displays the player's knowledge of how characters feel about each other and the player. Question marks indicate unknown knowledge and are replaces with the appropriate facial expression when players interact with characters.

$$\Delta x_{l,s} = \frac{x_{l,o} x\prime_{s,o}}{k_1} \tag{1}$$

$$\Delta x_{l,o} = \frac{x_{l,s} x\prime_{s,o}}{k_2} \tag{2}$$

Fig. 3. Equations that govern the change in opinion of a character when listening to another character's opinion in *Gossip* [7]. $x_{a,b}$ is a's actual opinion of b. $x\prime_{a,b}$ is a's declared opinion of b. l is the listener, s is the speaker, and o is the object (character) being gossiped about.

Calculating character relationships can also be as simple as summing the effects of various relationship factors. *City of Gangsters* and Crusader Kings II NPCs calculate their opinions as a linear combination of relationship modifiers (traits, events, succession law, and their relative positions of power). This approach keeps the math simple and instead relies on the data structure of the modifiers to provide expressivity and non-linearity to relationship development.

Lyra [3] calculates characters' opinions on topics of discussion based on their internal bias, private/public opinions, and uncertainty on the topic. Characters are then influenced by their proximity to the clusters of the opinions of all simulated characters.

Talk of the Town calculates character relationships over time as a function of the personality compatibility between characters, elapsed time since their last interaction, and each character's personality. This feature results in asymmetric relationships that evolve organically and reflect differences in character personalities [28].

8   Social Interaction

The last major component in the social simulation toolbox is the model of social interaction. As it implies, social interactions are how NPCs and players interact. Social interaction is usually defined by actions, each with specified preconditions and effects. Executing actions should change the current social state in accordance with the social dynamics (discussed in the previous section). The chosen social interaction model can be inspired by sociological theory or a designer's vision of players' core interaction loop with NPCs.

8.1   Models from Sociology and Social Psychology

Versu uses the concept of social practices derived from Schankian Scripts [33] to define what actions are available to characters in a given situation and how other characters should react to those actions. Social practices are triggered automatically when certain preconditions are met, and players and NPCs are free to choose actions from all the actively engaged practices. *Prom Week* does something similar but uses the concept of social games, multi-character social interactions intended to modify the social state. Social games are based on Goffman's dramaturgical analysis and encode patterns of behavior based on how characters present themselves and how they want others to perceive them [18]. In the case of *Versu*, social practices were used to encode the rules of etiquette for historical Rome for the game *Blood and Laurels*. In comparison, *Prom Week* encodes all the many social conventions one would see in an American high school.

8.2   Designer-Constructed Models of Desired Experience

Commercial games aim to provide players with a specific experience rather than focusing on operationalizing a particular theory. In their 2018 Game Developer Conference talk, *Crusader Kings II* lead designer, Henrik Fåhraeus, states that *Crusader Kings II* revolves around the concept of "dubious morality". Characters choose actions based on their agendas for power. In their discussion of social modeling in *City of Gangsters*, Robison et al. outline the core mentality for playing the game as "You gotta know a guy". That translated to players needing positive interactions with characters to increase their relationship score and gain favor points [26]. These favor points could then get exchanged to increase the player's relationship score with someone in the NPC's immediate social network. The entire experience involves leveraging the NPCs in the player's social network to expand their territory and gain new allies. *Middle Earth: Shadow of War* lets players build revenge relationships with orcs as they kill each other over multiple encounters. While each example does not directly call on sociological or social psychological theories, as we explained with *Gossip*, they can be derived upon closer inspection.

8.3   Action Selection

Action selection is part of the social interaction design and defines how NPCs decide what social actions to take. Actions selection blurs the line between social modeling and traditional autonomous AI techniques. Since readers can find more comprehensive explanations of the following action selection mechanisms, we will not go into much detail.

Relationship Threshold-Based. Relationship thresholds are probably the easiest to implement as characters make decisions based on the current valence value of the relationship. *Crusader Kings II* and *City of Gangsters* employ this approach when determining when to cooperate or oppose the player. Decisions can be made on a simple threshold of "if friendship is greater than X do Y", or they can connect the relationship value to a probability distribution for how likely a character is to take a specific action.

Rule and Utility-Based Methods. Utility methods score potential actions based on how well they benefit the character. They tend to consider multiple factors about the character's state, resulting in more believable behavior than strictly greedy action selection methods. *The Sims 4* uses utility AI to make characters seem more life-like. Sims make decisions based on basic needs like comfort, social, hunger, hygiene, and energy. When AIs select actions based on utility, they score each action, then choose the highest or from among the highest scoring. *Prom Week* uses a rule-based system and scores different social games based on rules that define how much a character wants to perform the action [18].

Limited Look-Ahead. Limited lookahead simulates the side-effects of taking actions to determine their utility. *Versu* and *PsychSim* use a form of lookahead. Characters in *Versu* simulate each action on the ground-truth state of the simulation, one step into the future, and weigh the action based on how many of the character's wants are satisfied. For instance, if a character wants to annoy another, and an action is available to achieve that goal, they are more likely to pick it. On the other hand, Characters in *PsychSim* simulate the effects of their actions using their internal theory of mind models of how characters might react.

Weighted Random with Preconditions. This method assigns preconditions that characters need to meet before executing an action. Perhaps, they need to be an unemployed adult living with their parents before they may execute the *move out of parents* action [29]. In addition to these preconditions, a random probability also determines if an action takes place. *Talk of the Town* and *Kismet* feature this form of action selection. At times it does border on utility-based. For example, *Kismet* uses character personalities and traits to determine which actions a character is most likely to take.

9 Discussion

9.1 Limitations of the "physics Engine" Analogy

The analogy works well for data modeling and mathematical processes (characters, relationships, social dynamics functions) but becomes stretched as we consider character autonomy. The analogy was initially chosen to reference physics games like *Angry Birds* and *Cut the Rope* in which the *player* takes actions, and the game responds, via a physics engine, in a systematic but non-prescripted way. Similarly, social simulation games provide this combination of systematicity and emergent dynamics. In this paper, we are building on this previously employed metaphor to make it more rigorous and highlight where it becomes problematic.

9.2 Accounting for Time and Space

Time and space were two domains that were not mentioned in the core DSA. However, they can be essential factors for social dynamics and character knowledge. Our definition of CBSS states that character relationships evolve over time. Time within a social simulation system can be used to track chronicles of events, decay relationship strength over periods of inactivity, or gate social rules based on the time period of the simulation.

Spatial representations offer context to characters' actions, determine the availability of actions, define socially acceptable actions, delimit what actions are observable to third parties, and limit with whom characters may interact. Space can be represented continuously in 2D/3D or as discrete spaces where the distance between entities is not represented. In *Crusader Kings II* and *City of Gangsters*, space is a limited resource, and characters battle for control over territory. *Kismet* and *Talk of the Town* divide the world into discrete locations where characters may be present. Each location lets characters know who is available to interact with, their role, and their available actions. *Versu* uses a similar representation to represent multiple rooms rather than different buildings within a town. *Versu* and *Kismet* allow designers to make interactions between characters visible to proximal, uninvolved third parties. These actions, of course, cannot be observed by characters in other places. *The Sims 4* also used a type of region system to determine how characters join ongoing social activities and interact with objects and other sims.

9.3 Comparing Social Physics Engines

As one motivation for developing a taxonomy of social simulations, Azad and Martens state that currently, there are no standard evaluation methods for social simulation systems [4]. They acknowledge the challenge of comparing systems that afford the same social interactions to players but model those interactions differently behind the scenes. For example, betraying someone in *Prom Week* and betraying someone in *Crusader Kings II* are handled differently by each

Table 1. Chosen social simulation samples

Title	Type	Description
Crusader Kings II	Commercial	Set in the middle-ages, *Crusader Kings II* has players fight for power against hundreds of NPCs as they lead their dynasty on a conquest for power and influence. Players need to leverage their own character attributes and the attributes of others to sway opinions an make their dynasty last.
The Sims 4	Commercial	The classic virtual dollhouse game, where players create and guide their cast of Sims through their virtual lives, making friends, having families, and achieving life goals.
Shadow of War	Commercial	Set in the world of Lord of the Rings, players engage in revenge-loops with casts of procedurally generated Orcs. The Nemesis System simulates an Orc military hierarchy, with specific Orcs gaining and losing power based on their battles against the player.
Gossip	Commercial	Made for the Atari, players are tasked with trying to become the most popular among a cast of characters by exchanging opinions about characters.
Talk of the Town/Bad News	Academic	Talk of the Town (TotT) simulates the 140-year history of a procedurally generated small American town town. Character live their lives on routines, making friends, lovers, families, rivals and more. Bad News is live-acting game that leveraged TotT for generating characters. Players play as a morticians assistant tasked with finding the next of kin of a recently deceased town resident.
Dwarf Fortress	Commercial	Players manage a fortress of Dwarves in a procedurally generated fantasy world. Dwarves interact with other Dwarves, having families, and pursuing life goals.
Comme il Faut (CiF)/Prom Week	Academic	CiF is a social physics engine that models characters engaging in social games. Prom Week is *CiF*'s accompanying game where players have to help a character achieve their relationship goals before the Prom by manipulating a social landscape of cool/lame and various personal relationships.
Versu/Blood and Laurels	Commercial	Blood and Laurels was an interactive fiction game on the iPad that let players observe or engage in an unfolding story generated by a cast of autonomous characters interacting based on personal goals. Versu was the engine that powered Blood and Laurels.
Lyra	Academic	Simulates opinion change between characters by modeling group beliefs, personal beliefs, and the influence of groups on individual identity.
PsychSim	Academic	Models *theory of mind* taking into consideration their internal beliefs about other characters beliefs when selecting actions.
City of Gangsters	Commercial	Set in prohibition America, players leverage their relationships with characters to gain favors that grow their business and territory.
Kismet	Academic	Kismet is a small language for authoring social simulations that can be used like modules of content in tabletop role-playing games. Characters are cast into roles and their roles determine the actions they can take and how they interact with others

system. *Prom Week* does not have the same type of Opinion system that drives the NPCs of *Crusader Kings*.

We believe that our design space shows why system comparisons are difficult. Translating theoretical social dynamics into code is an exercise in interpretation. There are no objectively-right answers, and multiple competing theories explain why people act the way they do. Traditional rigid-body physics engines share an agreed-upon set of dynamics equations and have collision detection and resolution as two standard bases for comparison. Social simulations, however, do not have a globally agreed-upon set of social dynamics for how humans interact. Also, the model of social interaction depends on the type of experience players should have and the emergent scenarios that designers want to create. Do characters enter into nemesis-style relationships over the course of multiple encounters? Do they need to reason about diplomatic relations with surrounding countries? Do they need to leverage a series of social games to make other characters see them as popular?

So what can we do? Our model provides multiple levels for evaluating social simulations. We could also evaluate systems based on their expressivity. How well can someone encode new social rules within the constraints of the abstractions? Finally, how believable are the social behaviors exhibited by the characters? Yes, this method depends on a final end-user media experience, but it is important to evaluate how legible the social rules are to the player. Making informed predictions about the effects of one's actions on the game is core to a player's feeling of agency and ability to perform social reasoning.

9.4 Feasibility and Challenges of Implementing Systems in Practical Settings

There are very few social simulation tools for commercial game engines. It is unclear if this results from the tools being challenging to design or social simulation being an afterthought during game design. A way to investigate this problem is employing *Research through Design* [39] methods. Future work should aim to develop tools, get them in the hands of developers (or direct stakeholders), observe how they use them, and take note of what they like/dislike. We are currently working on a lightweight tool inspired by *Crusader Kings'* opinion system to test this hypothesis.

10   Conclusion

In this paper, we propose a design space for social physics engines in games based on the design of traditional rigid-body physics engines. Our model has three layers: Character/Relationship Modeling, Social Dynamics, and Social Interaction. Social physics engines have many concepts that they could choose to represent, such as persuasion, self-concept, social mobility, group dynamics, and more. Their job is to provide game makers with a toolbox to leverage social intelligence in their game worlds. Ideally, they would empower people to make games that explore how sociocultural norms can affect people differently in society or how they can lead to population-level phenomena. Our proposed design space gets us closer to a reality where social physics engines are off-the-shelf solutions that game developers can add to their games like any other plugin.

References

1. Adams, T., Adams, Z.: Dwarf fortress. [Linux, macOS, Microsoft Windows, Macintosh operating systems, Classic Mac OS] (2009)
2. Aylett, R.: Narrative in virtual environments-towards emergent narrative. In: Proceedings of the AAAI Fall Symposium on Narrative Intelligence, pp. 83–86 (1999)
3. Azad, S., Martens, C.: Lyra: simulating believable opinionated virtual characters. In: Proceedings of the AAAI Conference on Artificial Intelligence and Interactive Digital Entertainment, pp. 108–115 (2019)
4. Azad, S., Martens, C.: Little computer people: A survey and taxonomy of simulated models of social interaction. In: Proceedings of the ACM on Human-Computer Interaction CHI PLAY (2021)
5. Barone, E.: Stardew valley. [Nintendo Switch, Android, PlayStation 4, macOS, iOS] (2016)
6. Cone, J.: It is rocket science. https://www.gdcvault.com/play/1024972/It-IS-Rocket-Science-The
7. Crawford, C.: Gossip. [Unpublished Atari 8-bit] (1983)
8. DeKerlegand, D., Samuel, B., Treanor, M.: Pedagogical challenges in social physics authoring. In: Proceedings of the International Conference on Interactive Digital Storytelling, pp. 34–47. Springer (2021). https://doi.org/10.1007/978-3-030-92300-6_4
9. Digital, P.: Gran turismo 7. [PlayStation 4, PlayStation 5] (2022)
10. Eladhari, M.P.: Re-tellings: the fourth layer of narrative as an instrument for critique. In: Proceedings of the International Conference on Interactive Digital Storytelling, pp. 65–78. Springer (2018). https://doi.org/10.1007/978-3-030-04028-4_5
11. Emily Short: Blood and laurels. [iPad OS] (2014)
12. Evans, R., Short, E.: Versu-a simulationist storytelling system. IEEE Trans. Comput. Intell. AI Games 6(2), 113–130 (2013)
13. Kaiser, R.: The surprising design of Crusader Kings II. gamedeveloper.com, January 2013. https://www.gamedeveloper.com/design/the-surprising-design-of-i-crusader-kings-ii-i-
14. Kreminski, M., Samuel, B., Melcer, E., Wardrip-Fruin, N.: Evaluating AI-based games through retellings. In: Proceedings of the AAAI Conference on Artificial Intelligence and Interactive Digital Entertainment, pp. 45–51 (2019)
15. MacLean, A., Young, R.M., Bellotti, V.M., Moran, T.P.: Questions, options, and criteria: elements of design space analysis. In: Design Rationale, pp. 53–105. CRC Press (2020)
16. Mateas, M., Stern, A.: Procedural authorship: a case-study of the interactive drama façade. Digital Arts and Culture (DAC) 61 (2005)
17. Maxis: The Sims 4. [PlayStation 4, Xbox One, macOS, Microsoft Windows, Macintosh operating systems, Classic Mac OS] (2014)

18. McCoy, J., Treanor, M., Samuel, B., Reed, A.A., Wardrip-Fruin, N., Mateas, M.: Prom week. In: Proceedings of the International Conference on the Foundations of Digital Games, pp. 235–237 (2012)

19. McCoy, J., Treanor, M., Samuel, B., Tearse, B., Mateas, M., Wardrip-Fruin, N.: Authoring game-based interactive narrative using social games and Comme il Faut. In: Proceedings of the International Conference & Festival of the Electronic Literature Organization (2010)

20. Monolith Productions: Middle Earth: Shadow of War. [PlayStation 4, Xbox One, iOS, Microsoft Windows] (2017)

21. Nintendo: Animal crossing: New horizons. [Nintendo Switch] (2020)

22. Paradox Interactive: Crusader Kings II. [macOS, Microsoft Windows, Linux, Classic Mac OS] (2012)

23. Psyonix: Rocket league. [PlayStation 4, Nintendo Switch, Xbox One, Microsoft Windows, Macintosh operating systems, Linux] (2015)

24. Pynadath, D.V., Marsella, S.C.: Psychsim: modeling theory of mind with decision-theoretic agents. In: Proceedings of the International Joint Conference on Artificial Intelligence, pp. 1181–1186 (2005)

25. Ravio Entertainment: Angry Birds. [Android, iOS] (2009)

26. Robison, E., Viglione, M., Zubek, R., Horswill, I.: AI design lessons for social modeling at scale. In: Proceedings of the AAAI Conference on Artificial Intelligence and Interactive Digital Entertainment, pp. 213–219 (2021)

27. Ryan, J.: Curating Simulated Storyworlds. Ph.D. thesis, University of California, Santa Cruz (2018)

28. Ryan, J., Mateas, M., Wardrip-Fruin, N.: A simple method for evolving large character social networks. In: Proceedings of the Social Believability in Games Workshop (2016)

29. Ryan, J., Summerville, A., Mateas, M., Wardrip-Fruin, N.: Toward characters who observe, tell, misremember, and lie. In: Proceedings of the AAAI Conference on Artificial Intelligence and Interactive Digital Entertainment, pp. 56–62 (2015)

30. Samuel, B., et al.: Playing the worlds of prom week. In: Narrative Theory, Literature, and New Media, pp. 87–105. Routledge (2015)

31. Samuel, B., Reed, A.A., Maddaloni, P., Mateas, M., Wardrip-Fruin, N.: The ensemble engine: next-generation social physics. In: Proceedings of the International Conference on the Foundations of Digital Games, pp. 22–25 (2015)

32. Samuel, B., Ryan, J., Summerville, A.J., Mateas, M., Wardrip-Fruin, N.: Bad news: an experiment in computationally assisted performance. In: International Conference on Interactive Digital Storytelling, pp. 108–120. Springer (2016). https://doi.org/10.1007/978-3-319-48279-8_10

33. Schank, R.C., Abelson, R.P.: Scripts, Plans, Goals, and Understanding: An Inquiry into Human Knowledge Structures. Psychology Press (2013)

34. Smith, A.M., Mateas, M.: Computational caricatures: probing the game design process with AI. In: Proceedings of the Artificial Intelligence in the Game Design Process Workshop at the 2011 AAAI Conference on Artificial Intelligence and Interactive Digital Entertainment (2011)

35. SomaSim: City of Gangsters. [Microsoft Windows (2021)

36. Studios, T.: Forza Horizon 5. [Xbox One, Xbox Series X/S, and Windows 10] (2021)

37. Summerville, A., Samuel, B.: Kismet: a small social simulation language. In: Proceedings of the Casual Creator Workshop at the 2020 International Conference on Computational Creativity (2020)

38. Wiltshire, A.: How Crusader Kings 2 makes people out of opinions, November 2016. https://www.rockpapershotgun.com/crusader-kings-2-characters

39. Zimmerman, J., Forlizzi, J., Evenson, S.: Research through design as a method for interaction design research in HCI. In: Proceedings of the SIGCHI Conference on Human Factors in Computing Systems, pp. 493–502 (2007)
40. Zubek, R., Horswill, I., Robison, E., Viglione, M.: Social modeling via logic programming in City of Gangsters. In: Proceedings of the AAAI Conference on Artificial Intelligence and Interactive Digital Entertainment, vol. 17, pp. 220–226 (2021)

Twine Screen Reader: A Browser Extension for Improving the Accessibility of Twine Stories for People with Visual Impairments

Luowen Qiao and Anne Sullivan(⊠) (iD)

Georgia Institute of Technology, Atlanta, GA 30332, USA
{lqiao35,unicorn}@gatech.edu

Abstract. In this paper, we describe the design, evaluation, and results of a screen reader created to improve the interactive fiction (IF) experience for people with visual impairments. Our screen reader was designed for IF written with Twine 2 using the Harlowe and SugarCube story formats. As a starting framework, we use the IF accessibility guidelines to address three major shortcomings of screen readers when used with Twine IFs: 1. Improving page content extraction with Twine-specific HTML elements; 2. Adding sound notifications and read out for page updates (commonly used by Twine); and 3. Adding keyboard commands to navigate between interactive elements. Running small-scale user evaluations of our screen reader with novice and expert screen reader users allowed us to refine our screen reader and highlight some ongoing challenges in this area. Finally, we posit that to improve the overall accessibility of interaction fiction requires the contribution of the entire IF community.

Keywords: Screen reader · Interactive fiction · Interactive digital narrative · Accessibility · Twine · Visual impairment

1 Introduction

According to the 2018 National Health Interview Survey (NHIS), approximately 32.2 million adults in the United States (or about 13% of US adults) have difficulty seeing or cannot see at all [1]. Despite this, web accessibility for those with visual impairments is quite low.

As the web has evolved, the structure and content of web pages has become more complex over time. Although complex content and structures may display more information or look more aesthetically pleasing, it increases difficulty for people with visual impairments to interact with, and gain information from, those web pages [2]. While there are guidelines such as the Web Content Accessibility Guide (WCAG) [3] and free tools such as WAVE [4] available for evaluating the accessibility of web content, much of the web remains inaccessible. The WebAIM Million – an annual accessibility analysis of the top one million homepages – reports that 96.8% of the web sites surveyed contain issues that have "notable end user impact" on accessibility [5]. Furthermore, the study

© The Author(s), under exclusive license to Springer Nature Switzerland AG 2022
M. Vosmeer and L. Holloway-Attaway (Eds.): ICIDS 2022, LNCS 13762, pp. 577–589, 2022.
https://doi.org/10.1007/978-3-031-22298-6_37

found that "users with disabilities would expect to encounter errors on 1 in every 19 home page elements with which they engage." With an average of 886 elements on a home page, this is close to 50 errors per home page.

While these numbers represent the current state of the web in February 2022, this level of inaccessibility is not new. A study by Loiacono and McCoy found that only 9% of companies had accessible home pages in 2004 [6]. With more than 1 in 10 people in the US having visual impairments and almost all web pages having accessibility issues, it's clear that accessible web experiences is an important area of research [7, 8].

When considering web-based interactive fiction (IF)[1], web accessibility is compounded by IF-specific challenges for screen readers. For example, IF text can change dynamically without triggering the screen reader, sidebar information may not read out in an understandable way, and many games made with the IF editors such as Twine [9] have custom HTML tags that are not recognized by screen readers. These issues combine to make IF experiences largely inaccessible for people with visual impairments.

To address this issue, we created a screen reader browser extension which works specifically with IFs created in Twine with the Harlowe or SugarCube story format. We evaluated the screen reader in two IRB-approved user studies, updating the software based on the user feedback. In this paper we detail the necessity for a screen reader for Twine games, then describe our design, evaluation results, and our conclusions.

2 Background

2.1 Screen Readers

There are various tools for people with visual impairments to interact with the web pages for both input and output, with screen readers being the most common output technology. Other tools include magnifiers, alternative keyboards and pointing devices, speech recognition, eye tracking, and Braille displays [8]. As the most commonly used tool, a number of mainstream screen readers exist, with the most popular being listed in Table 1.

Table 1. The most popular screen readers, platform they run on, and type of license they use.

Product	Platforms	License
NVDA [10]	Windows	Free
JAWS [11]	Windows	Commercial
Apple VoiceOver [12]	Mac OS, iOS	Free (Embedded)
Orca [13]	Linux	Free
ChromeVox [14]	ChromeOS, Chrome Browser	Free (Embedded)

---

[1] While interactive fiction (IF) is now more inclusively referred to as interactive digital narratives (IDNs) in this field, we use the legacy term "IF" in this paper to avoid confusion, as the tools and organizations we discuss still use the term IF.

For our project we studied the most common screen readers listed above, and also surveyed a selection of screen readers that provide different user interactions: WebAny-Where [15], a web-based screen reader; Vizlens [16], an interactive mobile app screen reader for real-world interfaces; Access lens [17], a gesture-based screen reader for real-world documents; and Capti-speak [18], a speech-enabled screen reader. These applications provided information as to the breadth of interactions available for screen-reader tools.

IF-Specific Screen Readers. In our survey, we found only two screen reader tools created specifically for Interactive Fiction (IF). The first is audio IF, a mobile app which plays Z-code (also known as Infocom format) games [19]. The application has a built-in screen reader and interactions designed to be accessible for people with visual impairments. The second is IF Interpreters, an NVDA-specific add-on which allows the NVDA screen reader to work with a set of supported Windows-based IF interpreters [20]. Neither of these applications work with Twine games, nor do they work beyond the OS they were built for. Additionally, neither of these tools has been updated since 2019.

Screen Reader Limitations. A published study of 100 blind users using screen readers highlighted common issues with screen readers [21]. The top causes of frustration reported in the study were:

- page layouts causing confusing screen reader feedback
- conflicts between screen readers and applications
- poorly designed/unlabeled forms
- no alt text for pictures
- misleading links
- inaccessible PDFs
- screen reader crashes

The results from this study highlight that content creators, web developers, and screen reader developers must all consider accessibility to meet the needs of those using screen readers.

2.2 Twine Games and Accessibility

The IF community has made strong progress on creating tools and output that are widely accessible [22]. However, much of the work is still nascent, consisting mainly of recommendations [23] and pages collecting lists of accessible games [24–26].

To extend this work, we focused on creating a tool that would provide access to the library of existing interactive fiction experiences, while considering the screen reader limitations above and recommendations from the IF community. To constrain the scope of the initial project, we chose to focus on the accessibility of Twine games specifically. Twine 2 [9] is open source, which allows us to inspect the code, and it is free, which means a sizeable library of experiences is already available. Additionally, Twine outputs the stories as web pages, which allows for easier integration with a browser-based screen reader.

Because Twine 2 is open source, we initially considered modifying Twine itself to output screen reader compliant HTML. However, because different story modes are available which create different tag structures and formats, we would need to modify each story format, and work with different third parties which maintain and create story formats. This is the ideal long-term solution, and one that we hope this work might encourage. However, for an initial step, we chose to make an extension that could manage two of the most common story formats. The extension also provides support for the tens of thousands of Twine stories that are already available online, so it provides accessibility in ways that modifying Twine directly could not.

3 Screen Reader Design and Implementation

3.1 Screen Reader Performance on Twine Games

To understand the current state of accessibility, we tested two popular screen readers, chosen based on the computer systems we had available: Apple VoiceOver and ChromeVox. We tested the screen readers on *Twine of Access*, a Twine game created specifically for testing accessibility with Harlowe and SugarCube story formats [27, 28].

When creating an IF with Twine, authors choose a story format to use. Each story format provides different default visual layouts and specialized author. Of particular note, each story format also has different standards for the HTML it generates, meaning that some story formats work better with screen readers than others.

During our testing, we found two dominant issues faced by the screen reader when playing Twine games. The first is that Twine games rely heavily on page updates (instead of page loads) for their interactions. However current screen readers don't provide update notifications, so the user will not know that the text has changed or what it has changed to.

Additionally, Twine-generated HTML can include Twine-specific elements and properties which screen readers do not know how to parse. For example, in the Harlowe version of *Twine of Access,* the first passage HTML includes elements such as: `<tw-link>`, `<tw-expression>`, and `<tw-include>`. This is problematic for screen readers because they typically read out the type of element before reading the content. For instance, a screen reader will say "Link" (denoted in the HTML with an `<a href>` tag) before reading out the link or say "Header 1" before reading a top-level header (denoted in the HTML with an `<h1>` tag). When elements are included in the HTML that the screen reader does not recognize, it cannot let the user know what that type of element is which may reduce the accessibility of the page.

The number of Twine-defined tags created is based on which story format is chosen. Harlowe (the default story format in Twine 2) and SugarCube are both story formats which create custom elements, and both are popular choices for designing Twine-based experiences. For this reason, we chose to focus on the Harlowe and SugarCube story formats for our screen reader.

3.2 Interactive Fiction Accessibility Guidelines

In 2019, the Interactive Fiction Technology Foundation (IFTF) released results from a survey regarding the current state of accessibility of IF platforms, including Twine [23]. The report provided 15 recommendations for the IF community around increasing accessibility, including accessibility for those with visual impairments. For our research, we are particularly focused on the guidelines which could be addressed specifically by a screen reader.

To identify the screen-reader specific guidelines, we first categorized the IFTF recommendations based on whether they were best addressed by IF authors versus IF tool creators. Two of the fifteen guidelines could be addressed by either authors or tool creators and are therefore included in both lists. What is most apparent by splitting the list in this way is that accessibility truly requires the effort of both authors and tool developers and cannot be achieved by one group alone.

Author Recommendations. Below is the list of IFTF guidelines that we identified as best addressed by IF authors, as authors have the knowledge and access to the content required to meet these guidelines.

1. Use alt text for all non-textual content (including "text art")
2. Offer quick-travel and other in-game shortcuts
3. Offer hints and walkthroughs
4. List content warnings, when applicable
5. List obvious exits and objects
6. List frequently accessed information in separate panes
7. Avoid assuming able-bodied life experience

Of the above recommendations, 2 and 7 exist on the Tool Developers list as well, as these issues can be addressed by both the content and the tools. While these recommendations are for many types of accessibility, based on our experiences with the screen readers we tested, we found recommendations 1, 2, 5 and 7 to be particularly salient for IF authors wishing to improving accessibility for those using a screen reader.

Tool Developer Recommendations. Below is the list of IFTF guidelines that we identified as best addressed by IF tool creators, as they require adding features to the tools themselves. Of the recommendations below, 4 and 8 exist on the Author Recommendations list as well, as explained in the previous section.

1. Offer prominent volume/mute controls
2. Allow the player to set text preferences, including "dark mode"
3. Pair special updates with sounds
4. Offer quick-travel and other in-game shortcuts
5. Offer an Undo command
6. Parser IF should offer a separate "training ground" for new players
7. Prominently display a command guide
8. Avoid assuming able-bodied life experience

9. Longer games should offer saving
10. Add accessibility awareness to creation tools

As we were creating IF tools, we used this list for guidance in our design. We identified guidelines 1, 3, and 4 as a focus for our screen reader implementation. Given that screen readers are an audio format, we prioritized including volume control within our extension (guideline 1). As mentioned earlier in this paper, Twine often makes use of page updates instead of page loads – this means that the text will update but the screen reader has no knowledge of it. Therefore, it was particularly important that we addressed this issue (guideline 3). Finally, we designed the screen reader to contain keyboard shortcuts to easily move between interactive objects (guideline 4).

3.3   Screen Reader Design and Implementation

Because Twine games are web-based, we chose to create a Chrome browser extension, as Chrome is widely available on most operating systems. Based on the IFTF recommendations [23], the results of our initial screen reader tests, and the feedback from our user studies, we designed and created the extension with the following features:

Read-Out Functionality

- HTML elements - including Twine-specific elements
- Interactive elements - e.g., links, buttons, checkboxes, etc.
- Twine-specific information – e.g., current selection, hints, sidebar contents, etc.
- Page updates - with audio cue

Keyboard and Voice Controls

- Select
- Read
- Interact/Click
- Interaction navigation
- Open/close tutorial
- Open/close settings

Settings

- Speech volume
- Speech rate speed
- Enable/disable keyboard control

- Enable/disable voice control

Tutorial

- Written in Twine
- Covers voice and keyboard controls

The screen reader is written in Javascript, with a manifest version 3.0 file in JSON format as the settings for the extension. The entire project is available at: https://github.com/luowenqiao/Screen-Reader-for-Twine. To run, the user opens the extension in Chrome, while closing the extension stops execution.

The extension detects the currently active web page on the browser. If the current page is not a recognized Twine game, the screen reader will sleep until a new web page is activated. If the current page is detected to be a Twine game, the screen reader will notify the user that a Twine game has been detected and extract the page content, while starting to listen for keyboard or voice input.

The user can use the controls listed above to navigate the experience. The screen reader also listens for page updates, notifying the user if an update has happened and re-extracting the page content. A video of the screen reader in use is available at https://www.youtube.com/watch?v=eamI58cufn8.

4   User Evaluation

We performed two sets of small-scale qualitative user studies, both with IRB approval. The first user study focused on the clarity of the screen reader i.e., whether the read out of the story made sense. The second user study focused on the overall experience of interacting with the screen reader.

In the first evaluation we tested whether the screen reader could be used to experience a Twine game without confusion. Many users of screen readers have adapted to the confusing way screen readers present web page [21]. However, this does not mean that clarity should not be a goal. To bypass any experiential bias, we recruited novice screen reader users for our first study to test their level of confusion during a Twine game.

After addressing the issues that arose from the first user test, we performed a second round of evaluation in which we worked with screen reader experts to better understand how the browser extension would perform in practice.

4.1   Evaluation of Screen Reader Clarity

For the initial evaluation, we wanted feedback on how easy it is to follow the Twine game using our screen reader. We conducted in-person user tests and interviews with three novice screen reader users, to avoid pre-existing screen reader expertise masking areas of confusion.

The user study was made up of an initial interview to assess the participant's experience with content being read to them, an ~15-min usability test, and a follow-up interview regarding their experience using the tool. During the usability test, the participants were asked to use the screen reader extension to play the Twine game, *Twine of Access* [27, 28]. The participants were unable to see the screen while testing our screen reader, and we used a think aloud protocol during the usability test. The researcher took field notes of their observations and participant feedback. Figure 1 displays a screenshot of the first session prototype.

Fig. 1. A screenshot of the first prototype. For the first iteration, the list of commands was not yet integrated into Twine, nor were there voice commands available.

Results

We observed that our prototype successfully fulfilled basic functionality. The screen reader could correctly read out the page content, as well as content properties, and could support keyboard control. The feedback was generally positive regarding the overall experience and clarity of the screen reader. However, based on our observations and participant feedback, we made the following refinements:

1. All participants interpreted the page update notification sound as sound that the computer acknowledging their input (as page updates generally follow participant input). They rated this as a positive thing, which led us to incorporate more audio feedback on input in our second prototype.
2. Participants wanted to be able to access the tutorial (or list of commands) as necessary, not just at the beginning. To address this, we updated the tutorial to make it optional, repeatable, and integrated it into the Twine experience for consistency.
3. Related, we observed the keyboard commands were difficult to remember. However, many simpler key-bindings are reserved for the operating system, browser, and general screen readers, so we added a voice control option along with easier access to the tutorial as listed above.
4. The participants noted they'd like to have keyboard shortcuts to move quickly among the interactive objects. This is consistent with Tool Developer guideline 4

(see Sect. 3.2). Therefore, we added keyboard commands for navigation between interactive elements.

5. Participants asked for a way to distinguish between read out of HTML elements versus page content. To address this, we added two distinct voices in the screen reader – one reads out HTML elements, the other reads page content.

4.2 Evaluation of the IF Screen Reader Experience

After making the refinements from our first evaluation, we ran a second set of interviews to evaluate our screen reader with people who have screen reader experience. We recruited five total participants: two participants who are legally blind and regularly use a screen reader, one expert on accessibility and screen readers, one screen reader researcher, and one novice screen reader user for comparison. Four of the studies were done remotely and one was held in person. A screenshot of the tutorial for the screen reader used in the second user study is shown in Fig. 2.

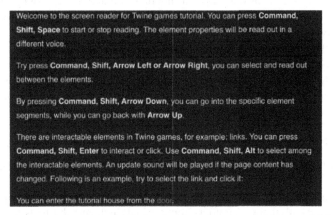

Fig. 2. The prototype of the screen reader for the second user study. The tutorial is now shown as a Twine game with all of the keyboard commands listed in the text, and a small interactive experience included to test the commands out.

The testing session included 2 steps:

1. A 10- to 15-min usability testing. The participants were asked to use the screen reader extension to play *Twine of Access* [27, 28] using a think aloud protocol. The researcher took field notes of their observations and what the participants said during this phase.
2. A 10-min interview reviewing the participant's thoughts about the experience. The researcher also asked follow-up questions based on their observations.

Results

Our results highlighted things that worked well with our screen reader as well as areas for future work.

Positives

1. All participants gave positive feedback that the screen reader extension helped them understand the page content, and they found the notification sounds useful.
2. All participants found the different voices removed confusion between what was page content versus HTML element notification.
3. All of the participants found the keyboard commands helpful.

Refinement. Through our observations and interview feedback, we were able to identify areas which would be ideal for refinement:

1. While the keyboard commands were generally positively regarded, four out of five participants spent a significant amount of time learning the commands. While this would diminish with use, it is still worth considering keyboard commands that have a lower barrier to memorization.
2. Because the voice control option was not on by default, most of our participants did not have a chance to try it. Another test of the voice controls is therefore needed to draw any conclusions.
3. Two of the participants suggested the tutorial for using the screen reader commands should be opened automatically, as opposed to requiring the participant to open it manually. This makes sense given that it requires a possibly unknown keyboard commands to open the tutorial. Adding a skip or hide option would help keep this from being intrusive.

Additional Considerations. In our second session, we became aware of issues that arose between using a generalized screen reader and our extension simultaneously.

1. The participants who used a screen reader regularly were used to the keyboard short-cuts they already know. Conflicts between our keyboard shortcuts and the general screen readers needs to be addressed.
2. When a user's generalized screen reader was left open, both screen readers would attempt to read the page at the same time, requiring the participant to find and mute the generalized screen reader. Finding a way to navigate this challenge more smoothly is required.

5   Discussion and Future Work

Based on our evaluations, there is still much work to be done with our screen reader as well as in the area of general IF accessibility. For our screen reader, another user study is necessary to test the voice control implementation more fully and gain insights into its functionality. Additionally, we need to address the conflicts between general screen readers and our more specialized one. There are two major issues:

1. Keyboard command conflicts and confusion.

2. Dealing with the generalized screen reader and our screen reader both reading content at the same time.

For the first issue, screen readers use different keyboard shortcuts depending on the program and the OS being used. Therefore, instead of attempting to standardize to a specific screen reader, it would be best to include customizable keyboard shortcuts. Additionally, adding presets tailored to the most popular screen readers would allow users to find a shortcut set that they are used to.

One way to address the second issue is implementing application or tab switching support in our screen reader so users can switch easily between the screen readers and mute/unmute as needed. A longer-term solution would be allowing communication between the screen readers, so they no longer compete.

IF-Specific Issues. In this study, we primarily focused on the technical issues involved with creating a screen reader for Twine. However, much research remains around IF-specific aspects of screen readers. When interviewing experts, we found that they were accustomed to a computerized voice reading out the text. For general web content this may suffice, but when reading narrative-based experiences, it was often at odds with the content. This ranged from the absurdity of reading out emotionally charged content in a computerized voice to user difficulty with distinguishing between different characters' dialogs.

As we touched on in Sect. 3.2, accessibility is something that must be considered by authors, tool developers, and screen reader developers. We hypothesize that one way the community could work together is to create an IF authoring tool that allowed creators to tag content for different voices and/or emotions, paired with a screen reader with voice libraries that support voice tonality. This would allow authors, tool developers, and screen reader developers to work together to vastly improve the IF experience for people with visual impairments.

6 Conclusion

In this paper, we discussed the creation of a screen reader extension for Chrome that was built specifically for Twine games. We ran two user studies; one with novice screen reader users to evaluate clarity of Twine game output, and the second with screen reader experts to evaluate the experience when used by our target audience. Based on our research we came to the following conclusions:

1. A specific screen reader for Twine games can address some accessibility issues and allow gamers with visual impairments to enjoy Twine gaming experiences. Noticeable improvement was made by refining page content extraction of Twine-specific pages, adding audio notifications on page updates, and creating keyboard shortcuts for moving between interactive elements.
2. To promote the overall accessibility of the interactive fiction experience, the responsibility lies not just with the screen reader developers, but also with the IF tool developers and IF content creators. Creating a more accessible space requires the contribution of the entire community.

It is the hope of the authors that this screen reader will be useful to people with visual impairments, while also promoting awareness of the accessibility issues that still exist with IF experience. Our screen reader and this paper are offered as the beginning of a discussion, not the end of one.

Acknowledgements. We thank the Interactive Fiction Technology Foundation (IFTF), Georgia Tech Center for Inclusive Design and Innovation (CIDI), and Center for Visually Impaired (CVI) for their help and guidance regarding this research.

References

1. Blewett, L.A., Drew, J.A.R., Griffin, R., King, M.L., Williams, K.C.: IPUMS Health Surveys: National Health Interview Survey, Version 6.3. Integrated Public Use Microdata Series, Minneapolis (2018)
2. Hackett, S., Parmanto, B., Zeng, X.: Accessibility of Internet websites through time. In: Proceedings of the 6th International ACM SIGACCESS Conference on Computers and Accessibility, pp. 32–39 (2003)
3. Caldwell, B., et al.: Web content accessibility guidelines (WCAG) 2.0. WWW Consortium (W3C) **290**, 1–34 (2008)
4. Kasday, L.R.: A tool to evaluate universal Web accessibility. In: Proceedings on the 2000 Conference on Universal Usability, pp. 161–162 (2000)
5. WebAIM: The WebAIM Million - The 2022 report on the accessibility of the top 1,000,000 home pages. https://webaim.org/projects/million/. Accessed 30 July 2022
6. Loiacono, E., McCoy, S.: Web site accessibility: an online sector analysis. Information Technology & People (2004)
7. Slatin, J.M., Rush, S.: Maximum Accessibility: Making Your Web Site More Usable for Everyone. Addison-Wesley Professional, Boston (2003)
8. Paciello, M.: Web Accessibility for People with Disabilities. CRC Press, Boca Raton (2000)
9. Twine/An open-source tool for telling interactive, nonlinear stories. http://www.twinery.org/. Accessed 30 July 2022
10. About NVDA. https://www.nvaccess.org/about-nvda/. Accessed 30 July 2022
11. JAWS® – Freedom Scientific. https://www.freedomscientific.com/products/software/jaws/. Accessed 30 July 2022
12. Accessibility – Vision. https://www.apple.com/accessibility/vision/. Accessed 30 July 2022
13. Orca Screen Reader. https://help.gnome.org/users/orca/stable/index.html.en. Accessed 30 July 2022
14. Use the built-in screen reader - Chromebook Help. https://support.google.com/chromebook/answer/7031755?hl=en. Accessed 30 July 2022
15. Bigham, J.P., Prince, C.M., Ladner, R.E.: WebAnywhere: a screen reader on-the-go. In: Proceedings of the 2008 International Cross-Disciplinary Conference on Web Accessibility (W4A), pp. 73–82 (2008)
16. Guo, A., et al.: Vizlens: a robust and interactive screen reader for interfaces in the real world. In: Proceedings of the 29th Annual Symposium on User Interface Software and Technology, pp. 651–664 (2016)
17. Kane, S.K., Frey, B., Wobbrock, J.O.: Access lens: a gesture-based screen reader for real-world documents. In: Proceedings of the SIGCHI Conference on Human Factors in Computing Systems, pp. 347–350 (2013)

18. Ashok, V., Borodin, Y., Puzis, Y., Ramakrishnan, I.V.: Capti-speak: a speech-enabled web screen reader. In: Proceedings of the 12th International Web for All Conference, pp. 1–10 (2015)
19. Red Rossi Studios: audio IF (2019)
20. Stockton, N.: IF Interpreters (2019)
21. Lazar, J., Allen, A., Kleinman, J., Malarkey, C.: What frustrates screen reader users on the web: a study of 100 blind users. Int. J. Hum.-Comput. Interact. **22**, 247–269 (2007)
22. Accessibility for players with low vision – IFWiki. https://www.ifwiki.org/Accessibility_for_players_with_low_vision. Accessed 30 July 2022
23. Accessibility Testing Report. http://accessibility.iftechfoundation.org/. Accessed 30 July 2022
24. The Infocom Documentation Project - Blind-Friendly Manuals. http://infodoc.plover.net/screenread/index.html. Accessed 30 July 2022
25. Kitchensinc - Jim's Kitchen. https://www.kitchensinc.net/. Accessed 30 July 2022
26. Home. https://www.game-accessibility.com/. Accessed 30 July 2022
27. twine-of-access-harlowe. http://accessibility.iftechfoundation.org/testing_website/Twine%20of%20Access/twine-of-access-harlowe.html. Accessed 30 July 2022
28. Twine of Access – SugarCube. http://accessibility.iftechfoundation.org/testing_website/Twine%20of%20Access/twine-of-access.html. Accessed 30 July 2022

Storygraphia: The Constrained Tool for IDN Authoring Education

Vincenzo Lombardo[✉][iD]

CIRMA and Dipartimento di Informatica, Università di Torino, Turin, Italy
vincenzo.lombardo@unito.it

Abstract. This paper presents the authoring tool Storygraphia, for interactive digital narratives. The editor is a graph-based editor that works with a story graph, augmented with metadata for tagging and agents. The authoring tool is oriented to the didactics of interactive storytelling and the major novelty is the implementation of classic constraints for the story engines, namely Propp functions, precondition-effect for story units, tension value.

Keywords: Graph-based editor · Authoring tool · Story editing

1 Introduction

Authoring tools support the creation of interactive digital narratives (IDNs) by making the creative process easier and avoiding technical skills. Authoring tools implement some design model and, sometimes, also implement the superimposition of constraints or principles on the IDN structure. IDN authoring tools have been proliferating in the last decades. They are not limited to text-based editors, but address some form of interactive digital media. For example, Ren'Py supports the creation of visual novels, Korsakow of interactive videos, and Unity3D of narrative games. This proliferation has been commented as "every researcher builds his/her own tool" [1].

Abstracting from the specific media, in Fig. 1 we present a general schema for identifying the components of an authoring tool (adapted from [2]). The story world includes some explicit or implicit description of the world of the story. This is an abstraction of what is represented in the authoring tool, possibly expressed formally.

The dynamic elements consist of an archive of the entities that are explicitly created by the author and/or are manipulated by the engine (below). They are typically the characters, with their behaviors and emotions, and the narrative units, with their metadata and aggregations. The elements can be augmented with attributes that are used by the authors to organize the story. For example, the basic actions that an agent can perform; the chapters or scenes to be sequenced for a hypertext narrative.

The engine is an algorithm that generates from scratch and sequences events, actions, and behavior. It takes into account the rules of the story world, the narrative logic and the user interactions.

M. Vosmeer and L. Holloway-Attaway (Eds.): ICIDS 2022, LNCS 13762, pp. 590–597, 2022.
https://doi.org/10.1007/978-3-031-22298-6_38

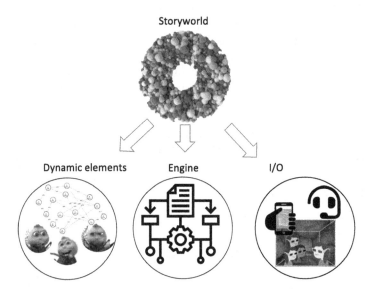

Fig. 1. Interactive storytelling model.

The I/O represents the manifestation of the story, together with the devices for the reception of the story and the interaction with the public.

The authoring tool presented in this paper, named Storygraphia[1], has been developed with a didactic goal in mind. It employs narrative units as dynamic elements; tags and participating agents can augment their representation, to provide an easier control to the authors. The engine implements a number of constraints that are useful for the didactics of some classic solutions to inter-active storytelling, namely, Propp's functions, constraints on preconditions and effects of units, alignment with a dramatic arc. Finally, I/O is text-based and a navigation mode allows the author to explore the graph of units and detects anomalies and cycles. After the description of the tool we briefly report on a comparison with related tools and testing with users.

2   The Editor Storygraphia

Storygraphia is a programme developed in Processing (download at https:// processing.org) that implements the editing and visualization of an interactive story graph. Storygraphia provides a GUI for editing a story graph and analyzing the stories that are compiled from it. In the following we intend that

- A story graph is a graph where nodes are units of the story and edges are transitions over units.
- A unit is a graph node, consisting of an identifier and a text (visualized through layover in the interface).

---

[1] Storygraphia can be downloaded at https://www.cirma.unito.it/storygraphia/.

- A graph edge consists of an identifier and a label, a free text corresponding to some branching point of the story.
- Unit metadata are tags and agents. Tags form a vocabulary created by the author according to some strategy for characterizing the content of units; agents are the entities that participate into the story and have intentions.

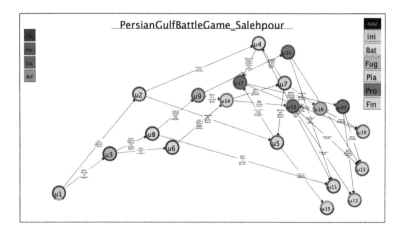

Fig. 2. Example of an interactive story graph (Courtesy of Shiva Salehpour).

2.1   The Graph Structure

The basic component of the software implements the creation of a graph-based narrative, with nodes and edges on a 2D surface that can be zoomed in/out and translated. A node is created in the center of the screen and then can be moved somewhere else, either manually (in case no constraint system is applied) or automatically (through the setting of some value, corresponding to some constraint system, see below). An edge is created by selecting the tail (a node) and then the head (another node). Figure 2 is a screenshot of the Storygraphia application for a story (top-middle is the title and author).

A typical attribute is the tagging of the units: tags are related to a list of terms that are significant for the story. A simple list is {Beginning, Middle, End}, distinguishing the units that can be the beginning of the story, its end, or the middle part. More meaningful tags can be found in the example of Fig. 2: while "Ini" and "Fin" are obvious identifiers for terms "Initial" and "Final", respectively, the others refer to "Battle", "Escape", "Plan", "Proposal", respectively, and correspond to relevant phases of the story. The tool fills the unit nodes with the color of the tag selected for the node (one per node) and the total list of tags is reported in the right of the screen (Fig. 2).

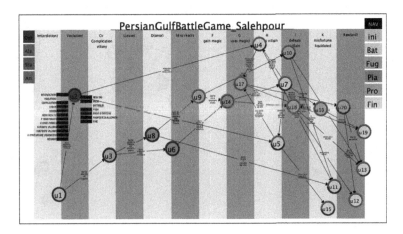

Fig. 3. The story graph of Fig. 2 in the Propp function interface.

Agents are a relevant component of a story. Though Storygraphia is not an agent-based editor, it is possible to annotate the agents that act in some unit. The total set of agents that populate the story is reported in a vertical list on the left (Fig. 2); the same color is reported in the border of the unit, possible segmenting the circumference based upon the number of agents that are assigned to some unit. So, for example, in Fig. 2, the unit "u9", in the middle of the screen is only related to one agent, namely "Darius", while "u17", on its right, is related to two agents, namely "Darius" and "Stateri" (each color spans half circumference).

2.2 Engine Constraints

When an author creates a story, he/she must take into account the constraints posed by the story engine. Storygraphia implements three types of constraints. Following the well-known Propp morphology, each unit can be assigned one of the relevant functions, namely: "Int(erdiction)", "Vio(lation)", "Complication", (the complete list is in Fig. 3). The screen is segmented into 12 parts and, when a unit is labelled with some function, the tool assigns the unit an horizontal position that is related to the corresponding Propp function. So, in Fig. 3, the selected unit "u2" has been assigned the "Violation" function and is located in the 2nd column.

The second constraint is the well-known dramatic arc, related to Freytag and several other scholars in the literature on drama and narrative. The idea implemented by the tool is to assign a vertical position to a unit labelled with some tension value, namely an integer from 1 to 100. Figure 4 reports the same example of Fig. 2 and we can notice that the distribution of units approximates the arc depicted in the background, to ease the work of the author.

Finally, logical states can characterize the behavior of the unit in terms of preconditions that must hold for the unit to be selected for a continuation and effects that hold after some unit has come into play. The tool interface offers two

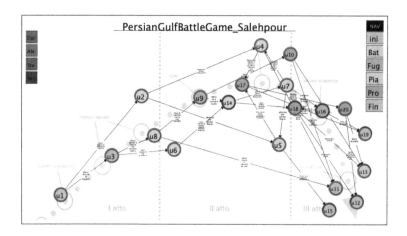

Fig. 4. The story graph of Fig. 2 in the dramatic arc interface.

modalities to insert such constraints: one is called "sculpture", that is all the units are connected unless the unit requires some precondition state to hold; in this case, other units, to be connected, must achieve the same state as an effect. The alternative method is called "painting", that is all units are disconnected unless some effect-precondition link is inserted into the story graph. In this constraint, edges are added automatically and not explicitly by the author.

In all the three cases, the tool allows for overwriting constraints through the free creation of nodes and edges. The tool does not disable the standard commands when we enter a constraint mode. However, we are thinking of an option switch for didactic reasons.

2.3   Interface and Functioning

Stoyrgraphia provides a basic editing mode, working with mouse and keyboard. Each action is triggered through key press: for example, keyboard press "a" adds an agent to a unit (the agent appears on the left side and can be selected for further assignments). The tag menu appears at a node selection: tags can be introduced from scratch or selected from previous insertions (appearing on the right side). Pressing "h" ("help") prints a list of commands.

The workflow with Storygraphia proceeds as follows. After launched the programme, the user is invited to select a work modality. The author can start a new story graph from scratch ("the white page") or upload a story graph that we have conceived in a text file, one unit per row (edges are to be created manually later). A story graph is saved in a JSON file and loaded subsequently. When loading a story graph, we can select one of the constraints that we like to apply during story creation, namely Propp functions, preconditions-effects in painting or sculpure mode, respectively, and tension values.

The save of a story graph also implements a visit of the graph to compile all the possible paths, for checking consistency and interest. The tool prints a text

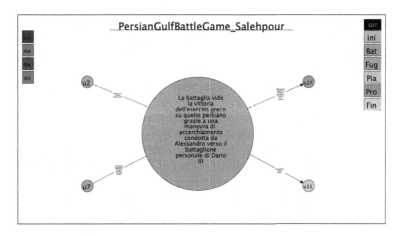

Fig. 5. The story graph of Fig. 2 in NAVigation mode.

file with all the possible linear stories. This also allows to provide some statistics about the ratio between the number of units and the existing continuations. For example, in the case of the story in previous figures, we have 37 potential linear stories, with a ratio of 1.85 between the number of units and the number of linear stories. Finally, Storygraphia also includes a NAVigation mode (Fig. 5): starting from any selected unit, one can follow backward and forward branchings to verify the consistency of the story. Navigation and Editing modes work alternatively to support the authoring process.

3 Testing the Editor in an Interactive Storytelling Course

We have employed the software Storygraphia in a course on Interactive Story-telling, by inviting students to elaborate a narrative and exploit the constraints implemented by the system. The recommendations were for 20–30 units, tagged with a consistent vocabulary to indicate the main parts of the story and including agent marking. The 34 students from the University of Torino had a background in humanities: media studies, book science and technology, historic studies, extra-european cultures. Some had attended narratology courses and knew about Propp's morphology and Freytag's arc. Different stories should result from the graph navigation, in order to maximize the ratio of the story graph. Also, we required to check the consistency of the generated linear stories by reading the "storyprint" file and indicate the three best linear stories that emerged.

We collected 36 narratives on several topics (to mention a few examples, interactive rewriting of WWII events, Germanic mythology, elfs' adventures, sport chronicles). The average number of units was 23.89, with 6.16 tags and 4.86 agents (max 15). The average number of stories generated was 340.38, with average ratio of 11.50^2. Students who committed to constraints (one third, 13) mostly used the Propp functions (9) and the tension value (8), also together (in 3 cases), while only in two cases they implemented the logic constraint. This can be explained with the fact that most of the effort was devoted to learn operating with the tool; the ones who were familiar with Propp and Freytag used the related constraints (it was already an effort to transit from theory to the encoded practice); only two were so brave to encode the logic constraints (rather unfamiliar for humanistic backgrounds).

The tool has revealed to be very usable, though its basic interface, in the final interviews; some students also benefitted from the direct intervention on the JSON file with a text editor or the import of a preliminary text file, which were generally considered (especially the latter) as useful features. Some students complained about the impossibility of having loops in Storygraphia-edited IDNs. Others have requested the integration of other media to produce multimedia stories, though the declared statement to operate at the treatment level.

4   Related Tools

Storygraphia, being a graph-based editor, shares this representation format with many other tools (also see the classification in [3]).

As Storygraphia, Twine[3] is an open source tool, that can be used with a graphical interface (no programming is needed). Differently from Storygraphia, it can include multimedia and interactivity cprogramming (through variables, conditional logic, images, CSS and JavaScript). For playback, while Storygraphia has its own internal navigation mode, Twine generates an HTML marking, to be displayed in a web browser. Twine does not offer support for narratological or logic constraints, though they could be enforced through programming. Most of the considerations listed for Twine also holds for the open-source version of the Ink tool[4], with minor differences on formats and choices.

Unlike Storygraphia, Storyspace[5] is a commercial system that exports into XML format (Storygraphia is currently missing an exporter). The Storyspace interface allows the author to activate and deactivate the links between the units, during a navigation phase. Deactivation is more flexible than delete, as per the current development of Storygraphia. Graph creation can proceed both with the manual connection and by licensing sequences from connected graphs. These modes recall the painting and sculpting modes of Storygraphia, though not referring to logic constraints. From a technological point of view, Storyspace also includes a *reader* of the interactive story, which can be distributed with the work.

---

[2] These data go down to 138.72 and 3.02, respectively, if we exclude an extreme case with 7600 stories and 316 ratio.
[3] https://twinery.org, visited on 10 Oct 2022.
[4] https://www.inklestudios.com/ink/, visited on 10 Oct 2022.
[5] http://www.eastgate.com/storyspace/, visited on 10 Oct 2022.

The Korsakow system[6] is a software available on the Web (which is free for small productions) for the creation of interactive films (K-films), through an HTML interface, that supports the marking of association rules to the units, namely video clips. So, differently from Storygraphia, the target is the video medium embedded into HTML format. Rather than an explicit graph, possibly constrained in some form, Korsakow associates the smallest narrative units, or SNUs, with metadata including, among others, "initial" or "final" marking, the number of times the unit can appear, the likelihood that some clip is connected to other clips. The behavior of the system is therefore much more complex than an explicit hypertext, as in Storygraphia, because of probabilities and markings. On the other hand, Korsakow does not support overall constrained systems, of narratological or computational origin.

5   Conclusions

We have presented the authoring tool Storygraphia, a IDN editor oriented to the creation of story graphs, with units augmented with tagging and agents to control the story development. The tool, mostly employed in teaching, implements a number of constraints for the simulation of story engine, namely Propp functions, precondition-effect states, and tension values. Storygraphia is employed in the didactics of interactive storytelling and a test with classes has produced interesting results on the usability of the tool.

Some limitations are due to the impossibility of creating loops and the impossibility to export multimedia IDNs. We are thinking of introduce a loop control, by signaling the author the number of traversed cycles and the possibility of control them, and an export to Twine format to exploit the HTML5 possibilities for multimedia.

Acknowledgements. I wish to thank Antonio Pizzo, for having discussed some of the features and tested the preliminary releases of Storygraphia, and Yotam Shibolet for pointing out some literature on authoring tools. I thank Shiva Salehpour for the screenshots of Storygraphia at work.

References

1. Koenitz, H.: Three questions concerning authoring tools. In: Proceedings of the International Conference on Interactive Digital Storytelling (ICIDS 2017) (2017)
2. Pizzo, A., Lombardo, V., Damiano, R.: Interactive storytelling: a cross-media approach to writing, producing and editing with AI. Routledge (forthcoming)
3. Shibolet, Y., Lombardo, V.: Resources for comparative analysis of IDN authoring tools. In: Proceedings of the International Conference of Digital Interactive Storytelling (ICIDS) (2022, to appear)

---

[6] http://www.korsakow.com, visited on 10 Oct 2022.

Virtual Worlds, Performance, Games and Play

Identification and IDNs in the Metaverse: Who Would We Like to Be?

Jonathan Barbara[1,2](✉) and Mads Haahr[1]

[1] School of Computer Science and Statistics, Trinity College Dublin, Dublin, Ireland
{barbaraj,haahrm}@tcd.ie
[2] Saint Martin's Institute of Higher Education, Hamrun, Malta

Abstract. One's digital identity on the Metaverse is critical enough to warrant EU regulation. Suggesting Interactive Digital Narratives as having a role to play in the Metaverse, we focus on the identity of the Virtual Reality interactor in such virtual spaces, and the potential impact this may have on the self-identity of the interactor. Building upon the notions of identity and the interactor's construction of their narrative identity, we revisit identification in the context of VR Interactive Narratives (VRINs) and explore authenticity and character similarity as its dimensions. We interpret the construction of a narrative identity in VR as a vehicle for identity shift between the interactor's self-identity and identification with the character. Based on the theoretical framework, we present a conceptual model for identity shift in VRINs which we then apply to a number of case studies to exemplify its utility and provide some guidelines for VRIN authors in how to use this model.

Keyword: Virtual reality · Interactive narrative · Identity · Authenticity

1 Introduction

The next generation of social media platforms are touted to be less of an asynchronous consumption of text and video posts as known from current platforms, like Facebook, YouTube, Twitter and TikTok, and more of an immersive experience in Virtual Reality (VR) of which Microsoft's AltSpaceVR and Meta's HorizonWorlds are typical exemplars. Coined by Neal Stephenson in his dystopian science-fiction novel *Snow Crash* [1], the term 'Metaverse' was subsequently adopted by the tech industry as an amalgam of Web 2.0 and video games in a roadmap presented by a cross-industry public foresight project looking into pathways to the 3D Web [2], then labeled as 'Web 3.0'. In their historical analysis of social media, Sajithra and Patil [3] presented Web 3.0 as an extension of Web 2.0's participatory technologies and social networks into 3D space. In this 3D space, identity is crucial for trust and reputation, as the EU's regulation on a digital identity[1] shows, while "identity experimentation, self-revelation, and roleplay [may be supported] [in] theme-based game worlds and less popular social [virtual worlds]" [2].

---

[1] https://ec.europa.eu/info/strategy/priorities-2019-2024/europe-fit-digital-age/european-digital-identity_en.

M. Vosmeer and L. Holloway-Attaway (Eds.): ICIDS 2022, LNCS 13762, pp. 601–615, 2022.
https://doi.org/10.1007/978-3-031-22298-6_39

Since its initial proposal, the focus of Web 3.0 seems to have shifted towards blockchain, cryptocurrencies, big data and artificial intelligence to build the 'semantic web' [4], but Meta's push towards the Metaverse as a social VR platform surely puts the technology as one of the main drivers of Web 4.0 [5].

For the ICIDS community in 2022, in its perspective on Speculative Horizons, the Metaverse may not be a total transition from asynchronous social media posts and websites to a 3D virtual world where visitors synchronously interact through their digital avatars. As an interim stage, IDNs may become a platform through which a poster's wall is presented as an asynchronous interactive experience for their VR visitors: a more personalized social media experience that allows the visitor to focus on information that they find more relevant to themselves, as represented by their online social identity. Just as Web 1.0 was dominated by commercial websites in comparison with Web 2.0 which empowered the general public to have their own online presence, likewise we expect the first wave of the Metaverse to be commercially driven, with already blossoming development of platforms that allow the general public to have their own 3D space. While we leave this speculative role of IDNs in the Metaverse for discussion elsewhere, we bring our attention to the identity of the VR interactor in such virtual spaces and also the potential impact this may have on the self-identity of the interactor. The recent reports of sexual violence and harassment on Metaverse platforms [6] draws attention to the interactor-avatar bond in relation to which scholarly research so far has focused more on presence and embodiment [7–10] and less on the transformational effects on the victim as interactor. The latter focused more on VR's supposed empathy-inducing abilities [11–13], a troublesome concept for IDN scholars [13–16] as VR by itself is not empathy-inducing without proper narrative techniques [17]. Instead, we shift our perspective onto an understanding of the relationship between the VR interactor's self-identity and their virtual identity by presenting a conceptual model that positions the narrative identity, constructed through the VR Interactive Narrative (VRIN) by the interactor, between their self identity and the author's intended character's identity. The conceptual model presents this relationship as a continuum between self-identity and character identification along the dimensions of authenticity and similarity and presents a few case studies that are discussed and projected onto this continuum to explain its use.

2   Background

2.1   Identity and Narrative Identity

Ricoeur [18] presents identity as the self-reflective ipse-identity (a selfhood that can change) and the external self, judged in terms of quality and structure, the idem-identity (sameness). Seeing narrative as "a crucial component for the creation of personal identities" [19] narrative-identity is presented as a bridge between the ipse- and idem- identities [20], representing both change and permanence [21].

Gee [22] presented three identities based around his relationship with his half-elf avatar in the game *Arcanum* (2001) as James Paul Gee as Bead Bead. James Paul Gee as himself is presented as the real identity, Bead Bead as his half-elf character is the virtual identity, and the prepositional "as" between these two identities as the projective identity in which Gee projects himself onto Bead Bead the half-elf - matching the above definition of identification.

From the personal narratives perspective, Wilt et al. [23] extend the narrative identity's function as a bridge by defining it as "the evolving life stories that connect one's past with the present day and imagined future" (pg. 8). Hallford and Mellor [24] claim that "the meaningful integration of positive and negative, congruent and contradictory experiences" (pg. 1) is a function of this narrative identity, drawing parallels with the Jungian "self" as "the sum of everything we are now, and everything we once were, as well as everything we could potentially become... that which we are as a totality" [25].

These competing identities were also addressed by Carl Jung through his notion of archetypes. Firstly, Jung claimed that identity was mainly the responsibility of our ego, the conscious mind comprising the thoughts, memories, and emotions of which a person is aware. However, Jung claimed that the ego is a "highly complex affair" that can be defined as "a relatively constant personification of the unconscious itself" [26]. Jung augmented the Freudian concept of the (personal) unconscious - repressed, unacknowledged mental material - with the notion of the collective unconscious that is common across the human species and in which he identified several archetypes, amongst them the persona, the anima/animus, and the self [26]. The persona archetype represents roles that we fulfill and the behavior expected out of them. Jung defines it as "the individual's system of adaptation to, or the manner he assumes in dealing with, the world" and it may happen that one becomes the persona, "that in reality one is not, [but] which oneself as well as others think one is" [27].

This compliance with expected behavior may explain questions about the notion of a single inner true self [28, 29]. Renowned psychologist Jerome Bruner proposes that "there is no such thing as an intuitively obvious and essential self to know" but "we constantly construct and reconstruct ourselves to meet the needs of the situations we encounter" [29]. By looking at how individuals use computers to work around their identity issues and develop intimacy with others, Turkle [28] sees computers as virtual realities in themselves, enabling the self to reflect on its own nature as well as explore its social context. As players seek to build different versions of themselves, already in the text-based versions popular in the 1990s, but more so in the visual realism offered today, a multitude of the self, rather than the single identity, results. Schlenker [30] had provided a suggestion that these alternate personae are in response to the environment and the audience within, while Bruner [29] later commented on how one's self-narratives attempt to find balance between autonomy and commitment to others.

2.2 Identification

These differences between the self and the personae cause identification to happen; otherwise, we have identity [31]. Thus, identification "is an imaginative experience in which a person surrenders consciousness of his or her own identity and experiences the world through someone else's point of view [vicarious experience]." [32]. It is "mediated by a psychological process in which the reader takes on the characteristics of the fictional character" [33]. "Identification leads to the (temporary) adoption of an external point of view and to viewing the world through an alternative social reality. The varying intensity of identification reflects the extent to which one exchanges his or her own perspective for that of another and is able to forget him- or herself" [32].

Identification has a greater chance of happening when certain antecedent conditions are met, including cognitive and social-science oriented elements. Cognitive elements, as suggested by Oatley [33], include enactment (adopting the goals of the protagonist), virtual worlds (presenting an imaginary world), addressing the player via parasocial interaction (PSI) (speech acts for the reader) and narrative consistency (the potential for constructive integration of disparate elements) (also cf [34]). Elsewhere, Busselle and Bilandzic [35] find strong correlation between Narrative Engagement and Identification. Drawing from social-science oriented research, Cohen [32] claims that narrative genres (such as drama and comedy) should elicit identification with a target character more than non-narrative genres (such as talk shows and news) as the latter address the audience and are more conducive to PSI. Cohen [32] also claims that in identification there is no PSI (with the target character) because as the interactor becomes the character, there is no interaction between them (as it requires them to be separate). However, we argue that, in the case of interactive narratives, PSI on the target character's behalf with other characters would enhance identification, as supported by Oatley [33] above.

Another antecedent condition is the target character's similarity to the reader in terms of appearance, culture, attributes, or situation and, subsequently, the character's perceived realism in relation to reality or stereotypical views [7, 32]. Klimmt et al. [36], amongst others, have considered the notion of identification in games. They define identification as "a temporary shift in players' self-perception" (p. 235) as the players fulfill the role of the character assigned to them in the game. They suggest that video game enjoyment is dependent on the assigned character's greater similarity to themselves (cf "mirror hypothesis"[2]) or to the player's ideal preferred self in relation to their own self-perception (cf "magic mirror hypothesis"). This latter similarity presents a "wishful identification" [7] as the player seeks to reduce their self-discrepancy (cf "self-discrepancy theory" [37]) by identifying with the character [8].

A counter-example is provided by *Grand Theft Auto IV* (2008), in which the narrative identity built through the player's actions is dissimilar to both the player's (hopefully) non-criminal own identity as well as the intentions of the played character Nico Bellic, as conveyed through the game's narrative. This lack of similarity to the narrative's character and discrepancy relative to the player's own identity causes discomfort with the gameplay [38].

Later research has explored different forms of identity and identification. Barker criticizes the concept of identification with on-screen characters in blockbuster movies based on a research carried out with viewers of The Lord of the Rings trilogy finding non-conclusive understanding of what identification really is [39]. Shaw, albeit based on research with two female individuals, claimed that identification requires that players see the video game character/avatar as separate from themselves [40]. However, she draws attention to media-specificity: "all attempts to describe identification in games must be more attentive to how specific games promote different types of connections

---

[2] 'The mirror hypothesis' in relation to the moving image is that viewers will tend to relate favorably to those onscreen who are either like themselves (the mirror) or who represent what the viewer would like to be like (the magic mirror).

and differences between player and avatar" [40]. In the context of Virtual Reality, where the interactor views and engages with the virtual world through the eyes and body of their avatar, the gap between the interactor and avatar is much reduced and shaped by what affordances the virtual world allows the interactor's character to do. This closeness of bodies, of the physical with the virtual, not only allows for the embodiment of the real into the virtual [41] but also facilitates an impact of the virtual onto the real [55].

In their work, Wilt et al. explored authenticity and inauthenticity in narrative identity by having undergraduate students write descriptions of situations where they felt authentic (e.g. expressing one's true nature, being content and relaxed, taking ownership of one's choices, not giving in to external pressures, and having open and honest relationships) and inauthentic (e.g. being phony, conforming to others' expectations, suppressing one's emotions, and denigrating the self) [23]. Authenticity, thus, reflects the salience of the self-concept in one's behavior while inauthenticity reflects the influence of the situation and audience on one's behavior [30].

For example, in *We. The Revolution* (2019) the interactor is faced with the choice of playing a gambling dice game with high stakes in the narrative. Should the player share any propensity to gambling like the main character, they ought to find it easier - authentic - to choose the gambling choice as opposed to those who are reluctant to gamble in real life and feel inauthentic living up to the character's gambling traits.

2.3 Identity Shift

Turkle had urged us to "[w]atch for a nascent culture of virtual reality that underscores the ways in which we construct gender and the self, the ways in which we become what we play, argue about, and build" [28].

This suggested an identity shift in computer mediated environments which refers to how communicators may become the self that is portrayed in public online contexts [and] how public online self-presentation influences individuals to embrace the traits performed in front of an audience [42].

While a study on the effect of self-identity on the VR interactor by Peña and Hill [43] did not support the phenomenon with statistically significant results, it suggests that such a shift is more pronounced in the presence of non-player characters (NPCs) and more so in the presence of other players' avatars - as suggested by Schlenker [30] as well as Jung [27] in the psychopathological phenomenon of personality transformation when the individual becomes one of the assigned personas in front of an audience.

Gupta et al.'s shift away from the freedom of choice offered by branching narratives and choice-based AI systems towards a scripted performance may be such an exemplar [44]. They present a participatory VR theater experience where the interactor is expected to play out the role of an actor on a stage in a piece of scripted theater, rather than have the level of agency that features regularly in the work of the ICIDS community. Their findings include participants who shifted their identity to the roles they played: "*I felt like Calliope!*" and felt deep connections to her sister Minerva. The identity shift was reported in another finding: "*Beyond knowing they were Calliope, the mirror also helped them visually transform into Calliope and leave their own identity behind*" [44].

Such identification can result in the Proteus Effect, when people, in their online behavior and attitudes, conform to their avatar's characteristics [45]. More interestingly, if the interactor's online behavior is felt to be inauthentic (see [23] above), does it cause some identity shift of the interactor towards that inauthentic self?

In *A Way Out* (2018), the players may have put their law-abiding identity aside in order to comply with the escaped convict nature of their character. However, towards the end of the narrative, one of the characters turns out to be a covert police officer and both players are tasked to shoot at their partner in order to progress the game. For the player identifying with the newly found police officer, this role, which may well be closer to their law-abiding nature, jars against the persona that would have been developed throughout the game's narrative and makes the player feel reluctant to betray it [46].

2.4   Identification in VR

What does all this tell the author of IDNs in VR?

For starters, identification with the player character has been deemed to be a determining factor of narrative immersion [47] and video game enjoyment [48–50]. Immersion has been categorized based on sources of pleasure in games into challenge-based immersion, imaginative immersion, and sensory immersion [50]. More pertinently, imaginative immersion has been defined as the dimension "in which one becomes absorbed with the stories and the world, or begins to feel for or identify with a game character" [50]. Hefner et al. argue that this identification is facilitated when interaction is provided in a rich audiovisual representation of the game world (cf sensory immersion, [50]), that enables a sense of Presence ("a perceptual illusion of non-mediation" [51]), which is inhabited by intelligent agents that address the player (cf para-social interaction, [52]), and is backed up by narrative elements ([49]; cf [35]). Presence has been considered as the highest level of immersion [53] to the point of often being "used as synonyms to each other" [50]. Perceptual (sensory) and Psychological (engagement, engrossment - cf [53]) Immersion are presented as one of the conceptualizations of Presence [51] together with social richness, realism (also a factor of sensory immersion, [50]), transportation, and para-social interaction. Presence is highly facilitated by VR technology, which provides high levels of sensory immersion and, by its affordance of telepresence [54], accommodates the metaphor of transportation.

Meanwhile, Slater is critical of using Presence as an element of engagement and presents three illusory components [55] to clarify its definition of "being in a virtual environment" that had been given in an earlier work [56]. The first is Place Illusion, and refers to the illusion of being in a virtual environment, even though one knows that they are not. The second element is Plausability Illusion which refers to the illusion that the events happening in the virtual environment are really happening. Such realism is dependent on actions and reactions, particularly those directed at the interactor [55] but also those carried out by the interactor [57]. The third element is Body Ownership Illusion, the illusion that the virtual body is one's own body particularly as it responds to the physical body's movement as well as the interactor's reaction to actions directed towards their body, as if it was their own.

Presence is also a motivational construct in Self Determination Theory together with autonomy, relatedness and competence [58]. Autonomy provides interactors with freedom of agency as afforded by the virtual world. Relatedness refers to feeling relevant and useful to the needs of others, as one's actions influence the state of others. Competence refers to the interactor's ability to achieve the intended outcomes, assuming clear goals and feedback are provided to help them progress towards their goal. Within this context, Presence is provided as a synonym for immersion, but the paper emphasises the interactor's agency in the virtual world as a predictor for presence [58].

We find Slater's Place Illusion in agreement with Biocca and Levy's definition used above [51]. We also think that Plausability Illusion corresponds well with Hefner et al.'s argument that a rich audiovisual representation of the game world facilitates identification [49]. Finally we see Kilteni et al.'s Body Ownership Illusion [41] as an important media-specific connection between player and avatar that facilitates identification in VR [40].

Studies found a positive correlation between, and a significant positive effect of, Presence and enjoyment within a virtual museum experience [59], VR Tourism [60] and 360 virtual tours [61]. Moreover, VR Interactive Narratives (VRINs) provide narrative elements to enrich the experience while the use of non-player characters (NPCs) to engage with the player provide social richness through parasocial interaction.

However, as VR technology blocks out the perception of the real world in favor of immersion into the virtual environment, interactors have their self-concept at a disadvantage. Presence, particularly understood as Place Illusion, may cause the interactor to feel freed from the expectations of the real world but at the same time pressured to live up to the expectations of the virtual world. Plausability Illusion, in the form of realism of the virtual environment and presentation of a virtual audience, may impinge upon their identification, potentially causing an identity shift into their virtual avatar and its characteristics. While the Body Ownership Illusion facilitates identification - the presence of the interactor in the virtual body - the attribution of the virtual body to the self may cause the mind to confuse the virtual body for its own and start living up to its expectations, particularly if it is perceived to be closer to one's ideal self [8, 45]. As Slater claims, "Virtual Reality can transform not only your sense of place, and of reality, but also the apparent properties of your own body" [55].

This identity shift is further affected by the level of freedom of choice provided in order to support the feeling of "being–in-the-world" [57]. AI-driven VRINs that provide greater freedom of choice and facilitate player-driven narrative may lead to authentic interactor experiences as the player is allowed to play in their own style. On the other hand, experiences that force an authored narrative may result in inauthentic experiences, as the interactor plays out the narrative identity expected by the situation (cf. Jung's persona) and virtual audiences - who may be virtually present, viewing through live stream, or viewing a recorded gameplay later. Hefner et al. suggest that games can have a better entertainment value if they can "evoke the perception in players that they can occupy the role they identify with successfully" [49]. Thus, inauthentic experiences that problematize identity shifts may jeopardize the quality of the experience.

3 Conceptual Model

We now present a conceptual model (see Fig. 1) which is intended to summarize the above literature and present narrative identity on a continuum from self-identity to character identification along the dimensions of authenticity and similarity. We theorize that VR interactors who ask "who am I that acts?" may sense a deeper level of Presence (1) if they are able to shift their identity (2) to the player character (3) whose role they are expected to fulfill (4) in the virtual experience, moderated by their similarity to the character (5). This can be aided by consistent narrative elements (6) and being addressed by the virtual world's inhabitants (9) which help construct a narrative identity (7) that may feel otherwise inauthentic to the player (8). High levels of enjoyment (10) are thus provided by identification and Presence.

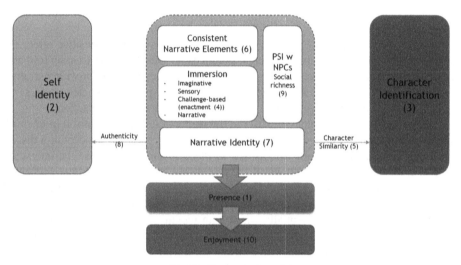

Fig. 1. Conceptual model

This conceptual model helps us situate the narrative identity created by the interactor's agency within a VRIN on a continuum between their own self-identity and the identity attributed by the author to the played character. Depending on the distance between one's identity and the target character's identity, there ought to be an inverse correlation between the similarity of the narrative identity to target characterization and its authenticity to the interactor's own identity. The greater the distance, the more inauthentic one's narrative identity will feel as they attempt to live up to the character's expected behavior.

This may be the expected outcome when the interactor is fulfilling a preset character persona, but may cause loss of presence, and thus enjoyment, if the interactor is led to believe that they are themselves in the virtual experience but are then forced to behave inauthentically to themselves, or are rewarded for it. An intermediate stage may occur when the interactor is not cast as a ready-made persona, but allowed to create their own character within a target storyworld. This makes it possible for the interactor to create an ideal self, relative to the given circumstances and available options, that satisfies their self-discrepancy (between their real self and their desired self). This often boils down to the customisation of the character's aesthetics [62], which are visible when looking into a virtual mirror but also from other interactors' reaction to one's appearance. Identification, however, goes beyond aesthetics and will reflect in the interaction process with the IDN where similarity to the desired self will again determine presence and enjoyment.

4 Case Studies

We shall now consider this conceptual model by applying it to six VR interactive narratives and positioning them along the dimensions of authenticity and character similarity (see Fig. 2).

The Spider-Man: Far from Home VR experience (2019) presents an interesting case study. The Spiderman narrative already has a character, Peter Parker, who identifies with a public-facing character, the Spider-Man, projecting his special abilities through the masked persona. The VR experience presents two gameplay modes. In the free play mode, the player has nothing to do with Peter Parker or his friends, and is urged to put on the mask and become Spider-Man. Through the spider-like abilities afforded by the Spider-Man, the player is able to identify with the superhero, shooting cobwebs and swinging from building to building throughout the city. Casting Spider-Man as the role model, in this game the player identifies with the character overcoming their self-discrepancy while retaining their authenticity. In the story mode, the player is expected to identify with Peter, whose voice we hear as a voice-over as he chats with his friend Ned over a digital communication platform. Putting on the mask when instructed, the player gets to look in the mirror and see themself as the Spider-Man. Egged on by Ned, the player is tasked to stop a robotic behemoth causing mayhem in the city's streets while bringing down flying droids serving as obstacles to the task. As Ned urges Peter to hurry up repeatedly throughout the game, the player is compelled to live up to expectations of his double persona (as Peter as Spider-Man) causing identification - but with who? As the Peter Parker persona lies in between the player and the Spider-Man, but as a character they are closer to the superhero, then the player is compelled to identify with Peter as he is closer to the role model. Identifying with a well-established character results in low authenticity and low character similarity. This is also explained by Self Determination Theory [58], as the constant urging by Ned coerces the player to act as the game wants them to, thus limiting their freedom of action and thus providing limited autonomy, resulting in low authenticity.

The Book of Distance (2020) goes to great lengths to build a bond between the anonymous character played by the interactor - so much so that there's nothing stopping you from identifying as yourself, resulting in a high character similarity - and the protagonist of the story, the narrator's grandpa, Yonezo Okita. However, halfway through the narrative, you are faced by a lever with which, upon interacting with it, fences in Yonezo into an internment camp, making the player feel inauthentic to their role identified with so far in the story. Indeed, the experience was an intention of the designers to prevent any identification for the interactor [63].

In *A Fisherman's Tale* (2019), a VR puzzle where the player's character owns a scale model replica of his room complete with a little character representing himself, the triple representation of the character (because the player's character is also a scale model of a gigantic version of himself) adds distance between the player and his character, introducing an element of parasocial interaction and reducing character similarity. The player helps the smaller character solve his puzzle, and in so doing, the gigantic character solves the puzzle for the player's character. Such a design diminishes identification as it externalizes the persona onto the smaller and larger characters while providing medium authenticity.

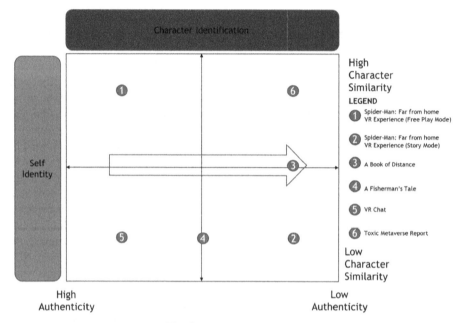

Fig. 2. Case study mapping

VRChat (2014) is an online VR social platform that allows users to embody an identity in the form of avatars. These are 3D characters over whose representation users have substantial control through its customization. While many users attempt to recreate their physical appearance on the avatar, others seek to create a representation of who they would like to be. Asshoff's study presents an ethnographic study that reports on the experience of embodiment as reported by about 20 participants. Amongst them were participants who were able to present themselves in the gender they identified with. For individuals whose physical appearance is a source of misgendering, the avatar allows them to be seen for who they feel they really are. This presents an example that offers high authenticity even if their avatar is dissimilar to their physical self [9].

This model also gives us an opportunity to understand the sexual harassment reportedly suffered in the Metaverse [6]. The virtual character embodying the SumOfUs researcher was made to act in a manner that was neither authentic to the researcher's own identity nor similar to the character they wished to project. While there was no physical body contact between the researcher and the perpetrator, the imagined behavior was shared by both in their physical brain and the degrading utterances of the perpetrator were heard by the auditory system of the researcher. Since there was no well-developed character being identified with by the researcher, there was high character similarity between interactor and avatar. Moreover, due to the affordances of the virtual reality, "identification collapsed into identity" [31] and whatever was being "suffered" by the avatar was suffered by the researcher interactor, a situation in which she did not feel authentic to herself at all. Thus the danger of a shared online and offline identity is that the social structures in place in the real world are absent in the Metaverse unless we, as IDN authors, put them into place to protect from such behavior - just like attempting to flirt with the wife in *Facade* (2003) results in the player being thrown out of the apartment.

5   Guidelines

Having developed this conceptual model, and seen some of its application in a few VR experiences, we are now in a position to suggest some guidelines for future VRIN authors with respect to identification, all open to empirical confirmation to which the ICIDS community is invited. We categorize our guidelines based on who the VR author wishes the interactor to identify with.

1. A well-known established character within an established virtual world
2. An unknown established character within an established virtual world
3. A customizable character within an established virtual world
4. Themselves within an established virtual world

Having a well-known established character presents the largest distance between the interactor and the character, as the interactor will project unto the character any prior knowledge they have about them, such as that gained from other media experiences. The interactor will be expected to push their narrative identity furthest away from themselves towards the character, potentially increasing inauthenticity and diminishing the enjoyment of the experience if they fail to live up to expectations of fulfilling the role of the character. This mode will be most pertinent to VRINs within established franchises. Hence, if you have an established franchise with highly defined characters, be aware of the limited identification possible as it will be a significant challenge to provide a genuinely enjoyable VRIN experience.

Having an unknown but established character presents an easier expectation that is free from prejudice but still demanding in fulfilling whatever expectations conveyed to the interactor through the experience itself. This could be a sidekick to an established protagonist [64]. Whatever is left untold is assumed to be as close to the interactor as possible (cf "principle of minimal departure", [65]). This may however result in inconsistencies later on in the experience as the interactor finds themselves continuously adjusting their narrative identity to remain similar to the target character, which is likely to reduce their feeling of authenticity. This choice of identification will be most fitting for new franchises expanding onto VR platforms as part of a transmedia marketing campaign. In this case, if you wish to minimize the reduction of authenticity during the experience, make sure to explain the character as fully as possible. This will help avoid having the interactor filling any knowledge gaps by projecting their own attributes onto the target character and then discovering and correcting these inaccuracies piecemeal throughout the experience.

Having a customizable character, whether based off a template character or built from scratch, allows the interactor to create a model of their ideal self, allowing them to reduce their self-discrepancy by identifying with the character. This is the category most relevant to IDNs in the envisaged Metaverse social platform, as virtual visitors will customize their character as befits the particular platform, just as we pick different profile pictures for different Web 2.0 social media platforms, like Facebook, LinkedIn, and Instagram, to present ourselves as befits the expectations. The ease of identification depends on the afforded customizability – not only in terms of form but also in terms of function. Therefore, a high level of customizability in VRINs will help achieve higher authenticity, not only in the character's appearance but also in the afforded agency. A particular challenge for platform developers is to find the right balance between high flexibility in the available functions and ethical issues, such as the provisioning of a safe virtual environment for everyone.

Having the interactor bring their own identity to the virtual world, filtered by the affordances of the technology, may still bring in issues of authenticity when such affordances limit their ability to react in line with their own physical identity. This category will be most pertinent where one's offline identity is needed for trust purposes, such as interacting with a commercial entity's VR presence and enacting financial transactions, say. If the interactor does not have sufficient trust in the platform, then they might not feel comfortable enough to fully populate their character details with their own, thus not providing an authentic representation of themselves. Thus, in situations where the interactor's real identity is expected to be represented in the virtual environment, measures should be in place to build the necessary trust for them to feel comfortable to share these details.

6   Conclusion

Identification with the player character has attracted academic interest in the past but the recent emphasis on virtual reality as a social media platform, and the potential for IDNs to become a means to provide asynchronous interaction with one's social media presence attracts renewed attention to the notion of identity in VRINs. EU regulation on digital identity and reported harassment on online platforms further warrant understanding and attention to the topic at hand.

Considering the dual identity of the interactor as avatar, while they construct their narrative identity as they interact with the VRIN, we revisit identification in terms of two dimensions: authenticity and character similarity. We interpret the construction of a narrative identity in VR as a means for identity shift between the interactor's self-identity and character identification. Based on a comprehensive theoretical framework, we presented a conceptual model for identity shift in VRINs along the aforementioned dimensions of authenticity and character similarity. We then applied the model to a number of VRIN case studies to exemplify its utility and extract some guidelines for VRIN authors in how to use this model with four different types of avatars in an established virtual world.

Further work may also consider the application of this model to non-established worlds that the interactor may create themselves. How does putting an established character into an interactor's world affect the identification along its similarity and authenticity dimensions? Are these qualities higher when an interactor's customized character, or maybe even themselves, are situated within the player's own created world?

References

1. Stephenson, N.: Snow Crash: A Novel. Bantam Books (1992). ISBN 0-553-08853-X
2. Smart, J., et al.: A cross-industry public foresight project. In: Proceedings of the Metaverse Roadmap Pathways 3DWeb, pp. 1–28 (2007)
3. Sajithra, K., Patil, R.: Social media–history and components. J. Bus. Manag. **7**(1), 69–74 (2013)
4. Hendler, J., Berners-Lee, T.: From the Semantic Web to social machines: a research challenge for AI on the World Wide Web. Artif. Intell. **174**(2), 156–161 (2010)
5. Menor, D.: Web 4.0 Explained – Defining the Next Big Leap in Tech. Hashdork (2021). https://hashdork.com/web-4-explained/
6. SumOfUs. Metaverse: another cesspool of toxic content (2022). https://www.sumofus.org/images/Metaverse_report_May_2022.pdf
7. Van Looy, J., Courtois, C., De Vocht, M., De Marez, L.: Player identification in online games: validation of a scale for measuring identification in MMOGs. Media Psychol. **15**(2), 197–221 (2012)
8. Praetorius, A.S., Görlich, D.: How avatars influence user behavior: a review on the proteus effect in virtual environments and video games. In: International Conference on the Foundations of Digital Games, pp. 1–9 (2020)
9. Rasmus, A.: Welcome to VRChat: an ethnographic study on embodiment and immersion in virtual reality. Thesis. Stockholm University (2022). http://su.diva-portal.org/smash/record.jsf?pid=diva2%3A1676200&dswid=-3145
10. Lynch, T., Matthews, N.L., Gilbert, M., Jones, S., Freiberger, N.: Explicating how skill determines the qualities of user-Avatar bonds. Front. Psychol., 828 (2022)
11. Nakamura, L.: Feeling good about feeling bad: virtuous virtual reality and the automation of racial empathy. J. Vis. Cult. **19**(1), 47–64 (2020)
12. Bujić, M., Salminen, M., Macey, J., Hamari, J.: "Empathy machine": how virtual reality affects human rights attitudes. Internet Research (2020)
13. Raz, G.: Rage against the Empathy Machine Revisited: The Ethics of the Empathic Affordances of Virtual Reality (2022)
14. Rouse, R.: Someone else's story: an ethical approach to interactive narrative design for cultural heritage. In: Cardona-Rivera, R.E., Sullivan, A., Young, R.M. (eds.) ICIDS 2019. LNCS, vol. 11869, pp. 47–60. Springer, Cham (2019). https://doi.org/10.1007/978-3-030-33894-7_6
15. Rouse, R.: Against the instrumentalization of empathy: immersive technologies and social change. In: Augmented and Mixed Reality for Communities, pp. 3–19. CRC Press (2021)
16. Barbara, J., Koenitz, H., Bakk, Á.K.: The ethics of virtual reality interactive digital narratives in cultural heritage. In: Mitchell, A., Vosmeer, M. (eds.) ICIDS 2021. LNCS, vol. 13138, pp. 288–292. Springer, Cham (2021). https://doi.org/10.1007/978-3-030-92300-6_27
17. Murray, J.: Not a film and not an empathy machine. Blog Immerse. news (2016)
18. Ricoeur, P.: Oneself as another. Translated by K. Blamey. University of Chicago Press. (1992). Originally published as Soi-même comme un autre. Paris: Éditions du Seuil (1990). ISBN 0-226-71328-8
19. Ricoeur, P.: Narrative identity. Philos. Today **35**(1), 73–81 (1991)

20. Ricoeur, P.: Time and Narrative, vol. 3 (1998). Translated by K. McLaughlin & D. Pellauer. University of Chicago Press, originally published as Temps et Récit, vol. 3. Paris: Éditions du Seuil (1985). ISBN 0-226-71335-0 (v. 3)
21. Crowley, P.: Paul Ricoeur: the concept of narrative identity, the trace of autobiography. Paragraph **26**(3), 1–12 (2003)
22. Gee, J.P.: Learning and Identity: What Does It Mean to Be a Half-Elf? (2007)
23. Wilt, J.A., Thomas, S., McAdams, D.P.: Authenticity and inauthenticity in narrative identity. Heliyon **5**(7), e02178 (2019)
24. Hallford, D.J., Mellor, D.: Development and validation of the awareness of narrative identity questionnaire (ANIQ). Assessment **24**(3), 399–413 (2017)
25. Stead, H.J.: 4 Carl Jung Theories Explained: Persona, Shadow, Anima/Animus, The Self, Personal Growth (2019). https://medium.com/personal-growth/4-carl-jung-theories-explained-persona-shadow-anima-animus-the-self-4ab6df8f7971
26. Jung, C.G.: The Archetypes and the Collective Unconscious, Collected Works, vol. 9. (1959). Trans. RFC Hull. New York: Princeton UP. (2014)
27. Jung, C.G.: Mysterium Coniunctionis, Collected Works, vol. 14. (1977). Trans. By RFC Hull (1989)
28. Turkle, S.: Constructions and reconstructions of self in virtual reality: playing in the MUDs. Mind Cult. Act. **1**(3), 158–167 (1994)
29. Bruner, J.: The narrative creation of self. In: The Handbook of Narrative and Psychotherapy: Practice, Theory, and Research, pp. 3–14 (2004)
30. Schlenker, B.R.: Self-identification: toward an integration of the private and public self. In: Baumeister, R.F. (ed.) Public Self and Private Self, pp. 21–62. Springer, New York (1986). https://doi.org/10.1007/978-1-4613-9564-5_2
31. Butler, J.: Precarious life: The powers of mourning and violence. Verso (2004)
32. Cohen, J.: Defining identification: a theoretical look at the identification of audiences with media characters. Mass Commun. Soc. **4**(3), 245–264 (2001)
33. Oatley, K.: A taxonomy of the emotions of literary response and a theory of identification in fictional narrative. Poetics **23**(1–2), 53–74 (1995)
34. Barbara, J.: Towards measuring consistency across transmedial narratives. In: Schoenau, H., Bruni, L.E., Louchart, S., Baceviciute, S. (eds.) ICIDS 2015. LNCS, vol. 9445, pp. 243–250. Springer, Cham (2015). https://doi.org/10.1007/978-3-319-27036-4_2
35. Busselle, R., Bilandzic, H.: Measuring narrative engagement. Media Psychol. **12**(4), 321–347 (2009)
36. Klimmt, C., Hefner, D., Vorderer, P., Roth, C., Blake, C.: Identification with video game characters as automatic shift of self-perceptions. Media Psychol. **13**(4), 323–338 (2010)
37. Higgins, E.T.: Self-discrepancy theory: what patterns of self-beliefs cause people to suffer? In: Advances in Experimental Social Psychology, vol. 22, pp. 93–136. Academic Press (1989)
38. Kampmann, B.: Using ludo-narrative dissonance in grand theft auto IV as pedagogical tool for ethical analysis. In: Liapis, A., Yannakakis, G.N., Gentile, M., Ninaus, M. (eds.) GALA 2019. LNCS, vol. 11899, pp. 3–12. Springer, Cham (2019). https://doi.org/10.1007/978-3-030-34350-7_1
39. Barker, M.J.: The lord of the rings and 'identification' a critical encounter. Eur. J. Commun. **20**(3), 353–378 (2005)
40. Shaw, A.: Rethinking game studies: a case study approach to video game play and identification. Crit. Stud. Media Commun. **30**(5), 347–361 (2013)
41. Kilteni, K., Groten, R., Slater, M.: The sense of embodiment in virtual reality. Presence Teleoper. Virt. Environ. **21**(4), 373–387 (2012)
42. Gonzales, A.L., Hancock, J.T.: Identity shift in computer-mediated environments. Media Psychol. **11**(2), 167–185 (2008)

43. Peña, J., Hill, D.: Examining identity shift effects in virtual reality. Cyberpsychol. Behav. Soc. Netw. **23**(10), 697–701 (2020)
44. Gupta, S., Tanenbaum, T.J., Muralikumar, M.D., Marathe, A.S.: Investigating roleplaying and identity transformation in a virtual reality narrative experience. In: Proceedings of the 2020 CHI Conference on Human Factors in Computing Systems, pp. 1–13 (2020)
45. Yee, N., Bailenson, J.: The Proteus effect: the effect of transformed self-representation on behavior. Hum. Commun. Res. **33**(3), 271–290 (2007)
46. Roth, C., van Nuenen, T., Koenitz, H.: Ludonarrative hermeneutics: a way out and the narrative paradox. In: Rouse, R., Koenitz, H., Haahr, M. (eds.) ICIDS 2018. LNCS, vol. 11318, pp. 93–106. Springer, Cham (2018). https://doi.org/10.1007/978-3-030-04028-4_7
47. Reyes Redondo, M.C.: Interactive fiction in cinematic virtual reality: epistemology, creation and evaluation. Ph.D. thesis at Universita' Degli Studi di Genova (2019). https://123dok.org/document/4zp76p0z-interactive-fiction-cinematic-virtual-reality-epistemology-creation-evaluation.html
48. Ermi, L.: Fundamental components of the gameplay experience: Analysing immersion (2005)
49. Hefner, D., Klimmt, C., Vorderer, P.: Identification with the player character as determinant of video game enjoyment. In: Ma, L., Rauterberg, M., Nakatsu, R. (eds.) ICEC 2007. LNCS, vol. 4740, pp. 39–48. Springer, Heidelberg (2007). https://doi.org/10.1007/978-3-540-74873-1_6
50. Mäyrä, F., Ermi, L.: Fundamental components of the gameplay experience. Digarec Ser. **6**, 88–115 (2011)
51. Lombard, M., Ditton, T.: At the heart of it all: the concept of presence. J. Comput.-Mediated Commun. **3**(2), JCMC321 (1997)
52. Horton, D., Richard Wohl, R.: Mass communication and para-social interaction: observations on intimacy at a distance. Psychiatry **19**(3), 215–229 (1956)
53. Brown, E., Cairns, P.: A grounded investigation of game immersion. In: CHI 2004 Extended Abstracts on Human Factors in Computing Systems, pp. 1297–1300 (2004)
54. Biocca, F., Levy, M.R.: Virtual reality as a communication system. In: Communication in the Age of Virtual Reality, pp. 15–31 (1995)
55. Slater, M.: Place illusion and plausibility can lead to realistic behaviour in immersive virtual environments. Philos. Trans. Royal Soc. Lond. Ser. B Biol. Sci. **364**(1535), 3549–3557 (2009). https://doi.org/10.1098/rstb.2009.0138
56. Sanchez-Vives, M., Slater, M.: From presence to consciousness through virtual reality. Nat. Rev. Neurosci. **6**, 332–339 (2005). https://doi.org/10.1038/nrn1651
57. Zahorik, P., Jenison, R.L.: Presence as being-in-the-world. Presence **7**(1), 78–89 (1998)
58. Grasse, K.M., et al.: Using self-determination theory to explore enjoyment of educational interactive narrative games: a case study of academical. Front. Virt. Real., 74 (2022)
59. Sylaiou, S., Mania, K., Karoulis, A., White, M.: Exploring the relationship between presence and enjoyment in a virtual museum. Int. J. Hum Comput Stud. **68**(5), 243–253 (2010)
60. Tussyadiah, I.P., Wang, D., Jung, T.H., Tom Dieck, M.C.: Virtual reality, presence, and attitude change: empirical evidence from tourism. Tour. Manage. **66**, 140–154 (2018)
61. Yang, T., Lai, I.K.W., Fan, Z.B., Mo, Q.M.: The impact of a 360 virtual tour on the reduction of psychological stress caused by COVID-19. Technol. Soc. **64**, 101514 (2021)
62. Turkay, S., Kinzer, C.K.: The effects of avatar-based customization on player identification. In: Gamification: Concepts, Methodologies, Tools, and Applications, pp. 247–272. IGI Global (2015)
63. Oppenheim, D., Okita, R.L.: The book of distance: personal storytelling in VR. In: ACM SIGGRAPH 2020 Immersive Pavilion, pp. 1–2 (2020)
64. Larsen, M.: Virtual sidekick: second-person POV in narrative VR. J. Screenwriting **9**, 73–83 (2018). https://doi.org/10.1386/josc.9.1.73_1
65. Ryan, M.L.: Fiction, non-factuals, and the principle of minimal departure. Poetics **9**(4), 403–422 (1980)

The Impacts of Design Elements in Interactive Storytelling in VR on Emotion, Mood, and Self-reflection

Austin Wolfe[✉], Sandy Louchart, and Brian Loranger

Glasgow School of Art, Glasgow G3 6RQ, UK
a.wolfe1@student.gsa.ac.uk, {S.Louchart,B.Loranger}@gsa.ac.uk

Abstract. Storytelling entertains, educates, and inspires people of all ages and a compelling story has the power to motivate, elicit emotions, behavioural change, and inspire self-reflection. Interactive Digital Narratives (IDN) offer, arguably, a greater potential for impact on their audience due to the participative nature of interaction whilst storytelling in Virtual Reality (VR), benefits from high levels of immersion. This work focuses on the design and development of compelling narrative elements towards a non-narrated and unguided VR experience aimed at portraying and evoking emotions, moods, and self-reflection. We explore how the combined elements of light, colour, shape and music can play a role in creating compelling stories and influence users within an immersive VR experience. Finally, this article presents an extensive study of relevant literature, the design of an impactful immersive VR narrative experience and an exploratory practice-based study.

Keywords: Immersive Storytelling · Interactive Storytelling · Self-Reflection

1 Introduction

From childhood to adulthood, stories are part of everyday life and represent an important way to connect and influence with any audience whether they are told, written or shown. "Stories have a transformative power to allow us to see the world in a different way than we do if we just encounter it on our own. Stories are an entry point to understanding a different experience of the world" [1]. It gives people the opportunity to learn and it can shape, strengthen or question their opinions and values. When a story captures a person's attention and captivates them, they are more likely to absorb the message and meaning. Similarly, if a person can experience a world in the way others might perceive it, emotions such as empathy or fear can be elicited [1].

Like traditional storytelling, virtual reality has played a pivotal role in influencing and impacting people's lives through its immersive nature. Immersion is the perception of a physical presence in a non-physical world. In contrast to traditional storytelling, where the recipient is the passive witness of the characters, VR allows the user to become a character. In essence, VR transforms the storytelling experience through having a presence in the world, and by becoming part of the narrative environment, VR. This

M. Vosmeer and L. Holloway-Attaway (Eds.): ICIDS 2022, LNCS 13762, pp. 616–633, 2022.
https://doi.org/10.1007/978-3-031-22298-6_40

immersive narrative experience has the potential to put across powerful messages and connect an audience emotionally as illustrated in Nonny de la Peña's work such as Hunger in Los Angeles [2] which invites the participant to experience poverty while waiting in line at a food bank, or Across the Line [3], a production focused on pro-choice and abortion legal rights. Additionally, Aardman Animations' We Wait follows a Syrian family seeking asylum in Greece, and the hopes and fears that follow [4]. VR storytelling projects such as the ones presented above have the potential to trigger strong emotional reactions from their audience and can connect people visually and emotionally in ways that other media cannot. As such, we argue that there is growing potential for impactful VR production targeted at emotional well-being and self-reflection interventions.

Emotional well-being is inextricably linked to mental health and a positive emotional well-being can help people make better decisions, be optimistic, be more productive, and influence physical health [5]. Self-reflection, on the other hand, is the ability to think about one's own feelings and behaviours and the reasons behind them. Engaging in practices that exercise these abilities lead to many benefits, including increased compassion, self-acceptance, and self-confidence, as well as improving the quality of life and the reduction of stress-related health disorders [6].

The aim of this research is to investigate the potential of unguided immersive storytelling on emotional wellbeing and self-reflection. Against this background, we pro-pose to provide a critical review of previous implementations of immersive storytelling for emotional and behavioural therapies, investigate how immersive storytelling can produce emotional and psychological outcomes and identify key aspects of compelling storytelling towards the development and assessment of an immersive narrative VR experience (The Journey). Whilst providing a practical illustration through which to explore participants' experiences, we hope this work can provide a foundation onto which future immersive stories can build upon towards facilitating better emotional and behavioural therapies.

2   Affect and Storytelling

This section focuses on emotional regulation, self-reflection, general well-being, and mindfulness through storytelling. In particular, the emotional outcomes and impacts on mindfulness and the self in non-goal-oriented, story-based virtual environments. Our aim is twofold and consists in exploring emotional and physiological outcomes associated with immersive experiences (i.e. presence, avatars) and investigating the emotional impacts of immersion in natural environments, and the narrative elements supporting emotional connection and self-reflection. Immersive and otherwise participatory storytelling in a virtual environment offers not only the opportunity to share a story, but also to support meditation [7] and to improve understanding of empathetic responses to stimuli [8]. Studies suggest that even casual video games have had positive emotional influences, including improved perceived mood and lowering stress [9]. In view of this knowledge, it is reasonable to continue to use these interdisciplinary effects of virtual reality beyond the entertainment industry. If casual games have the ability to positively influence social and emotional well-being, then it is reasonable that targeted, serious virtual environments could have the same, if not greater, impact.

2.1 Emotional Responses in Immersive Environments

Immersion in an alternative, but similar and understandable world, which allows for free exploration and opportunity for meaningful problem solving and interaction, often has several positive social and emotional effects. Much research on mood and social emotional well-being focuses on casual video games (CVG) and massively multiplayer online role-playing games (MMORPG). However, these research results are equally applicable to both virtual and serious gaming. Consider the following example:

Russoniello, O'Brien, and Parks [9] set out to determine if casual video games had an impact on players' mood outside of the game, specifically positive perceived mood and/or a decrease in stress. 134 participants were randomly assigned to a control group or to the game. Together with brainwave and heart rate data, all participants completed the Profile of Mood States [10] before and after the study to determine whether mood changes occurred before and after the tasks. Participants were given a choice of three CVGs to play, while the control group completed internet searches on a health topic. "The POMS scores on Total Mood Disturbance significantly changed for all three games, supporting the theory that while there were effects on brain wave activity in different parts of the brain, the end result was improved perceived mood" [9]. Moreover, measuring empathetic responses to virtual avatars [8] and animals [7] deepen our understanding of what empathetic responses are, on a physiological level, but also about the dynamic nature of self-awareness and im-portance of self-reflection and personal growth.

2.2 Physiological Connection and Presence

Given a simple virtual scenario of a hand at a desk, researchers Fusaro, Tieri, and Aglioti [8] set out to compare the "behavioural and physiological reactivity of participants who observed pain and pleasure stimuli delivered to the body of an embodied avatar when viewed from an egocentric perspective [8]. Participants in the study, were seated at a desk in an unadorned room with their right hand on the desk to align with their avatars'. Participants were then told that their avatar's hand would experience three different types of stimuli from a first and the third-person perspective. Researchers fitted the participants with Oculus sets and electrode systems to monitor the heart rate (ECG) and skin conductance responses (SCR). The stimuli in the virtu-al environment used were needle penetration, a caress from another hand, and a ball gently touching. Respectively, this translated to pain, pleasure and neutral stimuli. The scene was devoid of any facial cues, and participants observed only the hands on the desk. After each stimulus, participants were asked to respond with the visual analog scale 0–100 for illusory ownership, intensity, and (un)pleasantness. Illusory ownership was found higher in first rather than third person perspectives. Ownership also gained a marginal increase in relation to the pain stimuli vs the pleasure.

The results of possession and presence were more significant between the first and third perspectives, but the physiological responses were only marginally different, possibly due to variations in personal perspective and cultural background about physical touch. Further clarity about the pleasure stimulus, and perhaps a more diverse stimulus, is needed to assess whether pain really has a greater empathetic re-sponse than pleasure.

Additional research could also examine response variations in various virtual environments, especially from the first person within a complete environment in which the player has little to no control over the scenarios. If participants have the ability to empathize with a disembodied hand on a desk without any other context, then it is reasonable to conclude that a deeper empathetic response and potentially more connected presence would be experienced in a saturated, precisely created environment.

2.3 Compassion Based Interventions

Compassion-based interventions (CBIs) can be effective for increasing empathy and compassion, and reducing stress, anxiety, and depression [11]. With this background in mind, researchers Cebolla et al. [11] compared the efficacy of immersive technologies versus casual meditation systems using modified virtual reality and casual meditation procedures with regard to self-compassion. Notably, the VR experience also included a post meditation body-swap experience that 'allows participants to see themselves from a third perspective and have the illusion of touching themselves from outside' [11]. The 16 participants in the study were assigned randomly to either the usual meditation (CAU) or Meditation the Machine to Be Another (TMTBA-VR). Both groups used the same audio guidance for either medication method. The Cebolla et al. [11] study found that while there was some variance in outcome, both groups showed similar and impactful increases in positive self-image. Prior to the Cebolla et al. [11] study, Falconer et al. [12] looked deeper into the concept of self-compassion in VR. This was achieved comparing first and third person perspectives in participatory virtual reality. As with the Cebolla et al. Study [11], participants were immersed in a simple room visually matching their actual surroundings. Recordings of head movement and physiological responses were taken during the trial. First, they proceeded through a scenario of a crying child to elicit compassion responses in a third person view, and then were immersed in the story again in first person as the child. The key finding from the Falconer study was that VR had an additional effect of positively increasing self-compassion in naturally self-critical individuals [12].

2.4 Using Music, Colour, Shape and Light in Design to Affect

While the potential of influence of emotional responses and mood can be deduced from the previously mentioned studies, the environment of the experience can play a significant role in aiding this, particularly on the concepts of music, color, shape and light.

The Musical Mood Induction Procedure (MMIP) has been used in music research for over thirty years [13]. Overall, research shows that music does have an impact on emotion, but due to variation in self-reporting and other extrinsic factors it is difficult to know with certainty what is truly altered and what is situational. Therefore, the use of technology has been implemented by the use of functional magnetic resonance imaging (fMRI) and positron emission tomography (PET). A review of current studies in music showed that evoked emotions, fMRI and PET based studies identified areas of the brain activated during specific songs or sounds. Interestingly, fMRI shows emotional response as energy, while PET shows the same response on a molecular level. Regardless of the music sampled, participants showed autonomic response [14]. Västfjäll [13] mapped variations of musical elements and their likely emotional responses. Slow tempo produces seriousness, sadness, anxiety and even serenity, while a higher tempo can evoke humour, happiness or excitement. Low pitches tend to evoke seriousness, sadness and fear, while medium and higher pitches evoke serenity, humour, happiness and excitement. [13, 14]. With this knowledge in mind, the creators of serious games and immersive experiences will be better able to refine their musical choices to induce certain emotional responses in the average player.

As with music, creators of impactful serious games and immersive realities must also make use of colour theory to create the intended ambiance of a scene or story. Anecdotally, colour matters, but Wilms and Oberfeld [15] explored the physiological responses to colour, hue and saturation along with perceived mood. 62 participants viewed 27 chromatic colours and 3 achromatic colours for 30 s each and rat-ed their emotional state while skin conductance and heart rate were measured continuously. "The emotion ratings showed that saturated and bright colours were associated with higher arousal. The hue also had a significant effect on arousal, which increased from blue and green to red." [15]. For creators, the impact of this knowledge is clear. In order to create scenes and serious games with high emotional impact, colour saturation and hue are key.

Another crucial element is shape. Shape has long been used in art to convey emotions and personalities in stories. Regarding the psychology of shape, Arnhiem [16] suggested that shapes are simplified into three categories:

- Circle: innocence, youth, energy, femininity
- Square: maturity, stability, balance, stubbornness
- Triangle: aggression, masculinity, force

Psychologically, people associate with these shapes and their corresponding cocepts due to real-life experience and the sense of touch. Through touch, people visually assess the characteristics of objects based on experience (angular = sharp = harmful). These shapes can be used to influence an individual's perception of certain elements in a VR environment, and in extension affect their mood through that per-ception.

Finally, the use of light is an invaluable asset in VR. Light can influence the psychophysical wellbeing of an individual as it affects their perception of the world [17]. According to Tomassoni [17] light may stimulate perception through type and range of exposure and its colours can induce specific emotional states or behaviour. This stimulus is able to "excite, move, impress, communicate, heal and generate wellness, and create a sense of harmony and syntony." The strategic layout and modulation of lighting by VR designers may influence the perceiver's mood, creating a sense of calm and rest, or add mystery and suspense.

Practices of mindfulness and self-reflection are well-known to have positive effects and change on an individual's well-being and the above studies indicate that immersive experiences are able to connect people visually and emotionally in a way that TV, books and other forms of entertainment may not. Moreover, the creation of an immersive natural world inevitably leads to a deeper emotional response; howev-er, eliciting this response requires a degree of openness and awareness on the part of the participant. In other words, emotions are influenced by past emotional states or pre-existing individual characteristics, dispositions and context factors [18, 19].

3 The Journey and Evaluation

3.1 The Virtual Reality Experience

Story plays a strong role in the emotional connection and involvement of people in all of the media in which it is represented. It was therefore an integral part of creating the immersive experience. Therefore, a storyboard was used to capture the overall movement of the scenes as well as base colours, and to set written guidelines for the story sequence. For this project (see Fig. 3), our approach was oriented more towards a cinematic quality than one of pure game play and we developed an immersive virtual reality in Unreal [20], based on the composition of marine elements from reference images of ocean ecosystems. The models used were selected on a scientific basis of animals that co-existed in nature, interacted regularly with each other, and were native to specific locations in the Pacific [21]. The project consisted of a total of seven scenes. The scenes were conceptualized in order to elicit different emotions, namely, scene 1 (Joyful), scene 2 (Worry), scene 3 (Sad), scene 4 (Anxious), scene 5 (Mysterious), scene 6 (Calm) and scene 7 (Relief). Each scene ranged from a minimum of 1:30 min to 2:30 min, depending on the music/animation involved. Each scene flowed into the next in a continuous manner, separated by a 3 s fade to black to mark the scene change. To influence the targeted emotions/moods of each scene, the concepts of music, color, shape and light were implemented.

The story structure of each scene attempted to follow these emotions as well. In scene 1(joyful) the user observed a playful mother whale and calf swimming together and around the user. Scene 2 (worry) showed a murkier scene, with the mother and calf swimming higher overhead. In this scene a fishing boat comes along and captures the mother with the calf swimming and calling after it. Scene 3 (sad) has the calf swimming up to the user with a fin tangled in rope that the user must remove. In scene 4 (anxious) the calf encounters and is chased by several sharks, swimming tightly around the user. In Scene 5 (mysterious) the user floats along with the calf through a dark cave with glowing corals and fish. Scene 6 (calm) has the user again moving with the whale but joined with a large array of slow-moving sea turtles. Finally, scene 7 (relief) shows the calf finding and joining another pod of whales.

Using the aforementioned research on the influence of music, the animation, story, and movement of each scene were all created to revolve around the music. It needed to enhance and, in some instances, cause the change of mood as the story progressed. Therefore, the tempo, volume, rhythm, and harmony were carefully chosen for each scene [13, 14]. To demonstrate, music was catorgorised as having tempo range (high, medium, low), a pitch range (high, medium, low), a volume range (high, medium, low), and a rhythm range (fast, medium, slow) Thus, the music was applied in the following manner (Table 1):

Likewise, ambient whale sounds played a pivotal role. Raw whale audio vocalisations were added through the story to convey emotional aspects of the whales. For instance, the 2nd scene included a whale crying out for its mother to evoke worry, while the final scene includes the inviting sounds of a pod of whales, calling out and welcoming the young calf in to join them to evoke the emotion of relief.

Table 1. Scene music

Scene	Tempo	Pitch	Volume	Rhythm
Joyful	High	High	High	Fast
Worry	Low	Low	Medium	Medium
Sad	Low	Low	Medium	Slow
Anxious	High	High	High	Fast
Mysterious	Low	Medium	Medium	Medium
Calm	Low	Medium	Medium	Slow
Relief	High	Medium	Medium	Medium

As mentioned previously, colour is a powerful tool that can be used to influence mood and emotions. Consequently, the psychology of colour was carefully applied throughout the project and was at the forefront of the design process. Since each scene was broken down into a target emotional response, colour was added according to the mood. To give an example, the first scene was meant to have a jovial, energetic ambience, therefore oranges and yellows were used in more abundance as these colours tend to elicit feelings of enthusiasm and excitement. Conversely, the third scene was designed with a solemn and lonely atmosphere, and as a result, deep blues and desaturated colours were used instead [22].

Light and fog were implemented per scene to fit the corresponding targeted moods. An illustration of this would be the second scene in the story. This scene was a pivotal point in the story, one that involves tragedy and loss. Hence, there is a greater amount of fog and murkiness, framing the shapes in the distance to appear unsettling and slighting out of focus. Additionally, the sunlight did not shine as brightly through the surface of the water as it had in the previous scene. This in turn helped create a general sense of uneasiness and foreboding.

For the table below, *Colour* notes the dominate colour; *Saturation* notes the intensity of the saturation of the colour, and *Visibility* documents the clarity in which the scene elements were visible in the scene (Fig. 1).

Finally, shape theory was also applied to the environment of the experience. This was achieved by adding softer, rounder elements (such as rocks and coral) in the beginning scenes, and as the mood and narrative became more tense, harsher, sharper elements were introduced to surround the viewer (Table 3).

3.2 Measurements Protocol

After the completion of the project, a study was conducted using self-reporting measures. For each participant, these questionnaires were used and collected via an online link. These were applied in two phases: the baseline and the reflection.

For the baseline phase, the questionnaires were implemented before the playthrough of the experience to establish their natural baselines. These questionnaires consisted of

Table 2. Scene colour

Scene	Colour	Saturation	Visibility
Joyful	Oranges and yellows	Full	Clear
Worry	Blues	Low	Low
Sad	Blues and greys	Low	Medium
Anxious	Reds	Full	Clear
Mysterious	Blues, purples, oranges	Full	Medium
Calm	Greens and blues	Medium	Medium
Relief	Blues, yellows, oranges	Medium	Clear

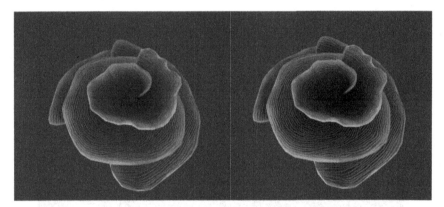

Fig. 1. Colour change: Joyful (left); Sad (right)

Table 3. Scene shape

Scene	Primary shapes	Texture
Joyful	Round	Mixture soft/rough
Worry	Mixture of round and complicated, angular	Rough/sharp
Sad	Round	Soft
Anxious	Complicated, angular	Rough/sharp
Mysterious	Round	Rough
Calm	Round	Soft
Relief	Mixture of round and complicated, angular	Mixture soft/rough

Fig. 2. Round soft shape Vs complicated/angular sharp shape

Fig. 3. A screenshot of the Immersive VR Narrative "The Journey" for scene 3. The project is available for download at the following location (https://drive.google.com/file/d/12az6FCSVJtc lQ0fQUqLRvixuFL6IR41o/view?usp=sharing).

a mood evaluation (MQ), the Positive and Negative Affect Schedule (PANAS), and the modified Five Factor Mindfulness Scale (FFMQ-15).

The (MQ) required participants to rate how they feel at this moment in time on a 7-point Likert scale (where 1 = not at all to 7 = extremely), with reference to each of the moods measuring Happiness, Sadness, Anger, Surprise, Disgust, Anxiety, and Quietness. The (PANAS) was composed of a list of 20 adjectives used to describe 10 positive emotions (which compose the global Positive Affect Score) and 10 negative emotions (which compose the global Negative Affect Score). Respondents are required to indicate the extent they experience the emotions included on the schedule "in the past week" on a five-point scale (where 1 = very slightly or not at all, to 5 = extremely). The (FFMQ-15) is the short form of the 39-item FFMQ [23]. It includes the same five facets at the long form: Observing, Describing, Acting with Awareness, Non-Judging of inner experience, and Non-Reactivity to inner experience. This measure is composed of a list of 15 statements used to describe the participants. Respondents are required to indicate the extent the statement is true to themselves on a five-point scale (where 1 = Never, or very rarely, to 5 = Very often or always true).

For the reflection phase, participants completed questionnaires after the completion of the VR experience. During this phase, these questionnaires were applied per each scene to assess each targeted emotion. These were the (MQ), (PANAS), emotional storytelling questions (ESQ), and the modified Slater-Usoh Steed Questionnaire (SUS-3). The (ESQ) rates how connected participants felt to the story at the moment of the scene on a 5-point scale (where 1 = not at all to 5 = extremely), with reference to targeted responses per each scene. Participants were asked three scene specific questions pertaining to their emotional connection. The (SUS-3) measures presence on a 7-point Likert scale asked the questions per each scene:

Table 4. VR (SUS-3) Questionnaire.

SUS1	"To what extent were there times during the experience when the environment was reality for you?"
SUS2	"Rate your sense of being in the specific environment?"
SUS3	"During the time of the experience, which was the strongest on the whole, your sense of being in the environment, or of being elsewhere?"

4   Results and Discussion

4.1   Experiment

Ten virtual reality equipment owners took part in the experiment. Participants did not receive any payment or credit for their collaboration and were all volunteers. All users of the application experienced the VR experiment in their own homes and without supervision. Participant demographics consisted of persons between the ages of 20 to 50, with normal or corrected vision and hearing. Although owners of the equipment, participants had little experience of VR or other VR applications. There was no limit in regard to geographical location of this study, as it was conducted online. Therefore, the participants ranged from locations in the US to areas in England, Scotland and Sweden.

The virtual program was run on the participants' home headset and personal computer. The headset was required to be an Oculus, either the Rift, Rift S, or the Quest, with the latter requiring Oculus Link. The PC to operate the program was expected to have a graphics card equivalent to a GeForce Nvidia 1060 or similar compatible card, as well as at least one controller. As the physical space was unable to be regulated, each participant was advised to have a standing room area of at least 1.5 m by 1.5 m. The experiment was then divided into three main phases: baseline, navigation, and reflection. This was due to Covid restrictions, as at the time in person studies were unable to be conducted. The study consisted of four phases: Baseline, Navigation, Reflection, and Analysis.

Baseline phase. For the first phase, participants were invited to complete the MQ, PANAS, and FFMQ-15 questionnaires to assess their baseline emotional and mindfulness state. It is important to note that the administration of the FFMQ-15 was only administered in this phase. This measurement was meant as an indicator for the user's proclivity towards mindfulness, so that it may be assessed for the accuracy of their ability to recall their emotions/moods upon the completion of the program. These questionnaires were completed online via a provided link to each participant. At the end of the questionnaires, participants were provided with one link to download the project and a second link providing the final set of questionnaires to be completed after the VR program.

Navigation phase. Once the participants had downloaded the program, it was then played through to its entirety. Navigation for the user in each scene was open to their available standing room and lasted about 2 min per scene, with the user having little influence on the progression of the story. At the end of the seventh scene, the credits rolled, and provided a passcode for the user. This passcode was then used to access the post questionnaires. This was made to ensure that the participants fully completed the program before being able to access and answer the final survey.

Reflection phase. After the completion of the VR experience, participants returned to the link previously provided in the baseline phase to complete the final set of questionnaires. The MQ, PANAS, ESQ, and SUS-3 were provided per each of the seven scenes in order to assess their emotional state, presence, and emotional story connection elicited by each environment. Each scene was marked with a description and thumbnail of a screenshot per scene to assist users in their recollection of each scene, as each scene was markedly different.

Table 5. Scene descriptions

Scene	Description
Joyful	Intro scene with mother and calf
Worry	Fishing boat
Sad	User must grab the rope off the calf
Anxious	Sharks swimming around you
Mysterious	The glowing cave
Calm	Swimming with sea turtles
Relief	Final scene with multiple whales swimming

Analysis. The analysis began with scoring calculations for the standard questionnaires to assess the effectiveness of virtual environments in evoking emotions. The PANAS, MQ, SUS-3, and ESQ were all scored with direct scoring, and the FFMQ-15 with a combination of direct and reverse scoring. This resulted in a mean (M) and a standard deviation (SD) based on sample size (Fig. 4).

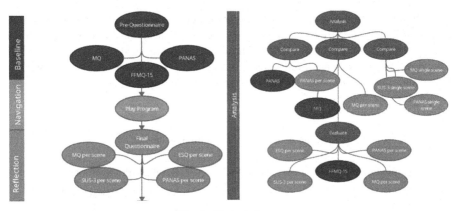

Fig. 4. Project phases

4.2 Results

A comparison was carried out to explore the changes of the mood states (PANAS and MQ) before (baseline) and after the first scene of the application. As the baseline PANAS measured the participants' mood over the past week compared to at this moment of the first scene, the data showed different significant changes. The first scene indicated a reduction in the positive affect and the negative affect schedules (see Table 2). The initial intention behind using the in the last week as opposed to at this moment was to get an indication of the total range of moods from the participants. In contrast, the MQ was measured both as at this moment before and after the first scene. Consequently, it showed an increase/decrease as expected. The scene significantly increased happiness and surprise, while reducing sadness and anxiety (see Table 6).

Table 6. Comparison of mood states.

PANAS	Baseline (Pre-questions)	Scene 1 (Joyful)
Positive affect	M = 33.8/SD = (1.16)	M = 28.8/SD = (1.33)
Negative affect	M = 18.8/SD = (1.21)	M = 11.1/SD = (.35)
Mood (MQ)		
Happiness	M = 4.8/SD = (1.03)	M = 5.7/SD = (1.25)
Sadness	M = 1.6/SD = (.69)	M = 1/SD = (0)
Anger	M = 1.1/SD = (.32)	M = 1.2/SD = (.63)
Surprise	M = 1.6/SD = (1.07)	M = 2.8/SD = (1.87)
Disgust	M = 1.1/SD = (.32)	M = 1.2/SD = (.63)
Anxiety	M = 3/SD = (1.6)	M = 1.3/SD = (.67)
Quietness	M = 3.9/SD = (2.56)	M = 3.3/SD = (2.31)

In addition, the FFMQ-15 was analysed to determine a general mindfulness/self-reflection factor of the participants before the experience. This was divided into its five factors and assessed accordingly. These subscales are rated with a range of 3–15. The highest score was achieved with a mean (M) of 11.9 in Observing, followed by Describing (11.1). The lowest levels were noted in Acting with Awareness (9.18) and Non-Reactivity (9.00) (see Table 7).

Table 7. Baseline of mindfulness factors.

Five facet mindfulness questionnaire (FFMQ-15)	Baseline (Pre-questions)
Observing	M = 11.9 (3.93)/SD = (1.05)
Describing	M = 11.1 (3.70)/SD = (.98)
Acting with awareness	M = 9.18 (3.06)/SD = (1.14)
Non-judging	M = 10.90 (3.63)/SD = (.92)
Non-reactivity	M = 9.00 (3.00)/SD = (1.08)

Following the preliminary survey, separate analyses of mood and emotion were carried out from each of the seven scenes.

First, the PANAS was considered across all seven scenes. The positive affect schedule showed some variation through all scenes, with the lowest recorded at 21.4 and the highest at 28.7. In contrast, the negative affect schedule showed a significant difference between the lowest (11.0) and the highest (22.9). As expected, scene 6 (calm) and 7 (relief) lead the highest levels on the positive affect schedule, (28.4) and (28.7) respectively. Similarly, scenes 2 (worry), 3 (sad), and 4 (anxious) marked the highest increases on the negative schedule at 22.9, 18.9, and 22.1 (see Table 4). It is also noted that the highest levels all exceed the previously recorded baseline at 18.8 (see Table 2).

Table 8. Difference PANAS across 7 scenes.

PANAS	Scene 1 (Joyful)	Scene 2 (Worry)	Scene 3 (Sad)	Scene 4 (Anxious)	Scene 5 (Mysterious)	Scene 6 (Calm)	Scene 7 (Relief)
Positive affect	M = 28.8 SD = (1.33)	M = 21.6 SD = (1.35)	M = 23.9 SD = (1.40)	M = 21.4 SD = (1.42)	M = 27.4 SD = (1.44)	M = 28.4 SD = (1.56)	M = 28.7 SD = (1.51)
Negative affect	M = 11.1 SD = (.35)	M = 22.9 SD = (1.37)	M = 18.9 SD = (1.25)	M = 22.1 SD = (1.45)	M = 11.5 SD = (.61)	M = 11.0 SD = (.50)	M = 11.1 SD = (.39)

Next the mood questions (MQ) were evaluated across all scenes. As presumed, happiness was recorded at its highest at 6.1 in scenes 1 (joyful), 5 (mysterious), 6 (calm), and 7 (relief). Scenes 2 (worry), 3 (sad), and 4 (anxious) marked a significant decrease in happiness at 1.7, 2.3, and 1.7. Similarly, sadness markedly increased for scenes 2, and 3, at 5.1 and 5.9, with a reduction in scenes 1 (1) and 6(1). Anger and surprise also have notable increases in scenes 2 and 3, the highest being in scene 2 with anger at 3.5 and surprise at 4. Finally, anxiety increased in scenes 2, 3, 4 at 4.4, 3, and 5 respectively. Interestingly, quietness varied from 2.7 to 5 with no discernible pattern, and with the largest standard deviations compared to all other moods (see Table 5) (Table 9).

Table 9. Difference of mood states across 7 scenes.

Mood (MQ)	Scene 1 (Joyful)	Scene 2 (Worry)	Scene 3 (Sad)	Scene 4 (Anxious)	Scene 5 (Mysterious)	Scene 6 (Calm)	Scene 7 (Relief)
Happiness	M = 5.7 SD = (1.25)	M = 1.7 SD = (1.56)	M = 2.3 SD = (2.06)	M = 1.7 SD = (1.25)	M = 5 SD = (1.69)	M = 5.6 SD = (1.57)	M = 6.1 SD = (1.1)
Sadness	M = 1 SD = (0)	M = 5.1 SD = (2.08)	M = 5.9 SD = (1.1)	M = 2.2 SD = (1.75)	M = 1.2 SD = (.42)	M = 1 SD = (0)	M = 1.3 SD = (.94)
Anger	M = 1.2 SD = (.63)	M = 3.5 SD = (2.41)	M = 3.2 SD = (1.81)	M = 2.2 SD = (2.29)	M = 1 SD = (0)	M = 1 SD = (0)	M = 1.3 SD = (.94)
Surprise	M = 2.8 SD = (1.87)	M = 4 SD = (1.33)	M = 3 SD = (2.21)	M = 2.8 SD = (1.75)	M = 1.8 SD = (1.31)	M = 2.4 SD = 1.16	M = 1.9 SD = (1.28)
Disgust	M = 1.2 SD = (.63)	M = 2.7 SD = (2.06)	M = 1.6 SD = (.96)	M = 1.5 SD = (.97)	M = 1 SD = (0)	M = 1 SD = (0)	M = 1 SD = (0)
Anxiety	M = 1.3 SD = (.67)	M = 4.4 SD = (2.17)	M = 3 SD = (1.76)	M = 5 SD = (2.4)	M = 1.5 SD = (1.26)	M = 1 SD = (0)	M = 1.4 SD = (.96)
Quietness	M = 3.3 SD = (2.31)	M = 2.9 SD = (2.18)	M = 4 SD = (2.0)	M = 2.7 SD = (2.49)	M = 5 SD = (2.31)	M = 4.9 SD = (1.72)	M = 3.5 SD = (2.54)

Lastly, results gathered to test emotional connections were assessed. On the 5-point Likert scale, all scores remained above 3 during all scenes. Interestingly, there was an unexpected drop in emotional connection during scene 2 (worry), at the lowest recorded (3.43), as well as recording the largest standard deviation. However, as expected, it increased to 4.56 in scene 3 and recorded highest in scene 5 at 4.83 (see Table 6 and Fig. 2) (Table 10).

Table 10. Emotional story connections – emotional story questions (ESQ).

	Scene 1 (Joyful)	Scene 2 (Worry)	Scene 3 (Sad)	Scene 4 (Anxious)	Scene 5 (Mysterious)	Scene 6 (Calm)	Scene 7 (Relief)
ESQ	M = 4.2 SD = (.92)	M = 3.43 SD = (1.65)	M = 4.56 SD = (.81)	M = 4.1 SD = (1.49)	M = 4.83 SD = (.87)	M = 4.63 SD = (.76)	M = 4.63 SD = (.61)

After finding that the scenes in the story were able to induce the expected mood states and emotion, the association between presence and emotion was investigated. The data (see Table 7) showed a constant level of presence above 5.6 on the 7-point Likert scale. Furthermore, the level of presence was highest in scene 6 (calm) at 6.36 (Table 11).

To better investigate the possible relationship between emotion and presence, two scenes between the presence level (SUS-3) and the PANAS and MQ were analysed (see Table 8). These scenes were scene 6 and scene 2, which had the highest and lowest values of presence respectively. Scene 6 (calm) recorded the 2nd highest level on the

Table 11. Presence level between 7 scenes

	Scene 1 (Joyful)	Scene 2 (Worry)	Scene 3 (Sad)	Scene 4 (Anxious)	Scene 5 (Mysterious)	Scene 6 (Calm)	Scene 7 (Relief)
SUS (Presence)	M = 5.9 SD = (1.03)	M = 5.6 SD = (1.27)	M = 6 SD = (1.31)	M = 6.06 SD = (1.14)	M = 6.03 SD = (1.51)	M = 6.36 SD = (1.24)	M = 6.16 SD = (.91)

positive affect schedule (28.4) and the lowest level on the negative affect schedule (11.0). Furthermore, scene 6 indicated the 2nd highest level of quietness (4.9) and the 3rd highest of happiness (5.6). In contrast scene 2 (Worry) with a presence of (5.6) indicated the 2nd lowest on the positive affect schedule (21.6) and the highest on the negative (22.9). In addition, it had the lowest level of happiness (1.7), the highest level of anger (3.5), disgust (2.7), anxiety (4.4) and surprise (4), with the second highest degree of sadness (5.1) (Table 12).

Table 12. Comparison of presence and mood

PANAS	Scene 2 (Worry)	Scene 6 (Calm)
Positive affect	M = 21.6 SD = (1.35)	M = 28.4 SD = (1.56)
Negative affect	M = 22.9 SD = (1.37)	M = 11.0 SD = (.50)
Mood (MQ)		
Happiness	M = 1.7 SD = (1.56)	M = 5.6 SD = (1.57)
Sadness	M = 5.1 SD = (2.08)	M = 1 SD = (0)
Anger	M = 3.5 SD = (2.41)	M = 1 SD = (0)
Surprise	M = 4 SD = (1.33)	M = 2.4 SD = 1.16
Disgust	M = 2.7 SD = (2.06)	M = 1 SD = (0)
Anxiety	M = 4.4 SD = (2.17)	M = 1 SD = (0)
Quietness	M = 2.9 SD = (2.18)	M = 4.9 SD = (1.72)
SUS (Presence)	M = 5.6 SD = (1.27)	M = 6.36 SD = (1.24)

5 Conclusion

The driving force of this project was the ability to create an immersive story in VR that would effectively portray emotions and induce emotional responses. This endeavour was undertaken by the careful review of storytelling elements, as well as the analysis of relevant immersive models on mindfulness, self-reflection, and emotional impact. While the development of the experience took considerable time to implement, the data recorded suggests a successful execution. The values regarding presence (SUS-3) showed a consistently high rate across all scenes, indicating a high degree of immersion. Furthermore, the ESQ gross values showed an above average emotional connection to the specifics in each scene, as well as the individually evaluated values.

Likewise, as recorded in the results, the targeted MQ followed a distinct pattern across all scenes, with the values indicating the expected targeted emotions for each scene. The exception to this was the quietness value of the MQ. Dissimilar to the other factors, quietness did not have a discernible pattern, and had a larger standard deviation. This may be due to different interpretations of the word. Whereas happiness and sadness are easy to identify with, it is possible that quietness is too complex to connect with, (especially across cultures) suggesting the need to change the word used. If, for instance, the word had been changed to calmness, based on the other MQ values, it would have been expected to have a more recognisable pattern.

Additionally, the PANAS was significantly successful in showing positive values in the scenes deemed to have positive emotions, and negative values in the scenes with negative emotions, so much so that the negative values outweighed the baseline values of participants for the past week. To surmise, the creation of an immersive VR story that portrays and induces emotions is deemed as successful by this study.

The self-reflection after the experience does not have a measured outcome in this study. The use of the FFMQ-15 before the experience set out an overall value of mindfulness and self-reflection values. On average, the participants were in the above average to high range on this scale. However, the success of self-reflection is evident based on the success of the other data recorded after the experience. Participants were required to experience all seven scenes before filling out the final questionnaire. Therefore, participants had to critically reflect on each scene in terms of their emotions, moods and presence, after the entire experience. Since the recorded data followed the projected result, one can assume that the experience was successful in depicting and evoking emotions. Thus, if the experience in this aspect was meaningful enough for the user to remember and record its effects, one can infer that this high degree of impact corresponds to a high degree of self-reflection.

In addition, based on the expected results of the questionnaire, it was concluded that the combined narrative elements in VR (colour, shape, light and music) could success-fully evoke and represent emotions. The literature identified several elements that create a compelling emotional connection in storytelling: colour, shape, music and light. On the subject of music, the ESQ did create a strong connection to participants, when asked "the music made me feel…" Additionally, as mentioned in the previous section, the PANAS noted a higher positive affect in scenes that featured saturated bright colours, and a negative affect with desaturated colours. However, colour, shape, and light were not individually evaluated by the user. Instead, they were combined as a stealth element to influence an emotional connection in the storytelling. In this aspect, it is believed to be effective, as the data recorded (ESQ) high emotional connection across, and the expected changes in the PANAS. With that in mind, while these elements are effective combined, further exploration is needed to assess the individual elements pertaining to successful emotional connections in stories. Nevertheless, it is recommended that more specific research be carried out on each element to determine the individual effects and effectiveness, either through qualitative or quantitative methods.

References

1. The Health Foundation. The power of storytelling. In: The Health Foundation (2016). https://www.health.org.uk/newsletter-feature/power-of-storytelling. Accessed 11 June 2020
2. Emblematic. Hunger in L.A. In: Emblematic (2012). https://emblematicgroup.com/experiences/hunger-in-la. Accessed 22 July 2020
3. Emblematic. Across the Line. In: Emblematic (2016). https://emblematicgroup.com/experiences/across-the-line. Accessed 22 July 2020
4. Aardman. We Wait. In: Aardman.com (2016). https://www.aardman.com/work/we-wait. Accessed 28 July 2020
5. Fiocco, A., Mallya, S.: The importance of cultivating mindfulness for cognitive and emotional well-being in late life. J. Evid.-Based Complem. Altern. Med. **20**, 35–40 (2014). https://doi.org/10.1177/2156587214553940
6. Bennett-Levy, J., Lee, N.: Self-practice and self-reflection in cognitive behaviour therapy training: what factors influence trainees' engagement and experience of benefit? Behav. Cogn. Psychother. **42**, 48–64 (2012). https://doi.org/10.1017/s1352465812000781
7. Ahn, S., Bostick, J., Ogle, E., et al.: Experiencing nature: embodying animals in immersive virtual environments increases inclusion of nature in self and involvement with nature. J. Comput.-Mediat. Commun. **21**, 399–419 (2016). https://doi.org/10.1111/jcc4.12173
8. Fusaro, M., Tieri, G., Aglioti, S.: Seeing pain and pleasure on self and others: behavioral and psychophysiological reactivity in immersive virtual reality. J. Neurophysiol. **116**, 2656–2662 (2016). https://doi.org/10.1152/jn.00489.2016
9. Russoniello, C., O'Brien, K., Parks, J.: The effectiveness of causal video games in improving mood and decreasing stress. J. Cyberther. Rehabil. **2**(1), 53–66 (2009)
10. McNair, D.M., Lorr, M., Droppleman, L.F.: Profile of mood states. Educational and Testing Industrial Testing Service, San Diego (1981)
11. Cebolla, A., Herrero, R., Ventura, S., et al.: Putting oneself in the body of others: a pilot study on the efficacy of an embodied virtual reality system to generate self-compassion. Front. Psychol. (2019). https://doi.org/10.3389/fpsyg.2019.01521
12. Falconer, C., Slater, M., Rovira, A., et al.: Embodying compassion: a virtual reality paradigm for overcoming excessive self-criticism. PLoS ONE **9**, e111933 (2014). https://doi.org/10.1371/journal.pone.0111933
13. Västfjäll, D.: Emotion induction through music: a review of the musical mood induction procedure. Music. Sci. **5**, 173–211 (2001). https://doi.org/10.1177/10298649020050s107
14. Schaefer, H.: Music-evoked emotions—current studies. Front. Neurosci. (2017). https://doi.org/10.3389/fnins.2017.00600
15. Wilms, L., Oberfeld, D.: Color and emotion: effects of hue, saturation, and brightness. Psychol. Res. **82**(5), 896–914 (2017). https://doi.org/10.1007/s00426-017-0880-8
16. Arnheim, R.: Art and Visual Perception, pp. 10–444. University of California Press, California (1954)

17. Tomassoni, R., Galetta, G., Treglia. E.: Psychology of light: how light influences the health and psyche. Psychol. [e-J.] **6**(10), 1216–1222 (2015). https://doi.org/10.4236/psych.2015.610119
18. Verduyn, P., Brans, K.: The relationship between extraversion, neuroticism and aspects of trait affect. Pers. Individ. Differ. **52**, 664–669 (2012). https://doi.org/10.1016/j.paid.2011.12.017
19. Kim, S., Park, G., Lee, Y., Choi, S.: Customer emotions and their triggers in luxury retail: understanding the effects of customer emotions before and after entering a luxury shop. J. Bus. Res. **69**, 5809–5818 (2016). https://doi.org/10.1016/j.jbusres.2016.04.178
20. Epic Games Unreal Engine. https://www.epicgames.com/site/en-US/home
21. NOAA Fisheries. All Species Directory Page. In: Fisheries.noaa.gov (2020). https://www.fisheries.noaa.gov/species-directory. Accessed 10 Apr 2020
22. Cherry, K.: Can Color Affect Your Mood And Behavior? (2020). Verywell Mind. https://www.verywellmind.com/color-psychology-2795824. Accessed 17 Apr 2020
23. Baer, R., Smith, G., Hopkins, J., et al.: Using self-report assessment methods to explore facets of mindfulness. Assessment **13**, 27–45 (2006). https://doi.org/10.1177/1073191105283504

Myth, Diegesis and Storytelling in Perennial Games

Bjarke Alexander Larsen$^{(\boxtimes)}$ and Elin Carstensdottir

University of California, Santa Cruz, USA
{balarsen,ecarsten}@ucsc.edu

Abstract. Perennial games—ongoing, live games—are a form of games that often seem at odds with storytelling through their temporality, repetition and strange diegesis. This paper proposes a reframing of storytelling in perennial games as *myth* to alleviate these problems. Two layers of myth are presented, the first as the constructed fictional layer, and the second as the lived experience of the communities and people engaging with the game. This avoids the traditional player/author split, often seen as problematic in perennial games, by not focusing on authorship or control of these layers. Rather, it focuses on what each layer is affecting about the experience, how both authors and audience can engage with each layer, and how these layers affect each other. Three additional problems with perennial storytelling are identified that this reframing as myth helps alleviate. Framing the play of perennial games as myth shows how players are a part of a greater mythological experience in a disenchanted world. It explains the repetitive nature of perennial games as re-enactment and ritual, instead of as a logic-breaking repetition of story events. Furthermore, mythology has an inherently complicated relationship with truth and fiction, and this fits naturally with a similar relationship of perennial games and diegesis. Through this recontextualisation, we can improve understanding of how players are experiencing and engaging with perennial stories with a holistical understanding of their play and development.

Keywords: Perennial games · Mythology · Myth · Repetition · Diegesis · Play

Perennial games—live, ongoing games with continuing stories—consistently account for some of the most popular games in the current media landscape [46,78] and include games like Minecraft [56], League of Legends [67], Fortnite [20], and Destiny [12]. Perennial games are expansive and often massive in scope, and their storytelling often sees content distributed across long periods of time, potentially spanning years. It is important to understand how these narratives are designed because of the presence and popularity of storytelling in perennial games. We should explore how perennial games enable interactive stories to be experienced on a different scale and scope than that seen from most other digital narrative experiences. However, narrative in perennial games has remained relatively underexplored in the literature outside of work focusing on storytelling in MMOs [7,42,46,50].

The perennial nature of storytelling in these games gives rise to a number of potential issues and conflicts in their design and how they are experienced. These include concerns about diegesis and repetition, such as how storytelling and diegetic framing is supported if key moments of the story are required, by design, to be repeatable and are engaged with multiple times by the same players. For example, how would an individual match of League of Legends make sense to players in relation to the lore? Are repeated runs of a raid in World of Warcraft separate from its place in the overarching story? Is this a concern for players? Another significant concern lies in the realm of the diegesis [35] (what is a part of the fictional world) and what constitutes "true" (i.e. canon) events. It is often unclear to players what is part of the storyworld and what is not, and it is likewise not often clear whether the actions of individual players matter. When a fictional character overtakes the official Bungie twitter account and talks in-character [60,84], is this part of the storyworld of Destiny? Authorship is a major point of contention in this context, when the actions of players can either become fictionalised, or be ignored. When players randomly dancing in Destiny becomes immortalized through in-game text [9], authorship cannot be said to lie entirely in the hands of the developers. Thus, the traditional split of author and player often falls apart in perennial storytelling. New approaches and perspectives are needed to describe and explore this phenomenon in greater detail.

We propose using *myth* as a lens through which we can understand perennial games and their storytelling. Many of the biggest events in perennial games already feel mythical. Take the example of the Fall of Dalamud from Final Fantasy XIV (FFXIV). On August 24, 2013, a moon crashed into the world, to fictionally wipe out the old world and replace it with the new "A Realm Reborn". The new game takes place 5 years after this "Calamity", and many of its events occur because of this originating event. And furthermore, the old world is no longer accessible to anyone: It *actually* got destroyed by the moon, and can only be seen today through videos, screenshots and retellings. This is a great example of a myth that propagated through a community and shaped its sense of identity, belonging and heritage. It is, literally, an origin myth[1]. And it was also something players lived through. It is, as a developer said, *"a myth that actually happened"* [62].

Understanding perennial stories as *myths* reframes the context for what the story tries to achieve, its reason for and method of being told. Recontextualising something as myth allows us to re-interpret some fundamental assumptions about its purpose and design. Repetition is treated quite differently in myth than it is in many other forms of storytelling [25,42]. Authorship, too is treated differently [2,15,25,42]. Using myth will therefore give us a different perspective on these key problems in interactive storytelling design. Further, it allows the use

---

[1] As defined by Eliade [19, p. 21] as stories that *"tell how the world was changed"*.

of myth as a tool for reframing interactive storytelling in perennial experiences, which will help recontextualize and improve understanding of how players are experiencing and engaging with perennial stories.

This helps us go beyond *solving* difficult problems and challenges, such as those posed by repetition or diegesis, and instead, shifts the perspective so they are not problems, but rather, meaningful aspects of the design that can be used, applied, and subverted.

Crucially, we propose looking at the play and development of perennial games as myth holistically. We argue that it is necessary to see the whole scope of the play, from an individual player grinding loot by themselves, to the community-wide activites such as The Gates of Ahn'Qiraj [68,89], to the background lore written by writers months before a player sees it. All of these elements are neccesary and involved in the storytelling experience of a perennial game. Using myth as a lens for these experiences enables a holistic view of these elements, as well as highlights their relevance for mythmaking. In this paper, we will show how the core aspects of play help construct the complete myth of a perennial game.

1 Related Work

1.1 Mythology

As Segal [76] explains, a common understanding of "myth" has become as a falsehood: A story that was once believed to be true but is false [76]. This is not what we mean by myth. Folklorist Honko [31] defined myth as *"a story of the gods, a religious account of the beginning of the world, the creation, fundamental events"* [31], and some folklorists still consider myths to be stories of this kind exclusively [76, p. 5]. However, the structuralist reinterpretation of myths by influential scholars like Levi-Strauss [47,48], Bronislaw [53], Campbell [13] or Jung and Eliade [25,76], contributed to a more modern understanding of myth as something that can *"teach us a great deal about the societies from which they originate"* [48] rather than as ground truths in and of themselves, and to help discover universal truths hidden beneath each untrue story [17]. Later, this understanding got challenged, as myth has lost many of its religious connotations [76] and expanded its form. Examples include mythology as modern cinema [29], as social contexts [6], as political strategy [34] or in the play of video games [2,25, 42]. This is not just meant in the sense that these media "contain" mythologies (or "lore bibles" etc.), but that we can view the construction and play of these stories as *mythmaking*. J.R.R. Tolkien, as raised by Aupers [3], advocated for *the active construction* of myths, using the term "mythopoeia" (mythmaking), to call for the powerful yet deliberate construction of secondary worlds that nevertheless speak to our own. We consider myth in both contexts: Myths are stories[2] by and for communities, to explain the world they inhabit, and these

---

[2] Story is here seen in the perspective of Abbott and Ryan [1,72], as a series of events, in contrast to a narrative, which is these events told through a discourse. A told myth is thus a narrative, and carries with it discoursal properties.

stories communicate their shared history, values, norms, and perspectives, and mythmaking is thus the active construction of these stories by the community[3] telling, re-enacting, retelling, or experiencing those stories with each other.

1.2 Myth in Games

Myth is not a stranger in game studies. Several scholars, including Krzywinska [42,43], Rusch [69], Asimos [2] and several others [3,15,21,22,25,28,86] have applied various aspects of myth to games, such as in the fiction, social contexts, rituals, shared history, and personal stories.

Mythology is heavily used in the worldbuilding of games. Games like World of Warcraft, Mass Effect, or Shadow of the Colossus *have* mythology [25,42,69], i.e. they have history and "lore" [66], ancient beliefs and stories of gods that impact the world. Furthermore, games allow, as Geraci [25] and Krzywinska [42] point out, players to exist *within* that mythological space, to exist in "an epic cosmos" [25] and partake in the epic narratives. The actions of a player are given meaning through their mythological context: Players are not just inputting actions to make a blank slate's health to go 0, they are slaying *Arthas, The Lich King*, a character with mythological meaning built up over years, and that has great impact to its audience [25]. Surprisingly, despite these strong connections to storytelling, myth has seen little play in interactive storytelling communities. The word myth has mostly been used in the sense of a falsehood [36,39,71], or as inspiration for storyworlds [49], or single references to Campbell or Levi-Strauss [39,58,80,83]. To our knowledge, myths have otherwise rarely been used specifically to understand interactive storytelling or interactive narrative systems.

However, myth has been used in other ways in game scholarship more broadly. One example is viewing both the game and the play of the game as mythic in itself. Harrington [28] uses Barthes' Mythologies—seeing social contexts as a kind of mythology that affects how the players view the world—to inspect the notion of the "4X Gamer" and how this specific genre of game has established its own mythology on how it is played and talked about. Rusch [69] sees games as potential guides to a meaningful life, just as traditional mythology would have, leaning on the psychological aspects from Campbell and Jung, to how games can affect contemplation and reflection in a player.

Cragoe [15] inspects the mythological relations to tabletop roleplaying games and finds several similarities between myths and RPGs. The most important ones here are "communication of expected norms", "providing a sense of solidarity through shared history", and "creating a system of mastery and ownership over the heritage and characteristics of the society" [15]. These all strongly relate to the amount of work done on the relationship between games and religion [4,25,27,65,88], showing how the practices of each overlap in forming social rituals and connections. Aupers [3,74], too, shows how games can be a place to experiment with religion. This is not directly the same as mythology, but there is an undeniable connection between myth and religion [25,76]. These sources all

---

[3] Authors are here seen as part of the community. See Sect. 3.1.

show how the play of games can be compared to religious activities, and mythical storytelling is one of those.

Asimos [2] is inspired by Levi-Strauss' explicit and implicit myths. The "explicit myth" of games can be seen as the written, authored mythologies of the world, and the "implicit" myth, as the personal, ritual action of myth, which in games is understood both as the active play experience and the personalized narrative. This split might strike a familiar chord in interactive storytelling communities to that of the authored versus player story [37,38,40,44,59,70] or emergent narrative [5,18,33,40,45,51,52,70,79,87]. The relationship between perennial games, myth, and emergent narrative, while fascinating, is unfortunately out of scope for this paper.

2   The Layers of Myth in Perennial Games

Existing literature on perennial games mentions myth briefly, but does not go into much detail on the power of this connection. As discussed in Sect. 1.2, myth is predominantly something that happens in *communities*, through social connections and customs, and *over time*, through rituals and repetition. Perennial games are perpetual, have a continuous temporality with the real world, and their narrative is shaped by a community and the authors at run-time [46]. Therefore, perennial games have mythmaking aspects built-in since they are, by definition, communal storytelling experiences that create systems and rituals of play. Unsurprisingly, their construction of myth is as a result highly complicated, especially as it relates to question of authorship and diegesis. Therefore, it is important to clarify how myth can be used in the context of perennial games and how it is constructed. To accomplish this, we define two inter-connected layers of myth in perennial experiences (seen in Fig. 1).

The first layer is the *fictional* myth. This is the realm of creative invention by authors [24], that create the myths inside games. It is the fiction, the lore, the backstories and fabric of the fictional universe. The fictional myth is the "canon" of the universal chronicle [46] of a perennial experience. This mythmaking is closely related to J.R.R. Tolkiens "mythopoeia" [3], which is the careful and deliberate construction of new fictional mythology that aims to say something about the world. This layer is Bungie authoring narratives in Destiny, by creating the gods and their domains. This layer is what the actions of players gain meaning by [25,42], and where we can view their lore and cosmology as revealing about their creators and the people who play them, as in traditional mythological studies [13,47,48]. However, it is not only the domain of authors, as the players and audience play with the fiction, too, and through fanfiction, deliberation, and play, they affect and create new fiction. Crucially, the role of the audience is also often to *maintain* the fiction, to deliberate it and hold it to account, to update wiki sites and discuss narrative developments. Blaseball [81] is a prime example of the audience directly participating in and maintaining the fiction through their own actions, and the developers responding to this through future authored events. Characters started with no more than a randomly generated

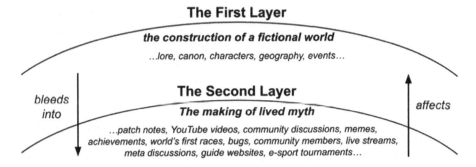

Fig. 1. The two layers of myth in perennial experiences. The first layer is the construction of the fictional world through text and lore and deliberation, and the second is the lived myth that develops as a consequence of play.

name, and the fans alone created the backstories that influenced future events [41,54].

The second layer is looking at the game as an object of myth-making *in play*[4]. This includes everything that is part of its play, and which is inherently *"non"-fiction* as it is stories lived by real people. All player activities in a game, such as questing, grinding, and raiding, and socializing and inventory management are included in its play and this sits in context to the mythical meaning established by the first kind of myth, even kinds of play that are not seen as traditionally narrative[5]. Asimos shows an example of how two kinds of Let's Plays both create myths [2], despite only one of them engaging overtly with the fictional element of the game. Krzywinska shows how the play of the game is affected by previous players, even without direct influence: Battles play out differently based on experience, based on best practices or the current "meta", that affect a player's given choices, even if established outside the game [42]. The second layer of myth is more expansive than in-game activities only. It includes everything that is part of the play of a game, even that which is not directly "playing the game": Patch notes, YouTube videos, community discussions, memes, achievements, world's first races, bugs, prominent community members such as YouTubers and live streamers, meta discussions, guide websites, esports tournaments[6]) etc.

The intention here is not to state that these aspects are inherently mythical, but highlighting that these are the tools with which the myths can be made. The second layer is powerful because it highlights those aspects of a game that are not typically seen as "narrative", and frames it as part of the narrative

---

[4] Here, Sicart's broad notion of play [77] is useful, as it encompasses the wide-ranging possibilities of play.

[5] One useful comparison to emergent narrative here is James Ryan's notion of emergent narrative as nonfiction or lived experience [70], as the case is similar: These are both stories created (curated) from a wealth of material events.

[6] Esports could be viewed as its own mythology, as a sports narrative on its own, but that discussion is beyond the scope of this paper.

experience by framing it as mythological. The creation of a "meta" in any game is a good example already mentioned by Krzywinska: We must submit to the *"powers that be"* [42] if we are to play efficiently—or intentionally counterplay against it, in any case, we reflect on the established myth. A meme, such as the infamous "Leeroy Jenkins" from early World of Warcraft [75] is part of the community's shared understanding of the game: It is part of the experience and used and reused as people play together. This *is* the enchantment of the world (see Sect. 3.2). We are able to take something fictional and *play* with it, make it real, and thus feel like we can make our lives a little more magical. This is often seen as the activity of the audience, although authors can and will participate, and in fact, any update to the game can be seen as a part of this mythmaking, a further event to create myths out of. This is the second layer of myth.

These two layers can help illustrate something crucial how perennial games function. The most cited examples of perennial games are MMOs or similar games with a strong fictional element. However, live service games like Rocket League [64] or Counterstrike: Go [85] or Minecraft [56] are perennial games under the strict definition given in the previous paper [46] as well, as they receive continuous updates perpetually. However, the two layers showcase a clear difference in the contents of the universal chronicle. As an illustrative example, a game like Rocket League has very little fictional content—its first layer of myth is thin—but it does still have a clear perennial experience in terms of its temporality, and has plenty of myth in the second layer. Take an example like the "flip reset" [63], a technique that was discovered by the community that has no definition in the game's rules, that over time was developed, practiced and then popularized to the point where it is a common and expected part of high-level play. This development over time is a story that is part of the mythology, the universal chronicle of Rocket League. The difference between this and the type of perennial experience that happens in Destiny, where the perennial developments are about fictional characters and events, is that in Rocket League, there is no discussion of what is true. When a fictional element enters the game, suddenly, there are elements that are up for debate and it is here the diegesis becomes muddy and where the layers begin to interact. Yet, it cannot be said that Rocket League has no presence in the first layer, as there is always the possibility for people to create a layer of fictionality where none is intended (see how players create lore of Minecraft despite being given very little to work with [82] or the story of "Herobrine" [57]).

As seen from this example, the second layer of myth is clearly created and maintained through play. However, the first layer of the fictional world is not exempt from play: It is in large part through "narrative play" that these myths are upheld, through retellings and mythic repetition, etc. It is also the first layer of myth that *draws* the player in, entices them with the promise of magic: Here in this world, you can be a wizard (or a rocket powered car, and who doesn't want to be that?). The first layer can also affect the second through establishing accepted norms or preferred play patterns through the fictional myth, which are then upheld (or subverted) by the community in the second layer.

These two kinds of myth cannot be separated, and it is where both kinds of mythmaking combine that perennial games shine. In particular, when the second layer of mythmaking can become *about* the first, and the first is *affected* by the second. Leeroy Jenkins, originally a person from a comedic video of a raid gone wrong that became a meme because of his recognizable shout, was later introduced in Hearthstone [8] on the same level as any fictional character in World of Warcraft. The Fall of Dalamud, mentioned in the beginning of this paper, is another great example of a myth that functions in both layers inherently, through its conception. It is both a scripted and authored event by the developers that is part of the fictional fabric of the universe of FFXIV, but it is also an event uplifted and retold to mythological status by its players. Destiny has countless examples of players engaging in an activity and then that becoming "canonized" through the game's lore acknowledging such actions later [46].

This is the true magic of perennial games, as it relies on perenniality to function: Mythmaking takes *time*, and it is only possible to affect the first layer of mythmaking, the fictional world, if there is a built-in affordance to change it, and that can only happen over time. The mythmaking of the second layer can emerge from any game, and the first layer happens in traditional fiction, but it is only in perennial games that we see *both simultaneously*. Players create new myths in the moment that alter the fictional world, and reflecting upon them and how they affect their play in the same moment. This is something that can only exist with perenniality and fiction combined. We do not argue that this is entirely unique to perennial *games*, as the examples that Saler [73] brings up also show signs of this kind of experience, and American wrestling, as discussed by us [46], also include fiction and perenniality. But what is unique about perennial *games* is rather why and how they work so effectively as perennial experiences.

3 How Myth Helps Perennial Games

There are four main advantages to viewing perennial games through the lens of myth: First, it avoids assuming a false player/author split that is frequent when studying storytelling in perennial games. Second, it helps to explain why we play perennial games and the immediate attraction of *playing with* myth. Third, mythology has an inherently complicated relationship with truth and reality that also fits well with the complicated diegesis of perennial games. Finally, it solves what has been perceived as a major issue with storytelling in perennial games, namely that of repetition.

3.1 The Author/Player Split

Myth provides an inherent binding between the traditionally narrative and the traditionally ludic. Krzywinska emphasizes how WoW situates its fiction firmly in the mythic, through its creation of an illusion of a coherent world in cultural, spatial, and temporal terms, yet this has gameplay consequences: *"Through a web of intertextual and intratextual signifiers, the game invites players to read the world and gameplay tasks as "myth," and like myth these have allegorical and material dimensions"* [42]. Krzywinska and Geraci show how the practices and play of games can be seen as mythological or sacred. Since the actions in games have mythological meanings (in the second and first layer), the individual actions of players become intertwined with the myth, and cannot be entirely separated from it. As Krzywinska says, *"it is common for players to understand the quest format in both narrative and other, more functional and experiential terms (e.g., a means of gaining better equipment and experience points); one is not reducible to the other, but instead they create a gestalt that better reflects in conceptual terms the multifaceted experience of playing the game"* [42]. In other words, the play of a perennial game affects both layers of myth at once, and they cannot be separated easily. This has implications for understanding the relationship between players and authors.

The two layers proposed in this paper might sound similar to the split mentioned in related work by Asimos (Sect. 1.2), of explicit and implicit myth. However, explicit myth was authored and implicit was personal for a player, and this is not where the split of the two proposed mythological layers is placed. It might seem natural to assume that the first layer of myth is for authors and the second layer is for the audience, but as already shown in examples in the previous section, there are counter-examples to both of those assumptions. Players affect the fictional myth and authors affect the lived experience. In fact, authors are as much part of the lived experience as any audience member, as they are also experiencing the development of the lived myth first-hand alongside the audience. It cannot be said that any layer belongs to any specific participant.

Even when you look at "both", as Asimos does, it will inevitably lead to separation of author and player stories. Instead the power of myth is that it is able to, in a single phrase, encompass a more holistic view of the narrative play that happens in perennial games, that does not talk about a played or designed narrative but rather something else. The two layers of myth are perhaps orthogonal, or at least divergent, to players or authors. Both the audience and authors have the capability to affect, be part of, and engage with both layers of myth. One example of this is Destiny's Loot Cave, which was an unintended exploit the developers later turned into a part of the story, and eventually part of future experiences [23,26,32].

The two layers of myth do not show who is in control of the mythmaking process, but rather what part of the experience it affects. These two layers are what is *at play* in a perennial game, it is what everyone changes when they engage with it. Even actions as simple as reading about the fiction helps enforce it, maintain it and strengthen its power, just as listening to a myth would help propagate it through society.

This is not to say that authors and audience members have the same kind of control over the perennial story—they are very different roles, still, but the roles are more complicated. The two layers show *what is*, not how it comes to be, and who is in control of what. The advantage of this is that it avoids the assumption that players are static "consumers" of the myth or that the authors are entirely the "gods" of the myth, as neither is the case.

3.2   Why We Play

Myth provides a very strong case for why perennial games are so enticing to play, and so successful as products.

Krzywinska [42] and Geraci [25] discuss how MMOs inherently invoke the "hero's quest"-aesthetics, and let the player "be part of something greater" or give them a chance to exist in *"a cosmos of epic meaning"* [25]. Geraci and Aupers [3] note how this is a response to Weber's old notion of the "disenchanted world", also referenced by others [3,73]. To summarize Weber's argument, the modern (mostly western) world has become increasingly secularized and non-religious, non-mystical and non-magical [3,25,73]. Virtual worlds, to Geraci and Aupers, offer a chance at living, if ever briefly, in a world that once again has something that the modern world is missing: A sense of purpose. As Geraci said: *"myths are the thing through which character's (and thus players) actions make sense"* [25]. This idea of dealing with a disenchanted world through fantastical media is not new. Saler's [73] historical account of turn-of-the-century (1900–1940) literature shows how fantastic media creations such as Sherlock Holmes stories and The Lord of the Rings gained a lot of traction at the time precisely because of their ability to inject enchantment into a world that was becoming increasingly rationalised. Saler covers in great detail how the fan communities that developed from this media communicated, in similar ways to that we see around perennial experiences, just using physical letters or debate clubs rather than forum posts and chat servers. They were, in another word, *playing* with their stories. What digital media offers today, however, is that is the possibility to "enter" these worlds, as the very object that is being mythologised *is* what people play inside.

And the notion of *play* is important. Aupers [3] shows how it is specifically the voluntary, inconsequential, non-important attitude of play that allows this experimentation and exploration. We can *play* with myth in perennial experiences because "it is only" a game. Players are well aware that they are not materially affecting the outside reality, but it is precisely this awareness that allows them to play with the fictional reality. As Saler [73] showed, in response to a disenchanted world, players needed fantasy to be pointless (yet sensible) to allow themselves to engage with it in a world increasingly funded on rationality. Because the world of Destiny takes place in a video game, it is acceptable for many to pretend to be a god-slaying space wizard. And furthermore, the promise of being part of an ever-evolving, *lived* myth, being *there when it happens* is something that perennial games excel at, through their temporality, and ability for players to inhabit spaces [25,61].

3.3   Real-not-real

To Geraci, this playing in an "epic cosmos" only works *because* virtual worlds have "real histories", which the players can reference and situate themselves in: Life goes on in a virtual world when a player does not engage with it, and a real sense of place is established through this passage of time. It is not *just* play. As

Krzywinska also said, *real* things happen in these worlds [42], and while they happen in mythological contexts, the events are not "fake" or "unreal", but in fact quite actual. Hong calls this notion *"real enough"* [30], focusing on the idea that these worlds are real enough for us to meaningfully get something out of them.

We have previously noted how the "diegetic muddiness"—the sense that what is part of the world is open to discussion at run-time—is part of the appeal of perennial games [46]. This echoes this exact "real-not-real" nature of myth that is also present in these games. They are fake enough to be fictional and exist within play (and is thus safe and inviting, non-dangerous and explorative), but are real enough that it matters (people care about it, find meaning and connection with it—it is more than frivolous). Hong [30] has valuable insight here: Using discussions on the real by Žižek [90], they conclude: *"I refer to it here as a sense of "real enough": We are able to play as if we believe this could have been real. The desire for the real does not take the form of earnest angst, but a willingness to dive knowingly into video game spectacles of "when life mattered."'* and later *"the invocation of a mythic time when life mattered comes hand in hand with a postmodern attitude of real enough. [...] what is at stake is not the "realness" of games, but a politics of engagement with the real writ large."* [30].

Mythology, too, has a complicated relationship with truth. It is baked into the very word (and the source for the meaning of the word as falsehood) that mythological stories are *false*, and yet there is still a grain of truth to them. Furthermore, traditional mythologies contradict themselves a lot [14], and have inconsistent logic or timelines. This is the case for MMOs and perennial games too. Different parts of a community can have multiple, co-existing explanations for events, and Destiny is a prime example of whole lore books with intentionally false accounts of happenings [10,11]. One does not need to spend a long time in any "lore" community to notice their frequent obsession with "the canon" [16,55]—knowing what is true and what is false. Multiple versions of the same story are rarely accepted, and rejected upon discovering one of them as a lie. "Retconning"[7] can be seen as a great sin and consistency often as a great virtue. This is perhaps ironic, as traditional mythology was often contradictory and illogical: Timelines are blurry and the state of the world is inconsistent from one story to the next. Yet, it is precisely this contradiction—the discussion of what is real given a complicated foundation—that is fundamental to perennial experiences. There is a built-in tension with the mythological and the audience's desire for knowledge, and this is, once again, *part* of the perennial experience. What happens in a perennial game is both real and not real, and it is impossible to define it fully as either.

---

[7] "Retroactive continuity": Changing a previously established truth about the world to serve a new narrative purpose. This could be innocuous, like changing the previous off-screen location of a character, to severe, such as reviving them from death.

3.4 Repetition

The fact that events in perennial games repeat has been a major point of criticism for their efficacy as storytelling media for a long time [7,42,46,50]. Events in MMOs happen over and over again as players repeat events ad infinitum: Even important story characters like Arthas are killed every day. How can storytelling make sense in such a world? To Krzywinska and Geraci, this does not spell the demise of storytelling in WoW. Rather, through the mythical lens, we can see a power in it. Krzywinska notes how *"as with retellings of myths, battles are fought over and over again, and in this there is a cyclical/recursive organization of time"*.

Geraci recalls Mircea Eliade's work how participation in a religious society is about ritually retelling or reliving the stories again and again. Rather than treating this as a break in the narrative construction of the world, we can instead see repetition as a "retelling" itself. Players relive mythos of World of Warcraft through their play, and thus ritually repeat the great events of its history. As we would retell a great myth over and over again, so too, does the players of any perennial game reenact its events. Each repetition can be viewed as a retelling or a *re-enactment* of the event. A ritual, performed over and over by the players, to commemorate and immortalize the event itself, much as ritual serves myth in religion—as re-enactment. Rituals and repetition are in religion a primary way through which the myths are experienced [19,76]. Similarly, we experience perennial games by (perennially) playing their content over and over again, and this is how their myths are absorbed, created and take form. Naturally, these re-enactments and retellings have the power to change what we think about the original event, as well. Repetition is thus not a byproduct but a necessity to establishing the myth of perennial games.

And just as rituals change over time in religion, the *powers that be* affect the second layer of myth, to affect how the ritual is performed every time. New strategies are discovered and new reasons to go through the raid may be found or implemented into the game. Nevertheless, each subsequent repetition is not the same as the event itself, but a reflection, a re-enactment.

4 Conclusion

In this paper, we propose using myth to reframe understanding of storytelling in perennial games. Doing so allows us rethink elements that are often thought to be in contention with successful storytelling in perennial games. Namely, it allows us to rethink the meaning of repetition as re-enactment and ritual, and think of the diegesis as mythological and thus both real and not real at the same time. Myth also helps contextualise perennial games, to understand how being part of a greater mythological cosmos is attractive. Two layers of myths in perennial games were presented that avoids splitting the storytelling across a player/author axis, but rather have a layer of the fictional myth and the lived myth created through play and creation. This showcases the two major kinds of myth perennial games play with, and how they can and will interact when they are both present.

This interaction between these layers, across players and authors, is the core of how myths are made, maintained, and altered in perennial games.

Reframing perennial games as myth allows new questions to come to the forefront, as the storytelling experience can be understood in a holistic way. It raises questions about how mythmaking operates in perennial games and how its aspects impact and shape the player and development experience, such as: How are myths created, deliberated, and maintained in perennial games, and by whom? What activities are repeated by players and how does that correspond with the fictional mythology? How does the developer respond to community actions, both those prescribed and those not?

The mythology of a perennial game must be understood in context to its play, its development, and its community as a whole, and thus we must ask questions that encompass the entire mythmaking process. This is the core of what framing it as myth gives us: We cannot help but acknowledge a holistic view of perennial games when we understand them as mythmaking processes, and thus we get a much more complete picture of the experience of playing them.

References

1. Abbott, H.P.: Story, plot, and narration. In: Herman, D. (ed.) The Cambridge Companion to Narrative, pp. 39–51. Cambridge Companions to Literature, Cambridge University Press (2007). https://doi.org/10.1017/CCOL0521856965.003
2. Asimos, V.: Playing the myth: video games as contemporary mythology. Implicit Religion 21(1) (2018)
3. Aupers, S.: Spiritual play: encountering the sacred in world of warcraft. Playful identities, p. 75 (2015)
4. Aupers, S., Schaap, J., De Wildt, L.: Studying religious meaning-making in MMOs. Methods for studying Video games and religion (2017)
5. Aylett, R.: Narrative in virtual environments-towards emergent narrative. In: Proceedings of the AAAI fall symposium on narrative intelligence, pp. 83–86 (1999)
6. Barthes, R.: Mythologies 1957. Trans. Annette Lavers. New York: Hill and Wang pp. 302–06 (1972)
7. Bartle, R.A.: Designing virtual worlds. New Riders, 201 West 103rd Street, Indianapolis (2004)
8. Blizzard Entertainment: hearthstone (2014)
9. Bungie: lore tab of the electronica ghost shell. Lore entry on Ishtar, https://www.ishtar-collective.net/entries/electronica-shell, as well as in Destiny 2. It describes Guardians (players), and how frequently they dance (2017)
10. Bungie: truth to power (2018), lorebook from Destiny 2, hosted on https://www.ishtar-collective.net/categories/book-truth-to-power
11. Bungie: the chronicon (2019), lorebook from Destiny 2, hosted on https://www.ishtar-collective.net/categories/book-the-chronicon
12. Bungie and Activision: destiny (2014)
13. Campbell, J.: The hero with a thousand faces, vol. 17. New World Library (2008)
14. Cornell, P., Orman, K.: Two interviews about doctor who. In: Pat Harrigan, N.W.F. (ed.) Third Person, chap. 3, pp. 33–41. MIT Press (2009)
15. Cragoe, N.G.: RPG mythos: narrative gaming as modern mythmaking. Games Cult. 11(6), 583–607 (2016)

16. Destinypedia: canon policy. The Canon Policy Guide for "Destinypedia" the unofficial Destiny wikipedia (2022). https://www.destinypedia.com/Destinypedia: Canon_policy. Accessed 16 July 2022
17. Dorson, R.M.: Mythology and folklore. Ann. Rev. Anthropol. **2**, 107–126 (1973)
18. Eladhari, M.P.: Re-Tellings: the fourth layer of narrative as an instrument for critique. In: Rouse, R., Koenitz, H., Haahr, M. (eds.) ICIDS 2018. LNCS, vol. 11318, pp. 65–78. Springer, Cham (2018). https://doi.org/10.1007/978-3-030-04028-4_5
19. Eliade, M.: Myth and reality. Harper & Row (1963)
20. Epic Games: fortnite (2017)
21. Ford, D.: The haunting of ancient societies in the mass effect trilogy and the legend of zelda: breath of the wild. Game Studies 21(4) (2021)
22. Ford, D.: That old school feeling (indeterminable year, after 2020)
23. Gach, E.: They brought back destiny's loot cave, but not the loot. Kotaku article (2020). https://kotaku.com/they-brought-back-the-loot-cave-but-not-the-loot-1845638914. Accessed on 30 Apr 2021
24. Genette, G.: Fiction & diction. Cornell University Press (1993)
25. Geraci, R.M.: Virtually sacred: Myth and Meaning in World of Warcraft and Second Life. Oxford University Press, Oxford (2014)
26. Good, O.S.: Here's how to find destiny's 'loot cave' and plunder it for endless riches. Polygon article (2014). https://www.polygon.com/2014/9/21/6760715/destiny-loot-cave-engrams-farming. Accessed 30 Apr 2021
27. Gregory Grieve, Kerstin Radde-Antweiler, X.Z.: Special issue: current key perspectives in video gaming and religion (2015). Panel debate. https://www.gamevironments.uni-bremen.de/issues-2015/
28. Harrington, J.: 4x gamer as myth: understanding through player mythologies. In: DiGRA/FDG (2016)
29. Hirschman, E.C.: Movies as myths: an interpretation of motion picture mythology. Marketing and semiotics: new directions in the study of signs for sale, pp. 335–74 (1987)
30. Hong, S.H.: When life mattered: the politics of the real in video games' reappropriation of history, myth, and ritual. Games Cult. **10**(1), 35–56 (2015)
31. Honko, L.: The problem of defining myth. Sacred narrative: readings in the theory of myth, pp. 41–52 (1984)
32. Hornshaw, P.: Destiny 2 grasp of avarice dungeon is hilariously salty about a 7-year-old exploit. Gamespot Article about the Grasp of Avarice Dungoen and how it ties to the Loot Cave (2021). https://www.gamespot.com/articles/destiny-2-grasp-of-avarice-dungeon-is-hilariously-salty-about-a-7-year-old-exploit/1100-6499082/. Accessed 6 Jun 2022
33. Jenkins, H.: Game design as narrative architecture. Computer **44**(3), 118–130 (2004)
34. Kjellgren, A.: Mythmaking as a feminist strategy: Rosi Braidotti's political myth. Feminist Theor. **22**(1), 63–80 (2021). https://doi.org/10.1177/1464700119881307
35. Kleinman, E., Carstensdottir, E., Seif El-Nasr, M.: A model for analyzing Diegesis in digital narrative games. In: Cardona-Rivera, R.E., Sullivan, A., Young, R.M. (eds.) ICIDS 2019. LNCS, vol. 11869, pp. 8–21. Springer, Cham (2019). https://doi.org/10.1007/978-3-030-33894-7_2
36. Knoller, N.: Agency and the art of interactive digital storytelling. In: Aylett, R., Lim, M.Y., Louchart, S., Petta, P., Riedl, M. (eds.) ICIDS 2010. LNCS, vol. 6432, pp. 264–267. Springer, Heidelberg (2010). https://doi.org/10.1007/978-3-642-16638-9_38

37. Koenitz, H.: Interactive Digital Narrative: History. Routledge, Theory and Practice (2015)
38. Koenitz, H.: Towards a specific theory of interactive digital narrative. In: Interactive digital narrative, pp. 107–121. Routledge (2015)
39. Koenitz, H., Di Pastena, A., Jansen, D., de Lint, B., Moss, A.: The Myth of Universal' Narrative Models. In: Rouse, R., Koenitz, H., Haahr, M. (eds.) ICIDS 2018. LNCS, vol. 11318, pp. 107–120. Springer, Cham (2018). https://doi.org/10.1007/978-3-030-04028-4_8
40. Kreminski, M., Mateas, M.: A coauthorship-centric history of interactive emergent narrative. In: Mitchell, A., Vosmeer, M. (eds.) ICIDS 2021. LNCS, vol. 13138, pp. 222–235. Springer, Cham (2021). https://doi.org/10.1007/978-3-030-92300-6_21
41. Kreminski, M., Mateas, M.: Toward narrative instruments. In: Mitchell, A., Vosmeer, M. (eds.) ICIDS 2021. LNCS, vol. 13138, pp. 499–508. Springer, Cham (2021). https://doi.org/10.1007/978-3-030-92300-6_50
42. Krzywinska, T.: Blood scythes, festivals, quests, and backstories: world creation and rhetorics of myth in world of warcraft. Games Cult. 1(4), 383–396 (2006)
43. Krzywinska, T.: Arachne v. Minerva: the spinning out of long narrative in buffy the vampire slayer and world of warcraft. In: Third Person. MIT Press (2008)
44. Larsen, B.A., Bruni, L.E., Schoenau-Fog, H.: The story we cannot see: on how a retelling relates to its afterstory. In: Cardona-Rivera, R.E., Sullivan, A., Young, R.M. (eds.) ICIDS 2019. LNCS, vol. 11869, pp. 190–203. Springer, Cham (2019). https://doi.org/10.1007/978-3-030-33894-7_21
45. Larsen, B.A., Bruni, L.E., Schoenau-Fog, H.: The story we cannot see: on how a retelling relates to its afterstory. In: Cardona-Rivera, R.E., Sullivan, A., Young, R.M. (eds.) ICIDS 2019. LNCS, vol. 11869, pp. 190–203. Springer, Cham (2019). https://doi.org/10.1007/978-3-030-33894-7_21
46. Larsen, B.A., Carstensdottir, E.: Wrestling with destiny: storytelling in perennial games. In: Mitchell, A., Vosmeer, M. (eds.) ICIDS 2021. LNCS, vol. 13138, pp. 236–254. Springer, Cham (2021). https://doi.org/10.1007/978-3-030-92300-6_22
47. Lévi-Strauss, C.: The structural study of myth. J. Am. Folklore 68(270), 428–444 (1955)
48. Lévi-Strauss, C.: Structuralism and myth. Kenyon Rev. 3(2), 64–88 (1981)
49. Lieto, A., Damiano, R.: Building narrative connections among media objects in cultural heritage repositories. In: Koenitz, H., Sezen, T.I., Ferri, G., Haahr, M., Sezen, D., Catak, G. (eds.) ICIDS 2013. LNCS, vol. 8230, pp. 257–260. Springer, Cham (2013). https://doi.org/10.1007/978-3-319-02756-2_33
50. Lohmann, B.: Storytelling in Massively Multiplayer Online Games. Master's thesis, IT University of Copenhagen (2008)
51. Louchart, S., Aylett, R.: Narrative theory and emergent interactive narrative. Int. J. Contin. Eng. Educ. Life Long Learn. 14(6), 506–518 (2004)
52. Louchart, S., Swartjes, I., Kriegel, M., Aylett, R.: Purposeful authoring for emergent narrative. In: Spierling, U., Szilas, N. (eds.) ICIDS 2008. LNCS, vol. 5334, pp. 273–284. Springer, Heidelberg (2008). https://doi.org/10.1007/978-3-540-89454-4_35
53. Malinowski, B.: Magic, science and religion and other essays. Read Books Limited (1954)
54. Manning, C.: I am all love blaseball (and you can too). Personal blog on Cat Manning's website, a prominent Blaseball community member. I Am All Love Blaseball (And You Can Too) (2020)

55. McSpazz: an overly long post talking about lore, canon, and headcanon (tm). Forum post on the City of Heroes: Homecoming forums. Presented as a guide for how to talk about canon and lore (2022). https://forums.homecomingservers.com/topic/34598-an-overly-long-post-talking-about-lore-canon-and-headcanon-tm/

56. Mojang: minecraft (2011)

57. Morton, L.: The story of herobrine, minecraft's decade-old creepypasta mystery. PC Gamer Article (2021). https://www.pcgamer.com/minecraft-herobrine-story-creepypasta-explained/ Accessed 16 Oct 2022

58. Murray, J.H.: Why paris needs hector and lancelot needs mordred: using traditional narrative roles and functions for dramatic compression in interactive narrative. In: Si, M., Thue, D., André, E., Lester, J.C., Tanenbaum, T.J., Zammitto, V. (eds.) ICIDS 2011. LNCS, vol. 7069, pp. 13–24. Springer, Heidelberg (2011). https://doi.org/10.1007/978-3-642-25289-1_2

59. Murray, J.H.: Hamlet on the holodeck: the future of narrative in cyberspace. Simon and Schuster (1997)

60. Murray, S.: The witch queen is roasting players in destiny 2 twitter takeover. Article on thegamer.com (2022). https://www.thegamer.com/the-witch-queen-savathun-roasting-destiny-2-twitter/. Accessed 16 July 2022

61. Nitsche, M.: Video game spaces. Image, Play, and Structure in 3D Worlds. Massachussets: MIT Press (2008)

62. Noclip: final fantasy xiv documentary part #3 - "the new world" (2017), https://www.youtube.com/watch?v=ONT6fxiu9cw. Quote in question is at 16:15, spoken by Michael Christopher Koji Fox

63. Pilkin, W.: The story of how flip resets evolved... YouTube Video, showcasing the history of the Flip Reset, by a Rocket League community member (2022). https://www.youtube.com/watch?v=0Q6fLpd4NUc&ab_channel=WaytonPilkin. Accessed 17 July 2022

64. Psyonix: rocket league (2015)

65. Radde-Antweiler, K., Waltmathe, M., Zeiler, X.: Video gaming, let's plays, and religion: The relevance of researching gamevironments. gamevironments (2014)

66. Rimington, E., Blount, T.: Lore v. Representation: narrative communication of power with regard to gender in league of legends. In: CEUR Workshop Proceedings, vol. 1628, pp. 1–5 (2016)

67. Riot Games: league of legends (2009)

68. Rousseau, S.: World of warcraft recreates one of its biggest events, including broken servers (2020). https://www.vice.com/en/article/ep4wqj/world-of-warcraft-recreates-one-of-its-biggest-events-including-broken-servers. Accessed 17 Jan 2021

69. Rusch, D.C.: 21st century soul guides: Leveraging myth and ritual for game design. Transgression, and Controversy in Play, University of Bergen, Norway, DiGRA Nordic Subversion (2018)

70. Ryan, J.: Curating Simulated Storyworlds. Ph.D. thesis, UC Santa Cruz (2018)

71. Ryan, M.L.: Beyond myth and metaphor: narrative in digital media. Poetics Today 23(4), 581–609 (2002)

72. Ryan, M.L.: Avatars of Story. University of Minnesota Press, 111 Third Avenue South, Suite 290, Minneapolis (2006)

73. Saler, M.: As if: Modern enchantment and the literary prehistory of virtual reality. Oxford University Press (2012)

74. Schaap, J., Aupers, S.: Gods in world of warcraft exist: religious reflexivity and the quest for meaning in online computer games. New Media Soc. 19(11), 1744–1760 (2017)

75. Schreier, J.: The makers of 'leeroy jenkins' didn't think anyone would believe it was real. Kotaku article describing the meme. https://kotaku.com/the-makers-of-leeroy-jenkins-didnt-think-anyone-would-b-1821570730 Acessed 5th of June 2022. Upload of the original video can be seen at https://www.youtube.com/watch?v=mLyOj_QD4a4 (2017)

76. Segal, R.A.: Myth: a very short introduction. OUP Oxford (2004)

77. Sicart, M.: Play matters. Playful Thinking, MIT Press (2014). https://books.google.com/books?id=ys06BAAAQBAJ

78. Statt, N.: Fortnite is now one of the biggest games ever with 350 million players. The Verge (2020). https://www.theverge.com/2020/5/6/21249497/fortnite-350-million-registered-players-hours-played-april Accessed on the 21th of January 2021

79. Swartjes, I.M.T.: Whose story is it anyway? How improv informs agency and authorship of emergent narrative. Ph.D. thesis, University of Twente, The Netherlands (2010)

80. Szilas, N., Estupiñán, S., Richle, U.: Qualifying and quantifying interestingness in dramatic situations. In: Nack, F., Gordon, A.S. (eds.) ICIDS 2016. LNCS, vol. 10045, pp. 336–347. Springer, Cham (2016). https://doi.org/10.1007/978-3-319-48279-8_30

81. The Game Band: blaseball. https://www.blaseball.com/ (2020)

82. theatakhan: A detailed theory on minecraft's lore. Reddit post by user "theatakhan" (2016). https://www.reddit.com/r/GameTheorists/comments/4uxh18/a_detailed_theory_on_minecrafts_lore/. Accessed 7 Jun 2022

83. Thue, D., Bulitko, V., Spetch, M., Webb, M.: Exaggerated claims for interactive stories. In: Iurgel, I.A., Zagalo, N., Petta, P. (eds.) ICIDS 2009. LNCS, vol. 5915, pp. 179–184. Springer, Heidelberg (2009). https://doi.org/10.1007/978-3-642-10643-9_23

84. Valle, C.G.D.: Destiny 2 twitter, facebook taken over by villain caiatl; zavala storyline cutscene leaked [video]. Techtimes article https://www.techtimes.com/articles/257864/20210309/destiny-2-twitter-facebook-taken-over-villain-caiatl-zavala-storyline.htm Article has images of tweets in question with corresponding avatar icon and name (the acconut has since been rebranded back to "Destiny 2" https://twitter.com/DestinyTheGame. Also see Reddit thread from the time https://www.reddit.com/r/DestinyTheGame/comments/m0kggb/destinythegames_twitter_profile_has_changed_his/ and community conversation about it at https://twitter.com/MyNameIsByf/status/1369991874539311104 (2021)

85. Valve: Counter-strike: global offensive (2012)

86. Wallin, M.R.: Myths, monsters and markets: ethos, identification, and the video game adaptations of the lord of the rings. Game Stud. 7(1) (2007)

87. Walsh, R.: Emergent narrative in interactive media. Narrative **19**(1), 72–85 (2011)

88. de Wildt, L., Aupers, S.: Creeds, souls & worlds of worship: Players' appropriations of religious worldviews through game forums. In: 1st International Joint Conference of DiGRA and FDG. Citeseer (2016)

89. Ziebart, A.: Wow archivist: the gates of ahn'qiraj (2011). https://www.engadget.com/2011-04-19-wow-archivist-the-gates-of-ahnqiraj.html. Accessed 17 Jan 2021

90. Žižek, S.: Welcome to the desert of the real! Verso (2002)

Bringing Stories to Life in 1001 Nights: A Co-creative Text Adventure Game Using a Story Generation Model

Yuqian Sun[1]([envelope]) [ID], Xuran Ni[2] [ID], Haozhen Feng[3] [ID], Ray LC[4] [ID], Chang Hee Lee[5] [ID], and Ali Asadipour[1] [ID]

[1] Computer Science Research Centre, Royal College of Art, London, UK
yuqiansun@network.rca.ac.uk,ali.asadipour@rca.ac.uk
[2] London, UK
[3] New Drama, Beijing, China
[4] School of Creative Media, City University of Hong Kong, Hong Kong, China
LC@raylc.org
[5] Affective System and Cognition Lab, KAIST, Daejon, South Korea
changhee.lee@kaist.ac.kr

Abstract. How can the stories we tell be turned from abstractions in our own minds into concrete elements in a digital environment that we can interact with? To immerse everyday storytelling into digital interactions, we created a game that turns entities in a story into digital assets that have functional roles. Taking the classic folklore as inspiration, we created 1001 Nights, a co-creative, mixed-initiative storytelling game using an existing AI creative writing system. In this game, Shahrzad (driven by the player) tells stories through a dialogue interface, while the King (driven by the AI model) continues the player's story in turn. Text from the story is used in the game mechanics, so that if the player enters keywords such as 'sword' and 'shield', they are turned into equipment that can be used in battles. Players who are more engaged with the game, measured by the length of their inputs, are rewarded with better achievements. The game aims to facilitate player engagement and creativity through natural language interactions in an empowering setting. This paper presents the game design, a breakdown of the development process and an analysis of user data, including instrumented gameplay data from 2055 players and comments from 422 players. The player feedback indicates that they enjoyed the creative interactions, the game mechanics and the narratives they constructed.

Keywords: Game AI · Intelligent narrative · Conversational agent · Game design · NCP-player interactions · Interactive storytelling

1 Introduction

Humans are fundamentally storytellers. From advancing in our careers to making pepperoni pizzas, stories infuse every part of our lives. The ability of machines to

---

X. Ni—Unaffiliated

© The Author(s), under exclusive license to Springer Nature Switzerland AG 2022
M. Vosmeer and L. Holloway-Attaway (Eds.): ICIDS 2022, LNCS 13762, pp. 651–672, 2022.
https://doi.org/10.1007/978-3-031-22298-6_42

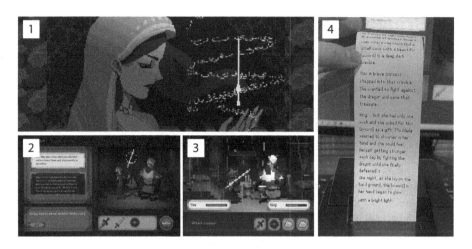

Fig. 1. (1) Shahrzad, the player character, who has a magical ability to turn language into reality. (2) The storytelling phase, where the player writes stories with the King, an AI character. Weapon words like 'sword' can be turned into real in-game weapons. (3) The turn-based combat phase, where the player can fight with the king in battles. (4) The printer prints the story when a weapon word is triggered. This matches with the core concept of the game: bringing storytelling into real life.

generate coherent text has allowed stories to be told in new ways by mechanising the writing process, through collaborative writing tools [1–3] or even directly talking to fictional characters [11,12]. Can text-based dialogue between human and machine be used as part of the game mechanics? As a metaphor for the storytelling process, we turned to the story of Shahrzad, who determined her fate by telling stories in real life. We created a game that uses the conceit of storytelling akin to The Thousand and One Nights to motivate real-life writing of stories.

Inspired by the classic folklore, we created the game 1001 Nights[1] (illustrative screenshots shown in Fig. 1), a co-creative, mixed-initiative storytelling game driven by an existing AI creative writing system. The core concept is 'bringing storytelling to real life' in game form: entities in storytelling are not just words and descriptions but can be turned into real assets to change the reality of a video game setting.

In this game, Shahrzad (controlled by the player) uses a dialogue interface to tell part of a story, and then the King (driven by the AI model) continues the player's story in turn. When the King's continuation contains weapon keywords like 'sword', 'knife' or 'shield', Shahrzad can use her special ability to turn words into real weapons and use them to fight with the king, creating game mechanics out of the player's own writing. This leads to an alternative ending of the original

---

[1] The game is available for download at: https://cheesetalk.itch.io/one-thousand-and-one-night.

story: the female storyteller and heroine, Shahrzad, defeats the tyrannical King and puts an end to his heinous crimes.

With this game, we expanded existing creative writing tools to create a playable storytelling experience in a familiar narrative setting. We believe that combining natural language interactions with a classic story can help players to explore and engage more in the game by expressing themselves. The efforts they put into imagination and creativity are rewarded with positive and adaptive content generation by the AI model.

We showcased a Chinese version of this game in several art exhibitions and received 12030 records of story inputs from 2055 players. This paper aims to investigate if the AI system can encourage players to contribute more collaboratively through engagement. The results demonstrate that those players who are more engaged (measured by the number of their inputs) in the game are rewarded with better achievements, as intended. Comments collected from winning players (n = 422) show positive feedback towards various aspects of the game, including the game mechanics and the stories created. Some of their feedback also shows a cultural connection through creative work: some players expressed their own interpretations of characters in the folklore, and were able to include characters and plots from their own cultural backgrounds.

2   Related Work

2.1   Natural Language Processing

Previous studies have investigated the use of natural language processing (NLP) for many different applications, including creative tools [1–3]. Some projects have developed collaborative AI writers focused on specific genres, for example Shelly [4], a crowd-sourced horror writer.

Similar approaches have been used in academic research for content generation. Murder mystery generation [5] generated murder mysteries for adventure games, using structured information about real-world people mined from Wikipedia articles. Designing for Narrative Influence [6] trained a language model to generate micro-fiction that promotes sustainable public health guidelines. Martin et al. [7] presented a series of experiments that connected ancient procedural techniques to modern technologies like language generation models.

Other studies have applied NLP to dialogue systems. Scheherazade's Tavern [8] and Prom Week [9] tried to develop deeper NPC interactions for a natural social simulation experience. Talk to Ghost [10] adapted Shakespeare's work to improve high school students' interest in reading by turning stories into interactive conversations with virtual characters.

In this work, we describe a hybrid experience that sits between creative writing and a game. Some of our main influences are CharacterChat [11] and BanterBot [12], dialogue systems that allow writers to talk with characters they have created. This extends writing assistance to an intelligent agent, turning the context of the interactions into a more familiar social setting. We designed the dialogue interface in 1001 Nights as a special scenario: two people telling each other stories. Through this, we hope players can easily understand the narrative context, and overcome a barrier to creativity documented by Kreminski and Wardrip-Fruin [13]: the fear of the blank canvas.

2.2   Game Interactions Using NLP

Through the use of NLP, emerging text adventure games give players more control over games compared with traditional games, which give players a limited number of fixed choices. For instance, *Interview With The Whisperer* [14] and *Mystery Of Three Bots* [15] let players explore mysterious stories with natural language text input through Semantic ML, a tool for semantic analysis developed by Google [16]. Fraser et al. [17] developed open-domain social conversational AI using emotion detection. In recent years, experimental games like *AI Dungeon* [18] even allow players to fully generate their text adventure with natural language input. The main goal of such games is to enhance the game playing experience by providing an immersive and engaging experience, similar to Sali's work [19], which has shown that natural language interfaces, while difficult to use, can reward players with high levels of engagement and enjoyment.

By creating conversational interactions through free-input dialogue systems, NLP has also been used in parts of commercial games such as *KuilciXi* [20], *Event [0]* [21] and *Bot Colony* [22]. These games use a natural dialogue system as the primary means to push the plot forward.

2.3   Natural Language Generation in Stories

Among these NLP-driven projects, only a few have used a natural language generation model, for example personaChat [25] in CharacterChat [11] or OpenAI's GPT-3 in AI Dungeon [18]; most other projects have implemented NLP for a specific task like parsing player utterances into logical statements [8,26] or finding the closest response from a database [14,15]. The main reason for this is that the use of a natural language generation model risks producing content that is out of topic, and these projects need to find a balance between player freedom and content quality. Accordingly, even when players can use natural language input, these games set very fixed storylines and backgrounds that cannot be intentionally changed by player inputs. Off-topic input will either lead to confusing responses, which are frequently discussed in the player community of AI Dungeon [27–29], or get limited by the customised module, like in Facade's Global Context Pool [30], which tried to maintain players' suspension of disbelief (their belief in the fictional story for the sake of enjoyment) even when their input was out of bounds. Another example is that, in Scheherazade's Tavern [8], when a player mentions a topic that is not in the knowledge module, the AI agent will repeat a word and then change the topic. These control mechanisms are methods to ensure output quality.

This led us to think about the possibility of letting players decide the game's plot and generating mechanics corresponding to the narrative framework of their story. To avoid quality pitfalls faced by other games, we set a clear goal – the player must lead the AI king to mention weapons – to restrict the output and keep it on topic. We assume the natural language model's creative ability has space to improve under the game environment: when it can generate adaptive content according to player's input, and let players' choices define components of the story (such as equipment and scenes), the full gameplay will become more dynamic, and bring co-authored creative artifact in the same time.

2.4   Dynamic Feedback Beyond Text

In games based on NLP, it is difficult to give dynamic feedback beyond the text. The text can adapt to the player's natural language input, but the rest of the game cannot. It is very time-consuming for creators to prepare assets, such as character animations and background scenery, that are synchronous with text output. For instance, in the development of *Facade* [30], two authors spent two years preparing the character reactions and assets for a 20-minute game with a single scene [30]. Some projects have started to use other AI generation models to provide adaptive content, like the GAN-generated images in *AI Dungeon* [18]. Our focus is on the text modality, but our contribution is to map text to another part of the game world: equipment. We were inspired by word-typing [31,32] games, where players must quickly type specific words to release character skills. However, these games do not have semantic relationships between the words and the skills or world environment, while keywords in 1001 Nights will always be part of stories and created through human-AI interactions.

We designed game mechanics to create a rich AI system: understanding the player's actions and responding intelligently, through which a player can attempt many different strategies in the game and find that they are equally supported by the system [33]. Accordingly, with weapon words as the main target, we can map infinite creations from players to limited instances, and then we can provide dynamic interactions with prepared assets, including 3D models and visual effects when a keyword is triggered.

3   Game Design

This section presents the design and development of the game.

The game is made up of two parts: storytelling and battles. Figure 2 illustrates the game mechanics: the player needs to keep telling stories to lead the King to produce story continuations that mention the important items for battle. In the first phase (Fig. 2 bottom left), Shahrzad (driven by the player) and the King (driven by the AI model) take turns continuing the story. In this game, Shahrzad has a special ability to turn words into reality: when another person utters keywords like 'sword', 'knife' or 'shield', those items materialise and drop to the ground. The player's goal in this phase is to lead the King to tell more stories that contain keywords and collect weapons.

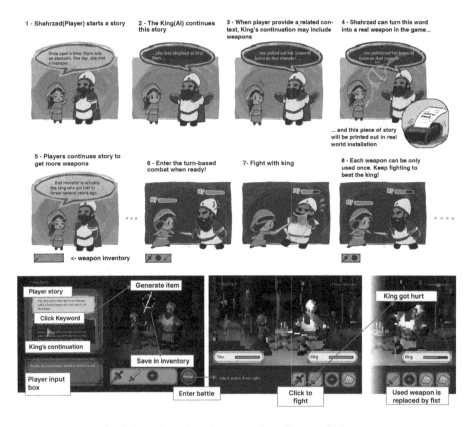

Fig. 2. (Up) Storyboard of the gameplay. (Bottom) Game process

After collecting enough weapons and pieces of armour, the player can enter the turn-based battle phase (Fig. 2 bottom right) to fight with the King. In this phase, the player can use the weapons collected during the last phase to fight the King. The Player's goal in this phase is to beat the King and free Shahrzad. This is a different ending from the original folklore.

We attempt to combine all components of the game into a coherent experience. The story background links to the mechanics: Shahrzad needs to create stories to survive. The AI system allows the player to be creative and explore different parts of the story.

3.1 Game Art

To encourage players to focus on the gameplay, we use a pixel art visual style. Most pixel art games, like *Terraria* [34] and *Red String Club* [35], use 2D hand-drawn images for all game assets. However, to save time while keeping the fluent aesthetic, we used 3D-to-2D techniques as in *A Short Hike* [36]. With this method, there is no need to manually draw character animations; instead, we used existing action animations from open source libraries like Mixamo [37]. The resulting game art is still in the traditional 2D pixel art style but with a reduced development time. The low-resolution art that blurs character faces also matches the feel of the ancient story and leaves room for the players' imagination.

3.2 Battle System

The aims of the battle system (illustrated in Fig. 3) are (1) to make the game interesting and challenging and encourage players to write more stories; and (2) to balance the difficulty – a player should not feel that it is too easy or too hard to win. For these purposes, we decided to require players to write at least two stories that trigger valid responses to win the game, that is, a player needs two attack weapons to win.

However, if two attacks are enough to defeat the King, a player will only click twice to win the battle. Hence, the time spent in this phase will be too short. The battle phase needs to be exciting for players, and they may meet failures before the victory. Thus, we implemented the following rules:

1. Each weapon collected in phase one can only be used once. Once used, this weapon will be replaced by a fist (punch) icon. The fist can also be used for attacking, but it deals much less damage. Shahrzad can only attack with a punch when she has no weapon in her hands, as in real life.
2. Some equipment is for defence rather than attack, such as 'shield' and 'armour'. They cannot hurt the king but enrich the game experience by preventing king from dealing damage during his turn. This effect is also realistic.
3. The maximum inventory space is four. Equipment exceeding this limit is not saved for battle but is recorded in the backend to confirm the player's achievement of obtaining weapons. If the inventory is not full, the empty spaces are replaced by the first in the battle phase.

By these rules, once players collect two attacking weapons (like 'sword' and 'dagger'), they can use them and then punch with their fist twice. These combinations will lead to victory. If players only have defending equipment, they can not defeat the King, since the only method of attack is a punch.

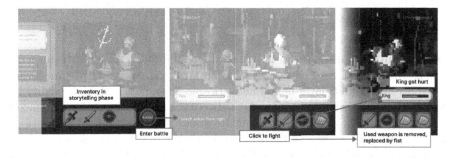

Fig. 3. Battle in game

3.3 AI Development

Demo 1 and Keywords. We designed four offensive weapons – the sword, knife, blade and dagger – and two defensive weapons – the shield and armour. These are keywords that yielded over 50 matching paragraphs when we searched for them in the Guttenberg Short Story collection [38], a dataset extracted from the portal of Project Gutenberg, a library of over 60,000 eBooks. Meanwhile, these are also weapon words that match with the ancient narrative setting of 1001 Nights. Within the original 94 MB Gutenberg short story dataset [38], we located each paragraph with a matching keyword and extracted the previous five paragraphs, yielding a smaller 16.24 MB dataset. In the first prototype, the King's AI model was trained on the extracted dataset using the GPT-2 medium model [39] with 6000 steps, so that it would be familiar with common tropes in various adventure stories. The text generation temperature was set to 0.8. Here are several 200-word examples of the results:

Example 1. Player: The princess tried to find her magic sword in the forest
    AI: ...and at last through sword at once hid it in her breast; whereupon the beast – a common creature – pretended to understand all she said, and then proceeded to strangle her for a good while. The princess fought with it, till the beast relaxed, took its sword, and set off home. 'They are the daughters of Snaxen,' said the young man, passing by to his friends.
    Player: 'Do you know them?' The princess asked.
    AI: 'I knew them,' answered Javelin. 'I was called about twenty years ago, and the King of Thessaly picked me up for the defense of the south against the armies of the Chilkatrachels. He gave me orders, and I carried them, and soon learned to toss my sword, and to wait for the return of the Sun, so that I might meet him face to face in the courtyard of my honor...

Stories generated in this manner are full of leaps and bounds, and develop logical holes as the story goes on. Although the training model might be improved using a larger dataset, this process would be time-consuming. Even if the model were improved, the story-continuation ability may not be flexible enough for modern players. Since the original story collection includes many old books, the model may struggle to understand players when they write in a more modern style. This may result in low-quality and confusing stories. To fix this problem, we sought alternative solutions.

English and Chinese Demo 2. We used Dreamily.ai [2] to reinforce our game design. Dreamily.ai is a creative writing platform using a modified transformer (a self-attention multi-layer neural network) model trained with high-quality fiction. Both its English and Chinese datasets consist of open access fan fiction and ebooks on the web, and both datasets are about 100 GB in size. This platform has over one million users of the Chinese version and 200 thousand users of the English version. Although the model is not suitable for all tasks (e.g. writing official documents or code), it is well suited to story generation. To use the model, it is only necessary to call the application programming pnterface and send the title and prompt to dreamily.ai's server [45].

This generation model with a large dataset was able to produce results similar to Demo 1, except for the keywords part. To implement our game mechanics, we designed the structure of requests for the model as in Fig. 4. With this design, dreamily.ai produces flexible stories that closely correspond to player input. The past five inputs are added to the prompt to ensure fluency. Records are refreshed when the player starts a new game or moves to the battle phase. When King's response does not include a keyword, Shahrzad sends a notification message to provide a hint to the player that they should tell a more relevant story. This helps to relieve confusion and the Tale-Spin effect [40], in which a system makes people feel it is less intelligent than it actually is due to insufficient explanation of the underlying processes.

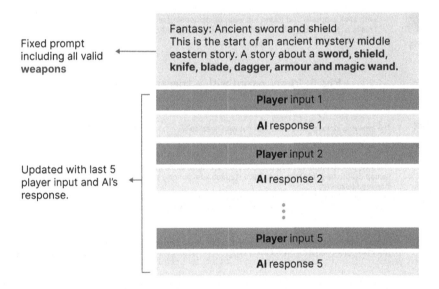

Fig. 4. Requests for the AI model

The player is allowed to mention keywords (like 'sword') in the input phase. This may increase the chance of obtaining stories that mention the corresponding weapons in some way, but it will not guarantee it. In contrast, an input that creates a suitable context without a weapon word can still lead to a valid response that contains keywords. Figure 5 shows an example of this. However, as illustrated in Fig. 6, due to the randomness of the AI system and the limited word list, a player may mention weapon words repeatedly, but may still fail to trigger a weapon. Some players may ask questions in conversations with the king, as shown in Fig. 7, but the king will still give adaptive responses. This can sometimes make the stories appear out of context.

Player

A fallen chief knight of an army of knights wanders through the Dark Forest with his cherished **sword** ...

Mentioned valid weapon word: **sword**

King

He was not happy that his army had been wiped out by the enemy, but his weapons were pretty much destroyed. "Holy knight lord, I would join your order, please take me in, if you will take me in then I would give anything just to be kept alive." ...

No trigger keyword

Player

The knight was cold and hungry; he had not had decent food for a week. Then a huge crow flew in and asked, "What good things do you have in your hand, human?"

No mentioned weapon

King

The raven smelt him and put its beak close to the tip. The raven took a breath and found his weapon appetising and said, "This is a good lance, a rare weapon with [blades], although it's broken ...

Trigger keyword [blades]

Fig. 5. Player record with a triggered weapon

Player

The little dog in the green suit rushed out with a red **spear**

Mentioned invalid weapon word: **spear**

King

The little children were terrified and fled in all directions while the other two rushed over to help, but they were still a step too late and only two of them managed to survive.
One of them, a young boy, looked to be about ten years old, his face covered in beads of sweat, but with a look of stubbornness in his eyes. ...

No trigger keyword

Player

He had heard a legend about magical swords, that if you grew a year older, you would gain a different **sword** every day

Mentioned valid weapon word: **sword**

King

and every day there would be a potion that would change his physique, so he wanted to have it all.
The other little girl, who seemed to be very weak, not yet an adult, but whose eyes revealed a resolute look, did not seem to care about anything ...

No trigger keyword

Player

He had heard a legend about magical **swords**, that if you grew a year older, you would gain a different sword every day

Mentioned valid weapon word: **sword**

King

The girl, however, was not at all afraid of the boy, but looked at him calmly, knowing that he must be her future husband, so she did not show any signs of panic.
The two of them supported each other to the depths of the valley, under an ancient tree, when a figure came out from the side ...

No trigger keyword

Fig. 6. Player record with no triggered weapon

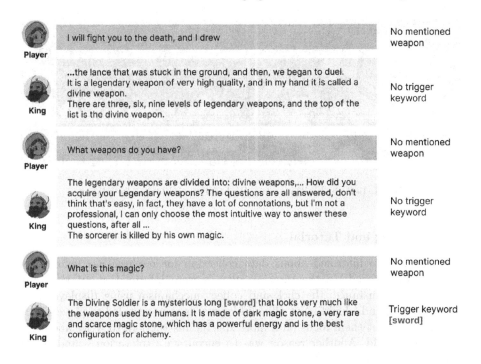

Fig. 7. Player record with out-of-context inputs

All these examples, translated from Chinese, are taken from play test records during exhibitions, which are discussed in the next section.

4 Evaluation Study

4.1 Experimental Setup

We were invited to showcase our work at three exhibition sites in China, to research a range of players and collect feedback. All three were in different cities, but they all shared the same digital and analogue setup, including a vintage monitor (to match the ancient setting of the story), a printer, and a workstation using the Windows 10 operating system. A tutorial leaflet (a screenshot of the help page in the game) was on the table for players to read.

A mini-printer was used during a two-month offline exhibition in Beijing to emphasise the concept of 'invading language' and to improve public engagement. Each time a keyword was triggered, the current piece of the story was printed out. In this game, the keywords are the materialised language that becomes part of the 'reality', and to players, the printed text is tangible output from the game to the real world. This feature encouraged people to spend more time at the exhibition since they could keep a hard copy of their stories.

Fig. 8. Left: Exhibition setup Right: Tutorial leaflet for players

4.2   Opening and Tutorial

All players were informed about data collection for research use before they entered the tutorial. In the tutorial, players were informed about the game dynamics, for instance, the click and collect mechanism using displayed keywords 'sword' and 'shield'. Not all valid keywords were revealed to players. One reason was to let them focus on a more specific instruction: to write about the sword and shield. Another reason was to encourage exploration – finding the valid keywords is also part of the gameplay.

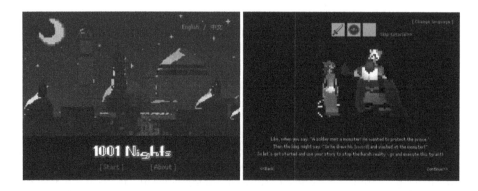

Fig. 9. Left: Opening screen Right: Screenshot of tutorial

5   Results and Findings

Since the core system in the game is the story generation model, this inevitably adds randomness to the results, which cannot be fully limited by rules. When analysing the player data, we aimed to confirm if the AI system can encourage players to engage and contribute more collaboratively in play.

Following the aim of this game – collaborative storytelling with clear goals – 'engagement' can be regarded as how much time and energy players want to spend, and 'contribution' means the quality of their inputs: whether the sentences make sense or not and whether they are directed towards obtaining weapons. Accordingly, the AI system should give positive feedback to players in the form of responses containing weapon keywords, which become the items that lead to success. If the AI system works effectively, then when a player engages and contributes more in collaborative storytelling, they should receive more weapons, making them more likely to win the game.

When evaluating player contribution, we met some difficulties. We had large amounts of player data (2065 players with 12030 inputs), so it was not feasible to evaluate the quality of all story content. Additionally, since the data were collected during exhibitions, the playing time might have been influenced by unpredictable factors, like the queue length or the number of visitors on that day. Thus, we decided to use average inputs per play to evaluate player engagement, and compare this with their achievements in the game. To be specific, 'play' is defined as reaching the end: success in defeating the king, failure to defeat the king, restarting or ending the game. Further evaluation like thematic analysis of stories and play tests without time limitations are left for future works.

To evaluate the level of achievements, we categorised players into three groups, as shown in Table 1: non-winner (G1, n = 299), journeyman (G2, n = 1106), and winner (G3, n = 650). These groups are independent of each other, but the level of progress raised from G1 to G3: non-winners (G1) did not collect any weapons or win the game, journeymen (G2) acquired at least one weapon but did not win, and winners (G3) defeated the king in one or more plays. All players had a chance to familiarise themselves with the game with printed screenshots and integrated tutorials prior to the game, with an identical experimental setup in all three locations.

Table 1. Grouping players by their achievements

Definition	G1	G2	G3
Collected at least one weapon	No	Yes	Yes
Defeated the King at least once	No	No	Yes

5.1 Analysis

This study aims to investigate the impact of engagement in storytelling (average inputs per play) on overall achievement level (from G1 to G3) made by players and to understand any potential trends between the groups. Hence, a Levene test is used to check the homogeneity of variances among engagement of each group, $F_{(2, 2055)} = 32.02$, $p < .05$. We believe that players that make little progress on average are more likely to experience frustration, meaning that the distribution of inputs per play in G1 (M = 2.59, SD = 2.05) is more influenced by the players' propensity to lose patience. Meanwhile, the distribution of inputs per play in G2 (M = 4.51, SD = 3.61) and G3 (M = 6.30, SD = 3.85) may also be influenced by the players' luck in finding the right inputs. This distinction may explain the difference in variances. Figure 10 shows the distributions in each group.

A non-parametric Kruskal-Wallis test, as an alternative to one-way ANOVA, is used to evaluate the correlation between player engagement and overall achievements. Players' achievements in this game were reported to be affected by engagement, H(2) = 328.295, p <.05. The results show that players are more likely to achieve a better outcome by making more contributions to the storyline. Also, a positive trend (shown in Fig. 11) is observed and reported by the Jonckheere-Terpstra test. Since the shape and variability assumption is violated, the obtained Welch's adjusted F ratio was used F(2, 1012.54) = 191.85, p <.001. Hence, we can conclude that at least two of the three groups differed significantly in their overall achievements in this game.

In general, the randomness of story generation sometimes influences the gameplay: high engagement (more inputs per play) does not guarantee victory, and fewer inputs may also lead to enough valid keywords for the player to win. However, as shown by the previous analysis, this randomness does not impact the overall performance of game design. In conclusion, the game encourages players to engage in storytelling: the more they engaged, the better achievements they would reach in the game.

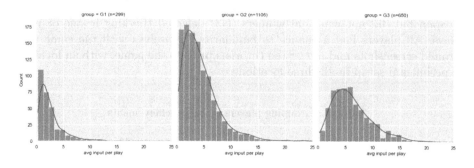

Fig. 10. Average input per play distributions per group

5.2   Comments from Winners

Since this game was only exhibited in China, although it received some feedback in English, the following section will only focus on feedback in Chinese. Only players in G3 (winners) were allowed to leave feedback after victory for the following reasons:

1. Players played this game during an exhibition, so not all of them had enough interest to reach the end. Sometimes there was a queue to play this game.

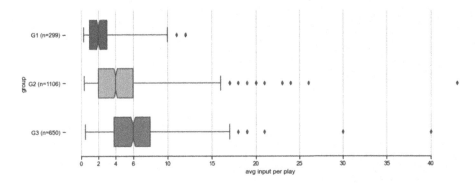

Fig. 11. Positive trend in overall achievements by average contributions made

2. We wanted to encourage players who were defeated to try again until they achieved victory, so that they went through the full gameplay. If we showed the ending page (Fig. 12 left) to all players, including ones who were defeated by the King, they may have regarded it as an ending and left.
3. We assume that players who were patient enough to win gained a deeper experience in this game, which is helpful for us to identify its weaknesses.

We received winners' records (n = 650) and removed those who did not leave comments (n = 226). We also removed two records from players who met technical difficulties during the experience (the printer was not working).

Finally, with thematic analysis, one of us developed a set of initial codes. After discussion with colleagues, the rest of the remaining feedback (n = 422) was identified and classified into nine categories (shown in Fig. 12 right). In future work, we hope to include multiple coders and inter-rater reliability calculations.

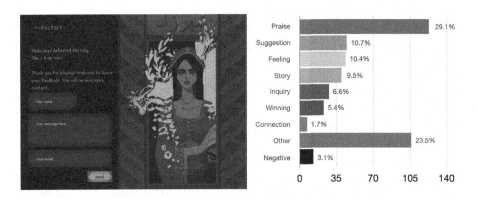

Fig. 12. Feedback page appears when a player achieves victory (left), categorised feedback (right)

Category	Description	Example	Number
Praise	General positive comments toward the game	Great game!/ I enjoy it	123 (29.1%)
Suggestion	Suggestions about gameplay	I think it should include more weapons/ hope it to be easier	45 (10.7%)
Feeling	Specific impression and feeling towards the gameplay, character, etc	This king is smarter than me/ It's an adult version of the folklore/ Feels like I'm teaching this AI	44(10.4%)
Story	Retell or comment specifically on the stories they created	The king ate too much deer meat and died in A's sword / A brings B to beat the king and get revenge!	40 (9.5%)
Inquiries	Ask questions about the game	Will it be published on Steam(a game platform)? / How can I get more weapons?	28 (6.6%)
Winning	Comments on their victory	I'm a king among kings!/ So easy, nobody can be my rival!	23 (5.4%)
Connection	Connected personal experiences outside the game	I hope I can become Shahrzad in real life and fight for freedom/ It reminds me of my memory of writing stories with friends when I was in high school.	7 (1.7%)
Criticism	Points out unsatisfied points	This is a bad game/ The king is too stupid.	13 (3.1%)
Others	Other unclassifiable comments	Oh yeah!!/ But he indeed lost language skills	99(23.5%)

Fig. 13. Comments categories

General. Positive feedback like 'Good game (P10)' or 'Interesting (P60)' are in the praise category. This type makes up the largest share of results (29.1%, n = 123). Feedback in other categories shows various focuses. 10.7% (n = 45) of players made suggestions. Together with 6.6%(n = 28) of players who left inquiries, 8 of them expressed willingness for further development and publishing on a commercial game platform like Steam. These comments made us notice several perspectives that we ignored before. About half of the players (n = 25) who left suggestions, and some from the inquiry category (n = 7) asked for the inclusion of more weapons. Although some of them (n = 5) mentioned weapons like guns that do not fit into the narrative setting, we do recognise the benefits of improving weapon choices and better player guides. Several players (n = 13, 3.1%) were unsatisfied with or disliked this game, which is expected for a game at an early stage of development.

Immersion in the Game and Story. 10.4%(n = 44)players shared personal feelings towards gameplay, like 'we should always believe in love and magic (P326)', 'It's interesting and immersive. Players are invited to save a character and feel strength (P511)' and 'we choose free rather than love (P261)'. Some also expressed thoughts about AI: 'Humans reach consensus with AI (P586)' and 'Humans are those who think beyond AI (P561)'. These suggest our game can provoke reflections about freedom, strength and the agency of AI. P624 gave a good summary that matches our motivation: 'It's interesting. The game mechanics of hidden triggers also brought 'freedom' to players, not only to Shahrzad.' The more interesting fact is that nearly one-third of this group (n = 14) shared their impressions about the king, like 'This king sounds like a gastronome (P564)' and 'The king can become a good writer in his next life (P542)'. A player even said 'There is not only betrayal and injury but also warmth and protection, in the hope that the defeated King in prison can understand what he has, treasure what he has, do not ask the past (P491)'. Even though we did not add any personal lines to the king, some players showed empathy toward this character. To some degree, this feedback shows the potential attraction of intelligent characters driven by NLP technology. A character can give reasonable responses even without detailed design work, and the player's interpretations can fill the gap in the story. The players' feedback was more varied than expected. We expected to receive general praise and suggestions – the most surprising result is that 9.5% (n = 40) of players talked specifically about the stories they created. Most of them (n = 29) mentioned the characters they included in their stories and described the plot in detail, like 'Summon the beasts' success! ! The black cat is turned to the witch, and it turns into a magic hat (P395)' and 'Princess Li finally defeated the evil emperor with high ideal (P230)'. This provides evidence that many players are highly engaged in the stories they created.

While some players were immersed in the stories they created, some players receive more pleasure from their victory. 5.4% (n = 23) of players gave highly positive feedback describing their feelings of victory, like 'AI cannot defeat human Shahrzad! (P30)' or 'I am very smart! I'm the smartest princess(P138)'. In general, this feedback suggests our game can bring both an entertaining experience and creative collaboration between humans and AI.

Cultural Connection. Among players who commented on the story they created, many of them were inspired by personal interests that matched with the mysterious background, like 'I want to lit the fire of renaissance in the darkness (P234)', 'No matter what, Sword Soul, Shield Sprite and Gun Sprite will always be good friends! (P637)' and 'Mountain Boots Puss and Iliad, Hit, the three live together forever and inherit the throne of Snow Mountain. (P540)'

Since the testing was performed in exhibitions in China, some of the players put aspects of their cultural background into their stories, which became creative artifacts through human-AI collaboration that show possibilities in cultural blends. For example, 'Awesome! How to play the sequel? I want to chat more with the old ancestor Ye who fought with the shovel in Luoyang and the witcher who fought with the lich... What happened to the Prince? (P350)' 'Shovel in Luoyang' here is one of the most important tools in Chinese archaeology, and is usually mentioned in grave robbing stories. Another player (P148) put a character from pop culture in the story: 'A Liang, the youth who left the factory, can beat the king.' This character 'A Liang' comes from the pop song 'About Life' by the 'Wutiaoren' [41], a popular band in China who are famous for their attention to the current situation of Chinese rural youth and for the strong humanistic feelings in their music.

Reflection on Reality. It was observed that a few players (n = 7, 1.7%) even connected this game to their experiences and feelings in real life, like someone who felt encouragement from Shahrzad: 'I am a student, I also want to be free, be as brave as the heroine in-game once (P451)' and 'I love this world, I also want to create valuable works. (P46)'

We also received very detailed feedback about previous personal experiences: 'Thank you for reminding me of my favourite game I played with my friends in class during my reading time. In those days we used to write a story on a large piece of scratch paper, one at a time. No one knows what will happen next, and we tend to avoid stories that fall into a rut, creating more and more mysterious adventures for it. Good memories. That's a good game. (P11)' This feedback suggests this game may have potential ability as an educational game for story writing.

Fig. 14. Exhibition photos. Left: A 11-year old boy kept playing for half an hour Right: Official photo from exhibition

6   Discussion

This study investigates how the AI system can reward players to motivate collaboration in writing stories. The results show a significant difference between at least two groups' overall achievements based on the level of engagement in storytelling. Players with higher engagement were more likely to reach improved achievements in the game. This is aligned with the hypothesis that our game design did encourage players to explore and collaboratively interact in the game, and the AI system could reward them with creative feedback.

Even when we did not ask players to rate their experience, in comments from players (n = 422) who won the game, players showed a high level of enjoyment and interest throughout the game, where they contributed their own stories to be part of it. Supported by the AI system, the same character and interface may bring different stories and experiences based on the players' personal choices, and they can immerse themselves in the game, exploring their own interests. Similar to previous studies [42], the unexpected but logical text generated by AI may make the story more exciting than the player's intention.

Players expressed their own interpretations of characters in the folklore and were able to include characters and plots from their own cultural backgrounds. For them, the king could be a coward, a peace lover or a gastronome, and these are reflections through the creation, rather than the line the creators set. They could introduce a character from a pop song in their story, or link the game to current social news. This suggests a potential chance to alleviate the creator's burden to develop games. Players' autonomy and imagination may fill in the gaps that developers leave blank. This is similar to the finding of Aljammaz et al. [8] that a player may view the repeated responses as the NPC's own personality.

7   Limitations

The creators faced common barriers in developing 1001 Nights. Like similar studies on dialogue interfaces, we found that open dialogue systems are a double-edged sword. They contribute to a sense of freedom but face the risk of going off track, and to limit that requires a large amount of authoring and design work.

Current weapon keywords are specific and limited. In future work, we plan to use semantic similarity detection to extend the range of valid keywords. For instance, in WebVectors [44], the sword is similar to the scimitar, rapier and broadsword. Less similar but closely related words, like hilt and scabbard, may become fragments that can be used to form actual weapons later.

Furthermore, due to the large playtest data, the current AI system was not able to evaluate the quality of player input. Consequently, we could only evaluate player performance through engagement (number of inputs per play). In future we hope to analyse the quality of inputs and responses received from the King. To see the impact of the game environment, we also hope to analyse how the results differ for players who directly use the story generation model and those who play the game in a version without keywords. In future work, participants will be able to download and play the game in their preferred environment, without the time pressure of physical exhibitions.

Meanwhile, when the player input includes some components that do not fit well in the setting of The Thousand and One Nights (like 'computer' or 'rifle gun'), the king can still continue the story, which may reduce player immersion, since an ancient king should not know about modern technologies. This could be improved by future enhancements, like keyword detection or neural classifiers.

Overall, as a game in its early stage, we received encouraging results. We started with the concept of 'bringing storytelling to life', and it was surprising to see that many players could naturally blend their own life into the game. We also suggest future investigation on using NLP models like OpenAI's GPT-3 [43] in more storytelling games.

8   Conclusion and Future Work

To extend storytelling to real-life contexts beyond the language, we created the game 1001 Nights, a co-creative storytelling game that leverages story writing into actual game mechanics, based on an existing story generation model. We have shown that 1001 Nights facilitates player engagement and creativity through natural language interactions in a well-known folklore setting. Our data suggest that higher player engagement generally leads to better achievements in the game, which demands further investigations.

Potential extensions of this research include multiple coder thematic analyses of players' stories and comments, and asking them to evaluate their engagement and interest on a Likert scale. This is key to evaluating the quality of inputs via a hybrid approach using NLP algorithms like text perplexity and domain experts. The game design could be improved to enhance replay value. For example, a weapon index could be added that documents the stories behind the triggered items. Furthermore, with emerging text-to-image technologies like DALL-E [46], it may even be possible to change the appearance of a weapon or character based on the corresponding sentences or change the background scenery over the course of the story. Beyond 1001 Nights, supported by text generation models, similar mechanics that set clear goals for players could be extended to more games, like suggesting a non-player character to spill a secret location that hides treasure.

References

1. Swanson, R., Gordon, A.S.: Say anything: a massively collaborative open domain story writing companion. In: Spierling, U., Szilas, N. (eds.) ICIDS 2008. LNCS, vol. 5334, pp. 32–40. Springer, Heidelberg (2008). https://doi.org/10.1007/978-3-540-89454-4_5
2. ColorfulClouds Tech, Dreamily.ai. https://dreamily.ai/. Accessed 16 Oct 2022
3. Coenen, A., et al.: Wordcraft: a human-AI collaborative editor for story writing. arXiv:2107.07430 (2021)
4. Yanardag, P., Cebrian, M., Rahwan, I.: Shelley: a crowd-sourced collaborative horror writer. Creat. Cogn. (2021). https://doi.org/10.1145/3450741.3465251
5. Barros, G.A.B., Liapis, A., Togelius, J.: Murder mystery generation from open data. In: L-Università ta' Malta (2016). https://www.um.edu.mt/library/oar/handle/123456789/47474
6. LC RAY, Mizuno, D.: Designing for narrative influence: Extended Abstracts of the 2021 CHI Conference on Human Factors in Computing Systems (2021). https://doi.org/10.1145/3411763.3450373
7. Pichlmair, M., Putney, C.: Procedural generation for divination and inspiration. Int. Conf. Found. Digit. Games (2020). https://doi.org/10.1145/3402942.3402950
8. Aljammaz, R., Oliver, E., Whitehead, J., Mateas, M.: Scheherazade's Tavern: a prototype for deeper NPC interactions. Int. Conf. Found. Digit. Games (2020). https://doi.org/10.1145/3402942.3402984
9. McCoy, J., et al.: Prom week: designing past the game/story dilemma. In: Foundation of Digital Games (FDG) (2013)
10. Jackson, D., Latham, A.: Talk to the ghost: The Storybox methodology for faster development of storytelling chatbots. Exp. Syst. Appl. 190, 116223 (2022). https://doi.org/10.1016/j.eswa.2021.116223
11. Schmitt, O., Buschek, D.: CharacterChat: supporting the creation of fictional characters through conversation and progressive manifestation with a chatbot. Creat. Cogn. (2021). https://doi.org/10.1145/3450741.3465253
12. Banter bot by Google Creative Lab - experiments with google. In: Google. https://experiments.withgoogle.com/banter-bot. Accessed 16 Oct 2022

13. Kreminski, M., Wardrip-Fruin, N.: Generative Games as Storytelling Partners. In: Proceedings of the 14th International Conference on the Foundations of Digital Games (2019). https://doi.org/10.1145/3337722.3341861
14. deconstructeam, Interview with the Whisperer. In: itch.io. https://deconstructeam. itch.io/interview-with-the-whisperer. Accessed 16 Oct 2022
15. (2020) The Mystery of the Three Bots. https://google.github.io/ mysteryofthreebots/. Accessed 16 Oct 2022
16. (2021) Semantic ML. In: Google. https://github.com/google/making_with_ml. Accessed 16 Oct 2022
17. Fraser J, Papaioannou, I., Lemon, O.: Spoken conversational AI in video games. In: Proceedings of the 18th International Conference on Intelligent Virtual Agents (2018). https://doi.org/10.1145/3267851.3267896
18. AI Dungeon. https://play.aidungeon.io/main/home. Accessed 21 Oct 2021
19. Sali, S., et al.: Playing with words. In: Proceedings of the Fifth International Conference on the Foundations of Digital Games - FDG 2010 (2010). https://doi.org/ 10.1145/1822348.1822372
20. Xi, Y., et al.: Kuileixi: a Chinese open-ended text adventure game. In: Proceedings of the 59th Annual Meeting of the Association for Computational Linguistics and the 11th International Joint Conference on Natural Language Processing: System Demonstrations (2021). https://doi.org/10.18653/v1/2021.acl-demo.21
21. Event[0] on Steam. https://store.steampowered.com/app/470260/Event0/. Accessed 27 Oct 2020
22. Bot Colony in Steam. https://store.steampowered.com/app/263040/Bot_Colony/. Accessed 27 Mar 2022
23. Kobzošová, K.: The changing value of the thousand and one nights and its influence on modern and contemporary Arabic literature, p. 16 (2012)
24. Enderwitz, S.: Shahrazâd is one of us: practical narrative, theoretical discussion, and feminist discourse. Marvels Tales **18**(2), 187–200 (2004). https://www.jstor. org/stable/41388707
25. Zhang, S., et al.: Personalizing dialogue agents: I have a dog, do you have pets too? (2018). https://arxiv.org/abs/1801.07243
26. Villar, S.O.: SHRDLU (2022). Accessed 27 Mar 2022. https://github.com/ santiontanon/SHRDLU
27. Realistic Net 1799: No comment, just some goofy AI stuff., r/AIDungeon 04 Apr 2022. www.reddit.com/r/AIDungeon/comments/twbpvw/no_comment_just_some_ goofy_ai_stuff/. Accessed 04 Apr 2022
28. TrovianIcyLucario, A.I Dungeon nonsense I've collected: Part 2, r/AIDungeon 03 Apr 2021. www.reddit.com/r/AIDungeon/comments/mj11bt/ai_dungeon_ nonsense_ive_collected_part_2/. Accessed 04 Apr 2022
29. Wank my Butt: New player. All of my stories derail into nonsense almost immediately. Is this normal?, r/AIDungeon 16 Jan 2022. www.reddit.com/r/AIDungeon/ comments/s53ywr/new_player_all_of_my_stories_derail_into_nonsense/. Accessed 04 Apr 2022
30. Mateas, M., Stern, A.: Façade: An experiment in building a fully-realized interactive drama (2003)
31. Steam - God of Word. https://store.steampowered.com/app/467320/God_of_ Word/. Accessed 04 Apr 2022
32. Steam - Orbi's chronicles. h. https://store.steampowered.com/app/1492190/ Orbis_chronicles/. Accessed 04 Apr 2022
33. Eladhar, M.P., Sullivan, A., Smith, G., McCoy, J.: Ai-based game design: enabling new playable experiences (2011)

34. Steam Terraria. https://store.steampowered.com/app/105600/Terraria/. Accessed 03 Apr 2022

35. Steam - The Red Strings Club. https://store.steampowered.com/app/589780/The_Red_Strings_Club/. Accessed 03 Apr 2022

36. Steam - A Short Hike. https://store.steampowered.com/app/1055540/A_Short_Hike/. Accessed 03 Apr 2022

37. Mixamo. https://www.mixamo.com/#/. Accessed 06 Apr 2022

38. Chatterjee, S.: 1002 short stories from project Guttenberg. In: Kaggle (2020). https://www.kaggle.com/shubchat/1002-short-stories-from-project-guttenberg. Accessed 16 Oct 2022

39. openai/gpt-2. OpenAI, 2020. Accessed 01 May 2020. https://github.com/openai/gpt-2

40. Wardrip-Fruin, N.: Three Play Effects-Eliza, Tale-Spin, and Sim City. Digital Humanities, pp. 1–2 (2007)

41. About Wutiaoren. https://wutiaoren.info/. Accessed 04 Apr 2022

42. Yang, D., Zhou, Y., Zhang, Z., Li, T.J.J., LC, R.: AI As an active writer: interaction strategies with generated text in human-AI collaborative fiction writing. In: Joint Proceedings of the ACM IUI Workshops 2022 (vol. 10) (2022)

43. GPT-3 Powers the Next Generation of Apps. OpenAI, 25 Mar 2021. https://openai.com/blog/gpt-3-apps/. Accessed 06 Apr 2022

44. Fares, M., Kutuzov, A., Oepen, S., Velldal, E.: Word vectors, reuse, and replicability: towards a community repository of large-text resources. In: Tiedemann, J. (ed.) Proceedings of the 21st Nordic Conference on Computational Linguistics, NoDaLiDa, Linköping University Electronic Press (2017)

45. Dreamily API. In: Dreamily API - CaiyunWiki. https://open.caiyunapp.com/Dreamily_API. Accessed 17 Oct 2022

46. OpenAI Dall·E 2. In: OpenAI. (2022) https://openai.com/dall-e-2/. Accessed 17 Oct 2022

A New Research Agenda: Writing for Virtual Reality Interactive Narratives

Joshua A. Fisher[1](✉) ⓘ, Mirjam Vosmeer[2] ⓘ, and Jonathan Barbara[3] ⓘ

[1] Ball State University, Muncie, IN, USA
joshua.fisher@bsu.edu
[2] Amsterdam University of Applied Sciences, Amsterdam, The Netherlands
m.s.vosmeer@hva.nl
[3] Saint Martin's Institute of Higher Education, Ħamrun, Malta
jbarbara@stmartins.edu

Abstract. Scriptwriting for Virtual Reality Interactive Digital Narratives (IDN) derives insights from writing for linear or cinematic Virtual Reality (VR). However, due to the lack of agency in linear VR, insights from the scholarship that might improve the writing process are limited. Therefore, this paper suggests a new research agenda to explore scriptwriting for VR IDN. The paper establishes insights and challenges writers for VR IDN may encounter while composing. These challenges include scripting the body, movement as action, environmental storytelling, and guiding the interactors' gaze. A research agenda is proposed that categorizes these compositional insights and challenges within different levels of the System-Process-Product model.

Keywords: Virtual Reality · Writing · Interactive digital narrative · Scriptwriting · Composition studies · SPP-model

1 Introduction

Writing Interactive Digital Narratives (IDN) is a widely explored, ever-expanding domain in which emerging interactive technologies present new authorial challenges for writers [1, 2]. This paper addresses these challenges of writing IDN for Virtual Reality (VR). Janet Murray and Nonny de la Peña declare that a VR narrative begins with a body in space, pointing out the centrality of the interactor's embodiment in VR IDN [3–5]. This embodiment offers novel modes of user engagement that have new authorial challenges [6]. While in the recent third-wave revival of VR [7], both filmmakers and game developers have taken steps to define the grammar of VR storytelling, there is not a consensus on scriptwriting [8–11].

The practice of writing scripts for VR productions is a barely explored field. In *Cinematic Virtual Reality: A Critical Study of 21st Century Approaches and Practices*, scholar and filmmaker Kath Dooley uses the term "scripting the virtual" for this process of writing for VR IDN [6]. Insights derived from writing video games, theater, and cinema are only partially valuable as they help guide a writer to consider the hermeneutic

© The Author(s), under exclusive license to Springer Nature Switzerland AG 2022
M. Vosmeer and L. Holloway-Attaway (Eds.): ICIDS 2022, LNCS 13762, pp. 673–683, 2022.
https://doi.org/10.1007/978-3-031-22298-6_43

strip [12] while achieving ludo-narrative harmony [13, 14]. However, the immersive, embodied, first-person experience that is characteristic of VR makes storytelling more complex than it does for traditional, more *frame-bound* media. Although writing for non-interactive 360° experiences already poses considerable challenges for authors, writing IDN for VR confronts them with more complications.

To that end, we suggest a new research agenda for exploring scriptwriting techniques, formats, and methods for VR IDN. Our proposed research tracks are based on current discussions in the IDN and VR communities. Synthesizing these discussions, while building on lessons from cinematic and linear VR experiences, suggests domains for future work that we hope practitioners and scholars will explore.

1.1 Building upon Cinematic and Linear Virtual Reality

The limited contemporary scholarship on writing for cinematic, mostly linear VR and 360° video, provides some initial insights into the writing challenges for VR IDN [6, 10, 15–20]. We recognize cinematic VR as VR that is recorded with a 360° camera and understood by audiences as a surrounding video. These experiences are usually explored as 3-Degree-of-Freedom (3DoF) experiences, giving the user the ability to look around but providing a linear narrative with little to no dramatic agency or interaction. In these experiences, writers expect the interactor to gaze in different directions to explore the story space and process the narrative.

Creators usually make VR IDNs using game development engines such as Unity or the Unreal Engine. These experiences are frequently 6-Degree-of-Freedom (6DoF) experiences where the interactor can move and interact using their body and different modalities such as controllers or gaze interaction. This active, embodied participation of the interactor in the narrative is the most distinguishing difference between linear VR and VR IDN. In addition, these experiences provide dramatic agency and may offer the possibility to explore non-linear or kaleidoscopic narratives [21].

VR scholar Jeremy Bailenson has noted this as an important distinction between traditional storytelling and VR storytelling: while the first is largely about control, as exercised by the narrator, VR is about exploration, as practiced by the interactor [8]. While scholars derive many insights from linear VR for VR IDN, the latter's affordance for dramatic agency—resulting in narrative complexity, perception, and variability—presents compositional challenges for writers. Accordingly, VR IDN scriptwriters need to learn how to use embodiment to meet the expectations of dramatic agency. The branching structures of VR IDN—structures such as Marie Laure Ryan's textual archi-tectures, which account for this agency [22, 23]—encourage new modes of composition. While these structures and accompanying theories [24–27] are fruitful domains for con-sideration, their impact on the composition process for VR scriptwriters is ambiguous [10].

1.2 The Systems-Process-Product Model as a Research Agenda Framework

The Association for Interactive Digital Narratives has proposed to use the Systems-Process-Product model (SPP) as a framework for conceptualizing, analyzing, and approaching IDNs [1, 28–31]. Approaching scriptwriting through this framework, using the SPP model as a lens to consider compositional aspects of writing for VR IDN, further affirms its utility. We propose that the model directs researchers' attention to the various facets of writing a script for a VR IDN. Further, its structure helps to delineate different steps in the inception, deployment, and engagement with an IDN experience that script writers need to consider. For example, writers are already familiar with thinking up all the different aspects of their story, a component of the system level, but they might not be familiar with its other component, how all these aspects fit together through software and hardware. An appreciation of the latter may lead to more creative and compelling scripts that take advantage of VR's affordances.

2   Insights and Challenges

First, this paper addresses insights and challenges that authors of VR IDN should consider in their scripts, taking the interactor's embodiment into account and their novel modes of dramatic agency. Subsequently, we will discuss connections to the SPP model, aiming to align the different insights and challenges within the model's levels.

2.1   Scripting the Body

As noted earlier, VR writing must start with the body and how its position and possible movement within the story space may enact the plot. Writers for more traditional screen-based media already have a non-canonical industry standard for this kind of scripting. Sebastian Byrne refers to the cinematic version of this as "scripting with the body." While writers know that choreographing actors' movements can be a part of plot development [32, 33], Byrne claims that the focus on character development in most screenwriting manuals has drawn attention away from the physical nature of the actor's body and how the character's psychology should impact that enacted physicality [34].

Byrne's recognition of how physical performance and enactment lead to character development draws our attention to how VR writers might write detailed stage directions for interactions. As Seymour Chatman states, "for psychological narratives, actions are 'expressions' or even 'symptoms' of personality, hence 'transitive'" [35]. VR writers might construct moments for these gestures that inform the psychology of the characters their interactors are embodying. They can compose character development through external interactions enacted by the interactor during moments of dramatic agency. As part of a research agenda on writing for VR IDN, scholars may explore how the internal psychologies of characters might be enacted externally through interactor gestures. Such gestures can be a significant driver of character development and inform an interactor's identification with their avatar.

The writer of a traditional screenplay might use previsualization methods that "extend the screenplay by foregrounding the actor's mobility, physicality and tactility, while achieving greater choreographic precision and intimacy in the relationship between the camera and actor" [34]. However, VR writers describe an enactment for an interactor's body that is not meant for an audience but is composed as the interface through which an interactor enacts the narrative. While, hypothetically, it could be helpful to also script the interactor in VR through in-situ previsualization, the hypermediacy of such instruction will likely be distracting, thus breaking narrative immersion [36]. VR writing, like theater, "must use its languages of expression to create a space in which the words that are spoken can become part of the multiplex transformational processes through which the performance realizes itself." Scripting the body without previsualization methods and putting plot enactments through designed interactor experiences in writing will require a new mode of stage direction.

2.2 Embodiment and Movement

When scriptwriting for VR IDN, it is essential to consider that in VR, the gap between the interactor and the character they may embody is at a minimum. The character's perception is rendered in front of the interactor's eyes, occupying their whole field of view while synchronized to the interactor's head and body movement. This immediacy causes high feelings of embodiment [37] and presence [38], leading to identification with the avatar [39]. This identification may even result in a temporary identity shift for the interactor, perceiving their embodied character's experience as their own [40], which may result in longer-term impacts on the interactor [41].

In other examples of VR, however, the interactor may be invited to engage through virtual embodiment without any form of narrative enactment. In the experience *Evolution of Verse* (2016) by Chris Milk, for example, there are no protagonists and no dialogue. Nevertheless, the production entails a story and a distinct notion of embodied engagement. Milk tells the story through the eyes of the interactor, and the VR director guides the user's sense of narrative engagement through the illusion of physical movement. Milk unfolds this affordance by introducing a train in the distance. After a short while, the train turns and approaches the interactor at an alarmingly high speed. The connection to the Lumiere brothers is witty. After the train collision, the interactor enters a new mode of narrative engagement in which they no longer observe the train's movement in the distance. Instead, the interactor is now being moved through the scene, riding through a fantasy sky, by the experience.

At this moment, their virtual physicality is the defining agent of the narrative. This story is not about encounters with characters but the relationship between the interactor, the agent that sees, and what is seen. With this short experience, Milk demonstrates how VR directors can manipulate a user's embodiment through the illusion of physical movement. VR IDN writers may consider this relationship of disembodied but physically present presence. This simulated, embodied, non-interactor-enacted-physical-presence requires further study regarding how it is composed within scripts and its effect on narrative perception [53]. For example, would a writer script this moment—from the point-of-view of a character? would the user's physicality need to be considered? how does ignoring the user's physical embodiment impact their Sense of Presence (SoP) and immersion? how can this be communicated to a design team?—are just a few questions fruitful for exploration.

2.3 Acknowledgement

Writers can choose to involve the interactor with the characters of the story world or put them in the position of a witness. Matt Burdette of Oculus Story Studio speaks of the uncomfortable sensation of being unacknowledged in the cinematic VR space. In his report on *Henry* and *Lost* [42], Burdette describes how the team initially felt a distinct lack of connection to the characters and environment, and in turn, to the story. This ghost-like lack of acknowledgment, the sensation of having no tangible relationship with one's surroundings despite feeling present, was coined the 'Swayze Effect' by Burdette in reference to the classic movie *Ghost*. With *Henry*, the team discovered that the 'Swayze Effect' could be partially eliminated by having the character look right into the camera to lock eyes with the interactor. When dramatic characters and fantasy figures directly address the viewer, this is often referred to as 'breaking the fourth wall' [42–44, 52].

Breaking the wall is constructive for VR IDN; characters engage with the interactor to open space for dramatic agency [37, 38, 45]. For example, in the final scene of *The Changing Same: An American Pilgrimage: Episode 1*, is a 13-foot Black woman named Harriet surrounded by white [46]. She confronts the interactor about the history of injustice they have witnessed in the experience. She suggests that the interactor, "take that thing," referring to the VR headset, off their head if they cannot take the truth of the history. However, "if you are game, though" she encourages the interactor to dance to the music as it starts to get louder. This powerful dynamic encourages interactor agency, dramatic and otherwise, through a confrontational acknowledgement. The ways in which other forms of acknowledgement impact interactor's perception and enjoyment of the VR narrative requires further exploration. In VR IDN, VR writers should be aware of this dynamic, deciding beforehand how they will involve the interactor, to what degree, and how to construct their stories accordingly.

2.4 Guiding the Interactor's Gaze

In a VR environment, the interactor can miss subtle story details that may be of great value for plot development. Therefore, guiding the interactor's gaze in cinematic VR is critical to story development and for the user to process the experience as a narrative. As stated, VR is about exploration as practiced by the interactor, and therefore writing for VR IDN is writing from an interactor's field of view. The Trap of 180°, as discussed by writer Gérard Bernasconi, keeps storytellers and writers within 180° of the interactor's originating point-of-view [47]. The Trap can be heard in the phrase, "In real life, nothing happens behind you." Realistically, there is an unknown number of dramatic moments happening behind someone. Research has shown that traditional theatrical techniques such as movement, noise, light, color, and the absence of these aspects can be applied to direct the user's attention. Script writers can write these as stage directions, suggesting how to inspire the interactor to look around the story space to access different beats in the story [19, 34, 39]. Scholars of IDN have suggested using guideposts through stationary or animated narrative clues to guide dramatic agency. These guideposts are not necessarily nodes or beats. Instead, they draw attention to or away from Points-of-Interest related to the story in the IDN.

VR filmmakers have explored various techniques to balance exploration with storytelling and mapped an undiscovered country between gameplay and linear narrative [12]. In a VR IDN, interactors have more agency, capacities, and modalities to process and shape the narrative. Bernasconi suggests that by eliminating the Trap of 180°, storytellers introduce audiences to the idea that multiple playthroughs, or viewings, enhance cinematic VR experiences. So that, through each viewing new meaning can be processed within the narrative. To encourage replay, writers construct multiple narrative clues of different types—stationary and direct or moving and disruptive—to weave together different paths in a VR experience. Upon replay, new paths result in a deeper understanding of the narrative [48]. However, VR IDN has more profound opportunities for narrative meaning-making through proceeding playthroughs. Partially because in a VR IDN, a writer accounts for more potential interactions in an array of modalities. Accordingly, the potential interactions are more diverse and complex, which makes scripting the body even more critical.

Further, a writer must also contend with an interactor that is not paying attention. Therefore, they must write structures that re-script the interactor into enacting the narrative. Finally, how a writer communicates these structures and interactions through a script requires further attention.

2.5   Environmental Storytelling

Another intriguing element of embodied storytelling for VR is the interactor's entrance into the storyworld and their exit. The consideration of "crossing the threshold" exists in previous media forms—cinema and theater, for example—but has renewed attention for VR. Dramaturgs or producers often prime their audience for a stage or screen performance through environmental storytelling in the lobby or the theater before the story begins. Environmental storytelling was first developed within the theme park industry, referring to the ways that, in theme parks, visitors are already warmed up to the attraction that they are about to experience by a carefully designed thematic surrounding for the entrance [49]. With VR, a user puts on a headset and is immediately immersed in another world. This immediate transition into the storyworld is considerably more overwhelming than the gradual transition from a lobby to a theater. To address this threshold in a VR IDN, Oculus Story Studio developed the concept of the *antechamber* to prime the narrative and position the user in the proper position for a room-scale experience [27, 42]. How VR writers might take this very functional moment—the donning of the VR headset—and make it narrative—entering the story-world as an embodied character—is another challenge worthy of exploration. A VR writer might use this functional transition to impart narrative meaning through additional environmental storytelling.

3   The Research Agenda

For the proposed research agenda, we explore how the SPP model may help categorize the different kinds of insights and challenges that scriptwriters for VR IDN may encounter. In doing this, we investigate how the tool might assist the writing process.

3.1   The Systems-Process-Product Model

The SPP model is a media-specific perspective that identifies three broad categories for the analysis of IDN artifacts, reflecting its different stages: *system*, the digital artifact; *process*, the interactive experience of a system; and *product*, the result of the experience.

At the *system* level of SPP, all the software and hardware combinations needed to run the IDN exist. Further, all the individual potential narratives that the interactor might experience exist at this level. Koenitz refers to these as protostories—they contain the ingredients for creating a narrative. At the *process* level, the interactor enacts these various narratives through ludo-narrative interactions at moments charged with dramatic agency. The *product* level of the SPP discusses anything the interactor may take away from an experience. It might be a retelling [48], a material artifact like a recording [31], a cognitive model of a complex idea [50], or a knowledge product [51].

Roth, Nuenen, and Koenitz [14] state that "through the *process* of the player's engagement with the interactive narrative *system* by choices and other behavior—her performance—a concrete and personal narrative *product* is instantiated." From a writer's perspective, this could be interpreted by stating that the writer is firstly involved with the system—the narrative design of the protostory. Decisions on the intended hardware and software also connect to this level: whether the VR experience will be produced using a 360° camera, volumetric capture technology, or a game development engine will impact aspects of the protostory.

Writing in the Systems Level for Virtual Reality Interactive Digital Narrative. At the *systems* level, a writer may be concerned with all aspects of the protostory and how they can use media assets, software, and hardware combinations to realize their authorial vision.

1. VR scriptwriters need to explore new methods for 'scripting the body'. Different compositional modes for stage direction need to be explored to assess how well the writer's vision was communicated to the design team, and how the interactor interprets their enactment of these stage directions. This exploration should include how the writer utilizes the interactor's poise, gestures, body language, and orientation as units of an IDNs protostory. Writing at the system level also includes how the hardware will capture and process an interactor's input. Communicating these technical expectations and written directions to a larger design team needs further attention.

2. VR scriptwriters must script for the body's movement through story spaces and worlds. In VR IDN, scriptwriters compose these spaces to encourage interactor action. How a writer communicates their vision for these spaces and their situated movements through writing requires formalization. Writers can rely on movement as part of an interactor's narrative progression because locomotion positively impacts an interactor's SoP and immersion. At the system level, a writer should consider how the interactor will move through space.

Writing in the Process Level for Virtual Reality Interactive Digital Narrative. At the *process* level, the writer may want to guide the interactor through the experience by subtly pointing out the intended 'optimal' course through the narrative.

3. Therefore, a research agenda on writing for VR IDN needs to explore and verify the methods available to direct the interactor's attention. Accordingly, this research agenda should establish a canonical style for script writing to communicate these practices.

4. Also, investigating the practices that ensure optimal levels of embodiment and engagement, for instance, through scripted acknowledgment and simulated physical experience, need to be included in the research agenda.

Writing in the Product Level for Virtual Reality Interactive Digital Narrative.
At the *product* level, a writer may be concerned with the intended narrative outcome for the interactor as a result of the experience:

5. VR writers might consider replay and how to use the product to create a deeper understanding of the narrative. Further research is needed into the opportunities for narrative meaning-making that this may entail for VR IDN. Writing for embodiment and spatial cognition concerning IDN's affordance of transformation is of particular interest.
6. VR writers are already exploring ways to use onboarding, environmental story-telling, and egress to drive home the product of their IDN. As part of this agenda, design knowledge should be developed on the utility of these moments for narrative progression and their overall interactive experience.

The SPP model provides a helpful way to conceptualize a research agenda for writing VR IDN. However, further attention and practice are required to comprehend the scope of the SPP model as a compositional scaffold for writing structures within this medium. For example, the scriptwriter's position concerning the SPP model needs to be established. However, the SPP model provides a direction: a writer may explore potential protostories at the *system* level while they ideate. However, as discussed, the field needs to explore a canonical approach. At the *process* level, a writer might address the previous point of embodied and engaged interactors. Again, how this would look on the compositional page or screen is unknown. Compositional approaches at the *system* and *product* levels require further attention and practice. Such work helps expand the SPP model's utility as a compositional tool.

In conclusion, to develop a research agenda, we have investigated the challenges facing a writer composing a script for a VR IDN. Our agenda, organized around the SPP model, is based on insights from cinematic and linear VR. There are diverse challenges ahead. They include how to write these scripts, what stage directions look like, how they are communicated to a production team, how well they render authorial vision through interactor enactment, and more. We cordially invite the ICIDS community to discuss and further explore this research. We believe that addressing the insights and challenges mentioned in this contribution might also help to develop the broader field of IDN.

References

1. Roth, C., Koenitz, H.: Towards creating a body of evidence-based interactive digital narrative design knowledge: approaches and challenges. In: AltMM 2017 - Proceedings of the 2nd International Workshop on Multimedia Alternate Realities, co-located with MM 2017, pp. 19–24 (2017). https://doi.org/10.1145/3132361.3133942
2. Carey, B.P.: The Architect of Forking Paths: Developing Key Writing Strategies for Interactive Writers (2018)

3. Murray, J.: Did it make you cry? creating dramatic agency in immersive environments. In: Subsol, G. (ed.) ICVS 2005. LNCS, vol. 3805, pp. 83–94. Springer, Heidelberg (2005). https://doi.org/10.1007/11590361_10

4. de la Peña, N., et al.: Immersive journalism: immersive virtual reality for the first-person experience of news. Pres.: Teleoper. Virtual Environ. **19**, 291–301 (2010). https://doi.org/10.1162/PRES_a_00005

5. de la Peña, N.: Embodied digital rhetoric: soft selves, plastic presence, and the nonfiction narrative. In: Digital Rhetoric and Global Literacies: Communication Modes and Digital Practices in the Networked World, pp. 312–327. IGI Global (2014)

6. Dooley, K.: Cinematic Virtual Reality: A Critical Study of 21st Century Approaches and Practices. Springer, Heidelberg (2021). https://doi.org/10.1007/978-3-030-72147-3

7. Belisle, B., Roquet, P.: Guest Editors' Introduction: Virtual reality: immersion and empathy (2020)

8. Bailenson, J.: Experience on Demand: What Virtual Reality is, How it Works, and What it Can Do. WW Norton & Company, New York (2018)

9. Vosmeer, M., Schouten, B.: Interactive cinema: engagement and interaction. In: Mitchell, A., Fernández-Vara, C., Thue, D. (eds.) ICIDS 2014. LNCS, vol. 8832, pp. 140–147. Springer, Cham (2014). https://doi.org/10.1007/978-3-319-12337-0_14

10. Reyes, M.C.: Screenwriting framework for an interactive virtual reality film interactive fiction in cinematic virtual reality: epistemology, creation and evaluation view project interactive media for e-learning view project (2017). https://doi.org/10.3217/978-3-85125-530-0-15

11. Vosmeer, M., Roth, C., Koenitz, H.: Who are you? Voice-over perspective in surround video. In: Nunes, N., Oakley, I., Nisi, V. (eds.) ICIDS 2017. LNCS, vol. 10690, pp. 221–232. Springer, Cham (2017). https://doi.org/10.1007/978-3-319-71027-3_18

12. Karhulahti, V.M.: Double fine adventure and the double hermeneutic videogame. In: ACM International Conference Proceeding Series, pp. 19–26 (2012). https://doi.org/10.1145/2367616.2367619

13. Seraphine, F.: The rhetoric of undertale: ludonarrative dissonance and symbolism. In: DIGRA JAPAN Conference. 8th Proceedings (2019)

14. Roth, C., van Nuenen, T., Koenitz, H.: Ludonarrative hermeneutics: a way out and the narrative paradox. In: Rouse, R., Koenitz, H., Haahr, M. (eds.) ICIDS 2018. LNCS, vol. 11318, pp. 93–106. Springer, Cham (2018). https://doi.org/10.1007/978-3-030-04028-4_7

15. Zhang, A., Research Online, G.: Developing a cinematic language for virtual reality filmmaking thesis type (2020). https://doi.org/10.25904/1912/4021

16. Dooley, K.: Scripting the virtual: formats and development paths for recent Australian narrative 360-degree virtual reality projects (2018)

17. Dooley, K.: Storytelling with virtual reality in 360-degrees: a new screen grammar. Stud. Aust. Cinema **11**, 161–171 (2017). https://doi.org/10.1080/17503175.2017.1387357

18. Damiani, J., Southard, D.: Writing for VR: the definitive guide to VR storytelling – VRScout. https://vrscout.com/news/writing-vr-definitive-guide-vr-storytelling/. Accessed 09 July 2022

19. Tuason, I.: Screenwriting for Virtual Reality. https://www.dimensiongate.com/post/2015/05/12/screenwriting-for-virtual-reality. Accessed 09 July 2022

20. Henrikson, R., de Araujo, B., Chevalier, F., Singh, K., Balakrishnan, R.: Multi-device storyboards for cinematic narratives in VR. In:Proceedings of the 29th Annual ACM Symposium on User Interface Software & Technology, pp. 787–796 (2016). https://doi.org/10.1145/2984511.2984539

21. Murray, J.H.: Research into interactive digital narrative : a kaleidoscopic view through the kaleidoscope, and across the decades. In: Rouse, R., Koenitz, H., Haahr, M. (eds.) International Conference on Interactive Digital Storytelling, pp. 1–16. Springer, Cham (2018)

22. Ryan, Marie-Laure.: Interactive narrative, plot types, and interpersonal relations. In: Spierling, U., Szilas, N. (eds.) ICIDS 2008. LNCS, vol. 5334, pp. 6–13. Springer, Heidelberg (2008). https://doi.org/10.1007/978-3-540-89454-4_2

23. Ryan, M.: Avatars of story: 1. narrative, media and modes. In: Avatars of Story, pp. 3–29 (2006). 9780816646869

24. Blankenburg, S., Palma, J.G., Tregenna, F.: Structuralism. In: Durlauf, S.N., Blume, L.E. (eds.) The New Palgrave: Dictionary of Economics, pp. 6425–6430. Palgrave Macmillan UK, London (2008). https://doi.org/10.1007/978-1-349-58802-2_1639

25. Attebery, B.: Stories About Stories: Fantasy and the Remaking of Myth. Oxford University Press, Oxford (2014)

26. Koenitz, H., Di Pastena, A., Jansen, D., de Lint, B., Moss, A.: The myth of 'Universal' narrative models. In: Rouse, R., Koenitz, H., Haahr, M. (eds.) ICIDS 2018. LNCS, vol. 11318, pp. 107–120. Springer, Cham (2018). https://doi.org/10.1007/978-3-030-04028-4_8

27. Ballantyne, J.: The Problem with Reality. https://www.oculus.com/story-studio/blog/the-problem-with-reality/. Accessed 06 July 2021

28. Koenitz, H., Roth, C., Dubbelman, T., Knoller, N.: Interactive narrative design beyond the secret art status: a method to verify design conventions for interactive narrative. matlit Materialities Liter. **6**, 107–119 (2018). https://doi.org/10.14195/2182-8830_6-1_7

29. Koenitz, H.: Towards a specific theory of interactive digital narrative. In: Interactive Digital Narrative: History, Theory and Practice, pp. 91–105 (2015). https://doi.org/10.4324/978131 5769189-8

30. Koenitz, H.: Towards a theoretical framework for interactive digital narrative. In: Aylett, R., Lim, M.Y., Louchart, S., Petta, P., Riedl, M. (eds.) ICIDS 2010. LNCS, vol. 6432, pp. 176–185. Springer, Heidelberg (2010). https://doi.org/10.1007/978-3-642-16638-9_22

31. Koenitz, H., Eladhari, M.P., Louchart, S., Nack, F.: INDCOR white paper 1: a shared vocabulary for IDN (Interactive Digital Narratives) (2020)

32. Garg, A., Fisher, J.A., Wang, W., Singh, K.P.: ARES: an application of impossible spaces for natural locomotion in VR. In: Conference on Human Factors in Computing Systems - Proceedings (2017). https://doi.org/10.1145/3027063.3048416

33. Cattrysse, P.: The protagonist's dramatic goals, wants and needs. J. Screenwrit. **1**, 83–97 (2010). https://doi.org/10.1386/josc.1.1.83/1

34. Byrne, S.: Embodying character: psychological and bodily performance and the cinematic construction of the character in goal-driven narrative cinema (2011)

35. Chatman, S.B.: Story and Discourse: Narrative Structure in Fiction and Film. Cornell University Press, Ithaca (1980)

36. Bolter, J.D., Grusin, R.: Immediacy, hypermediacy, and remediation. In: Remediation: Understanding New Media, pp. 20–50 (2000)

37. Kilteni, K., Groten, R., Slater, M.: The sense of embodiment in virtual reality. Pres. Teleoper. Virtual Environ. **21**, 373–387 (2012)

38. Hefner, D., Klimmt, C., Vorderer, P.: Identification with the player character as determinant of video game enjoyment. In: Ma, L., Rauterberg, M., Nakatsu, R. (eds.) ICEC 2007. LNCS, vol. 4740, pp. 39–48. Springer, Heidelberg (2007). https://doi.org/10.1007/978-3-540-74873-1_6

39. Klimmt, C., Hefner, D., Vorderer, P.: the video game experience as "True" identification: a theory of enjoyable alterations of players' self-perception. Commun. Theory **19**, 351–373 (2009). https://doi.org/10.1111/j.1468-2885.2009.01347.x

40. Goldstein, N., Cialdini, R.: The spyglass self: a model of vicarious self-perception. Association for Consumer Research (2007)

41. Steinemann, S.T., Mekler, E.D., Opwis, K.: Increasing donating behavior through a game for change: the role of interactivity and appreciation. In: CHI PLAY 2015 - Proceedings of the 2015 Annual Symposium on Computer-Human Interaction in Play, pp. 319–330. Association for Computing Machinery, Inc. (2015). https://doi.org/10.1145/2793107.2793125

42. Burdette, M.: The swayze effect (2016). https://storystudio.oculus.com/en-us/blog/the-swayze-effect/
43. Collins, K.: Breaking the fourth wall? user-generated sonic content in virtual worlds. In: The Oxford Handbook of Virtuality, pp. 351–363. Oxford University Press, Oxford (2014)
44. Ko, Dong-uk, Ryu, H., Kim, J.: Making new narrative structures with actor's eye-contact in cinematic virtual reality (CVR). In: Rouse, R., Koenitz, H., Haahr, M. (eds.) ICIDS 2018. LNCS, vol. 11318, pp. 343–347. Springer, Cham (2018). https://doi.org/10.1007/978-3-030-04028-4_38
45. Shafer, D.M., Carbonara, C.P., Korpi, M.F.: Exploring enjoyment of cinematic narratives in virtual reality: a comparison study. Int. J. Virt. Real. **18**, 1–18 (2018)
46. Yasmin, E., Brewster, J., Stephenson, M.: The Changing Same: Episode 1 "The Dilemma". Rada Studios, New York City (2021)
47. Bernasconi, G.: Writing Immersive Contents: Comments and Suggestions about Narration in VR.AR.XR. Gérard Bernasconi (2022)
48. Eladhari, M.P.: Re-Tellings: the fourth layer of narrative as an instrument for critique BT - interactive storytelling. Presented at the (2018)
49. Carson, D.:. Environmental storytelling: creating immersive 3D worlds using lessons learned from the theme park industry. Gamasutra. com, vol. 1 (2000)
50. Knoller, N.: The complexity triad and two+ systemic models of IDS/N (2020)
51. Fisher, J.A.: Epistemic rhetoric in virtual reality factual narratives. Front. Virt. Real. **3** (2022). https://doi.org/10.3389/frvir.2022.845489
52. Vosmeer, M., Roth, C.: Exploring Narrative Novelties in VR. In: Mitchell, A., Vosmeer, M. (eds.) ICIDS 2021. LNCS, vol. 13138, pp. 435–444. Springer, Cham (2021). https://doi.org/10.1007/978-3-030-92300-6_44
53. Gödde, M., Gabler, F., Siegmund, D., Braun, A.: Cinematic narration in VR – rethinking film conventions for 360 degrees. In: Chen, J.Y.C., Fragomeni, G. (eds.) VAMR 2018. LNCS, vol. 10910, pp. 184–201. Springer, Cham (2018). https://doi.org/10.1007/978-3-319-91584-5_15

Visionary Virtual Worlds

Storytelling via Digital Architecture in NaissanceE

Gabriele Aroni[✉] [iD]

Xi'an Jiaotong-Liverpool University, Suzhou 215123, Jiangsu, China
`Gabriele.Aroni@xjtlu.edu.cn`

Abstract. The narrative and worldbuilding of digital games are often constructed through their architectural design. This paper analyzes how virtual architecture can enable interactive digital storytelling through the case study of the game *NaissanceE* (Limasse Five 2014), which displays particularly imaginative architectural spaces within the panorama of digital games. *NaissanceE*'s architecture will be looked at through the lenses of 18th century visionary architecture, such as the works of Italian engraver Giovanni Battista Piranesi and French architect Étienne-Louis Boullée, as well contemporary mangaka Tsutomu Nihei, in order to understand which architectural elements carry the narration, how they are employed, and how they are understood by players.

Keywords: Architecture · Narrative · Visionary · Piranesi · Boullée · NaissanceE

1 Introduction

There is hardly any architecture more virtual than the one we can find in digital games, but designing "virtual" buildings, as in, structures invented for the sake of experimentation rather than with the purpose of being actually built – the so-called *paper architecture* – is hardly new. Architects have for millennia indulged in pushing their imagination with fantastic buildings, not just for mere exercise, but also as symbols and narrative devices.

Digital games provide an imaginary space made of virtual architecture, whereby a fictive composition of forms represents imaginary locales. Even when based on existing locations, digital game environments are adapted to suit and work with the gameplay. Thus, we can argue that every digital game is an exercise in visionary architecture, thence what is the relationship between visionary *paper* architecture and digital games architecture? How does the architectural vision enable and enhance digital storytelling?

As a predominantly visual medium, digital games spaces attracted the attention of scholars since the inception of game studies. Janet Murray affirmed that digital games "are characterized by their power to represent navigable space" (2016, p. 79), and Espen Aarseth considered spatiality "the defining element in computer games" (2001, p. 154). However, architectural analysis is relatively new to the medium, as most of the literature regarding digital game architecture focused on the broad concept of "space" rather than specifically architecture (Wolf 2001; Adams 2003; Tobin 2012; Murray 2016), or on

M. Vosmeer and L. Holloway-Attaway (Eds.): ICIDS 2022, LNCS 13762, pp. 684–696, 2022.
https://doi.org/10.1007/978-3-031-22298-6_44

more specific issues of level design (Totten 2014, 2017), or the relationships between architecture and games, rather than the architecture *in* games (Borries et al. 2007).

Recently, more attention has been given to digital games architecture. Architect Gregory Whistance-Smith, in his recent book on video game spaces, argues that "virtual environments, like their physical counterparts, have the ability to evoke narratives for their visitors while not necessarily being narrative works in any conventional sense" (2022, p. 34), and Gabriele Aroni likens virtual architecture to architectural *capricci*, a painting genre popular in the 17th and 18th centuries depicting fantastic and imaginary architectural landscapes, placing it within a longstanding tradition of fictive architectural representation (2022, p. 2).

In this paper, we are going to look at the world of the game *NaissanceE* (Limasse Five 2014), a first-person exploration and platform game set in a foreboding gigantic structure, without characters, dialogue, nor texts, where the narration is carried by the architecture alone. These spaces will be investigated through the works of 18th century visionary architects such as Étienne-Louis Boullée, Giovanni Battista Piranesi and contemporary mangaka Tsutomu Nihei, who was a direct reference for *NaissanceE*'s author Mavros Sedeño.

2   The Semiotics of Digital Games Architecture

Similarly to real world architecture, we can assume that digital games architecture fulfills two main roles: one functional, and one representational. Semiotician Umberto Eco affirmed that architectural objects denote a primary function, and connote a secondary "ideology of the function" (Eco 1997, p. 178). The denotative function is based on the mechanical, physical aspect of the architectural object. For instance, a door allows us to pass through a wall in virtue of its height and form and our understanding of the space around us. However, an architectural sign can also connote a symbolic meaning, through its design, materials, scale, etc. The definitions of "primary" and "secondary" function are not to be seen in order of importance, but rather on the fact that the secondary, connotative function rests "on the denotation of the primary function" (1997, p. 179). A door will always be a door first, denoted by its primary function, even if its connotative function is the main reason why it was built and designed in a certain way, rather than its mere functional aspect.

In digital games, architectural signs work in a similar fashion, whereas the primary function denotes the gameplay. For instance, a door still needs to be large enough for allowing players to pass through. The secondary function connotes the narrative, where the same door can be large or small, ornate or bare, depending on the mood, setting and worldbuilding the game artists are aiming for.

In the following analysis, we will see how the architectural elements of the game *NaissanceE* are utilized as gameplay signs to guide players, as well as connotative signs to deliver the silent narrative of the game.

3   NaissanceE

NaissanceE is a first-person exploration and platform game developed by Limasse Five, a one-man team composed of Mavros Sedeño, in 2014. Despite its small development size, the game has received considerable media coverage, primarily due to its stark and unconventional environment design. Indeed, it became a cult game amongst architectural enthusiasts as one of the prime examples of environmental storytelling – it is in fact on the cover of the two most recent books on digital games architecture, Whistance-Smith's *Expressive Space* (2022) and Aroni's *The Semiotics of Architecture in Video Games* (2022) – whereby the whole narrative and worldbuilding aspects of the game are carried out by its architecture alone, rather than through characters and dialogues.

The importance of architectural design in *NaissanceE* is stated by its very author, who claims that: "architecture is the basic element of games. Because games are almost always a process of going from one point to another. And in-between you have doors, you have puzzles, and it is always a journey, always a progression through space. Except in pure puzzle games, or text adventures, but in the majority of games it is the architecture you are experimenting with, though with new rules: with different gravity, with different ways to move. It's the essence of games. I played with this notion when I came to make *NaissanceE*." (Sedeño 2017, p. 100).

The stark beauty of *NaissanceE*'s environments was largely praised in reviews at the time of release (Rubbini 2014; Rossignol 2014), what Nick Capozzoli dubbed "the architecture of the unwelcome" (2014). The world of *NaissanceE* is completely artificial and inhuman, a sort of dystopian *capriccio* composed of gigantic textureless megastructures. Unlike usual postapocalyptic game worlds, the reasons for the look of the environment in *NaissanceE* is completely obscure. It is not the result of a nuclear war as in the *Fallout* series (Interplay Entertainment et al. 1997–2018), or a global pandemic as in *The Last of Us* (Naughty Dog 2013). The human element is almost completely discarded, since there is not the destruction brought forth by war, or the ruins of a disappeared civilization. As a matter of fact, we are not made aware if this is the result of some kind of apocalypse at all, or when the game is chronologically set. In fact, Sedeño designed the environment to be purposefully alienating to players (2017, p. 95).

The beginning of the game sees players dropped in a gigantic megastructure with no introduction nor explanation, save a cryptic message informing that they are chased by a mysterious presence. The environments are composed of bare, seemingly interminable corridors with incredibly high ceilings, which take considerable time to be traversed, especially for a digital game, where uneventful movement through space is a rare occurrence.

One of the most striking features of the alien structures that compose the landscape of *NaissanceE* is the lack of any textures and colors, or any difference in materials (see Fig. 1). Sedeño explains the reason for this design choice: "NaissanceE uses simple texture-less shapes combined in such a way that leads to rich and complex environments. This paradoxical association creates an unusual visual style helping to give this world its particular mood. In addition, the almost colour-less ambiance re-enforces the feeling of desolation and abandonment the player experiences when exploring the endless gigantic structures of NaissanceE." (Sedeño 2014).

The main inspiration for the visual design of *NaissanceE* was contemporary Japanese mangaka Tsutomu Nihei, in particular his manga *Blame!*, still, they both fit within a long-standing tradition of visionary architecture, as architecture has always been an effective device to represent cultures and civilizations. Moreover, architecture can be used as

Fig. 1. A corridor in *NaissanceE* © Mavros Sedeño 2014.

the visual metaphor for a social system, for instance in Ambrogio Lorenzetti's cycle of frescoes, *The Allegory of Good and Bad Government* (1338), in the Palazzo Pubblico of Siena, Italy, where a rendition of the city of Siena displays the effects of good and bad government. A well-maintained city is the symbol of the good government, whereas crumbling and neglected buildings embody the opposite.

4 Visionary Architecture

4.1 Giovanni Battista Piranesi

Having grandiose ideas not meant to be realized has been a long-standing passion for architects of all times and places. Dinocrates (4th century BCE) proposed to Alexander the Great to build a whole city in the hand of a colossal statue to be sculpted in place of mount Athos in Greece. While the idea was obviously discarded, Alexander appreciated Dinocrates' taste for grandiose plans, and welcomed him in his entourage (Vitruvius 1931, bk. II, 1). Particularly related to *NaissanceE* are the works of 18th century Italian engraver Giovanni Battista Piranesi, especially his *Imaginary Prisons* series which portray grim maze-like underground environments (see Fig. 2), and have been unsurprisingly compared to the game's environments (Sedeño 2014; Capozzoli 2014).

Piranesi's work is also relevant when looked at together with the main inspiration for *NaissanceE*, the manga *Blame!*. Albeit not cited as a direct inspiration by Sedeño nor Nihei, the influence of Piranesi is evident, as his works have been catalytic to architectural experimentation for centuries, from French, English, and German Neoclassical architects, to contemporary Deconstructivist movements (Kirk 2006, p. 239).

Piranesi rose to fame for his etchings of Roman *vedute*, but he always displayed a particularly imaginative style, due to his training as a theater set designer in Venice. Even

Fig. 2. Giovanni Battista Piranesi, *Scale, arcate e capriate*, etching, mm. 410x545 (1761) ©
Roma, Istituto centrale per la grafica, courtesy of the Ministry of Culture.

among his *capricci*, i.e. renditions of imaginary landscapes and monuments, including the aforementioned *Prisons*, he displayed a more visionary style, compared to his
contemporaries such as Panini and Canaletto (Selena 2016, p. 97). Both *NaissanceE*
and *Blame!* are set in environments that, despite the lack of precise temporal references,
look ancient and unchanging. Piranesi's etchings of Roman ruins had a similar approach,
whereby together with topographically accurate renditions of temples and aqueducts,
he added gigantic monuments of an imaginary Rome, with minuscule figures walking
by to underline their enormous size. The *Prisons* in particular, with their dungeons full
of interconnecting narrow passages, stairs and bridges, resemble an ancient version of
NaissanceE's levels.

Importantly, much akin to *NaissanceE*, Piranesi's compositions use architectural
signs to evoke a sense of contradiction to bewilder the viewer. In the words of eminent
architecture historian Rudolf Wittkower: "He reverses the traditional meaning of architectural structure in general and of the single parts. A pediment, on which the structural
emphasis of the building is usually laid, is degraded by him to a decorative detail; orna-
mental frames, on the other hand, became structural features; one architectural feature
is placed in front of another in such a way that the different planes of the building are
confused" (1938, p. 156).

4.2 Étienne-Louis Boullée

18th century French architect Étienne-Louis Boullée's works are particularly relevant for the analysis of the digital narrative of *NaissanceE* through architecture, not just because he was one of the most influential visionary architects, but because the gigantic structures he designed resemble *NaissanceE*'s environments in scale and look, and use similar design choices to convey feelings in the audience. The bare environments of *NaissanceE*, completely devoid of life, resemble sepulchers, and they indeed follow the indications that Boullée gives for the design of funerary monuments: "in order to produce sad and dark images, as I tried to do with funerary monuments, we need to present the skeleton of architecture as an imposing wall, completely bare" (Boullée 2005, p. 33). Boullée's most famous work, the *Cénotaphe de Newton* (1784) would in fact not be out of place in a *NaissanceE* level: a colossal sphere on a pedestal, where at the center of its empty interior, a light is lit during nighttime, while during daylight small holes in the shell let light filtrate to simulate the starry sky, in an artificial reversal of the natural cycle (see Fig. 3).

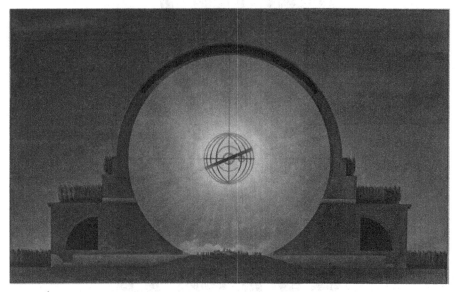

Fig. 3. Étienne-Louis Boullée, *Cénotaphe de Newton* (1784). Courtesy of the Bibliothèque nationale de France, département estampes et photographie.

The choice of size, textures, and forms are not arbitrary, but rather deliberate in order to fulfill a narrative objective by conveying meaning through architectural forms. For Boullée it is "impossible to conceive something sadder than a monument consisting of a smooth, bare and plain surface, made with a light-absorbing material, completely devoid of details and whose decoration is an assemblage of shadows delineated by even darker shadows." (2005, p. 89).

4.3 Blame!

As mentioned, Tsutomu Nihei's manga *Blame!* was the main visual source of inspiration for *NaissanceE*. *Blame!* is about the adventures of protagonist Killy, who is tasked with finding the "Net Terminal Genes", and who needs to wander the gigantic "City", an enormous megastructure whose size is never specified save for the mention of a 3,000-km staircase and a 143,000-km spherical room (Nihei 2017, pp. 67, 85). Especially in the first volume, it is the architectural design that carries the narrative of *Blame!*, for as in *NaissanceE* dialogues are almost completely absent (see Fig. 4).

Fig. 4. A plate from Blame! Master Edition Volume 1, p. 105 © Tsutomu Nihei/ Kodansha Ltd.

Much like the ancient ruins of Piranesi, and the timeless spaces of *NaissanceE*, Killy's voyages in *Blame!* lack a precise timescale. Due to the artificial nature of the protagonist, and the enormous distances involved, it is implied that Killy's trip lasts years if not centuries. This inhuman timescale is mirrored in the inhuman scale of architecture, with its immutable and ancient aspect.

5   NaissanceE's Narrative Design

There is not much in *NaissanceE* that communicates to players, save its architecture, and a particularly stark and bare architecture at that, composed mainly of simple geometric forms and textureless surfaces. Nonetheless, *NaissanceE* manages to convey a narrative to players. Not only in terms of giving instructions to players on how to proceed in the game, but also to narrate the context in which the game is set and its story. The author Mavros Sedeño explains that "there is a large range of abstraction in the environments, from pure visual to more representative constructions. These many variations, however still homogeneous on a large scale, are in correlation with the several games mechanics the player will encounter, like sections where lights and shadows are used to alter the perception of space and rhythmically structure the player progression." (2014).

The primary denotative function of architecture is thus carried by the geometry of the environment and understood by players through the movement capabilities of the avatar. Size and distance of architectural elements semiotically communicate to players what they can do and where they can go: seemingly random parallelepipeds protruding from walls invite to jump on them, and indicate the path to follow. In a game such as *NaissanceE*, where there are hardly any architectural elements that we can directly associate to real world ones, we can assume that the secondary connotative function of architecture is hardly expressed. On the contrary, due to the absence of conventional narrative devices such as dialogues, architectural forms – as abstract as they might be – are semiotically relevant and structure the narrative of *NaissanceE*.

Much a like a sepulcher designed by Boullée, the first room of the game is completely bare, sporting only grey featureless walls and an opening, which has the obvious denotative function of allowing players to exit the room. As players progress through the game, they encounter larger corridors displaying more elaborate structures, and the openings in the walls themselves start resembling doors, rather than simple cuts in the walls. More familiar elements, such as recognizable staircases, and even furniture start appearing, albeit always strictly geometric and textureless.

This dichotomy between the recognizability of some architectural elements and their strangeness or cyclopic scale communicates to players that the forms they witness in the game are not there only for their connotative role of allowing gameplay, but that a link exists between the architecture of the world of *NaissanceE* and the real world – as feeble as it might be – and this is what carries the "narrative" connotative function of its architectural design. A feature similar to what we can see in the manga *Blame!*, where most of its architecture is built theoretically for humans, but by machines who have lost their initial purpose, and thus create forms and scales which have little of human left. Moreover, very much like the deserted sepulchers of Boullée, and the lone voyage of Killy in *Blame!*, players in *NaissanceE* are always alone throughout the game.

As players progress through the game, the architectural elements change, from simple rooms and corridors to more elaborate structures. In the second chapter of the game, players encounter structures that resemble human settlements for the first time. However, these familiar sights always have some uncanny element, such as interconnected mazes of stairs with no handrails nor landings, which seem straight out of a Piranesi *Prison*, rather than a practical design (see Fig. 5). Here, the connotative function of architecture is to strengthen in players the impression of being in a strange place. Indeed, Sedeño comments: "When you see these ridiculous, impractical stairs, you really wonder what they are used for. I thought it would be interesting to give it a meaning, but as a game element, reinforcing the feeling of both being in a dangerous place and being unsure that the way you are taking is a good one to progress." (2017, p. 97).

Fig. 5. A maze-like environment in *NaissanceE* © Mavros Sedeño 2014.

These elements tell players that they are in a strange and unsettling place, as explained by Sedeño: "the reason I used some recognizable shapes and places, but also very unusual spaces, was to get a good mix between the symbolic and the abstract. And so to let the personal experience of the player make the experience of the game. Depending on your references in games, art, and architecture, and in life in general, you have a different experience." (2017, p. 102).

This dichotomy between the extraordinary and the mundane is accentuated by the scale. The human-sized openings between cyclopean structures feel out of place, a characteristic also present in the manga *Blame!* (see Fig. 6).

As we progress in the game, the scenery becomes larger. Once players reach the first open vista, they realize that what looked like the "outer wall" until now, was just one of the numerous megastructures that stretch to the horizon, in a subversion of scale that will be repeated later on in the game.

The game then alternates between abstract and more real, closed and open interior spaces, until players reach a cityscape that resembles an actual city more than anything else before it. Again, the expectation of normality is broken by geometric shapes that surround the player, creating a simple white room that looks exactly like the one at the beginning of the game.

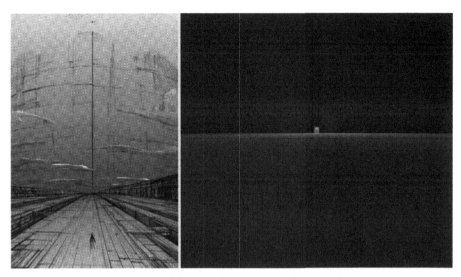

Fig. 6. A plate from *Blame!* Master Edition Volume 3, p. 193 © Tsutomu Nihei/ Kodansha Ltd (left) and a screenshot from *NaissanceE* © Mavros Sedeño 2014 (right).

Until now, the architecture in *NaissanceE* has been completely featureless, not just because of its bare grey material, but also for the complete absence of any sign of use, neglect, or wear. A broken tile on the floor is the first sign of change happening in the game. The perfectly incorruptible and immutable architecture can indeed be broken.

The game proceeds with more and more abstract sections, aptly titled *Deeper into Madness*, where the architecture returns to more abstract, haphazardly assembled forms. The entrance to the level is in fact marked by a door composed of disjointed cubes, unlike anything in the orderly level that precedes it (see Fig. 7). The architecture connotes that we are moving from a place of order to one of chaos, until, at the end of the level, where we are progressively back to the "familiar" spaces of *NaissanceE*, with sleek surfaces and clear-cut openings.

Subsequently, an *Interlude* brings players back to normality through a display of more human architectural forms, such as bridges and arches, telling us that the *Madness* has passed. The scene with a bridge crossing a deep canyon with lightings is a direct reference to *Blame!* and it also communicates that by crossing the bridge players are moving away from the world of madness and abstract geometrical forms, towards more familiar grounds. We cannot see the bottom of the canyon, but the ceiling of the structure is visible, a clear boundary that can be crossed by climbing the seemingly endless staircase on the other side.

Here, yet another subversion of scale takes place, where players are welcomed by the first real, open, natural space in the game, only to look up and see an infinite number of identical megastructures hanging from the ceiling, telling them that the ceiling that they just climbed is only the top of one of many other similar structures (see Fig. 8).

Fig. 7. The corridor leading to the level "Deeper into Madness".

Fig. 8. The "ceiling" of the megastructure and the first "natural" landscape of *NaissanceE* © Mavros Sedeño 2014.

As such, after having reached the "top" – or having believed to have reached it – players are forced to jump down again in order to progress, falling into a deep well surrounded by arches and buildings straight from a Piranesi etching or a Nihei plate, which leads to the final area of the game, again artificial, flat, and bare. In this last section of the game, players are confronted by The Host, an entity that "dismantles architecture entirely, tearing away exterior to reveal an endless void of inner space" (Sedeño 2017, p. 68) from which they have to run, until reaching a door which rewards with the enigmatic words "The Beginning".

6 Conclusions

As visionary architecture has done for centuries, *NaissanceE* is capable of narrating its story without additional aids save for its environments. The architecture in the game exists not only as a visual counterpoint to the gameplay, to instruct players how to proceed and what to do, but also as a storyteller in a silent world with no characters nor texts. The narrative architecture of *NaissanceE* builds upon our previous knowledge and understanding of architectural signs, given the absence of characters or other reference points. Which is why it is important to always relate virtual architecture to real architecture – even if only *paper architecture* – as this is one of the layers of our understanding of the world around us, and one of the most powerful that can be used in digital storytelling.

References

Aarseth, E.: Allegories of Space: The Question of Spatiality in Computer Games. In: Eskelinen, M., Koskimaa, R. (eds.) Cybertext Yearbook 2000, pp. 152–171. University of Jyväskylä, Jyväskylä, Research Centre for Contemporary Culture (2001)

Adams, E.: The construction of ludic space. In: Proceedings of the 2003 DiGRA International Conference: Level Up (2003)

Aroni, G.: The Semiotics of Architecture in Digital Games. Bloomsbury Academic, London (2022)

Borries F von, Walz SP, Boottger M (eds) Space time play: computer games, architecture and urbanism: the next level. Birkhäuser, Basel (2007)

Boullée, É.-L.: Architettura. Saggio sull'arte. Einaudi, Turin (2005)

Boullée, É.-L.: Cénotaphe de Newton (1784)

Capozzoli, N.: NaissanceE Review. Starkitecture. In: GameSpot (2014). https://www.gamespot.com/reviews/naissancee-review/1900-6415686/. Accessed 8 Sep 2019

Eco, U.: Function and sign: the semiotics of architecture. In: Leach, N. (ed.) Rethinking Architecture: A Reader in Cultural Theory, pp. 173–193. Routledge, London (1997)

Interplay Entertainment, Black Isle Studios, Bethesda Game Studios, Obsidian Entertainment (1997–2018) Fallout (series)

Kirk, T.: Piranesi's poetic license: his influence on modern Italian architecture. Mem. Am. Acad. Rome Suppl. Vol. **4**, 239–274 (2006)

Limasse Five. NaissanceE (2014)

Lorenzetti, A.: Allegoria ed effetti del Buono e del Cattivo governo (1338)

Murray, J.H.: Hamlet on the Holodeck: The Future of Narrative in Cyberspace, 2nd edn. Free Press, New York (2016)

Naughty Dog: The Last of Us (2013)

Nihei, T.: BLAME!, Master Vertical Comics, New York (2017)

Rossignol, J.: Wot I Think: NaissancE. In: Rock, Paper, Shotgun (2014). https://www.rockpapershotgun.com/2014/03/06/naissance-review-pc/. Accessed 14 Sep 2019

Rubbini, A.: Prima che la vita cominci. Ammira, immagina, sopravvivi. In: Multiplayer.it (2014). https://multiplayer.it/recensioni/128776-naissancee-prima-che-la-vita-com inci.html. Accessed 8 Sep 2019

Sedeño, M.: A Conversation with Mavros Sedeño (2017)

Sedeño, M.: Style is King footnotes #5: Limasse Five's NaissanceE (2014)

Selena, S. (ed.): : Patronage in the Golden Age of the Capriccio. In: The Architectural Capriccio: Memory, pp. 82–99. Fantasy and Invention. Routledge, London (2016)

Tobin, S.: Time and space in play: saving and pausing with the Nintendo DS. Games Cult. **7**, 127–141 (2012). https://doi.org/10.1177/1555412012440313

Totten, C.W.: An Architectural Approach to Level Design. CRC Press, Boca Raton (2014)

Totten, C.W. (ed.): Level Design: Processes and Experiences. CRC Press, Boca Raton (2017)

Vitruvius, M.P.: On Architecture. Harvard University Press, Cambridge (1931)

Whistance-Smith, G.: Expressive Space: Embodying Meaning in Video Game Environments, 1st edn. De Gruyter, Boston (2022)

Wittkower, R.: Piranesi's "Parere su L'Architettura." J. Warburg Instit. **2**, 147–158 (1938)

Wolf, M.J.P.: Space in the video game. In: Wolf, M.J.P. (ed.) The Medium of the Video Game, pp. 51–75. University of Texas Press, Austin (2001)

Build Your World – Meaningful Choices in a Hybrid Stage Play

Nils Gallist, Manuel Lattner, Michael Lankes⊙, and Juergen Hagler(✉)⊙

University of Applied Sciences Upper Austria,
Hagenberg Campus, 4232 Hagenberg, Austria
{nils.gallist,manuel.lattner,michael.lankes,
juergen.hagler}@fh-hagenberg.at
https://www.fh-ooe.at/campus-hagenberg

Abstract. This paper examines the design of meaningful choices for theater audiences embedded in a hybrid play using digital tools and systems. A case study is presented that is established on a hybrid stage performance called *ALIENATION* based on the so-far unpublished eponymous novel by Corinna Antelmann, which premiered in early 2022 at the *Landestheater Linz*. The audience could take part in the performance via a real-time rendering engine. Apart from describing the case study in detail, we outline further applications and opportunities to facilitate audience participation and engagement. In general, *ALIENATION's* design and production positively impacted the audience's attention, especially regarding younger demographics.

Keywords: Digital theater · Performance · COVID-19 pandemic · Game mechanics · Interactive storytelling · Computer games

1 Introduction

Social gatherings were broadly restricted in many countries during the COVID-19 global pandemic. Concerts or TV shows were canceled or postponed; museums, theaters, and other cultural institutions were closed. To rapidly overcome these challenging times, many events took place remotely. Significantly, the theater and its adjacent culture department were eager to adopt and implement new forms of media, storytelling approaches, and technologies for their live performances. With the implementation of novel technologies, such as Virtual Reality (VR) headsets or video conference platforms, new ways of storytelling emerged that allowed novel experiences and theatre audiences to interact with the performers.

Live streaming over the internet proved to be the most common solution for cultural institutions, as the technology is widely accessible and reliable for audiences and creators [19]. By moving the stage plays to a digital environment through live streaming, the providers gain a variety of new opportunities on how audiences can interact or influence the performance (i.e., chat system or emojis). Furthermore, the limitations of what is possible on a physical stage are lifted. Creating and using digital set extensions that would have exceeded the physical

© The Author(s), under exclusive license to Springer Nature Switzerland AG 2022
M. Vosmeer and L. Holloway-Attaway (Eds.): ICIDS 2022, LNCS 13762, pp. 697–704, 2022.
https://doi.org/10.1007/978-3-031-22298-6_45

space on stage made it possible to enhance the director's storytelling and the play performance. This approach drastically reduces common restrictions such as space and do-ability regarding "stage props" and stage design, as digital spaces are not bound to the law of physics.

The ability to open entirely new scenes at the press of a button or generate a stage in a different visual style by combining real-world footage with cartoonish styling allows the director to include more complex visual context into the performance. These options can be expanded even further when various systems of virtual production are taken into consideration by adding concepts such as *live tracking*, *live keying* or the ability to *layer video footage* on top of each other.

For the proposed application, our goal was to expand the benefits of digitization beyond the visual representation. With *ALIENATION*, we explored many new ways to integrate the audience into the performance. The adaption of game mechanics and the usage of game engines like *Unreal Engine* or *Unity* has proven to be particularly suitable.

The paper provides the following contributions: it presents a use case that enables audiences to participate in a stage play through decisions within the given boundaries. Furthermore, the work offers insights into what constitutes a meaningful choice in an interactive and hybrid performance.

2 Related Work

Choices in interactive media have already been subject to various studies [5,8,18], which outline the significance of holding the audience's attention by giving them the ability to make decisions to influence the content they are watching. Video games, for instance, often feature the possibility of giving the player multiple choices that affect the experience to a certain degree [9].

The question of 'what constitutes a choice that makes the player feel emotions?' has been the subject of numerous studies and papers [4,11,16,20]. Similar to reading an exciting and very moving book or watching a gripping movie, the emotions that are being evoked by choice do not necessarily have to be positive for the choice to be experienced as a *positive experience* [1]. Such decisions or choices in video games can lead to experiencing positive and negative emotions similar to the experience of emotions when watching a movie, reading a book, or visiting a theater play [17]. The main advantage of video games over other media such as film and paper is the high degree of interactivity.

Such choices may start as early as the ability to visually customize the playable character by implementing a character creator system or a simplified system that already contains predefined characters. Enabling players to make such choices increases the degree of experienced immersion [13], as well as deepening the connection with the playable character. Furthermore, interactive storytelling in *Augmented Reality* (AR) theater performances has also been investigated [2], which significantly aided this project's preparation phase. Moving away from the fully digital implementation of this topic in AR to *Mixed Reality*

(MR), shows another prototype and option on how to create compelling experiences for a live audience using both analogous and digital technology for an interactive storytelling experience [3].

Drawing inspiration from video games promised to be a solid starting point for research that can be translated into getting an audience to engage in a theater during a live performance [12]. Since recent years many theaters started exploring how to use immersive technologies and involve the audience in virtual theaters.[1] Due to the COVID-19 pandemic, video communication platforms (e.g., zoom or MSTeams) or VR/metaverse environments (e.g., Mozilla Hubs or Spatial.io) have proven particularly useful for virtual and hybrid theatres. These platforms offer various possibilities (e.g., chat, emojis, avatars) to interact with the audience. In recent years many theatres created digital twins of their stages [7] or established new virtual theaters, e.g., *Netzbühne - Landestheater Linz*[2] or *Digital Raum Bühne - Theater Dortmund*[3]. Besides the integrated interaction features of these platforms, communication via smartphone is a suitable way to reach a larger audience. A current example is the interactive play *1984 : Ministry of Love*[4]. The audience and the actors can communicate via mobile voting and chatting app, which allows them to influence the storyline.

Guidelines and foundations of essential concepts of what constitutes a choice and how to correctly implement the decision-making process into the performance have already been subject to numerous studies [4,6,14]. Besides, previous attempts to integrate live audiences into various forms of performance have been taken into consideration during the conception phase of this case study [15,21].

3   ALIENATION

ALIENATION is a stage play about a teenage girl called "Nikola" who takes us on a trip into her own world, premiered at the *Landestheater Linz*[5], on 17 January 2022. Nikola's world is upside down: Her co-students act like brainless zombies, and her parents decided to move into another city without prior notice. These decisions made her feel like an alien, which is exactly why she decided to dive into a new world: the internet. The protagonist seeks like-minded people and a place to feel at home. But can someone you only know through chat be trusted? The play aims to appeal to a younger target audience and is predominantly available for school classes with a particular focus on primary schools. Therefore the targeted age bracket can be narrowed down to the ages 9–13, especially during the performances reserved for schools only.

ALIENATION is a live streamed stage play on Vimeo in which the actor performs on a stage set and interacts with the audience with the support of a mobile voting app to navigate through a virtual stage. The first part of the play

---

[1] https://play-on.eu/.

[2] https://www.landestheater-linz.at/jungestheater/netzbuehne.

[3] https://www.theaterdo.de/produktionen/detail/digital-raum-buehne/.

[4] https://www.ludowy.pl/pl/spectacle/1984-ministerstwo-milosci/.

[5] https://www.landestheater-linz.at/.

Fig. 1. The protagonist Nikola is chatting with a stranger.

Fig. 2. Nikola plays the video game *Build your World*.

takes place in the teenage room of the protagonist Nikola (see Fig. 1). This room is a physical set akin to other stages found in traditional plays. This physical stage is where most of the acting takes place. The second part is called *Build your World*, a virtual world developed specifically for this stage play (see Fig. 2). As the performance was live streamed to Vimeo, the stagehands were able to utilize existing live streaming software such as Open-Broadcaster-Software (OBS)[6] to layer the video feed of the actress and of the video game (see Fig. 2). The last part consists of a series of pre-produced smartphone videos played during different parts of the performance. These video sequences were also prepared and fed into the live stream-video feed using OBS.

In collaboration with the director of the stage play, Nele Neitzke, we designed and developed the virtual stage *Build your World*, a video game to identify the potential of interactive media in a theatre context. In *ALIENATION*, this video game is the protagonist's digital and personal retreat. In the performance context, *Build your World* can be seen as a digital set extension, which fits the narrative of the stage play and gives the actor an additional space to perform. Furthermore, we added a system that allowed the audience to vote for different options how the play should proceed. The script gave the diverging paths and options during specific play points. An additional way to interact with the performers was set in place by the react voting system via emojis that could be voted on during any time of the performance.

3.1   Audience Interaction

The technological-mediated dialogue between the actor and the audience forms one cornerstone regrading the experience of *ALIENATION*. Via these tools, the audience should decide, how the story unfolds. In consultation with the *Landestheater Linz*, we chose the streaming platform Vimeo because of its automated chat moderation function. The test group's participants extensively used these functionalities to communicate with each other and the performers. The goal here was to provide a relatively high degree of freedom for the communication process. However, the amount of moderation needed to ensure a safe and

---

[6] https://obsproject.com/.

fitting environment for all participants across a specific age range was too much work for the duration of the stage play. The interaction between the audience members themselves shadowed their attention to the performance and was distracting to others. Apart from the distraction, it had to be made sure that the communicative acts related to the play.

These early tests led to disabling the chat functionality as a whole for the implementation and using a third-party application called *reaction-link*[7] for handling the decisions made by the audience. This solution was less work-intensive to moderate. Besides, the built-in chat function of the streaming provider was deactivated to increase performance.

This third-party application could be accessed anytime during the play by scanning a QR code that can be seen on the live stream. This allows the viewer to send emotes by choosing and clicking one of the five pre-chosen emojis (*thumbs-up, thumbs-down, clown, rocket, heart*). The *thumbs-up* reaction signaled a general liking of the current situation; *thumbs-down* was typically used for the opposite reason. The emojis *rocket, heart* and a *clown* could be freely interpreted by the audience as well as by the performer. These emojis did not appear on stream or in chat. However, the number of clicks was kept track of and displayed beneath the corresponding symbols. By choosing this way of interaction, we kept the distraction to a minimum for viewers who didn't want to express themselves while giving feedback to every viewer actively responding to the play.

However, the use of emoticons was merely an addition to the application. The emojis were not used in relevant situations but were implemented to keep the audience's attention on the performance. Their meanings were not dictated by the performers and directors but were left to be freely interpreted by the actress and the audience. Ultimately, it was decided to have a clear structure by offering the audience concrete choices in every relevant scene [10] in the form of a voting system within the same application that the audience already used for emoticon interaction. In total *Build your World* offers three different worlds and, in each world, three further branches. This voting mechanic was also revealed when the aforementioned QR code was scanned. Therefore, the complete interaction system consists of an always accessible emoji voting system which had no direct effect on the performance, and a more straightforward and clear single-choice voting system. The last mentioned system was made accessible to the user by scanning the on-screen QR code that was visible during key moments of the play and directly influenced the play.

Short discussions with the audience right after the performance revealed positive feedback about being able to add their own decisions to a live performance.

With close to 12400 registered voting reactions and 0.9 clicks per minute, distributed to over 200 students, the engagement was phenomenal! We have learned a lot throughout this project and are working on expanding our possibilities in integrating more interaction into our performances.
- *Nele Neitzke*

---

[7] https://www.reactionlink.de/.

The audience emphasized how they would have wished for even more opportunities to influence the play. Furthermore, the desire for more direct feedback has emerged from the discussions. The audience and staff members' feedback outlined this case study's positive aspects. The video game used in this hybrid performance was adequate and fit smoothly with the rest of the play. One way to increase the immersion of the audience or their participation would be to open the possibility of exploring these set extensions on their own devices, which would result in giving the audience a chance to influence the performance more directly.

3.2   Development

The video game *Build your World* was created in the *Unreal Engine*. The script of *ALIENATION* serves as the basis for the computer game. The play offers various possibilities to decide how the action can continue. The audience was free to choose between different predefined digital worlds at specific points. Besides, they were able to define the protagonist's visual appearance during the play. These decisions did not only have consequences on the performance's narrative (i.e., how the play proceeds) but had an impact on the play's visuals (i.e., tape of environment, visual representation of the avatar). Multiple variants of avatars and stage assets were created to offer a diverse set of options to choose from.

In detail, the audience could choose between different landscapes, ranging from desert to woodlands and mountains (see Fig. 3-4). The player starts in a vast and empty field that gets more populated as the performance progresses. Additionally, every world features a landmark building chosen by the audience to provide some form of visual reference. Finding a suitable way for the audience to interact with the play was more challenging than anticipated.

Fig. 3. *Build your World* - Sand.   **Fig. 4.** *Build your World* - Paradise.

4   Conclusion

The engagement in the stage play was received very well by the audience. This case study outlined one of many possibilities for actively encouraging the theater audience to participate in a hybrid stage performance. While this project was viewed as a proof of concept, many new ideas were generated that could take the deferred notion to a new level. For the run time of this performance, the performers and artists found ever more ways to include the decisions and emoticon votes into the stage play. The remaining question is: How far can these interactions be taken while maintaining control over the narrative structure? With the concept and ideas of improvisational theater, in which way can a performance benefit from interaction while still being distraction-free?

Research for more concept-expanding projects has already started. It will give insight into what constitutes meaningful choices in a stage performance (i.e., exploring other forms of interaction and finding cross-sections between the analogous and digital). The past years have outlined the potential benefits of merging theater with technology. This combination can be a beneficial symbiosis if done correctly. The following years will be a playground for many similar ideas and projects to test the waters of 'what is possible and what makes sense when combining theater with a digital addition?'

References

1. Bopp, J.A., Mekler, E.D., Opwis, K.: Negative emotion, positive experience? emotionally moving moments in digital games. In: Proceedings of the 2016 CHI Conference on Human Factors in Computing Systems, pp. 2996–3006. CHI '16, Association for Computing Machinery, New York, NY, USA (2016). https://doi.org/10.1145/2858036.2858227
2. Braun, N.: Storytelling in collaborative augmented reality environments. UNION Agency (2003)
3. Charles, F., Cavazza, M., Mead, S.J., Martin, O., Nandi, A., Marichal, X.: Compelling experiences in mixed reality interactive storytelling. In: Proceedings of the 2004 ACM SIGCHI International Conference on Advances in Computer Entertainment Technology, pp. 32–40. ACE '04, Association for Computing Machinery, New York, NY, USA (2004). https://doi.org/10.1145/1067343.1067347
4. Crawford, C.: Chris Crawford on Interactive Storytelling. Pearson Education (2004)
5. Georgios Floros, K.S.: Patterns of choices on video game genres and internet addiction. Cyberpsychol. Behav. Soc. Netw. **15**(8), 417–424 (2012). https://doi.org/10.1089/cyber.2012.0064
6. Glassner, A.: Interactive storytelling: techniques for 21st century fiction. CRC Press (2017)
7. Hagler, J., Lankes, M., Gallist, N.: Behind the curtains: comparing mozilla hubs with microsoft teams in a guided virtual theatre experience. In: 2022 IEEE Conference on Virtual Reality and 3D User Interfaces Abstracts and Workshops (VRW), pp. 19–22. IEEE (2022)
8. Iten, G.H., Steinemann, S.T., Opwis, K.: To save or to sacrifice? understanding meaningful choices in games. In: Extended Abstracts Publication of the Annual Symposium on Computer-Human Interaction in Play, pp. 495–502. CHI PLAY '17 Extended Abstracts, Association for Computing Machinery, New York, NY, USA (2017). https://doi.org/10.1145/3130859.3131309

9. Iten, G.H., Steinemann, S.T., Opwis, K.: To save or to sacrifice? understanding meaningful choices in games. In: Extended Abstracts Publication of the Annual Symposium on Computer-Human Interaction in Play, pp. 495–502. CHI PLAY '17 Extended Abstracts, Association for Computing Machinery, New York, NY, USA (2017). https://doi.org/10.1145/3130859.3131309

10. Jensen, K.: Designing tangible interfaces for collective decision making in interactive theatre. In: Aaltodoc (2015)

11. Johnson, D., Gardner, J.: Personality, motivation and video games. In: Proceedings of the 22nd Conference of the Computer-Human Interaction Special Interest Group of Australia on Computer-Human Interaction, pp. 276–279 (2010)

12. Kirschner, F., Kirschner, H.: Modding the stage. In: Abend, P., Beil, B., Ossa, V. (eds.) Playful Participatory Practices. PGS, pp. 95–109. Springer, Wiesbaden (2020). https://doi.org/10.1007/978-3-658-28619-4_6

13. Kolesnichenko, A., McVeigh-Schultz, J., Isbister, K.: Understanding emerging design practices for avatar systems in the commercial social VR ecology. In: Proceedings of the 2019 on Designing Interactive Systems Conference, pp. 241–252 (2019)

14. Lindinger, C., Mara, M., Obermaier, K., Aigner, R., Haring, R., Pauser, V.: The (ST) age of participation: audience involvement in interactive performances. Digital Creativity **24**(2), 119–129 (2013)

15. Maynes-Aminzade, D., Pausch, R., Seitz, S.: Techniques for interactive audience participation. In: Proceedings of the Fourth IEEE International Conference on Multimodal Interfaces, pp. 15–20 (2002). https://doi.org/10.1109/ICMI.2002.1166962

16. Švelch, J.: The good, the bad, and the player: the challenges to moral engagement in single-player avatar-based video games. In: Ethics and game design: teaching values through play, pp. 52–68. IGI Global (2010)

17. Tavinor, G.: Video games, fiction, and emotion. In: Proceedings of the Second Australasian Conference on Interactive Entertainment, pp. 201–207. IE '05, Creativity & Cognition Studios Press, Sydney, AUS (2005)

18. Thue, D., Bulitko, V., Spetch, M., Wasylishen, E.: Interactive storytelling: a player modelling approach. Proceedings of the AAAI Conference on Artificial Intelligence and Interactive Digital Entertainment **3**(1), 43–48 (2021). https://ojs.aaai.org/index.php/AIIDE/article/view/18780

19. Timplalexi, E.: Theatre and performance go massively online during the COVID-19 pandemic: implications and side effects. Homo Virtualis **3**(2), 43–54 (2020). https://doi.org/10.12681/homvir.25448, https://ejournals.epublishing.ekt.gr/index.php/homvir/article/view/25448

20. Triberti, S., Villani, D., Riva, G.: Moral positioning in video games and its relation with dispositional traits: the emergence of a social dimension. Comput. Hum. Behav. **50**, 1–8 (2015)

21. Vosmeer, M., Ferri, G., Schouten, B., Rank, S.: Changing roles in gaming: twitch and new gaming audiences. In: Proceedings of 1st International Joint Conference of DiGRA and FDG, pp. 1–2 (2016)

Author Index

Printed in the United States
by Baker & Taylor Publisher Services